T0332773

Handbook of Research on Gamification Dynamics and User Experience Design

Oscar Bernardes
ISCAP, ISEP, Polytechnic Institute of Porto, Portugal & University of Aveiro, Portugal

Vanessa Amorim
ISCAP, Polytechnic Institute of Porto, Portugal

Antonio Carrizo Moreira
University of Aveiro, Portugal

A volume in the Advances in Web Technologies
and Engineering (AWTE) Book Series

Published in the United States of America by
    IGI Global
    Engineering Science Reference (an imprint of IGI Global)
    701 E. Chocolate Avenue
    Hershey PA, USA 17033
    Tel: 717-533-8845
    Fax: 717-533-8661
    E-mail: cust@igi-global.com
    Web site: http://www.igi-global.com

Library of Congress Cataloging-in-Publication Data

Names: Bernardes, Oscar, 1978- editor. | Amorim, Vanessa, 1992- editor. |
   Moreira, Antonio Carrizo, 1961- editor.
Title: Handbook of research on gamification dynamics and user experience
   design / Oscar Bernardes, Vanessa Amorim, and Antonio Carrizo Moreira,
   Editors.
Other titles: Research on gamification dynamics and user experience design
Description: Hershey, PA : Engineering Science Reference, [2022] | Includes
   bibliographical references and index. | Summary: "This research book of
   contributed chapters considers the importance of gamification in the
   context of organizations' improvements and seeks to investigate game
   design from the experience of the user by providing relevant academic
   work, empirical research findings, and an overview of the field of
   study"-- Provided by publisher.
Identifiers: LCCN 2022014834 (print) | LCCN 2022014835 (ebook) | ISBN
   9781668442913 (hardcover) | ISBN 9781668442920 (ebook)
Subjects: LCSH: Gamification--Research. | Organizational behavior. | User
   interfaces (Computer systems) | Video games--Design.
Classification: LCC HB144 H366 2022 (print) | LCC HB144 (ebook) | DDC
   519.3--dc23/eng/20220603
LC record available at https://lccn.loc.gov/2022014834
LC ebook record available at https://lccn.loc.gov/2022014835

This book is published in the IGI Global book series Advances in Web Technologies and Engineering (AWTE) (ISSN: 2328-2762; eISSN: 2328-2754)

British Cataloguing in Publication Data
A Cataloguing in Publication record for this book is available from the British Library.

All work contributed to this book is new, previously-unpublished material. The views expressed in this book are those of the authors, but not necessarily of the publisher.

For electronic access to this publication, please contact: eresources@igi-global.com.

Advances in Web Technologies and Engineering (AWTE) Book Series

Ghazi I. Alkhatib
The Hashemite University, Jordan
David C. Rine
George Mason University, USA

ISSN:2328-2762
EISSN:2328-2754

Mission

The **Advances in Web Technologies and Engineering (AWTE) Book Series** aims to provide a platform for research in the area of Information Technology (IT) concepts, tools, methodologies, and ethnography, in the contexts of global communication systems and Web engineered applications. Organizations are continuously overwhelmed by a variety of new information technologies, many are Web based. These new technologies are capitalizing on the widespread use of network and communication technologies for seamless integration of various issues in information and knowledge sharing within and among organizations. This emphasis on integrated approaches is unique to this book series and dictates cross platform and multidisciplinary strategy to research and practice.

The **Advances in Web Technologies and Engineering (AWTE) Book Series** seeks to create a stage where comprehensive publications are distributed for the objective of bettering and expanding the field of web systems, knowledge capture, and communication technologies. The series will provide researchers and practitioners with solutions for improving how technology is utilized for the purpose of a growing awareness of the importance of web applications and engineering.

Coverage

- Software agent-based applications
- Mobile, location-aware, and ubiquitous computing
- Integrated user profile, provisioning, and context-based processing
- Web user interfaces design, development, and usability engineering studies
- Ontology and semantic Web studies
- Quality of service and service level agreement issues among integrated systems
- Web systems performance engineering studies
- Data and knowledge capture and quality issues
- Knowledge structure, classification, and search algorithms or engines
- Strategies for linking business needs and IT

IGI Global is currently accepting manuscripts for publication within this series. To submit a proposal for a volume in this series, please contact our Acquisition Editors at Acquisitions@igi-global.com or visit: http://www.igi-global.com/publish/.

Titles in this Series

For a list of additional titles in this series, please visit: http://www.igi-global.com/book-series/advances-web-technologies-engineering/37158

3D Modeling Using Autodesk 3ds Max With Rendering View
Debabrata Samanta (CHRIST University, India)
Engineering Science Reference • © 2022 • 291pp • H/C (ISBN: 9781668441398) • US $270.00

Advanced Practical Approaches to Web Mining Techniques and Application
Ahmed J. Obaid (University of Kufa, Iraq) Zdzislaw Polkowski (Wroclaw University of Economics, Poland) and Bharat Bhushan (Sharda University, India)
Engineering Science Reference • © 2022 • 357pp • H/C (ISBN: 9781799894261) • US $270.00

Handbook of Research on Opinion Mining and Text Analytics on Literary Works and Social Media
Pantea Keikhosrokiani (School of Computer Sciences, Universiti Sains Malaysia, Malaysia) and Moussa Pourya Asl (School of Humanities, Universiti Sains Malaysia, Malaysia)
Engineering Science Reference • © 2022 • 462pp • H/C (ISBN: 9781799895947) • US $380.00

Security, Data Analytics, and Energy-Aware Solutions in the IoT
Xiali Hei (University of Louisiana at Lafayette, USA)
Engineering Science Reference • © 2022 • 218pp • H/C (ISBN: 9781799873235) • US $250.00

Emerging Trends in IoT and Integration with Data Science, Cloud Computing, and Big Data Analytics
Pelin Yildirim Taser (Izmir Bakircay University, Turkey)
Information Science Reference • © 2022 • 334pp • H/C (ISBN: 9781799841869) • US $250.00

App and Website Accessibility Developments and Compliance Strategies
Yakup Akgül (Alanya Alaaddin Keykubat University, Turkey)
Engineering Science Reference • © 2022 • 322pp • H/C (ISBN: 9781799878483) • US $250.00

IoT Protocols and Applications for Improving Industry, Environment, and Society
Cristian González García (University of Oviedo, Spain) and Vicente García-Díaz (University of Oviedo, Spain)
Engineering Science Reference • © 2021 • 321pp • H/C (ISBN: 9781799864639) • US $270.00

Integration and Implementation of the Internet of Things Through Cloud Computing
Pradeep Tomar (Gautam Buddha University, India)
Engineering Science Reference • © 2021 • 357pp • H/C (ISBN: 9781799869818) • US $270.00

701 East Chocolate Avenue, Hershey, PA 17033, USA
Tel: 717-533-8845 x100 • Fax: 717-533-8661
E-Mail: cust@igi-global.com • www.igi-global.com

Editorial Advisory Board

List of Contributors

Table of Contents

Detailed Table of Contents

Alessandro Rogora, Politecnico di Milano, Italy
Paolo Carli, Politecnico di Milano, Italy
Alessandro Trevisan, Politecnico di Milano, Italy

The chapter concerns a research experience related to the design and online publication of The Imitation Game (TIG), a game whose goal is to identify sustainable behaviors and interventions on a local scale, increasing both the degree of awareness and the level of intangible assets, available to an established community. The game allows to experiment and share different scenarios through adopting specific technologies and behaviors, evaluating their effect on a transformation project. It can be played at the community level (municipality, neighborhood, etc.) and the building or group of buildings level. The transposition of the game results takes place through shared urban, building, and social transformation projects. In addition to a quantitative evaluation of the impacts, the game allows the evaluation of the established community's potential happiness (Hy).

Kristy de Salas, University of Tasmania, Australia
Lindsay Wells, University of Tasmania, Australia
Michael Quinn, University of Tasmania, Australia
Jenn Scott, University of Tasmania, Australia
Ian Lewis, University of Tasmania, Australia

Gameful interventions (including serious games and gamification) are a popular tool to motivate and engage users towards improved behavioural outcomes. However, such interventions often fail due to poor design, specifically due to a fundamental lack of understanding of the audience and the required behavioural outcomes, and the consequent uninformed selection of potentially inappropriate game elements by designers. This chapter describes exploring the behaviour change wheel (BCW) method as a tool to augment gameful intervention design and selecting appropriate game elements to action gameful intervention strategies. This exploration is undertaken in the context of developing a gameful intervention targeted toward energy conservation. Within this context, the BCW is shown to assist the designers in understanding the audience and the intervention's behavioural outcomes, which has led to a theoretically informed and rigorous selection of game elements that better support the achievement of the targeted behavioural outcomes.

Chapter 3

Gamification has demonstrated significant potential for the support of innovation processes and change initiatives in organizations. There are numerous examples of its application to employee idea crowdsourcing and internal platforms for innovation management in for-profit enterprises and government organizations, where it has fostered increased participation and engagement. A detailed overview of RE-PROVO—a game prototype designed to assist government practitioners in analyzing functional requirements during legacy IT system replacement projects—is an example of how gamification can further promote innovation by being applied to key business processes and practices. The evaluation of the prototype highlights the need for greater operational embeddedness of gamification and the added value of stakeholder participation in gamification design.

In recent years, the concept of gamification, and escape rooms (ER) as one of its methods, has become very popular. ER has been shown to be widely applicable for numerous target groups and contexts. This chapter presents explorative testing of two different ER contexts that have rarely been reported in the literature so far: one for needs analysis in a business setting (n = 21) and one as a tool for science communication in society (n = 63). Participants evaluated the ER with a 5-point Likert rating scale questionnaire (containing 12 respectively 11 items). The results confirm the entertaining nature of the method and show that the ER succeeded in raising awareness of the respective topics. Comparing the rooms provided valuable findings regarding different fields of application. It offers insights into developing this innovative method and conceptualizing future ER. Further implications and limitations are discussed.

Chapter 5

The gamification of different work tasks remains an area where studies have focused mainly on conceptual considerations. This chapter focuses on the gamification process in facility services jobs – cleaning and maintenance. In general, gamification can improve productivity and workplace well-being. Better motivation is supposed to lead to better results and more enjoyable work. This chapter describes the process of gamifying facility services jobs, from the interviews of the staff to the implementation of the custom-made application, WorkAI. Eighteen employees participated in the pilot study, filled in a questionnaire, and attended semi-structured end-interview sessions. This chapter shows how personnel perceived the gamified solution and its possible effects on the employees and their work. Based on the results, the gamified solution must be easy to adapt and should not disturb work routines. This application's main benefit lies in the employee's self-reflection and self-evaluation.

Breno José Andrade de Carvalho, Catholic University of Pernambuco, Brazil
Ammanda Cavalcanti Silva, Neurotech, Brazil & Catholic University of Pernambuco, Brazil
Carla Guedes Porfirio Cavalcante, Catholic University of Pernambuco, Brazil
Gil Vicente de Brito Maia, Catholic University of Pernambuco, Brazil

The results presented in this chapter come from a case study of gamification at Neurotech, a company located in Porto Digital, Recife, Pernambuco, Brazil. The objective was to develop a solution to improve the productivity and satisfaction rates of the company's clients. In general, the authors used contributions on gamification from Patrício, Moreira, and Zurlo; Burke; Costa and Marchiori; and Vianna et al. to which they added Mastrocola's playful learning, Huizinga's magical circle, Bartle's player profile, and engagement in the organizations of the Gallup Institute. For the experiment, the Gamification Canvas and the Trello tool were used to develop and monitor the "Kingdom of Satisfaction" activities. Among the results achieved, a significant increase in cooperation between teams and participants was identified, in addition to reaching a 100% customer satisfaction rate.

Antonio Córdoba-Roldán, University of Seville, Spain
María Jesús Ávila-Gutiérrez, University of Seville, Spain
Susana Suarez-Fernandez de Miranda, University of Seville, Spain
Francisco Aguayo-González, University of Seville, Spain

This chapter proposes a framework to develop a gamification platform for the activities, processes, and tasks executed by the stakeholders who participate in each stage of life cycle engineering (LCE). For this purpose, a review is made of the most significant aspects of gamification for its application in the LCE of the product. The stakeholders in the LCE must be known and classified to make a gaming experience. It is proposed to establish the relationship between the gameful and playful experiences expected by the stakeholders and the game design elements that allow the introduction of attractive game mechanics in the phases of the product design process. For this goal, it is proposed to gamify through a Kansei Engineering System. This methodology allows incorporating all the potential of the digital and organizational facilitators of Industry 4.0 and developing a cyber-physical holonic platform for the gamification of the LCE.

Maha Khemaja, ISSAT, University of Sousse, Tunisia
Syrine Khelifi, ISSAT, University of Sousse, Tunisia

This chapter tackles the difficulty of implementing agile methodologies in enterprises, especially for teams who are used to traditional working methods. Therefore, this work attempts to provide ways to engage better and motivate team members to embrace the use of agile methodologies. One such way has considered using gamification or serious games principles with agile/scrum activities. The main contribution of the present work is threefold. First, it provides a novel blended approach that combines agile principles with gamification mechanics and gameplay. Second, an adaptation approach is provided to adapt all gamification aspects such as gamification purpose and fun applied to agile/scrum activities to consider the enterprise's context, the specificities of the project, and those of the working teams. Finally, the proposed approaches have been instrumented through a mobile app. Experimentation of the approaches allowed the authors to draw interesting findings.

Chapter 9

While academic interest has grown in using gamification in training different aspects of cybersecurity, the research remains sparse on the design and development of games that focus on integrated concepts of security and sustainability. This chapter builds on a previously presented framework for designing serious games and develops and evaluates an instantiation of a game aimed to promote secure and sustainable behavior in digital ecosystems. It describes the theoretical foundation of the game, giving a detailed account of its game design process. Then, it provides the preliminary evaluation in which significant qualitative evidence of security and sustainable behavior is observed regarding progressive system thinking and anticipatory and problem-solving competencies. The results show that gamification facilitated learning the concepts and changing behavior towards sustainability transitions. Further investigation, with larger sample size, is required using other game elements that promote cooperation and critical thinking competencies.

Chapter 10

This chapter builds on Hansen and Scheier by further examining the intersection of game-based learning and digital health promotion apps. The intersection of digital technology and health promotion is an intriguing space given that cost-effective technologies backed by strong theory and implementation science can advance health promotion strategies. Gamification extends asynchronous computer-mediated communication by creating a sense of immersion in the virtual space, socially interacting, and experiencing strong social identifications. This produces feelings of "flow" reported as a stoppage of time and mitigating surrounding intrusive events. Avatars provide pedagogical supports to increase situational awareness, deepening their presence in the digital game world. Players can learn from these interactions, building rapport and developing social connections that might otherwise not be possible in different contexts. Gamified digital technology capitalizes on instructional technology, learning theory, and social identification in ways that can advance health behavior change.

    Leonardo da Conceição Estevam, Federal University of Pará, Brazil
    Lúcio Leandro Cruz de Oliveira, Federal University of Pará, Brazil
    Fernando Augusto Ribeiro Costa, Federal University of Pará, Brazil
    Marcos César da Rocha Seruffo, Federal University of Pará, Brazil

This chapter presents the Covid-Game, a serious game developed out of the difficulties that various societies, specifically the Brazilian, have faced with the advent of the current COVID-19 pandemic. Such difficulties are not restricted to health or economic issues but unfold into problems such as the dissemination of untrue information about the virus, the disease, the ways of prevention, and the treatments available to the population, including immunization through vaccines. Using techniques already consolidated in the state of art of serious games and gamification, this proposal innovates by aiming to disseminate correct information about COVID-19 playfully and considering the players' age, regional, and cultural aspects. This chapter demonstrates its viability, versatility, and convenience in these times of dissemination of countless false information that endangers human life itself.

    David Kessing, Bergische Universität Wuppertal, Germany
    Tim Katzwinkel, Bergische Universität Wuppertal, Germany
    Manuel Löwer, Bergische Universität Wuppertal, Germany

Gamification is an emerging approach to designing motivational strategies for many different applications. To maximize their efficiency, gamification strategies need an in-depth analysis of the users' behavior and appropriate gamification mechanics for implementation. Hence, gamification designs include a deep understanding of human interaction with the product and different motivational aspects during usage. This advantage offers product development opportunities to design more customer-oriented products using gamification methods. This chapter introduces an improved product development process regarding the design-to-customer aspect within the phases of customer analysis, mechanic ideation, and feature design. Each phase includes the integration of specific methods taken from established gamification frameworks. The new process is evaluated with a project on developing gamification strategies for the German Corona-Warning-App.

    Marcos Aurelio Domingues, State University of Maringá, Brazil
    Leonardo A. Alves, Federal University of Goiás, Brazil
    Rogerio Salvini, Federal University of Goiás, Brazil
    Dante Carrizo, University of Atacama, Chile
    Diego Issicaba, Federal University of Santa Catarina, Brazil
    Mauro Rosa, Federal University of Santa Catarina, Brazil

In this chapter, the authors propose a guideline to develop a mobile platform to collect data that makes it possible to predict energy consumption in residences in developing countries. The platform consists of a game that can be played individually or by a team (i.e., a family) that lives in the same house. From time to time, a person or family members will receive some challenges (i.e., some questions) that must be reached (i.e., answered) to collect the energy consumption habits data. The context of the game is in an aquarium, where a small fish will evolve or not during the game. The fish will live in this environment that starts very clean, and with the actions of the user concerning the challenges, may suffer an evolution or degradation. By using gamification techniques, the challenges will persuade the person or family members to provide directly or indirectly the energy consumption habits data for each electronic device. All data collected with the game platform can be analyzed through different types of analysis by using a dashboard.

Chapter 14

Buildings are responsible for 40% of the EU's total energy consumption and 36% of greenhouse gas emissions. Although difficult to quantify, individuals' attitudes to energy use significantly impact the energy consumed in households. In this context, serious games provide an opportunity to enhance buildings' energy efficiency through changes in users' behaviour. This chapter presents the results obtained in the EnerGAware-Energy Game for Awareness of energy efficiency in social housing communities project (2015–2018), funded by EU H2020. The project developed a serious game for household energy efficiency called "Energy Cat: The House of Tomorrow." The game was deployed and tested in a UK social housing pilot for one year. Cost-benefit analysis in the energy, environmental, and economic domains prove that serious gaming is among the most cost-effective energy efficiency strategies for households on the market.

Chapter 15

Gamification is increasingly utilized in modern organizational environments to increase motivation and compliance toward organizational goals. To improve its effectiveness in achieving behavioral change, designers routinely design and implement specially designed information systems (IS) that effectively enable the interaction between employees and game elements and ultimately define the nature of the gamified experience. Such gamified IS have already been put to practice, with positive results regarding usability, user engagement, and enjoyment, and—more importantly—actual energy savings have been recorded during their usage. Apart from an introduction to this very interesting field of application for gamification in organizations, more importantly, this chapter also provides insight and specific guidelines that researchers, as well as practitioners in this field, may need to bear in mind in their efforts to design and implement gamified IS for energy-saving in organizational environments.

    Luís Afonso Maia Rosa Casqueiro, ISCTE, University Institute of Lisbon, Portugal
    Tiago Espinha Gasiba, SIEMENS AG, Germany
    Maria Pinto-Albuquerque, ISCTE, University Institute of Lisbon, Portugal
    Ulrike Lechner, Universität der Bundeswehr München, Germany

Vulnerabilities in source code, when left unpatched, can potentially be exploited by a malicious party, resulting in severe negative consequences. These negative consequences can be significant if the vulnerable software is part of critical infrastructure. Previous studies, however, have shown that many software developers cannot recognize vulnerable code. One possible way to ameliorate the situation is by increasing software developers' awareness of secure programming techniques. In this chapter, the authors propose a serious game, the Java Cybersecurity Challenges, that presents secure programming challenges to the participants in a competitive scenario. They describe and analyze the tools required to implement these challenges and perform an empirical evaluation of the game with more than 40 software developers from the industry. The work contributes to the growing knowledge on the design of serious games and provides valuable information for industry practitioners who wish to deploy a similar game in their environment.

    Evangelos Chaskos, University of Peloponnese, Greece
    Jason Diakoumakos, University of Peloponnese, Greece
    Nicholas Kolokotronis, University of Peloponnese, Greece
    George Lepouras, University of Peloponnese, Greece

Defending against cyber threats is an essential procedure for an organization, and professional training is an important factor for the prosperity of an organization against sophisticated and multi-vector cyber-attacks. The background knowledge is needed from the employee to face and prevent incidents, as well as a level of awareness and experience. Towards this training, cyber security training platforms can significantly raise the trainees' knowledge, perspective, and incident handling. However, gamification mechanisms are implemented and embedded in such systems as an educational procedure to increase the engagement of the trainees. In this chapter, a description of different platforms and their mapping with their corresponding gamification mechanisms will be presented, and the specific gamification elements resulting from this review that are commonly used across all platforms and can have a more significant impact on a fast and meaningful gamified learning procedure will be pointed out.

    Tetiana Luhova, Odessa Polytechnic State University, Ukraine

The research aims to develop a method of creating moral and ethical scenarios for educational computer games based on stories from the cycle of robotic futurology by S. Lem. The result of the study revealed a correspondence between the directorial script and game design document; the critical components of

Lem's story "Trurl's Machine" were formalized considering the moral and ethical conflicts of the plot; the authors created a map of the action scene, game mechanics, and UML based on the story "Trurl's Machine." Considered the issues of transforming plots of classical literature into the game design of educational computer games with an emphasis on the development of the moral and ethical scenarios and the spiritual values formation in students, the rules of the "Mechanical Robots AlgorithmsAda Board Game" as a video game prototype have been rethought with pedagogical impact.

Open and distance learning became a global household term as it came to the forefront of education and work due to the proliferation of remote emergency teaching imposed by the pandemic's social distancing. Virtual reality (VR) is a technology that can transform distance education by overcoming the shortcomings of 2D web-based systems such as learning management systems and web-conferencing platforms. VR-powered teaching can support educators in implementing game-based methods, such as playful design, gamification, and serious games (e.g., educational escape rooms that promote intrinsic motivation towards sustainable engagement for durable, deeper learning). However, a transition from 2D to 3D teaching in the context of the Metaverse is not straightforward or intuitive as it requires a mental and paradigm shift. This chapter presents practical examples of applications and recommendations for practitioners.

Serious games (SGs), which support the player to achieve learning targets and engage in learning activities through a fun experience, have been a flourishing field of research over the last decades. Their dual role as an educational and entertainment tool contributes to their widespread adoption and dissemination. Emotions play a key role in SGs and can be used in various ways to improve a player's experience and their learning outcomes or even contribute to a holistic UX evaluation. Even though SGs have several applications in the cultural heritage (CH) field and GLAMs (galleries, libraries, archives, and museums) institutions to improve their services, their impact has not been adequately studied. This chapter focuses on affective SGs and their use in GLAM institutions to contribute to improving their services. A review of SGs and aspects related to the integration of affective computing (AC) for developing affective SGs are also presented.

Preface

Game definitions often include games and video games in the same category. Most definitions were established after video games became a representative synonym of cultural strength and innovative industry with significant growth (Arjoranta, 2019). Esposito (2005) states, "a videogame is a game which we play thanks to an audiovisual apparatus and which can be based on a story." In this sense, the concept of a video game can also be defined as "a mode of interaction between a player, a machine with an electronic visual display, and possibly other players, that is mediated by a meaningful fictional context, and sustained by an emotional attachment between the player and the outcomes of her actions within this fictional context," according to Bergonse (2017). However, there are elements whose presence is essential to determine a game context: the fictitious activity, the unpredictability, the rules existence, and the temporal and spatial limits, without any mandatory character (Esposito, 2005).

The growing attractiveness in the video game market is verified through several studies and statistics, which determine that a casual user plays on average 4.59 days – male – and 2.48 days – female; the average number of hours dedicated to games per day is 2.37 hours – male – and 1.98 hours – female; the average daily duration of a single game session is 79.42 minutes – male – and 68.6 minutes – female – and the average time spent searching for video games is 25.88 minutes – male – and 24.61 minutes – female (Kapalo et al., 2016). Thus, games provide higher levels of engagement and intrinsic motivation in their users, contributing to the achievement of cognitive, emotional, and social benefits (Xi & Hamari, 2019).

The success of the video game market has contributed to the application of the gamification concept in several areas. Now, gamification represents one of the most significant technological tendencies of the last decade, given the interest shown by organizations (Xi & Hamari, 2020). The literature presents several definitions of the concept (Deterding et al., 2011; Huotari & Hamari, 2012; Hamari et al., 2014). Thus, it is further described in the literature that gamification represents a "process of applying elements of game design to a non-game context, where the interaction between the game mechanisms and personal disposition results in a fun and enjoyable experience" (Tobon et al., 2020).

Its distinction from the serious games (SGs) concept is fundamental in defining the gamification concept. In this sense, it is necessary to consider first the differences between the elements of gamification and the design of games that compose each of these typologies. While gamification uses game elements in non-game contexts, SGs use various game elements to build a game for purposes unrelated to fun or entertainment, such as educational learning, human resources management, or other fields (Georgiou & Nikolaou, 2020; Chow et al., 2020). However, according to the literature, SGs and gamification jointly seek changes in their users' behaviors through pleasant interactions using different levels of motivation to offer the best overall experience to their users (Ponce et al., 2020; Chow et al., 2020).

Gamification uses numerous game elements to obtain a response or behavior from users within a specific context in which it is applied (Klock et al., 2020). Thus, one can consider that the process of designing gamified strategies is different from the design of a game structure, given that in gamification, the goal is to enhance the interaction of its users with a particular purpose or behavior, while in the gaming industry the aim is to create fun and entertainment for its players (Nasirzadeh & Fathian, 2020). According to Zainuddin et al. (2020), gamification elements allow for an excellent way of learning because it enables a better orientation to individual objectives.

Game designers prepare the design of gamified experiences based on frameworks developed and studied by various authors that allow them to have a greater overall understanding of the strengths and weaknesses that can determine the success of a given gamified system (Kusuma et al., 2018). In this context, the frameworks also enable the design and development of a gamified approach, considering the entire project life cycle between planning, designing, and marketing (Briciu & Filip, 2018).

This comprehensive and timely publication aims to be an essential reference source, building on existing literature in the Gamification Dynamics and User Experience Design field while providing additional research opportunities in this dynamic and growing field. Thus, the book aims to reflect on this critical issue, increasing the understanding of the importance of the topics and providing relevant academic work, empirical research findings, and an overview of this relevant field of study. It is hoped that this book will provide the resources necessary for academicians, interdisciplinary researchers, advanced-level students, technology developers, managers, and government officials to adopt and implement solutions for a more digital world. The book comprises 20 chapters, where every chapter explains different implementations of gamification from a cross-discipline view.

The first chapter, "The Imitation Game: Games as an Experience of Participation, Knowledge, Evaluation, and Sharing of Design," concerns a research experience related to the design and online publication of The Imitation Game, a game whose goal is to identify sustainable behaviors and interventions on a local scale, increasing both the degree of awareness and the level of intangible assets, available to an established community.

The next chapter, "The Behaviour Change Wheel to Support the Design of Gameful Interventions: An Exploratory Study," calls for attention that gameful interventions often fail as a result of poor design, precisely due to a fundamental lack of understanding of the audience and the required behavioral outcomes. In this context, the chapter explores the Behaviour Change Wheel method as a tool to augment gameful intervention design and select appropriate game elements to action gameful intervention strategies.

"Gamification for Organisational Change and Innovation" addresses a detailed overview of RE-PROVO – a game prototype designed to assist government practitioners in analyzing functional requirements during legacy IT system replacement projects. This chapter offers the possibility to understand how gamification can further promote innovation by being applied to critical business processes and practices.

The chapter "The Use of Escape Rooms in Society and Business Environments: Two Exploratory Studies on the Potential of Gamification" aims to evaluate two different Escape Rooms contexts that have rarely been reported in the literature so far: one for needs analysis in a business setting and one as a tool for science communication in society. The results confirm the entertaining nature of the method and show that the Escape Rooms are succeeded in raising awareness on both topics.

Chapter 5, "WorkAI: Raising Work-Related Self-Awareness With Gamified Approach," focuses on the gamification process in facility services jobs – cleaning and maintenance – and describes the process of gamifying facility services jobs from the interviews of the staff to the implementation of the custom-made application, WorkAI. The authors emphasize that the main benefits of this application consist of the employee's self-reflection and self-assessment.

The following chapter, "The Kingdom of Satisfaction: Case Study of Gamification at Neurotech," considers the results of Neurotech, a Brazilian company responsible for developing a solution to improve the productivity and satisfaction rates of the company's clients. The results demonstrate a significant increase in cooperation between teams and participants and a customer satisfaction rate of 100%.

"Gamification for Stakeholders in the Product Life Cycle: Holonic Platform With Kansei Engineering" is the title of Chapter 7, which proposes a framework to develop a gamification platform for the activities, processes, and tasks executed by the stakeholders who participate in each stage of Life Cycle Engineering.

Chapter 8, "GaminScrum an Adaptive Gamification Approach Applied to Agile Processes," highlights the difficulty of implementing agile methodologies in enterprises, especially for teams who are used to traditional working methods. Within this scope, this research attempts to provide ways to engage better and motivate team members to embrace the use of agile methodologies.

"Promoting Secure and Sustainable Behavior in Digital Ecosystems Through Gamification" intends to build on a previously presented framework for designing SGs and develop and evaluate an instantiation of a game aimed to promote secure and sustainable behavior in digital ecosystems. The results demonstrate that gamification facilitated learning the concepts and changing behavior towards sustainability transitions.

In Chapter 10, "Gamified Digital Apps and their Utilization to Improve Health Behaviors in the 21st Century: Gamified Digital Health Behavior Interventions," the authors further explore the study of Hansen and Scheier (2019) and study in detail the question of the intersection of game-based learning and digital health promotion apps, which can advance health promotion strategies.

The next chapter, "COVID-Game: A Serious Game to Inform About Coronavirus," presents the Covid-Game, a serious game developed out of the difficulties that various societies, specifically the Brazilian, have faced with the advent of the current COVID-19 pandemic. According to the authors, this proposal innovates by aiming to disseminate correct information about COVID-19 playfully and considering the players' age, regional, and cultural aspects.

Chapter 12 is entitled "Integration of Gamification Methods to Improve Design-to-Customer in Product Development: Use Case – The German Corona-Warning-App." It introduces an improved product development process regarding the Design-to-Customer aspect within the phases of customer analysis, mechanic ideation, and feature design. The new process is then evaluated with a project on developing gamification strategies for the German Corona-Warning-App.

Chapter 13, "A Guideline to Develop a Game Platform to Collect Energy Consumption Data From Residences in Developing Countries," explores a guideline to develop a mobile platform to collect data that makes it possible to predict energy consumption in residences in developing countries. The results of this platform indicate that the challenges will persuade individuals to provide directly or indirectly the energy consumption habits data for each electronic device.

The following chapter, "Gamification and Household Energy Saving: Insights From the EnerGAware Project," argues that SGs provide an opportunity to enhance buildings' energy efficiency through changes in users' behavior. The results emphasize that serious gaming is among the most cost-effective energy efficiency strategies for households on the market.

"Gamified Information Systems as a Means to Achieve Energy-Saving at Work Through Employees' Behaviour" is the title of Chapter 15. This chapter highlights the importance of information systems, which can have positive results regarding usability, user engagement, enjoyment, and energy savings. This chapter also provides insight and specific guidelines for researchers and practitioners in this field.

Chapter 16, "Increasing Developer Awareness of Java Secure Coding in the Industry: An Approach Using Serious Games," proposes a serious game, the Java Cybersecurity Challenges, that presents secure programming challenges to the participants in a competitive scenario. This chapter contributes to the growing knowledge on the design of SGs and provides valuable information for industry practitioners who wish to deploy a similar game in their environment.

Chapter 17 is entitled "Gamification Mechanisms in Cyber Range and Cyber Security Training Environments: A Review." It presents a description of different platforms and their mapping with their corresponding gamification mechanisms and the specific gamification elements resulting from this review that are commonly used across all platforms and can have a more significant impact on a fast and meaningful gamified learning procedure will be pointed out.

"Moral and Ethical Scenarios for Educational Computer Games Based on the Robotic Futurology by Stanislaw Lem" composes Chapter 18 and reveals a correspondence between the directorial script and game design document; the critical components of Lem's story "Trurl's Machine" were formalized considering the moral and ethical conflicts of the plot; created a map of the action scene, game mechanics, and UML based on the story "Trurl's Machine."

Chapter 19, "Sustainable Engagement in Open and Distance Learning With Play and Games in Virtual Reality: Playful and Gameful Distance Education in VR," emphasizes that open and distance learning became a global household term as it came to the forefront of education and work due to the proliferation of remote emergency teaching imposed by the pandemic's social distancing. In this context, Virtual Reality is considered a technology that can transform distance education.

Emotions play a crucial role in SGs and can be used to improve a player's experience. The chapter "Affective Serious Games for GLAMs Institutions" focuses on affective SGs and their use in GLAM – Galleries, Libraries, Archives, and Museums – institutions to contribute to improving their services because their impact has not been adequately studied.

We hope that this book provides an enjoyable reading experience.

Oscar Bernardes
ISCAP, ISEP, Polytechnic Institute of Porto, Portugal & University of Aveiro, Portugal

Vanessa Amorim
ISCAP, Polytechnic Institute of Porto, Portugal

Antonio Carrizo Moreira
University of Aveiro, Portugal

REFERENCES

Arjoranta, J. (2019). How to Define Games and Why We Need to. *The Computer Games Journal*, 8(3), 109–120. doi:10.100740869-019-00080-6

Bergonse, R. (2017). Fifty Years on, What Exactly is a Videogame? An Essentialistic Definitional Approach. *The Computer Games Journal, 6*(4), 239–255. doi:10.100740869-017-0045-4

Briciu, C.-V., & Filip, I. (2018). Applying Gamification for Mindset Changing in Automotive Software Project Management. *Procedia: Social and Behavioral Sciences, 238*, 267–276. doi:10.1016/j.sbspro.2018.04.002

Chow, C. Y., Riantiningtyas, R. R., Kanstrup, M. B., Papavasileiou, M., Liem, G. D., & Olsen, A. (2020). Can games change children's eating behaviour? A review of gamification and serious games. *Food Quality and Preference, 80*, 103823. Advance online publication. doi:10.1016/j.foodqual.2019.103823

Deterding, S., Dixon, D., Khaled, R., & Nacke, L. (2011). From Game Design Elements to Gamefulness: Defining "Gamification." *Proceedings of the 15th International Academic MindTrek Conference on Envisioning Future Media Environments - MindTrek '11*. 10.1145/2181037.2181040

Esposito, N. (2005). A Short and Simple Definition of What a Videogame Is. *Proceedings of the 2005 DiGRA International Conference: Changing Views: Worlds in Play*, 1-6.

Georgiou, K., & Nikolaou, I. (2020). Are applicants in favor of traditional or gamified assessment methods? Exploring applicant reactions towards a gamified selection method. *Computers in Human Behavior, 109*, 106356. Advance online publication. doi:10.1016/j.chb.2020.106356

Hamari, J., Koivisto, J., & Sarsa, H. (2014). Does gamification work? - A literature review of empirical studies on gamification. *Proceedings of the Annual Hawaii International Conference on System Sciences*, 3025–3034. 10.1109/HICSS.2014.377

Huotari, K., & Hamari, J. (2012). Defining Gamification-A Service Marketing Perspective. *Proceeding of the 16th International Academic MindTrek Conference on - MindTrek '12*. 10.1145/2393132.2393137

Kapalo, K. A., Dewar, A. R., Rupp, M. A., & Szalma, J. L. (2016). Individual Differences in Video Gaming: Defining Hardcore Video Gamers. *Proceedings of the Human Factors and Ergonomics Society Annual Meeting*, 878–881. 10.1177/1541931215591261

Klock, A. C. T., Gasparini, I., Pimenta, M. S., & Hamari, J. (2020). Tailored gamification: A review of literature. *International Journal of Human-Computer Studies, 144*, 102495. Advance online publication. doi:10.1016/j.ijhcs.2020.102495

Kusuma, G. P., Wigati, E. K., Utomo, Y., & Putera Suryapranata, L. K. (2018). Analysis of Gamification Models in Education Using MDA Framework. *Procedia Computer Science, 135*, 385–392. doi:10.1016/j.procs.2018.08.187

Nasirzadeh, E., & Fathian, M. (2020). Investigating the effect of gamification elements on bank customers to personalize gamified systems. *International Journal of Human-Computer Studies, 143*, 102469. Advance online publication. doi:10.1016/j.ijhcs.2020.102469

Ponce, P., Meier, A., Méndez, J. I., Peffer, T., Molina, A., & Mata, O. (2020). Tailored gamification and serious game framework based on fuzzy logic for saving energy in connected thermostats. *Journal of Cleaner Production, 262*, 121167. Advance online publication. doi:10.1016/j.jclepro.2020.121167

Tobon, S., Ruiz-Alba, J. L., & García-Madariaga, J. (2020). Gamification and online consumer decisions: Is the game over? *Decision Support Systems, 128*, 113167. Advance online publication. doi:10.1016/j. dss.2019.113167

Xi, N., & Hamari, J. (2019). Does gamification satisfy needs? A study on the relationship between gamification features and intrinsic need satisfaction. *International Journal of Information Management, 46*, 210–221. doi:10.1016/j.ijinfomgt.2018.12.002

Xi, N., & Hamari, J. (2020). Does gamification affect brand engagement and equity? A study in online brand communities. *Journal of Business Research, 109*, 449–460. doi:10.1016/j.jbusres.2019.11.058

Zainuddin, Z., Chu, S. K. W., Shujahat, M., & Perera, C. J. (2020). The impact of gamification on learning and instruction: A systematic review of empirical evidence. *Educational Research Review, 30*, 100326. Advance online publication. doi:10.1016/j.edurev.2020.100326

Chapter 1
The Imitation Game:
Games as an Experience of Participation, Knowledge, Evaluation, and Sharing of Design

Alessandro Rogora
Politecnico di Milano, Italy

Paolo Carli
Politecnico di Milano, Italy

Alessandro Trevisan
Politecnico di Milano, Italy

ABSTRACT

The chapter concerns a research experience related to the design and online publication of The Imitation Game (TIG), a game whose goal is to identify sustainable behaviors and interventions on a local scale, increasing both the degree of awareness and the level of intangible assets, available to an established community. The game allows to experiment and share different scenarios through adopting specific technologies and behaviors, evaluating their effect on a transformation project. It can be played at the community level (municipality, neighborhood, etc.) and the building or group of buildings level. The transposition of the game results takes place through shared urban, building, and social transformation projects. In addition to a quantitative evaluation of the impacts, the game allows the evaluation of the established community's potential happiness (Hy).

INTRODUCTION

The impact of human behavior on the environment far outstrips our planet's capacity to absorb and metabolize it. We consume far more resources than the ecosystem is able to regenerate, with disastrous consequences in terms of the pollution of the planet and the depletion of living species, in both number

DOI: 10.4018/978-1-6684-4291-3.ch001

and variety. Nevertheless, a significant chunk of the human population lives below the absolute poverty line, with difficulty accessing adequate quantities of food and water, as well as a lack of sufficient energy and material goods. This situation makes it very clear that there is a need to drastically reduce our consumption levels and the impact resulting from the lifestyles of more developed countries in order to facilitate the development of populations that are in dire need - as opposed to bringing the point of deficit of natural resources even closer than it has been for quite some time - and thus allow for an attempt to rebalance the ratio of available resources to consumption on a global scale.

Global efforts to reduce energy consumption and CO_2 emissions have not had the desired effects, despite significant increases in the energy efficiency levels of the manufacture of individual products and the provision of services. The policy initiatives promoted by governments have not proven capable of reversing the global trend, and there are very few concrete actions at the local level that attempt - even in their own small way - to address the overall problem of emissions and consumption by providing virtuous models to be followed.

Each of us, in our capacity as citizens, is aware of the need to change our behavior with a view to increasing environmental sustainability, but it is difficult - if not outright impossible - for any of us to gain an accurate idea of the real-world effect of each individual choice that we make. Even when we are working as planners or administrators - in other words, whenever we are making choices outside our personal sphere - despite the existence of participatory planning tools, we struggle to accurately discern the degree of social acceptability of our operations and weigh up the available alternatives.

Although on the one hand, there is now widespread use of advanced simulation tools that allow us to make conscious choices with respect to specific issues (e.g. energy consumption) as they affect individual objects or services (cars, buildings, etc.), the available options for predicting the degree of acceptability of these choices by the general population, as well as their interaction at the scale of the settled society, highlights a chronic lack of tools for assessment and representation (Rogora 1997, Clementi, 2019).

The search for impact prediction tools that can be used by administrators, planners and citizens alike and that involve and engage all stakeholders in deciding what action to take is the foundation of this research project: The Imitation Game.

This chapter reports the results of a more in-depth look at this approach, thanks to the research the Imitation Game, applying it to the specific issue of actions in a local area that are oriented towards *deep sustainability* objectives, where the framework of available environmental resources is clear.

The peculiarity of the game proposed by The Imitation Game research lies in the need to modify the behavior of individual players in order to make operational certain project choices. The choice to adopt soft mobility solutions, for example, will be mandatory for the entire duration of the game for the player that selects to use the bicycle. This will allow to bring out potential conflicts between sustainability and social acceptability and to identify possible solutions to the problem.

The basic experiment underpinning the research involves applying the logic of role-playing and simulation games and assessing their effectiveness in shared decision-making for sustainable planning choices which require significant changes to the lifestyle of those involved. This approach also represents a highly innovative method in terms of teaching and teacher-student interaction.

It offers a game experience in which the participants can simulate transformation scenarios within a set of limited available resources (time, money, water, energy, productive land, food, etc.) and in which the players represent the real-life stakeholders of the context in which it is set. This makes it possible to simulate the effects and define the countermeasures to be adopted in order to arrive at shared solutions with explicit, measurable effects.

The idea of interacting with students (or citizens) as one would in a large-scale "role-playing game" makes it possible to simulate both the social acceptability and the environmental consequences of a series of options for transforming the built environment, making the effects and weight of the choices implemented clear and explicit. The main objective is to change the users' behavior by increasing their level of awareness in order to build new shared values of sustainability.

The field of play consists of a real setting, suitably simplified (in the experiment, the Municipality of Rescaldina in northern Milan was used), for which various pieces of information are available, including the geo-referenced data relating to the locally available resources, the information about the population's consumption (ISTAT data), and an up-to-date GIS-based map (Ronchi, Arcidiacono, Pogliani, 2021). Where certain data required for the evaluations is missing, national average values or values available in literature are used.

The various design choices, technical solutions and behaviors adopted by the players (architecture students, in our case) continually alter the results, making explicit the consequences of their choices with respect to two parameters: the amount of land needed to produce the basic materials required to sustain the lifestyles of the settled population, and the amount of CO_2 emitted for their processing and use.

The game is structured into six 'impact sections', with some subsections: *clothing*, *mobility*, *food*, *energy: heating*, *energy: electricity*, *energy: DHW* and *cooking*, *leisure* and *communication*, *education*, *health* and services, for each of which impact values are given in terms of m² of surface area used and amount of CO_2 emitted.

The structure of the game requires the proposed behaviours to be adopted by the players in real life in order to be effective (e.g. if a player selects the 'vegetarian' option, that player must actually eat vegetarian for the entire duration of the game). The game must last long enough for the players to fully grasp the complexity of adopting the new behaviours involved and, consequently, to identify the design and planning actions required to make them possible. In the case of games played with students, the duration of the game was set to last as long as their term in the workshop.

The Imitation Game is a convivial game for architects, architecture students, administrators and even ordinary citizens who are interested in experimenting with approaches to local self-sustainability.

The Imitation Game can be played on a 'Building' or 'Community' scale. The 'Building' scale refers to a 'real-life' condition in which a collection of users is faced with a localised and defined building or set of buildings, whilst the 'Community' scale simulates the shared transformations undergone by a settled society with regard to its own local area and way of life. As such, the field of play at the Community scale must be a significant unit for planning purposes, typically a municipality or consortium of municipalities, a mountain community, etc.

The aim of the research is to define a simplified procedure to roughly estimate the effect of the behavior of people in a given area in terms of land necessary to support their lifestyle. To calculate the amount of land required, all the consumptions have been converted into biomass (wood, biofuel, food, …) and then into land surface to produce such biomass. The Imitation Game was structured as a board game in which players (typically students) can gain extra points performing specific activities (i.e., reading books on the topic, performing activities), can play technological choices (available as cards in a deck of cards) and can modify their behavior to affect the final results. A Web site with the rules and examples for the Imitation Game has been prepared for the students.

The user manual for the game, as well as specific instructions for players and playing groups on how to fill in the calculation spreadsheets, can be found at: http://www.imitationgame.rf.gd/home-general/index.html.

As already mentioned, the main scope of the chapter is to fully illustrate the various phases and activities, and the possible margins for improvement, of the "serious game", right now only for students and teachers, produced during the research The Imitation Game, as well as the critical issues, found during its gaming sessions.

Therefore, starting from a state of the art with respect to the application of game dynamics to the decision-making processes of territorial planning, with particular reference to environmental aspects (saving energy and resources, decreasing of CO_2 production, reduction of own impacts), the chapter is structured following the scheme of the game itself, in order to explain its mechanisms and, above all, the basic choices, highlighting the importance of the player's active role in relation to the possibility of positively affecting the environment by modifying one's behavior and lifestyles.

BACKGROUND

Although nowadays, "serious games" are understood to exist in a strictly digital format, their origins date back to the first half of the 20th century, when strategic board games were used for war simulations. The purpose of these games is not purely fun or entertainment; instead, they revolve around educational elements aimed at creating an effective and enjoyable learning experience. Over the last twenty years, they have developed in leaps and bounds, mainly in the area of video games, but in the wake of these, we have also seen innovations in the areas of board games and role-playing games (Patrício, et al., 2018). The Imitation Game falls into the category of serious games in that it brings about a modification of reality through concrete actions in a real -albeit simplified - context.

There are many examples of simulation games, with the more complex ones such as SimLife or SimCity ("world management games" designed by Maxis, a division of video game publisher Electronic Arts) allowing the player to simulate the birth and development of life on a planet and the rise and fall of a city, respectively. These simulation games have reached extremely refined levels of representation and can be used to faithfully simulate certain transformations in the real world (traffic flows, financial flows, property market trends, etc.). Despite their complexity, however, they are not capable of simulating the behaviour and personal commitment of their users, and therefore fall short of being educational and effective from this perspective.

One particularly interesting game is Polygame, developed by Profs. S. Caserini and R. Casagrandi at the Politecnico di Milano. Polygame aims to study energy conversion solutions capable of reducing the emission of climate-changing gases by using a blend of solutions (biomass power stations, improving the energy efficiency of buildings, modification of transportation systems, etc.), and can be played by groups of students, whose goal is to achieve a good degree of consensus within the group before convincing the players of the other teams of the validity of their playing strategies.

Another gaming experience for educational use is Metro Game, developed by Prof. A. Contin, also at the Politecnico di Milano. Metro Game is a board game in which the participants discuss possible intervention strategies and choose those which they agree upon from a limited number of options, receiving feedback in terms of certain short- and long-term sustainability indicators at several points.

The simulative approach can be understood as a teaching/learning methodology that involves the players taking an active part in the game (and, ultimately, in the decision-making process) by influencing the shape and nature of their environment, with a view to prompting them to act according to a logic of limiting the consumption of resources and making the proper use of increasingly rapid development opportunities, as well as establishing a balanced relationship between economic development and an appropriate approach to the environmental components at stake.

Educational games and simulations can be effective ways of motivating students to learn by experiencing first-hand the behaviours involved in them, or by allowing them to explore areas to which they have no access in real life. The use of simulation games can also help students to correct errors or misunderstandings in their own way of thinking, allowing them to test out hypotheses or develop familiarity with a certain activity before actually engaging in it; indeed, experience says that the use of simulations allows students to be more confident in their abilities when they are subsequently faced with the real materials and situations in question.

Generally speaking, simulation allows us to compare the effects of adopting specific behaviors, but not the actual acceptability of these behaviors, nor does it allow us to compile the blend of solutions capable of garnering the highest degree of acceptance by a resident population, indicate the set of problems and conflicts that the adoption of these behaviors results in, or provide the set of solutions that must be adopted in order to tackle them (Patrício et al., 2021).

DESCRIPTION OF THE ACTIVITY

Initial Hypothesis and Problems Encountered During the Research Project

The structure and organization of The Imitation Game are rooted in the assumption that without a profound shift in the behaviors of individuals - and therefore in the values of a settled society - any given collection of technical solutions is not sufficient to bring us closer to the sustainability goals that are considered necessary to keep humanity's impact on the planet within sustainable limits.

The first hypothesis of the research was to represent this impact using a single parameter, namely the surface area needed to support any given lifestyle in order to make the discrepancy with the available surface area per capita in the defined environment immediately clear. The main problem was a double-edged sword: how to simplify the complexity of the real world to make the game playable, whilst at the same time maintaining its complexity to allow for specific, localized design operations.

In The Imitation Game, the evaluations and transformations that take place only affect the residential area, whereas the impact of production and service activities has been indirectly included in the consumption categories that refer to the production of goods and services. Whilst this choice undoubtedly represents a major simplification of reality, it stems from the awareness that, on average, the impacts of a settled community constitute the main environmental burdens weighing on its local area. This choice also makes sense in terms of playability, because residential activities are the only ones we can easily circumscribe and analyze - something which is impossible for industrial activities, which involve input and output flows on a much larger scale, almost always of a supra-local nature and with data that is difficult to obtain and assess.

Certain assumptions were made with regard to the information, specifically that the municipal maps, the data as surveyed by ISTAT and the actual situation were all congruent, that this information was available for all the census sections of the municipality in question, and that quantitative information was available on the consistency and consumption patterns of the various subjects present in the local area. In reality, despite the decision to use a municipality with a newly created PGT [Area Zoning Plan] and up-to-date GIS-based maps for the tests, the problems encountered in terms of the availability and reliability of the data were significant.

In addition to the difficulty in obtaining some data - as well as the inconsistency of the information provided on the same data point by different sources - there were inconsistencies between the information given in the graphic documents (e.g., the number of buildings present in a given census section), the official data available (e.g., the information collected and processed by ISTAT), and the actual situation as observed in situ. In some cases, the inconsistencies were so obvious that they proved 'embarrassing' due to the obvious discrepancy with the actual values.

These difficulties emerged clearly during the first round played with the students involved in the workshop at the Construction and Sustainability Design Studio. As such, for subsequent rounds of the game, only certain census sections for the municipality were selected as the focus for the simulations, with others left out because they were obviously unusable.

The original hypothesis of being able to represent consumption of all kinds in terms of surface area of land used proved to be extremely difficult as, whilst the relationship with the amount of land used was immediately clear for certain impact categories, in other cases it proved totally impossible to find a simple relationship between the two that would be meaningful to the player. If we take the "Food" impact category as an example, it is relatively simple to define the amount of land needed to feed a person, and thus the portion of land required depending on the type of diet being followed. However, attempts to do the same with services that have a minimal impact in terms of the area they directly take up (e.g. a hospital or a library), but which are indirectly responsible for significant impacts, proved much more difficult. To better describe the effects of these elements, the amount of CO_2 emitted to produce any given good or service has been taken into account, combining it with the amount of land used for the production of the primary goods involved for a more comprehensive picture of its impact (Berners-Lee 2020).

For the first round of the game, we attempted to convert the amount of CO_2 emitted in these transformation processes into the area of forest land required to absorb it, but the discussions had, and criticisms received in our dialogues with the researchers met at one of the conferences at which we presented our work convinced us to go back on our decision, instead evaluating the two parameters separately.

Experimentation and Experiences with the Game

The first round played (September 2019 - January 2020) proved to be particularly complex due to the continuous changes and corrections that had to be made as a result of the various problems that arose when moving from the initial declarations of intent to their actual implementation as part of the project. More specifically, we found it exceedingly difficult to obtain and process the data, and that the use of the spreadsheets for the impact calculations proved somewhat cumbersome; as a result, we sought to reduce their number and simplify them for subsequent rounds. Another serious flaw was the substantial lack of quantitative information on the effects of the behaviors and on the individual technical solutions in terms of their impact on the local area. Particularly during the course of the game, we realized that playing at the community level presented some significant differences compared to the building scale. When playing at the urban (or community) scale, the players represent a percentage of the population with average starting behaviors (and as such, potentially very different from their own). whereas when playing at the building scale, the players impersonate themselves (or their 'real-life' family) in a much more precise context, with reference consumption values linked to a tangible context that can therefore be completely different from the average (i.e. an existing building with specific performance values).

As a result, the game was subsequently organized with the same structure, but keeping the Community (urban) and Building levels separate, with different procedures and calculation files for each.

We then worked on reducing the overall number of calculation files involved, taking them down from over ten initially to four (three general ones, plus a spreadsheet for calculating heat loss), in which we sought to maintain a uniform structure to reduce the risk of errors when completing them.

Whilst the procedure proved to be long and complex, the experience of the first round was interesting nonetheless, with the results presented at two international conferences - MED (Florence) and SEB 2020 (Split) - for discussion with other researchers.

The first round also made it clear that the professors at the workshop still needed to carry out further in-depth work on preparing the information and data relating to the field of play before proceeding. The round played in the Construction and Sustainability Design Studio with primarily foreign students shed light on both the difficulty of the language involved and the fact that the players came from very different cultures, with not insignificant problems in decoding the information.

One final and highly necessary area for in-depth review was the definition of the "Playing Deck", i.e. the preparation of the set of playable actions available to the students, divided into Behavior cards and Technical Solution cards. The development of the playing deck proved to be particularly lengthy and demanding, and unfortunately presents problems that remain partly unresolved. Not all the cards can be used in the same way, as they sometimes refer to individuals, sometimes to families, and sometimes to groups of families sharing a given good or service, requiring calculation methods that can differ significantly.

Organization and Structure of the Game at the End of the Research Project

The structure of The Imitation Game, as used in the round played February - March 2021, is described below. The round was played at the urban level, covering three census sections of a total of 38 in the municipality. The decision to use just three sections, but representative of the entire urban environment in question, was prompted by the complexity (and continuous modification) of the assessments of the built environment that led us to prioritize the verification of the game's structure over a comprehensive analysis of the built environment, which would have represented nothing more than a repetition of the procedures used for the sample sections.

The structure of The Imitation Game consists of various calculation spreadsheets and a database connected to them (Card DB) and is organized around the Game file (Figure 1), which contains the general data relating to the field of play, receives the data from the individual players and the playing group, and processes this data by returning its evaluation of the choices made. Linked to the Game file are two other files, the Player and Design files, which describe the behavioral choices of the individual players and the design choices made by the playing group, respectively.

The first activity involves entering any potentially missing information from the playing groups to determine the initial average impacts into the Game file. From an educational point of view, it was preferable to have the students carry out these activities, but in the event of a round to be played with the inhabitants of a municipality, all these initial operations could be carried out by the organizers of the game.

Once the average consumption values associated with the six impact sections have been established and inserted into the Game file, the initial situation is displayed with regard to land consumption in both absolute terms (m2 of productive land required) and relative terms, as compared with values associated with the land actually available in the local, regional and national area in question (i.e. how many municipalities, regions and countries are required) in order to sustain the lifestyle adopted. Similarly, the

Figure 1. Game structure and relationship between the different game files. Source: The Imitation Game project, 2020

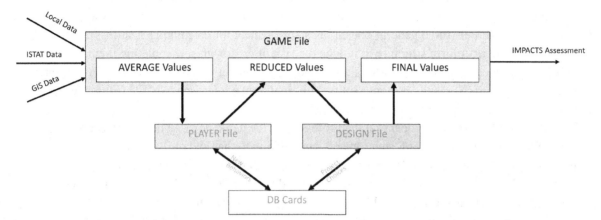

average CO_2 emissions related to the given lifestyles are displayed, indicating the difference between these values and the sustainability target of 5 tons/person (AA.VV., 2018).

Once the average values have been defined, we move on to the declarations of behaviors by each of the individual players of the playing group, who choose which changes to implement, selecting them from the available options in the Database (Playing Deck) or adding new ones. In the event that they wish to introduce new behaviors, incorporating them into the database, these must be described with an indication of the economic cost and time required to implement them, as well as their effects in terms of CO_2 emitted and land area impacted. In order to maintain the internal consistency of the information contained in the behavior cards and make them easier for the users to describe, each player must denote a specific household composition of reference, with their decisions reflected in households of different types as per the method indicated by the ISTAT. Any new behaviors described by the players are incorporated into the Database and immediately become available to any other players who also wish to adopt them. Each individual player's modification of their behaviors results in reduced impact values, which are then reported and processed in the Game file, subsequently flowing into the Design file, where the resulting design choices will then be described and evaluated.

The design choices describe the proposed transformation actions and the resulting effects thereof.

In more detail: the game is played using a computer, a tablet or a smartphone to access the site, where players can download the latest files containing the data relating to the specific field of play that they intend to use. The files are available as Microsoft Excel spreadsheets, and the game starts at the urban level, with the players filling in the *"URBAN GAME"* file, which contains:

- The *general data sheet*, which contains conversion factors, national reference costs, data on the population and land area of Italy, national average consumption values, and data on average monthly expenditure by household type for the consumption categories *clothing, mobility, food, energy: heating, energy: electricity, energy: DHW and cooking, leisure and communication, education, health and services*. The data for these consumption categories are based on ISTAT calculations relating to the average monthly expenditure of Italian households living in the northwestern area of the country. Average national per capita consumption values are expressed as the amount of land occupied in order to produce the goods in question and tons of CO2 emitted to transform the goods and provide the required services.

- The *municipality data sheet*, which contains all the data relating to the municipality selected as the field of play. In addition to the data on the number of residents and overall land area, this breaks down the composition of the population by age group and household type, as well as providing data on any renewable energy sources used in facilities already installed in the area. The average monthly expenditure figures as per the ISTAT, found in the previous spreadsheet, are here applied to the entire municipality and contribute to the definition of the budget for the game.

- The *census section data sheet*, which is used on a provisional basis to carry out certain simulation operations concerning the residential building stock of the whole municipality, based on the data obtained and calculated from a limited number of census sections.

- The *average sheet*, with the average impact values for the settled community, applying national average values for habits and behaviors and energy consumption for heating the residential buildings in the field of play, as well as the use of electricity, domestic hot water and energy for cooking: all information based on the distribution of household types according to ISTAT data. Through graphs, this sheet displays the values of land area occupied and CO2 emitted by the specific community in question; an example below shows the average sheet from the last round played before the end of the research project (Figure 2).

Figure 2. Graphical representation of the land area occupied, and the CO_2 emitted by a community adopting the average behaviors game structure and relationship between the different game files. Source: The Imitation Game project, 2020

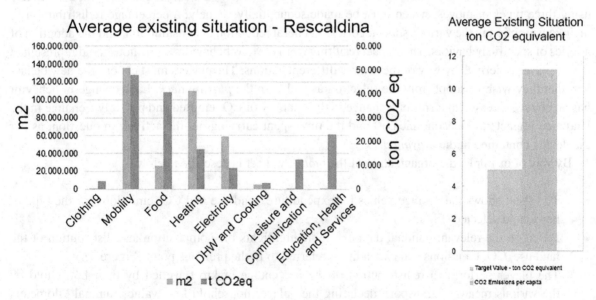

- The *behaviors sheet*, which shows the variations resulting from the changes in the behaviors of the various players across the various impact categories, expressed in units of land area, tons of CO_2 emitted, money spent and time spent; the total of all the players in a given playing group defines the new overall global behavior. The data contained in this sheet comes from the Player files filled in by each player in the playing group.

- The *design sheet*, with the variations resulting from the technical solutions adopted by the entire playing group. The data contained in this sheet comes from the Design file filled in by the playing group.
- The *results sheet*, which contains the original impact values compared with the final ones, following the individual players' variations in behavior and the decisions made as a playing group.

In summary, in the "*URBAN GAME*" file, players will find all the information they need to play the game, as well as the means to create a graphical representation of their results.

Each player then proceeds to fill in the "*PLAYER*" file and, by defining certain behaviors, alters the habits of a certain section of the population. The "*PLAYER*" file consists of:

- The DATA sheet, which contains some general values taken from the "*PLAYER*" file, in which players must insert their name and the numerical composition of their household, i.e., the family/household that they will represent for the purposes of the game.
- A series of 8 sheets, divided up by category, namely: *clothing, mobility, food, energy: heating, energy: electricity, energy: DHW and cooking, leisure and communication, education, health and services*.
- The *results sheet*, with a summarized overview of the player's behaviors to be entered into the respective section of the behaviors sheet within the "*URBAN GAME*" file.

In each thematic sheet pertaining to a specific impact category, the player plays out their behaviors using three types of moves, which must be made sequentially, namely: a percentage redistribution of their consumption in the various subcategories, a general reduction in consumption, and the adoption of a series of specific behaviors. The impact resulting from the new behaviors of the household represented by the player is defined by way of these three different actions. The players must choose the new behaviors that they wish to adopt from the selection available in the *playing deck*. Each change in behavior has an effect expressed in terms of a change in the quantity of CO_2 emitted and possibly a change in the land area impacted, the economic cost and the time spent carrying out the activity in question, as per the details contained in the *playing deck*.

By way of example, the organization of the *mobility* sheet is described below:

- The sheet shows the average values for expenditure, land use and CO_2 emissions for the type of household selected (Figure 3).
- Based on the relevant national data, the table highlights the composition and distribution of the land use, CO_2 emissions and expenditure referred to in the previous point (Figure 4).
- The player performs a redistribution of the percentage of km travelled by their household by the various means of transport, declaring the "player household km" values (annual kilometers travelled by the household). In this case, the total number of kilometers travelled by the average citizen remains unchanged, but the means of transport used varies.
- The player can subsequently reduce their total impact of their travel (changing distance and/or means of transport), thus committing to adopt this behavior for the duration of the game. The player can also declare if they believe that the replacement rate of their vehicle is higher than the

average time stated, thus resulting in a reduction in the number of new vehicles bought on average every year by the segment of the population represented (Figure 5).

- The final operation has to do with the behaviors - as contained within the *playing deck* - that the player intends to adopt. This part of the spreadsheet lists the cards played and shows, for each variation, the values that can be deduced from each card chosen. (Figure 6)
- Finally, a summarized overview shows the average values of expenditure, land use and CO_2 emitted pertaining to the type of household declared and following the redistributions, reductions and behaviors played (Figure 7).

Figure 3. View of the table showing the average values for expenditure, land use and CO_2 emissions for the type of household selected. Source: The Imitation Game project, 2020

MOBILITY		
Type of family	**4**	**Persons**
	per person	**per family**
Land use per person [mq]	**8.291**	**33.164**
CO_2 Emitted [t CO_2]	**3,43**	**13,72**
Monthly Expenditure [€]		**531**

Figure 4. Tabular view of the data that contribute to the formulation of the previous table. Source: The Imitation Game project, 2020

	% kilometres	km	occupied m2	tCO2	€	kWh
Private Mobility - Cars [KM]	72,73%	28.336	29.753	3,77	3400 €	
Private Mobility - Motorcycles [KM]	6,32%	2.464	1.423	0,23	246 €	
Long Distance Mobility Airplanes [KM]	3,09%	1.204	1.264	0,72	361 €	
Pullmann [KM]	1,75%	680	371	0,05	136 €	
Subway and Tram [KM]	1,17%	456		0,02	91 €	91
Local and Regional Trains [KM]	11,15%	4.344		0,28	869 €	869
Long Distance Mobility Trains [KM]	2,05%	800		0,1	160 €	240
eMobility - Cars [KM]	0,23%	88		0,00	4 €	11
eMobility - Motorcycles [KM]	0,51%	200		0,00	6 €	10
eMobility - eBike and eMicro Vehicles [KM]	0,00%	0		0,00		-
Bicycle [KM]	1,00%	390				
TOTAL		**38.962**	**32.811**	**5,17**	**5.274 €**	**1.221**
Purchase, Management and Maintenance				8,55	1.101 €	

In each thematic sheet pertaining to a specific impact category, the player plays out their behaviors using three types of moves, which must be made sequentially, namely: a percentage redistribution of their consumption in the various subcategories, a general reduction in consumption, and the adoption of a series of specific behaviors. The impact resulting from the new behaviors of the household represented by the player is defined by way of these three different actions. The players must choose the new behaviors that they

Figure 5. Tabular view of the data related to the reduction of impact travels depending by the behaviors shift during the game. Source: The Imitation Game project, 2020

Mobility Remodeling	Modified % of km	km	m2	tCO2	€	kWh	km per Family-player
Private Mobility - Cars [KM]	35,71%	13.915	14.611	1,85	1.670 €		20.000
Private Mobility - Motorcycles [KM]	0,00%	0	0	0,00	- €		0
Long Distance Mobility Airplanes [KM]	17,86%	6.957	7.305	4,13	2.087 €		10.000
Pullmann [KM]	0,00%	0	0	0,00	- €		0
Subway and Tram [KM]	1,07%	417		0,02	83 €	83	600
Local and Regional Trains [KM]	34,29%	13.358		0,87	2.672 €	2.672	19.200
Long Distance Mobility Trains [KM]	5,36%	2.087		0,25	417 €	626	3.000
eMobility - Cars [KM]	0,00%	0		0,00	- €	-	0
eMobility - Motorcycles [KM]	0,00%	0		0,00	- €	-	0
eMobility - eBike and eMicro Vehicles [KM]	0,00%	0		0,00	- €	-	0
Bicycle [KM]	5,71%	2.226					3.200
TOTAL	100,00%	38.962	21.916	7,12	6.930 €	3.381	56.000
Purchase, Management and Maintenance				8,55	1.101 €		

Reduction	Quantity	Variation of kWh/year	Variation of m2	Variation of tCO2			Variation of €
Car purchase time variation (standard = 10 years)	20%			-1,140			-334 €
General reduction of conventional mobility (excluding cycling and walking)	-5%	-169	-1.096	-0,356			-346,48 €

Figure 6. Views of part of the play deck, related to mobility, showing the values that can be deduced from each card chosen. Source: The Imitation Game project, 2020

ACTIONS Behavior
Speed reduction and smooth driving - M
Convert a vehicle to gas - L

Variation of kWh/year	Variation of m2	Variation of tCO2	Declared usage factor
	- 1644	-0,208	49%
	-	-0,680	49%

Variation of €	Variation of Spent time
-156 €	64,0
-536,00 €	0,0

Figure 7. An overview showing the average values of expenditure, land use and CO2 emitted in relation to the type of household declared and the shifting of player's behaviors. Source: The Imitation Game project, 2020

SUMMARY OF FINAL IMPACTS		
Family	**4**	**Persons**
Land	**20.013**	m2
CO2	**5,19**	t
Money	**7.011**	€
Time	**31,4**	Hours

After having filled out their personal "*PLAYER*" files, the players then insert the values relating to their behaviors in the "*URBAN GAME*" file to obtain the overall impact of the segment of the population represented.

The final step involves the playing group as a whole filling in the "*DESIGN*" file.

The "*DESIGN*" file consists of 10 sheets, the first of which contains the general data concerning the field of play and the consumption values for each of the impact sections, as influenced by the reductions resulting from the behaviors implemented by the players; it also shows the quantities of Time and Money resources available to the playing group following the behaviors chosen by each of them individually, as well as a summary illustrating the behavior of the *average inhabitant*, which takes into consideration the different percentages of influence held by each player as compared with both the whole population and their specific household composition.

The structure of the "*DESIGN*" file is largely similar to that of the "PLAYER" file: it lists the urban design actions (i.e., those relating to the entire field of play) and highlights all the changes brought about in terms of land use, CO_2 emissions, and time and money spent.

The "*DESIGN*" file ends with the results sheet, which summarizes the results for the various impact categories following the implementation of the design actions; this data must be copied into the project sheet of the "*URBAN GAME*" file so that the variations achieved over the course of the game can be displayed in the results sheet of the same file.

The calculations are performed automatically and provide a comparison with the sustainability targets defined (Figure 8):

- at the national level - with a National Sustainability Index ≤ 1.
- at the global level - with CO2 emissions ≤ 5 tons/person.

These indices allow for a comparison between various rounds of the game and the definition of the winning group, namely whichever has proven to be capable of coming as close as possible to reaching sustainability on a local scale by identifying and adopting strategies, technical solutions and shared behaviors that minimize the impact of their lifestyles on the area, using only the available resources.

Below is a graphical representation of the results obtained when playing an example round of the game, using the municipality of Rescaldina as the field of play (Figure 9).

As clearly shown by the calculation files, at this stage of the research project, given that this was a game played by architecture students, priority was given to the analysis of consumption related to buildings and to energy consumption for heating spaces, electricity consumption and transportation. With reference to energy consumption for heating, historical thresholds were established for 1945, 1975, 1990 and 2015, for which the transmittance values of the building shell elements were identified (Dall'ò et Al., 2008); these values were subsequently processed with a piece of software known as ProCasaClima to verify the effectiveness of the evaluations obtained through the dedicated calculation file (Urban Heating) for estimating urban energy consumption.

Following an initial assessment in terms of the energy required to heat each square meter per individual building for a year, we moved on to a more analytical approach to the assessment, capable of determining figures for heat loss through the transmittance values of the building shell elements, each categorized by historical threshold and, consequently, attributed to the actual geometrical dimensions of said elements.

Figure 8. Representation of the impacts in the different sectors. Source: The Imitation Game project, 2020

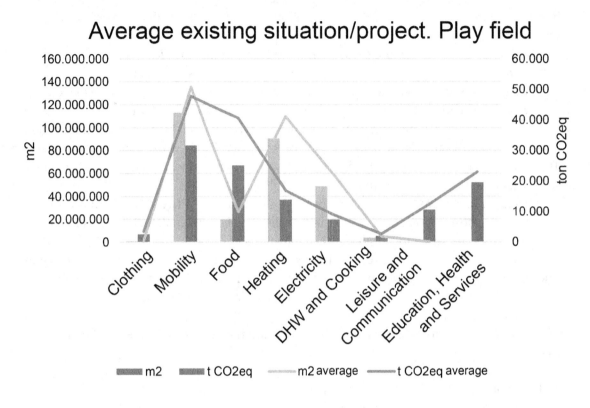

Figure 9. Graphical representation of CO$_2$ emissions and impacts in terms of land area used over the different phases of the project (initial, intermediate, final). Source: The Imitation Game project, 2020

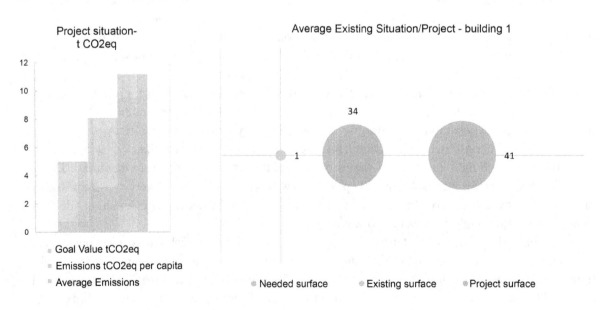

Alongside the evaluation carried out with the ProCasaClima software, a selection of different primary shell stratigraphies were simulated (roof, ground floor, perimeter walls, windows) following the shifts in construction techniques characteristic of different historical periods or coinciding with the introduction of energy-related regulations that resulted in their performance differing.

In addition to the transmittance values, other parameters were also given, relating to the incidence of thermal bridges, air exchange and system efficiency. It should be noted that the hourly values for air exchange are higher than established by regulations due to the fact that the construction methods of the time allowed for the occurrence of ventilation-related losses that did not depend on the user.

The data input procedure takes into account every single building in the local area, inserting their actual geometrical dimensions obtained semi-automatically, in other words by manually inserting only the information on the number of residential floors in the building and its classification in the framework of the historical thresholds, as defined previously (Figure 10).

Figure 10. Average transmittance values for building shell elements in w/m2k divided by historical threshold. Source: The Imitation Game project, 2020

Average Values	Before 1945	1945 - 1975	1975 - 1990	1990 - 2015	After 2015
Roof slab	0,92	0,92	0,48	0,32	0,24
Ground slab	1,00	1,00	1,63	0,62	0,29
Walls	1,64	1,07	0,48	0,32	0,28
Windows	4,90	4,90	2,80	1,80	1,40
Thermal bridges	15%	10%	20%	15%	15%
Exchanges/Hour	1,2	1,0	0,8	0,7	0,5
Plant efficiency	0,6	0,6	0,7	0,8	0,9

These values, each of which refers to their historical threshold, were applied to the geometrical characteristics of each individual building in order to provide an analytical breakdown of their heating requirements. Using GIS information deducible from the shapefiles (at the "building footprint" level) referring to the field of play (municipality or census section) available from Geoportale Lombardia, it is possible to determine the overall heat loss figures for the buildings present in the area.

Once the procedure had been established, the operation itself proved to be relatively simple, albeit rather lengthy due to the time required to retrieve the data. Three census sections were identified as representative of the 'field of play' which, in the case of the municipality of Rescaldina, were: section 1 (characterized by rows of terraced buildings located in the historical center), section 19 (notably featuring recently built multi-story residential blocks) and section 28 (mainly consisting of detached houses).

The transposition of the GIS data (values for ground footprint and perimeter for merged buildings), together with the number of floors and the relevant historical threshold (both deduced through visual survey), made it possible to determine the overall heat loss values for heating with regard to each of the individual sections examined automatically by simply inserting the values of area, perimeter and number of floors into the Urban Heating file (data available from the GIS shapefiles). By using the three sample sections as a reference, it was possible to estimate the total value for the heat loss of all the buildings in the municipality (Figure 11; Figure 12).

Figure 11. Locations of the three census sections analyzed and focus shot of CS 1 (historical center), highlighting the perimeters of the buildings and the GIS identification codes corresponding to the "building footprint" level. Source of data: Geoportale Regione Lombardia, 2020

Definition of Possible Changes in Behaviors and Technical Actions to be Undertaken

All of the behavioral modification actions and technical solutions that can be used in the game are contained in a database of cards describing the specific ways in which each action can be applied, as well as the costs and results that each action entails. The maps allow the players to estimate the environmental performance (land consumption to support the behaviours and CO_2 emitted) of these actions, all of which fall into one of 6 impact categories: *clothing, mobility, food, energy: heating, energy: electricity, energy: DHW and cooking, leisure and communication, education, health and services.* Following the evolution of the research project, we focused more on the categories of clothing (*clothes*) (Fig. 13),

Figure 12. Summary of the heat loss by transmission in reference to CS 28 - Most of the data is from the GIS Database, whilst the portions highlighted in yellow show the additional data collected via visual survey. Source: The Imitation Game project, 2020

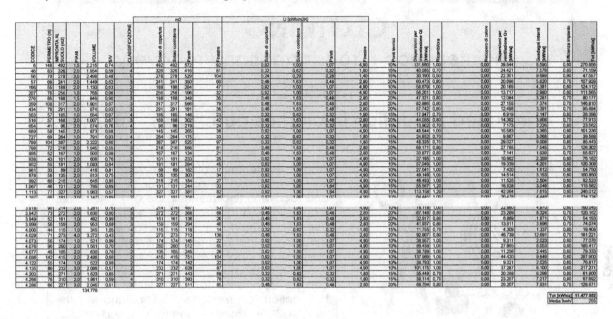

food, energy (electricity, DHW and cooking). The "*CARDS*" describe the environmental effects of the technical action or behaviour in question, but also the cost of implementing it in terms of Time and Money spent. The possibility of at least partially self-implementing many of the measures, or delegating their implementation with appropriate financial compensation, was considered. Obviously, the choice of whether these actions are implemented by the individual or by someone else substantially modifies both the time and Money commitments required.

Many of the behaviours related to the individual impact categories were divided into three value scales of applicability: L (*Light*), M (*Medium*) and S (*Strong*), thus offering three possible levels of commitment to each issue by the player (Figure 14).

In some cases, when drawing up certain *CARDS* - such as, for example, those shown here - it was not possible to define the economic variations brought about by their applicability in a linear way with respect to the ISTAT data, the information found in the literature, or even the various household compositions, and they were instead evaluated by establishing an estimate of the fixed costs and one of the variable costs; the latter were informed by an effective, albeit hypothetical, applicability of the behaviour implemented.

Different *CARDS* were drawn up for the same category, each referring to different, specific actions that can have a cumulative effect (Figure 15).

Finally, some *CARDS* were drawn up indicating the path towards a possible reduction in impact by means of upgrading commonly used devices with better-performing products. In this case, the card type is U (Unique) and its playability is contingent on both the presence (or absence) of such devices and a financial cost which is, however, deemed to be "amortizable" over a fixed period of time, corresponding to the type of device (e.g. washing machine = 10 years, refrigerator = 15 years) (Figure 16).

Figure 13. Example of a "model" card with an indication of the relative values of time, money, land area and CO$_2$. Source: The Imitation Game project, 2020

CLOTHING
maintenance / transformation / recovery
mode L
induced reduction in clothes purchase: -10%

Proper maintenance of clothes (washing, drying, ironing, etc.) as well as their repair, adjustment and recovery, finalizes their use at longer times than usual and therefore can lead to a general decrease in the purchase of the same.

The size of these operations is subject to the operational capabilities of the users and the time they can dedicate to it. These activities and time can be delegated to others without reducing the action of reduction on purchases, the related CO2e emissions and the needed land.

executive methods / effects	autonomous	delegated
cost (€.) - 1 p.	-53	-28
Cost (€.) - 2 p.	-92	-67
Cost (€.) - 3 p.	-119	-69
Cost (€.) - 4 p.	-148	-98
Cost (€.) - 5 p.	-169	-94
Cost (€.) - 6 p. e +	-195	-120
Time (h/y) – 1 p.	+50	+10
Time (h/y) – 2 p.	+50	+10
Time (h/y) – 3 p.	+55	+11
Time (h/y) – 4 p.	+55	+11
Time (h/y) – 5 p.	+60	+12
Time (h/y) – 6 p. e +	+60	+12
CO2e (t) p.p.	-0,018	-0,018
Used land (m2.) p.p.	-6	-6

Figure 14. Example of changing the level of commitment required to play the "care/maintenance of clothing" card. Source: The Imitation Game project, 2020

CLOTHING	CLOTHING
maintenance / transformation / recovery	maintenance / transformation / recovery
mode **M**	mode **S**
induced reduction in clothes purchase: -15%	induced reduction in clothes purchase: -20%

Figure 15. Examples of cards that can be played in the same category. Source: The Imitation Game project, 2020

CLOTHING	CLOTHING
maintenance / transformation / recovery	maintenance / transformation / recovery
mode **L**	mode **L**
induced reduction in clothes purchase: -10%	induced reduction in clothes purchase: -10%

The purchase of classic and / or sports clothes, not linked to the trend of the moment and of controlled quality, despite having an economic burden on the purchase, have greater durability and lead to a reduction in expenditure which is therefore considered overall similar to that normally carried out. The reduced access to purchases involves the relative reduction of CO2eq emissions, as well as the necessary land attributed to the production of products and a saving of time dedicated to this activity.
Activities and time that cannot be delegated.

The purchase of classic and / or sports clothes, not linked to the trend of the moment and of controlled quality, despite having an economic burden on the purchase, have greater durability and lead to a reduction in expenditure which is therefore considered overall similar to that normally carried out. The reduced access to purchases involves the relative reduction of CO2eq emissions, as well as the necessary land attributed to the production of products and a saving of time dedicated to this activity.
Activities and time that cannot be delegated.

Once the *CARDS* had been formalized as described above, we went back over a round that had already been played (with manual calculations) in order to check the usability of the cards and test out the impact reductions linked to both the behavioral actions chosen (a reduction brought about by the individual player) and the possible design actions identified on an urban scale.

The test was carried out at the Community level. This operation was carried out through the use of the "Urban Game" file, in which the cards tested included "Replacement of internal combustion vehicles with electric vehicles", "Cycle lanes", "Bicycle parking station", "Bicycle repair workshop" and "Building insulation", "Installation of PV panels", etc.

FUTURE RESEARCH DIRECTIONS

As users, the goal is to achieve and maintain conditions of adequate environmental comfort (thermal conditions, lighting, health and wellbeing, but also clothing and nutrition) and social qualification (demonstration of a certain social status through the possession of goods and access to services that are consider adequate). Very broadly speaking, it could potentially indicate the former as elements of a physical nature and the latter as elements of a symbolic nature (Los, 2013), which must be satisfied "without compromising the ability of future generations to meet their own needs" (Brundtland, 1987; p. 16).

Figure 16. Example of a 'U' card which can be played as a single choice within a specific category, and which cannot be adjusted according to different value options. Source: The Imitation Game project, 2020

ELECTRICITY
replacement of appliances
WASHING MACHINE
from A class to A+++ class
mode U
induced reduction in EE: -3.40%

The replacement of household appliances in use with others, which are equal in performance and use characteristics, but of class A +++ leads to energy savings, especially if the household appliances in possession are older than 5 years.
Attention to this aspect in the use of low-performance technologies and therefore their correction can lead to both economic savings and a decrease in CO2e emissions and neede land, and this without increasing time.

effects	saving/burden
cost (€.) - 1 p.	+11
cost (€.) - 2 p.	+2
cost (€.) - 3 p.	-6
cost (€.) - 4 p.	-12
cost (€.) - 5 p.	-19
cost (€.) - 6 p. e +	-25
CO2e (t) p.p.	-0,022
Used land (m2) p.p.	-144

On the other hand, the designers tend to provide a specific response to problems involving changes to an environment (on scales from a local area to a specific building), at times favoring the needs of a physical nature, at others those of a symbolic nature, generally without having a clear insight into the effects that the choices have on the environment and without being required to illustrate these effects to the clients.

The result is often that the building transformations are extremely efficient in terms of an individual problem (e.g. the conservation of thermal energy) without worrying about the amount of energy consumed to create the set of elements, systems and components needed to achieve the energy-saving objective (the building LCA); in much the same way, often also the urban organization solutions are relatively efficient as regards the capture and production of energy (e.g. detached houses) which, however, have a significant impact in terms of mobility, land consumption, etc.

These analyses provide numerical results of the amount of energy needed for a given purpose or the carbon dioxide emissions avoided after making a set of choices. However, these numerical values are information that is often only understandable to industry professionals and difficult to translate into visible quantities, making it hard from them to provide any helpful indication of proximity to a general global sustainability target.

Attempts to shift from spot analyses of an effect to analyses that include multiple sets of parameters are by no means new, but such attempts are generally oriented towards providing assessments of integrated comfort for single individuals or environments, whilst at the extreme other end of the scale, other methods have been developed to assess such values for whole nations and populations (GDP, Happy Planet Index, etc.). The lack of an intermediate scale for assessing impacts - especially one in relation to environmental effects which encourages shared, informed design choices - has led the research team to work towards creating one; indeed, this issue represents an interesting field of work for the near future and has links with recent work on the subject (Clementi, 2019).

CONCLUSION

Over these first two years, the research project has revealed a great deal of growing potential. Development at this early stage largely focused on outlining the general structure of the game, seeking to simplify it more and more as the level of complexity increased.

We noted that moving the solution to a problem from a REMOTE level to a LOCAL one increases the degree of Resilience of the system, even though we have not yet found a way to exemplify and incorporate these considerations into the game. In addition, we have not differentiated the effects of Money spent locally (Local Money) as against expenditure elsewhere, nor have we clearly defined the extent of the impact of goods and services being produced locally, which would bring about a further improvement in terms of closing the cycles involved.

As regards the initial objectives of the research project, we did not deal with the calculation of the level of Intangible Assets available, nor their variation within the context of the game. We strongly believe that an increase in the level of Intangible Assets of a settled society represents an initial indicator for estimating said society's level of Potential Happiness (Hy), but this part has yet to be fully developed.

Bonuses for each of the impact categories were also established. These Bonuses can be obtained by engaging in independent training, informational and practice activities:

- Possible training activities include: reading texts, attending seminars or online training courses on local sustainability issues, participating in training courses for manual skills (weaving, carpentry, cooking, sewing, etc.) or artistic skills (singing, music, dance, painting, etc.).
- Possible informational activities include: organizing social activities, promoting and disseminating knowledge online, writing blogs, promoting manual or artistic activities, etc.

- Possible practice activities include: gentle exercise (qigong, yoga, tai chi, Nordic walking, etc.), meditation, bike fixing, enjoying the arts (painting, sculpture, music, theatre), hobbies (manual activities, etc.), etc.

The value of the achievable Bonuses cannot exceed the threshold value of 6% for each individual impact category, but this feature has not yet been fully implemented in the calculation spreadsheets.

Aside from criticality and possible improvements of the dynamics of playability and, above all, of a modelling as likely as possible of the impacts and their measurement, The Imitation Game remains mainly a serious game developed in the academic field for didactic-demonstrative purposes for students. Even if its ability to affect the lifestyles of active players, who therefore decide to accept the challenge of the game by changing their personal habits in favor of the common good for the community, has proved to be a powerful lever, so much so that it is worth trying to scale it also in other audiences of players, such as, for example, public administrators.

ACKNOWLEDGMENT

This research project, The Imitation Game, was carried out over the period spanning March 2019 - March 2021, most of which was affected by the spread of COVID-19 and the consequent restrictions and limitations. As such, the activities initially proposed in the research agenda, as well as the dissemination activities, were significantly disrupted due to it being impossible to travel, meet up and work alongside the students for the practical activities involved. The uncertainty surrounding the development of the pandemic, which long led to hopes of a possible return to normality and in-person teaching and research, made it even more difficult to carry out the activities, as they were moved and postponed multiple times before ultimately being modified and adjusted to suit an online platform.

This research was supported by the Dipartimento DAStU of the Politecnico di Milano through the internal competitive call "ex-FARB".

REFERENCES

AA.VV. (2018). *Das 2000-Watt-Areal*. Retrieved July 26, 2022, from http://www.2000watt.swiss

Abt, C. C. (1987). *Serious games*. University Press of America.

Berners-Lee, M. (2020). *How bad are bananas? The carbon footprint of everything*. Profile Books.

Brundtland, G. H. (1987). Our common future—Call for action. *Environmental Conservation*, *14*(4), 291–294. doi:10.1017/S0376892900016805

Clementi, M. (2019). *Progettare l'autosostenibilità locale, strumenti e metodi di supporto alla progettazione ambientale integrata* [Designing Local Self-Sustainability, tools and Methods to Support integrated Environmental Design]. Edizioni Ambiente.

Dall'ò, G., Silvestrini, G., & Gamberale, M. (2010). *Manuale della certificazione energetica degli edifici* [Building Energy Certification Manual]. Edizioni Ambiente.

Djaouti, D., Alvarez, J., & Jessel, J. P. (2011). Classifying serious games: the G/P/S model. In P. Felicia (Ed.), *Handbook of research on improving learning and motivation through educational games: Multidisciplinary approaches* (pp. 118–136). IGI Global. doi:10.4018/978-1-60960-495-0.ch006

Los, S. (2013). *Geografia dell'architettura. Progettazione Bioclimatica e disegno architettonico* [Geography of Architecture. Bioclimatic Design and Architechtural Design]. Il Poligrafo.

Morganti, M., Vigoni, V., Currà, E., & Rogora, A. (2020). Energy Retrofit Cost-Optimal Design Solutions in Social Housing: The Case of Three Tower Buildings of the 1980s. In A. Sayigh (Ed.), *Green Buildings and Renewable Energy* (pp. 221–235). Springer. doi:10.1007/978-3-030-30841-4_16

Patrício, R., Moreira, A. C., & Zurlo, F. (2018). Gamification approaches to the early stage of innovation. *Creativity and Innovation Management*, 27(4), 499–511. doi:10.1111/caim.12284

Patrício, R., Moreira, A. C., & Zurlo, F. (2021). Enhancing design thinking approaches to innovation through gamification. *European Journal of Innovation Management*, 24(5), 1569–1594. doi:10.1108/EJIM-06-2020-0239

Patti, I. (2018). *Serious Game Design: storia e teorie sull'esperienza ludica applicata* [Serious Game Design: History and Theories on the Applied Play Experience]. Franco Angeli.

Petruzzi, V. (2015). *Il potere della Gamification* [The Power of Gamification]. Franco Angeli.

Ronchi, S., Arcidiacono, A., & Pogliani, L. (2021). The New Urban Plan of Rescaldina Municipality. An Experience for Improving Ecosystem Services Provision. In A. Arcidiacono & S. Ronchi (Eds.), *Ecosystem Services and Green Infrastructure* (pp. 141–152). Springer. doi:10.1007/978-3-030-54345-7_11

UNESCO. (2010). *Tomorrow Today*. Tudor Rose.

Viola, F. (2011). *Gamification - I Videogiochi nella Vita Quotidiana* [Gamificatio – Video Games in Everyday Life]. Arduino Viola.

Chapter 2
The Behaviour Change Wheel to Support the Design of Gameful Interventions:
An Exploratory Study

Kristy de Salas
University of Tasmania, Australia

Lindsay Wells
University of Tasmania, Australia

Michael Quinn
University of Tasmania, Australia

Jenn Scott
University of Tasmania, Australia

Ian Lewis
University of Tasmania, Australia

ABSTRACT

Gameful interventions (including serious games and gamification) are a popular tool to motivate and engage users towards improved behavioural outcomes. However, such interventions often fail due to poor design, specifically due to a fundamental lack of understanding of the audience and the required behavioural outcomes, and the consequent uninformed selection of potentially inappropriate game elements by designers. This chapter describes exploring the behaviour change wheel (BCW) method as a tool to augment gameful intervention design and selecting appropriate game elements to action gameful intervention strategies. This exploration is undertaken in the context of developing a gameful intervention targeted toward energy conservation. Within this context, the BCW is shown to assist the designers in understanding the audience and the intervention's behavioural outcomes, which has led to a theoretically informed and rigorous selection of game elements that better support the achievement of the targeted behavioural outcomes.

DOI: 10.4018/978-1-6684-4291-3.ch002

INTRODUCTION

Gameful interventions (including gamification and serious games) employ game elements such as challenges, narrative, goals, and badges to reward and incentivise players and engage them in a playful way to prolong a desired target behaviour. As such, gameful interventions are a form of persuasive technology that can serve as a powerful tool for encouraging positive behaviour in fields as diverse as defence, health, education, and corporate training (Larson, 2020; Sipiyaruk et al., 2019; Rapp 2019). The market for gameful interventions is predicted to register an impressive growth of 32% to reach $40 billion by 2024 (TechSci Research, 2019; Xi & Hamari 2019). Yet, despite the proliferation of games in many fields, the landscape of gameful technologies designed to persuade users to change is "riddled with the carcasses of failed projects" (Fogg, 2009). Research on gamification and serious games still faces a variety of empirical and theoretical challenges to understand this contradiction (Rapp, 2019; de Salas et al., 2022).

Gameful interventions have been reported to improve student learning and attitudes (Bodnar et al., 2016; Chapman & Rich, 2018) and the productivity of disengaged employees (Oprescu et al., 2014), increase user compliance with health interventions (Sardi et al., 2017), and support the uptake of pro-environmental behaviours (Medema, et al., 2019). However, Rapp (2019), in leading a special issue on gamification research, found that most studies are often not evaluated empirically. De Salas et al.'s 2022 systematic review of gameful interventions targeted toward environmental outcomes confirms this finding, indicating that in their review 17% of studies reporting on gameful interventions included no evaluation, while the remaining interventions were evaluated for a vast range of outcomes, and so contributed to a lack of comparability across studies. Rapp (2019) further noted that those scarce empirical studies typically focus narrowly on evaluating and understanding individuals' short-term interactions with the system, ignoring more difficult-to-measure outcomes.

It stands to reason then that these reportedly 'successful' implementations must be more rigorously explored with regards to their design, their evaluation, and their impact, and that gameful studies would benefit from wider use of theories to account for the complexity of human behaviour (Rapp, 2019; Derksen, et al., 2020; de Salas et al., 2022). Indeed, Gartner Research asserts that 80% of gameful interventions fail in achieving their outcomes primarily due to poor design (Burke, 2014; Rapp 2019). Recent reviews of gameful interventions highlight that specific to this poor design is the *lack of behavioural insight built into the design* of these interventions, as many gameful interventions did not undertake to understand existing behaviour prior to the game's design or test the likelihood of a game-changing an identified behaviour (Rapp, 2019; Derksen, 2020; de Salas et al., 2022). Indeed Purwandari.et al., (2019) and Ferreira-Brito, et al., (2019) note that the justification for many of the gameful interventions included in their systematic reviews were merely "because others had used games in the past", and that they were perceived as cost-effective and readily available, although no exploration or substantiation of these claims was made.

Furthermore, existing gameful systematic reviews show *no evidence that the selection of game elements was mapped to evidence-based behaviour change techniques* to ensure that these would serve as 'active ingredients' in the intervention and achieve the targeted behaviour (Manzano-León, et al., 2021; Ávila-Pesántez, et al., 2017; Ferreira-Brito, et al., 2019; Lopes, et al., 2019; de Salas et al., 2022). As such, designers persist in selecting those elements most obvious and easy to implement, such as points, badges, and leaderboards (Rapp, 2019; Valencia, 2019; Ferreira-Brito, et al., 2019), rather than those that have been mapped as likely to bring about a specific and targeted behavioural outcome (de Salas et al., 2022).

This uninformed selection and application of game elements means that the target audiences of these gamified solutions not only do not benefit from the opportunities afforded by playfulness, but also that considerable resources are wasted on poorly designed systems (Purwandari.et al, 2019; Lopes, et al., 2019). In the worst case, these interventions can cause harm to the target audience (Rapp, 2019; Ferreira-Brito, et al., 2019, de Salas et al., 2022).

It can be concluded therefore that to bring about targeted behaviour change, gameful interventions could benefit from insight in the field of behavioural psychology which entails understanding people and what affects their behaviour (Purwandari et al., 2019; de Salas et al., 2022). Gameful intervention design must include strategies to *better understand the audience and targeted behaviours* that the intervention seeks to influence, as well as a more rigorous method to *guide the selection of game elements* that are likely to bring about this change (Lopes, et al., 2019; de Salas et al., 2022). In the following sections of this chapter, the authors explore a tool that has the potential to support these twin goals. Through its implementation in a case example of gameful design, they explore and report on its potential contribution to gameful intervention design methodology.

BACKGROUND: PRIOR WORK TO IMPROVE UNDERSTANDING OF USERS AND GAME ELEMENT SELECTION

Work towards the twin goals of *better understanding the audience and targeted behaviours* that the intervention seeks to influence, and more rigorous method to *guide the selection of game elements* that are likely to bring about change outcomes, has been underway since 2014. Mohr, et al., (2014) proposed the Behavioural Intervention Technology Model (BiTM) as a mechanism to guide the development of Behavioural Intervention Technologies (BITs), such as gameful interventions. This model suggests that technical intervention designers need to describe:

- the treatment goal or intervention aims;
- the methods used to attain clinical and use aims;
- the corresponding technical elements; and
- the frequency of delivery of each of these elements.

As a general premise, this model provides a set of points to guide developers in *what* to explore and indeed supports the work of others who agree with the need to identify intervention aims and technical elements. However, this model is limited in its description of *how* gameful intervention designers practically work through each of these stages and develop a deep understanding of the target behaviours, thus limiting its direct practical applicability the process of gameful intervention design.

Similarly, in 2016, the Behavioural Economics Team of the Australian Government (Ames & Hiscox 2016) suggested nine guiding questions related to the discovery and diagnosis phases that were required when developing behavioural interventions. Three questions particularly relevant to the design of gameful interventions are:

- what is the outcome of interest? – Any behavioral project should be organized around understanding and intervening in the behaviors driving specific, identified outcomes;
- what behavior is leading to the outcome? – Any intervention should investigate the most important behavioral challenges that may be driving the target behavior, and which are likely the most important barrier to good choices in this context; and
- what interventions might influence the target behavior? – Any behavioral intervention should understand the option or behavioral dimensions to impact the target behavior.

However, like the issues inherent in Mohr, et al., (2014)'s BiTM, no practical guidance towards developing this behavioural insight is forthcoming. Thus, designers of gameful interventions remain in the dark about how best to practically develop this required insight and guide their selection of game elements to bring about change.

Indeed, de Salas et al., (2022)'s recent review of environmentally-focused gameful interventions continues to identify that "our review has identified a lack of comprehensive articulation of the behavioural design elements to guide the intervention, including an absence of information regarding the process undertaken to gain an understanding the target behaviour and audience; a lack of justification for the selection of intervention functions; and a failure to substantiate the use of a game as an appropriate delivery mode for the intervention" (p25).

There remains an apparent need to provide a series of steps to practically guide designers towards developing insight about the audience, behaviour, and active ingredients of a target intervention as "academic research on gamification has been slow to improve the techniques and methods through which gamified systems and services are designed" (Rapp, 2019).

Given that the goals of gamification and serious games are to influence behaviours, the authorship team posits that behavioural psychology might provide a source of insight to support gameful intervention design. As is the nature of exploratory research, the authors seek to explore the potential opportunities to be offered by behavioural intervention theory within gameful intervention design. They seek not to provide conclusive results, but to develop a basis for future research connecting these fields of research together towards the development of a best-practice gameful intervention design methodology, and to improve the achievement of intervention outcomes.

To this end, this chapter introduces the Behaviour Change Wheel (BCW) (Michie, et al., 2011) and explores its potential to support gameful intervention design. The BCW is a method that is well-established in behavioural intervention literature, and provides a step-by-step guide for intervention designers, taking them through the first challenge of developing an understanding of the audience and the behaviour being targeted, as well as the second challenge of selection of the 'active ingredients' required to bring about that outcome.

THE BEHAVIOUR CHANGE WHEEL

The BCW is the result of a synthesis of 19 existing frameworks of behaviour change identified in a systematic literature review (Michie et al., 2011; Michie, et al., 2013) and describes a methodology by which intervention designers can systematically examine the behaviours that an intervention aims to target. The aim of the methodology is to improve the design and implementation of evidence-based practice and was born from the need to consolidate the plethora of individual frameworks of behaviour change into one framework that was practically useful to intervention design practitioners.

The methodology can be used for *evaluating* existing interventions, *categorising* interventions in a domain, and, of interest to this chapter, *designing* interventions. The purpose of the BCW is to allow intervention designers access to a systematic method for reviewing the full range of options available to them so that they may arrive at the most suitable and efficacious strategy.

Designers utilising the BCW are prompted to begin by thinking about the behaviour they wish to change through the lens of the *COM-B* model (Capability, Opportunity, Motivation, and Behaviour model - described in the following section), then about which intervention functions are appropriate (e.g. educating people, persuading people, modelling behaviour), followed by which approaches for changing behaviour are promising, and finally to consider the content of the intervention (Figure 1).

Figure 1. Stages of the BCW methodology relevant to gameful intervention design (Adapted from Michie, et al., 2013)

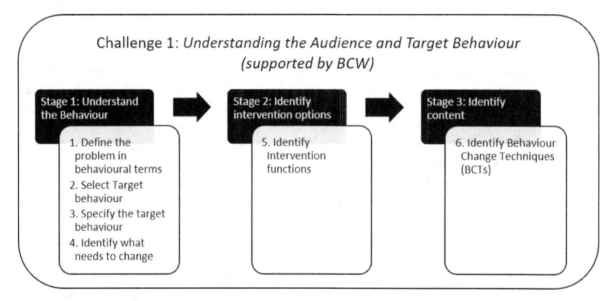

Stage 1: Understand the Behavior

The BCW design process consists of three main stages. The first is to define the problem in behavioural terms. Good behavioural definitions will provide a description of the problem, any specific condition(s)/ setting(s) under which the problem is likely to occur, and information about the frequency, intensity, duration, or other dimensions of relevance (Michie, et al., 2011). Having a clear definition also allows clarity in ensuring that all stakeholders are working on the same problem and with the same parameters. The method prompts designers to consider a long list of possible target behaviours relevant to the overarching problem. This list is then prioritised based upon the extent of their impact on the overarching problem, the likelihood of changing the behaviour, the likelihood of spill-over effects onto other behaviours, and how easy it is to measure the behaviour. This stage also prompts designers to analyse the target behaviour(s) within the COM-B model of behaviour (Michie, et al., 2013). COM-B is the core behavioural theory behind the BCW, and includes the components of:

- capability: an individual's capacity to engage in the activity concerned, which can be psychological (comprehension, reasoning, etc.) or physical (strength, skill, etc.);
- opportunity: all factors that lie outside the individual that make the behavior possible or prompt it, which can be physical (environmental) or social (afforded by culture, and what is socially acceptable); and
- motivation: all those brain processes that energize and direct behavior, not just goals and conscious decision-making, which can be reflective (evaluation, planning to do something, etc.), or automatic (involving emotions, impulses, etc.).

Stage 2: Identify Intervention Options

Once the areas of change have been identified using the COM-B model, the second stage in the BCW identifies promising intervention functions for these areas. The intervention functions or categories of interventions defined by the BCW are education, persuasion, incentivisation, coercion, training, restriction, environmental restructuring, modelling, and enablement (Michie, et al., 2011).

Evaluation of these functions within the intervention context is then undertaken, not only in terms of potential effectiveness, but also with consideration of the relevant social context. To facilitate this process, the APEASE criteria for evaluating options is applied, which includes an assessment of: affordability, practicability, effectiveness, acceptability, side-effects, and equity as it relates to the specific intervention context (Michie, et al., 2014).

Stage 3: Identify Content and Behavior Change Techniques

The next stage in the BCW process is to identify Behaviour Change Techniques (BCTs). A BCT is defined as "an active component of an intervention designed to change behaviour" (Michie, et al., 2014; Michie, et al., 2013). At this point, designers can select BCTs that are appropriate (based upon the APEASE criteria) for the intervention functions. This is aided by the Behaviour Change Technique Taxonomy (v1) (Michie, et al., 2013) which identifies 93 hierarchically organised techniques drawn from a wide range of fields, and the BCW links these to the different intervention functions (Michie, et al., 2013).

In brief, the BCW methodology allows designers to gain a better understanding of the behaviours that an intervention is targeting by prompting them to consider components of the behaviour and the proposed intervention systematically and within a social context using the APEASE criteria. While not specifically developed with gameful interventions in mind, the authorship team posit that this methodology can assist in developing insight into the specific behaviours that games are being developed to support.

To illustrate the authorship team's exploration of the application of the BCW to the design of a gameful intervention, the following section presents the design of *Energy Explorer*, a gameful intervention aimed to bring about a reduction in household energy use. Through *Energy Explorer*, the authorship team provide a practical example of the application of the BCW to support the designer's understanding of the audience and target behaviours required to bring about behavioural change. Further, the BCW is explored as a starting point to guide an evidence-based selection of game elements within this design, and thus overcoming the twin issues identified by literature as significantly inhibiting the successful design of gameful interventions.

APPLYING THE BCW IN THE DESIGN OF A GAMEFUL INTERVENTION: ENERGY EXPLORER

Australia's Commonwealth Scientific and Industrial Research Organisation (CSIRO) seeks to promote the reduction of household energy use, as energy conservation is a core area of concern worldwide. In order to augment their traditional non-technology-based interventions towards this goal (Grozev, et al., 2016), CSIRO had noted that games had been applied to the domain of energy conservation in the past, for example, Kukui Cup (Brewer, 2013), PowerAgent (Gustafsson, et al., 2010), PowerHouse (Reeves, et al., 2015), JouleBug (Elliott, 2012), and OPower (Laskey & Kavazovic, 2011) to bring about a conservation effect (Wells, 2018). However, despite the proliferation of games towards energy conservation, they all report varying levels of success in achieving their goal, and when they are reviewed and compared to identify what might have led to their specific outcomes, it becomes apparent that they differ in methodological approach, both in terms of design and evaluation, and further, they do not fully articulate that any review of the potential target audience or review of target behaviours were undertaken. This field therefore exhibits the same problems in gameful intervention design as other fields identified in the introduction section of this chapter.

The authorship team was commissioned by CSIRO to explore how a game focused towards a behavioural outcome of energy conservation might be designed to ensure that it was theoretically-informed, and could be methodologically replicated. To this end, the design of *Energy Explorer*, a gameful intervention to promote the reduction of household energy (Wells, 2018) was created, with its design informed by the BCW methodology. The following sections describe the exploratory application of the BCW within this specific context, and how this method guided practice to overcome the twin obstacles previously identified in gameful intervention design.

Overcoming Gameful Design Challenge 1 – Understanding the Audience and Target Behavior

As a first step to understand the outcome of interest and the behaviours leading to the targeted outcome, the authorship team employed the BCW, via a step-by-step process described throughout the following sections.

Stage 1: Understand the Behavior

BCW Step 1: Define the problem in behavioral terms

As described previously, this first stage of the BCW encourages the definition of the problem so that all stakeholders have a shared understanding of what the problem being focused on was, where the problem was most likely to occur, and who was likely to be exhibiting the problem behaviour being exhibited. In the context of *Energy Explorer*, the focus identified by the CSIRO was as follows:

- What? The need to reduce household energy consumption.
- Where? Within the home.
- Who? Household members with variation in authority and capability (i.e., some may own the home while others may be renting, some may be adults, and some may be children).

BCW Step 2: Select the Target Behaviour

The BCW points out that behaviours are not isolated, and indeed work within the context of other behaviours, and so the next step in the process is to identify all relevant behaviours and select those that are most relevant to solving or alleviating the overarching problem. This commences with the generation of a 'long list' of all the potential behaviours that may have been relevant to the problem identified in step 1, and then short-listing these issues for further investigation based on the criteria of: *the centrality of the behaviour* in the system of behaviours; *the likely impact* if the behaviour were to be changed; *the likelihood of changing* the behaviour; and *the ease of measurement* of the behaviour.

Subject matter experts at CSIRO, coupled with the research literature on energy conservation behaviours provided insight that within the domain of energy conservation, many behaviours can bring about reduced energy consumption (Grozev et al., 2014). A commonly used dichotomy in energy conservation behaviours is the distinction between curtailment behaviours (which are generally every-day actions that are repeated with each instance of the action bringing about a small conservation effect and are low in cost) and efficiency behaviours (which are generally once-off or irregular actions with a large conservation effect and can sometimes be high in cost).

A list of 24 curtailment and efficiency energy behaviours was compiled from CSIRO subject matter experts and published sources (Dietz, et al., 2009; Fielding, et al., 2010; Gardner & Stern, 2008; Karlin, et al., 2014), which was then assessed (in according with Michie et al., (2011) advice) for the *impact*, *likelihood of change*, *centrality* to other behaviours (i.e. if a person exhibited this behaviour, how likely it would be that other positive behaviours would occur), and *ease of measurement*. Table 1 provides a sample view of this process, with only 15 of the 24 behaviours shown for brevity (for a full analysis, see Wells (2018).

As shown in Table 1, "Turning off lights in unoccupied rooms" was assessed as: *very promising* regarding the likely impact on the outcome as it is a very common behaviour, *very promising* with regard to the likelihood of changing the behaviour due to the simplicity of the behaviour, and *promising* with regard to the measurability of the behaviour as some houses isolate lighting to a separate circuit measured by their smart electricity meter, and thus was selected as a target behaviour.

Conversely, "Waiting until the dishwasher is full to run" was assessed as *unpromising* regarding the likely impact on the outcome, *promising* with regard to the likelihood of changing the behaviour, and *unpromising* with regard to the centrality of the behaviour. Thus, this behaviour was not selected as a target behaviour to pursue.

As an example of the utility of this BCW step, within the *Energy Explorer* design, three behaviours that were ranked highest to pursue were identified from the original list of 24 opportunities, and thus the design team was able to focus their efforts towards encouraging households to:

1. Turn off lights in unoccupied rooms;
2. Reduce standby electricity consumption; and
3. Adjust air conditioner usage.

Table 1. Analysis of potential behaviors to reduce household energy consumption

Potential Behaviours	Impact	Likelihood of change	Centrality of Behaviour	Ease of Measurement
Turning off lights in unoccupied rooms	*VERY PROMISING*	*VERY PROMISING*	Promising	*VERY PROMISING* (light circuits)
Reducing standby electricity consumption	*VERY PROMISING*	*VERY PROMISING*	Promising	Promising (change in resting energy consumption)
Adjusting air conditioner usage (thermostat setbacks)	*VERY PROMISING*	*VERY PROMISING*	Promising	*VERY PROMISING* (air conditioner smart meter channel)
Switch off unused appliances	Promising	Promising	Promising	Promising (electricity)
Use cold water to wash	Promising	Promising	Promising	Unpromising (water)
Switch off computers when not in use	Unpromising	Promising	Promising	Promising
Purchasing energy efficient light bulbs	Promising	*VERY PROMISING*	Promising	Unpromising (installation, automatic detection)
Wait until dishwasher is full to run	Unpromising	Promising	Unpromising	Unpromising (water)
Shorter showers	Promising	Unpromising	Unpromising	Unpromising (water)
Line drying	Unpromising	Promising	Promising	Unpromising
Purchasing energy efficient appliances	Promising	Promising	Promising	Unpromising (installation, automatic detection)
Weatherization	Promising	Unpromising	Promising	Unacceptable (installation)
Low rolling resistance tires	Promising	Unpromising	Promising	Unacceptable (transport, installation)
Fuel-efficient vehicle	Promising	Unpromising	Promising	Unacceptable (transport)
Add insulation in the home	Promising	Unpromising	Promising	Unacceptable (installation)

Each of these three target behaviours were then examined and analysed through the lens of the remaining BCW steps to determine a set of techniques that might be selected to include in the intervention. For the purposes of brevity however, the assessment of only one of these three target behaviours will be described in the remaining sections of the BCW method: *Adjusting air conditioner usage* (for full coverage of all three, see Wells (2018).

BCW Step 3: Specify the Target Behavior

Step 3 of the BCW guided the authorship team to further specify the behaviour in appropriate detail and in its context. A set of six questions focused their understanding of the behaviour of *Adjusting air conditioner usage*, represented in Table 2.

In specifying the need to adjust air conditioning further, the authorship team was able to identify some preliminary requirements for the design including the *audience* for the gameful intervention, the *contexts* in which the game would be deployed, the *frequency* that users were likely to engage with the game, and other direct *stakeholders* that the intervention might need to support.

Table 2. Specifying the target behavior: Adjusting air conditioner usage to reduce household energy consumption

Who needs to perform this new behaviour?	Household members (where the household has an air conditioner)
What do they need to do differently?	(If they have temperature control) • On hot days increase air conditioner temperature by at least 2 degrees (C) • On cold days decrease air conditioner temperature by at least 2 degrees (C) • On average temperature days do not use the air conditioner • During peak times adjust the temperature by at least 2 degrees (C)
When will they do it?	Event days (hot days, cold days, holidays) peak times, average days
Where will they do it?	In the home
How often will they do it?	Every day, in the morning and night
With whom will they do it?	Other household members should be considered and included in the decision to change the temperature

BCW Step 4: Identify What Needs to Change

For the authorship team to achieve the desired change in this target behaviour, they needed to identify and understand what needed to change in the person and/or the environment where the behaviour occurred. To overcome the limitations of previous gameful interventions and address the challenge of understanding the audience and target behaviour, the BCW guided the team to use the COM-B model (Michie et al., 2013, see Figure 2) to build an understanding of whether the household members had: the *capability* to adjust their air conditioners (both physically and psychologically); the *opportunity* to adjust their air conditioners (supported by a conducive physical and social environment); and a sufficiently strong *motivation* to adjust their air conditioners.

Figure 2. COM-B Model (Michie et al,. 2013)

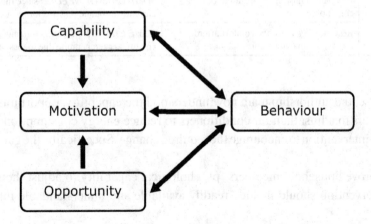

Assessing the target behaviour against this COM-B model, the authorship team were able to identify which attribute (capability, opportunity, or motivation) would need to change in households to support them to adjust their air conditioners to achieve reduced energy usage (described in Table 3).

Table 3. Identifying what needs to change to adjust air conditioner usage to reduce household energy consumption

COM-B Components	What needs to happen for the target behaviour to occur?	Is there a need for change?
Physical capability	Have the physical skill to adjust the temperature	No change is needed as most household members have the physical capability to use the air conditioner controls (possible exceptions include children)
Psychological capability	Can set the temperature to an amount relatively higher or lower than they normally do, depending on the current outside temperature	*SOME CHANGE NEEDED* as some people lack the ability to keep track of the usual temperature settings of their air conditioner, or the ability to acknowledge that a day is not hot enough to warrant use
	Can recognize when it is currently a peak time for air conditioner usage	*SOME CHANGE NEEDED* as many people are not aware of peak times
Physical opportunity	Be able to accept the impact of a change in room temperature on individual comfort, considering current physical health status	No change is needed as methods other than an air conditioner can be used to adjust an individual's temperature (most notably, change in clothing)
	Physical access to air conditioner controls	No change is needed, as controls are usually remote
Social opportunity	See others with similar houses adjusting their air conditioner usage on event days	*SOME CHANGE NEEDED* as this information is not readily available in a reliable and understandable fashion.
	Being able to adjust the temperature of the air conditioner appropriately even with guests in the house	*SOME CHANGE NEEDED* as there is social pressure when guests are in the household to ensure their comfort
Reflective motivation	Hold the belief that adjusting air conditioner temperature will make a monetary difference	No change is needed as many know that better air conditioning usage should result in lower power bills
	Hold the belief that adjusting air conditioner temperature will make an environmental difference	*SOME CHANGE NEEDED* as many hold a belief that their contribution to Climate Change is negligible
	Hold the belief that adjusting the temperature of the air conditioner will not have a negative impact on comfort	*SOME CHANGE NEEDED* as many are resistant to changing air conditioner temperature due to potential negative impact on comfort
Automatic motivation	Routinely adjust the temperature of the air conditioner daily	*SOME CHANGE NEEDED* since this behaviour is not currently a routine practice for most residents
	Resist the desire for the comfort afforded by a stable room temperature	*SOME CHANGE NEEDED* as many resist changing air conditioner temperature due to loss of comfort

From this exercise, the authorship team now understood the capability, opportunity, and motivation of household members to adjust their air conditioners to reduce energy consumption and what must be present in a gameful intervention to encourage the required change. Specifically, the gameful intervention:

- needed to improve household members' psychological capability to adjust their air conditioners, and so the intervention should include readily available and understandable information on how to do so;
- needed to improve the social opportunity to adjust their air conditioners, and so the intervention needed to include evidence-based support for reducing energy through this means; and
- needed to improve household members' reflective and automatic motivation to adjust their air conditioners, and so the gameful intervention should include an ability for a household member to track their energy use practically and easily.

Stage 2: Identify Intervention Options

BCW Step 5: Identify and Select Intervention Functions

With the identification of the COM-B components, the authorship team then commenced determining the mechanisms by which the intervention could change behaviour, known as Intervention Functions (IFs). Michie et al., (2013) suggests a relationship exists between elements of the COM-B model and IFs, and that there is a specific set of intervention functions that actively support different elements of the COM-B model (Figure 3).

Figure 3. Linking Intervention Functions to COM-B components (Michie et al., 2013). Filled cells indicate a relationship where an intervention function may actively support the relevant COM-B component

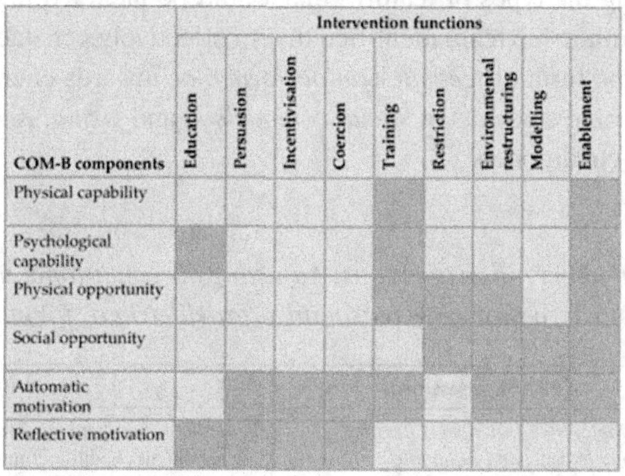

The authorship team were guided by Michie et al.,'s (2013) mapping and so identified intervention functions that could support the achievement of improved capability, improved opportunity, and improved motivation to adjust air conditioners among household members. For example, to adjust air conditioner usage, the authorship team could implement strategies of:

- *Restriction, Environmental restructuring, Modelling,* and *Enablement* to improve the social opportunity for change;
- *Education, Persuasion; Incentivization,* and *Coercion* to improve the reflective motivation for change;
- *Persuasion, Incentivization, Coercion,* and *Training* to enhance automatic motivation for change; and
- *Education, Training,* and *Enablement* to improve the psychological capability for change.

It should be noted here that while this mapping allowed the authorship team to identify a list of *possible* intervention functions to be applied to a target behaviour, not all intervention functions were deemed *appropriate* in the context of the behaviour. Rather than making use of all identified intervention functions, the BCW suggests filtering them by applying the previously-mentioned APEASE criteria, assessing the suitability of each candidate and identifying those that should be selected as targeted intervention functions.

For example, Table 5 shows that persuasion was assessed as *affordable, practical, effective, acceptable, safe,* and *equitable* by CSIRO subject matter experts and was subsequently selected as an appropriate intervention function. In contrast, coercion was assessed as *not practical* and *not acceptable* by CSIRO subject matter experts, and thus was not selected as an intervention function to pursue further in this context.

At the completion of step 5 of the BCW, the authorship team now understood that to improve social opportunity, reflective motivation, automatic motivation, and psychological capability amongst the target households, the intervention functions of *persuasion* and *incentivisation* were the most appropriate to employ in the design of the gameful intervention (as seen in Table 5).

In selecting appropriate intervention functions of *persuasion* and *incentivisation*, the authorship team was able to start identifying the types of features that would be included in the gameful intervention design. For example, the authorship team identified that to effectively persuade the audience to engage in the target behaviour some form of *feedback on performance* towards energy reduction would need to be provided, as well as some elements of *social comparison* and *virtual rewards* to incentivise them towards adjusting their air conditioners.

Table 5. Assessing potential intervention functions: Adjusting air conditioner usage to reduce household energy consumption. For brevity, a shortened reasoning is provided here, for more detail see Wells (2018)

Intervention Function	APEASE assessment	Reason
Restriction	*Affordable, NOT Practical, Effective, Acceptable, Safe, and Equitable*	Not practical as there are no options to restrict access to the household air conditioner in this context
Environmental Restructuring	*Affordable, NOT Practical, Effective, Acceptable, Safe, and Equitable*	Not practical as options to restructure the environment are costly (e.g. installing insulation).
Modelling	*Affordable, NOT Practical, Effective, Acceptable, Safe, and Equitable*	Could provide a demonstration of the ideal behaviour, but not practical
Enablement	*Affordable, NOT Practical, Effective, Acceptable, Safe, and Equitable*	Not practical in this context as individuals already have all the physical and psychological skills required to perform the behaviour
Education	*Affordable, Practical, NOT Effective, Acceptable, Safe, and Equitable*	Education on how to reduce air conditioner settings is unlikely to be effective as many are already aware of how to adjust their air conditioner
Persuasion	*Affordable, Practical, Effective, Acceptable, Safe, and Equitable*	Can be used to provide feedback on performance for comparison
Incentivisation	*Affordable, Practical, Effective, Acceptable, Safe, and Equitable*	Can provide feedback on performance, and social rewards
Coercion	*Affordable, NOT Practical, Effective, NOT Acceptable, Safe, and Equitable*	Can identify a discrepancy between current behaviour and goals, and can remove rewards for failing to perform the ideal behaviour, but not practical and not acceptable in this context

Stage 3: Identify Content and Behavior Change Techniques

BCW Step 6: Identifying BCTs

To provide a more comprehensive approach to the selection of specific technical elements in the design, the authorship team were again informed by the work of Michie, et al., (2013), who introduce the concept of a behaviour change technique (BCT). A BCT is the "active component" of an intervention designed to change behaviour - that is an observable, replicable, and irreducible component of an intervention designed to change behaviour (Michie, et al., 2013).

According to Michie et al., (2013), there are 93 defined BCTs that are often used to activate specific intervention functions, and so the authorship team mapped Michie's BCTs to the selected intervention functions of *persuasion* and *incentivisation*, as evidenced in Table 6. For example, *persuasion* can be actioned by providing individuals with *feedback on their energy use behaviour, comparison to others' usage, and information about social consequences of their usage*, among others. Similarly, *incentivisation* can be actioned by providing individuals with *feedback on behaviour, social rewards, incentives, and rewards for specific outcomes*. Following this step of the BCW, the authorship team identified a set of 11 BCTs, mapped directly back to the target behaviour of adjusting air conditioning.

Table 6. Selecting appropriate BCTs to support adjusting air conditioner usage to reduce household energy consumption

Persuasion:	Incentivisation:
• Feedback on behaviour • Social comparison • Identity associated with changed behaviour • Information about others' approval • Identification of self as role model • Salience of consequences • Information about social and environmental consequences	• Feedback on behaviour • Social reward • Incentive • Reward (outcome)

Summarizing the BCW Contributions Towards the Design of Energy Explorer

The six steps of the BCW offered by Michie et al., (2011) allowed the authorship team to rigorously investigate the target audience of the proposed gameful intervention, explore the behaviours that were being targeted for change, and identify appropriate mechanisms to add to the game that were likely (as supported by intervention design theory and theory) to bring about that change.

Repeating this process across the remaining two energy conservation target behaviours identified in Step 2, the authorship team was adequately equipped with a set of techniques mapped directly back to each target behaviour that could be built into the game to support the achievement of the target behaviours. For example, the authorship team now understood:

1.   that there were three behaviors to target (turning off lights in unoccupied rooms, reducing standby electricity consumption, and adjusting air conditioner usage);
2.   that these behaviors could be influenced by persuasion and incentivization; and

3. persuasion and incentivization in turn could be actioned by 14 specific BCTs that could be embedded in the design of the intervention to bring about these targeted changes (for a full description of the BCW applied to these additional two behaviors, see Wells (2018).

Specifically, the authorship team now knew that the following features should be included in the energy conservation game to impact the behavioural outcomes required:

*   Feedback on energy use behavior
*   Virtual forms of social comparison
*   Allowing the development of a new identity associated with changed behavior
*   Provision of information about others' approval
*   Opportunities to identify self as a role model
*   Provision of information about social and environmental consequences
*   Provision of information about relevant consequences
*   Personal rewards
*   Social rewards
*   Personal incentives
*   Descriptions of the discrepancy between current behavior and the goal
*   Virtual punishment
*   Recognition of behavior cost
*   Opportunities to avoid future punishment

Given one of the most significant limitations of previous gameful intervention designs that inhibited their success was a lack of comprehension of the target audience, the behaviours that needed to change, and how they could be actioned, the authorship team was confident that the BCW allowed them to overcome this challenge in the design of *Energy Explorer*. Specifically, the BCW allowed the identification of a set of BCTs that could be embedded into the design of the gameful intervention to bring about the required behaviour changes.

Overcoming Gameful Design Challenge 2 – Selecting Game Elements

While, for the purpose of this intervention design, the role of the BCW ends at the point of identifying appropriate behaviour change techniques and thus overcomes one of the core limitations of existing gameful intervention design, a second core challenge still remains – how to address the apparent *ad hoc* selection of game elements and the over-reliance on the more easy-to-implement elements of points, badges, and leader boards which may not act as enablers for change (as noted by many sources such as Deterding, et al., (2011) and Bogost (2015)). The following section provides insight into how the authorship team were able to use the insights formed from the BCW steps to undertake an informed selection of game elements to be implemented into *Energy Explorer* (Figure 4).

Figure 4. Understanding the Audience and Target Behavior to better support the Selection of Game Elements

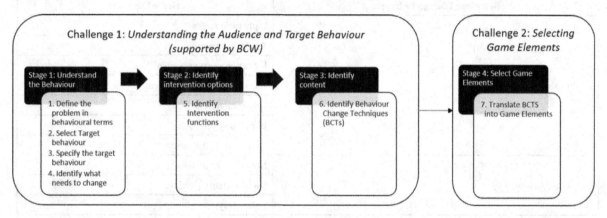

Stage 4: Select Game Elements

Step 7: Translate BCTs into Game Elements

A significant limitation facing the successful use of gameful interventions to persuade users to change behaviour is that developers do not understand how game elements impact behaviour, and thus the design of games for targeted behavioural outcomes is compromised. In previous work, the authorship team assessed 22 systematic reviews of serious game use across multiple disciplines. Each review urgently called for a stronger evidence base to substantiate game element selection (see for example: Lau, et al., (2017); Edwards, et al., (2016); Alanne (2016); Antonaci, et al., (2019); Bodnar, et al., (2016); Cechetti, et al., (2017) and Silva, et al., (2019); de Salas et al., (2022)). While this work continues within the design and academic communities and the authorship team await the results eagerly, the use of the BCW allowed the authorship team to immediately improve the rigour of their game element selection by mapping their identified BCTs against game elements that exhibit similar characteristics.

Armed with an understanding of 14 different techniques that had the potential to bring about energy conservation behaviour, a process of translating these BCTs to similarly focussed game elements was undertaken. Specifically, lists of game elements were drawn from academic sources (Deterding, et al., (2011); Chou & Ting, (2003); Rapp, (2017); Reeves & Read, (2009), and Johnson, et al., (2017)), and game design subject matter experts, to determine which game elements might match a particular BCT. For example, game elements of 'Daily login screen', 'Statistics screen', and 'Notification system', might reasonably reflect the need to provide 'Feedback on behaviour', as a BCT to incentivise and to persuade. Table 7 provides an example of the translation of BCTs into practical game elements that could be integrated into the game design.

From insights gained from applying the BCW methodology, the authorship team now had a practical method to guide their selection of game elements, that was more than just the *ad hoc* selection of points, badges, and leaderboards, as has been the limitation of much gameful intervention design to date (Bogost, (2014); de Salas et al., (2022)). These game elements now became the active ingredients in the practical design of the game *Energy Explorer*.

Table 7. Translating BCTs to game elements

Behaviour Change Technique	Game Elements
Feedback on behaviour	Daily login screen
	Statistics screen
	Impact on game resources
	Impact on game environment
	Notification System
	Level-up system
	Normative leaderboards
Social comparison	Normative leaderboards
	Social system (friends)
	Level-up system
Identity associated with changed behaviour	Avatar
Information about others' approval	Narrative (dialog)
Identification of self as role model	Normative leaderboards
Information about social and environmental consequences / Salience of consequences	Impact on game resources
	Impact on game environment
Reward	Daily login screen (reward)
	Quests (rewards)
	Checklist (rewards)
	Level-up system
Social reward	Normative leaderboards (rewards)
	Quests (dialog)
Incentive	Daily login screen (reward)
	Quest (reward)
	Checklist
	Normative leaderboards (rewards)
Discrepancy between current behaviour and goal	Quests (progress)
Punishment / Behaviour cost	Impact on game resources
	Impact on game environment
	Quests (failure)
Future punishment	Quests (failure)

BUILDING ENERGY EXPLORER WITH INSIGHTS FROM THE BCW

In line with our goal of exploring how the BCW might provide a practical contribution to gameful intervention design, the previous sections have described how the authorship team applied the BCW methodology to the domain of energy conservation, outputting a set of BCTs which were subsequently linked to game elements to overcome the two core challenges of gameful intervention design: *Understanding the Audience and Target Behaviour*, and *Selecting Game Elements*.

Armed with these evidence-based BCTs and their translation into game elements, a gameful intervention incorporating these elements titled *Energy Explorer* was developed (see Figure 5).

Figure 5. Building Energy Explorer from insights gained from the BCW and Translating BCTs into Game Elements

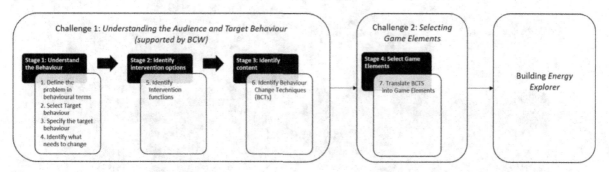

Energy Explorer is a 2D top-down exploration game, linked to data sourced from energy smart meters in the player's household (Wells, 2018). The game reads this data in the form of a number expressed in kilowatt hours (kWh) for overall consumption during a period of time, as well as for different channels representing portions of the participant's home such as their air conditioner, lighting circuitry, and various rooms.

Energy use in the home is reflected in the game as environmental conditions and exploration opportunities – for example, good energy use in the home registered by the smart meters translates to open skies, and access to resources and new areas within the game; while poor energy use in the game translates to stormy or snowy conditions, and fewer resources and access, making exploration and questing more difficult (See Figure 6).

The player controls an avatar that traverses a procedurally generated world populated with characters and animals that can be interacted with. They are provided with a large checklist of tasks to complete in the world and the aim of the game is to explore as much as possible.

Regarding the target behaviours identified in the BCW methodology, these are integrated as data sourced from the smart meters, for example, adjusting air conditioner usage can be assessed by a specific channel of the smart meter, and thus any negative directional change can be measured and reflected into the game as more icy conditions that inhibit the players' exploration.

With regards to the BCTs and game elements previously described energy conservation in the household results in better weather throughout the game and allows access to new characters and items. While initially inaccessible, these characters and items are made visible to show the player what improving the weather will help them access and incentivise them to conserve energy. This novel mechanic of tying real-world energy usage to in-game resources and the game environment was deemed to reflect the BCTs of *feedback on behaviour, information about social and environmental consequences of poor energy usage behaviour resulting in fewer resources, salience of consequences, punishment, and behaviour cost.*

Figure 6. Screenshots of the Energy Explorer game, showing the different weather conditions in the game (dictated by real-world energy consumption). Screenshots are of procedurally generated areas of the game

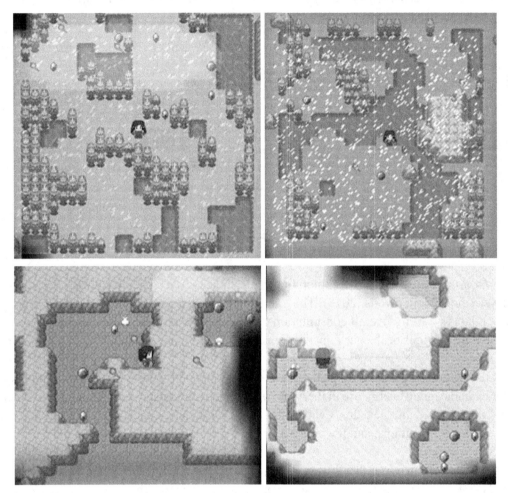

Furthermore, when the player begins a session of *Energy Explorer*, they are provided with exploration resources as part of the daily login screen (Figure 7). They are provided with a base amount of each of the resources and an additional amount based upon their energy savings as recorded by the smart meter. This game element implements the BCTs of *feedback on behaviour, reward,* and *incentive*.

Almost every interaction in the game rewards the player with a certain amount of a resource named experience points (XP) which is based upon the frequency and difficulty of the action. The XP resource directly influences the player's level in the game, which is visible to other players through a social system, and the player's XP level influences the aspects of the game that are available to them. The level-up game and social elements operationalize the *reward*, *social comparison*, and *feedback on behaviour* BCTs.

Finally, characters in *Energy Explorer* provide the player with quests to complete (Figure 7). In total, 43 quests were implemented for the game, providing an extensive but simple storyline for players to engage with. Procedurally generated quests are also included in the game, with requirements for completion which link directly to real-world energy consumption (e.g., if the player has high air conditioner consumption, the game detects this and presents a quest which requires the ice resource which is linked directly to the air conditioner channel on the smart meter). Characters and quest game elements were key to implementing many of the BCTs previously identified in Table 7.

The above provides only some examples of the full range of game elements employed within *Energy Explorer* for brevity. Many other game elements are included to both incentivise and persuade the player to display the identified target behaviours and are fully explained in Wells (2018).

Figure 7. Screenshots of the Energy Explorer game, showing resource availability and quests

Preliminary Feedback on Energy Explorer

The purpose of this chapter, and indeed the goal of the CSIRO in commissioning this research, was to introduce and explore the BCW as a pragmatic method to gain insight into the audience and target behaviour for a gameful intervention and show a practical path from those insights to the selection and deployment of game elements. The previous sections have provided this illustration and thus have met these exploratory goals.

However, as gameful interventions will invariably be required to bring about a change to a target behaviour as their development commence, an obvious question will be: did *Energy Explorer* bring about a reduction in household energy use?

While evaluation of *Energy Explorer* game was not the core goal of this exploratory study, to date, *Energy Explorer* has been preliminarily deployed to a pilot intervention group of 19 participants previously recruited into an existing CSIRO research program that had given permission for an EcoPulse smart meter to be placed in their home to allow CSIRO to monitor their energy use (with data compared to a control group with the same smart meters who were not given the game, n=149).

Over a period of 3 months, a household's individual energy consumption data was collected via the smart meter at one-minute intervals to form the baseline data source for game. Realtime usage and comparison to this baseline data (with changes in temperature controlled for) was used for the operation of the game.

Player usage of the game in the form of analytics was recorded, including session logs within the game, logs of when the game notifies players (game-initiated actions), and tracking of player-initiated actions within the game such as viewing of various screens, or character actions. All metrics were time-stamped, which allowed for exploratory analysis of energy consumption changes after certain actions within the game. A total of 1,666 game actions were recorded (on average 83.3 actions per player; SD = 89.0)

An analysis of the household energy use 14 days prior to accessing the game, coupled with an analysis of 14 days after the completion of the experimental phase was undertaken. Analysis of this data showed a small but significant difference in change in conservation effect 14 days pre-test and 14 days post-test was observed in the intervention group ($U = 1567$, $n_{control} = 128$, $n_{intervention} = 19$, $M_{control} = 0.234kWh$, $M_{intervention} = -0.043kWh$, $p = 0.043$). Figure 8 provides a representation of the difference in conservation effect for the 19 players of *Energy Explorer* compared to the other members of the original CSIRO research project that did not participate in this pilot over the same period of time.

These preliminary results provide positive indications that *Energy Explorer*, as informed by the BCW, has the potential to bring about a reduction in household energy use, however further insights will require a more in-depth deployment and evaluation of this gameful intervention amongst participants not already engaged in a CSIRO energy conservation research program, to which ceiling effects might impact outcomes.

Figure 8. Change in Conservation Effect Pre-test/Post-test for Number of Days Before and After

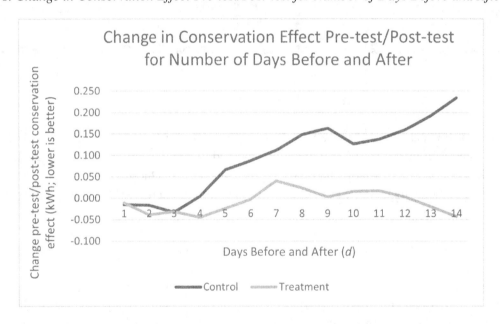

FUTURE RESEARCH DIRECTIONS

The opportunities offered by the procedural focus of the BCW have been explored in disciplines outside behavioural psychology, for example, Deleris & Mac Aonghusa (2020) describe their application of the BCW to design behavioural interventions related to the development of a sharing economy, noting that this methodology helped to guide novices with the need for intervention design insight, and Huang, et al., (2017) employed the BCW to build an intervention to encourage office workers to take regular micro-breaks at work, noting that it proved useful to elicit theory-based design recommendations. However, the adoption of this methodology remains novel in the field of gameful intervention design.

The intent of exploratory research is to investigate a topic that has not been previously studied in-depth and indeed, this study has innovatively connected the ideas and practice offered by the BCW to the questions inherent in games intervention design. Exploratory research is the initial research, which forms the basis of more conclusive research and indeed this study is only the first step towards its further exploration and adoption more broadly in this field. For example, it is too soon to be able to extrapolate these pilot results to be able to claim that the authorship team have changed the behaviours targeted in this intervention as interventions require time to assess the longer-term achievement of the goals and to date, *Energy Explorer* has not yet been deployed for sufficiently long periods to make this assessment. Further work will continue to assess the longer-term effects of this intervention, however the BCW has clearly assisted the design team in being able to substantiate design choices, which is often missing in reports of gameful intervention design, and thus limits replicability.

The authorship team now calls for further case examples of the application of the BCW to games interventions and further investigation of its characteristics not yet explored in this study. For example, one recommendation of the BCW methodology not explored in this study was to analyse the possible modes of intervention delivery appropriate to the audience once the intervention had been designed. In the context of this study, CSIRO had determined their delivery mechanism was to be a game, and so no analysis of this was required. However, de Salas et al.,'s (2022) recent work in systematically reviewing gameful interventions indicates "a compelling justification for the selection of a game was generally absent" (p14), and where a reason was provided, it was that games were perceived as 'efficient' and 'engaging', despite no justification being provided, nor any analysis of their suitability to their audience being explored. The authors now encourage investigation of this additional feature of the BCW to assist in building justification for the selection of games as the delivery mechanism in future studies.

CONCLUSION

This exploratory research has been undertaken to explore the usefulness of the BCW, a behavioural intervention design methodology, to inform the design of gameful intervention design. Literature reports that gameful interventions suffer from a multitude of heterogeneous designs and evaluation approaches, as well as a lack of audience and behavioural insights, which has resulted in the failed achievement of their targeted outcomes.

The exploratory application of the Behaviour Change Wheel methodology within the case context of *Energy Explorer* has supported the design team to overcome two common design pitfalls of gameful interventions related to designing with an understanding of the target audience and behaviour being targeted, and substantiated selection of game elements to include in the intervention. In following the BCW steps identified in Figure 1, the team developed insight into the core problems being experienced by CSIRO, namely: 1) the potential behaviours to target in an intervention and the specifics of each energy-saving target behaviour; 2) the capability, opportunity, and motivational attributes that were required to be changed in the target group; 3) the intervention functions that would bring about those changes, and 4) the behaviour change techniques that would be implemented into the intervention as action and interaction elements. Specifically, the authorship team learned that:

- The need to reduce household energy consumption was a problem related to behaviours within the home and the actions of household members who varied in authority and capability.
- Three behaviours that were very promising to pursue were: turning off lights in unoccupied rooms; reducing standby electricity consumption; and adjusting air conditioner usage.

- To change these behaviours, users would need readily-available and understandable information, support for challenging their existing behaviours, and the ability to track their energy use practically and easily.
- Users could be persuaded and incentivised to change their behaviour if they were exposed to a range of 14 specific activities and information sources through the intervention, including, for example, feedback on behaviour, social comparison, and rewards.
- These 14 specific behavioural activities could be translated into equivalent game elements that the players of *Energy Explorer* would encounter within the game, such as daily statistics, in-game impact visualisations, normative leader boards, and quests.

While it is not the intent of exploratory research, nor indeed this chapter, to conclusively prove that the application of the BCW is the salve to all gameful intervention design problems, the authorship team believe that their use of the BCW has fundamentally improved the rigour in the design of their gameful intervention, and results point to a promising short-term improvement in the targeted behavioural outcomes.

The BCW is a rigorous methodology that consolidates 19 different intervention design frameworks. While the BCW has received some criticism within its home discipline of Health Psychology as simplifying intervention design by reducing the variability in approach (Ogden 2016), researchers and practitioners in disciplines with less experience in intervention design continue to find this guided approach accessible and relevant to their needs (Deleris & Mac Aonghusa (2020) and Huang, et al., (2017)).

Similarly, the work described in this chapter suggests that while the BCW may be reductionist in its approach to intervention design, it has been a very useful tool to guide the development of a gameful intervention, designers of which traditionally have very limited experience in understanding behaviour (de Salas et al., 2022). The authorship team's experience suggests that the BCW can indeed assist designers of gameful interventions to become better informed of their audience, their behaviours, and approaches to selecting technology elements that are more rigorous and theoretically informed, while recognising further investigation is now required to build a more generalisable set of examples and practice.

In reference to other models that have been published to guide gameful design, such as Mohr et al.,'s (2014) Behavioural Intervention Technology Model, the introduction of the BCW may serve to provide a practical method of provide insight into the goals they propose such as: develop understanding the treatment goal or intervention aims; understand methods used to attain clinical and use aims; and select the corresponding technical elements. Furthermore, the use of the BCW may also support the Behavioural Economics Team of the Australian Government's (Ames & Hiscox, 2016) guidelines on the discovery and diagnosis phases required when developing behavioural interventions, in that the BCW can provide a practical method to answer their questions of: *what is the outcome of interest?, what behaviour is leading to the outcome?, and what interventions might influence the target behaviour?*

In summary, and as stated previously, given that market for 'gameful' interventions is predicted to register an impressive growth of 32% to reach $40 billion by 2024 (TechSci Research 2019), a more theoretically informed and rigorous approach to their design can result in significant benefits including increased engagement by target users and improved behavioural outcomes. The authorship team has introduced the BCW as a potential practical mechanism for building this insight and rigour, and now invites further investigation of this methodology and its application in additional gameful intervention design case studies.

REFERENCES

Alanne, K. (2016). An overview of game-based learning in building services engineering education. *European Journal of Engineering Education, 41*(2), 204–219. doi:10.1080/03043797.2015.1056097

Ames, P., & Hiscox, M. (2016). *Guide to developing behavioural interventions for randomised controlled trials: Nine guiding questions*. Department of the Prime Minister and Cabinet.

Antonaci, A., Klemke, R., & Specht, M. (2019, September). The effects of gamification in online learning environments: A systematic literature review. *Informatics (MDPI), 6*(3), 32. doi:10.3390/informatics6030032

Ávila-Pesántez, D., Rivera, L. A., & Alban, M. S. (2017). Approaches for serious game design: A systematic literature review. *The ASEE Computers in Education (CoED) Journal, 8*(3).

Bodnar, C. A., Anastasio, D., Enszer, J. A., & Burkey, D. D. (2016). Engineers at play: Games as teaching tools for undergraduate engineering students. *Journal of Engineering Education, 105*(1), 147–200. doi:10.1002/jee.20106

Bogost, I. (2014). Why gamification is bullshit. *The gameful world: Approaches, issues, applications*, 65-80.

Brewer, R. S. (2013*). Fostering sustained energy behavior change and increasing energy literacy in a student housing energy challenge* (Doctoral dissertation). University of Hawai'i at Manoa.

Burke, B. (2014). *Gamification Trends and Strategies to Help Prepare for the Future*. Available at: https://www.gartner.com/it/content/2191900/2191918/november_28_gamification_bburke.pdf?userId=61080590

Cechetti, N. P., Biduki, D., & De Marchi, A. C. B. (2017, June). Gamification strategies for mobile device applications: A systematic review. In *2017 12th Iberian Conference on Information Systems and Technologies (CISTI)* (pp. 1-7). IEEE. 10.23919/CISTI.2017.7975943

Chapman, J. R., & Rich, P. J. (2018). Does educational gamification improve students' motivation? If so, which game elements work best? *Journal of Education for Business, 93*(7), 315–322. doi:10.1080/08832323.2018.1490687

Chou, T. J., & Ting, C. C. (2003). The role of flow experience in cyber-game addiction. *Cyberpsychology & Behavior, 6*(6), 663–675. doi:10.1089/109493103322725469 PMID:14756934

Connolly, T. M., Boyle, E. A., MacArthur, E., Hainey, T., & Boyle, J. M. (2012). A systematic literature review of empirical evidence on computer games and serious games. *Computers & Education, 59*(2), 661–686. doi:10.1016/j.compedu.2012.03.004

De Salas, K., Ashbarry, L., Seabourne, M., Lewis, I., Wells, L., Dermoudy, J., Roehrer, E., Springer, M., Sauer, J. D., & Scott, J. (2022). Improving Environmental Outcomes with Games: An Exploration of Behavioural and Technological Design and Evaluation Approaches. *Simulation & Gaming*, (July), 1–43. doi:10.1177/10468781221114160

Deleris, L., & Mac Aonghusa, P. (2020). Behaviour Change for the Sharing Economy. In *Analytics for the Sharing Economy: Mathematics, Engineering and Business Perspectives* (pp. 173–187). Springer. doi:10.1007/978-3-030-35032-1_11

Derksen, M. E., van Strijp, S., Kunst, A. E., Daams, J. G., Jaspers, M. W. M., & Fransen, M. P. (2020). Serious games for smoking prevention and cessation: A systematic review of game elements and game effects. *Journal of the American Medical Informatics Association: JAMIA*, *27*(5), 818–833. doi:10.1093/jamia/ocaa013 PMID:32330255

Deterding, S., Dixon, D., Khaled, R., & Nacke, L. (2011, September). From game design elements to gamefulness: defining" gamification". In *Proceedings of the 15th international academic MindTrek conference: Envisioning future media environments* (pp. 9-15). 10.1145/2181037.2181040

Dietz, T., Gardner, G. T., Gilligan, J., Stern, P. C., & Vandenbergh, M. P. (2009). Household actions can provide a behavioral wedge to rapidly reduce US carbon emissions. *Proceedings of the National Academy of Sciences of the United States of America*, *106*(44), 18452–18456. doi:10.1073/pnas.0908738106 PMID:19858494

Edwards, E. A., Lumsden, J., Rivas, C., Steed, L., Edwards, L. A., Thiyagarajan, A., Sohanpal, R., Caton, H., Griffiths, C. J., Munafò, M. R., Taylor, S., & Walton, R. T. (2016). Gamification for health promotion: Systematic review of behaviour change techniques in smartphone apps. *BMJ Open*, *6*(10), e012447. doi:10.1136/bmjopen-2016-012447 PMID:27707829

Elliott, J. (2012). *Development of an Energy-Information Feedback System for a Smartphone Application*. Academic Press.

Ferreira-Brito, F., Fialho, M., Virgolino, A., Neves, I., Miranda, A. C., Sousa-Santos, N., Caneiras, C., Carriço, L., Verdelho, A., & Santos, O. (2019). Game-based interventions for neuropsychological assessment, training and rehabilitation: Which game-elements to use? A systematic review. *Journal of Biomedical Informatics*, *98*, 103287. doi:10.1016/j.jbi.2019.103287 PMID:31518700

Fielding, K. S., Thompson, A., Louis, W. R., & Warren, C. (2010). *Environmental sustainability: understanding the attitudes and behaviour of Australian households*. Academic Press.

Fogg, B. J. (2009, April). A behavior model for persuasive design. In *Proceedings of the 4th international Conference on Persuasive Technology* (pp. 1-7). Academic Press.

Gardner, G. T., & Stern, P. C. (2008). The short list: The most effective actions US households can take to curb climate change. *Environment*, *50*(5), 12–25. doi:10.3200/ENVT.50.5.12-25

Grozev, G., Garner, S., Ren, Z., Taylor, M., Higgins, A., & Walden, G. (2016). Modeling the Impacts of Disruptive Technologies and Pricing on Electricity Consumption. In Future of Utilities Utilities of the Future (pp. 211-230). Academic Press. doi:10.1016/B978-0-12-804249-6.00011-7

Gustafsson, A., Katzeff, C., & Bang, M. (2010). Evaluation of a pervasive game for domestic energy engagement among teenagers. *Computers in Entertainment*, *7*(4), 1–19. doi:10.1145/1658866.1658873

Huang, Y., Benford, S., Hendrickx, H., Treloar, R., & Blake, H. (2017, April). Office workers' perceived barriers and facilitators to taking regular micro-breaks at work: A diary-probed interview study. In *International Conference on Persuasive Technology* (pp. 149-161). Springer. 10.1007/978-3-319-55134-0_12

Johnson, D., Horton, E., Mulcahy, R., & Foth, M. (2017). Gamification and serious games within the domain of domestic energy consumption: A systematic review. *Renewable & Sustainable Energy Reviews*, *73*, 249–264. doi:10.1016/j.rser.2017.01.134

Karlin, B., Davis, N., Sanguinetti, A., Gamble, K., Kirkby, D., & Stokols, D. (2014). Dimensions of conservation: Exploring differences among energy behaviors. *Environment and Behavior*, *46*(4), 423–452. doi:10.1177/0013916512467532

Larson, K. (2020). Serious games and gamification in the corporate training environment: A literature review. *TechTrends*, *64*(2), 319–328. doi:10.100711528-019-00446-7

Laskey, A., & Kavazovic, O. (2011). Opower. XRDS: Crossroads. *The ACM Magazine for Students*, *17*(4), 47–51.

Lau, H. M., Smit, J. H., Fleming, T. M., & Riper, H. (2017). Serious games for mental health: Are they accessible, feasible, and effective? A systematic review and meta-analysis. *Frontiers in Psychiatry*, *7*, 209. doi:10.3389/fpsyt.2016.00209 PMID:28149281

Lopes, S., Pereira, A., Magalhães, P., Oliveira, A., & Rosário, P. (2019). Gamification: Focus on the strategies being implemented in interventions: A systematic review protocol. *BMC Research Notes*, *12*(1), 1–5. doi:10.118613104-019-4139-x PMID:30795806

Manzano-León, A., Camacho-Lazarraga, P., Guerrero, M. A., Guerrero-Puerta, L., Aguilar-Parra, J. M., Trigueros, R., & Alias, A. (2021). Between level up and game over: A systematic literature review of gamification in education. *Sustainability*, *13*(4), 2247. doi:10.3390u13042247

Medema, W., Mayer, I., Adamowski, J., Wals, A. E., & Chew, C. (2019). *The potential of serious games to solve water problems: Editorial to the special issue on game-based approaches to sustainable water governance*. Academic Press.

Michie, S., Atkins, L., & West, R. (2014). *The behaviour change wheel. A guide to designing interventions*. Silverback Publishing.

Michie, S., Richardson, M., Johnston, M., Abraham, C., Francis, J., Hardeman, W., Eccles, M. P., Cane, J., & Wood, C. E. (2013). The behavior change technique taxonomy (v1) of 93 hierarchically clustered techniques: Building an international consensus for the reporting of behavior change interventions. *Annals of Behavioral Medicine*, *46*(1), 81–95. doi:10.100712160-013-9486-6 PMID:23512568

Michie, S., Van Stralen, M. M., & West, R. (2011). The behaviour change wheel: A new method for characterising and designing behaviour change interventions. *Implementation Science; IS*, *6*(1), 1–12. doi:10.1186/1748-5908-6-42 PMID:21513547

Mohr, D. C., Schueller, S. M., Montague, E., Burns, M. N., & Rashidi, P. (2014). The behavioral intervention technology model: An integrated conceptual and technological framework for eHealth and mHealth interventions. *Journal of Medical Internet Research*, *16*(6), e146. doi:10.2196/jmir.3077 PMID:24905070

Ogden, J. (2016). Celebrating variability and a call to limit systematisation: The example of the Behaviour Change Technique Taxonomy and the Behaviour Change Wheel. *Health Psychology Review*, *10*(3), 245–250. doi:10.1080/17437199.2016.1190291 PMID:27189585

Oprescu, F., Jones, C., & Katsikitis, M. (2014). I PLAY AT WORK—Ten principles for transforming work processes through gamification. *Frontiers in Psychology*, *5*, 14. doi:10.3389/fpsyg.2014.00014 PMID:24523704

Purwandari, B., Sutoyo, M. A. H., Mishbah, M., & Dzulfikar, M. F. (2019, October). Gamification in e-Govemment: A Systematic Literature Review. In *2019 Fourth International Conference on Informatics and Computing (ICIC)* (pp. 1-5). IEEE. 10.1109/ICIC47613.2019.8985769

Rapp, A., Hopfgartner, F., Hamari, J., Linehan, C., & Cena, F. (2019). *Strengthening gamification studies: Current trends and future opportunities of gamification research*. Academic Press.

Reeves, B., Cummings, J. J., Scarborough, J. K., & Yeykelis, L. (2015). Increasing energy efficiency with entertainment media: An experimental and field test of the influence of a social game on performance of energy behaviors. *Environment and Behavior*, *47*(1), 102–115. doi:10.1177/0013916513506442

Reeves, B., & Read, J. L. (2009). *Total engagement: How games and virtual worlds are changing the way people work and businesses compete*. Harvard Business Press.

Ricciardi, F., & De Paolis, L. T. (2014). A comprehensive review of serious games in health professions. *International Journal of Computer Games Technology*.

Sardi, L., Idri, A., & Fernández-Alemán, J. L. (2017). A systematic review of gamification in e-Health. *Journal of Biomedical Informatics*, *71*, 31–48. doi:10.1016/j.jbi.2017.05.011 PMID:28536062

Silva, R. J. R. D., Rodrigues, R. G., & Leal, C. T. P. (2019). Gamification in management education: A systematic literature review. *BAR - Brazilian Administration Review*, *16*(2), e180103. doi:10.1590/1807-7692bar2019180103

Sipiyaruk, K., Gallagher, J. E., Hatzipanagos, S., & Reynolds, P. A. (2018). A rapid review of serious games: From healthcare education to dental education. *European Journal of Dental Education*, *22*(4), 243–257.

TechSci Research. (2019). *Global Gamification Market*. Available at: https://www.techsciresearch.com/sample-report.aspx?cid=3892

Valencia, K., Rusu, C., Quiñones, D., & Jamet, E. (2019). The impact of technology on people with autism spectrum disorder: A systematic literature review. *Sensors (Basel)*, *19*(20), 4485.

Wells, L. F. (2018). *Energy Explorer: A theory-informed design for a serious game with the purpose of promoting energy conservation behaviours* (Doctoral dissertation). University of Tasmania.

Xi, N., & Hamari, J. (2019). Does gamification satisfy needs? A study on the relationship between gamification features and intrinsic need satisfaction. *International Journal of Information Management*, *46*, 210–221.

Chapter 3
Gamification for Organizational Change and Innovation

Assia Alexandrova
Accenture, Canada

Lucia Rapanotti
The Open University, UK

ABSTRACT

Gamification has demonstrated significant potential for the support of innovation processes and change initiatives in organizations. There are numerous examples of its application to employee idea crowd-sourcing and internal platforms for innovation management in for-profit enterprises and government organizations, where it has fostered increased participation and engagement. A detailed overview of RE-PROVO—a game prototype designed to assist government practitioners in analyzing functional requirements during legacy IT system replacement projects—is an example of how gamification can further promote innovation by being applied to key business processes and practices. The evaluation of the prototype highlights the need for greater operational embeddedness of gamification and the added value of stakeholder participation in gamification design.

INTRODUCTION

Global economic shifts, the COVID pandemic and climate change have all highlighted the need for a sustained approach to organizational change and innovation. Swift transformation and adaptation are key for the survival and successful performance of commercial and non-for-profit companies, government entities and scientific institutions alike.

Organizational gamification has evolved beyond the point of experimental applications and reached a stage where large enterprises are adopting it in more systematic ways, so that certain toolsets, like online training and sales, are being bundled with gamified options by default. As gamification is approaching maturity (Nacke & Deterding, 2017), it is increasingly considered a customary solution when enterprises need to boost innovation (Burke, 2012; Alsaad & Durugbo, 2020) employee engagement in

DOI: 10.4018/978-1-6684-4291-3.ch003

organizational change. Yet, a clear picture of current intra-organizational approaches and practices is still lacking. This gap motivates the content of this chapter, in which we review, analyses and critique existing and potential applications of gamification that promote or deal with organizational change and innovation in order to derive insights relevant to the study of organizational gamification. Alongside an analysis of the wider literature, we report on our own primary research on gamification to foster innovation in the public sector.

We work with the definition of gamification put forth by Kevin Werbach: "the process of making activities more similar to games" (Werbach, 2014), as in the case of organizational gamification the design process is of critical importance and gamification is not just an end-product. In this chapter, we focus on digital tools which incorporate elements, such as reward actions with badges or levels of achievement, as well as other electronic artefacts which position participants in playful competitive situations. We also consider applications constructed as missions or player journeys, where the completion of a series of tasks is at the heart of the online experience. However, business-focused social networking tools which use online identities and avatars for purposes of interaction and reaction to posts and content, are not treated as examples of gamification in our review (even if the aesthetics and feel of such tools may include elements of entertainment) and hence are out of scope.

This chapter is organized as follows. In Section 2, we review the literature on gamified solutions to foster organizational innovation and change, arguing that a gap exists in relation to gamified solutions utilized internally in public sector agencies. In Section 3 we present in detail RE-PROVO, our application of gamification designed to tackle legacy system replacement project issues in government agencies, as a specific, yet persuasive, case for the use of gamification elements in public sector organizational change. Key implications of our research are discussed in Section 4, in the context of related work and in relation to the need and benefits of embedding gamification in existing operations, and the importance of involving employees in organizational gamification design. In Section 5, we draw some overall conclusions.

BACKGROUND

Generating innovative ideas and iterating through them via a collective exercise in an open dialogue format is part of the general trend from closed narrow-sourced innovation to open innovation, which taps into communities outside individual departments or entire organizations. Methods such as workshops, skunkworks, focus groups or specialized R&D methods that require physical collocation and extensive resources are being replaced or augmented by online ideation management technologies (Dombrowski et al, 2007). These allow organizations to transition from potentially expensive discrete events and stand-alone contests to more cost-effective and ongoing competitions for stakeholders to provide suggestions on process and product improvement. However, engagement in mass innovation initiatives has been traditionally seen as problematic (Totterdill et al., 2016; Tidd & Bessant, 2005) for reasons spanning from inertia, a lack of desire to perform beyond one's job description, to skepticism about how ideas and feedback are ultimately handled by organizational management.

Gamification is seen as a remedy to such an engagement deficit. Already in 2012, Gartner predicted 'an explosion of gamified crowdsourced innovations by 2020' (Burke, 2012). In this section we consider the extent to which such a prediction has been rrealized and where gaps still exist.

Gamification in Enterprise Innovation

Embedding gamification elements in enterprise innovation platforms has become common in industry and is a key strategy to surface ideas that help companies stay competitive and promote incremental organizational change (Burke, 2016; Viberg et al., 2020). While externally focused innovation crowd-sourcing centers around product and service improvements (Witt et al., 2011), employee programs involve generating ideas about the enhancements to internal processes as well, which increases their prospective utility. Gamifying employee suggestion programs follows the successes of corporate community-building campaigns which generated consumer feedback and promoted customer brand loyalty while soliciting and collecting ideas for new product development and service improvement. Examples include the Virtual Idea Communities established by IBM, Starbucks, and BMW, among others (Scheiner et al., 2017), and notably a system implemented by Salesforce, the company whose focus is Customer Relationship Management platform development, which demonstrates the integration of consumer feedback and ideation with customer profiles to generate marketing data about product preferences (Schweitzer & Tidd, 2018). Idea crowdsourcing has thus informed companies' strategic approach to consumer experience management and has allowed them to gain market share. Similarly, the integration of internally facing ideation management tools with enterprise processes, such as talent identification, skill development, and collaboration platforms, has the potential to lead to strategic human resource management and continuous business process improvement.

A study of industry insights into gamified innovation (Breuer & Ivanov, 2020) identified several core themes around gamification in the context of intra-organizational innovation processes, namely providing a safe space for experimentation, overcoming a silo mentality, and enabling collaboration across organizational units. We highlight some examples from organizational practice as an illustration of those themes. Bank Nordea, a large Scandinavian financial institution, established a virtual platform where employees can share their own ideas, and comment on those proposed by others. The goal was not just to stimulate the development of new concepts and products, but also knowledge sharing among different departments of the company. The platform enabled posting of ideas on an ongoing basis, alongside the creation of time-based special campaigns with calls to innovate on a specific topic. Two versions of the platform were established and compared – one gamified, and one not. The gamified version, which included leaderboards, progress bars, a point system, and idea feedback was found to have a definite stimulating impact on innovation, although the findings were not conclusive due to research study limitations. Similar to other studies (Witt et al., 2011), the Bank Nordea example brought to light that, as extrinsic elements, gamification mechanisms must work in tandem with internal motivation and that gamification operates best in conjunction with additional organizational measures.

Other examples of internal innovation approaches include 'gamestorming' (Gray et al., 2010) and design thinking virtual workshops to involve employees in exploration of innovative solutions (Kumar, 2011). In his analysis of Deloitte India's Maverick program, Kumar notes that out-of-the-box thinking is structurally discouraged in many enterprises because employees are socialized into risk aversion. The Maverick program, much like games and innovation labs, provides a safe space for employees to experiment and fail without negative consequences.

ideaChef®, by Patricio & Morozumi (2018), is a gamified method and tool to strengthen the idea development phase and complement design thinking practices employed by firms. Its evaluation revealed that gamification effectively contributed to identifying ideas to address particular business challenges and also helped build action plans to support their implementation. This is a rare outcome, as recent research indicates that most uses of organizational gamification focus on earlier stages of ideation, and not on prototyping, evaluation or implementation of innovative ideas (Breuer & Ivanov, 2020; Patricio et al., 2018).

Gudiksen and Inlove review the potential benefits of games and gamification to address the lack of cross-functional communication in organizations. Wherever silos form and knowledge flows are hindered by organizational hierarchies and structures, decision cycles become extended, team cohesiveness is hampered and inefficiencies occur. The authors highlight the creation of a safe, neutral space where different parties can communicate better and improve their collaboration – referred to as "third space communication" (Gudiksen & Inlove, 2018) of which game mechanics are suitable enablers. Third space gamification is demonstrated in knowledge management, where gamification techniques have been used to supplement collaboration activities in enterprise knowledge systems: knowledge capture, sharing and transfer are incentivized (Shpakova et al., 2017; Ďuriník, 2015; Elm et al., 2016) with benefits including increased transparency and thus increased trust among representatives from different enterprise departments.

Gamification in Enterprise Transformation

Few notable examples exist of gamification applied to tackle specific domain problems and to improve the outcomes of organizational transition projects, including digital transformation or the adoption of new technologies and systems (Guinan et al., 2019; Gudiksen & Inlove, 2018; Shiralkar, 2016) and related changes to business process, which are a challenge for organizations of all sizes.

Shreekant Shiralkar (2016) reports on the use of a game based on the metaphor of a treasure hunt to acquaint employees with new technology concepts in a large global delivery software organization. The game participants find clues to a puzzle in software documentation and must absorb information about the new technology in order to progress in the game, gather clues, and ultimately find the treasure. In this fashion, the game incentivizes employees to read otherwise unappealing technical texts, by leveraging their competitive drive and curiosity.

Another illustration of Breuer and Ivanov's "gamification as experimentation enabler" can be found in Guinan et al.'s study of IT organizations. They position the ability to rapidly experiment, gain insights and learn as a main lever of the successful digital transformation team, with the agile development methodology (Highsmith & Fowler, 2001), design thinking (Brown, 2008) and gamification all seen as effective instruments organizations can use to support digital transformation initiatives. The core strength of gamification in this context is identified as its encouragement of positive risk taking, with the authors providing examples of themed innovation days with an entrepreneurial slant where new digital product and solution storyboards were awarded venture funding in the form of game points (Guinan et al., 2019).

Innovation in government organizations tends to occur at a slower pace than in commercial enterprises, due to their more bureaucratic and risk averse culture, as well as fewer market pressures. Gamified innovation has been touted as particularly suitable where behavior and attitude adjustments are required for a successful outcome, therefore, next we review case studies where gamification has been deployed to support organizational change in government bureaucracies, highlighting successes and limitations (Buheji, 2019; Al-Yafi & El-Masri, 2016; Sandoval-Almazan & Valle-Cruz, 2017).

While for-profit companies can choose whether or not to engage actors outside of their boundaries in innovation processes, public sector organizations must by definition involve their external stakeholders, particularly the general public, in order to achieve meaningful transformation. Hence civic engagement is paramount, yet problematic (Hassan, 2017), with multiple examples where only low numbers of constituents react to calls for feedback, attend city commission meetings, or engage in government-developed online discussion fora. Consequently, so far the majority of examples of gamification to promote innovation have targeted citizens, rather than government employees with only few examples of intra-organizational practices supported by gamification, primarily in internal ideation management and knowledge management processes.

A key obstacle to public sector innovation has been identified as the bureaucratic inclinations and inertia of government employees (Boyne, 2002), with gamification hailed as a means to instill and mobilize more pro-transformation attitudes (Hassan, 2017). As an illustrative example, the Swiss process exchange platform (Dargan & Evequoz, 2015) involves the internal sharing of Business Process Management (BPM) documentation among government workers, so that they can develop a more innovative mindset around BPM practices. This platform embeds gamification elements, such as badges, although in their evaluation Dargan and Evequoz observed that despite their universal use, badges, like all other virtual incentives, need to be highly contextualized in order to be effective, which poses specific challenges for the design of personalized rewards for wider audiences (Dargan & Evequoz, 2015).

In another example, from the first author's professional practice, the Miami-Dade County employee suggestion program was modernized with the use of gamification elements, such as upvotes and progress meters (Taylor, 2011). The resulting application – Idea Machine - was implemented on the municipal organization's employee portal and utilized the notion of open competition to promote ideas for detailed feasibility review and possible monetary rewards. This employee-centered application later evolved into MyGovIdea and was made more widely available for submissions by County residents. The visibility of ideas was a significant improvement over the old system, where employees submitted their suggestions as an email or a paper file and had no transparency and insights of the review process. Along similar lines, "Idea Street" was developed a gamified platform for collecting and sharing cost-saving ideas in the UK Department for Work and Pensions (Shpakova et al., 2019; Vezina, 2011).

Summary

While acknowledging the growing body of work on the use of gamification for organizational innovation, this can hardly be seen as the explosion in uptake predicted by Gartner almost a decade ago. The literature we have reviewed highlights some notable examples, demonstrating the possible benefits of using gamification in organizational settings, particularly around exploring potential innovations and organizational transformations in a context of safety from failure, to engage different organizational perspectives more effectively, or to inspire playful collaboration. However, both the extent these benefits can be realized by different organizations and their impact on practice remain unclear.

A notable gap exists when it comes to government organizations, where the focus so far has been on citizen engagement rather than surfacing employees' innovative ideas and stimulating internal process improvement. This is where our research focus lies: the development of RE-PROVO, described in detail in the next section, is our attempt to demonstrate and evaluate the potential of gamification to support organizational innovation and change in public sector agencies. This approach has been dubbed "gamification-as-induction" because it aims to induce innovative behaviors and processes though the use of game elements (Alsaad & Durugbo, 2020).

RE-PROVO: FOSTERING GAMIFIED INNOVATION IN THE PUBLIC SECTOR

An issue intrinsic to large bureaucratic institutions, and particularly severe in government agencies is their over-reliance on legacy IT systems (Halachmi, 2011). These tend to constrain an organization's ability to adapt to its continuously changing environment. Some argue that in order to enable innovation in government organizations, the best approach would be to replace legacy systems (Charette, 2020). However, legacy system replacement projects in government tend to be drawn out, expensive and ineffective. Hence, our research investigates whether gamification can contribute positively to public sector innovation through its application to legacy system replacement projects in a way which leverages Breuer and Ivanov's gamification innovation themes – safe space for experimentation, cross-unit collaboration and overcoming the silo mentality.

The 'Legacy Problem'

We have defined the 'legacy problem' (Alexandrova & Rapanotti, 2020) in the public sector, as the uncritical replication of legacy systems in the requirements for applications that supersede them. Such replication is intended to minimize the changes to business processes which were shaped by the technological constraints of those same legacy systems. Government organizations tend to resist moving away from anachronistic work practices supported by and embedded in legacy IT systems. One of the most fundamental ways in which the legacy problem manifests itself is in creating paralysis when organizations review potential changes to business processes, this paralysis being reinforced by the existence and proliferation of organizational rules that have often been developed as workarounds to limitations of the very same legacy systems. It results in missed opportunities for business process innovation in government agencies and in the replication of outdated institutional policies and procedures which limit organizational flexibility, and ultimately the ability to respond swiftly to meet constituents' needs and requests.

The legacy problem emerges primarily in the requirements activities undertaken during legacy replacement projects, where our research findings (Alexandrova & Rapanotti, 2020) indicate that legacy system features commonly become the direct requirements for how the technology replacing them needs to look and behave. Therefore, our research focuses on addressing the legacy problem through gamification at the requirements analysis phase of legacy system replacement projects.

Our research has followed design science research (DSR), a distinct research paradigm which contributes new knowledge via the design and construction of innovative and practically useful artefacts (Thuan et al., 2019): in other words, DSR is a research paradigm aimed at solving real-world problems in order to generate new knowledge about the problem or the solution or both (Gregor & Hevner, 2013). DSR is rooted in engineering and design scientific thinking (Simon, 1996) from the mid-90s, hence is relatively new and still evolving. However, there is broad agreement on its key activities (Hevner at al., 2004; Peffers et al., 2006) and research process cycles (Hevner, 2007), which span problem identification within real-world contexts (establishing relevance and fitness), artefact design and construction, and rigorous evaluation and knowledge generation. DSR is a broad methodology able to accommodate: the creation of all sorts of innovative artefacts, from algorithms to systems, processes, methods, etc. (Peffers et al., 2012); the application of diverse evaluation techniques, from logical argumentation to experimental work, to case studies and more (Peffers et al., 2012), both formative and summative (Venable et al., 2021); and the generation of different types of knowledge, from descriptive to prescriptive (Gregor &

Hevner, 2013). DSR is not prescriptive of which problem solving and design methods should apply to frame the problem or design and construct the solution artefact, expecting the researcher to select and justify the most appropriate approach based on the nature of both problem and solution. However, the process is expected to be iterative both in problem and solution spaces.

In our work we have applied DSR to the legacy problem outlined above, for which we have designed and evaluated a gamified tool (the artefact) called RE-PROVO ("provo" means "test" or "attempt" in the international language Esperanto and was chosen to emphasize the need for iterations in the act of deliberation). RE-PROVO is a requirements deliberation game designed to promote creativity during the analysis and critique of business requirements stemming from legacy systems. Its design was informed by three distinct DSR cycles, from inception to full design and evaluation, which we discuss next.

Inception

In the first DSR cycle, the root causes of the legacy problem were analyzed and two prevailing perspectives were identified as common to legacy systems replacement projects (Alexandrova & Rapanotti, 2020): risk aversion (also referred to as legacy, or heritage preservation) vs. innovation. Such perspectives informed the basic discussion-structuring mechanisms of RE-PROVO.

Triadic Game Design (Harteveld, 2011) principles were adopted to guide the RE-PROVO high level design. They distinguish between three main design areas: ontological, semiotic and ludic. The ontological aspects of a game encompass the underlying model of the real-world domain the game is based on. The semiotic design incorporates the elements and approaches that make the game meaningful and generate lessons and useful information that can be transferred to the "real-world". The ludic aspects cover the techniques which make a game interactive, challenging, fun and immersive. Well-designed games achieve a balance between these elements: without a strong ontological base, a game would be simplistic and suitable for basic education only; without the semiotic emphasis, the game would be mostly fun but not educational; and without the ludic elements, the game would be merely a training or simulation tool (Martens et al., 2008). With these principles in mind, we developed a mapping between game elements, requirements engineering concepts and organizational goals, so that we could introduce game elements purposefully and associate them with learning and pragmatic outcomes. Game components were included to support the ludic element of the design, specifically the basic Points -Badges-Leaderboards (PBL) model (Deterding, 2012), which is a standard gamification mechanism end users may already be familiar with from other games or software applications.

Finally, we adopted role-play as an enabler of creativity: since games create an artificial, fictional setting, participants can assume different roles, characters, or personas that allow them to explore a diverse set of behaviors and assumptions, and take symbolic actions, experiencing a disinhibition effect, overcoming personal barriers that may otherwise hinder participation in group discussions and collective activities (Aubusson et al., 1997).

The result was a first design involving a roleplaying activity governed by rules to enable s structured discussion of requirements along the two themes of heritage preservation and innovation, while providing a safe space for being creative and voicing opinions, or possibly dissent.

This early design was evaluated through a playtesting session (Chaffin & Barnes, 2010), a practice recommended for testing the viability of a game concept and for further evolving a game design: it does not require all game elements or technologies to be finalized and should be performed as early as possible in the development process. This is consistent with the DSR evaluation of an artefact construct via expert qualitative feedback (Peffers et al., 2012). The playtesting session involved a low fidelity try-out of the game by a team of five non-technical business experts at a municipal government agency in the United States. The purpose was to evaluate player roles, rules and dynamics for their adequacy in discussing requirements in legacy system replacement projects. It was intended to imitate the flow of the game using a generic online chat tool, without a specifically developed graphical user interface: the players were expected to discuss requirements by sending chat messages. Requirements from a fictitious IT system were used in the playtest.

While both intent and basic game design were deemed appropriate to foster innovation in legacy replacement projects, the session highlighted the need to improve game flow and to design a graphical user interface to enable group interactions. In particular, although the players understood and adapted their messages to their roles, they could not easily follow the group dialogue due to the lack of interface cues to prompt them to engage in the structured discussion. This informed the next design cycle.

PROOF OF CONCEPT DESIGN

In this cycle, the focus was on designing an interface able to support the game dynamics developed in the previous cycle, while enabling effective group dialogues. Further validation of roles and game dynamics was also sought, in line with DSR principles of iterative and incremental enquiry cycles.

In this cycle, the qualitative evaluation took the form of a focus group involving 18 expert participants from a graduate studies program in Public Administration in South Florida, who were also working professionals, and the requirements used were from an actual IT replacement project run by a public administration (focus group process reported originally in Alexandrova, 2018). Via an interactive presentation, the participants were guided through a hypothetical gameplay session supported by seven screen mock-ups. At each step, they were asked to comment on game design and gameplay, and on ways to make it more effective and engaging.

In this evaluation too, most participants acknowledged the great potential of the game as a tool for innovation, but also raised issues related to organizational dynamics and how such a game would be implemented and integrated within an organizational context.

Firstly, participants felt very strongly that anonymity was required for the game to be successful. Without anonymity, they were concerned that management could obtain the players' identities and see their comments and recommendations. They highlighted the need to assure absolute safety and freedom of expression for players, so that they could be honest in their suggestions and analysis.

How to reward participation was another key emerging theme. Reward elements inherent in the game, i.e, points, leaderboards and votes, were seen as insufficient motivators, with participants suggesting they should be linked to more tangible, real world rewards, like organizational recognition, or even paid time off work. This, however, would be difficult to achieve if players were to be kept strictly anonymous.

Participants were also concerned as to how IT system requirements developed throughout a game session would be communicated to decision makers within an organization, so as to be considered seriously as likely system changes or improvements, pointing to a need for the integration of gameplay within decision making processes. Notably, the focus group participants provided less feedback on the proposed graphical user interface than on organizational dynamics.

Game Design and Implementation

Early design and evaluation cycles fed into the final design and implementation of RE-PROVO. Specifically, in the game requirements are critiqued from the two dominant perspectives in legacy system replacement projects - those of risk aversion and innovation, within the following gameflow.

The game is seeded with a set of business requirements, which are entered as separate discussion threads in an online repository. Each player is assigned a play role of either a 'Heritage Keeper', or 'Innovator'. Players are asked to review and analyze the requirements. Those in the role of Heritage Keeper must issue a challenge to the requirements they think depart too much from the operational status-quo and are too risky for implementation. Those in the role of Innovator must issue challenges to the requirements which too faithfully reproduce legacy workflows and features, and thus do not take advantage of opportunities for innovation through new technologies or new system design (illustrated in Figure 1).

Once a requirement has been challenged, any player can respond to the challenge by proposing a modification to the requirement, i.e., by `morphing' it in a way that addresses the issues put forth in the challenge. Morphings can be challenged too, thus potentially producing several different versions of a requirement. At the end of an agreed upon timeframe (e.g., two weeks), the players vote on all proposed requirement morphings, and those with the most votes become the winning, or final, versions of the requirements. The lifecycle of a functional requirement in RE-PROVO is represented in Figure 2.

Players are awarded points based on their quantitative activity and engagement. They are rewarded for each challenge, morphing, comment, or requirement rating, and the player with the most points becomes the winner of the game.

The JIRA platform (by Atlassian) was used for the RE-PROVO implementation due to its flexibility of customization and the technical support offered by its development community. The platform is commonly used by small organizations and large enterprises alike to manage Agile projects and includes a number of functionalities that could be repurposed for the game implementation (although it is not a bespoke game development platform). In particular, JIRA's main programmatic object the "issue," which may represent a software error, feature, etc., and its core function is issue tracking. JIRA allows for different actions to be taken in response to an identified issue and automatically enables changes to the issue status through a workflow transition process.

However, it is not sophisticated enough to support the challenge-morphing cycle envisioned for RE-PROVO or the ludic elements of the the Points-Badges-Leaderboards model, so that a series of additional plugins developed by third-party companies were installed, customized and extended programmatically to approximate the RE-PROVO game elements. Figure 3 demonstrates a specific sequence of challenges and requirement morphing.

In relation to the organizational context, RE-PROVO is meant to be played before business requirements are delivered to a vendor, or service provider via a procurement document such as a call for tenders, request for proposals, or invitation to bid. In the case of bespoke development, the game should be played prior to commencing development efforts – i.e., before a finalized requirements specification is delivered to the software development team. In an agile development environment the game can be executed in parallel with the iterations or "sprints" taking place, and it can be consulted by product owners to finalize the formulation of user stories.

While RE-PROVO was designed for primary participation by business users, information technology staff or users with a technical background can also partake, as long as the discussion of technical details does not dominate the gameplay.

Figure 1. Example of Innovation Challenge

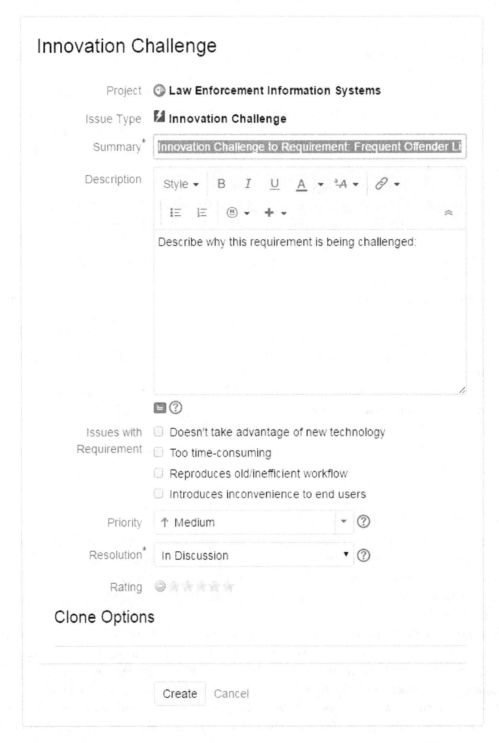

Figure 2. Requirement morphing cycle in RE-PROVO

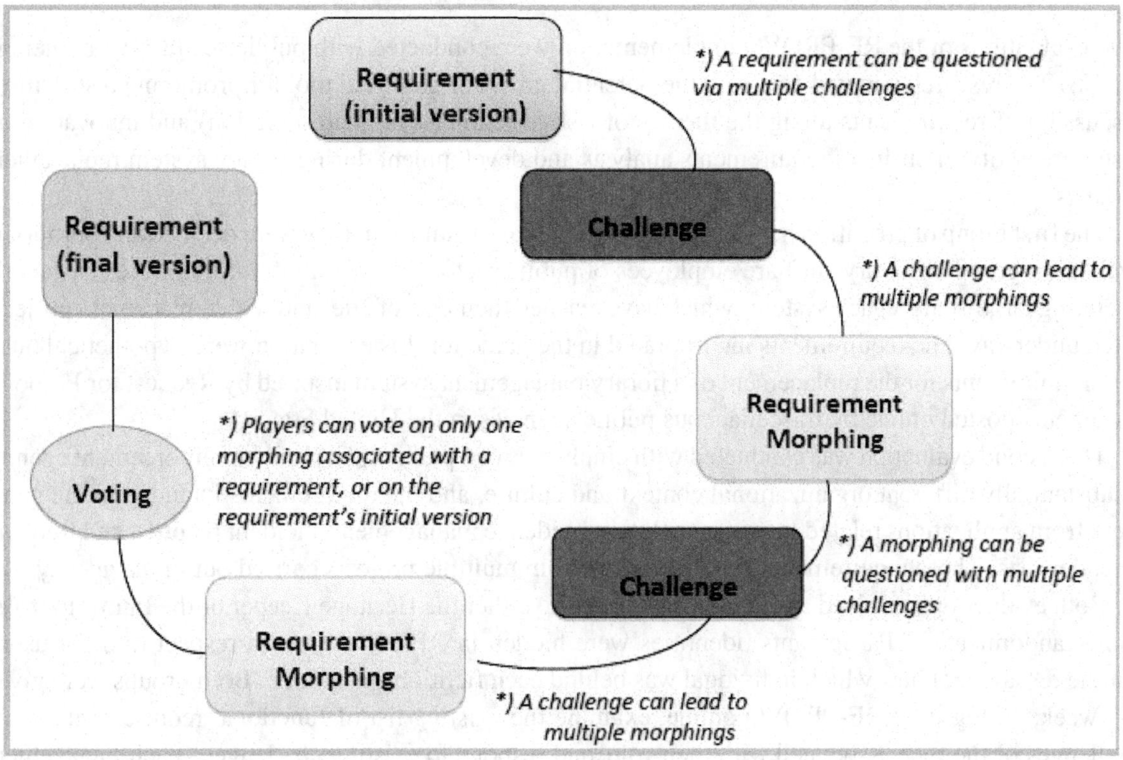

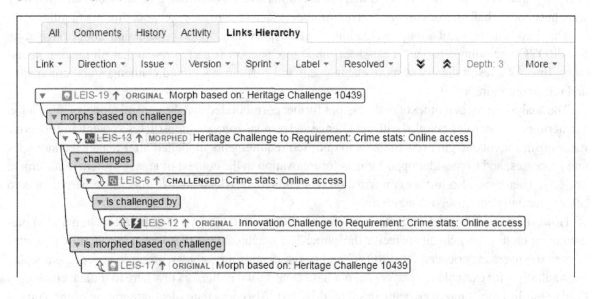

Figure 3. Example of Requirement Challenge tracking in RE-PROVO

Evaluation

Two evaluations of the RE-PROVO implementation were conducted with public sector practitioners in the US. The research aim was to assess the potential utility of gamified tool for promoting a structured discussion of requirements along the themes of risk aversion (legacy preservation) and innovation, to foster creativity in business requirements analysis and development during legacy system replacement projects.

The first group of practitioners was from a public library institution: they were deemed an appropriate evaluation group as library staff are employees of public sector organizations, with libraries frequently operating large-scale legacy systems which have reached their end-of-life, and with replacement projects often underway. The requirements incorporated in the game for this evaluation were hypothetical business requirements for the replacement of a library management system inspired by Request for Proposal documents posted online by miscellaneous public agencies in the United States.

The second evaluation was conducted with employees of a public safety and law enforcement agency, a substantially different organizational context and culture, and the requirements included in the game were from applications related to crime analytics, evidence management, incident records, and frequent offender lists. These requirements were compiled from multiple projects carried out in the agency.

Both evaluations involved assigning participants to either the Heritage Keeper or the Innovator roles using randomization. Participants' identities were hidden in RE-PROVO with respect to other users, but the researcher knew which individual was behind each fictitious username. Both groups were given 2-3 weeks to log in to RE-PROVO online, examine the existing list of functional requirements, issue challenges of the type associated with their role, and respond to existing challenges. Their engagement was evaluated in terms of the number of times they logged in, the number of challenges they issued, the comments they made, their page views of the points, badges and leaderboard tab, and the votes they cast.

The Public Library group evaluation was conducted first and registered minimal engagement. After follow-up interviews it was discovered that the user interface was confusing to the users, and that they were hesitant to challenge or comment on requirements for a system they were not directly familiar with.

The Law Enforcement group evaluation involved providing more information about navigating RE-PROVO, including a paper "cheat-sheet" and more support from the researcher on logging in and using Jira. As a result there was more engagement and participants issued challenges and comments, and registered more logins.

The analysis of the outcomes of both sessions further corroborated that the general model of innovation and heritage keeper roles, coupled with a challenge and response process, constitutes a potentially effective mechanism for encouraging practitioners to question requirements modelled after legacy technologies and processes, and to consider opportunities for innovation in the context of legacy system replacement projects. There was also further confirmation that anonymity is essential to encourage participants to offer potentially controversial suggestions.

However, as in the initial evaluation, findings highlighted the impact of software design and implementation on how participants perceive the game. The graphical user interface was a significant factor in how the users experienced RE-PROVO and in the case of the Library group it impeded gameplay substantially – for example the players did not have clear visual indicators of where to initiate challenges (due to the Jira tool's interface being dashboard-based). Also, less than ideal integration of the Points–Badges-Leaderboards elements within the JIRA platform (illustrated in Figure 4) led to these features rarely being sought out intentionally by participants.

Figure 4. Points-Badges-Leaderboard Tab in RE-PROVO (using the Jiraffe plugin for Jira)

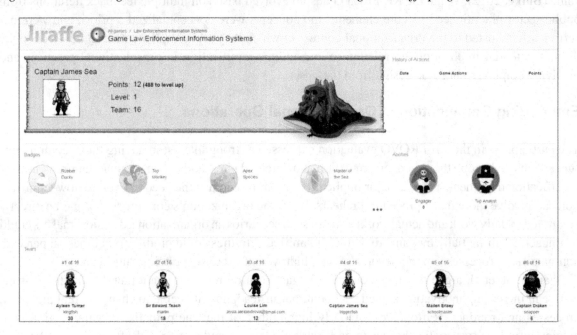

The findings further highlighted the importance of tailoring game user interface and features to actual organizational requirements and context in order to enhance the participants' experience and the overall effectiveness of the game. In the case of RE-PROVO, the game evaluation was undertaken for research purposes, and even though it contained real scenarios and requirements from actual ongoing projects, it was primarily an exercise in deliberation, and its outcomes had no guarantee of impacting agency decision makers. RE-PROVO has been, in effect, a rehearsal for future discussions. This echoes the notion of "procedural rhetoric" (Bogost, 2008), which posits that the main impact of games is to imply and teach a certain procedural model of the world. The innovation and idea management platforms discussed in Section 2 are also separate standalone systems dedicated specifically to ideation activities and processes. We will elaborate on the disadvantages of such a separation, and on opportunities for promoting gamification to operational processes in the next discussion section.

DISCUSSION AND RELATED WORK

Generally, our findings indicate that, despite the graphical interface shortcomings discussed, the fundamental RE-PROVO design and gameplay has potential for fostering innovation in legacy replacement projects, but that appropriate organizational contextualisation is essential to both participants' experience and game effectiveness. Such an organizational focus during evaluation suggests that perhaps details regarding the game elements might be less, or at least equally, important as the conversation and discourse surrounding how the game is executed in a government agency environment.

In fact, proper design and integration of game elements into business applications is an acknowledged top issue in gamification: Gartner analysts suggest that gamification's slip into the "trough of disillusionment" is precisely because poorly designed gamification applications have failed to deliver value (Burke, 2012). While the RE-PROVO design evolved based on multiple feedback iterations from public sector practitioners, its core elements and concepts were conceptualized a priori, and were not sufficiently adjusted to the organizational context in which they were implemented. In this section we discuss potential implications in relation to embedding gamification in organizational practices and involving employees in game design from the onset.

Embedding Gamification in Organizational Operations

The participants in the RE-PROVO evaluation expressed a strong interest in having their requirements suggestions go beyond the sphere of simulation and "pretend play" and become actual requirements in a specification document. Thus, a major implication of our research is the need to explore how gamification can involve more than "procedural rehearsals" of the organization's core processes and be directly integrated in daily work and actual workflows. In such scenarios an organization's decision-makers could be impacted substantially by game dynamics. Gamified activities could produce outcomes on par with non-gamified processes, and go beyond being a lightweight exercise, or being "just a game."

Warmelink et al. argue that a key question in gamification research is not merely whether it is effective in increasing motivation and engagement, but instead, how it is able to change actual practices, processes and routines. Raftopoulos similarly highlights that the true potential of gamification is in helping introduce systematic changes to how work is designed and managed (Raftopoulos, 2014).

Humlung and Haddara echo these notions in advocating a transition from gamification of ERP training to the incorporation of gamification techniques "into the business as a whole" (Humlung & Haddara, 2019). Such an augmented scope for gamification is not common, however, because it is more difficult to design and implement, as the specific business context to be gamified "provides operational requirements that limit the unlimited design space" regular games otherwise have (Morschheuser et al., 2018).

In our discussion in Section 2, we argued how in idea management platforms, idea competitions and workshops, the innovation aspect is in effect segregated from the other functional areas of the organization, but there is evidence in favor of embedding gamification in enterprise systems and operations. Introducing game elements in areas such as software engineering, testing and quality assurance (QA), project management, enterprise resource planning (ERP), logistics, etc. might offer tangible and improved support for organizational change by establishing less circuitous paths towards innovation (Nah et al. 2018; Humlung & Haddara, 2019). We highlight some examples in which this has happened.

A comprehensive literature review conducted by de Paula Porto et al. (2021) found multiple uses of gamification in software engineering practice. Gamification-induced user participation in requirements activities led to higher quality requirements (Lombriser et al., 2016). The application of gamification also resulted in improved programming practices (Foucault et al., 2019), up-to-date software product documentation (Sukale & Pfaff, 2014), decreased coding time (Tsunoda & Yumoto, 2018), fewer software bugs, improved code refactoring, and drove better adherence to agile software development principles. These cases, however, exemplify applications of gamification to software development activities where games can be readily integrated with existing development tools and where impact can be easily quantified, whereas examples of gamifying more complex and critical software engineering activities, such as software design, modelling and architecture, are still lacking. The benefits gamification can introduce to these areas stem from its noted strength in breaking down silos and promoting collaboration. The bird's eye view necessary to produce an effective enterprise architecture can be aided by measures that promote improved cross-department communication and knowledge sharing.

There are few examples from other industries. For instance, a cleaning services company sought to improve the process of building maintenance problem reporting by gamifying it (Rix et al., 2015). Its user research uncovered that points and badges might be insufficient to change the motivation of their workers to perform extra steps in their daily routines, so the resulting app was a combination of gamification and social collaboration: the tool reflected the staff's desire not for simple mechanical problem reporting (i.e., broken door, security issue etc.), but for more involved problem solving. Overall, this example reinforces the argument that gamification introduces positive changes when it augments a process, rather than when it acts to reduce, mechanize and simplify it.

Hense et al. introduced GameLog, a gamification of the logistics process of order picking aimed at increasing motivation in repetitive, error-prone tasks (Hense et al., 2013). The approach to designing GameLog was interdisciplinary and unique in analyzing and incorporating several different perspectives on motivation, rather than simply focusing on the classic divide between intrinsic and extrinsic motivation. The authors' research also focuses on using game elements other than the standard gamification package of points, badges and leaderboards (PBL), with the goal of recognizing the uniqueness of the labor context.

Gamification experiments have been conducted in manufacturing as well, where the typical patterns of visually highlighting achievements, e.g., a blinking indicator showing one has accumulated points, or allowing the user to press a "Like" button, have been modified (or removed) to prevent distraction in work sequences with safety implications (Korn & Schmidt, 2015). Gamifying work contexts other than online applications in office settings demonstrates the need to evolve the gamification experience as we know it, and rather than apply a one-size fits all model (e.g., the universal PBL model), to better focus on the specificity of organizational contexts, on the unique characteristics of the business or production processes being gamified, as well as on a more nuanced analysis of the motivations and interests of the concrete employee groups involved.

Employee Participation in Organizational Gamification Design

When participants in the RE-PROVO evaluations provided feedback on their experience, they had numerous suggestions on how the game could be improved. Many of them voiced specific ideas on better ways to gamify the requirements analysis process, on ways to incentivize players, on additional game elements. Some began sketching designs and thinking out loud how they would develop a game if it were up to them. In summary, they showed strong enthusiasm for the prospect of co-designing organizational gamification.

Engaging public sector practitioners in design reviews and playtesting was a critical step in our research process, and it streamlined and improved the RE-PROVO prototype through its multiple design iterations. However, the nature of the engagement was such that the basic design concepts were already established, and the main problem targeted for resolution was already defined, and practitioners responded with feedback and critiques. A more active participatory involvement of end-users (in this case of government agency employees) in RE-PROVO's design would have been beneficial not only from a user experience perspective, but also for purposes of setting end goals and integrating with organizational processes. Therefore, a key conclusion from our RE-PROVO research was that involving users in the gamification design process from its very beginning - in the definitional and ideation stages - would lead to the development and implementation of a more successful requirements analysis tool and to better organizational outcomes (participation in requirements engineering activities and overcoming of legacy system models in the requirements analysis phase of legacy replacement projects).

Indeed, interviews conducted by Morschheuser et al. related to methods of engineering gamification solutions indicated that development projects of gamified software often fail due to a lack of involving key stakeholders in the engineering process (Morschheuser et al., 2018), highlighting that a key success factor in such engineering efforts is a focus on employees' needs, goals and motivations. However, such a focus is usually sought through standard user-centered techniques such as user interviews, brainstorming, and ethnographic research, while direct involvement is rarely practiced, and only a few of the experts interviewed by Morschheuser et al. recommended it as essential.

The design of software artifacts traditionally involves techniques and practices in which the "users world" and the "software world" come together only in limited ways, and where the flow of ideas, the learning and discussions are largely unilateral (Muller & Druin, 2002). Participatory design, on the other hand, focuses on reciprocity and mutuality, and requires the combination of the user and the designer/developer perspectives (ibidem). This is generally realized during prototyping or ideation workshops – e.g., future workshops, where the focus is on establishing end-users as co-creators and collaborators throughout all phases of project development, and in multiple iterations (Scariot et al., 2012).

The benefits of participatory design are manifold. On the one hand, an improved user experience is produced, user requirements are better fulfilled, and user acceptance is increased. On the other, its participants are empowered with knowledge of the design and development process, and their ideas and opinions directly impact the artifact design, thus incorporating their goals, interests and preferences, and establishing a sense of ownership (Muller & Druin, 2002)

Our review of the literature on organizational gamification has found little evidence of engaging employees in the ideation and design of gamified solutions. Generally, end-users are recruited in the testing phase of gamification apps, or as participants in user research where they are either involved in evaluating graphical user interface elements, or asked solution-agnostic questions about their behaviors and motivations respectively. This follows the traditional design model in the domain of conventional entertainment games (Khaled & Vasalou, 2014). A study conducted by Vilarinho et al. concluded that the targeted end-users of gamification can be suitably involved in the ideation phase of gamification apps, and that they do participate in such sessions creatively and think out-of-the-box (Vilarinho et al., 2018). The study, however, did not revolve around an organizational application, but a mental wellbeing app. There is similar evidence of end-user involvement in participatory design primarily in the gamification of educational solutions, but not for gamification efforts in an organizational context.

Practitioners have commonly sought to ensure the fit between a gamified app and its end-users by analyzing their motivations and characteristics and aligning them with existing player typologies (Hamari & Tuunanen, 2013). Others have applied user-centered design concepts throughout the research/design and implementation process (Chen, 2019). In many studies user-centered design (UCD) and participatory design have been treated as synonymous, however a key difference is the involvement of employees in the actual design process. Whereas in user-centered design users' interests, motivations and context are considered the main driver of design decisions – in the words of E. Sanders "the user is not really a part of the team but is spoken for by the researcher" (Sanders, 2002), participatory design affords end-users more agency, and more constitutive functions, including design decisions.

There are reports of participatory design in serious game projects (Khaled & Vasalou, 2014) which outline unique challenges and the need for a tailored approach. In serious games the set of design elements is broader than those utilized in gamification, and the domain content is potentially more complex.

Due to the need for integration with an existing business process, gamification covers a more finite set of game design possibilities and is applied in a more formulaic manner - most commonly through the abstraction of a pointification logic that can be added "on top" of any information system component, or, as RE-PROVO demonstrated with Jira: the points can be associated with any standard system activity – closing an issue, commenting on an issue, self-assignment, an issue status change and so on. As a result, practitioners, consultants and companies that create and configure enterprise gamification tools and platforms risk resorting to a design element reductionism (Warmelink et al., 2021), where design revolves around a predefined set of user interface options, and the need for involved designs is effectively diminished. The implicit argument is that design is involved only when one must define which activities need to be rewarded with points, and what the rewards would look like. Representing gamification exclusively through the Points-Badges-Leaderboard triad is another reason for such a reductionist approach, which, perhaps, is the reason why we see so few examples of participatory design in gamification. Such an oversimplification must be challenged - there is the potential to produce more elaborate and holistic solutions (Thibault & Hamari, 2021). Engaging end-users to participate actively in the design of organizational gamification has the potential to expand the gamification design space and introduce a greater variety of game elements - not only the well-established points, badges and leaderboards.

While the need to establish competition, mark levels of accomplishment and quantify achievements are addressed by these core elements, there are examples of other components, such as avatars, boss fights, collections, social graph, virtual goods, combat, content unlocking, gifting, quests, teams (Werbach & Hunter, 2012), and surely enough other new elements which might be contributed by employees (who have the benefit of not being constrained by specific technological or conceptual frameworks), which allow for additional design possibilities and more creative applications.

Notwithstanding, even if points and rewards are the basic mechanisms adopted and deemed sufficient to fulfill the goal of a particular gamification project, involvement of employees is still merited to tackle issues of impact, appropriateness, and privacy. While it is attractive to use gamification to introduce organizational changes in a more palatable way, researchers see possibilities for employee manipulation and exploitation, because gamification is not intended/perceived as a spontaneous undertaking, but as a management tool (Bogost, 2013; Raftopoulos, 2014). Its design is therefore highly consequential in terms of ethics, equity, agency, privacy. Raftopoulos singles out possibilities for increased surveillance, coercion, manipulation, and misrepresentation among other risks, in what she dubs the "deadly sins" of gamification (Raftopoulos, 2014). Misrepresentation, specifically, refers to creating an illusion of change. While gamifying enterprise work processes might give employees the impression that the nature of their work is changing, in reality enterprise buyers of gamification tools are primarily interested in making existing workflows efficient or fulfilling immediate executive mandates, rather than fundamentally changing work processes. Hence, the companies developing gamification platforms respond to this demand and produce tools geared specifically towards these functions.

These issues of ethics and disempowerment can be explicitly addressed in participatory design sessions, and such sessions can for instance, be structured according to specific ethical concerns. The potential impact on power relations and existing hierarchies should also be tackled in design explicitly, with business process changes and implications for organizational culture addressed openly. However, in order to meet the need for employee involvement in participatory design and still allow efficient implementation, gamification solutions must either be bespoke, or gamification platforms must be sufficiently flexible and open to customization.

CONCLUSIONS

The application of gamification to generate employee suggestions for process improvement and organizational change is becoming mainstream in order to cultivate enterprise innovation. Directly asking employees to provide innovative ideas and incentivizing them with game elements is now common in corporations and public organizations alike and does not involve substantial resources to set up and maintain given readily available gaming platforms. Points, badges and leaderboards are standard gamification mechanisms applied to idea management systems and have achieved the objective of increasing engagement and participation in processes for idea solicitation and socialization, one of their key benefits. However, that they create a separate space where it is safe to pitch any idea and flesh out any concept, can also be seen as a drawback: when gamified ideation platforms are separated from other processes, and not integrated with daily workflows, may only contribute to surfacing an idea, rather than to generate and develop it, or to prototype and assist its implementation.

Embedding game elements in an enterprise's business processes has been demonstrated in the areas of software engineering, knowledge management, even in logistics and manufacturing, to a limited extent. When applied to actual daily work, gamification has the potential to act as a change agent by boosting collaboration, providing insights on employee motivation and behavior, and in certain cases enhancing conventional enterprise communication and decision-making paths. As the RE-PROVO research has illustrated, employees are interested in seeing the outcomes of their game sessions be made actionable and be assessed for inclusion in product or business process change proposals.

However, achieving positive change and innovation can only be realized if gamification is properly designed. The criteria for successful design established by gamification researchers have included alignment with organizational goals, meaningful rewards, and recognition of player motivations, with a more recent focus on ethics, privacy and other value-based considerations. Moreover, the RE-PROVO participant feedback suggested that employee involvement in gamification design would lead to improvements in the game experience and boost the transformational potential of the game elements when layered on top of an existing business process. However, the minimal evidence of participatory design in organizational gamification has underscored a common reductionist approach to the scope of gamification applications for organizational change, and a propensity to implement quick, standardized solutions in organizations, which is perhaps a reflection of low maturity of gamification.

In this respect, M. Raftopoulos identifies the highest maturity phase of organizational gamification as the creation of an integrated enterprise environment for innovation (as cited in Humlung & Haddara, 2019), which she recognizes to be a complex undertaking. Hence, she advocates going beyond the basic introduction of a game layer to a business process, stressing the need "to develop a renovated game design thinking method" when transforming enterprise structures and processes. Based on our research, we argue that this can only be achieved with proper employee engagement in the process of participatory gamification design and meaningful embedding of gamification in organizational practice.

REFERENCES

Al-Yafi, K., & El-Masri, M. (2016). *Gamification of e-government services: A discussion of potential transformation*. Association for Information Systems.

Alexandrova, A. (2018). *Digital government systems: tackling the legacy problem through a game-based approach to business requirements analysis* [Doctoral Dissertation, The Open University]. ProQuest.

Alexandrova, A., & Rapanotti, L. (2020). Requirements analysis gamification in legacy system replacement projects. *Requirements Engineering*, *25*(2), 131–151. doi:10.100700766-019-00311-2

Aubusson, P., Fogwill, S., Barr, R., & Perkovic, L. (1997). What happens when students do simulation-role-play in science? *Research in Science Education*, *27*(4), 565–579. doi:10.1007/BF02461481

Bogost, I. (2008). *The rhetoric of video games*. MacArthur Foundation Digital Media and Learning Initiative.

Bogost, I. (2013). Exploitationware. In Rhetoric/composition/play through video games (pp. 139-147). Palgrave Macmillan.

Boyne, G. A. (2002). Public and private management: What's the difference? *Journal of Management Studies*, *39*(1), 97–122. doi:10.1111/1467-6486.00284

Brown, T. (2008). Design thinking. *Harvard Business Review*, *86*(6), 84. PMID:18605031

Buheji, M. (2019). Re-inventing public services using gamification approaches. *International Journal of Economics and Financial Issues*, *9*(6), 48–59. doi:10.32479/ijefi.8803

Burke, B. (2012). Gamification 2020: *What is the future of gamification*. Gartner. *Inc.*, (Nov), 5.

Burke, B. (2016). *Gamify: How gamification motivates people to do extraordinary things*. Routledge. doi:10.4324/9781315230344

Chaffin, A., & Barnes, T. (2010, June). Lessons from a course on serious games research and prototyping. In *Proceedings of the Fifth International Conference on the Foundations of Digital Games* (pp. 32-39). 10.1145/1822348.1822353

Charette, R. N. (2020). *Inside the hidden world of legacy IT systems: How and why we spend trillions to keep old software going*. IEEE. https://spectrum.ieee.org/comp fluting/it/inside-hidden-world-legacy-it-systems

Chen, Y. (2019). Exploring design guidelines of using user-centered design in gamification development: A Delphi Study. *International Journal of Human-Computer Interaction*, *35*(13), 1170–1181. doi:10.1080/10447318.2018.1514823

Dargan, T., & Evequoz, F. (2015). Designing engaging e-Government services by combining user-centered design and gamification: A use-case. In *Proceedings of the 15th European Conference on eGovernment ECEG 2015 University of Portsmouth* (p. 70). Academic Press.

de Paula Porto, D., de Jesus, G. M., Ferrari, F. C., & Fabbri, S. C. P. F. (2021). Initiatives and challenges of using gamification in software engineering: A Systematic Mapping. *Journal of Systems and Software*, *173*, 110870. doi:10.1016/j.jss.2020.110870

Dombrowski, C., Kim, J. Y., Desouza, K. C., Braganza, A., Papagari, S., Baloh, P., & Jha, S. (2007). Elements of innovative cultures. *Knowledge and Process Management*, *14*(3), 190–202. doi:10.1002/kpm.279

Ďuriník, M. (2015). Gamification in knowledge management systems. *Central European Journal of Management, 1*(2). Advance online publication. doi:10.5817/CEJM2014-2-3

Elm, D., Kappen, D. L., Tondello, G. F., & Nacke, L. E. (2016). CLEVER: Gamification and enterprise knowledge learning. In *Proceedings of the 2016 Annual Symposium on Computer-Human Interaction in Play Companion Extended Abstracts* (pp. 141-148). Academic Press.

Foucault, M., Blanc, X., Falleri, J. R., & Storey, M. A. (2019). Fostering good coding practices through individual feedback and gamification: An industrial case study. *Empirical Software Engineering, 24*(6), 3731–3754. doi:10.100710664-019-09719-4

Gregor, S., & Hevner, A. R. (2013). Positioning and presenting design science research for maximum impact. *Management Information Systems Quarterly, 37*(2), 337–355. doi:10.25300/MISQ/2013/37.2.01

Gudiksen, S., & Inlove, J. (2018). *Gamification for business: Why innovators and changemakers use games to break down silos, drive engagement and build trust.* Kogan Page Publishers.

Guinan, P. J., Parise, S., & Langowitz, N. (2019). Creating an innovative digital project team: Levers to enable digital transformation. *Business Horizons, 62*(6), 717–727. doi:10.1016/j.bushor.2019.07.005

Halachmi, A. (2011). Imagined promises versus real challenges to public performance management. *International Journal of Productivity and Performance Management, 60*(1), 24–40. doi:10.1108/17410401111094295

Hamari, J. & Tuunanen, J. (2013). Player types: A meta-synthesis. *Transactions of the Digital Games Research Association, 1*(2).

Harteveld, C. (2011). *Triadic game design: Balancing reality, meaning and play.* Springer Science & Business Media. doi:10.1007/978-1-84996-157-8

Hassan, L. (2017). Governments should play games: Towards a framework for the gamification of civic engagement platforms. *Simulation & Gaming, 48*(2), 249–267. doi:10.1177/1046878116683581

Hense, J., Klevers, M., Sailer, M., Horenburg, T., Mandl, H., & Günthner, W. (2013). Using gamification to enhance staff motivation in logistics. In *International Simulation and Gaming Association Conference* (pp. 206-213). Springer.

Hevner, A. R. (2007). A three cycle view of design science research. *Scandinavian Journal of Information Systems, 19*(2), 4.

Hevner, A. R., March, S. T., Park, J., & Ram, S. (2004). Design science in information systems research. *Management Information Systems Quarterly, 28*(1), 75–105. doi:10.2307/25148625

Highsmith, J., & Fowler, M. (2001). The agile manifesto. *Software Development Magazine, 9*(8), 29–30.

Humlung, O., & Haddara, M. (2019). The hero's journey to innovation: Gamification in enterprise systems. *Procedia Computer Science, 164,* 86–95. doi:10.1016/j.procs.2019.12.158

Khaled, R., & Vasalou, A. (2014). Bridging serious games and participatory design. *International Journal of Child-Computer Interaction, 2*(2), 93–100. doi:10.1016/j.ijcci.2014.03.001

Liu, D., Santhanam, R., & Webster, J. (2017). Toward Meaningful Engagement: A framework for design and research of Gamified information systems. *Management Information Systems Quarterly*, *41*(4), 1011–1034. doi:10.25300/MISQ/2017/41.4.01

Lombriser, P., Dalpiaz, F., Lucassen, G., & Brinkkemper, S. (2016). Gamified requirements engineering: model and experimentation. In *International Working conference on requirements engineering: foundation for software quality* (pp. 171-187). Springer.

Martens, A., Diener, H., & Malo, S. (2008). Game-based learning with computers–learning, simulations, and games. In *Transactions on edutainment I* (pp. 172–190). Springer. doi:10.1007/978-3-540-69744-2_15

Morschheuser, B., Hassan, L., Werder, K., & Hamari, J. (2018). How to design gamification? A method for engineering gamified software. *Information and Software Technology*, *95*, 219–237. doi:10.1016/j.infsof.2017.10.015

Muller, M. J., & Druin, A. (2012). Participatory design: the third space in human–computer interaction. In *The Human–Computer Interaction Handbook* (pp. 1125–1153). CRC Press.

Myers, M. D., & Venable, J. R. (2014). A set of ethical principles for design science research in information systems. *Information & Management*, *51*(6), 801–809. doi:10.1016/j.im.2014.01.002

Nacke, L. E., & Deterding, C. S. (2017). The maturing of gamification research. *Computers in Human Behaviour*, 450-454.

Nah, F. F. H., Eschenbrenner, B., Claybaugh, C. C., & Koob, P. B. (2019). Gamification of enterprise systems. *Systems*, *7*(1), 13. doi:10.3390ystems7010013

Patrício, R., Moreira, A. C., & Zurlo, F. (2018). Gamification approaches to the early stage of innovation. *Creativity and Innovation Management*, *27*(4), 499–511. doi:10.1111/caim.12284

Patricio, R., & Morozumi, R. (2018). Gamification for service design and Innovation: ideaChef® method and tool. In *ServDes2018. Service Design Proof of Concept, Proceedings of the ServDes. 2018 Conference, 18-20 June, Milano, Italy* (No. 150, pp. 1212-1228). Linköping University Electronic Press.

Peffers, K., Rothenberger, M., Tuunanen, T., & Vaezi, R. (2012, May). Design science research evaluation. In *International Conference on Design Science Research in Information Systems* (pp. 398-410). Springer.

Pfeffers, K., Tuunanen, T., Gengler, C. E., Rossi, M., Hui, W., Virtanen, V., & Bragge, J. (2006). The design science research process: A model for producing and presenting information systems research. In *Proceedings of the First International Conference on Design Science Research in Information Systems and Technology (DESRIST 2006), Claremont, CA, USA* (pp. 83-106). Academic Press.

Raftopoulos, M. (2014). Towards gamification transparency: A conceptual framework for the development of responsible gamified enterprise systems. *Journal of Gaming & Virtual Worlds*, *6*(2), 159–178. doi:10.1386/jgvw.6.2.159_1

Rix, K., Zeihlund, T., & Long, T. (2015) Double the sharing- the effects of gamification at one of the world's largest employers. *Strategic industrial applications of games and gamification: proceedings of the International Gamification for Business Conference 2015.*

Sanders, E. B. N. (2002). From user-centered to participatory design approaches. In *Design and the social sciences* (pp. 18–25). CRC Press. doi:10.1201/9780203301302.ch1

Sandoval-Almazan, R., & Valle-Cruz, D. (2017). Open innovation, living labs and public officials: The case of Mapaton in Mexico. *In Proceedings of the 10th International Conference on Theory and Practice of Electronic Governance* (pp. 260-265). New York, NY: ACM. 10.1145/3047273.3047308

Scariot, C. A., Heemann, A., & Padovani, S. (2012). Understanding the collaborative-participatory design. *Work (Reading, Mass.), 41*(Supplement 1), 2701–2705. doi:10.3233/WOR-2012-0656-2701 PMID:22317129

Scheiner, C., Haas, P., Bretschneider, U., Blohm, I., & Leimeister, J. M. (2017). Obstacles and challenges in the use of gamification for virtual idea communities. In *Gamification* (pp. 65–76). Springer. doi:10.1007/978-3-319-45557-0_5

Schweitzer, F., & Tidd, J. (2018). *Innovation heroes: Understanding customers as a valuable innovation resource* (Vol. 31). World Scientific. doi:10.1142/q0158

Shiralkar, S. W. (2016). *IT through experiential learning: Learn, deploy and adopt IT through gamification*. Apress. doi:10.1007/978-1-4842-2421-2

Shpakova, A., Dörfler, V., & MacBryde, J. (2017). *Changing the game: a case for gamifying knowledge management. World Journal of Science, Technology and Sustainable Development*.

Simon, H. A. (1996). *The sciences of the artificial*. MIT Press.

Sukale, R., & Pfaff, M. S. (2014). QuoDocs: Improving developer engagement in software documentation through gamification. In CHI'14 Extended Abstracts on Human Factors in Computing Systems (pp. 1531-1536). ACM.

Taylor, C. (2011, June 6). Counties honored for Web 2.0 innovations. *NaCO County Newsletter*.

Thibault, M., & Hamari, J. (2021). Seven points to reappropriate gamification. In Transforming Society and organizations through Gamification: From the Sustainable Development Goals to Inclusive Workplaces (pp. 11-28). Palgrave Macmillan. doi:10.1007/978-3-030-68207-1_2

Thuan, N. H., Drechsler, A., & Antunes, P. (2019). Construction of design science research questions. *Communications of the Association for Information Systems, 44*(1), 20.

Tidd, J., & Bessant, J. R. (2005). *Managing innovation: integrating technological, market and organizational change*. John Wiley & Sons.

Totterdill, P., Dhondt, S., & Devons, N. (2016). The case for workplace innovation. Brussels: European Workplace Innovation Network (Euwin).

Tsunoda, M., & Yumoto, H. (2018). Applying gamification and posing to software development. In *2018 25th Asia-Pacific Software Engineering Conference (APSEC)* (pp. 638-642). IEEE. 10.1109/APSEC.2018.00081

Venable, J., Pries-Heje, J., & Baskerville, R. (2012). A comprehensive framework for evaluation in design science research. In *International conference on design science research in information systems* (pp. 423-438). Springer. 10.1007/978-3-642-29863-9_31

Viberg, O., Khalil, M., & Lioliopoulos, A. (2020). Facilitating Ideation and Knowledge Sharing in Workplaces: The Design and Use of Gamification in Virtual Platforms. In *International Conference on Human-Computer Interaction* (pp. 353-369). Springer. 10.1007/978-3-030-50506-6_25

Vilarinho, T., Farshchian, B., Floch, J., & Hansen, O. G. (2018). Participatory Ideation for Gamification: Bringing the User at the Heart of the Gamification Design Process. In *International Conference on Human-Centred Software Engineering* (pp. 51-61). Springer.

Warmelink, H., van Elderen, J., & Mayer, I. (2021). Game Design Elements: Understanding the bricks and mortar of gamification. In Organizational Gamification (pp. 40-60). Routledge.

Werbach, K. (2014). (Re) defining gamification: A process approach. In *International conference on persuasive technology* (pp. 266-272). Springer. 10.1007/978-3-319-07127-5_23

Witt, M., Scheiner, C. W., & Robra-Bissantz, S. (2011, October). Gamification of online idea competitions: insights from an explorative case. In GI-Jahrestagung (p. 392). Academic Press.

Chapter 4
The Use of Escape Rooms in Society and Business Environments:
Two Exploratory Studies on the Potential of Gamification

Tanja Kranawetleitner
University of Augsburg, Germany

Heike Krebs
University of Augsburg, Germany

Diana Pistoll
Medical School Hamburg, Germany

Julia Thurner-Irmler
University of Augsburg, Germany

ABSTRACT

In recent years, the concept of gamification, and escape rooms (ER) as one of its methods, has become very popular. ER has been shown to be widely applicable for numerous target groups and contexts. This chapter presents explorative testing of two different ER contexts that have rarely been reported in the literature so far: one for needs analysis in a business setting (n = 21) and one as a tool for science communication in society (n = 63). Participants evaluated the ER with a 5-point Likert rating scale questionnaire (containing 12 respectively 11 items). The results confirm the entertaining nature of the method and show that the ER succeeded in raising awareness of the respective topics. Comparing the rooms provided valuable findings regarding different fields of application. It offers insights into developing this innovative method and conceptualizing future ER. Further implications and limitations are discussed.

DOI: 10.4018/978-1-6684-4291-3.ch004

INTRODUCTION

Engaging and motivating (young) children to learn by using games is a common method that has been practiced around the globe (Borrego et al., 2017, p. 164). Lately, the idea of *play* in different settings has become a very popular way of encouraging active engagement with a given topic for adults as well. In this vein, the concept of gamification seems promising and effective. The introduction of cooperative learning situations in a game-like manner, for instance, for educational purposes, can be advantageous since the learner is thus given an active and more constructive role. The intrinsic reward system can be activated through curiosity or ambition without the component of the extrinsic compensation (Deci et al., 2001). In the following, the potential of the gamification approach will be analyzed regarding the specific example of Escape Rooms or Escape Games, which have become popular in recent years. This book chapter presents the explorative testing of two different Escape Rooms and their potentials in different institutions, settings, and from different disciplinary perspectives: a room in a business context as an initiation to a needs analysis and a STEM room as a tool for science communication in society. On the basis of these two pilot studies, the pursuit of both the common and specific purposes of the different Escape Rooms will be discussed comparatively.

BACKGROUND

Escape Games seem to have a versatile range of uses – not only linked to spare time activities. Diverse target groups, different (learning) goals and various forms of application are imaginable. The origin of Escape Games can be traced back to the year 2008. The Japanese entrepreneur Takao Kato once filled clubs and bars with hidden objects, riddles, messages, and codes. In these role models of modern Escape Games called "Riaru Dasshutsu Ge–mu (Real Escape Game)", a group of individuals had to escape the room by not only answering questions within a given timeframe, "but *identifying* them in the first place" (Corkill, 2009, para. 7).

These kinds of games have gained more and more popularity. One widespread definition of Escape Games – or Escape Rooms – is by Nicholson (2016). According to his understanding, they focus on solving riddles and require accomplishment of challenges in collaboration with other people under time pressure to complete a task successfully, like escaping the room (Nicholson, 2016, p. 1). During these "ludic activities" (Borrego et al., 2017, p. 162), a team works towards a joint goal. An alternative name could be "live-action adventure" (Nicholson, 2016, p. 1), because the term "escape" may be misleading, since the confinement or the getaway is often not a main characteristic of these games (Nicholson, 2016, p. 18).

Bakhsheshi (2019) points out that Escape Games can cover a wide range of different topics. Common to all variations is that players are supposed to become a part of a story and forget the real world while playing. This process offers considerable potential for using Escape Games in the educational context. "The learner then immersed in the context is ready to learn in the stream of practice and have the courage to get involved in the action, try to overcome the obstacles, and face the consequences, either positive or negative" (Bakhsheshi, 2019, p. 2). These *Educational Escape Rooms* are the latest trend to motivate learners (Borrego et al., 2017, p. 164). Therefore, Escape Rooms are also Serious Games, which can be designed to reach a specific educational objective rather than to have fun (Abt, 1987, p. 9). Compared to commercial Escape Rooms, the goal of educational ones "may not be to escape, but to understand and solve a problem" (Nicholson & Cable, 2021, p. 5).

In recent years, Educational Escape Games have been applied in various contexts to support enthusiasm as well as students' motivation and learning processes (Borrego et al., 2017, p. 164; Parra-González et al., 2020, p. 1). Hence, learners are able to engage deeper with the didactic content (Clark et al., 2017, p. 84). A visit can also be linked to an aim of shifting attitudes towards a specific topic (Glavaš & Staščik, 2017, p. 282).

Apart from achieving a concrete learning goal or the mediation of knowledge, other competences can be supported, for example, working in a team or communicating. Furthermore, riddles and task designs can offer the possibility to gain new competences, like decoding or translation skills (Nicholson, 2016, p. 16). Therefore, Escape Games own "the potential to be used both in serious gaming and as a serious game" (Bakhsheshi, 2019, p. 1). The concept of gamification can thus be accentuated within a learning process, which – in general – includes no playful context (López-Belmonte et al., 2020, p. 2). Gamification can thus be understood as the addition of gaming elements to non-game situations (Deterding et al., 2011, p. 10). Incentives often take the form of points, levels or rewards and are perceived to be more effective than just one final reward: "gamification uses this principle to promote short-term engagement with a long-term process" (Betts, 2013, p. 188). However, unlike in other examples of gamification, the "rewards" in Escape Games consist in the players approaching – and finally achieving – the learning/ story goal by solving various riddles or problems step by step. Individual and innovative answers and procedures support the process of the critical thinking rather than extrinsic motivation (Nicholson & Cable, 2021, p. 5).

COMPARING THE USAGE OF TWO ESCAPE ROOMS IN DIFFERENT SETTINGS

Using an Escape Room for Needs Analysis in a Business Setting

A detailed and realistic determination of the specific needs of small and medium-sized enterprises (SMEs) represents one of the most difficult but at the same time one of the most important steps for successful consulting. It contributes to the development of a sustainable adaptation of the business model towards a model incorporating the assessed requirements (Riedel, 2006, pp. 115–116).

In general, a needs analysis targets clarification of the discrepancy between a desired and a current state. It focuses on deficiencies and problems in the areas of education, support, and organizational development. The analysis is carried out in relation to an institution (e.g., company), to an activity as well as on an individual level (Becker, 2013, pp. 825–826). The needs analysis of the Escape Room to be described concentrates on knowledge and attitudes of the workforce. Apart from purely factual knowledge, it focuses on experiential and implicit knowledge. In addition, a needs analysis is intended to identify previously unmentioned and critical issues such as reservations, difficulties, and obstacles. The causes of these can be personal (lack of qualifications or motivation) or structural (need for organizational development) (Becker, 2013, pp. 826–827).

The selection of a suitable method for a needs analysis can ultimately determine the quality and validity of the data. Quantitative questionnaires are commonly used, although qualitative instruments of data collection are employed as well (Riedel, 2006, pp. 115–116). However, a methodological weakness both instruments can do little about is a partial confounding of the collected data due to biased response behavior (Häder & Kühne, 2009, pp. 175–176). Respondents' answers do not always refer to their actual subjective perception, but – depending on the social relevance of the respective topic – to a socially desirable and adapted behavior (Döring & Bortz, 2016, p. 437). The latter can lead to deviations in the understanding of individual fields of action, so the objective should be to minimize precisely these response tendencies.

Previous literature shows that a rather sterile setting with little emotional activation leads to less engagement and motivation, and – importantly – to higher social desirability (Holden, 2010). Hence, an atmosphere should be created that is both free of anxiety and motivating, thus encouraging the participants to express their opinions. This should also prevent respondents from answering superficially. Comprehensive analysis and the identification of needs as a result are the basis for ascertaining a realistic picture of the status quo. For this purpose, an emotionally charged Escape Room seems to be a promising approach; its playful component might lead the participants into an affective instead of a purely cognitive state of experience (Clark et al., 2016, p. 86). In addition, an innovative learning context enables participants to use different strategies and think *out-of-the-box* (Clarke et al., 2017). Creative problem-solving abilities are thus fostered (Patrício et al., 2020, p. 152).

To identify the real situation in a company, the project *Education 4.0 for SMEs* includes an Escape Room in the area of knowledge management in its needs analysis. The project focuses on knowledge transfer in connection with digital learning within a company. The knowledge transfer addressed in the business Escape Room is the one between different co-workers and departments within a company. Identifying existing knowledge as well as making it visible and usable is one of the goals of knowledge transfer in companies (Minbaeva et al., 2003, p. 587) and thus a main priority of the project. A meaningful and clear knowledge base, above all one that is actually used, is crucial in today's world. However, in most cases, there is no structured and thus efficient knowledge exchange; the search for information is time-consuming and there are only a few strategies and technologies for knowledge documentation, which often results in a loss of knowledge (e.g., Gold et al., 2001; KYOCERA Document Solutions, 2018).

The presented Escape Room introduces a needs analysis concerning knowledge management in companies and pursues several objectives. One of the main goals is to raise awareness for the importance of appropriate knowledge transfer within the company. This includes the understanding of knowing what one knows, the articulation as well as the transparent and comprehensible documentation of the knowledge in question. Learning more about the current difficulties in knowledge transfer and the status quo in the respective enterprise represents a further goal. Finally, the workforce should be encouraged to talk openly and freely about the experiences they are facing in their everyday working lives.

Requirements for the Business Context Escape Room

With regard to the objectives of the needs analysis, several requirements must be taken into account. In general, the participant groups consist of six to eight employees, who are chosen by the management according to specific criteria. Their background should provide the broadest possible insight into the workforce and therefore be as heterogeneous as possible, for example, in terms of department, length of service, hierarchical level, training, gender, and full-time or part-time employment. In addition, the playing time and the difficulty of the riddles need to be individually adjustable.

Since the Escape Room serves as an introduction to the needs analysis on the topic of knowledge transfer and both are integrated into a so-called *practical taster day*, the planned time for the entire part is one hour. Therefore, the playing time should not exceed 20 to 25 minutes. Correspondingly, control of the game from outside must be possible.

Furthermore, the Escape Room should be mobile and quick to set up, as it is played directly on site in the company. In addition, it has to be easy to adapt to the spatial conditions there. After all, a real working atmosphere is to be created in the Escape Room. Familiar problems and situations are supposed to help participants to talk honestly about the actual situation in their companies. Riddles resembling tasks in everyday work situations are also planned to support this open exchange.

Structure of the Escape Room in the Business Context

The storyline of the Escape Room revolves around a fictional medium-sized company named "DEM-MIC". The Escape Room takes place in a business setting right after a call from a customer complaining about a missing order. Now, the participants have to retrieve and forward it to the production department.

The story of the Escape Room serves as a worst-case scenario for internal knowledge management, since there is no coherent documentation of the work processes by their fictional colleagues and no use of common company standards such as using file servers. Additionally, the players find themselves in a cluttered working environment full of unnecessary items, like non-work-related magazines. Finally, most of the documents that can be found on the laptops of the Escape Room are outdated or even incorrect.

In total, there are six riddles with the option of a seventh, depending on how much time has already elapsed. The detailed structure of the Escape Room as well as the riddles and items which are needed to retrieve the missing order are shown in Figure 1. Various (hidden) clues that are found in the office setting unlock different laptops (riddles 1 to 4). These help the participants to get pieces of information which are relevant to find the lost order (riddle 5) and to subsequently solve the final riddle 7. After calling the production department (riddle 7), the participants have solved the problem and thus successfully completed the Escape Room.

In addition to the riddles, there are false clues hidden throughout the Escape Room in order to mislead the players and let them experience a feeling of frustration about unstructured knowledge management. Moreover, incorporating aberrations is also a common feature in commercial Escape Rooms (Nicholson, 2016, p. 15).

A gamemaster is aware of the participants' progress and can intervene from outside whenever needed. Hints are only provided via a smartphone the participants are handed in the beginning, so that they can immerse in the situation in the best way possible. An optional riddle (riddle 6) was introduced to control the playing time. Beyond that, depending on the progress of the players, the gamemaster can give more or less specific hints.

Pretest and Execution

Before the implementation in the pilot companies, the Escape Room was pretested twice. This helped to assess the time needed and difficulty of the riddles. The participants were able to achieve the story goal without external support within around 30 minutes. However, at one point, the test subjects had difficulties solving a puzzle, because they did not recognize some clues as such. This showed that some additional instruction was necessary. Due to individual on site conditions, for the actual execution it is important to explain exactly which items belong to the game and which do not.

Figure 1. Riddle flow chart of the Escape Room in the business context (inspired by Borrego et al., 2017)

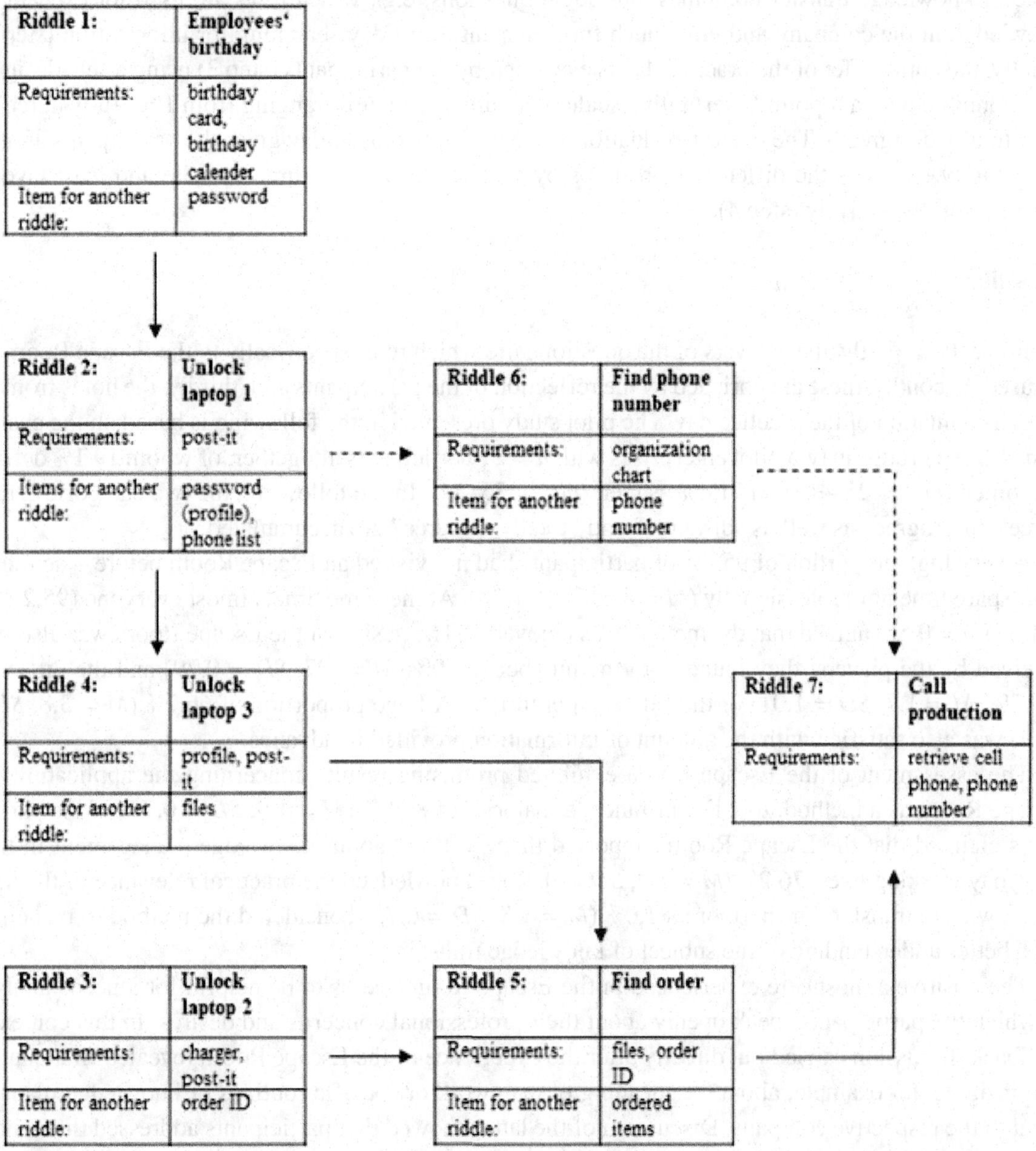

Riddle 1:	Employees' birthday
Requirements:	birthday card, birthday calender
Item for another riddle:	password

Riddle 2:	Unlock laptop 1
Requirements:	post-it
Items for another riddle:	password (profile), phone list

Riddle 6:	Find phone number
Requirements:	organization chart
Item for another riddle:	phone number

Riddle 4:	Unlock laptop 3
Requirements:	profile, post-it
Item for another riddle:	files

Riddle 7:	Call production
Requirements:	retrieve cell phone, phone number

Riddle 3:	Unlock laptop 2
Requirements:	charger, post-it
Item for another riddle:	order ID

Riddle 5:	Find order
Requirements:	files, order ID
Item for another riddle:	ordered items

In order to utilize the potentials of the gamification approach for the purpose of a needs analysis, it is reasonable to integrate it into a multi-level procedure. This combines different methods for the present purpose. The needs analysis starts with a guideline-based interview with the executive level to identify starting points (step 1). Based on these first results, one or two practical taster day(s) are individually organized for each company. They consist of several workshops including a needs analysis. The Escape Room serves as an introduction for said analysis on the topic of knowledge transfer. After the completed Escape Room, the participants can express their feedback. They are especially invited to consider in what way the game experience reflects in their everyday work. In addition, an interactive presentation on the topic of knowledge transfer combines individual questions, e.g., which tools are used for exchanging knowledge in the company and how much time is spent every day searching for information (step 2). Finally, the entire offer of the practice day is evaluated by the participants (step 3) using a self-designed questionnaire with a 5-point Likert rating scale (containing 12 items, ranging from 1 = "fully agree" to 5 = "totally disagree"). The overall evaluation at the end of the taster day gives the participants another opportunity to assess the different workshops by writing down their three favorite and least favorite experiences respectively (step 4).

Results

In this section, firstly, the answers of the questionnaire which refer specifically to the Escape Room are focused. Secondly, these are enriched by the reflection of the participants and, thirdly, the notes from the overall evaluation of the practice day. The pilot study presented in the following is based on the evaluation of three groups in two pilot enterprises with $n = 21$ participants altogether, of whom 19.1% defined as women ($m_{age} = 25$–44) and 71.4% as men ($m_{age} = 35$–54). In the following, the two categories "fully agree" and "agree" as well as "disagree" and "totally disagree" are accumulated.

A very high proportion of 95.2% of participants had not visited an Escape Room before – neither in their spare time nor professionally ($M = 4.6$, $SD = 1.20$). At the same time, almost everyone (95.2%; $M = 1.3$, $SD = 0.56$) agreed that the method was enjoyable. The design of the Escape Room was also well received by the players: they found both the number (81.0%; $M = 1.7$, $SD = 0.79$) and the difficulty (85.7%; $M = 1.7$, $SD = 1.01$) of the riddles appropriate. A large proportion of 66.7% ($M = 3.8$, $SD = 1.14$) was also satisfied with the amount of information provided in advance.

The assessment of the Escape Room exhibited promising results concerning the applicability of Escape Room as a method, too. For instance, a majority of 80.9% ($M = 1.9$, $SD = 0.77$) of the participants claimed that the Escape Room supported them to think about knowledge management in their everyday working lives. 76.2% ($M = 1.9$, $SD = 0.77$) acknowledged the practical relevance of the topic of knowledge transfer. Furthermore, 81.0% ($M = 1.8$, $SD = 0.75$) considered the method to be helpful for a better understanding of the subject of knowledge transfer.

The positive atmosphere experienced in the Escape Room seems to be helpful for a needs analysis in which the participants speak openly about their professional concerns and desires. In this context, a feedback discussion carried out directly after the experience of the Escape Room revealed first qualitative insights, for example, about the meaning of teamwork or specific routines of knowledge management in the respective company. Discussion of the latter showed that participants addressed the issue of knowledge management in an open way. They used the scenario for a reflection of individual and team routines, also mentioning critical cases like situations in which their knowledge management did not work as planned. In this respect, they for instance admitted that some parts of the displayed worst-case scenario seemed familiar and revealed their own routines despite the presence of an executive in one case. The issue of teamwork was mentioned by a participating employee without being prompted. The person explicitly claimed that they could not have solved the Escape Room without their colleagues. The interpretation of this remark touches upon the heterogeneous background of the participants, who are dependent on each other's expertise and profit from working as a team.

Apart from these content-related results which will be taken up in the comparative discussion below considering the usability of Escape Rooms for their specific purposes, the feedback also brought to light specific comments on the story. According to a sales representative, the logical structure of the scenario would not work in their company as it does not consider the regular chronology of the sales department. Comments like this are important clues for the future use and development of the Escape Room.

The overall impression of the Escape Room can also be concluded from statements in the evaluation of the whole practical taster day. The assessment includes an anonymous collection of positive and negative aspects of the day in terms of short, written statements. In this context, the method was specifically mentioned as an entertaining part of the program. Also, more generally, the participants praised the whole day for its "agreeable atmosphere" and the welcome change between sessions that provided more input and rather active parts. In this respect, one result also specifically judged the Escape Room as better than its subsequent theoretical counterpart with input on knowledge management.

Using an Escape Room as a Tool for Science Communication in Society

In recent years, knowledge transfer has started to play an increasingly important role. In the context of universities, the focus has shifted from information and technology transfer – which ideally should result in an application, a product, or a unique process (Siegel et al., 2003, p. 119) – to the so called *Third Mission*. This highlights the social function and responsibility to generate, reflect, collect, and present knowledge besides the two central duties of teaching and researching (Bayerische Staatsregierung, 2020).

The presentation of knowledge can – among other things – occur in different kinds of science communication. The goal is to distribute scientific knowledge and knowledge about science in society – therefore the term *science transfer* may seem more reasonable than *knowledge transfer* (Wodke, 2020) to accentuate the difference to the transfer focused on in the business Escape Room. Depending on the target group, the content and its complexity, various forms of communication are possible (Hochschulrektorenkonferenz, 2013, p. 31). Applying the paradigm of *Public Understanding of Science* (PUS), a knowledge deficit in society needs to be compensated so that scientific facts and processes can be understood. Knowledge should be presented in an understandable way (Bauer, 2017, p. 26; Bubela et al., 2009, p. 515). In this context, one fundamental component is the concept of *Public Awareness of Science* (PAS) which aims at promoting awareness and positive attitudes towards science (Burns et al., 2003, pp. 187–190).

However, the idea of this deficit approach is gradually neglected. Instead, science events are developed to allow for scientific staff and society to communicate and exchange knowledge on equal terms (Fähnrich, 2017, pp. 166–167). Science communication that uses events to promote science is called *"Scientainment"* (Science + Entertainment). Here, science is introduced in an entertaining way but this implies that scientific topics can only be treated superficially. During a *Scienceperience* event (Science + Experience), visitors gain first-hand insights into scientific work (Schreiber, 2012, pp. 108–109). The integration of narration or storytelling can serve as an easy access to convey the significance of scientific topics (Dahlstrom, 2014, p. 13618).

Lewenstein (2011, p. 820) shows that entertainment media, like movies or games, have already gained a permanent place in the field of science communication. A subcategory of games are Escape Games which can be operated as Scientainment or even Scienceperience events to create an introduction as well as to develop an understanding or attitude towards a specific scientific topic in a playful, interesting, and descriptive way.

Requirements and First Decisions for the STEM Escape Room

The point of origin for addressing the field of science communication in the ensuing study is the project *WiR*, which deals with knowledge transfer into society around Industry 4.0, digitalization, technology, science, and research. The project aims at designing, implementing, and evaluating various formats of science communication and knowledge transfer for society. In this context, the paradigm of gamification is of great interest to provide low-threshold and intelligible access to science and especially to STEM (Science, Technology, Engineering, Mathematics), not only because student performance in STEM-related subjects has been dropping steadily in recent years (acatech, 2020, p. 3). It is essential to deepen the understanding and appreciation of STEM to secure skilled labor in the future. With these ideas in mind, it was decided to create a STEM Escape Room to increase the awareness of this issue but also to test the idea of gamification in science communication. Due to the entertaining nature, which presents a short introduction to selected STEM topics and as participants actively experience scientific methods like experiments, the presented Escape Room can be classified as both Scientainment and Scienceperience.

The target group generally consists of the society, including different age groups (from children to elderly people) as the main variable, while other dimensions like gender or educational background are also considered. The Escape Room is designed to be part of a social program during different events or as a school lesson. Regarding this requirement, the Escape Room must be mobile with the option of transportation, quick setup, resetting, and removal. Hence, the set time limit per group (with about six to eight people) should not exceed 30 minutes. Due to these various determining factors, an open puzzle-structure allows the participants of a group to work on the riddles simultaneously, while still having to communicate and collaborate to solve the tasks (Nicholson, 2016, p. 9). Since the background and previous knowledge of the visitors are unknown and it is assumed that many of them have not perceived STEM subjects consciously, the (scientific learning) goal of the STEM Escape Room is to generate awareness of STEM in daily life, the scientific explanation for these phenomena, and why these subjects and the knowledge they convey are relevant.

The structure of the STEM Escape Room

The story goal depends on the setting, which can vary according to the target group. Adults, for example, will find themselves in an office needing to help a supervisor to unlock a tablet computer for a presentation, pupils must help the teacher to regain access to the digitalized school marks. This task can be solved with a code. The needed four digits are obtained by solving four riddles (one exemplary for each STEM area) and arranging them in the correct order. The code is the solution to the meta-puzzle of the open-puzzle structure. The gamemaster – in the role of the person requiring the code – provides hints if necessary.

The setting can be designed as an open-plan office or a study room. There are six areas decorated with books, pencils, cups, and notes, simulating someone's workspace or study. The four STEM riddles as well as the items and pieces of information which are necessary to solve the puzzles are distributed across the room. Posters, postcards, bookmarks, written notes, and other items indicate which of the STEM subjects is addressed, provide a scientific explanation for the experienced phenomenon, and lead to the solution of the riddle.

Figure 2. Riddle flow chart of the STEM Escape Room (inspired by Borrego et al., 2017)

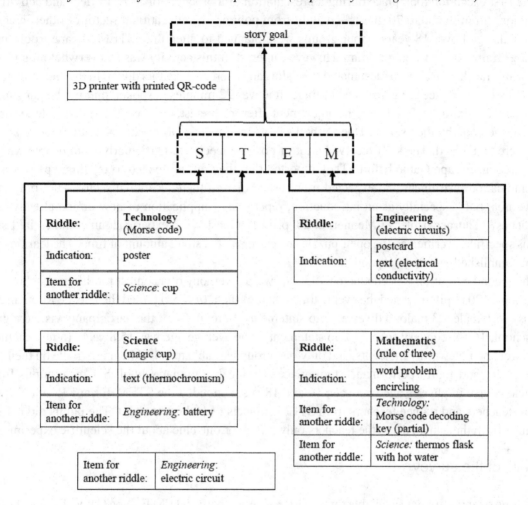

The riddle flow chart (Figure 2) depicts how the riddles, indications, and items are connected to each other, how they merge to the meta-puzzle, and finally the story goal – breaking out of the room is not part of the intended tasks.

Pretest and Execution

The STEM Escape Room has been conducted four times. Before the actual execution, the STEM Escape Room was pretested with six people. The focus of the pretest was to specifically evaluate the time taken, the perceived difficulty of the riddles, and thoughts about the setting. The group needed 27 minutes, which was within the intended time frame. Nothing was considered too difficult or too easy. Some scribbles and doodles which were implemented to foster the atmosphere distracted from the actual solution of the puzzles. The pre-test mainly revealed a problem with the sorting of the four digits into the correct order at the meta-puzzle. As a solution, it was decided to use less distractive elements and add a special lock screen on the tablet with four placeholders hovering over the term STEM.

The first execution took place during a presentation of a brochure of STEM offers and activities in the region. From the 60 to 70 guests – mainly from politics, the educational sector or other interested individuals aged over 18 years – four groups were planned to attend the STEM Escape Room in the two-hour frame of the social program. However, interest in this activity was so overwhelming that the mentoring staff had to allocate designated time slots and even turn visitors down. In the end, five groups were able to experience the game. The average time was 22 minutes, a spoken hint by the gamemaster was necessary six times. Even with the adjustment after the pretest, only one group was able to sort the digits of the code by themselves. Due to the lack of time, merely observations and random conversations were conducted. The staff received a lot of positive feedback, particularly from people who had not visited an Escape Game before. They reported that they felt motivated to try this type of science communication instrument and expected more usage of it in the educational sector – not only in the STEM area, but "especially as an introduction, repetition or application of new or/and already learnt substances" (Thurner-Irmler & Menner, 2020, p. 112). Guests with experience in commercial Escape Rooms specifically criticized the open-puzzle structure and the small amount of time. The learning goal was accomplished by every respondent.

The second execution was conducted after an award ceremony of a contest for different schools and age groups. 120 pupils attended the event, almost half of them ($n = 53$) joined the Escape Room in eight groups (25 female, 23 male, 0 diverse, 5 no statement). In total, 34 of the participants visited a grammar school, 16 a secondary school (3 no statement). The average age was 15.8 years (5 no statement). There were no noteworthy incidents, and only one group was able to solve the meta riddle on their own.

The third and fourth performance took place at a local grammar school. Six male pupils from a practical course in physics aged between 16 and 18 years attended the STEM-Escape Room, followed by four teachers and trainee teachers from STEM subjects (3 male, 1 female). The pupils did not need any hints from the gamemaster, the teachers only asked for one clue about the scientific experiment.

Results of the survey

There is no quantitative data available for the first execution of the STEM Escape Game. During the other three performances, in total $n = 63$ people voluntarily filled out a self-designed, printed questionnaire with a total of 16 items (not including questions about demographic data), which could be answered on a 5-point Likert rating scale (11 items ranging from 1 = "fully agree" to 5 = "totally disagree") and open questions (5 items). In these answers, favorable and adverse points could be added.

A total of 54.0% of the respondents specified that they had not visited an Escape Room before, 22.2% had experienced one once, 13.3% two or three times ($n_1 = 57$). The statement that they enjoyed (or enjoyed very much) the visit was confirmed by 84.2%. Only 3.2% were not pleased with the experience ($M = 1.9$, $SD = 0.73$). Similar results were noted for the item "I had fun in the STEM Escape Room", with 84.1% agreeing (or fully agreeing). 12.7% were not committed while 1.6% disagreed ($M = 1.8$, $SD = 0.74$, $n_2 = 62$). The collaboration of the team was perceived positively by 77.8%, neutrally by 15.9% and negatively by 4.8% ($M = 1.9$, $SD = 0.9$, $n_3 = 62$). 76.2% confirmed that they were able to take part actively in the solution processes of the riddles. However, 8% claimed that they could not participate in these actions ($M = 2.0$, $SD = 0.97$, $n_3 = 62$). About 90.5% agreed or agreed totally that illustrative experiments supported the understanding of the respective scientific topics or theories. Only 9.5% rated this item neutrally ($M = 1.7$, $SD = 0.65$). The addressed scientific topics in the STEM Escape Room

Table 1. Clustered mentions to the open question "What appealed to you specifically?"

"What appealed to you specifically?"	Mentions
Science experiment ("magic cup")	8
Many topics / riddles in a short amount of time	8
Engineering experiment ("electrical circuit")	6
Working together with other people	6
Technology experiment ("Morse code")	5
Practical experience	3
Searching and finding things	3
Understandable and solvable tasks	3
Working with digital tools	2
Mathematical riddle ("rule of three")	2
Pens	1
Time pressure	1

were perceived as being important or very important by 63.5%. 31.7% adopted a neutral position while 3.2% disagreed ($M = 2.1$, $SD = 0.84$, $n_3 = 62$).

The visitors were also asked about other conceivable topics for future Escape Rooms. The subject mentioned most often was physics (five times, three of which stemmed from the pupils from the practical course), followed by general knowledge (four mentions), language and biology (three mentions each), and technologies (two mentions). Topics like computer programming, music, history, chemistry, and environment were mentioned individually.

In the open questions part of the survey, the guests were asked what specifically appealed to them during their experience (Table 1). It was possible to refer to more than one element, so overall 48 aspects were mentioned. The scientific experiment as well as the number of topics and riddles in the scheduled time frame were mentioned eight times. The other experiments (engineering, technology, mathematics) also gained between two and six votes. The collaboration with other people was perceived as highly positive, as was gaining practical experience and the method of searching and finding things to complete understandable tasks.

Six people stated that they had not missed anything during their stay in the STEM Escape Room. However, five people criticized the independency of the riddles which resulted from the open-puzzle structure. Other mentions like the lack of more than one room or the small number of riddles are also linked to the conditions and embedding of the Escape Game.

COMPARATIVE DISCUSSION

Concluding, the comparison of the different versions of Escape Rooms shows some aspects they have in common, such as their entertaining character. Most participants stated that they enjoyed the Escape Room experience and had (a lot of) fun playing it. This result is particularly interesting since only a minority of players had visited an Escape Room before – not even in their spare time. The players' positive experience thus ties in perfectly with the application of the gamification approach, which relies on fun as a main feature of games. The participation in the Escape Room as part of the project *Education 4.0 for SME* could represent a certain obligation due to its embedding in a practical taster day in the company during working hours and the fact that the participating employees were selected by the management, yet playing the STEM Escape Room was voluntary. At least in the first and second executions at two events, this room was a supplementary offer. Only the two last ones (15.8% of the overall sample, STEM Escape Room) took place in a school context, which implied a certain obligation to participate.

Furthermore, the evaluations of both Escape Rooms confirm that they were successful in achieving their goals. They aimed at raising awareness for their respective topics. On the one hand, the Escape Room used for science communication successfully promoted the topic of STEM in daily life, the scientific explanation underlying the demonstrated phenomena, and the relevance of this knowledge. On the other hand, the business Escape Room supported its participants in recognizing the importance of appropriate knowledge transfer within the company. In addition, many players in companies considered the Escape Room method to be helpful for a better understanding of the subject of knowledge transfer and acknowledged its practical relevance. The illustrative and descriptively demonstrated experiments in the STEM Escape Room supported the participants' understanding of the respective scientific topics or theories. Finally, the Education 4.0 Escape Room pursued two further goals, which could also be attained. The positive atmosphere experienced during the game seems to be helpful for a needs analysis in which the participants voice their professional concerns and desires. This had the effect that also current difficulties in the area of knowledge management could be revealed. For instance, the participants admitted that they were acquainted with parts of the presented worst-case scenario themselves and openly discussed possible solutions.

Regarding the design of the rooms, the participants predominantly rated the number and difficulty of the riddles as appropriate. In the case of the STEM Escape Room, the various puzzles were also positively highlighted. Further favorable aspects of both were the Escape Room as a social event and the role of teamwork. In this respect, the collaboration as a team was mentioned as the most positive impression (STEM Escape Room). The participating company representatives also emphasized the meaning of teamwork during the game. This illustrates the collaborative potential of the method.

Since the target groups of both rooms were expected to be very diverse, decisions about the setting, puzzle organization, and story goal were made to be adaptable to a great variety of situations. Yet these choices were, concerning the STEM Escape Room, not perceived as positive as initially imagined. So, for the future, it should be tested whether a different (story) goal or setting might be more efficient in fostering action and excitement. The feedback discussion carried out directly after the experience of the Education 4.0 Escape Room showed that it was easy to transfer the fictional situation to one's day-to-day routines. It revealed first insights, for instance concerning the meaning of specific habits of knowledge management in the company or – as already mentioned – of teamwork. Nevertheless, criticism was also voiced in that the developed scenario was not considered realistic for the operative routines of the companies involved. In this case, as well, a different framework or a different task could enhance the link to real everyday working life.

Additionally, it is important to point out that the quality of the study design and thus the resulting data could have been improved by designing the questionnaires following probabilistic testing theory. This lack of a methodological basis is restricting to the validity of the data. At any rate, future research is necessary to design and evaluate an Escape Room which respects the needs, preferences, experiences, and previous knowledge of each target group through a test battery with a transparent methodological approach and the calculation of internal consistency for each item. Despite the obvious parallels between the pilot studies, the dissimilar number of participants (63 in science communication vs. 21 in needs analysis), which is due to the different conditions of both contexts as well as the various target groups, also limits the direct comparability methodologically. Nevertheless, the presented rooms are at a pioneering stage for gamified approaches, as both the combination of an Escape Room with a needs analysis in a company and its use as a tool for science communication in society are unprecedented to the authors' knowledge. Thus, future research is required to validate the first results of the exploratory studies. An expansion toward another focus is also conceivable regarding content or learning goal.

FUTURE RESEARCH DIRECTIONS

Most of the participants in the STEM Escape Room were students who were accompanied by (their) teachers. During the game, it was noticeable that the students first turned to the known teacher in case of uncertainties instead of looking for clues together with the other players or asking the gamemaster. In this context, the question arises what role the presence of the teacher(s) played. Also, in the business Escape Room, the participants might have behaved differently if they had known that the management was watching them solve the riddles. Hence, the role of the (indirect) presence of a person regarding (socially desirable) behavior of others during a gamification method would be an intriguing starting point for further research. Similarly, different backgrounds (e.g., previous experience, education) and social dimensions (e.g., gender, age) of different target groups offer a broad field for further research. Moreover, the study of players' interactions while solving the puzzles might be an interesting point of investigation. Especially in the presented areas, such as business or school, there are numerous approaches to the topic of team development or class networking, which could be considered in the light of gamification.

The research on evaluating game-based learning approaches so far seems to put an emphasis on the cognition and/or meta-cognition of its participants (see e.g., Woo, 2014). This is particularly true for Escape Rooms, where only a few studies have focused on delving deeper into the activation patterns and the understanding of underlying motivational processes. Although the present study did not collect data on the Escape Room's emotional impact, presumably, for a gamified needs analysis approach, a setting would be needed that puts the participants in specific (affective) states, so they would want to share personal and/or informal details and not just superficial or socially desired information. Affective states – which can be defined as perceived feelings concerning underlying emotions – have been proven to have an impact on the learning process and precisely on one´s motivation to learn and achieve a certain goal (see e.g., Lane, 2005; Pekrun, 2006). Both positive and negative emotions seem to be substantial parts of learning, as they can, for instance, steer cognition and uphold motivational processes (see e.g., Pekrun & Stephens, 2012; Schwarz, 2011).

Concerning the STEM Escape Room, it would be reasonable to assume that the induction of a specific set of emotions (e.g., curiosity) might render the covered topics more appealing. Different affective states might be induced through specific settings, which could, for the purpose of needs analysis, lead to the disclosure of new and subconscious information. The business case Escape Room, representing a worst-case scenario, was emotionally charged (e.g., frustration), too. Therefore, it might have enabled the participants to access information in a more flexible way (Ehrlich et al., 2020, p. 5). However, when evaluating the Escape Rooms, no emphasis was put on the emotionally inducing impact. Hence, this hypothesis can neither be falsified nor validated at this stage. This could be a worthwhile starting point for future research, which could examine participants' affective states by focusing on the interim inquiry or retrospective judgment methods, in order to examine and understand the effectiveness of these states more closely. Particularly, the connection between gamification approaches and emotion research seems a rather new and unexplored field.

CONCLUSION

The results seem to confirm the entertaining nature of the Escape Room itself and show that this method succeeded in raising awareness on the respective topics. Furthermore, the presented pilot studies offer valuable insights into two different applications of gamification and further research seems worthwhile. On the one hand, elaborating on the affective focus in needs analyses as a basis for creating an atmosphere of openness seems to be an intriguing contribution from a psychological perspective. On the other, the newly discovered utilization of Escape Rooms for science communication has provoked the need for further research involving areas such as pedagogics, media, or game studies. Such exploratory results could contribute to the creation of further target group-specific Escape Rooms on a wide spectrum of topics. Hence, the potential of the gamification approach cannot only be measured in concrete numbers of evaluative results but should also be considered in terms of its fruitfulness in fostering interdisciplinary collaboration.

ACKNOWLEDGMENT

The project *Bildung 4.0 für KMU* (Education 4.0 for SMEs, Grant number 01PA17014) is funded by the German Federal Ministry of Education and Research (BMBF) and the European Social Fund for Germany within the program Digital Media in Vocational Training.

The project *WiR* (Wissenstransfer Region Augsburg/Knowledge transfer region Augsburg, Grant number 03IHS040) is funded by the German Federal Ministry of Education and Research (BMBF) within the program Innovative University.

REFERENCES

Abt, C. C. (1987). *Serious Games*. University Press of America.

Acatech. (2020). *MINT Nachwuchsbarometer*. Gutenberg Beuys Feindruckerei.

Bakhsheshi, F. F. (2019). Serious games and serious gaming in escape rooms. *Proceedings of the 1st International Serious Games Symposium (ISGS)*, 1–6. 10.1109/ISGS49501.2019.9047019

Bauer, M. W. (2017). Kritische Beobachtungen zur Geschichte der Wissenschaftskommunikation. In H. Bonfadelli, B. Fähnrich, C. Lüthje, J. Milde, M. Rhomberg, & M. S. Schäfer (Eds.), *Forschungsfeld Wissenschaftskommunikation* (pp. 17–40). Springer. doi:10.1007/978-3-658-12898-2_2

Bayerische Staatsregierung. (2020). *Hochschulinnovationsgesetz schafft zuverlässigen Rahmen für zuku-nftsfähige Hochschulstrukturen*. https://www.bayern.de/hochschulinnovationsgesetz-schafft-zuverlssigen-rahmen-fr-zukunftsfhige-hochschulstrukturen/

Becker, M. (2013). *Personalentwicklung: Bildung, Förderung und Organisationsentwicklung in Theorie und Praxis*. Schäffer-Poeschel.

Betts, B. (2013). Game-based learning. In R. Hubbard (Ed.), *The really useful elearning instruction manual* (pp. 175–194). Jon Wiley & Sons Ltd.

Borrego, C., Fernández, C., Blanes, I., & Robles, S. (2017). Room escape at class: Escape games activities to facilitate the motivation and learning in computer science. *Journal of Technology and Science Education, 7*(2), 162–171. doi:10.3926/jotse.247

Bubela, T., Nisbet, M. C., Borchelt, R., Brunger, F., Critchley, C., Einsiedel, E., Geller, G., Gupta, A., Hampel, J., Hyde-Lay, R., Jandciu, E. W., Jones, S. A., Kolopack, P., Lane, S., Lougheed, T., Nerlich, B., Ogbogu, U., O'Riordan, K., Ouellette, C., ... Caulfield, T. (2009). Science communication reconsidered. *Nature Biotechnology, 27*(6), 514–518. doi:10.1038/nbt0609-514 PMID:19513051

Burns, T. W., O'Connor, D. J., & Stocklmayer, S. M. (2003). Science communication: A contemporary definition. *Public Understanding of Science (Bristol, England), 12*(12), 183–202. doi:10.1177/09636625030122004

Clark, D., Tanner-Smith, E., & Killingsworth, S. (2016). Digital games, design, and learning: A systematic review and meta-analysis. *Review of Educational Research, 86*(1), 79–122. doi:10.3102/0034654315582065 PMID:26937054

Clarke, S., Peel, D. J., Arnab, S., Morini, L., Keegan, H., & Wood, O. (2017). escapED: A framework for creating educational escape rooms and Interactive Games For Higher/Further Education. *International Journal of Serious Games, 4*(3), 73–86. doi:10.17083/ijsg.v4i3.180

Corkill, E. (2009). *Real escape game brings its creator's wonderment to life*. https://www.japantimes.co.jp/life/2009/12/20/general/real-escape-game-brings-its-creators-wonderment-to-life/#.Xocyd0pCQ2x

Dahlstrom, M. F. (2014). Using narratives and storytelling to communicate science with nonexpert audiences. *Proceedings of the National Academy of Sciences of the United States of America, 111*(Suppl 4), 13614–13620. doi:10.1073/pnas.1320645111 PMID:25225368

Deci, E. L., Koestner, R., & Ryan, R. M. (2001). Extrinsic rewards and intrinsic motivation in education: Reconsidered once again. *Review of Educational Research, 71*(1), 1–27. doi:10.3102/00346543071001001

Deterding, S., Dixon, D., Khaled, R., & Nacke, L. (2011). From game design elements to gamefulness: Defining "gamification". *MindTrek'11: Proceedings of the 15th International Academic MindTrek Conference: Envisioning Future Media Environments*, 9–15. 10.1145/2181037.2181040

Döring, N., & Bortz, J. (2016). *Forschungsmethoden und Evaluation in den Sozial- und Humanwissenschaften* (5th ed.). Springer. doi:10.1007/978-3-642-41089-5

Ehrlich, I., Filipenko, M., Kranawetleitner, T., Krebs, H., Löw, R., Pistoll, D., & Thurner-Irmler, J. (2020). Escaping the Everyday Chaos: Assessing the Needs for Internal Knowledge. Transfer in SMEs via an Escape Room. In *CERC proceedings 2020* (pp. 1–19). Collaborative European Research Conference.

Fähnrich, B. (2017). Wissenschaftsevents zwischen Popularisierung, Engagement und Partizipation. In H. Bonfadelli, B. Fähnrich, C. Lüthje, J. Milde, M. Rhomberg, & M. S. Schäfer (Eds.), *Forschungsfeld Wissenschaftskommunikation* (pp. 165–182). Springer. doi:10.1007/978-3-658-12898-2_9

Glavaš, A., & Staščik, A. (2017). Enhancing positive attitude towards mathematics through introducing escape room games. In Z. Kolar-Begovic, R. Kolar-Super, & L. Jukic Matic (Eds.), Mathematics education as a science and profession (pp. 281–294). Academic Press.

Gold, A. H., Malhotra, A., & Segars, A. H. (2001). Knowledge management: An organizational capabilities perspective. *Journal of Management Information Systems*, *18*(1), 185–214. doi:10.1080/07421 222.2001.11045669

Häder, M., & Kühne, M. (2009). Die Prägung des Antwortverhaltens durch die soziale Erwünschtheit. In M. Häder & S. Häder (Eds.), *Telefonbefragungen über das Mobilfunknetz.* VS Verlag für Sozialwissenschaften., doi:10.1007/978-3-531-91490-9_13

Hochschulrektorenkonferenz. (2013). *Wissenstransfer in die Mediengesellschaft: Situationsanalyse und Orientierungshilfen: Beiträge zur Hochschulpolitik 3/2013.*

Holden, R. (2010). Social desirability. *The Corsini encyclopedia of psychology*, 1–2.

KYOCERA Document Solutions. (2018). *Wissensmanagement im Mittelstand: Mit Dokumentenmanagement Wissen besser verfügbar machen.* https://www.kyoceradocumentsolutions.de/de/smarter-workspaces/ media-center/e-books/e-book-wissensmanagement-dms.html

Lane, A. M., Whyte, G. P., Terry, P. C., & Nevill, A. M. (2005). Mood, self-set goals and examination performance: The moderating effect of depressed mood. *Personality and Individual Differences*, *39*(1), 143–153. doi:10.1016/j.paid.2004.12.015

Lewenstein, B. V. (2011). Experimenting with engagement: Commentary on: Taking our own medicine: On an experiment in science communication. *Science and Engineering Ethics*, *17*(4), 817–821. doi:10.100711948-011-9328-5 PMID:22095058

López-Belmonte, J., Segura-Robles, A., Fuentes-Cabrera, A., & Parra-Gonzáles, M. E. (2020). Evaluating activation and absence of negative effect: Gamification and escape rooms for learning. *International Journal of Environmental Research and Public Health,* *17*(7), 1–12.

Minbaeva, D., Pedersen, T., Björkman, I., Fey, C., & Park, H. (2003). MNC knowledge transfer, subsidiary Absorptive Capacity, and HRM. *Journal of International Business Studies*, *34*(6), 586–599. doi:10.1057/palgrave.jibs.8400056

Nicholson, S., & Cable, L. (2021). *Unlocking the potential of puzzle-based learning. Designing Escape Rooms + Games for the classroom.* CORWIN.

Nicholson, S. (2016). *The State of the Escape: Escape Room Design and Facilities.* Paper Presented at Meaningful Play 2016. https://scottnicholson.com/pubs/stateofescape.pdf

Parra-González, M. E., López-Belmonte, J., Segura-Robles, A., & Fuentes-Cabrera, A. (2020). Active and emerging methodologies for ubiquitous education: Potentials of flipped learning and gamification. *Sustainability, 2020*(12), 602. doi:10.3390u12020602

Patrício, R., Moreira, A., Zurlo, F., & Melazzini, M. (2020). Co-creation of new solutions through gamification: A collaborative innovation practice. *Creativity and Innovation Management, 29*(1), 146–160. doi:10.1111/caim.12356

Pekrun, R. (2016). Academic Emotions. In K. Wentzl & D. B. Miele (Eds.), *Handbook of Motivation at School* (pp. 120–144). Routledge.

Pekrun, R., & Stephens, E. J. (2012). Academic emotions. In APA educational psychology handbook: Vol. 2. *Individual differences and cultural and contextual factors* (pp. 3–31). American Psychological Association.

Riedel, S. (2006). Bedarfe erheben oder Bedarfe wecken? Das Tiefeninterview der qualitativen Marktforschung – diskursanalytisch betrachtet. In M. Boenigk, D. Krieger, A. Belliger, & C. Hug (Eds.), *Innovative Wirtschaftskommunikation* (pp. 115–128). DUV. doi:10.1007/978-3-8350-9663-9_9

Schreiber, P. (2012). Kinderuniversitäten in der Welt – ein Vergleich. In B. Dernbach, C. Kleinert, & H. Münder (Eds.), *Handbuch Wissenschaftskommunikation* (pp. 107–115). Springer. doi:10.1007/978-3-531-18927-7_14

Schwarz, N. (2011). Feelings-as-information theory. In P. A. M. Van Lange, A. W. Kruglanski, & E. T. Higgins (Eds.), *Handbook of theories of social psychology* (pp. 289–308). Sage Publications Ltd.

Siegel, D. S., Waldman, D. A., Atwater, L. E., & Link, A. N. (2003). Commercial knowledge transfers from universities to firms: Improving the effectiveness of university–industry collaboration. *The Journal of High Technology Management Research, 14*(1), 111–133. doi:10.1016/S1047-8310(03)00007-5

Thurner-Irmler, J., & Menner, M. (2020). The Development and Testing of a Self-designed Escape Room as a Concept of Knowledge Transfer into Society. In M. Ma, B. Fletcher, S. Göbel, J. Baalsrud Hauge, & T. Marsh (Eds.), *Serious games. JSCG 2020* (pp. 105–116). Lecture Notes in Computer Science. Springer. doi:10.1007/978-3-030-61814-8_9

Wodke, P. (2020). *Wissenschaftskommunikation – Wissenschaftstransfer – Wissenstransfer. Im Dickicht der Begriffswelten.* https://kristinoswald.hypotheses.org/3044

Woo, J. C. (2014). Digital game-based learning supports student motivation, cognitive success, and performance outcomes. *Journal of Educational Technology & Society, 17*(3), 291–307.

ADDITIONAL READING

Bonfadelli, H. (2017). Handlungstheoretische Perspektiven auf die Wissenschaftskommunikation. In H. Bonfadelli, B. Fähnrich, C. Lüthje, J. Milde, M. Rhomberg, & M. S. Schäfer (Eds.), *Forschungsfeld Wissenschaftskommunikation* (pp. 83–108). Springer. doi:10.1007/978-3-658-12898-2_5

Ehrlich, I., Filipenko, M., Kranawetleitner, T., Krebs, H., Löw, R., Pistoll, D., & Thurner-Irmler, J. (2020). Escaping the Everyday Chaos: Assessing the Needs for Internal Knowledge. Transfer in SMEs via an Escape Room. In *CERC proceedings 2020* (pp. 1–19). Collaborative European Research Conference.

Kranawetleitner, T., Krebs, H., Kuhn, N., & Menner, M. (2020). Needs Analyses with LEGO® SERIOUS PLAY. In M. Ma, B. Fletcher, S. Göbel, J. Baalsrud Hauge, & T. Marsh (Eds.), *Serious games. JSCG 2020* (pp. 99–104). Lecture Notes in Computer Science. Springer. doi:10.1007/978-3-030-61814-8_8

Salen, K., & Zimmerman, E. (2004). *Rules of Play, Game Design Fundamentals*. MIT Press. https://gamifique.files.wordpress.com/2011/11/1-rules-of-play-game-design-fundamentals.pdf

Thurner-Irmler, J., & Menner, M. (2020). The Development and Testing of a Self-designed Escape Room as a Concept of Knowledge Transfer into Society. In M. Ma, B. Fletcher, S. Göbel, J. Baalsrud Hauge, & T. Marsh (Eds.), *Serious games. JSCG 2020* (pp. 105–116). Lecture Notes in Computer Science. Springer. doi:10.1007/978-3-030-61814-8_9

KEY TERMS AND DEFINITIONS

Escape Game/Room: A multiplayer game consisting of various contextualized riddles, usually set in one room. The riddles contribute to achieving the main goal – mostly escaping the room – while they or the Escape Game itself can have further educational goals.

Gamification: The principle of using game/gaming (design) elements in non-game contexts.

Knowledge Transfer: The passing on of knowledge of any kind, for example concerning processual structures, responsibilities, or factual knowledge.

Needs Analysis: An analysis to identify the needs of a company, for instance in terms of information flow, knowledge transfer, or digital tools.

Riddle Flow Chart: A chart that visualizes the connections of the interdependent riddles in an Escape Game.

Science Communication: Different kinds of communication about scientific knowledge or knowledge about science to designated target groups.

Serious Game: A game specifically conceptualized and designed for achieving an educational goal. Fun is no main characteristic, but an important element.

SME: The acronym describes small and medium-sized enterprises (SMEs) of less than 250 employees. The definition used in the chapter refers to the definition of the European Union.

STEM: An acronym for the subjects Science, Technology, Engineering, and Mathematics.

Chapter 5
WorkAI:
Raising Work–Related Self–Awareness With Gamified Approach

Pauliina Tuomi
https://orcid.org/0000-0001-9986-6426
Tampere University, Finland

Kati Fager
Crazy Town, Finland

Jari Multisilta
https://orcid.org/0000-0002-5636-6365
Satakunta University of Applied Sciences, Finland

ABSTRACT

The gamification of different work tasks remains an area where studies have focused mainly on conceptual considerations. This chapter focuses on the gamification process in facility services jobs – cleaning and maintenance. In general, gamification can improve productivity and workplace well-being. Better motivation is supposed to lead to better results and more enjoyable work. This chapter describes the process of gamifying facility services jobs, from the interviews of the staff to the implementation of the custom-made application, WorkAI. Eighteen employees participated in the pilot study, filled in a questionnaire, and attended semi-structured end-interview sessions. This chapter shows how personnel perceived the gamified solution and its possible effects on the employees and their work. Based on the results, the gamified solution must be easy to adapt and should not disturb work routines. This application's main benefit lies in the employee's self-reflection and self-evaluation.

DOI: 10.4018/978-1-6684-4291-3.ch005

INTRODUCTION

Gamification is often described as the use of video-game elements to improve user engagement and experience with non-game initiatives (Deterding et al, 2011, 1). Benefits of gamification have been widely acknowledged in recent years and it has been studied from several viewpoints. Gamification has been previously implemented for example in education (Landers & Landers, 2014; Clark, Tannersmith & Killingsworth 2015), data-collection (Downes-le Guin, Baker, Mechling, & Ruyle, 2012), health (Bellotti et al. 2010; Jones, Madden, & Wengreen, 2014), marketing (Hamari, 2013, 2015) and environmental protection (Gustafsson, Katzeff, & Bang, 2009).

Gamification in work has also been in the interest of research for a while now. (e.g., Arai, Sakamoto & Washizaki, 2014; Fernandes et al., 2012). It has been seen supporting user engagement and enhancing positive patterns in service use, such as increasing user activity, social interaction, or quality and productivity of actions (Hamari et al. 2014; Hamari 2013). Based on e.g., Hamari et al. (2014) research, these desired use patterns are considered to emerge because of positive, intrinsically motivating (Ryan & Deci 2000) "gameful" experiences (Huotari & Hamari 2012) brought by game/motivational affordances implemented into a service. (Hamari, Koivisto & Sarsa 2014)

According to Sailer, et al. (2017), game design elements can deliberately be used to modify non-game contexts such as working environments to address motivational mechanisms, especially when well designed and built upon well-established implementation models. (Sailer, Hense, Mayr & Mandi 2017, 378) gamification primarily aims to increase users' positive motivations towards given activities or use of technology (Hamari & Koivisto 2015; Huotari & Hamari 2016) It has been suggested that more and more of all organizations will have gamified parts in their processes in the future (Morschheuser, Werder, Hamari & Abe 2017)

Scholars in the field of workplace settings have argued that the use of game elements in the workplace setting might increase intrinsic motivation and thereby the meaning of work (Nicholson, 2012; Rosso, Dekas, & Wrzesniewski, 2010). Gamification is used to make work activities more enjoyable and interesting in schools, health care and business. Reward schemes can help achieve this through performance-dependent points, increasing levels of difficulties, leader boards, and achievement badges (Nicholson, 2015). However, there is still a need for empirically based knowledge on gamification and, it has not been studied elaborately in business organizations, i.e., real-life professional settings. (Obrescu et al. 2014; Hamari et al. 2014; Pogrebtsova et al. 2017; Lamberts et al. 2016; Hoffman et al. 2017).

In this study, the overall approach was to explore whether the gamified approach influences both the self-awareness and the knowledge acquisition of respondents during the pilot. The approach in this study is to use a gamified solution called WorkAI that aims to track the employee's daily routines and feelings through relevant thematical areas. WorkAI can then be seen as a tool for self-evaluation. There are studies concerning the gamificational approaches that deal with the idea of work personnel self-awareness in the workplace (Lamberts et al. 2016; sutton et al. 2015), acquisition of knowledge in information security (thornton & Francia 2014; Antonaci et al. 2017), sociocultural studies (sitas 2017), emotional level in stress management (Hofmann et al. 2017) and overall, in workplace well-being (e.g. Pogrebtsova et al. 2017; Alatalo et al. 2018). Organizations have become increasingly aware of the positive implications of promoting well-being at work. Well-being at work is a concept that can be associated with various aspects of workplace health promotion (Anttonen & Vainio 2010). In this study, the substance of the application is gathered to raise self-awareness and through the application the employee is able to visualize his/her current position in respect to the themes. The approach of self-measurement and self-evaluation can be seen as phenomenon of "the quantified self", term that was coined by Gary Woolf and Kevin Kerry in 2008. Nowadays it is possible to varying degrees to self-track and self-measure using smartphones, watches, and other wearable technologies. For example, physical activities are monitored and transformed into data, which can be used to generate statistics and can be shared on social networks (Maturo et al. 2016, 249.)

The study and the WorkAI application and its substance concentrates on the physical (workplace circumstances), psychological (self-evaluation and well-being & endurance at work) and social level (communication and cooperation). A view of this kind can be considered to refer to a holistic perspective on well-being at work (Alatalo et al. 2018, 226). However, in this project the aim is not to measure whether the actual well-being increases. The overall aim is to raise awareness how daily work processes influence the well-being, health and for example safety at the workplace.

Research questions:

1) How was the gamified application perceived by the respondents?
2) What affects, if any, WorkAI had in terms of self-awareness?

BACKGROUND

Kisa-Project

Kisa-project (2017-2018) was funded by the Finnish work environment fund (TSR). The aim of the project was to study how does gamification effect the facility services jobs – especially in real-estate maintenance and cleaning services. The overall process of this project included work engagement scale test, interviews with the staff, design process of the application based on the interview findings, implementation, and piloting and finally end-interviews. The cooperative organizations RTK-palvelu (cleaning services) and Porin Palveluliikelaitos (real-estate maintenance) were committed to take part in the project. (Fager, Tuomi & Multisilta 2018, 57)

Application

The application development process is a combination of adapting existing platform and using external developers. Application bases on "one by one" platform by Headai that is an AI - based interactive questionnaire form. Headai company operates on artificial intelligence (AI), and they blend cognitive psychology, machine learning and semantic computing1. The used user interface resembles Whatsapp or Messenger, but instead of messaging a person, a software robot (bot) is messaging to the user, who has certain answering options to message it back. The background work and the design of the used application is better described in the paper "'Gamifying facility service jobs - using personnel attitudes and perceptions for designing gamification" (Fager, Tuomi & Multisilta 2018), presented in the Gamifin 2018 conference. The conference paper focuses then on the design process of the application, while this chapter analyses the actual results of the study through interview and inquiry data. This book chapter manuscript then expands (by using totally different data & research focus) the previous work from a different perspective.

In the WorkAI application, the aim is to get the workers to self-evaluate different aspects of their work. The content of the application is on general level (not profession-specific), and it deals with work-related content widely, via themes described in Table 1. (Fager, Tuomi & Multisilta 2018, 60)

Table 1. The main themes of the application

Social	Physical	Psychological
Sense of community (1)	Safety in work (1)	Self-evaluation (2)
Information flow (2)	Work itself (1)	Feedback (3)
customer experience (2)	Working hours (2)	Learning (1)

All in all, WorkAI consists of fifteen different question patterns under nine themes. Fifteen was chosen because of three-week testing period (with five workdays a week) with dividing some themes into two or more categories. The categories are presented in table 1.

Using WorkAI goes as follows:

- At first you register in and create a software robot (bot). One can name the bot as one likes. Next step is to click "start" and the bot starts messaging to the user, explaining what the application is all about.
- One can then choose a theme to address. The bot introduces the theme and then gives one a claim, such as "I will say hello to five customers today" (communality) or "I will have a peaceful coffee break" (working hours) or "I got good feedback from my supervisor" (feedback). Some of the claims guide the worker to activity, some were just statements of how things are.
- The bot gives the answer scale (Likert): very often / often / seldom / not at all / does not concern me. One chooses the answer, and the bot gives feedback like "good!", "well done!" And then moves on to the next question. (Fager, Tuomi & Multisilta 2018, 59)

All the time one "plays", one can also choose to check how one has progressed from the learning map, check out the trophies one has earned or go back to the starting page. The nine themes and the questions of WorkAI can be found from Appendix 1.

RESEARCH METHODS AND DATA

The project operated within the action research (AR) framework. In KiSA-project the researcher and the organizational actors both participated interactively in the research. The approach was selected since it is particularly suitable when a study aims at improving a situation by making concrete changes to it (Toubolic & Walker 2016) and, at the same time, expanding scholarly knowledge providing deeper insights into the issues under consideration (e.g. Touboulic, & Walker 2016). Action research involves active participating in changing situation, often via an existing organization, whilst simultaneously conducting research. (Fager, Tuomi & Multisilta 2018, 56)

Figure 1. Screenshots from WorkAI application. On the left, caption from the conversation with the bot (in Finnish). In the middle, first badge/trophy given for progressing in the application. On the right, the learning map where participants can follow their own progress and/or choose themes. (Fager, Tuomi & Multisilta 2018, 60)

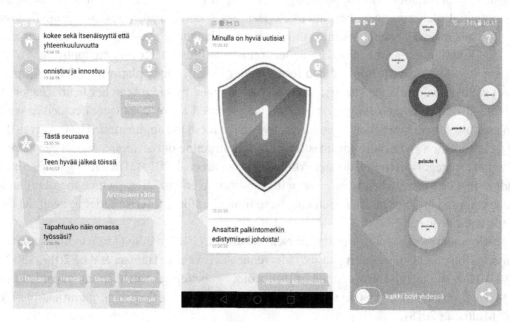

The data consists of a) semi-structured interviews before the pilot, which were utilized in designing the gamified application, b) the data collected by the application during the pilot and the researcher's observation on the usage of the application, and c) the questionnaire and semi-structured end-interviews after the pilot. In this chapter, the focus is on the results of the questionnaire and end-interviews.

Pre-interviews

The initial semi-structured theme interviews took place in both workplaces in spring 2017. Two researchers executed the interviews based on the thematic frame of questions that reflected with the previous research on work life research, work life well-being and gamificational aspects. Staff members were interviewed individually, and interviews were recorded. One interview took approx. 45 minutes. Interviews were transcribed afterwards and analyzed qualitatively using a thematic analysis. Overall, 18 staff members, 14 from RTK-palvelu and 4 from Porin Palveluliikelaitos, were interviewed. Two of the interviewees were managers. Three of them were male and fifteen were female. The interviewees were selected voluntarily, based on their interest to take part.

Design Process

The data from the initial interviews were utilized in designing the gamified application. The main result was that the application needed to be simple, easy and fast to use. There was also clear need to move from specific work-related tasks to more general user needs, since the tasks and work environment of the workers varied substantively (Fager, Tuomi & Multisilta 2018, 62). Themes from the interview data that operated on the physical, psychological, and social levels were detected. Themes were developed further into practical claims on the gamified application.

The gamified application was supposed to be developed by the research team but instead, already existing, potential platforms were benchmarked. Habitica2- communal, a rewarding application was tested, but it was rejected since it operated only in English language and had a complex user interface and also due to the unsureness of the data collection possibilities. After that an application of a local AI company was tested and it was decided to use their "One by One" platform and have it modified for project's purposes, while the specific content was designed by the researcher team. (Fager, Tuomi & Multisilta 2018, 59) By selecting the platform, the gamified approaches were decided as well. The platform uses a software robot (bot) as an interactive character in the application. The bot gives the user a feel of a conversation and softens the questionnaire-like structure of the application. It can be regarded as a story/theme category of motivational affordances (Hamari et al. 2014). The other gamified elements were badges that one gains when advancing in the application and progress, which the user can follow from the learning map. The gamified elements were limited in these three in order to keep the application simple and fast to use.

The development process reflects on the Morschheuser et al. (2017) method for designing gamification, which divides the process into seven phases. (Morschheuser, Werder, Hamari & Abe 2017, 1300-1301, 1303-1304) How the method was applied in this project is better described in the paper "Gamifying facility service jobs – using personnel attitudes and perceptions for designing gamification." (Fager, Tuomi & Multisilta 2018)

The Pilot Study

The pilot study (staff members using the gamified WorkAI application) was implemented in March-April 2018. Most of the participants were different than of the initial interviews. There were nine voluntary participants from RTK-palvelu (cleaning services) and nine from Porin Palveluliikelaitos (real-estate maintenance). The pilot study began with training sessions of both groups. The participants used the application during workdays for a period of 3 weeks (15 workdays). During the try-out phase, researcher was observing the use of application in the work environment.

End Interviews

In order to get the overall experiences and opinions towards the pilot study and application, semi-structured interviews were conducted with the pilot study participants. All 18 participants took part in them. The end-interviews were done in groups, in both workplaces individually. In the beginning of the interview, the participants were asked to fill-in the questionnaire forms. After that, there was a semi-structured end-interview based on the thematical areas of WorkAI and the participants were able to speak freely how they had perceived the use of application and its content. Gamification elements were discussed as well. The semi-structured interview questions can be found from Appendix 2.

RESULTS

End-Questionnaire and Interview Results

Both the end-questionnaire and - interview data were analyzed. The final interview results are in line with the questionnaire results and in addition to questionnaire the interview sessions gave the participants a possibility to speak freely about the content of the questionnaire and the pilot study itself. Since only two organizations were involved and the number of participants is rather small, the end-interview results are not identified on the organizational level, they are left anonymous. The results are presented by highlighting the number of participants, out of the overall amount of 18, in parenthesis. The options agree/disagree and strongly agree/disagree are combined.

Application

Based on the end-questionnaires, for the majority, the application and its usage were considered easy, well-adopted (18) and participants did not encounter major technical difficulties (17). The participants felt the use of application fun (15) and some felt it was beneficial (8). Majority (14) would like to use similar application with perhaps new thematical areas in the future. (See Table 2.)

Table 2. Application

	Strongly disagree	Disagree	Neutral	Agree	Strongly agree	No opinion
It was easy to start to use the application	0	0	0	2	16	0
The technical execution of the application was good	0	1	0	2	15	0
The application was easy to use	0	0	0	2	16	0
The application was fun to use	0	2	1	10	5	0
The application was useful to me	2	1	6	7	1	1
I would like to use a similar application in the future	1	1	2	5	9	0

During the end-interviews, majority of participants highlighted the easiness of the AI work application – both when starting the usage as well as during the experiment. No one encountered major technical difficulties nor felt assistance needed.

- "Easy to start using, there were no technical difficulties during the try-out"
- "The interface was really good, would be really suitable for people born in the 21st century – it also worked very well and was easy to use."

However, few remarks concerning the logic behind the application aroused during the end-interviews. This was mainly due to the AI logic and the preconditions of the applications. The problem was noted during development before the actual piloting, but due to the budgetary and schedule-related reasons the application could not be modified. The bot in WorkAI offered same thematical areas several times even when participants had done them already during the day. This lead to confusion time to time.

- "There were some repetitions in the questions. Made it hard to answer all the questions"

In addition to this, it would have been more beneficial if the bot would have been showing the already covered areas clearer by preventing participants to go through the same theme. This feature is probably one of the reasons why all the participants did not go through all the areas.

- "You didn't always know where you were, what areas had been completed."
- "Where's the logic? It didn't operate on numerical order?"

Substance

The application included nine different themes and based on the results, the participants executed the thematical areas as planned (one area per day) and considered themselves motivated to access the next stage/theme. The majority (13) did go through the whole 15 steps. The content of the thematical areas were seen both relevant (10) and irrelevant (4) to participants work. See Table 3.

Table 3. Substance of the application

	Strongly disagree	Disagree	Neutral	Agree	Strongly agree	No opinion
I used it one subject/theme at a time	3	3	0	8	4	0
I was looking forward to exploring the new theme	1	0	6	7	4	0
I went through all 15 topics	2	0	1	4	9	2
The content of the app seemed irrelevant and not related to my work	5	5	4	4	0	0

Despite this challenge, the perception of the application remained positive throughout the both interview sessions. 11 of the participants felt motivated to finalize one area and then accessing the next one. Based on the interviews, the intrinsic motivation was a key factor also behind the motivation to proceed – if the themes were felt important, they were perceived close to the participants work day, participants were motivated to go further and reach another area.

- "The themes arouse a lot of questions in my mind. I was easy to answer the questions since they related to my work"
- "All areas were relevant to my work and I considered them important"

Overall, the themes of the bot were considered mainly relevant, but during the interviews it was stated that it might be more effective to actually concentrate on one theme instead of covering them all. One suggested theme in both of the interview sessions was work safety.

- "The whole application could have concentrated on work safety"
- "Work safety is a very important theme that all employees should be reminded of – also the fact that all issues should be reported"

This aspect also brought up some critical feedback as well as suggestions how to improve the application in relation to work safety. The more interactive interface was proposed.

- "The application just revised the old knowledge I already had; it didn't however make it interesting since nothing actually happened"
- "Could the use of pictures/videos and more in-depth questions make the application on work safety more affective?"
- "It would have been nice to be able to actually provide my own answers (in text) and at least to explain and elaborate the questions choices I made."

Work safety was seen as a theme that a) would require daily attention and b) would be relevant to everyone. Of course, in this case, the content would have to be produced by an expert of a certain field e.g., work safety concerning cleaning maintenance's use of corrosive liquids.

Gamification

11 of the participants agreed that the trophies were seen as positive feature and 9 felt collecting them as motivating. Also, the map that highlighted the areas participants had gone through as well as their progress in general, was considered (15) a motivating feature. See Table 4.

Table 4. Gamificational elements

	Strongly disagree	Disagree	Neutral	Agree	Strongly agree	No opinion
I perceived the trophies positive	0	0	5	5	6	0
Collecting trophies motivated to move forward in the application	1	1	7	4	5	0
I was following my own progress on the map	2	0	1	5	10	0
I chose themes through the progress map	5	3	0	5	5	0
I wanted to go through all areas of the progress map	0	0	3	5	10	0

Also, in the end-interviews, the use of gamified elements was perceived positively. There were three elements used: the software robot (bot) as a story/theme element, badges that you gained when advancing in the application and progress, which the user can follow up from the learning map (Gamified elements in line with motivational affordances by Hamari, Koivisto & Sarsa. (Hamari et al. 2014, 3027)

The respondents liked the playful and interactive bot and its pleasant mode of talking was a liked feature.

- "The bot and its way of talking was smooth and funny!"

The use of the map where one can follow up his own performance and success was used a lot and it functioned as a visualisation of one's progress.

- "It was good that you were able to follow your progress through the map function"
- "I followed the progress map, but I liked the trophies better".

The use of map was also, based on the interviews, a feature that brought up collective efforts and communication. Both within the pilot group, but also with people outside the pilot experiment e.g. during the coffee breaks of the whole company.

- "The application made me talk to my colleagues more."
- "The questions enabled conversation (with colleagues) and the application worked as a good topic"
- "We browsed the application together with my colleague"
- "We used the application together and had conversations on the topic"

As a remark, it is evident that for the personnel that operate and work on their own on several locations, the sense of community is totally different than for the personnel that work together throughout the day. Also, the organizational cultures and ways to operate influence the sense of community, as well does the personality of the employee.

The collecting of the trophies was seen as a motivating feature. Participants felt that receiving a new trophy encouraged them to continue to pursue the next one. Participants said they felt proud when receiving a digital trophy on their phone.

- "The trophies were great!"
- "I waited my next trophy a lot"

Again, some ideas of improving the idea of trophies were presented during the end-interviews.

- "This is a great application for the youth. Would be great if the trophies could be earned through actual work tasks, not just for answering questions"
- "Would be great if you could post on Facebook every time you unlock a trophy"

However, it was also stated by the respondents that the application could have emphasized more gamificational elements and that the application was not perceived as a game as suspected.

- "It didn't really feel like a game, more like a questionnaire."
- "Would be nice if you could personalize and customize your own bot, appearance, looks etc."

The work-related requirements of having the application easy and fast to use affected the fact that the solution could not be more interactive and intense. The application had to appeal differently.

Effects on Work Routines

Based on the end-questionnaire, the use of application did not disturb the majority's work routines (14), and the use of application was fluent during the workday (13). Some (8) felt working more positive while using the application and a few (4) of the participants felt that the use of application helped them to improve their work. Some (8) felt as the application had taught something new. See Table 5.

Table 5. Effects on the workday and routines

	Strongly disagree	Disagree	Neutral	Agree	Strongly agree	No opinion
The use of application interrupted work routines	11	3	1	2	1	0
The use of application was smooth during the working day	1	1	2	3	10	1
Performing work assignments seemed more meaningful during the experiment	2	2	6	4	2	2
The arguments provided by the application helped to improve my work	2	4	7	3	1	1
I learned new ways to operate based on the claims applications offered	2	3	4	7	1	1

The participants highlighted also in the end-interviews that the application did not disturb their work routines and tasks. This was especially important for these particular work places – the main result of the pre-interviews was that the application needed to be simple, easy and fast to use and that using it shouldn't disturb the work routines. Participants described the use of application during the workday fluent and some of them even stated that working felt more positive with the application.

- "WorkAI didn't interrupt my working. On the contrary, it was fun to have the bot chatting and asking questions."
- "I liked the fact that WorkAI intercepted the workday a bit and I had something different to do for a while."
- "It (WorkAI) was pleasant, not 'stalkative'. (in the meaning of harassment)"

The Main Outcome: Self-Awareness

The main outcome of the gathered data was, all aspects mentioned combined, the factor that the application and substance got respondents to think about their own behaviour. The process of becoming more self-aware is shown in the transcript answers below. There were three areas that participants most frequently became aware of in relation to their own experiences and feelings. First theme was well-being and how to manage the workload. This is an important factor since the balance between workload and one's endurance affects the well-being at work. (Anttonen & Vainio 2010; Schaufeli et al. 2002).

Well-being & endurance (e.g., hurry, fatigue):

- "The work effectivity clearly declines in the afternoon; you just notice that you get tired. It is not stress-related, it is just that you slow down."
- "It would help me to endure working if I could have an impact, a possibility to suggest the order of the work tasks allocated for the day."
- "My endurance and effectiveness are day and week-based, but it was good to actually woke up to think about this."
- "I noticed while answering that how much does the badly slept night affect the following work day or how important it is to eat right."

The second theme was workplace environment and general feedback system at work. Also, these aspects are crucial for the employees feeling of control and succeeding in one's work tasks. Feedback can increase the feeling of occupational identity and empowerment when given constructively. (Anttonen & Vainio 2010) By getting feedback, the professional identity and self-confidence can be boosted, which affects the efficiency of the employee beneficially. (Askheim 2003, 230).

Workplace circumstances (e.g., safety, feedback system):

- "I just suddenly noticed that I actually get feedback every now and then"
- "(I awoke to) the fact work safety issues are not reported because there is sort of a mentality towards it. All the serious ones are reported of course, but the close-cases are rarely."
- Feedback-theme arouse most thoughts. I get negative feedback time to time, but it is a good thing since only through that we can make things better. Sometimes I feel that the negative feedback is also sometimes seen or perceived as a bigger thing that it actually is."

The third theme was social communication within the workplace. A positive atmosphere enables employees to share their feelings and knowledge which again may increase the feeling of empowerment. (Alatalo et al. 2018; Anttonen & Vainio 2010; Zimmerman 1995, 592)

Social communication (e.g., work colleagues, customers, superiors/employees).

- "Noticed that I don't necessarily talk a lot to others, could talk more, but always depends on the work situation, especially location."
- "The questions made me think that even if someone sometimes annoys or disturbs you, you should not react."
- "Made me think of how I work among the others, do I get nervous and do I let it show to others etc."

To conclude, the main preconditions from the pre-interviews – application needed to be easy and fast to adapt and use without disturbing work routines - were successfully implemented into the application used in the pilots. This was confirmed both through the questionnaire results and group end-interviews. Also, the reception towards gamified elements (bot, map and trophies) was promising. One of the most positive outcomes in respect to the whole study, from the design of the application to actual pilot experiments, is the fact that the clear majority would be willing to use a similar application in the future as well. The main benefit of this sort of application would lie in the self-reflection and self-evaluation. In order to feel empowerment, the employee must have a feeling of control of his/herself and work. (Askheim 2003, 230; Zimmerman 1995, 592).

- "Self-reflection was most beneficial in this experience!"
- "I thought every question precisely, I never answered lightly."
- "This could be arranged once a year in order to remind employees about these issues, motivation and well-being."

DISCUSSION

Overall, the pilot study was executed as planned. There are however few remarks concerning the process.

In a review of the literature, Hamari et al. state that most published gamification studies reported some positive effects, but they identified a number of methodological limitations that may have contributed to varying results. These limitations included small sample sizes, lack of control groups and very short experiment timeframes. A fourth limitation was that multiple game elements were often investigated in combination, but not individually, making it impossible to establish whether individual elements had measurable effects (Hamari et al. 2014).

When reflecting to these valid points gathered by Hamari et al 2014, it can be said that the amount of the respondents in this study is rather small so the findings cannot be generalized. However, within this project the approach was qualitative which aims to in-depth understanding of a certain, specified research theme, not on representativeness. The results cannot be generalized also due to the fact that there are lots of variety in the participants' background - ICT skills, technology used at work, attitudes towards games etc. The expectations towards games as well as the prior knowledge of the players can lead to different game experiences and learning outcomes within the same game. (e.g., Plass et al.2015). The working conditions vary since there are a lot of difference between the two organizations and within them. Unfortunately, also the idea of control groups was not applicable at this stage of the project.

There were three different gamificational elements within WorkAI, so it is not possible to say whether the appreciation of the application bases on the trophies, bot, progressive maps or even just on the functionality of the application and its themes. To point out, it would be difficult to come up with a gamificational solution with only one gamified feature. The three features in WorkAI were not adequate to some of the participants since they felt the solution not gamified enough. Nacke and Deterding (2017) state well while saying that at the heart of the gamification design process is the development of gameful systems, which are complex combinations and interactions between elements. To explain these systems, there is also a need for more complex explanations than the mere understanding of how each element functions individually (Nacke & Deterding 2017, 453). It is also problematic where to draw the line on what constitutes gamification in the given context (e.g., Warmelink et al.2018) and it should also be kept in mind that gamifying something does not make it automatically engaging – there needs to be enough value in the concept to want people to participate and play along (e.g., Kim 2015).

Also, in respect to the WorkAI and end-interview results, one particular theme area could have been chosen instead of using all of them as a content of the application. It could have concentrated on e.g., safety at work or well-being in order to give more intense and detailed insights to the participants. Also, the AI features of the platform could have been executed more properly. If used more effectively, AI would enable searches for information on certain topics that could be filtered to the application in wanted way. In the future studies concentrating on one theme and seeking the ways of using AI in gamification could produce more beneficial outcomes to the employees.

Also, at this stage only the data from the interviews was utilized as a background for the application. However, facility service jobs already produce lots of sensor-based data, often in the form big data. These could be for example the energy consumption of the buildings, satisfaction of the users of the buildings, cleanliness, and the fuel consumption of the work appliances. In the future, this sort of a data could be utilized in gamifying different work tasks. Then it would be possible to integrate gamified elements to already existing technical systems.

CONCLUSION

This chapter described the design process of a solution to gamify facility service work tasks. The used application bases on the pre-interview data and the design process were reported in line with Morschheuser's et al. (2017) theory on designing gamification (Morschheuser, Werder, Hamari J & Abe, 2017; (Fager, Tuomi & Multisilta 2018). The main findings of the pre-interviews were: a) the application for facility service work needed to be simple, easy and fast to use b) communal and rewarding elements were appreciated c) the participants' background and the working conditions varied a lot. This demanded the application to concentrated on the general user needs rather than specific work-related tasks. Nine work-related themes were detected from the interview data and the WorkAI application was built on them. The 3-week pilot study took place on spring 2018 and overall, 18 employees participated in the study. After the pilot study, participants filled in a questionnaire and attended semi-structured group interview sessions. In this chapter the focus was on the results of the questionnaire and end-interviews.

Based on these results, the answers to research questions are the following: 1) How was the gamified application perceived by the respondents? The attitudes after the pilot study were positive and the gamified features implemented in the application were positively perceived. Half of the respondents felt the use of application motivating, especially through the gamificational elements e.g., collecting of the trophies and progress map. Also, the use application did not interfere with respondents' work-routines during the pilot. As a promising result, due to the previous points, the majority would like to use similar solutions in the future. Based on the results, the gamified solution needs to be easy to adapt and it should not disturb work routines. Secondly, it should operate on relevant issues and offer new insights on e.g., well-being at the workplace. Thirdly, gamified elements play an important role when motivating respondents to use the solution daily. To conclude, the main preconditions – easy and fast to use and adapt without disturbing work - were successfully implemented into the application used in the pilots. This was confirmed both through the questionnaire results and group end-interviews. 2) What affects if any WorkAI had in terms of self-awareness? The main outcome of the research was clearly, all aspects mentioned combined, the factor that the application and substance got respondents thinking about their own behaviour. The end-interview data highlighted the fact that the thematical areas, the substance of the application evoke lots of thoughts that increased employees' self-awareness on the topics. The participants started to reflect their own attitudes, behaviour and working habits. Though personal development might appear to be an intrinsic outcome, as an incentive it is an extrinsic goal that can be achieved through the participation in the gamified process. As such, it is not the participation in the gamified process that motivates the participant, but the expectation of improved personal skills (Lamberts et al. 2016). Therefore, the main benefit of this sort of application would lie in the self-reflection and self-evaluation.

In the future it will be fruitful to measure the actual impact of the used application in the study group when compared to a control group without the application. Is there a clear difference when work engagement is measured for example through work engagement scale (UWES) by Schaufeli & Bakker (2003). The timeframe of three-week pilot study is short, but since the aim was to validate the application designed within the project, the period was feasible. In the future the application could be implemented as a feature that would run longer periods, as a part of normal work routines. Also, the aspect of managerial implications is interesting. Gamification, if employed successfully could be a tool for innovation and strategy. However, challenges might rise, in terms of data management. As most of the applications acquired user data, there is a need for management of such data, including security and ethical issues. Thus, gamification of management requires a management of gamification itself. (Wanick & Bui 2019, 14) According to Wanick & Bui (2019), the opportunities of gamification applied to management in businesses could be explored, such as management for environmental-related applications, sustainability, general education and training, team effectiveness, issues related to governmental practices and new policies, enterprise innovation and data management and protection. (Wanick & Bui 2019, 14) In all, a fun, engaging, gamificational experiment can be utilized for managers, staff, and leaders in global contexts, even the stakeholders involved in the process in a more engaging way and promoting more innovative outcomes. (Wanick & Bui 2009) As in KiSA-project, where both researchers and the organizational actors participated interactively in the project. This can be addressed since the idea and numerous opportunities around personalisation in different gamified applications.

ACKNOWLEDGMENT

This work was funded by the The Finnish Work Environment Fund (TSR).

REFERENCES

Alatalo, S., Oikarinen, E.-L., Reiman, A., Tan, T.-M., Heikka, E.-L., Hurmelinna-Laukkanen, P., Muhos, M., & Vuorela, T. (2018). Linking concepts of playfulness and well- being at work in retail sector. *Journal of Retailing and Consumer Services*, 43(C), 226–233. doi:10.1016/j.jretconser.2018.03.013

Antonaci, A., Klemke, R., Stracke, C. M., Specht, M., Spatafora, M., & Stefanova, K. (2017). Gamification to Empower Information Security Education. In P. Tuomi & A. Perttula (Eds.), *Proceedings of the 1st International GamiFIN Conference* (pp. 32-38). Pori, Finland: CEUR Workshop Proceedings.

Anttonen, H., & Vainio, H. (2010). Towards better work and well-being: An overview. *Journal of Occupational and Environmental Medicine, 52*(12), 1245–1248. doi:10.1097/JOM.0b013e318202f3bd PMID:21750472

Arai, S., Sakamoto, K., & Washizaki, H. (2014). *A gamified tool for motivating developers to remove warnings of bug pattern tools.* Paper presented at the IWESEP 2014, Osaka. 10.1109/IWESEP.2014.17

Askheim, O.-P. (2003). Empowerment as quidance for professional social work: An act of balancing on a slack rope. *European Journal of Social Work, 6*(3), 229–240. doi:10.1080/1369145032000164546

Bellotti, F., Berta, R., & De Gloria, A. (2010). Designing effective serious games: Opportunities and challenges for research. *International Journal of Emerging Technologies in Learning, 5*(SI3), 22–35. doi:10.3991/ijet.v5s3.1500

Clark, D. B., Tanner-Smith, E. E., & Killingsworth, S. S. (2015). Digital Games, Design, and Learning. A Systematic Review and Meta-Analysis. *Review of Educational Research, 86*(1), 79–122. doi:10.3102/0034654315582065 PMID:26937054

Deterding, S., Sicart, M., Nacke, L., O'Hara, K., & Dixon, D. (2011). Gamification. using game-design elements in non-gaming contexts. *Proceedings of the 2011 Annual Conference Extended Abstracts on Human Factors in Computing Systems*, 2425–2428. 10.1145/1979742.1979575

Dominguez, A., Saenz-de-Navarrete, J., De-Marcos, L., Fernández-Sanz, L., Pagés, C., & Martinez-Herráiz, J.-J. (2013). Gamifying learning experiences: Practical implications and outcomes. *Computer Education, 63*, 380–392. doi:10.1016/j.compedu.2012.12.020

Downes-Le Guin, T., Baker, R., Mechling, J., & Ruyle, E. (2012). Myths and realities of respondent engagement in online surveys. *International Journal of Market Research, 54*(5), 1–21.

Fager, K., Tuomi, P., & Multisilta, J. (2018). Gamifying facility service jobs – using personnel attitudes and perceptions for designing gamification. *GamiFIN 2018 - Proceedings of the 2nd International GamiFIN Conference Pori, Finland, May 22-23, 2018. WS-CEUR*, 55–64.

Fernandes, J., Duarte, D., Ribeiro, C., Farinha, C., Pereira, J. M., & Silva, M. M. (2012). iThink: A game-based approach towards improving collaboration and participation in requirement elicitation. *Procedia Computer Science, 15*, 66–77. doi:10.1016/j.procs.2012.10.059

Gustafsson, A., Katzeff, C., & Bang, M. (2009). Evaluation of a pervasive game for domestic energy engagement among teenagers. *Computers in Entertainment, 7*(4), 1–19. doi:10.1145/1658866.1658873

Hamari, J. (2013). Transforming Homo Economicus into Homo Ludens: A field experiment on gamification in a utilitarian peer-to-peer trading service. *Electronic Commerce Research and Applications, 12*(4), 236–245. doi:10.1016/j.elerap.2013.01.004

Hamari, J., & Koivisto, J. (2015). Why do people use gamification services? *International Journal of Information Management, 35*(4), 419–431. doi:10.1016/j.ijinfomgt.2015.04.006

Hamari, J., Koivisto, J., & Pakkanen, T. (2014). Do persuasive technologies persuade? — a review of empirical studies. In A. Spagnolli, L. Chittaro, & L. Gamberini (Eds.), *Persuasive Technology* (pp. 118–136). Springer International Publishing. doi:10.1007/978-3-319-07127-5_11

Hamari, J., Koivisto, J., & Sarsa, H. (2014). Does gamification work? A literature review of empirical studies on gamification. *System Sciences (HICSS) 2014 47th Hawaii International Conference on*, 3025–3034.

Hoffmann, A., Christmann, C. A., & Bleser, G. (2017). Gamification in stress management apps: A critical app review. *JMIR Serious Games*, 5(2), 13. doi:10.2196/games.7216 PMID:28592397

Huotari, K., & Hamari, J. (2012). Defining gamification: a service marketing perspective. *Proceedings of the 16th International Academic MindTrek Conference*, 17–22.

Huotari, K., & Hamari, J. (2017). A definition for gamification: Anchoring gamification in the service marketing literature. *Electronic Markets*, 27(1), 21–31. doi:10.100712525-015-0212-z

Jones, B. A., Madden, G. J., & Wengreen, H. J. (2014). The FIT game: Preliminary evaluation of a gamification approach to increasing fruit and vegetable consumption in school. *Preventive Medicine*, 68, 76–79. doi:10.1016/j.ypmed.2014.04.015 PMID:24768916

Kim, B. (2015). Designing gamification in the right way. *Library Technology Reports*, 51(2), 29–35.

Lamberts, B., Migchelbrink, K., Kaan, M., Burgers, M., & Ouweland van den, R. (2016). *Gamification of the workplace setting. An inquiry into the possibilities of gamification of the workplace setting for sustainable work by an exploration of gamification.* Interdisciplinair Honours program MA, Radboud University.

Landers, R. N., & Landers, A. K. (2014). An empirical test of the theory of gamified learning: The effect of leaderboards on time-on-task and academic performance. *Simulation & Gaming*, 45(6), 769–785. doi:10.1177/1046878114563662

Maturo, A., Mori, L., & Moretti, V. (2016). An ambiguous health education: The quantified self and the medicalization of the mental sphere. *Italian Journal of Sociology of Education*, 8(3), 248–268.

Morschheuser, B., Werder, K., Hamari, J., & Abe, J. (2017). How to gamify? Development of a method for gamification. *Proceedings of the 50th annual Hawaii international conference on system sciences (HICSS)*, 4–7.

Nacke, L., & Deterding, S. (2017). The maturing of gamification research. *Computers in Human Behavior*, 71, 450–454. doi:10.1016/j.chb.2016.11.062

Nicholson, S. (2012) A User-Centered Theoretical Framework for Meaningful Gamification. Paper Presented at Games+Learning+Society 8.0, Madison, WI.

Nicholson, S. (2015). A recipe for meaningful gamification. In T. Reiners & L. C. Wood (Eds.), *Gamification in business and education.* Springer. doi:10.1007/978-3-319-10208-5_1

Oprescu, F., Jones, C., & Katsikitis, M. (2014). I PLAY AT WORK—Ten Principles for Transforming Work Processes through Gamification. *Frontiers in Psychology*, 5, 14. doi:10.3389/fpsyg.2014.00014 PMID:24523704

Plass, J. L., Homer, B. D., & Kinzer, C. K. (2015). Foundations of game-based learning. *Educational Psychologist*, 50(4), 258–283. doi:10.1080/00461520.2015.1122533

Pogrebtsova, E., Tondello, G.F., Premsukh, H., & Nacke, L.E. (2017). Using Technology to Boost Employee Wellbeing? How Gamification Can Help or Hinder Results. *PGW@CHI PLAY.*

Rednic, E., Toma, A., & Apostu, A. (2013). Organize distributed work environments in a game-like fashion. In Z. Chen & E. Lopez-Neri (Eds.), *Recent Advances in Knowledge Engineering and Systems Science* (pp. 213–218). WSEAS Press.

Rosso, B. D., Dekas, K. H., & Wrzesniewski, A. (2010). On the meaning of work: A theoretical integration and review. *Research in Organizational Behavior, 30,* 91–127. doi:10.1016/j.riob.2010.09.001

Ryan, R. M., & Deci, E. L. (2000). Self-determination theory and the facilitation of intrinsic motivation, social development, and well-being. *The American Psychologist, 55*(1), 68–78. doi:10.1037/0003-066X.55.1.68 PMID:11392867

Sailer, M., Hense, J. U., Mayr, S. K., & Mandl, H. (2017). How gamification motivates: An experimental study of the effects of specific game design elements on psychological need satisfaction. *Computers in Human Behavior, 69,* 371–380. doi:10.1016/j.chb.2016.12.033

Schaufeli, W., & Bakker, A. (2003). *UWES Utrecht Work Engagement Scale, Preliminary Manual* [Version 1, November 2003]. Utrecht University: Occupational Health Psychology Unit.

Sitas, E. (2017). Gamification as tool to raise sociocultural awareness. *International Conference on Open & Distance Education, 9,* 275–281.

Sullivan, P. H. (1998). *Profiting from Intellectual Capital: Extracting Value from Innovation.* John Wiley & Sons.

Sutton, A., Williams, H., & Allinson, C. (2015). A longitudinal, mixed method evaluation of self-awareness training in the workplace. *European Journal of Training and Development, 39*(7), 610–627. doi:10.1108/EJTD-04-2015-0031

Thornton, D., & Francia, G. (2014). Gamification of Information Systems and Security Training: Issues and Case Studies. *Information Security Education Journal, 1,* 16–29.

Touboulic, A., & Walker, H. (2016). A relational, transformative, and engaged approach to sustainable supply chain management: The potential of action research. *Human Relations, 69*(2), 301–343. doi:10.1177/0018726715583364

Wanick, V., & Bui, H. (2019). Gamification in Management: A systematic review and research directions. *International Journal of Serious Games, 6*(2), 57–74. doi:10.17083/ijsg.v6i2.282

Warmelink, H., Koivisto, J., Mayer, I., Vesa, M., & Hamari, J. (2018). Gamification of the work floor: A literature review of gamifying production and logistics operations. *Journal of Business Research, 106,* 331–340. doi:10.1016/j.jbusres.2018.09.011

Zimmerman, M. (1995). Psychological empowerment: Issues and illustrations. *American Journal of Community Psychology, 23*(5), 581–599. doi:10.1007/BF02506983 PMID:8851341

ADDITIONAL READING

Gerdenitscha, C., Sellitscha, D., Besser, M., Burger, S., Stegmann, C., Tscheligia, M., & Kriglsteina, S. (2020). Work gamification: Effects on enjoyment, productivity and the role of leadership. *Electronic Commerce Research and Applications*, *43*, 100994. doi:10.1016/j.elerap.2020.100994

Hamari, J., Koivisto, J., & Sarsa, H. (2014). Does gamification work? A literature review of empirical studies on gamification. In *2014 47th Hawaii international conference on system sciences* (pp. 3025–3034). IEEE. 10.1109/HICSS.2014.377

Hammedi, W., Leclercq, T., Poncin, I., & Alkire, L. (2021). Uncovering the dark side of gamification at work: Impacts on engagement and well-being. *Journal of Business Research*, *122*(3). Advance online publication. doi:10.1016/j.jbusres.2020.08.032

Klasen, J. (2016). *Employees' experiences and perceptions of work gamification*. Theses and Dissertations. 677. https://digitalcommons.pepperdine.edu/etd/677

Kumar, H., & Raghavendran, S. (2015). Gamification, the finer art: Fostering creativity and employee engagement. *The Journal of Business Strategy*, *36*(6), 3–12. doi:10.1108/JBS-10-2014-0119

Mulcahy, R.-F., Zainuddin, N., & Russell-Bennett, R. (2020). Transformative value and the role of involvement in gamification and serious games for well-being. *Journal of Service Management*.

Newcomb, E. T., Camblin, J. G., Jones, F. D., & Wine, B. (2019). On the implementation of a gamified professional development system for direct care staff. *Journal of Organizational Behavior Management*, *39*(3-4), 293–307. doi:10.1080/01608061.2019.1632243

Wünderlicha, N., Gustafsson, A., Hamari, J., Parvinen, P., & Haffa, A. (2019). The great game of business: Advancing knowledge on gamification in business contexts. *Journal of Business Research*. Advance online publication. doi:10.1016/j.jbusres.2019.10.062

KEY TERMS AND DEFINITIONS

AI: Artificial intelligence.

Bot: Abbreviation of the term robot.

Gamification: Use of game design -based elements in non-game contexts.

Gamified Elements: Usually elements such as use of badges, score list, avatars that can be used in non-game contexts.

Productivity: A measure to determine the efficiency of a person completing a task.

Self-Awareness: Ability to reflect to one's feelings, thoughts, and actions.

Self-Evaluation: Ability to examine oneself to find out how much progress one has made.

Well-Being: The state of being comfortable, healthy, or happy, efficient.

ENDNOTES

[1]   Create Artificial Labour" https://www.headai.com/

[2]   Habitica- Gamify your Life: https://habitica.com/

APPENDIX 1

The content of WorkAI application

    Does this happen in your own work?

    Is this true for you?

    Does this happen in your work?

        very often / often / seldom / not at all / does not concern me.

Sense of Community

- I talk nicely to my co-worker
- I go to a workplace health promotion event with my co-workers
- I help my co-worker in his/her assignment
- My co-worker helps me in my assignment

Feedback 1

- I tell my superior how my workday has passed
- I thank my co-worker
- I thank myself for a job well done

Feedback 2

- I get feedback from a co-worker
- I get feedback from a customer
- I get feedback from a superior

Feedback 3

- I give feedback to a co-worker
- I give feedback to a customer
- I give feedback to a superior

Information Flow 1

- We brainstorm together to solve a problem
- I figure out a development idea and bring it forward
- I learn a new thing at work

Information Flow 2

- We learn a new thing together with co-workers
- I teach something to my co-worker
- My co-worker teaches me something

Safety at Work

- I notice a security lack in workplace and report it
- I follow safety in work guidelines fully
- I take the initiative to improve safety in work

Work Itself
- I perform quality work
- I am prompt at my tasks
- I use stairs instead of elevator

Learning
- I learn a new feature from a technical system
- I use new equipment/tool/cleaning agent
- I succeed in a hard assignment

Working Hours 1
- I don't lose my nerves even when I get bothered
- I manage despite of hurry
- I don't let hurry affect my mood
- I spend coffee break in peace

Working Hours 2
- I spend lunch break as planned and in peace
- I remember to use the monitoring of working hours correctly
- I stay on schedule
- I forget things and it slows down my working

Customer Experience 1
- I say hello to around five customers in a day
- I talk nicely to customers
- I respond to customer feedback in a factual matter

Customer Experience 2
- I say hello to around ten customers in a day
- I respond to customer feedback in a factual matter
- I help the customer (open the door etc.)

Self-Evaluation 1
- I stay on a good mood the whole day
- Some assignments remain undone
- A seemed-like-an-easy-job doesn't work out

Self-Evaluation 2
- I postpone a tedious assignment
- I have to cut corners to get the job done
- Work-related thing bother me even outside work

APPENDIX 2

End-interview questions

1. **All the nine themes were individually discussed:**
   - How did you feel on answering questions from this theme?
   - Did this theme awake any thoughts?
   - Any notions concerning your own work?
   - Did the theme change your behavior?
   - Did the theme make you think differently?
   - Do you feel you learned something from this theme?
2. **The overall experiences of the pilot study and the possible effects were discussed:**
   - Did WorkAI influence your work, how? (Motivation, endurance, enjoyment, etc.)
   - Did WorkAI influence the sense of community, how?
   - Did WorkAI influence your self-awareness, how?
   - Did you feel that WorkAI was useful for you, how?
   - Did you feel that participating on this pilot study was useful, how?
3. **The gamificational elements of the experiment were discussed:**
   - How did you perceive the gamificational elements (the bot, trophies & progressive map) of WorkAI?
   - Did the gamificational elements influence your usage of WorkAI, how?
   - Did WorkAI succeed as a gamificational solution and what did you appreciate and what would you change?
4. **General and free discussion concerning the pilot study, WorkAI and overall feelings of the participants.**

Chapter 6
The Kingdom of Satisfaction:
Case Study of Gamification at Neurotech

Breno José Andrade de Carvalho
https://orcid.org/0000-0002-4449-4036
Catholic University of Pernambuco, Brazil

Ammanda Cavalcanti Silva
Neurotech, Brazil & Catholic University of Pernambuco, Brazil

Carla Guedes Porfirio Cavalcante
Catholic University of Pernambuco, Brazil

Gil Vicente de Brito Maia
https://orcid.org/0000-0002-0870-194X
Catholic University of Pernambuco, Brazil

ABSTRACT

The results presented in this chapter come from a case study of gamification at Neurotech, a company located in Porto Digital, Recife, Pernambuco, Brazil. The objective was to develop a solution to improve the productivity and satisfaction rates of the company's clients. In general, the authors used contributions on gamification from Patrício, Moreira, and Zurlo; Burke; Costa and Marchiori; and Vianna et al. to which they added Mastrocola's playful learning, Huizinga's magical circle, Bartle's player profile, and engagement in the organizations of the Gallup Institute. For the experiment, the Gamification Canvas and the Trello tool were used to develop and monitor the "Kingdom of Satisfaction" activities. Among the results achieved, a significant increase in cooperation between teams and participants was identified, in addition to reaching a 100% customer satisfaction rate.

DOI: 10.4018/978-1-6684-4291-3.ch006

INTRODUCTION

We are living in a society which is undergoing various changes and transformations in the most varied sectors, and organizations, which are inserted in this context, depend on countless factors to achieve their goals and to solve the problems that occur daily in their environment.

Gamification is the concept presented in this chapter as one of the ways to solve some practical problems and awaken engagement among a specific audience by using game mechanisms. This practice has been increasingly applied by companies and entities from different segments as an alternative to traditional (teaching and learning) approaches. Its main objective is to encourage people to develop assertive behaviors that are more compatible with new digital technologies, thereby generally speeding up tasks that are considered very bureaucratic or repetitive.

This trend is due to including game designers from around the world in the training team. They have been dedicated to applying game principles in various fields, such as health, education, sports, public policy, marketing and business, the latter with the purpose of leveraging sales and/or increasing productivity.

This study was developed as an activity of the Gamification module of the Masters in Creative Industries at the Catholic University of Pernambuco in 2019 and the gamification process applied at the Brazilian company Neurotech. The Neurotech founded in 2000 by people with master's degrees and doctorates in computer science, mathematics and artificial intelligence. Its purpose is to intelligently connect data so as to make the future more predictable for its clients. It is a pioneer in creating advanced Artificial Intelligence solutions for the entire decision cycle in credit, fraud and risk operations, in various sectors such as: credit, finance, fintechs, retail and insurance. During its 20 years of activity in the market, Neurotech has built up a portfolio of more than 100 clients throughout Brazil and more than 1000 solutions have already been developed in the credit, retail, insurance and financial market segments.

By means of periodic surveys carried out in the company's Operations sector from 2017 to 2019, using the Net Promoter Score (NPS) methodology, a satisfaction survey which the client responds to during service/support, and by means of survey/conversations/visits to clients, it was found that customer satisfaction is increasing but still below expectations. In addition, in September 2019, as a result of making a critical analysis of Key Performance Indicators (KPIs) and restructuring the operations sector, with a focus on the centrality of the client, the possibility was identified of improving the indicators and engagement of employees who had been reorganized into new teams.

Therefore, in parallel with several actions mapped and in progress to improve the points listed above, with a focus on the centrality of the customer, what was considered as an alternative for engaging and motivating staff was to develop a pilot gamification process in a part of Neurotech's Operations sector. The objective of this chapter was to develop a solution to improve the productivity rate and the satisfaction rate of the company's clients.

This chapter is divided into five sections. In the first section, Background, a brief report will be presented about the problems that organizations have in engaging their employees or collaborators with a focus on delivering solutions to the demands of the business and this is also related to customer satisfaction. The second section, Gamification - state of the art presents some theoretical contributions about gamification and the playful learning context to be explored, and some cases of real companies that used gamification as an aid to solve problems are discussed. The third section, Experimental details, sets out the entire methodological process for developing the gamification process which is called "The Kingdom of Satisfaction" which has been applied at Neurotech. This ranges from the survey, which was conducted on employees to identify their motivations and player profiles, to constructing the gamification canvas and to applying it by using the tool called Trello. In the fourth section, Analysis of results, the analysis of the feedback from the participants, of the data obtained and of the results of the process is presented. Finally, in the fifth stage, Conclusions about the experiment in the business environment of Neurotech are presented as are future prospects.

BACKGROUND

In this scenario in which several Information Technology (IT) organizations deal with difficulties, including several related to delivery and satisfaction, gamification can help influence and motivate employees by improving the results that are obtained from employees and for customers.

Companies are inserted in a world that is being transformed and to achieve their goals and function effectively, they depend on several factors. One of them is that there are well-structured processes, which deliver quality products or services, via satisfied and qualified employees, and thus these generate satisfied customers. However, there are a number of challenges and issues that are commonly encountered in various companies and these affect their optimal functioning.

According to Marques (2019), the main challenges are: vision of the future, alignment, recognition, poor quality of delivery, unsatisfactory organizational climate, transparency in communication, knowledge sharing, ineffective management and gossip. Lack of recognition and an unsatisfactory organizational climate can impact employee productivity by reducing motivation and engagement. Regarding the poor quality of delivery of products or services offered to the market, the source of the problem may be in the employees, i.e., delivery of work outside the expected or staff without the necessary competences and skills occupying posts, or in the organization of internal processes, which will directly impact customer satisfaction.

According to Lederman Consulting & Education (2019), the 6 most common problems in companies are: lack of engagement of the members and dissatisfaction; the work delivered is not satisfactory; the atmosphere in the company is bad; the company does not know where it wants to go or how it wants to get there; lack of transparency in decisions; and inflexibility of knowledge management. As to the lack of the members' engagement and dissatisfaction, happiness or unhappiness directly interferes in the work delivered and consequently in customer satisfaction. As for undelivered work, incompetence or problems in the processes may explain the problem. For example, if the selection process is inefficient, people who are not suitable for posts or who do not meet expectations may be selected and end up not performing the role that the company's manager expects from them.

Another worrying factor for corporations is related to the low engagement of their teams and staff in carrying out their everyday activities and in searching for innovation, either to improve the work process or to create new products or services, thereby diversifying the business possibilities of the institution. According to information from the State of the Global Workplace (2017, p. 22), a study promoted annually by the Gallup Institute, the general scenario of organizations is that only 15% of employees worldwide feel engaged in their work. That is, 85% of employees may be wasting their potential for producing results (State of the Global Workplace, 2017).

The problems listed above reinforce how the quality of delivery and employees' motivation/engagement are important items for the success of an organization and, consequently, for customer satisfaction, one of the items that can be considered to measure the success of an organization.

Reinforcing the importance of the customer for the organization's success, Kotler and Armstrong (2003, p. 45) report that: companies need to focus on winning over new clients and delivering services or products with added-value to maintain them. In the competitive market, it is necessary to understand the needs and wants of clients, and after so doing, to satisfy them.

According to Rubini (2019), customer satisfaction is the result of a perception that originated from the customers' point of view and not from the supplier's point of view. Thus, companies need to focus on their customers' needs, desires and satisfaction. According to Rosa (2021), companies that create incredible experiences for their customers are able to obtain a competitive differential in relation to the competition. What happy and satisfied customers can generate for the company are: new sales, increased revenue, increased customer retention, reduced churn (customer churn rate) and an expansion of the customer base.

Thus, it would be expected that the more engaged in, and committed to, not only delivering satisfactory results, but also to proposing constant innovations and developments in processes that staff are, the more satisfied clients would be with the experience that they were offered.

Therefore, organizations must, together with their staff, seek alternatives that lead to staff becoming more involved in their company's activities. There are several tools that seem to offer the possibility of motivating staff to produce more and, consequently, to make an impact on consumers' experience. Gamification appears, therefore, to be an option that can help achieve this objective.

In the city of Recife, capital of the state of Pernambuco, Brazil, there is one of the largest technological hubs in the country, the Porto Digital. It includes several companies in the Information Technology - IT area that have been facing difficulties regarding the performance of internal teams in carrying out solutions and delivering, with quality, what clients want. This chapter presents the **case study** carried out in one of the companies located in the Porto Digital: Neurotech.

GAMIFICATION: STATE OF THE ART

Gamification

The term gamification, although it had been around for a while, was created in 2002 by British consultant Nick Pelling, and reached a critical mass of use only in 2010 (Vianna et al., 2013). The objective of the term was to describe the services of a start-up consultancy called Conundra Ltd.

On using mechanisms such as proposing challenges, rewards, interactivity, attribution of points and progress throughout the working day, gamification is regarded as a strategy that takes place using elements of games, to optimize contexts that are not those of games (Deterding, 2011; Galetta, 2013; Harwood & Garry, 2015; Piligrimiene, Dovaliene, & Virvilaite, 2015; Robson et al., 2015).

Gamification presents itself as a way to provide playful learning and entertainment to its participants. According to experts on the subject, gamification goes beyond fun activities performed in the workplace (Agogué, Levillain and Hooge, 2015; Dale, 2014; Kalinauskas, 2014). According to Brian Burke (2015), gamification induces an emotional connection in players, by enhancing contexts in different areas, especially in the organizational one. It is, therefore, a strong tool for achieving goals and motivating people.

According to Huizinga (2001), when an individual participates in an activity that provides entertainment, he/she feels in another universe, and thus forgets difficulties, problems, etc. The author calls this phenomenon the "magic circle".

When participating in a game or gamified processes, the participant finds him/ herself immersed in a mysterious atmosphere, in which everyday life is put aside. Even so, what happens within this magic circle impacts the real lives of those who participate in the experience.

In this sense, the authors Patrício, Moreira and Zurlo (2020) claim that games can improve productivity, user engagement and sustainable practices. The authors also claim that gamification is a powerful tool to sharpen people's innovative skills to carry out activities, above all, co-creation (Patrício, Moreira & Zurlo, 2018).

The authors AlSaad and Durugbo (2021) state that the use of gamification as innovation enables a value creation logic with a focus on collaborative behavior, process improvement, innovation and competition with rewards and process analysis. However, the authors warn that innovation through gamification may not be applicable to institutions, in addition to its being a challenge to understand this perspective (AlSaad and Durugbo, 2021).

According to Costa and Marchiori (2016), the applicability of gamification in organizations implies a return of competitiveness and information gain after gamified processes have been implemented. Hence, this results in players' greater engagement and an increased probability of achieving results that the organization has stipulated. Mastrocola (2012) also points out that the gamification process needs a playful learning context, and not just an automatic and cold process of setting goals and making gains. For him, the most adequate term is gamification.

There are several practical tools for implementing the gamification process in an organization. According to Ysmar Vianna et al. (2013), 8 steps can be followed to support development, namely: understanding the problem and context; understanding who the players are; identifying the guiding criteria and mission of the game; developing ideas for the game; defining the game and its mechanics; testing in low, medium and/or high fidelity (evaluation of the mechanics of the game, scoring and the concept) of the game; implementation and monitoring; and measurement and evaluation.

For some researchers, such as Flora Alves (2015), it is essential to be knowledgeable about the audience that will participate in the gamification process. Based on observation or research, the intrinsic and/or extrinsic motivations of the participants can be ascertained.

There is no ready-made recipe for a solution that uses gamification. However, being knowledgeable about the player's profile, making the planning and alignment of gamification more assertive in order to solve the problem, whether this be of an educational or corporate nature, is essential. The same technique may not be applicable to everything that needs to be taught, and hence the importance of identifying the objective you want to achieve (ALVES, 2015, p.115).

According to Teles (2018), game mechanics can be used as tools that contribute to the instructional strategy, but not for defining the instructional strategy as a whole.

Therefore, by using gamified processes, it is seen that game mechanisms can be used to build a narrative that results in an experience that impacts contexts that are not linked to the game. Thus, organizational environments are constituted as a space that allows gamification to be implemented, which can generate considerable gains for the company and for its clients.

Nevertheless, while this chapter shows that gamification has led to successful practices in a broad range of sectors that have benefitted companies and their employees, it should not be forgotten that any tool can be used not just for benign purposes that seek to achieve a balance between making work more enjoyable and engaging for employees and improving the performance and balance-sheet of companies, but tools can also be misused.

Regarding the benefits of using gamification, peer learning is observed (Romero-Rodríguez, Ramírez-Montoya and González, 2019) when working as congruent teams (Parjanen and Hyypiä, 2019) that solve difficult problems (Agogué, Levillain and Hooge, 2015), in addition to engaging in critical thinking (Agogué, Levillain and Hooge, 2015).

Companies may, wittingly or unwittingly, focus excessively on the benefits to them and lay themselves open to accusations of converting gamification into 'exploitation-ware' (Bogost, 2011) or using gamification as 'an electronic whip' (Allen, 2011). Moreover, there is evidence of gamification having been used by criminal, terrorist and other malign organizations. (Brachman and Levine, 2010; Ungerleider, 2011). Such negative examples point to the need for standards to be set for industry and commerce by professional bodies and for governments to monitor how gamification is being used and to introduce legislation that counteracts uses that are not in the public interest.

Gamification: Successful Cases

Regarding the results of using gamification in organizations, recent studies have analyzed market share data from 2020/2021 and presented various statistics that show benefits in the most diverse areas and sectors. One of the results listed is how gamification is changing the results in organizations (Jay, 2021), as shown in Figure 1. Google achieved 100% employee compliance after implementing a gamified travel expenses system. Astra Zeneca achieved 97% participation in training on medicines using gamification. Spotify succeeded in having 90% of its employees voluntarily participate in their annual reviews using a mobile phone game. And SAP found that there was a 58% increase in the generation of successful ideas after it introduced gamification.

Figure 1. Examples of organizational achievements using gamification. Adapted from Jay (2021) by the authors

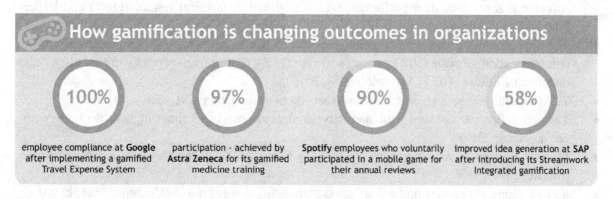

As to gamification in operation, according to Figure 2, the data show: a 700% increase in the conversion rate of companies that use gamification; 97% of employees over 45 agree that gamification would improve work; 87% of employees agree that gamification would make them more productive; 85% of employees like gamification software solutions at work; 50% of startups supposedly integrate gamification into their strategy (Chang, 2021).

Figure 2. Results of using gamification in operations. Adapted from Chang (2021) by the authors

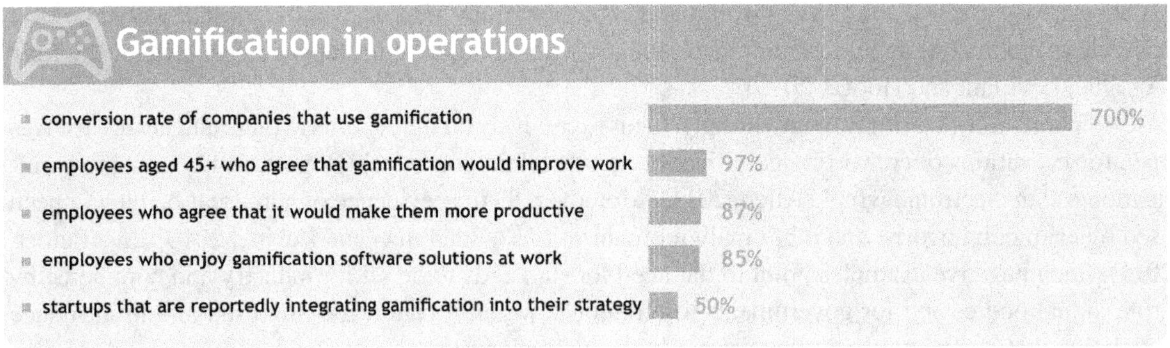

Still on Gamification in Operations, Jenny Chang (2021) presents some statistics reported by several researchers, professionals and companies, which were published on websites and digital platforms such as TalentLMS, Ceros, Review 42, eLearning Learning, eLearning Industry and ResearchGate. The statistics are:

- 89% of employees think they would be more productive at work if it were more like a game (Apostolopoulos, 2019).
- 88% of respondents say that gamification makes them happier at work (Apostolopoulos, 2019).
- 78% of respondents think companies would be more desirable to work for, if their recruitment process were gamified (Apostolopoulos, 2019).
- Game elements at work make 87% of employees feel more socially connected (Apostolopoulos, 2019).
- The most common gamification elements that employees encounter are badges (71%), an app or software that assesses their performance (59%), virtual or physical rewards (56%) and leader-boards (51%) (Apostolopoulos, 2019).
- The apps or work processes that employees would like to gamify are training software (33%), communication software (30%), contact software (15%), project management software (12%), and document software (10%) (Apostolopoulos, 2019).
- 72% of employees said gamification motivates them to work harder (Lynkova, 2021).
- The conversion rates of sites with interactive content are nearly six times higher than those without it (Ceros, 2019).
- Gamification can increase company productivity by up to 50% and employee engagement by 60% (Maske, 2019).
- 86% of young job seekers find gamification at work fun and enjoyable (Heimburger et al., 2019)
- 71% of employees believe that gamification leads to an increase in energy levels (Sharma, 2020).
- 66% of employees say gamification at work has reduced their stress levels (Sharma, 2020).

According to the points listed above, the benefits of gamification can be observed at various times in the working day of an employee in the organization. This ranges from candidates being more attracted to companies that have a gamified selection process to gains in happiness and motivation rates, reduction in stress and increased engagement and productivity at work due to being in contact with gamification.

In addition, a Gartner report (Growth Engineering, 2021) showed that 70% of companies on the Global 2000 list of companies have already adopted gamification. And this number is tending to increase as more companies implement gamification in their business operations. In the next five years, it is expected that 87% of companies will be using gamification techniques and half of these companies will have gamification as a priority.

Another example pointed out by Growth Engineering (2021) as to the successful application of gamification in organizations is L'Oréal's solution for the L'Oréal Travel Retail travel area. With the aim of improving its training for its beauty consultants, who are distributed across 18 countries and speaking six different languages, a gamified mobile app called *My Beauty Club* was developed in 2018 to train and involve them. As a result, L'Oréal exceeded its targets for engagement and customer satisfaction within one year of implementing the app.

There are also numerous other cases of using gamification successfully in organizations, such as described by Teles (2018): Samsung, which increased the number of users submitting product reviews on its global website by 66% and the number of these reviews by 447%, which prompted 34% of users to place 224% more items in shopping carts; Omnicare, which achieved a 100% participation rate from team members in its IT service desk; Deloitte, which reduced employee training time by 50%; Objective Logistics, which increased its profit margin by 40% by motivating its staff using behavioral rewards.

Trends related to the workplace show that the main benefits of gamification are that it increases employee engagement and their productivity. According to Growth Engineering (2021), the impact of using gamification results in some significant results for companies, namely: an increase in employee productivity of up to 90%; the majority of employees, about 69%, become more productive, and 95% of employees like using this approach.

Finally, given the success stories, statistics and results presented, the benefits that the application of gamification can generate for an organization in the most diverse sectors are evident.

EXPERIMENTAL DETAILS

During the Gamification module of the Master's course in Creative Industries, each team was asked to present a real problem to be solved. Among the difficulties of the Neurotech company, the issue presented was: "how to improve the performance in customer satisfaction and increase the engagement of employees in the Neurotech Operations sector?".

To solve the problem in part resulting from the level of engagement of employees with a focus on satisfying the organization's clients, this chapter presents the development, implementation and results of a gamification process carried out in the company in the second half of 2019. The objective was to encourage and improve the performance of individual and collective production processes among the employees, in addition to increasing customer satisfaction with the products offered.

The methodological process of the work is divided into three stages: the first was the investigation of the persona and the player profile of the employees in the operations sector of the chosen company, Neurotech. The second stage was the production of the Gamification Canvas for the production of the experiment. The third step was the application of gamification and its monitoring. Finally, the results were analyzed, and a new questionnaire was applied to obtain the participants' opinions about the fun-way-to-learn process. A breakdown of each step is presented below.

Step 1 – The Persona

The study began by investigating the player's profile; thus, a semi-structured questionnaire was drawn up to map and define the best gamification strategy and understand more deeply who the players are in order to build a Persona. According to Vianna et al. (2013), Building a Persona is a synthesis technique for a detailed understanding of the subject. It represents needs, motivations, desires, expectations and behavior, in addition to helping to develop ideas for the experience-oriented product and services.

First of all, a questionnaire was developed that included 13 questions based on the concept of player profile by Richard Bartle (1996b). According to Bartle (1996a), we can consider there are four profiles, i.e., types of players. In the 1990s, Richard Bartle conducted a survey of MUD (Multi-user dungeon) players in order to find patterns of motivation. The author described the player profiles he found and split them into four broad groups (Killers, Achievers, Socialisers and Explorers). As for the details of these profiles, the entrepreneurs (Achievers) are interested in acting in the world, i.e., in doing things in the game. The Explorers are interested in interacting with the world, i.e., in how the game surprises them. The Socializers are interested in interacting with other players and, finally, the Killers are interested in acting on other players, i.e., in doing things to people. This study by Bartle (1996a) is considered by several authors as the oldest and most popular study on players' profiles and is adopted by researchers and professionals to this day.

Profile of the Player

The questionnaire addressed the following aspects: age group; the movies they like the most; the books they like the most; what they do in their free time; whether they like games; and information related to preference in a game answered by eight of the fifteen participants. The age group of this group was as follows: 50% between 25 and 35 years old, 25% between 18 and 24 years old and 25% between 35 and 50 years old. Thus, it was possible to infer that for a relatively young audience there are certain types of more up-to-date game mechanisms that are more attractive than traditional ones.

Regarding personal tastes, the musical styles mentioned were quite diverse, such as Spanish music, pop/rock, samba, electronica, indie rock, rock, hip hop and *forró,* a form of folk music that is very popular in NE Brazil. The favorite movies cited by respondents comprised mostly fiction, action and adventure genres, e.g., AI Artificial Intelligence (Steven Spielberg), Labyrinth (1986), Indiana Jones and the Temple of Doom, Fast and Furious, Harry Potter, The Avengers, WALL·E, Gladiator, Captain Fantastic, I Am Legend, About Time, Into the Wild, The Perks of Being a Wallflower, Jurassic Park, The Matrix, and Robocop.

The most cited books also followed the genre preference observed in the movies and added strategy-oriented books which included: The Prince (Machiavelli), The Art of War, The Lord of the Rings, Harry Potter, Game of Thrones, The Hitchhiker's Guide to the Galaxy. Only one of the interviewees reported not liking books and another mentioned not being in the habit of reading. With regard to activities performed in their free time, these included reading, dancing, staying with the children, going out with friends, going to the beach or barbecue, traveling, playing electronic games (mentioned more than once), watching TV series and listening to music.

In answer to the question of whether they like games, 87.5% said yes, and among the most mentioned types of games are action and adventure, logic, construction, strategy and football. We highlight Multiplayer Online Battle Arena (MOBA - online games on a multiplayer platform that involve action and strategy); the RPG (Role Playing Game) style in which a narrative is developed for the beginning of games, and each player plays a character; the MMORPG (Massively Multiplayer Online Role-Playing Game), similar to RPG, but with the participation of a large number of players, whether in board or digital games.

Also, for the same percentage, 87.5% or seven of the participants pointed out that the number of missions that should be completed is more important in a game than the number of missions that must be achieved. In the same way, being involved in the story is more significant for 75% of them than getting rewards at the end although this is what 25% like better.

Going without playing and losing rewards are the worst situations that can occur related to games. Opinions about this item in the questionnaire were split 50:50.

In the item, what makes a game fun? 75% of the responses showed that it is more fun to have multiple missions in a game than to have the highest score among the players, in the question about what is better in a game. Solving a problem that no one can solve got 75% of responses while 25% said they preferred to focus on receiving rewards. In terms of winning points, 75% of participants prefer to pool points for a bigger reward and 25% prefer to receive several smaller rewards.

Step 2 – the Gamification Canvas

From the survey and analysis of the results of the questionnaire, the Persona to be adopted was created when constructing the Gamification Canvas. According to data analysis, the player profile is a young person, who likes interaction, fun and who seeks strategy games that have adventure and action with rewards. In addition, he/ she likes the universe of medieval games, made up of dialogues and characters such as wizards, sorceresses, archers and warriors.

In addition, although there is no specific question in the survey, the public is from the Information Technology area. It was also possible to consider the observation of one of the authors of this study who suggested developing a Persona, "Rodrigo", since he is a leader at Neurotech and already professionally works alongside the interviewees.

Rodrigo is a 27-year-old graduate in computer science. He is articulate, likes to talk, to go out to have fun, to listen to rock music and to watch fiction and action movies. He is an occasional reader who reads a variety of books. He likes strategy and RPG games that have many missions and for the story to be engaging and challenging with the possibility of adding points to get large rewards. He is communicative, has a team spirit and is cooperative. He is a persona defined as 'Socializer', according to the profiles described by Richard Bartle (1996).

By creating this persona, it was possible to proceed to the step of applying the Gamification Canvas, according to Vianna et al. (2013), so as to define what the rules, setting, scores, rewards, desired benefits and business and game objectives would be.

To assist designing the gamification to be proposed and understanding users, Canvas uses techniques derived from Design Thinking, which can be defined as a mental map or diagram designed to organize thoughts in a visual and textual way, thus helping to visualize different themes and allowing connections to be made between them.

The Canvas for a gamification process takes into account three aspects at this stage: the company culture, business objectives and, principally, understanding the user. The Gamification Canvas for the study was prepared following the topics detailed in Table 1 below:

Table 1. Canvas of gamification to Neurotech. Adapted from Vianna et al. (2013), by the authors

Topic	Detailed description
Strategic partnerships	Engagement of the coordinators and managers of the Squads participating in the gamification process, as well as the operations department who enable the app to be produced and assist in disseminating its importance and benefits.
Definition of general aspects of the game	The most suitable platform for the game was the computer, using the Trello app (player interaction) and Google Drive (keeping the scores).
	The process was applied for 4 days, from 09.12 to 12.12.
	The frequency of interaction with the Trello platform and Google Drive was daily.
Rules of the Game	Each player must choose a character within the narrative.
	Points are earned by obtaining rewards and completing general missions and challenges.
	Players will be able to come together to resolve a ticket and receive a higher score.
	Players must guarantee the completion of the ticket by the requester.
	Players must resolve the tickets within the Service Level Agreement (SLA).
	Points can be lost due to tickets from the requester not being attended to, being rejected, reporting dissatisfaction and out of the SLA at the end of the week.
	Points will be counted by the color of each card.
	Rewards will be awarded at the end of each day and/or week.
	Challenges will be counted at the end of the week.
	Penalties will be assigned at the end of the day according to the returns of the tickets: reopened, with a report of dissatisfaction, are outside the SLA and the requester is kept waiting for more than 5 days.
Activities that the player performs in the game	Attending to tickets registered in Neurotech's call receiving tool.
	Contact the requester to resolve the ticket and return of pending information to the service.
	Direct the requester to answer the satisfaction survey at the end of the service.
	Carry out the missions: 90% of the tickets resolved in the month must have the satisfaction survey answered; 90% of the tickets with an answered satisfaction survey must have a score of 4 or 5; 90% of tickets resolved within the SLA; 90% of tickets delivered without rejection.
Business objectives	Improved customer satisfaction.
	To encourage cooperation in Squads.
	Engagement of the service team to focus on the customer.
	Increased number of customer responses to satisfaction surveys.
Environmental setting of the game	Narrative of the "Realm of Satisfaction", based on RPG characteristics and defined according to the definition of the persona.
	Story: Once upon a time there was a happy kingdom, but one day its queen "Satisfaction" was kidnapped by "Dissatisfaction" and imprisoned in a castle far away. To save the queen, the representatives of the kingdom split into two teams to travel through the gloomy realms in search of the crystal pieces (quality, SLA, backlog and together we are+, satisfaction). The Queen will be saved by the team that gets the most pieces of the crystal to reach the castle, destroy "Dissatisfaction" and release "Satisfaction".
Player's characteristics	Young, socializer, computer student, enjoys strategy and RPG games, has team spirit, is communicative and cooperative.
Game objectives	Achieve the target of 90% of the customer satisfaction index in the period of applying the process.
Score and reward	Points according to the relevance of the ticket, penalties in negative cases and rewards.
Costs, difficulties, obstacles	Costs: Cards for representing characters, buttons, stickers, chocolates and mugs.
	Difficulties and obstacles: non-engagement of the team in the gamification process.
Expected benefits	Cooperation between Squads and collaborators.
	Engagement of the service team to focus on the customer.
	Increased number of customer responses to satisfaction surveys.
	Results will be measured using Trello.

Implementation in Trello

After drawing up the canvas, characters were created with characteristics inspired by the world of RPG games with a medieval theme. They were represented by cards that took into account their characteristics and powers, as shown in Table 2 below. Altogether, 12 types of characters were developed.

Table 2. Characters of the game. Compiled by the authors

Avatar	Characteristics and Powers
Griming – The leader **Gardlett – The leader**	Race: Human Powers: Strong leadership spirit, motivates his team to work together in pursuit of goals.
Niman – The Helper Woman **Hawise – The Helper**	Human race Powers: Due to their ability to help, they can motivate others around them and achieve goals. Any character that joins Niman or Hawise can get extra points. - Green Tag Tickets - 2 extra points for those who ask for help and 3 extra points for Niman or Hawise - Yellow or Pink Tag Tickets - 2 extra points for both - Blue or Purple Tag Tickets - 1 extra point for both Observations: 1. Tickets resolved with the help of Niman/Hawise, need: a comment from Niman/Hawise on the ticket (call receiving tool); addition of Niman/Hawise as a member of the card (Trello).
Mag – The Precise Woman **Igim – The precise**	Race: Dwarf Powers: Due to his ability of precision, Mag manages to perform a feat with absolute rigor and perfection, satisfying everyone. Any ticket resolved by Mag that is responded with satisfaction can generate extra points: - Green Tag Tickets - 2 extra points - Yellow or Pink Tag Tickets - 2 extra points - Blue or Purple Tag Tickets - 1 extra point Observations: 1. To obtain points, tickets must have a positive 5-star return.
Neadinus – The Counsellor **Gamon – The Counsellor**	Race: Wizard Powers: Due to his ability to advise, he manages to use his talent to negotiate, influence and mediate. Every ticket awaiting a requester that is settled or canceled after trading by Gamon/ Neadinus may generate extra points. - Green, Yellow or Pink Tag Tickets - 2 extra points - Blue or Purple Tag Tickets - 1 extra point Observations: 1. Tickets resolved with the help of Gamon/Neadinus, must have the previous status "waiting for requester". 2. Only Gamon/Neadinus will receive points for the settled or canceled ticket.
Elbor – The Solicitous One **Ra'lan – The Solicitous One**	Race: Elf Powers: Due to their ability to get things done quickly and quickly, they manage to complete activities on time. Every ticket settled within the SLA by Ra'lan/Elbor can generate extra points. - Green or Yellow Tag Ticket - 2 extra points - Blue, Purple or Pink Tag Ticket - 1 extra point
Thorra - The Proactive **Drud - The Proactive**	Race: Barbarian Powers: Due to their proactive ability, Thorra manages to anticipate future problems, needs or changes.

From then on, the gamification process was implemented using Trello, an app popularly used for project management and already used at Neurotech, but for other purposes. This tool was chosen due to the mobility of cards and the power-ups that allow information to be managed.

In the app, gamification was operationalized, with the creation of an environment for interaction between players, within the narrative that included history, rules, challenges, missions, penalties, rewards and scores that arise during a dispute to rescue a "Queen". The environment was called the "Kingdom of Satisfaction".

As shown below (Figure 3), several columns were created, each with the corresponding cards:

- The first, which is in relation to the administrators of the game who are deemed to be the Counsellors of the Kingdom, had three cards, each of which is assigned to one of the researchers;
  - The second has the story;
  - The third one contains the rules of the mechanism of the game.

Figure 3. Operationalization of the gamification in Trello: administrators, story, and rules. Compiled by the authors

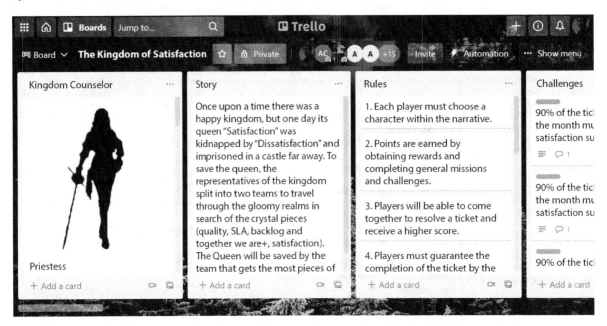

Soon after, columns with challenges, missions, penalties, rewards and scores were created, according to Figure 4 below. The score for each mission, challenge, penalty and reward is represented by different colored tags.

The control of points was conducted daily at the end of working hours using spreadsheets. During the day, players moved the cards according to the missions achieved. At the end of the day, cards were validated, and scores confirmed and adjusted as a result of penalties and rewards. Finally, after validation, the scores of the teams and each player were published in Trello, as shown Figure 5 below.

Figure 4. Operationalization of gamification in Trello: challenges, missions, penalties, rewards and scores. Compiled by the authors

Figure 5. Operationalization in Trello: scoring. Compiled by the authors

Application and Monitoring

The process was applied for four days from December 9th to 12th, 2019 in two of the squads of the Operations Directorate, with the participation proposal of 15 Neurotech employees, but one of them did not want to participate for personal reasons.

During the week, during office hours, the teams carried out their activities and fed the Trello with information about tickets attended to. At night, after the end of the working day, the organizers checked if what had been entered on Trello was in accordance with what was in the company's internal system. After this was checked, scores were tallied and posted to Trello for teams to check the next day.

The process was performed daily to count the score was difficult and complex, because validating the information posted to Trello and the information in the call receiving tool of Neurotech was done manually.

After this step, a new questionnaire was applied regarding on the participants' impressions of the gamification process.

ANALYSIS OF THE RESULTS

On the Results after Applying Gamification

After completing the gamification process, the data was compiled and the returns achieved were observed, translated into positive aspects for the teams and, consequently, for the customers served. The results were as follows:

A significant increase in cooperation between teams and between team members, due to the engagement to achieve missions and goals. Exceeding the target of 90% of surveys with 4 or 5 stars, i.e., the result of 100% customer satisfaction was obtained, as shown in Table 3.

Table 3. Customer satisfaction. Compiled by the authors

Stars	The Amount	Percentage (%)
1, 2, 3	0	0%
4, 5	13	100%

A 30% increase in the coverage of the satisfaction survey, i.e., a greater number of respondents, as shown in Table 4.

Table 4. Coverage of the satisfaction (drawn up by the authors)

Time	Coverage (%)	Increase
Before gamification	14.29%	-
After gamifications	18.57%	30%

Improvement or maintenance of the positive values of the Key Performance Indicators (KPIs) of the Service Level Agreement (SLA), of the Quality and Backlog (list of demands) of Neurotech's Operations area, as shown in Tables 5, 6, and 7.

Another piece of interesting data is that 81.43% of the completed demands were without customer feedback regarding the quality of delivery, as shown in Table 8.

Table 5. Service Level Agreement. Compiled by the authors

Team	SLA Before Gamification	SLA After Gamification
1	83.33%	95.86%
2	80.95%	88%

Table 6. Quality. Compiled by the authors

Team	Quality Before Gamification	Quality After Gamification
1	0% rejected calls	0% rejected calls
2	0% rejected calls	0% rejected calls

Table 7. Backlog. Compiled by the authors

Team	Backlog Before Gamification	Backlog After Gamification	Reduction Backlog
1	39	39	0,00%
2	88	81	-7,95%

Table 8. Customer feedback regarding the quality of delivery. Compiled by the authors

Time	Customer Feedback (%)	Without Customer Feedback
Before gamification	14.29%	85.71%
After gamifications	18.57%	81.43%

It was noticed that the indicators achieved when gamification was applied were higher than those of previous months, without using this playful approach that gamification has, which was very positive. The results achieved were as follows.

Increased cooperation between teams and between team members. Increased productivity for resolved demands by 20% for team 1 and by 78.26% for team 2, i.e., more calls were registered and resolved when the gamification process was applied, as shown in Table 9.

Table 9. Productivity of resolved demands. Compiled by the authors

Team	Productivity Before Gamification	Productivity After Gamification	Increase in Productivity
1	25	30	20%
2	23	41	78.26%

Improvement in the Backlog KPI. In the month prior to applying the process, there was an increase of 45% in this by team 1 and of 7% by team 2, while during the study period, the backlog of team 2 was reduced by 7.95% while team 1 maintained their performance without improving it, as shown in Table 10.

Table 10. Improvement in the Backlog KPI. Compiled by the authors

Team	KPI Backlog November 2019	KPI Backlog After Gamification
1	Increase 45%	Decrease 7,95%
2	Increase 7%	Stabilized

Improved KPIs of SLA, as shown in Table 5. Team 1 reached the target of 90% of completed demands within the SLA – their result was 95.86%, and team 2 achieved 88%. However, in the months prior to the experiment, the indicators were 83.33% and 80.95% respectively.

From the data and analysis of the results presented above, some positive and negative aspects can be identified, namely:

§ Positives
    ¡ Monitoring the performance of employees;
    ¡ Visualization of the quality of the employees' work among the participants;
    ¡ Increased teamwork;
    ¡ Increased customer contact.
§ Negatives
    ¡ 1 player who did not participate in the process, recording his activities;
    ¡ Difficulty in evaluating scores more efficiently, manual process performed daily;
    ¡ Complexity of counting the points.

Although there are negative points and improvements to be made, the business objectives were achieved, which ranged from improving customer satisfaction to team engagement, cooperation between squads and increasing the number of responses to satisfaction surveys by 30%.

Finally, the results were shared with the teams and symbolic prizes (mugs and sweets) were distributed to the team and the player with the highest score.

Feedback from Participants after Applying Gamification

At the end of the process, a questionnaire was generated to collect feedback from participants on the process applied. The questions addressed: previous knowledge and participation in gamification, past use of Trello and satisfaction with the tool during the process, satisfaction and difficulty with the gamification process, changes of the gamification at work.

As for the survey results, although 75% of respondents answered that they already knew about the concept, no-one had participated in a gamification process.

Of these, 62.5% indicated that they already used the Trello tool in their activities in the company to organize tasks or backlog, but not in gamification processes, the most common use being to manage tasks.

Regarding the satisfaction of using Trello for gamification, 75% said they were very satisfied and 25% that they were moderately satisfied. As to the gamification process, it was extremely satisfactory, as demonstrated by 87.5% of the answers and 12.5% said they were moderately satisfied.

Regarding motivation after starting gamification, 62.5% of participants reported being very motivated and 37.5% said they were moderately motivated.

Asked about the tool (Figure 7), 87.5% of respondents said it proved to be very useful while 12.5% found it moderately useful.

Figure 7. Feedback from participants about gamification. Compiled by the authors

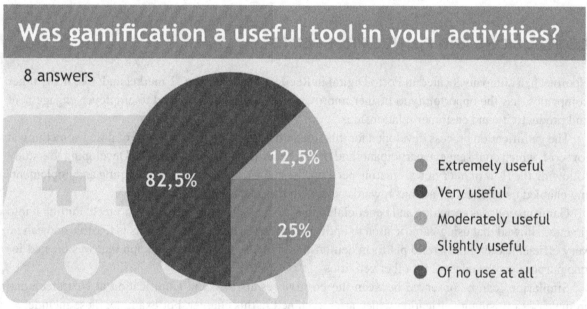

After completing the gamification, 100% of respondents reported their opinion about how their concept of it had changed, by means of various expressions of feedback:

- "I could see in practice the increased motivation to carry out daily activities".
- "It stimulates people's competitive spirit, causing a faster response in their activities".
- "It contributed to teamwork".
- "We were able to measure our performance based on the tickets, we can have feedback".
- "I didn't know that the practice of this particular concept could be so broad and positively impact our daily routine without taking the focus away from priority day-to-day activities".
- "I found the experience positive".
- "Very good, we were able to eliminate our backlog".
- "It was very interesting to get to know the gamification format and its benefits".
- "The experience was valid, we thought about a strategy to round off tickets, which reduced the backlog".
- "It had positive impact on the productivity of the team".

- "It was a new experience because we were able to work as a team, act with quality and speed. At the end of the day, we had feedback from the people who contributed, who succeeded in standing out. We also managed to organize the activities that were carried out".
- "It was very "mind-blowing", as a newcomer to the company, I realized that with this gamification people were eager to do their activities. I already knew Trello and had used it in other places, and this experience was way beyond that".
- "I started to look more attentively at the qualities of my teammates".

Finally, what could be seen was the enthusiasm of the participating teams, as a result of on-site observation and reports during the gamification process.

CONCLUSIONS AND FUTURE PROSPECTS

Neurotech, a company located in Porto Digital in Recife, operates in the IT market and, like many other companies, has the opportunity to further improve its KPIs which are linked to employee engagement and productivity and customer relationships.

The gamification process developed for this research began with the challenge of doing something at low cost, which could engage participants and obtain benefits for the organization. Developing this study following the flow of interviews, creating persona, the gamification canvas, prototyping and implementing enabled us to direct all actions towards achieving the goals and challenges.

Gamification was enriching and beneficial for players/collaborators and for Neurotech. Putting it into practice showed that using gamification to optimize processes and achieve results is feasible and can be very efficient. Using the Trello platform demonstrated that with creativity an app that was created for one purpose can be adapted for other activities.

Similarities can be observed between the positive results of using gamification at Neurotech and in the cases of using gamification which are mentioned in this chapter. For example, these include: an increase in employee productivity and a preference for using the gamification approach as presented by Growth Engineering (2021); increased coverage of customer responses to surveys, as occurred at Samsung (Teles, 2018); good participation rate of team members as occurred at Omnicare (Teles, 2018); high employee motivation rate by using gamification similar to the index presented by Chang (2021).

The results reinforce the arguments that gamification goes beyond just being fun activities performed in the workplace (Agogué, Levillain and Hooge, 2015; Dale, 2014; Kalinauskas, 2014), and has an influence on improving productivity (Patrício, Moreira & Zurlo, 2020).

Feedback from participants pointed out that gamification helped in processes, but also in teamwork and in the perception of each other's competences. Furthermore, even with symbolic prizes, the engagement and motivation of employees during the gamification process was very strong. Thus, we can see in this study that the motivation of employees is not linked to the value of the prize, but to the playful process that gamification addresses. The entire process drew the attention of other areas of the company who became eager to apply gamification to their needs and problems. The Neurotech board itself was very satisfied with the results achieved in the process and very interested in expanding its application to other sectors.

Finally, this analysis contributes to the reinforcement that the gamification process, when well structured, presents successful results in the engagement and motivation of people and contributes even more to its application in the business scenario, as demonstrated by this study carried out at Neurotech.

As a future study, it is intended to extend the period of application of gamification and the number of teams in Neurotech's customer satisfaction sector, to verify how the engagement of teams and each participant will take place, as well as whether the results will be maintained or can be further expanded.

REFERENCES

Agogué, M., Levillain, K., & Hooge, S. (2015). Gamification of creativity: Exploring the usefulness of serious games for ideation. *Creativity and Innovation Management, 24*(3), 415–429. doi:10.1111/caim.12138

Allen, F. E. (2011, May 3). Disneyland Uses 'Electronic Whip' on Employees. *Forbes.*

AlSaad, F. M., & Durugbo, C. M. (2021, August 19). Gamification-as-Innovation: A Review. *International Journal of Innovation and Technology Management, 18*(5). doi:10.1142/S0219877021300020

Alves, F. (2015). *Gamification: Como criar experiências de aprendizagem engajadoras, um guia completo: do conceito a prática.* Dvs Editora.

Apostolopoulos, A. (2019, August 19). *The 2019 Gamification at Work Survey.* TalentLMS. https://www.talentlms.com/blog/gamification-survey-results/

Bartle, R. (1996a). Players Who Suit MUDs. *Journal of MUD Research.* https://mud.co.uk/richard/hcds.htm

Bartle, R. (1996b). *The Bartle Test of Gamer Psychology.* https://matthewbarr.co.uk/bartle/

Bogost, I. (2011, October 21). *Persuasive Games: Exploitationware.* Gamasutra.

Brachman, J., & Levine, A. (2010, April 13). The World of Holy Warcraft: How al Qaeda is using online game theory to recruit the masses. *Foreign Policy.*

Burke, B. (2015). *Gamificar: como a gamificação motiva as pessoas a fazerem coisas extraordinárias.* Dvs Editora.

Ceros. (2019, March 9). *Interactive Content Marketing: A Beginner's Guide.* Ceros. https://www.ceros.com/resources/

Chang, J. (2021). *54 Gamification Statistics You Must Know: 2020/2021 Market Share Analysis & Data.* Finances Online. https://financesonline.com/gamification-statistics/

Costa, A. C. S. & Marchiori, P. Z. (2015). Gamificação, elementos de jogos e estratégia: uma matriz de referência. *InCID: Revista De Ciência Da Informação E Documentação, 6*(2), 44-65. doi:10.11606/issn.2178-2075.v6i2p44-65

Deterding, S. (2011). Situated motivational affordances of game elements: a conceptual model. *Workshop on Gamification: Using Game Design Elements in Nongaming Contexts, CHI 2011, Vancouver, BC, Canada. Proceedings*, 1-4. https://www.researchgate.net/publication/303084050_Situated_motivational_affordances_of_game_elements_A_conceptual_model

Exame. (2017, July 22). *Harter, do Gallup: emprego x felicidade*. https://exame.com/mundo/harter-do-gallup-emprego-x-felicidade

Galetta, G. (2013). The gamification: Applications and developments for creativity and education. Paper presented at conference on Creativity and Innovation in Education. 10.13140/RG.2.2.24817.68965

Growth Engineering. (2021, May 27). *19 gamification trends for 2021-2025: top stats, facts & examples*. Growth Engineering. https://www.growthengineering.co.uk/19-gamification-trends-for-2021-2025-top-stats-facts-examples

Harwood, T., & Garry, T. (2015). An investigation into gamification as a customer engagement experience environment. *Journal of Services Marketing*, 29(6/7), 533–546. doi:10.1108/JSM-01-2015-0045

Heimburger, L., Buchweitz, L., Gouveia, R., & Korn, O. (2019, June). Gamifying Onboarding: How to Increase Both Engagement and Integration of New Employees. *Advances in Social and Occupational Ergonomics, Proceedings of the AHFE 2019 International Conference on Social and Occupational Ergonomics*, 3-14. https://www.researchgate.net/publication/333655639_Gamifying_Onboarding_How_to_Increase_Both_Engagement_and_Integration_of_New_Employees doi:10.1007/978-3-030-20145-6_1

Huizinga, J. (2001). Homo Ludens: O Jogo como elemento da Cultura (5th ed.). Perspectiva, SP.

Jay, A. (2021). *12 Gamification Trends for 2021/2022: Current Forecasts You Should Be Thinking About*. https://financesonline.com/gamification-trends

Kotler, P., & Armstrong, G. (2003). *Princípios de Marketing* (9th ed.). São Paulo: Prentice Hall.

Lederman. (2019). *Os 7 problemas mais comuns nas empresas*. Lederman Consulting & Education. https://www.ledermanconsulting.com.br/educacao-corporativa/os-7-problemas-mais-comuns-nas-empresas

Marques, J. R. (2019). *Quais são os principais problemas organizacionais?* Instituto Brasileiro de Coaching - IBC. https://www.ibccoaching.com.br/portal/rh-gestao-pessoas/quais-sao-principais-problemas-organizacionais

Maske, P. (2019, June 10). *Benefits of gamification in training*. eLearning Learning. https://www.elearninglearning.com/gamification/statistics/?open-article-id=10681320&article-title=benefits-of-gamification-in-training&blog-domain=paradisosolutions.com&blog-title=paradiso

Mastrocola, V. M. (2012). *Ludificador: um guia de referências para o game designer brasileiro*. Independente.

Parjanen, S., & Hyypiä, M. (2019). Innotin game supporting collective creativity in innovation activities. *Journal of Business Research*, 96, 26–34. doi:10.1016/j.jbusres.2018.10.056

Patrício, R., Moreira, A. C., & Zurlo, F. (2018). Gamification Approaches to the Early Stage of Innovation. *Creativity and Innovation Management*, 27(4), 499–511. doi:10.1111/caim.12284

Patrício, R., Moreira, A. C., & Zurlo, F. (2020). Enhancing design thinking approaches to innovation through gamification. *European Journal of Innovation Management, 24*(5), 1569–1594. doi:10.1108/EJIM-06-2020-0239

Piligrimiene, Z., Dovaliene, A., & Virvilaite, R. (2015). Consumer engagement in value co-creation: What kind of value it creates for company? *The Engineering Economist, 26*(4), 452–460. doi:10.5755/j01.ee.26.4.12502

Robson, K., Plangger, K., Kietzmann, J. H., McCarthy, I., & Pitt, L. (2015). Is it all a game? Understanding the principles of gamification. *Business Horizons, 58*(4), 411–420. doi:10.1016/j.bushor.2015.03.006

Romero-Rodríguez, L. M., Ramírez-Montoya, M. S., & Gonzalez, J. R. V. (2019). Gamification in MOOCs: Engagement application test in energy sustainability courses. *IEEE Access: Practical Innovations, Open Solutions, 7*, 32093–32101. doi:10.1109/ACCESS.2019.2903230

Rosa, B. (2021). *Guia Completo de Customer Success (Sucesso do Cliente): Conceitos, Estratégias e Ferramentas: entenda a jornada do cliente no seu negócio.* Academic Press.

Rubini, P. (2019). *A Fórmula da Satisfação do Cliente: como conquistar e manter clientes rentáveis.* Editora Autografia Edição e Comunicação Ltda.

Sharma, A. (2020, January 26). *Back To Basics: How Gamification Can Improve Employee Engagement In 2020.* eLearning Industry. https://elearningindustry.com/how-gamification-improve-employee-engagement-2020

State of the Global Workplace. (2017). *Gallup's state of the Global Workplace.* https://fundacionprolongar.org/wp-content/uploads/2019/07/State-of-the-Global-Workplace_Gallup-Report.pdf

Teles, J. (2018). *O uso do Gamification como ferramenta de aprendizagem no treinamento e desenvolvimento de colaboradores.* Linkedin. https://www.linkedin.com/pulse/o-uso-do-gamification-como-ferramenta-de-aprendizagem-jenifer-teles/

Ungerleider, N. (2011, April 22). *Welcome To JihadVille.* Fast Company.

Vianna, Y., Vianna, M., Medina, B., & Tanaka, S. (2013). *Gamification, Inc. Como reinventar empresas a partir de jogos.* MVJ Press.

Chapter 7
Gamification for Stakeholders in the Product Life Cycle:
Holonic Platform With Kansei Engineering

Antonio Córdoba-Roldán
 https://orcid.org/0000-0002-0560-5696
University of Seville, Spain

María Jesús Ávila-Gutiérrez
 https://orcid.org/0000-0002-2801-1153
University of Seville, Spain

Susana Suarez-Fernandez de Miranda
 https://orcid.org/0000-0002-5757-3382
University of Seville, Spain

Francisco Aguayo-González
University of Seville, Spain

ABSTRACT

This chapter proposes a framework to develop a gamification platform for the activities, processes, and tasks executed by the stakeholders who participate in each stage of life cycle engineering (LCE). For this purpose, a review is made of the most significant aspects of gamification for its application in the LCE of the product. The stakeholders in the LCE must be known and classified to make a gaming experience. It is proposed to establish the relationship between the gameful and playful experiences expected by the stakeholders and the game design elements that allow the introduction of attractive game mechanics in the phases of the product design process. For this goal, it is proposed to gamify through a Kansei Engineering System. This methodology allows incorporating all the potential of the digital and organizational facilitators of Industry 4.0 and developing a cyber-physical holonic platform for the gamification of the LCE.

DOI: 10.4018/978-1-6684-4291-3.ch007

INTRODUCTION

Over the last decade, interest in gamification, its principles and the benefits derived from its application in contexts as diverse as education, business and social marketing, management, and others, has grown (Marcão et al., 2017; Mitchell et al., 2016). Gamification is described as the process of adding mechanical elements and principles of games and video games in non-playful scenarios. Gamification can enhance the creation of positive emotions, motivate, improve cognitive skills, create personal bonds and relationships, increase the sense of achievement, reduce stress and enhance engagement (Deterding et al., 2011; Granic et al., 2013).

A variety of authors propose principles of play in non-playful contexts among which the most representative are the following (Dicheva et al., 2015; Erenli, 2013; Kapp, 2012): achievement of goals and objectives, creation of rules and game mechanics, feedback, rewards, motivation and freedom of choice, facilitating engagement, raising success metrics.

The concept of gamification was originated by video game designer Nick Pelling in 2002 when he had to design an interface for ATM and vending machines using game mechanics (Christians, 2018). The interest in gamification goes hand in hand with the development of video games and the increase of gamers, with more users familiar with gamified game types, mechanics, dynamics and experiences.

Regarding the video games sector, the Entertainment Software Association (ESA) (Entertainment Software Association, 2017, 2020), states that young people who have not yet entered the world of work spend most of their time playing video games. It is essential to understand why people spend part of their time playing video games and what the game provides them with in their daily lives, as these same motivations can be extrapolated to a non-game context with similar objectives (Lee & Fonseca, 2021). From the point of view of the gamified experience, the ESA (2020) states that 80% of gamers experience mental stimulation as well as relaxation and stress relief (79%). Gamers express that video games help connect people, 65% of gamers share their gaming experience with other gamers online or in person, and 55% of gamers state that video games help them connect with people and friends. On the other hand, 63% think that video games have a big impact on their problem-solving skills.

It is important to know the behavioral trends as introducing gaming experiences in professional contexts today can have a greater acceptance among the agents that are part of a project, regardless of the benefits that can be obtained.

In terms of the incorporation of gamification in the field of business and social marketing, its objectives are to create states of engagement mainly in digital environments and to establish metrics and indicators for the evaluation of use, improve the quality of interaction and establish the level of commitment (Sarkum, 2018). For its application, it is proposed to establish three types of engagement related to a product design project:

- **Customer Engagement**: commitment and interaction dynamics of a customer towards a company throughout the Product Design Process (PDP).
- **Employee Engagement**: commitment in human and work terms that an employee has with the company to which he/she belongs.
- **User Engagement**: commitment and interaction dynamics of a user with a product or service throughout the Product Life Cycle (PLC), mainly in the use phase. It also considers interaction with the brand through communication channels other than the product.

Introducing gamification in professional contexts can generate interactive experiences of cooperation that help agents or stakeholders to interact with each other, solve problems, stimulate and foster a workspace based on cooperation with experiences similar or close to video games. The rise of technologies based on the Internet of Things (IoT), big data, machine learning and wearable sensors, among others, generate an ideal context for extrapolating gaming experiences to the professional world (L'Heureux et al., 2017).

In this framework it is especially important to consider the PLC and the different stakeholders in each of the stages, as well as the processes and activities they develop. In addition, a continuous process of learning and interaction with the different stakeholders is required, which allows the introduction and development of gamification in a holistic and integrated way in the value chain of all stakeholders. Hitch (2018) considers that in order to introduce gamification in companies and boost efficiency and productivity in all activities of an organization, it is necessary to use the combined effect of techniques and tools such as big data, data mining tools, IOT and other intelligent tools that help to evoke the natural competitive and cooperative instinct in the workplace (L'Heureux et al., 2017).

Currently, gamification is becoming a concept of interest for its incorporation into work or professional contexts. The objectives of this framework are to identify the stakeholders who participate in the different stages of the product's LCE (Life Cycle Engineering) and to engage them through an experience based on game mechanics in cyber-physical and intelligent digital environments such as those proposed in Industry 4.0. The use of gamification in digitized LCE can have a great impact on younger stakeholders and especially on those who will join in the future, target end users of the proposed gamification.

The main objective of the proposal is to introduce gamification in LCE possibility of classify stakeholders and improve their experience with real-time data to measure progress, in addition to introducing a sense of responsibility, commitment and competence (Hitch, 2018). To achieve this objective, it is proposed to apply Kansei Engineering (KE) as a methodology that allows and supports the incorporation of gamification. As a proposal for the projection of the gamification of the LCE, a holonic model will be presented which is in work in progress. The development of this framework has the following phases to propose:

- **Phase 1**: Identify and characterize the interest and viability of transferring experiences obtained in the gaming environment through gamification of professional activities developed by stakeholders in the life cycle of products and in the value chain of services.
- **Phase 2**: Establish the background on gamification and its development in the field of design and product development to provide concepts, definitions, frameworks, and incorporate points of view from others (literature review) to support the proposed framework.
- **Phase 3**: Identify and characterize LCE stakeholders based on types of gamification users to develop gaming experiences.
- **Phase 4**: Incorporate KE as a design methodology to gamify stakeholder experience in LCE using design elements and game mechanics.
- **Phase 5:** Propose a holonic model for the gamification of LCE in sustainable environments under the potential of the digital enablers of Industry 4.0, and artificial intelligence and neuroscientific methods.

In the field of engineering, particularly in the PDP, gamification is not widespread, considered just more that products proposal encapsulated in information technology (IT) applications based on interfaces.

The approach of gamified products can provide benefits to the user, as gamification brings new paradigms of user experience (Hoos, 2016; Robson et al., 2014). Understanding user emotions, behaviours and experiences will help to the implementation of a gamification strategy to improve the user engagement with the product (Sweetman, 2018). This gamified approach is focused on the PLC product use stage and the user-product relationship and interaction to provide exciting, pleasant experiences where new linkages are created between the company and product with the user (Nobre & Ferreira, 2017).

Beyond the perspective centred in gamified user experiences with the product where the user is implicated, in this study propose an extension of gamification principles to all stages of LCE, taking into account the totality of stakeholders involved in the development process of industrial products. Applied gamification during the PLC will generate attractive working experiences to engage and motivate stakeholders due to the implementation of game elements and principles.

This proposal develop the LCE in all stages the product or system pass through. LCE start from the phase of need and requirement identification and analysis, followed by the product design and development stage, industrialization, distribution and sale, stage of use and technical support, and lastly the recuperation or recovering stage and the end of the product useful life (Rozman et al., 2015). The main objective of this formal proposal is establishing a set of gamified tools for the user experience at every stage of the PLC, techniques and tools which generate exciting, pleasant and memorable experiences to the stakeholders involved in each stage. On the other hand, conceiving a gamified LCE will help to design, develop, use products with embedded gamification of personalised experiences according to the type of user and the motivations of use, creating new interactions and linkages with the products, packaging and company (Syrjälä et al., 2020), this strategies are especially useful thanks to the possibilities that offer intelligent products connected as Cyber-Physical Systems (CPS), supported in sustainable digital environments.

The gamification of the experience of the stakeholders in the PLC, integrates the internal stakeholders or integrated in the company (project management, product design and product development, manufacturing, marketing and sales) and the external stakeholders (suppliers, distribution, sales, use, after-sales service, reverse logistics and reverse manufacturing). These activities, processes and tasks are proposed under the sustainable development goals of the 2030 agenda.

BACKGROUND

In order to develop the background, firstly, an analysis will be made of the possible stakeholders involved in the lifecycle and the types of players proposed in a gamification project. The proposal will link the experiences and interests of stakeholders with types of players in order to provide a correct and personalized gamified experience in the different phases of the lifecycle. Therefore, secondly, the cognitive aspects of gamification will be analyzed. It is essential to understand and translate gamified experiences for stakeholders through design elements, mechanics and dynamics. The proposed application linking gamified stakeholder experiences with game elements will be developed using a Kansei Engineering System (KES), which will be adapted to meet the objectives of the study (Figure 1). The possibilities of incorporating numerical and artificial intelligence methods into KE will be analyzed. Finally, the possibilities of adapting and implementing the digital transformation of companies and the digitization of workplaces and products by configuring the product and company components as cyber-physical systems using embedded Key Enabling Technologies (KET) will be analyzed. The aim is to be able to

Figure 1. Incorporate a Kansei Engineering System (KES) for gamification transposition

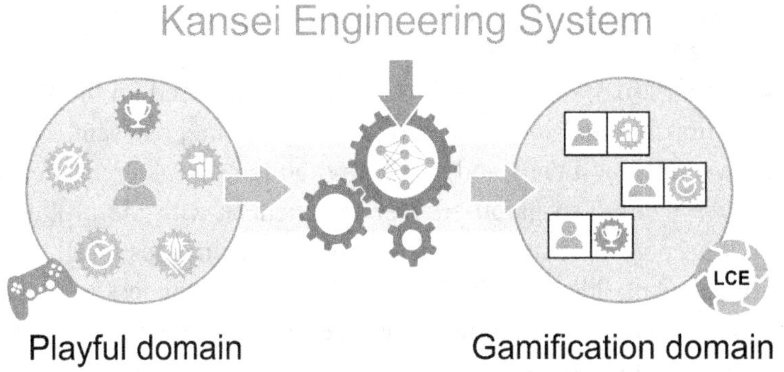

carry out the proposal in all phases and levels of the PLC, guaranteeing feedback between stakeholders and enabling the implementation of a system to generate gamified experiences.

Stakeholders in the Industrial Product Life Cycle and Types of Gamified Users

Throughout the whole PLC different stakeholders are involved, who can be any group or person that can affect or be affected by the objectives of the specific PDP (Freeman & McVea, 2005). In a PDP project it is crucial to involve both internal and external stakeholders as they can contribute to the success of the project. For their part the stakeholders should add value to the stages of the PLC, organizational processes and systems that can be adapted to their requirements and contributions and promote a communication system that enables them to achieve goals and manage conflict effectively (Kochan & Rubinstein, 2000).

The introduction to gamification in the stages of the PLC can make changes in the stakeholders' experiences benefit from the motivational aspects of behaviour through emotional reinforcements (Robson et al., 2015).

This life cycle model in PLC from the perspective proposed by ISO 14040:2006 can be divided into three main phases, the Beginnings-of-Life (BoL) which includes the planning, design and manufacturing stages; the Middle-of-Life (MoL) including distribution or external logistics, use and support and/ or maintenance; and the End-of-Life (EoL) where products are retired and can be disposed of, recycled, reused or remanufactured (Terzi et al., 2010).

At the BoL internal stakeholders mainly take action in the process, as the directive team, project managers, marketing, engineering teams and industrial designers. In this starting point is considered the project planning stage, needs/requirements analysis, the PDP and the manufacturing stage, in which can contribute as well eternal stakeholders as suppliers and the target user (market). In the MoL, distribution or logistics stages and the phase of use and maintenance, other external stakeholders take part of the process such as distributors, retail outlets and users. In the EoL stage contribute mostly the government, as the user that freedom of choice resulting in sustainable end of life (Aaltonen & Kujala, 2010; Moultrie, 2016; Smith, 2000). In Table 1, it is proposed to incorporate into the PLC, the project planning phases and the PDP that are not normally taken into account when referring to the PLC (Terzi et al., 2007). From the point of view of carrying out an industrial product engineering project, it is advisable to take into account the early stages of planning, market research, and design and development, as these phases involve various stakeholders whose experience must be taken into account in the proposal made

Table 1. Stakeholders on the proposed life cycle

PLC phases	Internal Stakeholders	External Stakeholders	Interests
Definition and planing	• Executives • Project Lead • Project Manager	• Investors • Sponsors	• Planning • Provide leadership • Management
Design and development	• Team Manager • Project team members (Design Engineers)	• Consultants	• Projcct cxccution • Engineering • Quality
Manufacturing	• Work teams (Manufacturers, Assembly, Quality…)	• Suppliers	• Execute tasks and activities • Provide products or services
Distribution and sales	• Logistics • Marketing manager • Sales	• Shipping • Storage • Vendors • Customers	• Distribute • User-company relationship • Facilitate the product to the user
Use	• Customer Service	• Users	• Satisfy user needs
End of life	• Supplies	• Government • Users	• Sustainable and social development

This framework focuses on the stakeholders' interest in the product design and development project, although factors such as importance, influence, level of interest, responsibility, objectives, communication, dependencies between each other, etc. must also be considered.

Once stakeholders are identified, the type of gamified experiences that can be generated and the role that stakeholders can play must be defined. Classification criteria will also be taken into account according to the six types of players explained by Marczewski (2015), who organized them depending on motivational factors, intrinsic or extrinsic factors. Thanks to that stakeholder classification, can be defined a relationship between the types of player/ stakeholders and the game design elements, for develop and potentiate a gamified experience (Tondello et al., 2016).

The stakeholder can construct their experience based on the two fundamental dimensions proposed by Pine & Gilmore (1999), the level of participation and the connection or relationship with the environment. On the other hand, Cobaleda & Aguayo (2011) propose a third dimension that represents the motor or motivation that would move the stakeholder to participate in the experience.

Robson et al., (2015) propose a classification of the gamified experience based on the dimensions of Pine & Gilmore (1999). Adapting the study to the present proposal, it is established that the level of participation of the gamified stakeholder is based on whether he/she actively or passively contributes or engages in the experience. The connection or relationship of the gamified stakeholder with the environment, whether physical or virtual, describes whether the experience takes place before the stakeholder (absorption) or the stakeholder is part of the experience itself (immersion). Based on the proposal of Cobaleda & Aguayo (2011) it is proposed that the gamified stakeholder will have an evocation experience when participating in the experience based on another previous experience, or on the contrary, an involvement experience when a satisfactory outcome is foreseen without having a previous experience reference.

Robson et al., (2015) defines in their framework "Mechanics, Dynamics, and Emotions" (MDE) that there are four types of experiences involved in a gamified environment: players, designers, spectators, and observers. Players are defined as the interpreters of the experience, as they have a level of active participation and their link with the environment is through immersion. Designers are those who have a gamified experience based mainly on decision making and supervision. The level of participation of a designer can change over time, having an active experience at the beginning because they configure the experience, and once the experience is designed, their level of participation would be passive and by absorption based on their relationship with the environment. On the other hand, there are the spectators, who are not an active part of the experience, but are part of the gamified environment, being immersed in the experience. Finally, observers are outside the gamified context (absorption) and participate in a passive way in the experience, however, they can have an influence on the popularity and acceptance of the gamified experience.

On the other hand, based on the studies of Xu et al. (2012), Marczewski (2015) proposes a model called Hexad that defines the existence of six gamification user types: achievers, players, socialisers, free spirits, disruptors and philanthropists. The main objective of achievers is to complete tasks in order to achieve greater progress and by taking on challenges, their main reward is internal. Players are motivated by achieving the goal and being the best, their main reward is external. Socialisers base their activity on generating social relationships that allow them to interact with each other. On the other hand, free spirits are autonomous and want to express themselves freely, create and explore without external control. Disruptors want to provoke positive or negative changes in the system and their behaviour tends to go beyond the limits, for example, to try to improve the system. Finally, philanthropists are altruistic and do not expect rewards for their achievements.

Dolatabadi & Budinskai's (2020) proposal analyses the engagement of the stakeholders in competitive markets by defining four types of players and their interaction in gamification strategy: Competitors, Researchers, Exterminator and Non-social. The authors base their classification on two dimensions: capabilities to create value for the organisation and interaction with the organisation. Competitors participate in the game competitively and have high level of expertise. Researchers learn to play, but do not interact, and seek to experience new dynamics. Exterminators play for their personal growth with little interaction and specialise in specific games. Finally, the non-social have low interaction and no expertise, they can be integrated into the game but do not add value to the game.

Frameworks for the Gamified Experiences

In order to develop the proposal, firstly, it is essential to know how to identify the types of gamified stakeholders that allow the gamified experience to be defined. On the other hand, the design elements with which this experience can be built must be identified. Once this relationship has been identified, the gamified experience must be provided.

Marczewski's Hexad model (2015) presents a segmentation of the users of the gamified experience based mainly on their motivations. The study by Diamond et al. (2015) proposes a questionnaire-based analysis method to assess and identify the user based on the six types of gamified users of the Hexad model. The proposed questionnaires include the evaluation of 30 items related to the types of gamers. Subsequently, it is analyzed through the scoring system which type of gamified user has obtained the highest score.

For the creation of gamified experiences, the MDE framework by Robson et al. (2015) is analyzed. The MDE framework defines the three gamification principles; mechanics, dynamics, and emotions; describing the relationship between them and illustrating how they can be applied together. The first

Table 2. Relationship between types of gamified users and design elements. Based on Marczewski (2015b) and Tondello et al. (2016)

User types	Motivation	Design Elements
Achievers	Competence	Challenges, certificates, learning new skills, quests, levels or progression, and epic chal- lenges
Players	Extrinsic rewards	Points, rewards or prizes, leaderboards, badges or achievements, virtual economy, and lotteries or games of chance.
Socialisers	Relatedness	Guilds or teams, social net- works, social comparison, social competition, and social discovery
Free Spirits	Autonomy	Exploratory tasks, nonlinear gameplay, Easter eggs, unlockable content, creativity tools, and customization
Disruptors	Change	Innovation platforms, voting mechanisms, development tools, anonymity, anarchic gameplay.
Philanthropists	Purpose	Collection and trading, gifting, knowledge sharing, and administrative roles

dimension to be defined is the mechanics are created by those responsible for gamification in a non-playful context.

For the development of the mechanics, the goals, the rules, the setting, the context, the types of inter-actions and the boundaries must be specified. In the MDE framework, three different types of mechanics are defined: setup mechanics, rule mechanics, and progression mechanics. On the other hand, gamification dynamics are defined through the player behaviour's when participating in the gamified experience, and describe the actions and strategies carried out by the player. Behaviours are generated based on the defined mechanics. For example, team-based mechanics generate cooperative dynamics and individual game mechanics generate competitive dynamics. It is complex to predict the dynamics that a player will follow since, in addition to the player himself, the dynamics can be modified by external factors such as the presence of other agents like observers or spectators. Finally, emotions are the affective state of the player that is evoked by the mechanics generating dynamics. The experience must be engaging for the user and fun (Leblanc, 2004).

Having identified the types of gamified users and the dimensions that define gamified experiences, Tondello et al. (2016) propose a link between the type of gamified user and experience with the design elements of gamification. The results of the study are summarised in Table 2, which shows the types of gamified users of the Hexad model, their motivations and the design elements suggested to generate the experience.

It is important to know the cognitive aspects of the experience in order to understand the emotions of the stakeholders classified on the basis of the Hexad model and to provide a methodological framework such as the KE to define a gamified experience domain that encompasses the dimensions proposed in the MDE framework and the main design elements.

Cognitive and Neuro Cognitive Aspects of Gamification

One of the bases for success in the application of gamified systems is the capacity to motivate and involve with engagement "players" in the task to develop, evoking both positive and negative emotions through gamification. Mullins and Sabherwal (2018) expose the lack of existing orientation in gamification about the creation of emotionally positive experiences through gamification.

At this point knowing the motivational process, from cognitive origin, is helpful to achieve the gamified objectives, apart from other cognitive processes such as the attention, memory, learning capacity, problem resolution and affections and emotions associated. Thanks to the advances of neuroscience in this study the authors analyse the relationship and integration of the emotion and cognition as neural processes which cause a determined pleasure conduct or behaviour (Carretié, 2011; Pessoa, 2013).

The specific emotions derived from the different design elements of the game should be analysed for the purpose of obtaining a positive gamified experience. The design elements of the game can, individually or in combination, evoke specific emotions to the user, and these emotions can be harnessed to promote the expected results of the gamified experience. Just few investigations exist currently focused on the analysis of emotional results of the gamified experience, since memorable experiences are not always achieved due to a wrong game design (Burke, 2014; Mullins & Sabherwal, 2018). Getting to know the desirable emotions to evoke to the user must be the starting point of the game mechanics proposal (configuration, rules, progression system) to get the adequate dynamics for the gamified experience (Mullins & Sabherwal, 2020).

With the rise of the application of neuroscientific techniques in the PDP, the possibilities of supporting gamification through neuroscientific techniques and tools are analysed (Przegalinska, 2015). In that field of study, neurophysiological techniques, such as electroencephalography (EEG), eye tracking, functional magnetic resonance imaging (fMRI) etc., can be included in order to collect data for the explanation of complex emotional procedures and decision making involved in the stakeholders actions during the process or "game", acting as support for the neuro feedback and enabling the neuro gamification in closed-loop (Soler-Dominguez & Gonzalez, 2021).

Gamification is a user-centred technique, so controlling the psychological component is crucial when designing a good strategy. In 1975, the psychologist Mihaly Csikszentmihalyi (1997) proposed the Flow Theory, whereby a person's mental state is totally immersed and absorbed by the activity they are performing. The flow state is reached when there is a perfect balance between the complexity of the task to be performed and the skills. The user's senses and energy are totally focused on the successful performance of the task. Once this level of immersion is reached, the subconscious is able to perform activities with muscle memory and movement in parallel with other activities related to creativity and strategy to accomplish the task. This flow state makes the experience of performing the task rewarding and invites the user to repeat it. Csikszentmihalyi (1991) defined eight flow dimensions to obtain optimal flow: clear goals and immediate feedback, equilibrium between the level of challenge and personal skill, sense of potential control, focused concentration, merging of action and awareness, loss of self-consciousness and self-rewarding experience.

Product Life Cycle and its Gamification in a Cyber-Physical System

Proposals have been made to incorporate gamification into the field of industrial product design and development, beyond products based on interfaces and applications (Kavaliova et al., 2016; Leclercq et al., 2017). On the other hand, the incorporation and use of Design Thinking (DT) techniques can help to generate the gamified experience through methodologies and tools that improve Project-Based Learning (PBL) and creative processes in the generated playful environment, such as agile methodologies (Hermanto et al., 2018; Leitão, 2019).

In order to support both the types of experiences generated and the methodologies and tools, it is proposed to use the resources proposed by the Industry 4.0 paradigm (Almeida & Simoes, 2019; Reis, Silva, et al., 2020). The digital transformation of companies and the digitization of industrial products makes it possible to generate a CPS to configure the constituent elements of the company and the product. These CPS are made up of the real elements in the work or operational context and their virtual digital twin in the cloud. The development of these systems is achieved through KETs or digital enablers and facilitators among which are: Big Data, Cloud Computing, Collaborative Robotics, machine learning, Deep learning, affective interfaces, CPS, visualization and dematerialization, ubiquitous connectivity, additive manufacturing, mass sensing, virtual assistants and avatars, co-design, prosumers, design and manufacturing in the cloud, etc. (Reis, Júnior, et al., 2020; Tsourma et al., 2019).

Previous research can be projected and inserted in the context of the digital transformation and is determined by the technological development that has led to the Industry 4.0. This new industry concept offers a major transformation to the classical concept of PLC, determining the digital transformation of the company's value chain (Forstner & Dümmler, 2014). Alongside the incorporation of technological KETs, companies are striving for the development of disruptive innovations incorporating edge knowledge, such as neuro design. These new organizational models can support the complexity that comes from digitalization and CPS through fractal (Sahnoun et al., 2019) and holonic (Pazzi & Pellicciari, 2017) organizational models. This incorporation of knowledge and emerging digital technologies enhances and supports the gamification approach, aligning it with the Sustainable Development Goals (SDGs) contained in the UN 2030 agenda and other ecological and energy transition strategies (Stock et al., 2018).

Consequently, of the digital transformation, the potential of KETs, the incorporation of emerging knowledge and the SDGs strategy of the 2030 agenda, the need arises to provide the LCE of products, product lines and product portfolio with all the potential for innovation and sustainability that comes from them, incorporating gamification as the axis of innovation that allows a memorable experience design for all stakeholders involved in the PLC. The following aspects are considered in the proposal formulated in sustainable environments: smart connected product as CPS, the Holonic conceptualization of the LCE and the incorporation of emerging knowledge for continuous innovation by co-design and prosumers that determine memorable experiences through gamification.

FRAMEWORK FOR STAKEHOLDERS GAMIFICATION

The gamification applied to the LCE through game elements, allow obtaining information from the stakeholders to generate experiences of motivation, satisfaction, engagement, similar to those offered by games in playful contexts for all types of players. In this framework it is proposed to apply the industrial design methodology called Kansei Engineering (KE) for the development of the gamification proposal (Nagamachi, 2011). Assisted numerical and artificial intelligence techniques such as artificial neural networks, deep learning and machine learning, and the full potential of digital enablers can be incorporated into the KE (Quan et al., 2018). In addition to allowing the use of biometric and neuroscientific techniques (Saeed & Nagashima, 2012)

The basic objectives of KES are to know and understand the emotional needs of users (called kanseis) and to know the design elements of the product that can satisfy those needs. The main objective is to link the needs of the users with the properties of the product through quantitative techniques to translate the emotions of the users into products with value for the user and the organization (Schütte et al., 2004).

Figure 2. Kansei Engineering System (KES) adapted for stakeholder gamification

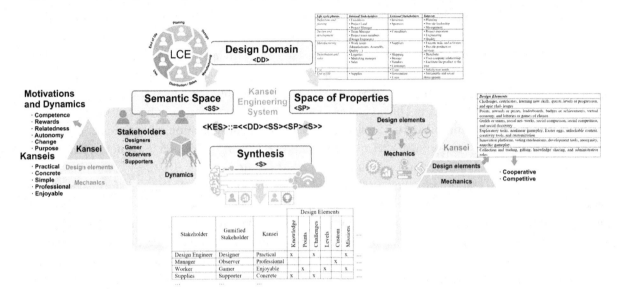

Creating a KES helps organizations to have a user-centered design orientation. The application of the KE is divided into four phases: choice domain, semantic space, space of properties and synthesis space (Figure 2).

- **Design Domain (DD)**: the project is defined from the business model, process, activity to the usability of the product. In this phase, the stakeholders involved in the PLC are identified.
- **Semantic Space (SS)**: the kanseis that the product embodies are established. In this case, the semantic space must include the stakeholder's gamified experience.
- **Space of property (SP)**: product design solutions, activity etc with different levels of solution are configured
- **Synthesis (S)**: using statistical techniques (PLS, ANOVA, Rough set.), soft computing techniques, machine learning, the property space is configured to evoke the kanseis defined in the semantic space

The KE provides a systematic methodological framework used in many successful contexts, especially in industrial product design. The advantage of applying KE in this context is that physiological measurements, unlike the case of cognitive measurements, can be recorded in real time. KE can extract data in real time and process it by supporting quantitative analysis techniques in the synthesis phase. The downside of applying KE in this context is that the methods described above can be intrusive and uncomfortable to extract stakeholder information (Bouchard & Kim, 2014). In addition to this, these information capture such as wearables and sensors based on EEG, eye tracking, etc. are expensive and can be influenced by environmental variables. In this case, it will also be necessary to have experts in this type of techniques and in the interpretation of the data.

In this framework, the application of a KES is proposed in a different application context, so the phases or spaces must be redefined. Table 3 shows the definition of the spaces of a KES in its traditional

Table 3. Original definition of KE spaces and proposed redefinition for its application for stakeholder gamification

KES phases	Product Design	Stakeholders gamification
Design Domain (DD)	• Selection of a target group • Selection market-niche • Specification of the new product	• Select stage of the LCE • Select stakeholders • Activity specifications
Semantic space (SS)	• Define Kanseis • Kansei measurement • Kanseis selection	• Classify the gamified stakeholders • Define the rol in gamified experience
Space of properties (SP)	• Identification of product properties • Determination of importance • Select a product that represents the selected properties	• Identify design elements • Select game mechanics • Establish gamified environments that represent the elements and mechanics of the game
Synthesis (S)	• Link the semantic space and the space of properties • Numerical and statistical treatments	• Link the gamified stakeholders with design elements and mechanics • Numerical and statistical treatments

application, product design and development, and the redefinition proposal for this framework, gamifying experiences for stakeholders.

The classification of gamified stakeholder types is proposed based on two dimensions. This dimension describes how important it is for the stakeholder to have a gamified experience. The importance dimension is a classic dimension for stakeholder classification and is derived from the classification strategies proposed by Project Management Institute (2017). In addition, the dimension of the level of participation in the experience is considered. This dimension is used to classify types of experiences, it is normally divided into active and passive; in this framework, it has been considered to use the levels of high and low, whether it is passive or active (Pine & Gilmore, 1999). With this proposal, the classic stakeholder classification and the classic experience classification are linked, to give rise to a classification of four types of gamified stakeholders as depicted in the Table 4: gamers, designers, supporters and observers. In future works, it is proposed to incorporate a third dimension that measures the level of previous experience of stakeholders as proposed by Cobaleda & Aguayo (2011) in their experiential design model.

In order to establish the proposed stakeholder classification, one of the problems was to define the term assigned to one of the types, gamer or player. In MDE framework proposed by Robson et al., (2015) and in Hexad model proposed by Marczewski (2015) use the term player, but in the context of

Table 4. Proposal for the classification of gamified stakeholder types

Importance of experience in LCE	High	**Designers** analyse stakeholders and select design elements and mechanics. They create and develop the gamified experience	**Gamer** is the stakeholder who participates in the experience. He explores the possibilities of experience through dynamics and wants to achieve the goal. They play a competitive role
	Low	**Observers** participate passively. They check that the mechanics and objectives are correct and the performance of the stakeholders. They can influence designers	**Supporter** participate in the experience and analyse its possibilities to help maintain the state of flow. They play a cooperative role with the gamer
		Low	*High*
		Participation in the experience in LCE	

videogames, the use of the term gamer is very frequent. The difference between terms is not clear, it is possible to say that a gamer is the person who plays games or participates in role-playing games, the term player being more generic as it can be used in sports and music. In the context of video or interactive games, the following distinction is proposed: the gamer is the person who participates in the playable experience and the player is the representation of the person in the game, a similar concept of avatar and the role it performs in the game experience. Therefore, in this framework, the term gamer will be used to refer to stakeholders who have a high participation and a high importance and interest in enjoying a gamified experience. In this case, the stakeholder is the gamer and the gamer's behavior as a player defines the game dynamics. The most important experience is that of the gamer, as they are the ones who really participate and enjoy the most complete gamified experience. Among this type, a second level classification proposal could be made on the basis of the Hexal model if it were necessary to specify or adjust the experience. (Tondello et al., 2016).

The designers have an active participation since they are mainly the agents who must make decisions in the project and participate in the design and development of the mechanics of the experience of all the stakeholders. Once the experience has been designed, their level of participation is passive, limited to managing and maintaining the experience, and they are responsible for analyzing that the stakeholders comply with the objectives of the gamified experience, being able to intervene in the experience to adapt it to the dynamics. The stakeholders classified as designers follow the proposal of the MDE framework. In the same way, the stakeholder observers of the MDE framework are incorporated to establish those stakeholders with a low and/or passive level of participation in the experience.

Finally, a type of gamified stakeholder called supporters is proposed to describe those stakeholders who participate in the gamified experience as part of the system, but do not play a competitive role based on individual objectives. Mainly they adopt a cooperative role with the rest of the stakeholder in an active way and keeping the state of flow, their experience is by evocation. In the same type of stakeholder there may be different types of gamified stakeholders; for example, the project team members, stakeholders of great importance in the LCE stage of product design and development. Within this project team, there may be different types of roles based on the desired gamified experience, for example the team manager may play the role of game designer, the design engineer may play the role of gamer, the marketer may play the role of supporters and the project manager may play the role of observers.

Obtain the kanseis of gamified stakeholderscan be carried out using psychological techniques such as surveys and biometric techniques with a neuroscientific approach such as EEG. Diamond et al. (2015) proposes the use of dichotomous response questionnaires to analyze the type of role in gamification like semantic differential. KE supports such techniques to analyze the stakeholder and apply classification analysis techniques such as cluster analysis. Dolatabadi & Budinskai (2020) propose the use of clustering algorithms to classify stakeholders, which is the most widespread technique. In order to establish the KE space of properties, a base of available game design elements as defined in Table 2 must be generated. The objective of this phase is to use the design elements to make proposals for mechanics that generate the gamified experience. Design elements establish mechanics, rules, and progression system. In this framework, the definition of the design elements and mechanics will not be detailed as they do not require adaptation to the application context. There are publications describing game design elements and mechanics which are valid for application in a gamified stakeholder experience in the LCE (Schell, 2008; Sicart, 2008; Tondello et al., 2016).

The synthesis space relates the motivational aspects and types of stakholdelders to the design elements and their mechanics. The game elements suitable in each stage include the game mechanics through the

Figure 3. Holonic architecture for product lifecycle engineering gamification platforms

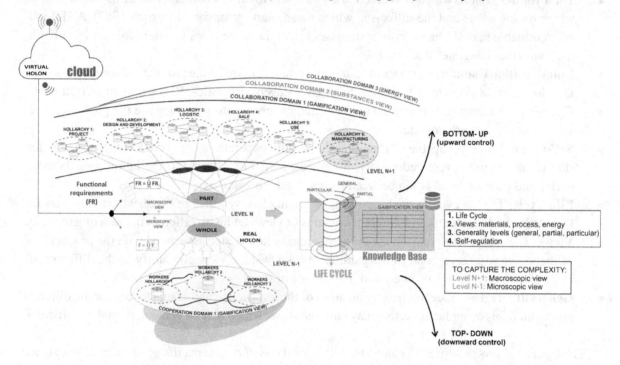

definition of goals, rewards, competitive game elements, progress analysis systems, definition of states, development of levels and scenarios, elections, comments, etc. The choice and design of game elements is key to designing game mechanics to generate an attractive gamified experience that motivates and engages stakeholders. In this phase, the relationship of the game elements and the stakeholder. In this phase, the full potential of statistical analysis and neural networks and machine learning can be incorporated to generate correlation models based on the data obtained.

HOLONIC ARCHITECTURE FOR LCE GAMIFICATION PLATFORMS

The main objective of the research was the stakeholder gamification proposal based on Kansei Engineering which has been developed previously. This section presents a proposal for an integrative model based on the Holonic paradigm. This proposal is part of a work in progress of which an advance is shown in this study.

PLE as an Intelligent CPS can be conceptualized from the Holonic paradigm, as the set of activities, processes and tasks that are deployed in the lifecycle. This is included in the product model as a CPS in the subsystem called life cycle, which is represented both in the physical product and in the virtual product in the cloud.

As shown in the Figure 3, the following elements can be distinguished in the product as a holon for the purposes of projecting them in the design of a platform for gamification, based in Ávila et al. model (Ávila Gutiérrez et al., 2020) .

This architecture is made up of the following components (Ávila Gutiérrez et al., 2020):

- The **Product Holon**: which is Whole/Part. The term Holon is a combination of the word Holos-, which means whole and the suffix -on, which means particle or part (Koestler, 1967). A Holon is an identifiable part of one or more systems and is, at the same time, a system formed by subordinate parts that integrates it as a whole.
- **Collaboration Domain**: These are the different scenarios in which the product collaborates: Design, Development, Manufacture, Logistics, Sale, Use, Reverse Logistics, Reverse Manufacturing, etc.
- **Cooperation Domain**: It is formed by the different subsystems that integrate the product. Power subsystem, user interfaces, etc.
- **Self-regulation**: it is capable of changing the way it cooperates to perform a function by conferring resilience to the required variety. It can be internal or external to the holon. Regulation is performed on the central holon between the part and the whole.
- **Life Cycle**: The life cycle is made up of the different phases of the life cycle, which integrates the knowledge and competence of different domains or views and with different degrees of generality.
- **Views**: The view corresponds to the different areas of knowledge associated with the product, one of the views will correspond to the gamification knowledge view, to gamify in the different life cycle phases and the agents interested in each one of them.
- **Generality degree**: refers to the specification of the knowledge and competences for the different product models or applications that may have the same, which may be general, partial or particular.

The figure 4 shows the different elements, which for the system the specific product has an existence as a real product, the physical product, and a digital twin or virtual product. It is in this virtual existence where it finds the artificial intelligence techniques and tools for data processing such as Big Data, Machine learning, deep Learning, Databases, which will allow us to support the gamification platform dynamically. Through connectivity with the physical model, gamification is enabled for the different agents associated with the tasks or activities of the life cycle.

Based on the conceptualization of the Smart Connected Product and its LCE as a holon, a platform for the development of gamification of the tasks performed by the different stakeholders in the PLC is formulated.

These include a generic product such as a CPS, the physical product and its digital twin, and in a special way:

a)   The collaboration domains that allow us to identify the different activities, processes and tasks as well as the executing agents, stakeholders, that would be involved in the gamification processes.

b)   The view of the gamification knowledge in the physical holon, which corresponds to the subrogated cloud gamification model to implement gamification in the different collaboration domains and users or workers, depending on the lifecycle phase.

c)   The knowledge of gamification under KE that will be carried out in the cloud with the data sensorized in edge or field of the different domains of collaboration and sent to cloud, which stored in databases and processed with big data, and techniques of Machine Learning and Deep Learning allows obtaining satisfaction measures through metrics of efficiency of gamification, as well as the establishment of gamification under kansei more accepted by workers or customised.

Figure 4 shows an example in the manufacturing stage of the LCE, where the gamified stakeholder types are established, an experience can be generated through the connected workstations and tools.

Figure 4. Example of a KE application for gamification the manufacturing stage of the LCE and its projection as holon

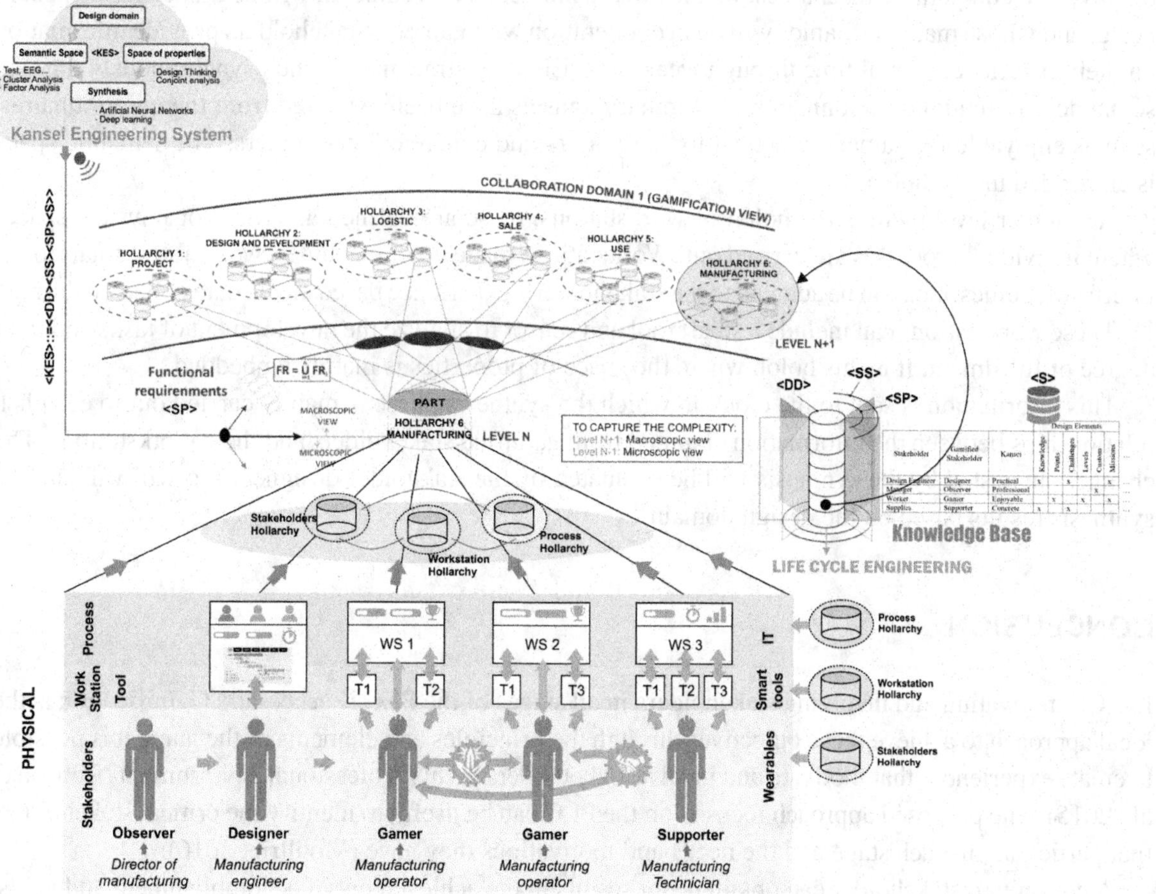

With wearables and sensors can be established the psychophysiological measures of the stakeholders as well as measures of the environment and tools. For example, the data of the connected tool such as the position of use, the force, the temperature, etc., together with the performance of the task, can generate performance metrics of the experience, which are transferred to the cloud to generate a virtual manufacturing environment. Based on these metrics, support can be given to help the gamer to improve their work experience. On the other hand, the designer can analyze and control to adjust the parameters of the gamer's experience to achieve the proposed challenge.

Explained how to proceed to establish the design domain, intends to present a preliminary conceptual example of early development on one of the holons, specifically the manufacturing holon. The development of the holonic framework will be presented in future works, in this case as an advance it is exemplified in the manufacturing phase of the LCE.

Manufacturing cooperation domain holon is made up of three main holarchies: stakeholders, workstations and process. The result of this collaboration will be the product object of manufacture.

First, it is proposed to identify four stakeholders and their gamified experience to form the manufacturing holon. Based on the classification proposed in Table 4, it is proposed that the Director of manufacturing have a gamified experience based on the role of observer. On the other hand, the manufacturing engineer will have a designer experience. The manufacturing operators will be the gamers who will mainly have competitive mechanics. Finally, the manufacturing technician will be associated with supporter and whose main mechanics will be in cooperation with gamers. Stakeholders provide information on their experience in real time through wearables (EEG, eye tracking…) and asynchronously through semantic differential questionnaires. Preliminary kanseis have been extracted from the questionnaires, such as enjoyable for gamers, practical for supporters and concrete for designers. The semantic space is embedded in this holon.

At another level there is the holon of workstations, these are defined as virtual or physical spaces where individual processes are carried out. Workstations made up of machines, worktables, smart tools, interfaces, guides, etc., can be adapted to the stakeholder's experience based on the data collected through IT. These workstations can include a smart tool and sensor to analyze the development of tasks and their degree of fulfilment. It is this holon where the space of properties is mainly embedded.

This information is sent to the cloud in which the synthesis phase is mainly carried out to establish relationships between the information obtained from gamified stakeholders and their Workstations. The changes suggested by the synthesis will be evaluated by the stakholder designer who will validate the synthesis results based on the design domain.

CONCLUSION

In LCE motivating and involving stakeholders in all stages of the PLC is necessary. Gamification is the ideal approach to achieve these objectives through the principles and elements of the game it is possible to create experiences that motivate and involve stakeholders in this professional environment (Robson et al., 2015). The proposed approach focused on the PLC can be useful to identify the critical stakeholders that participate in each stage and the needs and motivations they have (Moultrie, 2016).

A committed stakeholder can obtain better results in the achievement of accomplishment and goals, obtaining a cognitive and emotional connection with the effort made.

The introduction of gamification in the phases of the PLC presents an opportunity to increase motivation and engagement, develop skills or drive innovation from stakeholders. By establishing feedback loops, gamified experiences are generated for stakeholders that provide valuable engineering requirements for the PDP (Dalpiaz et al., 2017).

The holonic architecture for the gamification of LCE in sustainable environments under the potential of the digital enablers of Industry 4.0 based on the KE, allows for future developments and applications to be developed to test and verify the potential and impact on agents.

REFERENCES

Aaltonen, K., & Kujala, J. (2010). A project lifecycle perspective on stakeholder influence strategies in global projects. *Scandinavian Journal of Management*, 26(4), 381–397. doi:10.1016/j.scaman.2010.09.001

Almeida, F., & Simoes, J. (2019). The role of serious games, gamification and industry 4.0 tools in the education 4.0 paradigm. *Contemporary Educational Technology*, 10(2), 120–136. doi:10.30935/cet.554469

Ávila Gutiérrez, M. J., Martín Gómez, A., Aguayo González, F., & Lama Ruiz, J. R. (2020). Eco-Holonic 4.0 Circular Business Model to Conceptualize Sustainable Value Chain towards Digital Transition. *Sustainability, 12*(5), 1889. doi:10.3390u12051889

Burke, B. (2014). Gamify: How Gamification Motivates People to Do Extraordinary Things. Routledge.

Carretié, L. (2011). *Anatomía de la mente: Emoción, cognición y cerebro*. Ediciones.

Charness, N., & Boot, W. R. (2015). Technology, Gaming, and Social Networking. In *Handbook of the Psychology of Aging* (8th ed.). Elsevier Inc. doi:10.1016/B978-0-12-411469-2.00020-0

Christians, G. (2018). The Origins and Future of Gamification. *Senior Theses*. https://scholarcommons. sc.edu/senior_theses

Cobaleda, A., & Aguayo, F. (2011). *Mobiliario de recepción para un hotel boutique bajo diseño. experiencial* [Reception Furniture for a boutique hotel under Design Experiential]. Universidad de Sevilla. Escuela Politécnica Superior. https://fama.us.es/permalink/34CBUA_US/3enc2g/alma991009358809704987

Csikszentmihalyi, M. (1991). Flow: The Psychology of Optimal Experience. *Academy of Management Review, 16*(3), 636–640. doi:10.2307/258925

Csikszentmihalyi, M. (1997). Finding flow: the psychology of engagement with everyday life. *Choice Reviews Online, 35*(3). doi:10.5860/CHOICE.35-1828

Dalpiaz, F., Snijders, R., Brinkkemper, S., Hosseini, M., Shahri, A., & Ali, R. (2017). Engaging the Crowd of Stakeholders in Requirements Engineering via Gamification. In Gamification: Using Game Elements in Serious Contexts (pp. 123–135). Springer International Publishing. doi:10.1007/978-3-319-45557-0_9

Deterding, S., Dixon, D., Khaled, R., & Nacke, L. (2011). From game design elements to gamefulness: Defining "gamification." *Proceedings of the 15th International Academic MindTrek Conference: Envisioning Future Media Environments, MindTrek 2011*, 9–15. 10.1145/2181037.2181040

Diamond, L., Tondello, G., Marczewski, A., Nacke, L., & Tscheligi, M. (2015). The HEXAD Gamification User Types Questionnaire : Background and Development Process. *Workshop on Personalization in Serious and Persuasive Games and Gamified Interactions*.

Dicheva, D., Dichev, C., Agre, G., & Angelova, G. (2015). Gamification in education: A systematic mapping study. *Journal of Educational Technology & Society, 18*(3), 75–88.

Dolatabadi, S. H., & Budinskai, I. (2020). A New Method Based on Gamification Algorithm to Engage Stakeholders in Competitive Markets. *INES 2020 - IEEE 24th International Conference on Intelligent Engineering Systems, Proceedings*, 11–17. 10.1109/INES49302.2020.9147196

Entertainment Software Association. (2017). *Comments on the Global Digital Trade Study. Report #1*. Entertainment Software Association.

Entertainment Software Association. (2020). *2020 Essential Facts About the Video Game Industry*. Entertainment Software Association (ESA). https://www.prnewswire.com/news-releases/new-survey-2020-essential-facts-about-the-video-game-industry-301093972.html

Erenli, K. (2013). The impact of gamification: Recommending education scenarios. *International Journal of Emerging Technologies in Learning, 8,* 15–21. doi:10.3991/ijet.v8iS1.2320

Forstner, L., & Dümmler, M. (2014). Integrated value chains—Opportunities and potentials through Industry 4.0. *Elektrotechnik Und Informationstechnik, 131*(7), 199–201. doi:10.100700502-014-0224-y

Freeman, R. E. E., & McVea, J. (2005). A Stakeholder Approach to Strategic Management. SSRN *Electronic Journal.* doi:10.2139/ssrn.263511

Granic, I., Lobel, A., & Engels, R. C. M. E. (2013). *The Benefits of Playing Video Games.* doi:10.1037/a0034857

Hermanto, S., Kaburuan, E. R., & Legowo, N. (2018). Gamified SCRUM Design in Software Development Projects. *2018 International Conference on Orange Technologies, ICOT 2018.* 10.1109/ICOT.2018.8705897

Hitch, J. (2018, June 7). Gaming the Factory: Can Data Make Manufacturing Fun Again? *IndustryWeek.* https://www.industryweek.com/technology-and-iiot/article/22025774/gaming-the-factory-can-data-make-manufacturing-fun-again

Hoos, S. (2016). *Gamification in UX Design-one way to do it.* doi:10.18420/muc2016-up-0021

Kapp, K. (2012). The Gamification of Learning and Instruction: Game–based Methods and Strategies for Training and Education. John Wiley & Sons Inc.

Kavaliova, M., Virjee, F., Maehle, N., & Kleppe, I. A. (2016). Crowdsourcing innovation and product development: Gamification as a motivational driver. *Cogent Business and Management, 3*(1), 1128132. Advance online publication. doi:10.1080/23311975.2015.1128132

Kochan, T. A., & Rubinstein, S. A. (2000). Toward a Stakeholder Theory of the Firm: The Saturn Partnership. *Organization Science, 11*(4), 367–386. doi:10.1287/orsc.11.4.367.14601

Koestler, A. (1967). *The ghost in the machine.* Hutchinson.

L'Heureux, A., Grolinger, K., Higashino, W. A., & Capretz, M. A. M. (2017). A gamification framework for sensor data analytics. *Proceedings - 2017 IEEE 2nd International Congress on Internet of Things, ICIOT 2017,* 74–81. 10.1109/IEEE.ICIOT.2017.18

Leblanc, M. (2004). Game design and tuning workshop materials. *Game Developers Conference.*

Leclercq, T., Poncin, I., & Hammedi, W. (2017). The Engagement Process During Value Co-Creation: Gamification in New Product-Development Platforms. *International Journal of Electronic Commerce, 21*(4), 454–488. doi:10.1080/10864415.2016.1355638

Lee, J. P., & Fonseca, N. (2021). Video Gaming & Esports Taking Media and Entertainment to the Next Level An in-depth look at the investment case for video gaming and esports. Van Eck Associates Corporation.

Leitão, J. (2019). Concepts, methodologies and tools of gamification and design thinking. *Contributions to Management Science,* 85–127. doi:10.1007/978-3-319-91282-0_3

Marcão, R. P., Pestana, G., & Sousa, M. J. (2017). Gamification in project management. *Conference: 2nd International Conference On Economic and Business Management (FEBM 2017).* 10.2991/febm-17.2017.115

Marczewski, A. (2015a). Even Ninja Monkeys Like to Play: Gamification, Game Thinking and Motivational Design. In User Type Heaxd. CreateSpace Independent Publishing.

Marczewski, A. (2015b). Gamification mechanics and elements. In Even Ninja Monkeys Like to Play: Gamification, Game Thinking & Motivational Design (pp. 165–177). CreateSpace Independent Publishing Platform.

Mitchell, R., Schuster, L., & Drennan, J. (2016). Understanding how gamification influences behaviour in social marketing. *Australasian Marketing Journal.* Advance online publication. doi:10.1016/j.ausmj.2016.12.001

Moultrie, J. (2016). *Stakeholder analysis - lifecycle approach.* University of Cambridge. Management technology Policy. https://www.ifm.eng.cam.ac.uk/research/dmg/tools-and-techniques/stakeholder-analysis-lifecycle-approach/

Mullins, J. K., & Sabherwal, R. (2018). Beyond Enjoyment: A Cognitive-Emotional Perspective of Gamification. *Proceedings of the 51st Hawaii International Conference on System Sciences,* 1237–1246. 10.24251/HICSS.2018.152

Mullins, J. K., & Sabherwal, R. (2020). Gamification: A cognitive-emotional view. *Journal of Business Research, 106*(October), 304–314. doi:10.1016/j.jbusres.2018.09.023

Nagamachi, M. (2011). *Kansei / Affective Engineering.* CRC Press.

Nobre, H., & Ferreira, A. (2017). Gamification as a platform for brand co-creation experiences. *Journal of Brand Management, 24*(4), 349–361. doi:10.105741262-017-0055-3

Pazzi, L., & Pellicciari, M. (2017). From the Internet of Things to Cyber-Physical Systems: The Holonic Perspective. *Procedia Manufacturing, 11,* 989–995. doi:10.1016/j.promfg.2017.07.204

Pessoa, L. (2013). *The Cognitive-Emotional Brain. from Interactions to Integration.* MIT Press. doi:10.7551/mitpress/9780262019569.001.0001

Pine, J., & Gilmore, J. (1999). The Experience Economy. Harvard Business School Press.

Project Management Institute. (2017). *A guide to the Project Management Body of Knowledge (PMBOK guide)* (6th ed.). Project Management Institute.

Przegalinska, A. (2015). Gamification: Playing with Neuroscience. In Gamification Crital Approaches (pp. 40–55). University of Warsaw, Faculty of Artes Liberales.

Quan, H., Li, S., & Hu, J. (2018). Product innovation design based on deep learning and Kansei engineering. *Applied Sciences (Switzerland), 8*(12), 1–17. doi:10.3390/app8122397

Reis, A. C. B., Júnior, E. S., Gewehr, B. B., & Torres, M. H. (2020). Prospects for using gamification in industry 4.0. *Production, 30.* Advance online publication. doi:10.1590/0103-6513.20190094

Robson, K., Plangger, K., Kietzmann, J. H., McCarthy, I., & Pitt, L. (2015). Is it all a game? Understanding the principles of gamification. *Business Horizons*, *58*(4), 411–420. doi:10.1016/j.bushor.2015.03.006

Robson, K., Plangger, K., Kietzmann, J., McCarthy, I., & Pitt, L. (2014). Understanding the Gamification of Consumer Experiences. In A. Press (Ed.), Association for Consumer Research ACR North American Advances (Vol. 42, pp. 352–357). Academic Press.

Rozman, T., Maribor, S. S., Fistis, G., Luminosu, C., & Zwolinski, P. (2015). *Leadership in sustainability - Support your business towards sustainability - For educational purposes only. LeadSUS Project Group.* doi:10.13140/RG.2.2.20342.40001/1

Saeed, K., & Nagashima, T. (2012). *Biometrics and Kansei Engineering.* Springer-Verlag. doi:10.1007/978-1-4614-5608-7

Sahnoun, M., Xu, Y., Belgacem, B., Imen, B., David, B., & Louis, A. (2019). Fractal modeling of Cyber physical production system using multi-agent systems. *Proceedings - 2019 3rd International Conference on Applied Automation and Industrial Diagnostics, ICAAID 2019.* 10.1109/ICAAID.2019.8934976

Sarkum, S. (2018). *A Strategy Engagement in Marketing: A Reviews of the Literature.* 10.31227/ doi:osf. io/kw9uz

Schell, J. (2008). *The Art of Game Design: A book of lenses.* CRC Press. https://www.amazon.es/Art-Game-Design-book-lenses/dp/0123694965

Schütte, S., Eklund, J., Axelsson, J., & Nagamachi, M. (2004). Concepts, methods and tools in Kansei Engineering. *Theoretical Issues in Ergonomics Science*, *5*(3), 214–231. doi:10.1080/1463922021000049980

Sicart, M. (2008). Defining Game Mechanics. *The International Journal of Computer Game Research*, *8*(2).

Smith, L. W. (2000). Stakeholder analysis: a pivotal practice of successful projects. *Project Management Institute Annual Seminars & Symposium.* https://www.pmi.org/learning/library/stakeholder-analysis-pivotal-practice-projects-8905

Soler-Dominguez, J. L., & Gonzalez, C. (2021). Using EEG and Gamified Neurofeedback Environments to Improve eSports Performance: Project Neuroprotrainer. *Proceedings of the 16th International Joint Conference on Computer Vision, Imaging and Computer Graphics Theory and Applications (VISIGRAPP 2021).* 10.5220/0010314502780283

Stock, T., Obenaus, M., Kunz, S., & Kohl, H. (2018). Industry 4.0 as Enabler for a Sustainable Development: A Qualitative Assessment of its Ecological and Social Potential. *Process Safety and Environmental Protection*, *118*, 254–267. doi:10.1016/j.psep.2018.06.026

Sweetman, B. (2018, March 16). Increasing Engagement Using Product Gamification. *Headway.Io.* https://www.headway.io/blog/gamification-is-more-than-achievements

Syrjälä, H., Kauppinen-Räisänen, H., Luomala, H. T., Joelsson, T. N., Könnölä, K., & Mäkilä, T. (2020). Gamified package: Consumer insights into multidimensional brand engagement. *Journal of Business Research*, *119*(January), 423–434. doi:10.1016/j.jbusres.2019.11.089

Terzi, S., Bouras, A., Dutta, D., Garetti, M., & Kiritsis, D. (2010). Product lifecycle management - From its history to its new role. *International Journal of Product Lifecycle Management, 4*(4), 360–389. doi:10.1504/IJPLM.2010.036489

Tondello, G. F., Wehbe, R. R., Diamond, L., Busch, M., Marczewski, A., & Nacke, L. E. (2016). The gamification user types Hexad scale. *CHI PLAY 2016 - Proceedings of the 2016 Annual Symposium on Computer-Human Interaction in Play,* 229–243. 10.1145/2967934.2968082

Tsourma, M., Zikos, S., Albanis, G., Apostolakis, K. C., Lithoxoidou, E. E., Drosou, A., Zarpalas, D., Daras, P., & Tzovaras, D. (2019). Gamification concepts for leveraging knowledge sharing in Industry 4.0. *International Journal of Serious Games, 6*(2), 75–87. doi:10.17083/ijsg.v6i2.273

Wijman, T. (2020, June). *Three Billion Players by 2023: Engagement and Revenues Continue to Thrive Across the Global Games Market.* https://newzoo.com/insights/articles/games-market-engagement-revenues-trends-2020-2023-gaming-report/

Xu, Y., Poole, E. S., Miller, A. D., Eiriksdottir, E., Kestranek, D., Catrambone, R., & Mynatt, E. D. (2012). This is not a one-horse race: Understanding player types in multiplayer pervasive health games for youth. *Proceedings of the ACM Conference on Computer Supported Cooperative Work, CSCW, April 2015,* 843–852. 10.1145/2145204.2145330

ADDITIONAL READING

de Miranda, S. S. F., Córdoba Roldán, A., Aguayo González, F., & Ávila Gutiérrez, M. J. (2021). Neuro-competence approach for sustainable engineering. *Sustainability, 13*(8), 4389. Advance online publication. doi:10.3390u13084389

Martín Gómez, A., Ávila Gutiérrez, M. J., & Aguayo González, F. (2021). Holonic reengineering to foster sustainable cyber-physical systems design in cognitive manufacturing. *Applied Sciences (Basel, Switzerland), 11*(7), 2941. Advance online publication. doi:10.3390/app11072941

Nagamachi, M. (2018). History of Kansei engineering and application of artificial intelligence. *Advances in Intelligent Systems and Computing, 585,* 357–368. doi:10.1007/978-3-319-60495-4_38

KEY TERMS AND DEFINITIONS

Cyber-Physical System (CPS): Are networks of computer elements that work in conjunction to control a physical process. The structure of a CPS is composed of a real and a virtual part and aims to unite conventional technologies with ICT, so that humans, machines and products can communicate with each other, and the physical elements can be virtualized.

Experience: It is a form of knowledge or skill derived from observation, from the participation of an event.

Holon: The term Holon is a combination of the word Holos-, which means whole and the suffix -on, which means particle or part. A Holon is an identifiable part of one or more systems and is, at the same time, a system formed by subordinate parts that integrates it as a whole.

Kansei Engineering (KE): User-centered product design and development methodology. The methodology translates the user's psychological feelings and needs into the domain of product design using numerical and statistical methods.

Life Cycle Engineering (LCE): Is a sustainability-oriented engineering methodology that analyzes the ecological, economic, technical, and social impacts throughout the product life cycle.

Product Life Cycle (PLC): Are all the stages necessary to develop a product or system from its inception through engineering, design and manufacturing, as well as service and disposal of the product. The product design process (PDP) is contained in the first phase of the PLC.

Stakeholder: Refers to all those people or organizations affected by the activities and decisions of a company project.

Chapter 8
GaminScrum an Adaptive Gamification Approach Applied to Agile Processes

Maha Khemaja

https://orcid.org/0000-0002-6262-8528

ISSAT, University of Sousse, Tunisia

Syrine Khelifi

ISSAT, University of Sousse, Tunisia

ABSTRACT

This chapter tackles the difficulty of implementing agile methodologies in enterprises, especially for teams who are used to traditional working methods. Therefore, this work attempts to provide ways to engage better and motivate team members to embrace the use of agile methodologies. One such way has considered using gamification or serious games principles with agile/scrum activities. The main contribution of the present work is threefold. First, it provides a novel blended approach that combines agile principles with gamification mechanics and gameplay. Second, an adaptation approach is provided to adapt all gamification aspects such as gamification purpose and fun applied to agile/scrum activities to consider the enterprise's context, the specificities of the project, and those of the working teams. Finally, the proposed approaches have been instrumented through a mobile app. Experimentation of the approaches allowed the authors to draw interesting findings.

INTRODUCTION

Companies are increasingly facing rude competition and market positioning problems. The market is currently distinguished by increased dynamicity and rapid continuous change in consumer needs and requirements. To tackle this kind of problems, on the one hand companies must offer products and services which are reliable, robust, of high quality and which meet the needs of their customers without at the same time exceeding budget and deadlines. On the other hand, they are supposed to respond quickly to

DOI: 10.4018/978-1-6684-4291-3.ch008

this need through efficient development and management methods and processes. This is true for existing products or services as well as for development projects of new services and products. Particularly, to achieve their objectives, companies must develop their capacities to implement strategies and methods of planning and efficiently managing collaborative projects and teamwork.

Currently, two large families of project planning and management approaches do exist: classical approaches known as predictive (e.g., the Waterfall approach) and lean approaches as reported in Veretennikova and Vaskiv (2018) or agile approaches which are also called adaptive approaches (e.g., the Kanban approach (Lei et al., 2017)). This second family of approaches not only allows to plan and manage projects, but also to make teamwork the most effective.

The 14th study reported in ("14th-annual-state-of-agile-report", 2020) shows the value of adopting agile methodologies in projects' development. This study has shown the importance and the advantages of these methodologies over traditional ones as they allow to better manage changing priorities and risks and deliver quality products and products' releases on a regular basis and on time. These methods are also User-centric as they encourage end users' and clients' participation throughout all the project's development processes. This leads development teams to be more efficient and to more satisfy clients' needs. Finally, they allow flexible adaptation and agility to handle in time the changing and emerging needs of the client.

Several existing methods fall under the category of agile methods (Ozkan et al., 2020). Scrum is one example which additionally is considered as the most popular and used agile methodology with 58% of people adopting ("14th-annual-state-of-agile-report", 2020).

However, it seems that it is difficult to integrate and implement for many interrelated reasons. First, for many well and early established enterprises, teams working on project management are mainly used to traditional methods such as waterfall or Spiral. They therefore have difficulties to adopt and learn to use agile methods (Chan & Thong, 2009). Second, the resistance of those teams to change, the spread culture that is in contradiction with agile values, the lack of discipline and agile mindset, the lack of skills /experience with agile methods and finally the omnipresence of traditional development methods and their related tools do not favor implementation of agile ones. In situations where clients suggest instant reactivity and agility to changes, risks related to the non-adoption of agile methods and which result in neither delivering the product on time nor considering at the same time clients' needs change, becomes even more important. All these reasons require finding out different ways to better engage and motivate team members to embrace its use and hence learn and gain in agile skills such as problem solving, adaptability and reactivity to changes, capacity to negotiate and propose value added user stories and finally interpersonal, leadership and communication skills (Hidayati et al., 2020).

One such a way can be through serious games or gamification of Agile activities and principles (Stettina, et al., 2018) and (Ahmadi et al., 2016). Indeed, in the one hand, serious games are considered as a category of games that engage and motivate users and contribute to achieve prior defined objectives thanks to the game concept they introduce and their positive impact on people and teams (Susi et al., 2007), (Schuller et al., 2013), (Tanenbaum et al., 2013) and (Rumeser & Emsley, 2019).

On the other hand, Gamification uses game design theories and mechanics which define the main drivers that engage players, and which are based specifically on behavioral evidence (Caillois, 1967). These drivers are mainly classified by Caillois as Agon (Competition), Alea (Chance), Mimesis (Mimicry) and Ilinx (Vertigo or altered perception of the world with loss of control). Based on those drivers, game mechanics such as challenges, fun and rewards are used in Gamification to accurately and relevantly design and combine fun and serious aspects in order to enhance users' experiences in virtual as well as in real world contexts and help in solving problems and engaging audiences (Černezel & Heričko, 2013), (Asuncion et al., 2011), (Deterding et al., 2011), (Kappen & Nacke, 2013) and (Garett & Young, 2019).

Many attempts to use serious games in enterprises have been so far provided. Examples of such attempts are those realized within the GaLA project (Game and Learning Alliance, the European Network of Excellence on Serious games) and presented in (Riedel et al., 2013). These works assume that serious games may not only be used for training purposes but also for other kinds of projects such as those in the context of change management. According to the same works, Gamification constitutes the main approach for integrating serious games in enterprises. This concerns the use of game mechanics and gameplay to solve problems and engage all stakeholders. Typically, an enterprise system, process, project, or methodology define sets of activities that are designed and developed to target a specific purpose and specific actors. The Gamification approach applied to those activities should therefore consider the context of each actor and each activity. Very often, the Gamification approach and its purpose, rules, game mechanics and fun should be continuously adapted accordingly to that context, especially, when this latter is continuously changing (Korn et al., 2014; Dubois, 2012; Su, & Cheng, 2015; Khemaja & Buendia, 2017).

Considering Scrum as the most popular and used agile methodology, it is therefore chosen along the present work. The main contribution developed in this chapter is threefold. First, a novel blended methodology or approach is provided. This approach combines agile principles and specifically Scrum ones to Gamification mechanics and Gameplay. These are considered as motivating and engaging aspects that are added to Scrum activities, and which make it possible to encourage teams to better play their roles by helping them to positively change their behavior and modify their habits. Indeed, the main objectives of the adoption of Gamification is to influence the behavior of individuals and motivate them to change their habits while carrying Scrum driven projects (Caillois, 1967; Asuncion et al., 2011; Conill, 2016). At the same time this impacts their willingness to learn and acquire new skills such as relevant communication and negotiation as well as efficient teamwork.

Second, an approach is provided to adapt all Gamification aspects, that are applied to Scrum activities, such as Gamification purposes, behavior, rules, game mechanics and fun in order to consider the enterprise's context, the specificities of the project and those of the working teams.

Finally, the proposed approaches have been instrumented through a mobile app to answer to the lack of dedicated mobile Scrum tools that could be easily gamified and adapted. Moreover, this mobile app is considered as a main source of data related to teams working on real projects and which analysis can lead to draw better insights.

The methodology adopted in the present work is the Design Science Research Methodology (DSRM) (Wieringa, 2014). This methodology deals mainly with two kinds of activities which are respectively design and investigation of artifacts in context (Wieringa, 2014). Two intertwined kinds of contexts are considered: the social context and the knowledge context. In general, the DSRM when applied to a given domain, it iterates over solving design problems and answering knowledge questions.

A design goal addresses the problem of developing a new or improving an existing artifact to it better contributes to the achievement of stakeholders' goals or to solve their corresponding problems. An artifact can be an algorithm, a method, a software, a game, etc. It is the case, for example, of the design of a serious game to help students acquiring a new foreign language or employees acquiring a new working methodology. A knowledge goal addresses questions that should be answered through surveys, field experimentation, statistical data analysis, etc. A knowledge goal related to the previous example could be to answer to which extent the serious game has helped students respectively the employees to acquire the foreign language respectively the new working methodology?

Additionally, a knowledge goal may be refined into more detailed knowledge questions. These may be descriptive or explanatory, open, or closed and also about effect, trade-off, sensitivity and requirements satisfaction (Wieringa, 2014).

As a design science project iterates over designing and investigating activities, its design activity is itself decomposed into three tasks namely (1) Problem investigation which main aim is to know more about the problem, its knowledge context, the stakeholders' goals, etc, (2) Design of a solution or a proposal, and (3) Validation of the proposal.

The three tasks are called the design cycle which is considered as part of a more elaborated engineering cycle (Hevner, 2007) and (Wieringa, 2014). This latter includes amongst the tasks of the design cycle, other tasks that aim to implement and evaluate the proposal in a real context.

Generated results of a given iteration over a design science activity may be investigated and generalized among a set of similar projects, cases or designs. This generalization could be on its own a research problem that should be investigated and answered.

The rest of this chapter is an application of the DSRM design cycle. It is therefore organized into the following six sections besides the first section dedicated to the introduction:

The second section concerns the research problem investigation. It presents therefore the general background and related works about adoption and adaptation of Gamification for agile methodologies. The third section focuses on identification of requirements as well as their refinement and analysis. The fourth section presents the first and the third contributions, namely the application of Gamification approach for the Scrum methodology and its instrumentation through the mobile app.

In section five, the second contribution is presented. It deals with the adaptation approach and the main aspects that should be considered for adaptation.

In section six, the evaluation approaches are designed and carried on. Three dedicated evaluation approaches have been designed accordingly to each kind of contribution. These are mainly based on empirical data and their assessment by teams and end users. Finally, the section seven focuses on drawing conclusions about the proposal and highlighting its advantages by positioning and relating it to existing approaches. Future orientations of this work are also proposed in this section.

PROBLEM INVESTIGATION: BACKGROUND AND RELATED WORK ABOUT ADOPTION AND ADAPTATION OF GAMIFICATION FOR AGILE METHODOLOGIES

Problem Statement

As highlighted in the first section, the problem context of the present work concerns the miss use of Agile methodology processes within engineering projects. This is mainly due to the preference and familiarity of projects' engineers or development teams to work with classical methods, and their rigidity and nonmotivation to change habits and minds.

The design problem is therefore introduced as the following:

Improve and encourage the use of agile methodologies to reinforce development teams' efficiency as well as performance by designing a Gamification process that (1) considers the Gamification principles and (2) provides fun, challenging, motivating and engaging activities (3) creates the mechanics that allow teams communicate and collaborate better and (4) is flexible enough to be adapted accordingly to its context of use. This latter encompasses the kind and the domain of the project, the enterprises and teams' contexts as well as the specificities of the project. The ultimate goal of any kind of project's stakeholders is to enhance products' quality, avoid delays and reduce time to market.

More specifically the Gamification process considered in the present work should be instrumented and automated through a dedicated tool that could be used anytime and anywhere to allow end users to work independently from the location where they could be to follow up a given project. Moreover, The Gamification process and the way it is adapted could be applied to any kind of project including software engineering projects.

Scrum Conceptual Framework

An agile methodology is an iterative and incremental approach, which is carried out in a collaborative mindset (Gannod, et al., 2015). It generates a high-quality product while considering continuous changing customer needs (Messager Rota & Tabaka, 2009). Many existing methods fall under the category of agile methodologies. We can name for instance XP, Kanban, Cristal, ScrumBan, Agile UP and OpenUP (Anwer et al., 2017). Scrum is one example. Scrum constitutes a framework within which actors can address complex and adaptive problems, delivering efficiently and effectively creative products of the greatest possible added value (Sutherland & Schwaber, 2007; Sutherland & Schwaber, 2017).

The Scrum framework is made up of teams and their associated roles, events, artifacts, and rules (Schwaber & Sutherland, 2011). The different roles in a Scrum project are: the Product Owner (Lonchamp, 2015), the Scrum Master (Schwaber & Sutherland, 2011) and the development team member (Lonchamp, 2015).

Scrum Artifacts are organized around the product, to which one or several projects are defined each of which is organized in turn into sprints and tasks.

The main artifacts that are managed by the Framework are: the Product Backlog which is a list of items (user stories) that must be developed in decreasing priorities. Each item includes a definition, estimated effort and priority (Lonchamp, J., 2015). The other artifatcs are the sprint backlog (Sutherland, J., & Schwaber, K, 2017), the sprint burndown chart (Schwaber, K., & Sutherland, J., 2011) and the product burndown chart.

Scrum prescribes four formal events or ceremonies for inspection and adaptation which are the Sprint Planning, the Daily Scrum, the Sprint Review, and the Sprint Retrospectives (Marshburn, 2018; Lonchamp, 2015; Schwaber & Sutherland, 2011).

During the Sprint, no changes are made that would jeopardize the Sprint's Goal; the Quality goals do not decrease; and the Scope may be clarified and re-negotiated between the Product Owner and Development Team as well as the end user as more is learned.

Gamification Conceptual Framework

Several works have dealt with gamification either by defining it or by implementing it in non-ludic systems (Khemaja & Buendia, 2017). Among the definitions that have been given to Gamification and found in (Zichermann, & Cunningham, 2011) is the following: "Gamification is a process that uses game thinking and game dynamics to engage users and solve problems". In the present work the definition which is adopted is "The use of game design mechanics and techniques in a non-playful context, in order to solve real life problems, positively influence the behavior of individuals and finally engage and motivate them to do or achieve something". This definition highlights specifically, many interesting concepts that go hand in hand with the problem statement that have been defined previously especially aspects related to engaging people, influencing their behavior, and motivating them to do or achieve something such as adopting agile methodologies even though they were familiar with classical methods. In addition, the MDA (Mechanics, Dynamics, and Aesthetics) Framework defines, in this sense, three complementary facets of Gamification that the designer should consider (Hunicke et al., 2004). The "Mechanics facet" describes each element of the game with an emphasis on how it works, how it looks and what game logic it might be associated with.

Game elements and mechanics are a set of tools, which once used correctly in a gamified system, help to build user engagement and motivation. Indeed, these elements ensure the success of a system with its users be it digital or not (Juul, 2011).

As illustrated in the figure 1 that defines the Gamification Framework developed in (Khemaja & Buendia, 2017), rewards that should be compliant to a kind of rewarding system could be expressed as points, levels, badges, leaderboards, etc. These could be either virtual or not.

Figure 1. Gamification Framework including MDA facets

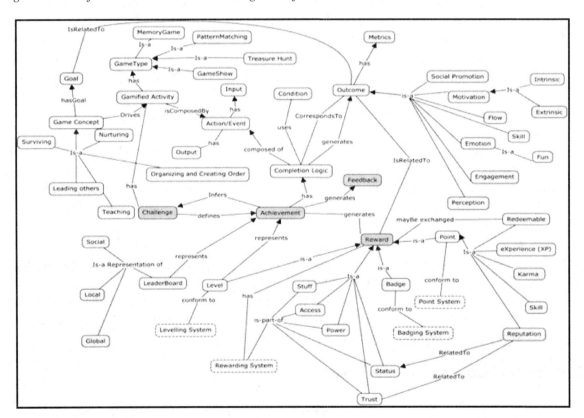

Points are considered one of the most popular items (Zichermann & Cunningham, 2011). There are different types of point systems such as Experience (XP), Redeemable, Skill, Karma and Reputation points. In most games, levels indicate to players their progress through the system. Experience points can also be used to indicate this progress.

Leaderboards designate the rank of a player among other players. Badges are simple virtual (or not) symbols that can be obtained after performing an action or completing a challenge. Challenges are missions or problems that a user must complete or solve to receive a reward (Zichermann & Cunningham, 2011). The engagement loop is made up of three main elements which are Motivation, Action and Feedback.

The "Dynamics facet" describes the possible interactions of users with the elements of the game (Hamari & Eranti, 2011).

Finally, the "Aesthetics facet" of the game makes it possible to define the results linked to the player's interactions with the mechanics of the game.

According to Bartle (2008), there exist many different types of personalities. In 1996, Richard Bartle established the Bartle's typology which has become one of the fundamental concepts of Gamification (Bartle, 1996). This typology classifies players into 4 categories which are: Achiever, Explorer, Socializer and Killer. Bartle has also associated percentages to each category of player in terms of their frequency within a given game.

Related Work

In this section, several research areas related to, gamification, application of Gamification to project management and Gamification adaptation are investigated. Therefore, works allowing to identify gamification characteristics, features, and concepts (Deterding, 2011; Challco et al., 2014, 2015) as well as those related to approaches, strategies, methodologies, and frameworks for defining gamification are considered (Darius & Robertas, 2014; Anton & Zsofia, 2008). Additionally, works having addressed adaptation to context either for Serious Games or Gamification are studied (Qamar et al., 2014; Alamri et al., 2013; Hardy et al, 2011; Edoh-Alove et al., 2013; Reichle et al., 2008). Works applied to project management approaches or for Scrum agile methodology are discussed. Finally, some agile tools are compared to check whether they presented motivating and engaging features or integrated gamification.

Works Related to Identification of Gamification Characteristics and Concepts

In Eliëns and Ruttkay (2008), authors have developed a framework for understanding Serious Gameplay. The approach exploited symbolic machinima by tracking and recording users' actions in virtual environments. Data collection and analysis aim to serve later for authoring alternative game scenarios.

In Deterding et al. (2011), authors have surveyed and situated current use of Gamification. Emerging definitions and related concepts have been identified such as gamefulness, playfulness, game thinking, game mechanics, playful design, etc. Comparison and characterization of those terms show that Gamification relates to games not to play and it always focuses on design elements for rule-bound, goal-oriented play (Deterding et al., 2011).

In Ašeriškis and Damaševičius (2014), authors attempted to extract and model gamification patterns from a set of known gamified systems. The work had also used the MDA (Mechanics, Dynamics and Aesthetics) framework.

Challco et al. (2014, 2015) provided an ontology that aims to gamify collaborative learning scenarios.

Works Related to Adoption of Gamification in Organizations and Project Management Activities

The following literature review considered in the present work is either related to systematic review about the use of Gamification in enterprise systems or in project management methodologies or related to the implementation of Gamification and its experimentation in real cases. Very few works have considered adaptation of Gamification or the use of full-fledged games in project management methodologies.

In Dubois and Tamburrelli (2013), authors proposed a methodology that seeks to choose the best gamification techniques to be applied at different stages of software development.

In Ašeriškis and Damaševičius (2014), authors analyzed, through a case study, the gamification of the Trogon Project Management System. The evaluation has focused on the System Usability Scale (SUS) to evaluate usability of gamification.

The research in Pedreira et al. (2015) consisted of a literature review for investigating the use of Gamification in software engineering. The focus was on the Gamification elements that were used.

In Pereira et al. (2016) Gamification experience is reported. This experience has been carried on computer research laboratories where almost of collaborators share time of their projects with other activities. Game mechanics were used to improve the commitment and performance of collaborators and encourage follow-up of events in the process.

In Souza et al. (2016), authors' aims were to study the gamification and the Scrum framework to find games' elements, which can be used during the software development and find where to put them in Scrum. Therefore, Game elements have been mapped to Scrum ones. Authors have also added rewards and levels. The mapping was done based on Role Playing Games. Collected data analysis made it possible to verify how the gamification use affected the team motivation, their on-time releases and the customer satisfaction.

In Conill (2016), the author highlighted issues related to dislocated projects. He presented RedCritter Tracker as the first project management software that introduces gamification techniques as a main feature to engage team members and to tackle issues of employee motivation and productivity.

In Pateiro Marcão (2017), the study has focused on the performance of the employee and its strong dependency on motivation. Therefore, the study identified techniques and concepts that allow to tackle motivation problems such as through gamification.

The study in Machuca-Villegas and Gasca-Hurtado (2018), considered a systematic literature review to understand the current state of gamification as a strategy for improving processes associated with software project management and to define future gamification in the same context.

The study in Patrício et al. (2018), focused on the use of Gamification in the early stage of innovation by making a cross-comparison of published case studies of firms where gamification was used to address innovation challenges.

The objective of the study presented in Marshburn and Sieck (2019), is to develop a full-fledged game to be used in Scrum retrospectives. Interesting aspects reported in this work are related to Game adaptation which have been applied to rules and the Scrum master instructions.

Work in Patricio et al. (2020) emphasized the impact of gamification approaches on co-creation in the development of new solutions through empirical case research studies. Synthesis of the presented works is illustrated by the Table 1.

Table 1. Adoption of gamification in enterprises

Proposal	Gamification/purpose	Domain	Adaptation	Authors
A methodology for best gamification techniques	Improve code quality/ Stimulate competition between teams			Dubois and Tamburrelli (2013)
Gamification of the Trogan Project Management system	Improve the Usability of the system	Project management system Interface		Ašeriškis and Damaševičius (2014)
Literature review	Identify Gamification elements	Software engineering		Pedreira et al. (2015)
Gamification experience	Improve the commitment and performance of collaborators/ improved tracking of agile management process	Computer research laboratories		Pereira, et al. (2016)
Mapping Game elements to scrum	Role playing Games/motivation and impact on releases time and customer satisfaction	Development environment		Souza et al. (2016)
RedCritter Tracker	Improve cohesion motivation, communication and engagement in virtual spaces	Dislocated software projects		Conill (2016)
Gamification model	Improve motivation that strongly impacts performance	Enterprises in general		Pateiro Marcão, (2017)
A systematic literature review	Gamification elements. The research methods. The industry sector.	Software Project Management		Machuca-Villegas and Gasca-Hurtado (2018)
Cross-comparison of published case studies (Analytical Framework)	Gamification to address Innovation challenges	Early stage of innovation		Patrício et al. (2018)
Full-fledged game	Engage participants Improve processes and team dynamics	Scrum retrospectives	Adaptation applied to rules and directions	Marshburn and Sieck (2019)
Empirical case research study	Gamified Method and tool/ Impact of Gamification	Co-creation in the development of new solutions		Patricio et al. (2020)

Works Related to Context Awareness and Adaptation of Serious Games or gamified apps

Concerning adaptation and context, authors in Hardy et al. (2011), added context awareness to games for sport and health. They proposed a Framework for Social Networks and Internet based Web services for capturing spatial and temporal context as well as vital parameters of a user.

In Alamri et al. (2013), authors provided a cloud based pervasive Serious Game Framework to support obesity treatment. The Framework aims to engage people for exercising by using exergaming while monitoring their bio-signals using body sensor networks.

Edoh-Alove et al. (2013) have combined Geomatics and Augmented Reality to improve the immersive aspects of Serious Games. For that aim a spatial context was developed and exploited with an Service Oriented Architecture based solution.

Authors in Qamar et al. (2014) have presented an e-Therapy Framework that collects live therapeutic context by analyzing body joint data in a noninvasive way. The system assumes that each patient is surrounded by a smart 3D space that identifies her context and tracks her gestures. A specific approach is provided to model and generate a set of high-level Serious Game based therapies by composing complex gestures models from different primitive gesture sequences.

Synthesis of the previous works is illustrated by the Table 2.

Table 2. Context awareness and adaptation

Kind of Context	What is adapted?	Domain	Authors
Spatial and temporal context and vital parameters of users	e-health service such as exergaming	Sport and health	Hardy, et al. (2011)
Bio-signals (Body Sensor Networks)	Exergaming accordingly to bio-signals	Obesity treatment	Alamri et al. (2013)
Spatial context	The user's immersion through augmented reality	Multiplayer serious games in general	Edoh-Alove et al. (2013)
Live therapeutic context (body joint data)	Gesture models composition	Gesture therapy	Qamar et al. (2014)

Existing Scrum tools features

Several Scrum tools have been developed to support users and scrum adopters while carrying on projects. These tools have been compared regarding their features (established in the first column of the table 3) and whether they have integrated gamification or other engaging aspects such as videoconferencing or advanced HCI such as those based on augmented reality or 3D spaces (Edoh-Alove et al., 2013).

Table 3. Existing Scrum tools comparison

Feature	iceScrum	ZohoSprints	Trello	Monday.com	Vivify Scrum
Sprint Planning	✓	✓	✗	✗	✗
Priority Definition	✓	✓	✓	✓	✓
Tasks management	✓	✓	✓	✓	✓
Backlogs management	✓	✓	✗	✗	✗
Burndown charts	✓	✓	Available as an external tool	✗	✗
Kanban cards	✓	✓	✓	✓	✓
Team management	✓	✓	✓	✓	✗
Videoconferencing	✗	✓	✗	✗	✗
Meetings management	✗	Professional Plan only	✗	✓	✗
Gamification	✗	✗	✗	✗	✗
AR or 3D Spaces	✗	✗	✗	✗	✗

As a conclusion out of the previously presented research, it is worth to highlight the following conclusions:

First, Gamification when accurately designed should be rule-bounded and goal-oriented (Deterding et al., 2011).

Second the use of Gamification patterns as good design practices such as those defined in the MDA Framework, could bring the desired impact on users, and have a valuable added value (Ašeriškis & Damaševičius, 2014).

Third, almost the presented works are related to the use of Gamification in domains such as project management, software development or also innovation management challenges. Purposes for using gamification were to improve aspects such as processes, code quality or usability of the system (Ašeriškis & Damaševičius, 2014). Some other aspects like engagement, motivation, commitment, and communication as reported in (Conill, R. 2016) have been targeted by Gamification. These strongly impact performance and team dynamics as reported in Marshburn & Sieck (2019) and in Pateiro Marcão (2017) as well as releases time and customer satisfaction pointed out in Souza et al. (2016). Gamification has been also used to stimulate competition between teams as shown in Dubois & Tamburrelli (2013) and to improve tracking of agile management process as reported in Pereira et al. (2016).

Fourth, even though some works have dealt with context and context-awareness, almost of them considered the e-health or sports domain with context models that are specifically dedicated to space, time, and bio-signals or body gestures of the users (Hardy, S., et al, 2011; Alamri et al., 2013; Qamar et al., 2014). None of the mentioned works have considered enterprises' contexts. Moreover, only the work of Edoh-Alove et al. (2013) has considered the adaptation of users' immersion using Augmented Reality. Only the work presented in (Marshburn & Sieck, 2019) and which proposed a fully-fledged game applied adaptation to rules and directions.

Fifth, very few works have considered tracking and recording of users' actions although this allows data collection and further data analysis and either authoring alternative gamification scenarios or adapting rationally Gamification elements.

Finally, the studied Scrum tools do not encompass all the scrum features, they do not provide Gamification, videoconferencing, and Augmented Reality features. Almost of them are not dedicated to mobile use which hampers their usability in projects that are run in physical environments where users are mostly mobile and where augmented reality features could bring additional assistance to its users.

Therefore, very few works have instrumented the use of Gamification through protypes or fully-fledged tools, although that these instruments might constitute a further step to collect and analyze Gamification resulting data. Indeed, having an automated tool that can identify each activity and store each result be it positive or negative could allow the system designer as well as decision makers to delve deeper into this data and to analyze it and make consequently further rational decisions and orientations about methodology adoption as well as gamification impacts.

Inferred Requirements

Based on the previous section findings, the solution goals that the present work aims to tackle, are to provide an approach that combines in a relevant way Gamification and agile or more specifically the scrum methodology. This approach should be enough flexible to be adapted easily. Moreover, it should be instrumented by a dedicated mobile tool that integrates videoconferencing as well as augmented reality.

The inferred requirements encompass therefore both Scrum methodology requirements as well as Gamification requirements. Hence, the intended solution should allow first to satisfy the following requirements that are classified accordingly to Scrum roles.

- Each user should have an identity in the system or the organization. Therefore, he should be allowed to have an account, a profile and corresponding character that illustrates his personality and which could be personalized.
- Each user should have the possibility to create or manage projects. In this case he gets the role of Product owner and hence could add collaborators, assign them either scrum master role or the team member role and accept user stories.
- The scrum master should have the possibility to manage and schedule meetings.
- Each collaborator could attend Meetings either in site or remotely. This could be even possible indoor or outdoor (field visit).
- Each collaborator should have the possibility to create sprints and to define user stories and tasks.

The figure 2 illustrates these requirements.

Figure 2. Scrum requirements

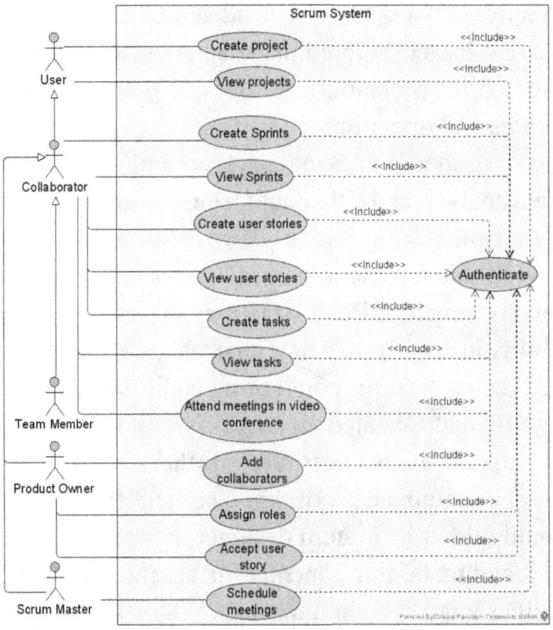

Second, regarding Gamification, as illustrated in the figure 3:

- A rewarding system should be defined to attribute relevant rewards to each completed action.
- Collaboration between teams' members as well as between teams is rewarded.

- Increased performance of collaborators such as finishing tasks before deadlines while keeping up good deliverables' quality is equally rewarded.
- Each collaborator can track his progress as well as the progress of the other collaborators.
- Gamification should be fun and engaging. It should provide good onboarding to a new collaborator, allow competition between teams, and allow good user experience by using AR and mobile videoconferencing.
- Finally, Gamification should be enough flexible and easy to be adapted, in order to take into account, the users' contexts as well the enterprises' context.

Figure 3. Gamification requirements

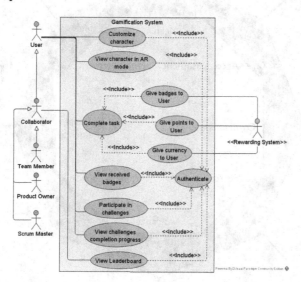

PROPOSAL

The proposal called GaminScrum, addresses three main contributions namely the Gamification approach that is applied to the Scrum methodology, a Gamification adaptation approach and finally a mobile app prototype that is used to instrument and evaluate the proposal. These three contributions are presented in the following sub-sections.

GaminScrum: Application of Gamification to the Scrum Methodology

To design a gamified Scrum system, first, the types of players should be identified. The focus had been on two types namely the Socializer and the Achiever since the main goal of Gamification application considered in this work is to help Scrum team members to better collaborate among each other's and to motivate them to accomplish the project's objectives. Once the personalities of the target users have been established, game mechanics are presented and implemented.

To implement the elements of Gamification in the Scrum methodology, the Octalysis framework is used (Chou, 2015, 2016). This framework presents 8 different motivational engines such as Epic Meaning and Calling, Development and Accomplishment, Empowerment of Creativity and Feedback, etc.

Motivation as shown in figure 4 has been classified into two categories: Intrinsic (Right Brain) and Extrinsic (Left Brain).

Figure 4. Intrinsic motivation and extrinsic motivation

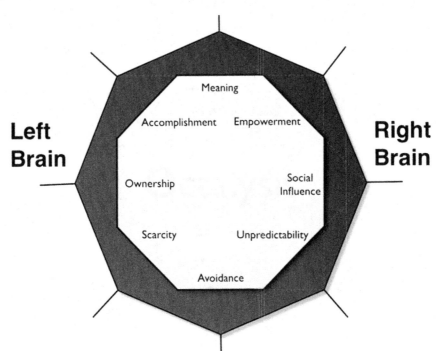

To gamify the Scrum methodology, the PBLVC elements (Points, Badges, Leaderboards and Virtual Currency) have been used as elements and mechanics. A progression system has been equally defined accordingly to the Octalysis Framework.

The Octalysis graph created thanks to the Octalysis tool (Chou, n.d) (see figure 5) shows the different motivational drivers chosen for GaminScrum as well as the corresponding game elements. Thanks to this tool, the 8 motivational drivers have received values between 0 and 10. The sum of these values allows to identify the Octalysis score and its analysis by the tool which indicates as a result whether the design is fair, and a balance do exist between intrinsic and extrinsic motivation. The figure 5 shows accordingly to the score analysis that GaminScrum presents a good balance between intrinsic and extrinsic motivators. Such a balance strongly impacts the system and allows users to keep engaged with it.

The PBLVC elements defined in GaminScrum work as follows:

- Points: Users of GaminSrcum will be able to receive points (Experience points and health points) for each action performed.

Figure 5. The Octalysis graph

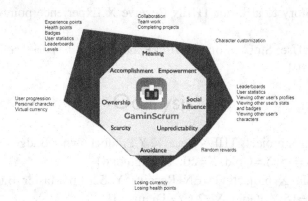

- Badges: Users are rewarded with 4 categories of badges: Bronze, Silver, Gold and Diamond to show the user's progress.
- Leaderboards: To instill a competitive spirit and use the power of social influence in the GaminScrum teams, Leaderboards are used. Users can therefore compare and situate their level to other team members.
- Level progression system indicates to the user his progress in GaminScrum. The user can level-up thanks to the experience points he has obtained. Each level has a minimal number of points required to reach it.
- Character Customization: GaminScrum users will be able to own a character which can be personalized thank to an AR based interaction.
- Health points or currency could be also lost or redeemed according to defined rules.

The previous gamification elements are controlled by several rules that should be understood by all the users engaged in the GaminScrum experience. Each defined rule is related to one or more element and gets triggered upon users' actions related to the Scrum activities such as User story or task creation. Therefore, they are classified into categories as Points & Currency, Badges and Estimation points for User story or task. In the following, examples of rules are defined according to their respective categories:

Points and Currency

1. IF Created new account in the application THEN Receive Y Gold coins WITH {Y=200}
2. IF Created project THEN Receive X Experience points, Y Gold Coins, Z diamonds WITH {X=200, Y=10, Z=5}
3. IF Added new collaborator to the project THEN Receive X Experience points, Y Gold Coins WITH {X=20, Y=10}
4. IF Created User Story THEN Receive X Experience points, Y Gold Coins WITH {X=200, Y=10}
5. IF Accepted User Story in Product Backlog THEN Receive X Experience points, Y Gold Coins WITH {X=60, Y=20}
6. IF Created a Task associated to a user story THEN Receive X Experience points, Y Gold Coins WITH {X=200, Y=10}

7. IF Created a Sprint THEN Receive X Experience points, Y Gold Coins WITH {X=200, Y=30}
8. IF Added a User Story to a Sprint THEN Receive X Experience points, Y Gold Coins WITH {X=50, Y=10}
9. IF Completed Task/User Story in time THEN Receive X*B Experience Points, Y*B Gold Coins WITH {X=20, Y=10}

Badges

10. IF Product Owner in X projects THEN Receive Y Product owner Badge WITH {X=5: Y=Bronze, X=10: Y=Silver, X=15: Y=Gold, X=20: Y=Diamond}
11. IF Scrum Master in X projects THEN Receive Y Scrum Master Badge {X=5: Y=Bronze, X=10:Y=Silver, X=15:Y=Gold, X=20:Y=Diamond}
12. IF Team Member in X projects THEN Receive Y Team Member Badge {X=5: Y=Bronze, X=10:Y=Silver, X=15:Y=Gold, X=20:Y=Diamond}
13. IF Created X User Stories THEN Receive Y Story Creator Badge {X=5: Y=Bronze, X=10:Y=Silver, X=15:Y=Gold, X=20:Y=Diamond}
14. IF Created X Tasks THEN Receive Y Task Creator Badge {X=5: Y=Bronze, X=10: Y=Silver, X=15:Y=Gold, X=20:Y=Diamond}
15. IF Completed X Tasks THEN Receive Y Task Completor Badge {X=5: Y=Bronze, X=10: Y=Silver, X=15:Y=Gold, X=20:Y=Diamond}
16. IF Collected X Badges THEN Receive Y Collector Badge {X=2:Y=Bronze, X=4:Y=Silver, X=10:Y=Gold, X=20:Y=Diamond}

X: Times completed an action
  Y: Level of the badge

Estimation points for User Story/Task

1. IF Completed Task/User Story before its due date THEN Increase Score multiplier by U and Receive U*X Experience points, U*Y Gold Coins for each completed action during A amount of time WITH {A=60, U=2, X=100, Y=20}
2. IF Due date of Task/User Story expires THEN Lose Y Gold Coins, W Health Points and eliminate any multiplier that is currently applied WITH {Y=200, W=10}
3. IF Another team buys a deliverable from the user's current team for Y Gold Coins and Z Diamonds, THEN all team members Receive Y Gold Coins and Z Diamonds WITH {Y=1000, Z=20}
4. IF Scrum Master creates meeting THEN Receives X Experience points, Y Gold Coins and Z Diamonds WITH {X=100, Y=200, Z=10}

U: Value of multiplier
  X: Value of Experience points
  Y: Value of Gold Coins
  Z: Value of Diamonds
  W: Value of Health Points
  A: Amount of time (Unit = minutes) during which the multiplier is applied.

The GaminScrum Adaptation Approach

According to foundations of the Gamification design adopted in the present work, which is compliant to the MDA Framework, the Octalysis Framework and Bartles's player types, all elements described in the Gamification Framework should be adaptable during a given Scrum play. For instance, challenges, actions, rewards, feedbacks, conditions, completion logic as well as game concepts could be adapted and therefore the Game aesthetics will be consequently changed.

The adaptation approach should, therefore, be enough flexible to allow easily to adapt all those Gamification elements to users' contexts as well as to enterprises' contexts. Indeed, depending on the kind of enterprise, the project's domain as well as the kind of users, the PBLVC elements are carefully defined for the first run. A further evaluation of the obtained results (i.e. the impact of the used gamification elements and rules) could drive or not an adaptation process.

Moreover, three adaptation manners could be adopted with different levels of users' control. This latter is either attributed entirely to users especially to the product owner or the scrum master or attributed to the system itself. For the first case the adaptation is considered as manual while in the other case it is either automatic or intelligent.

- The Manual adaptation introduces a kind of autonomy and freedom within users while at the same time it could introduce many negative effects or overestimated positive effects.

Examples of manually adapted rules are listed in the following:

1. IF Due date of Task/User Story expires THEN Lose Y Gold Coins, W Health Points and eliminate any multiplier that is currently applied; {Y=0, W=0}.
2. IF Another team buys a deliverable from the user's current team for Y Gold Coins and Z Diamonds, THEN all team members Receive Y Gold Coins and Z Diamonds; {Y=5000, Z=1500}.
3. IF Completed Task/User Story in time THEN Receive X Experience Points, Y Gold Coins WITH {X=20, Y=200}
4. IF Completed Task/User Story before its due date THEN Increase Score multiplier by U and Receive U*X Experience points, U*Y Gold Coins, U*Z Diamonds for each completed action during R amount of time {R=60, U=8, X=100, Y=600, Z=50}.
5. IF Purchased deliverable THEN decrease XP, Gold coins and Diamonds with Deliverable = 1000 XP, 3000 Gold Coins and 2000 Diamonds.
   - The Automatic adaptation is realized by a dedicated algorithm and can influence all game mechanics, dynamics, and effects. For instance, the adaptation algorithm uses the list of rules (stored in an XML file) as its input together with the action realized by the user and it result (success or failure). Each rule is composed of two sides: the condition or the left-hand side (before THEN) and the consequence or the right-hand side. If the rule's condition matches the action realized by the user and its result, then the rule is first fired and then it is changed in a second step by replacing the consequence by another possible one already defined by the gamification designer. This allows to change randomly the rules of the game and hence introduce more surprise effect.
   - Finally, the Intelligent adaptation uses intelligent rules and inferences to adapt in the most relevant manner the game elements, mechanics, dynamics, and effects. Details of this lat-

ter kind of adaptation could be found in (Khemaja & Buendia, 2017) where authors have provided Gamification as a set of intelligent services that could act on an external system to Gamify it or to adapt its already existing gamification. This set of services are based on a Gamification ontology and a set of inference rules.

Implementation of GaminScrum

To instrument the GaminScrum, a mobile app based on the Android system is implemented. Therefore, the executable. apk file can be deployed on any Android device (Smartphone or Tablet). GaminScrum also uses an external Firebase database, and an Agora real-time Video-Conferencing Framework, respectively. These are accessible in the Cloud as illustrated by figure 6.

Figure 6. Physical architecture of GaminScrum

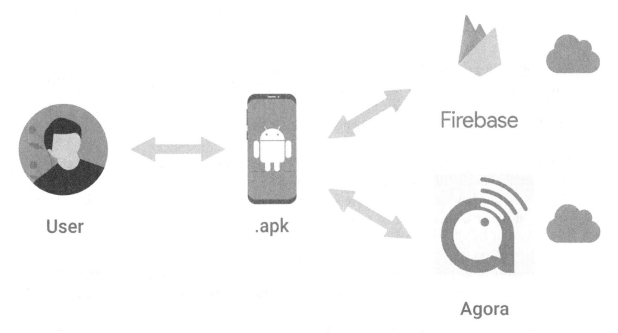

To run correctly, this uses the Unity3D engine and the Vuforia engine (a 3D game engine and an augmented reality library respectively) as well as the two client components Agora and Firebase. Agora provides the required API for the videoconferencing features while firebase constitutes the cloud database in which all the activities and traces of users are stored. This database constitutes a rich source of data that could serve for further analysis of the GaminScrum system and the interactions of users with it.

The logical architecture of GaminScrum is divided into 3 logical layers (See figure 7). The first concerns the presentation or view layer, the second layer is the application logic layer and finally the third layer concerns the interaction with external systems (the resource management layer).

Figure 7. The logical architecture of GaminScrum

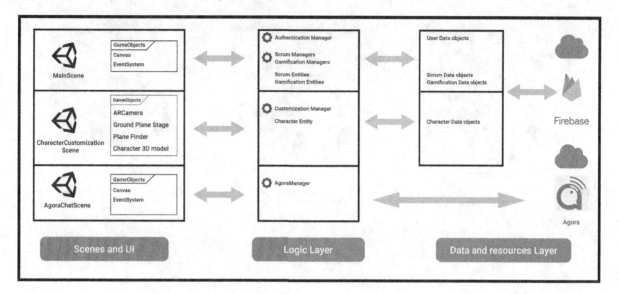

Many scenarios could be realized by a single user or a group of users. One typical scenario is when a user interacts with the application to create a project, to associate collaborators, to personalize his profile and then to visualize the rewards he owned after as a result of her/his previous actions.

The following figures illustrate an example of scenario with a set of possible activities performed in GaminScrum mobile app. Once connected to the GaminScrum app, the user can visualize his profile, his badges and his statistics (See figure 8).

The user can also personalize his character by activating the AR mode (See Figure 9). After Ground plane detection, the user can place his character on it and then customize it by changing some features.

Thanks to the "Video chat Agora", users will be able to join a meeting by video conference. With the initialization of the agora engine the local user's audio and video are activated. When another user joins the call, remote video and audio are enabled. At the end of the call all audio and videos are deactivated, and the engine is destroyed (See Figure 10).

Finally, the user can visualize all available badges, his leaderboard teams as well as his progress through the challenges (Figure 11).

THE EVALUATION APPROACH

The evaluation approach attempts to make both analytical and empirical evaluations of the interactions created by (1) Gamification and (2) Gamification adaption to the agile/scrum context (Wieringa, 2014).

First, GaminScrum as a mobile app constituted an instrument to evaluate the proposed approaches. The observational case study (experimentation) has been done with software engineering students, and the Gamification has been applied for scrum in software engineering domain.

Figure 8. Profile, badges, and statistics

Figure 9. AR Character customization

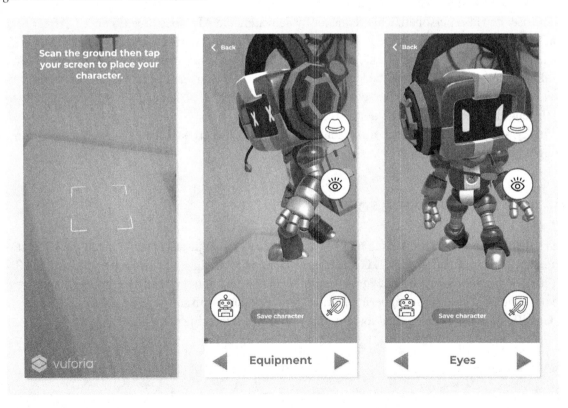

Figure 10. Scrum meeting ensured thanks to videoconferencing

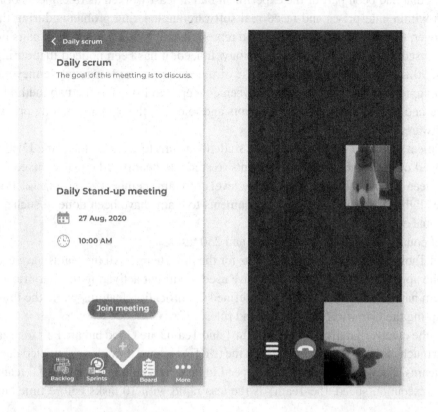

Figure 11. Leaderboards, badges and challenges

All students that had been part of the experiment had at least worked as freelancers or have carried many projects within enterprises and faced real software engineering problems during their years of studies. Moreover, these students constitute good representative candidates for their pairs in enterprises as they are not used to agile or scrum methodology. Indeed, it has been noticed that during their Capstone projects, 90% of the students claim the use of the scrum methodology while they end up by using a classical approach. Many confusions between concepts and steps of the two methodologies have been identified and rather than working on sprints and releases, the students mainly provide a bloc of developed software.

The experiment consisted on choosing three students' teams to work on the same J2EE project. The teams are formed of the same number of students (6 students /team) and equally mixed (3 girls and 3 boys aged between 22 and 24). The proficiency levels of team members regarding J2EE software development are slightly different, therefore assignments to teams have been done in such a way that all teams have global equivalent proficiency.

The project counts 4 sprints, 50 user stories and 250 tasks.

Table 4 and Table 5 show the obtained results for the three teams. All the teams have used the GaminScrum mobile app. However, the first team have used it without activating the Gamification features, the second team have used it by activating predefined Gamification features while the third team have used it by adapting the Gamification features and rules.

In Table 4., the quality of deliverables for Team1 and Team2 are Good but are Fair for Team3. Team3 has completed much more tasks before time then the two first teams, they also completed one more sprint then the first teams. They showed much more speed in tasks execution then the first 2 teams.

In terms of execution speed, the Team1 is the less rapid with 10 tasks before time and no sprints before time.

It seems that the predefined Gamification in GaminScrum has impacted positively the speed of Team2 while its absence has negatively impacted the speed of Team1.

However, there isn't any noticed impact on the quality of deliverables. For the case of Team3, Gamification has impacted positively the speed but negatively impacted the quality of deliverables.

Table 4. Scrum results of the three teams

Team	Tasks delays	Tasks completed in time	Tasks completed before time	Sprints delays	Sprints completed in time	Sprints completed before time	Quality of the deliverable
Team 1	20	220	10	2	2	0	Good
Team 2	10	220	20	1	2	1	Good
Team 3	10	210	30	0	2	2	Fair

The comparison between rewards obtained respectively by Team2 and Team3 shows that Team3 members have gained much more XP (experience points), Gold coins as well as Diamonds then the Team2. This is explained by the rules that have been modified by the Team3 (see rules defined in the "The GaminScrum adaptation approach section"). Another aspect that can allow the Team 3 gaining in speed is their possibility to purchase items from Team2 while the latter find themselves unable to purchase items from the Team3 as they do not have enough Coins, Diamonds or XP.

After the experimentation, the Team2 members reported that they felt bored after the sprint number 3 as the Gamification rules seem to be almost the same. Moreover, all team members reported their wishes to gain additional grades as a kind of reward.

Table 5. Gamification results of the three teams

Team	User's Role	Experience Points	Gold Coins	Diamonds	Health Points	Badges
Team1	PO1	0	0	0	0	0
	SM1	0	0	0	0	0
	TM11	0	0	0	0	0
	TM12	0	0	0	0	0
	TM13	0	0	0	0	0
	TM14	0	0	0	0	0
Team2	PO2	3300	1260	5	70	0
	SM2	9200	18600	920	70	0
	TM21	19350	2230	200	70	4
	TM22	19350	2230	200	70	4
	TM23	16500	6330	0	20	4
	TM24	16500	6330	0	20	4
Team3	PO3	3300	1260	5	70	0
	SM3	9200	18600	920	70	0
	TM31	16950	12900	0	70	4
	TM32	16950	12900	0	70	4
	TM33	28400	87700	6000	70	4
	TM34	28400	87700	6000	70	4

CONCLUSION

The present research has dealt with issues related to the implementation of agile methodologies and their adoption in enterprises. More specifically, it should be noted that the problems encountered during the implementation of agile methodologies are due to the resistance of the teams to change, the spread of a culture in contradiction with agile values, the lack of skills / experience with agile methods and the ubiquity of traditional development methods.

The main objective of this research was therefore to investigate a possible solution to those problems using Gamification. The research methodology that has been applied guided the work through 3 main steps. The first step focused on the problem investigation where related work has been examined and several requirements have been identified. The second step concerned the design of GaminScrum a generic Gamification approach and its adaptation. Both approaches have been applied to the scrum Methodology without considering a specific domain. Finally, both approaches have been implemented to provide a tool or instrument that distinguishes itself from other tools not only by the integration of gamification concepts but also by the integration of a very important communication feature for teams, namely Videoconferencing. In addition, the tool integrated augmented reality as an immersive Human Computer Interface which was applied for the user's profile customization.

Thanks to the GaminScrum tool, the gamification approach and its adaptation have been experimented and many insights have been drawn. Indeed, it was noted that Gamification when designed carefully could impact positively the adoption of agile methodologies and their implementation in enterprises. However, Gamification design and its adaptation should not be rendered possible for players. These latter could transform the system in such a way that it could jeopardize the considered agile project. Moreover, even though competition is considered as a good motivator, it should not be applied between the members of the same team to value actions that are not naturally collaborative or cooperative.

Another main important advantage of the GaminScrum mobile app is that it could represent a rich source of data that could be collected automatically and analyzed for better decision making about Gamification design. Indeed, every action realized by the user as well as the Gamification elements that are involved during the tool's execution, are stored in the Firebase database. Therefore, further works will consider this aspect related to intelligent data driven gamification by making use of deep learning and artificial intelligence.

REFERENCES

Ahmadi, M., Anisi, Y., Rad, B. B., & Rana, M. E. (2016). Using Serious Games to Replicate Scrum Framework in Daily Software Development Practices. *Proceedings of Int'l Conference On Data Mining, Image Processing, Computer & Electronics Engineering (DMIPCEE-16)*.

Alamri, A., Hossain, A. M., Hassan, M. M., Hossain, S. M., Alnuem, M., Ahmed, T. D., & el Abdulmotaleb, S. (2013). A cloudbased pervasive serious game framework to support obesity treatment. *Computer Science and Information Systems*, *10*(3), 1229–1246. doi:10.2298/CSIS120717046A

Anwer, F., Aftab, S., Waheed, U., & Muhammad, S. S. (2017). Agile software development models tdd, fdd, dsdm, and crystal methods: A survey. *International Journal of Multidisciplinary Sciences and Engineering*, *8*(2), 1–10.

Ašeriškis, D., & Damaševičius, R. (2014). Gamification of a project management system. In *Proc. of Int. Conference on Advances in Computer-Human Interactions ACHI2014* (pp. 200-207). Academic Press.

Ašeriškis, D., & Damaševičius, R. (2014). Gamification patterns for gamification applications. *Procedia Computer Science*, *39*, 83–90. doi:10.1016/j.procs.2014.11.013

Asuncion, H., Socha, D., Sung, K., Berfield, S., & Gregory, W. (2011). Serious game development as an iterative user-centered agile software project. In *Proceedings of the 1st International workshop on games and software engineering* (pp. 44–47). ACM. 10.1145/1984674.1984690

Bartle, R. (1996). Hearts, clubs, diamonds, spades: Players who suit MUDs. *Journal of MUD Research*, *1*(1), 19.

Bartle, R. A. (2008). Player types. *Jeannie Novak: Game Development Essentials*, 39-40.

Caillois, R. (1967). *Les jeux et les hommes Le masque et le vertige* [Games and men. The Mask and Vertigo]. Gallimard.

Chan, F. K., & Thong, J. Y. (2009). Acceptance of agile methodologies: A critical review and conceptual framework. *Decision Support Systems, 46*(4), 803–814. doi:10.1016/j.dss.2008.11.009

Challco, G. C., Moreira, D. A., Mizoguchi, R., & Isotani, S. (2014). An ontology engineering approach to gamify collaborative learning scenarios. In *Collaboration and Technology* (pp. 185–198). Springer International Publishing. doi:10.1007/978-3-319-10166-8_17

Challco, G.C., Andrade, F.R., de Oliveira, T.M., Mizoguchi, R., & Isotani, S. (2015). An Ontological Model to Apply Gamification as Persuasive Technology in Collaborative Learning Scenarios. *Anais do XXVI Simpósio Brasileiro de Informática na Educação (SBIE 2015)*.

Černezel, A., & Heričko, M. (2013). A user-centric approach for developing mobile applications. In *7th International Conference on Knowledge Management in Organizations: Service and Cloud Computing* (pp. 455-465). Springer. 10.1007/978-3-642-30867-3_41

Chou, Y. K. (2015). Octalysis: Complete Gamification Framework-Yu-kai Chou. Octalysis Media.

Chou, Y. K. (2016). *Actionable gamification*. Beyond Points, Badges, and Leaderboards.

Chou, Y. K. (n.d.). *Octalysis Tool*. https://www.yukaichou.com/octalysis-tool

Conill, R. F. (2016). Feeding the RedCritter: the gamification of project management software. In *The Business of Gamification* (pp. 43–61). Routledge.

Deterding, S., Dixon, D., Khaled, R., & Nacke, L. (2011). From game design elements to gamefulness: defining gamification. In *Proceedings of the 15th international academic MindTrek conference: Envisioning future media environments* (pp. 9–15). ACM. 10.1145/2181037.2181040

Domínguez, A., Saenz-de-Navarrete, J., De-Marcos, L., Fernández-Sanz, L., Pagés, C., & Martínez-Herráiz, J. J. (2013). Gamifying learning experiences: Practical implications and outcomes. *Computers & Education, 63*, 380–392. doi:10.1016/j.compedu.2012.12.020

Dubois, D. J. (2012). Toward adopting self-organizing models for the gamification of context-aware user applications. In *Proceedings of the Second International Workshop on Games and Software Engineering: Realizing User Engagement with Game Engineering Techniques (GAS)* (pp. 9-15). IEEE. 10.1109/GAS.2012.6225928

Dubois, D. J., & Tamburrelli, G. (2013). Understanding gamification mechanisms for software development. In *ESEC/FSE 2013 Proceedings of the 2013 9th Joint Meeting on Foundations of Software Engineering*. ACM. 10.1145/2491411.2494589

Eliëns, A., & Ruttkay, Z. (2008). Record, Replay & Reflect–a framework for understanding (serious) game play. *Proc Euromedia, 9*.

Edoh-Alove, E., Hubert, F., & Badard, T. (2013). A web service for managing spatial context dedicated to serious games on and for smartphones. *Journal of Geographic Information System, 5*(2), 148–160. doi:10.4236/jgis.2013.52015

Gannod, G. C., Troy, D. A., Luczaj, J. E., & Rover, D. T. (2015). *Agile way of educating. In Proceedings of IEEE Frontiers in Education Conference (FIE).* IEEE.

Garett, R., & Young, S. D. (2019). Health care gamification: A study of game mechanics and elements. *Technology. Knowledge and Learning, 24*(3), 341–353. doi:10.100710758-018-9353-4

Hamari, J., & Eranti, V. (2011). Framework for Designing and Evaluating Game Achievements. In Digra conference (Vol. 10, No. 1.224, p. 9966). Academic Press.

Hardy, S., El Saddik, A., Göbel, S., & Steinmetz, R. (2011). Context aware serious games framework for sport and health. In *Medical Measurements and Applications Proceedings (MeMeA). IEEE International Workshop* (pp. 248–252). IEEE. 10.1109/MeMeA.2011.5966775

Herzig, P., Ameling, M., & Schill, A. (2012). A generic platform for enterprise gamification. In *Software architecture (WICSA) and European Conference on Software Architecture (ECSA). Joint Working IEEE/IFIP Conference* (pp. 219–223). IEEE.

Hevner, A. R. (2007). A three cycle view of design science research. *Scandinavian Journal of Information Systems, 19*(2), 4.

Hidayati, A., Budiardjo, E. K., & Purwandari, B. (2020). Hard and soft skills for scrum global software development teams. In *Proceedings of the 3rd International Conference on Software Engineering and Information Management* (pp. 110-114). 10.1145/3378936.3378966

Hunicke, R., LeBlanc, M., & Zubek, R. (2004). A formal approach to game design and game research. *Proceedings of the AAAI workshop on challenges in game AI, 4*, 1.

Juul, J. (2011). *Half-real: Video games between real rules and fictional worlds.* MIT Press.

Kappen, D. L., & Nacke, L. E. (2013). The kaleidoscope of effective gamification: deconstructing gamification in business applications. In *Proceedings of the first international conference on gameful design, research, and applications* (pp. 119-122). 10.1145/2583008.2583029

Khemaja, M., & Buendia, F. (2017). Building context-aware gamified apps by using ontologies as unified representation and reasoning-based models. In *Serious Games and Edutainment Applications* (pp. 675–702). Springer. doi:10.1007/978-3-319-51645-5_29

Korn, O., Funk, M., Abele, S., Hörz, T., & Schmidt, A. (2014). Context-aware assistive systems at the workplace: analyzing the effects of projection and gamification. In *Proceedings of the 7th international conference on pervasive technologies related to assistive environments* (pp. 1-8). 10.1145/2674396.2674406

Lei, H., Ganjeizadeh, F., Jayachandran, P. K., & Ozcan, P. (2017). A statistical analysis of the effects of Scrum and Kanban on software development projects. *Robotics and Computer-integrated Manufacturing, 43*, 59–67. doi:10.1016/j.rcim.2015.12.001

Lonchamp, J. (2015). *Analyse des besoins pour le développement logiciel: Recueil et spécification, démarches itératives et agiles* [Needs analysis for software development: Collection and specification, iterative and agile approaches]. Dunod.

Machuca-Villegas, L., & Gasca-Hurtado, G. P. (2018). Gamification for improving software project management processes: A systematic literature review. In *International Conference on Software Process Improvement* (pp. 41-54). Springer.

Marshburn, D. (2018). Scrum retrospectives: Measuring and improving effectiveness. *Proceedings of the southern Association for Information systems conference.*

Marshburn, D., & Sieck, J. P. (2019). Don't Break the Build: Developing a Scrum Retrospective Game. *Proceedings of the 52nd Hawaii International conference on system sciences.* 10.24251/HICSS.2019.838

Messager Rota, V., & Tabaka, J. (2009). *Gestion de projet–vers les méthodes agiles* [Project Management Towards Agile Methods]. Eyrolles.

Ozkan, N., Gök, M. Ş., & Köse, B. Ö. (2020). Towards a Better Understanding of Agile Mindset by Using Principles of Agile Methods. In *Proceedings of the 15th Conference on Computer Science and Information Systems (FedCSIS)* (pp. 721-730). IEEE.

Pedreira, O., García, F., Brisaboa, F., & Piantinni, M. (2015). Gamification in software engineering –a systematic mapping. *Information ans Software Technology, 57,* 157–168.

Patrício, R., Moreira, A. C., & Zurlo, F. (2018). Gamification approaches to the early stage of innovation. *Creativity and Innovation Management, 27*(4), 499–511. doi:10.1111/caim.12284

Patricio, R., Moreira, A., Zurlo, F., & Melazzini, M. (2020). Co-creation of new solutions through gamification: A collaborative innovation practice. *Creativity and Innovation Management, 29*(1), 146–160. doi:10.1111/caim.12356

Pereira, I. M., Amorim, V. J., Cota, M. A., & Gonçalves, G. C. (2016). Gamification use in agile project management: an experience report. In *Brazilian workshop on agile methods* (pp. 28-38). Springer.

Qamar, A., Rahman, M. A., & Basalamah, S. (2014). Adding inverse kinematics for providing live feedback in a serious game-based rehabilitation system. In *Proceedings of the 5th International Conference: Intelligent Systems, Modelling and Simulation (ISMS)* (pp. 215–220). IEEE.

Reichle, R., Wagner, M., Khan, M. U., Geihs, K., Lorenzo, J., Valla, M., Fra, C., Paspallis, N., & Papadopoulos, G. A. (2008). A comprehensive context modeling framework for pervasive computing systems. In *Distributed Applications and Interoperable Systems* (pp. 281–295). Springer. doi:10.1007/978-3-540-68642-2_23

Marcão, R., Pestana, G., & Sousa, M. J. (2017). Gamification in project management. *Conference: 2nd International Conference On Economic and Business Management (FEBM 2017).*

Riedel, J. C., Feng, Y., & Azadegan, A. (2013). Serious Games Adoption in Organizations–An Exploratory Analysis. In *European Conference on Technology Enhanced Learning* (pp. 508-513). Springer.

Rumeser, D., & Emsley, M. (2019). Can serious games improve project management decision making under complexity? *Project Management Journal, 50*(1), 23–39.

Schuller, B. W., Dunwell, I., Weninger, F., & Paletta, L. (2013). Serious gaming for behavior change: The state of play. *IEEE Pervasive Computing, 12*(3), 48–55.

Schwaber, K., & Sutherland, J. (2011). The scrum guide. *Scrum Alliance, 21*(19), 1.

Stettina, C. J., Offerman, T., De Mooij, B., & Sidhu, I. (2018). Gaming for agility: using serious games to enable agile project & portfolio management capabilities in practice. In *2018 IEEE International Conference on Engineering, Technology and Innovation (ICE/ITMC)* (pp. 1-9). IEEE.

Souza, J. P., Zavan, A. R., & Flôr, D. E. (2016). Scrum hero: Gamifying the scrum framework. In *Brazilian Workshop on Agile Methods* (pp. 131-135). Springer.

Su, C. H., & Cheng, C. H. (2015). A mobile gamification learning system for improving the learning motivation and achievements. *Journal of Computer Assisted Learning, 31*(3), 268–286.

Sutherland, J., & Schwaber, K. (2017). *The Scrum Guide™ The Definitive Guide to Scrum: The Rules of the Game November 2017*. Academic Press.

Susi, T., Johannesson, M., & Backlund, P. (2007). *Serious games: An overview*. Academic Press.

Tanenbaum, T. J., Antle, A. N., & Robinson, J. (2013, April). Three perspectives on behavior change for serious games. In *Proceedings of the SIGCHI Conference on Human Factors in Computing Systems* (pp. 3389-3392). ACM.

Van Rozen, R., & Dormans, J. (2014). Adapting game mechanics with micro-machinations. In Foundations of Digital Games. Society for the Advancement of the Science of Digital Games. Springer.

Veretennikova, N., & Vaskiv, R. (2018). Application of the lean startup methodology in project management at launching new innovative products. In *2018 IEEE 13th International Scientific and Technical Conference on Computer Sciences and Information Technologies (CSIT)* (Vol. 2, pp. 169-172). IEEE.

Vermeulen, H., Gain, J., Marais, P., & O'Donovan, S. (2016). Reimagining gamification through the lens of Activity Theory. *49th Hawaii International Conference on System Sciences (HICSS)*. doi:10.1109/HICSS.2016.168

Wieringa, R. J. (2014). *Design Science Methodology for Information Systems and Software Engineering*. Springer.

Zichermann, G., & Cunningham, C. (2011). *Gamification by Design: Implementing Game Mechanics in Web and Mobile Apps*. OReilly Media, Inc.

Chapter 9
Promoting Secure and Sustainable Behavior in Digital Ecosystems Through Gamification

Mazaher Kianpour

 https://orcid.org/0000-0003-2804-4630
Norwegian University of Science and Technology, Norway

Stewart James Kowalski

 https://orcid.org/0000-0003-3601-8387
Research Institute of Sweden, Sweden

ABSTRACT

While academic interest has grown in using gamification in training different aspects of cybersecurity, the research remains sparse on the design and development of games that focus on integrated concepts of security and sustainability. This chapter builds on a previously presented framework for designing serious games and develops and evaluates an instantiation of a game aimed to promote secure and sustainable behavior in digital ecosystems. It describes the theoretical foundation of the game, giving a detailed account of its game design process. Then, it provides the preliminary evaluation in which significant qualitative evidence of security and sustainable behavior is observed regarding progressive system thinking and anticipatory and problem-solving competencies. The results show that gamification facilitated learning the concepts and changing behavior towards sustainability transitions. Further investigation, with larger sample size, is required using other game elements that promote cooperation and critical thinking competencies.

DOI: 10.4018/978-1-6684-4291-3.ch009

INTRODUCTION

Evolving malicious cyber activities and increasing cyber risks to individuals, organizations, and governments have made cybersecurity a significant challenge and core part of societal, political, and economic decisions (Anderson et al., 2019; Geer et al., 2020). The Global Risks Report 2021, published by the World Economic Forum, has categorized cybersecurity failures as clear and present dangers (McLennan, 2021). This category reveals concern about lives and livelihoods – among them infectious diseases, employment crises, digital inequality, and youth disillusionment. Moreover, the increasing value of tangible and intangible assets in cyber-physical systems is becoming more attractive to those who wish to penetrate systems for financial gains, psychological and reputational gains, or to cause instability. Therefore, ensuring cybersecurity through greater awareness, strong multi-stakeholder partnerships, and deep structural changes in key areas of institutional activities are crucial for having secure, sustainable hyper-connected societies that rely on digital infrastructure (Assembly, 2017).

The solution to many cybersecurity problems is to build and develop strong cybersecurity policies that enable the organizations to extend protection against cyber-attacks, and strategies that enable timely detection of risks, threats, and breaches, and allow the organizations to tackle them. Cybersecurity policies and strategies need to be sustainable, measurable, and offer actionable insights. In addition to security, therefore, this work focuses on a hard-to-quantify but vital concept known as sustainability.

Galaitsi et al. define sustainability as the ability to maintain a high level of functionality without inputs from external resources (Galaitsi et al., 2021).[1] This definition can be extended through interconnected domains, including society, technology, and economics. Secure, sustainable cybersecurity behavior in the presence of rapid-paced socio-technical changes in today's world compel the organizations and governments to deal with cyber threats potentially affecting them, to prioritize the defense of their digital and physical assets, decide what security measures should be implemented, and what operations need to be integrated into their daily routines.

Both of these concepts, security and sustainability, focus on both ordinary, repetitive threats and those that are extreme and rare. Therefore, consideration of security and sustainability goals together, reflection on current behavior, and engagement in more secure operations that lead to the formation of sustainable behaviors are the challenges that this work tackles. To tackle these challenges, the authors designed and developed a strategic simulation, also known as policy simulation or policy exercise. Strategic simulations are interactive, participatory methods to develop strategic insight that builds on selected representations of real-world structures and processes (Duke & Geurts, 2004). This approach allows individuals to explore real policy issues, using design elements known from serious games to structure communication (Geurts et al., 2007), as well as to include feedback that participants receive based on their decisions.

The current state of the art of gamification studies shows that integrated concepts of security and sustainability are not at the forefront of the design and execution of games initiatives, despite some awareness of security and privacy implications and developing skills. However, the uptake in the field of gamification in cybersecurity dictates a necessary shift from implementing a limited set of security measures to a more mature and holistic conception of security and sustainability as integral parts of digital ecosystems, starting at the very first stages of design. In many current reports on sustainable cybersecurity, these factors are only discussed in a limited fashion. (Sadik et al., 2020; Shackelford et al., 2016; Vasiu & Vasiu, 2018). This chapter does not aim to suggest that these initiatives are necessarily insufficient in this respect, but in general, it appears that the focus on the aspects related to security and sustainability is relatively peripheral.

This work is positioned and designed as an experimental instantiation of the framework presented by Kianpour et al. (Kianpour et al., 2019). The developed artifact investigates the individual behaviors in promoting secure, sustainable cybersecurity behavior through the use of situational assessments implemented as a strategic simulation game. To justify the use of strategic simulations, this work relies on the literature of sustainability transitions (i.e., specific processes of systemic, socio-technical change towards a sustainable environment (Fünfschilling, 2014)) and gamification. On the one hand, Holtz et al. discussed the benefits of modeling in sustainable transitions research by providing multiple examples of modeling to develop scenarios to examine transition narratives and explore their dynamics (Holtz et al., 2015). The use of simulation modeling to study system interactions and policymaking for sustainable transitions is also discussed by Papachristos (Papachristos, 2014). On the other hand, the literature of gamification points to the benefits of strategic simulations in terms of their potential to stimulate learning, (Wenzler & Chartier, 1999), building and improving relationships among stakeholders (Haug et al., 2011), fostering a holistic view of the problem (Toth, 1988), and stimulating thinking about the medium- to long-term future (Wenzler, 1993). Consequently, the objective of this chapter is to investigate how employing gamification this specific context enables the development of strong microfoundations of individuals' behavior and understanding the dynamics of transitions towards secure and sustainable digital ecosystems. This study evaluates the effectiveness of gamification for training the executive-level managers within an organization. It aims to go beyond lower cognitive levels (knowledge and comprehension) by focusing on high cognitive level learning tasks (synthesis and evaluation). Hence, the learning was assessed through tracing conceptual changes in a quasi-experimental design.

In the strategic simulation game presented in this chapter, attackers are internally rational that is, they maximize expected utility under uncertainty over an infinite horizon given dynamically consistent subjective beliefs about the future. The players take the defender role in the game. They are provided with a set of actions and quantifiable data. The data, such as the number of incidents, cost of cyber-attacks, percent of vulnerable systems, and mean time between incident discoveries empowers the player with practical insights and reveals the state of the system. A great number of problems in the first instance can be handled with such measures, so they will be used heavily in the management tools that are increasingly employed in many organizations. Although sometimes it is very difficult to obtain the required information, because it relates to sensitive process information, quantifiable data allow some benchmarking within an organization and further decomposed into Measures of Effectiveness, Measure of Performance, and Measure of Suitability (Gortney, 2012).

Although this word does not aim to identify an ideal or preferred approach, it supports players in the formation of sustainable, secure behaviors that are proportional to solutions to problems in the domain of cybersecurity decisions. The authors achieve this goal by building a game-based model to gamify the tasks (e.g., cybersecurity resource allocation, adoption of cyber insurance, information sharing, and incident response) related to sustainable, secure behaviors. The approach of this study to gamifying the interactions is to metrify the tasks with additional frame mechanics and elements of play. Metrification of tasks involves incorporating a measure of attainment upon which a concept of goal-directed movement is predicated.

This work contributes to the literature of employing gamification in cybersecurity in three ways: 1) showing how to use gamification for encouraging secure and sustainable behavior in digital ecosystems, aligned with Expansive Learning theory and principles, 2) design and development of situational assessments to evaluate high-order cognitive skills; and 3) using metrification to assess the impact of decisions, understanding trends, and scenario analysis.

The remainder of this chapter is structured as follows. The following section reviews the theoretical foundations of this work. The materials and methods section describes the general structure and procedures for design and implementation of the game. The results section reports the findings of this study based upon the information gathered as a result of the conducted experiments. The final section concludes the chapter by discussing the findings and outlining the limitations and proposes the future work.

THEORETICAL FOUNDATIONS

To develop specific learning outcomes needed to work on achieving secure and sustainable behavior, there is a consensus that individuals need to have certain key competencies that enable them to engage constructively and responsibly with today's societies. Competencies describe the specific attributes individuals need for action and self-organization in various complex contexts and situations (Rieckmann, 2017). Table 1 collects the key competencies that are crucial to advance secure and sustainable development within the context of cybersecurity. The current version of this game attempts to help the players to develop all the competencies but collaboration and critical thinking competencies.

Table 1. The key competencies to advance secure and sustainable behavior in digital ecosystems

Key Competencies	Description	Reference
System thinking competency	the abilities to recognize and understand relationships in complex socio-technical systems and to deal with uncertainty	(Zoto et al., 2019)
Adversarial thinking competency	the ability to look at system rules and think about how to exploit and subvert them as well as to identify ways to alter the material, cyber, social, and physical operational space	
Anticipatory competency	the abilities to understand and evaluate multiple possible and probable consequences of actions and to deal with risks and changes.	(Kianpour, 2020)
Integrated problem-solving competency	the abilities to apply different problem-solving techniques to complex security and sustainability problems and develop viable solution options that promote secure and sustainable developments.	
Normative competency	the abilities to understand and reflect on the security and sustainability norms and values that underlie one's actions in a context of trade-offs, uncertain knowledge, and contradictions.	(Wiek et al., 2011)
Self-awareness competency	the ability to reflect on one's own role in the local or global environments to continually evaluate actions and deal with feelings and desires.	(Østby et al., 2019)
Collaboration competency	the abilities to learn from others and understand their needs	(Rieckmann, 2012)
Critical thinking competency	the abilities to question security and sustainability norms and values and take a position in these discourses	(De Haan, 2010)

After identifying and recognizing the competencies that need to be learned, it is needed to choose a learning tool that empowers the players to develop such competencies. Educating decision-makers about the challenges of sustainability requires methods capable of fostering a systematic perspective, understanding complexity, and action competencies. Gamification has been an increasingly popular tool and technique for training and education across various domains such as energy, climate change, cybersecurity, and crisis management. It also has been introduced as an effective learning approach for encouraging sustainable behavior in different domains. Games demonstrate pedagogic effectiveness in this field, however, they need to comply with national, organizational, and individual strategies and characteristics. A well-designed game provides the players, individually or in groups, with an opportunity to develop their adversarial and system thinking skills to set up effective defenses. Different simulations and serious games have been developed to induce behavioral changes in specific subjects like risk management, resource management, and sustainability (Wanick & Bui, 2019). Facilitating the change in human attitudes and behavior is one of the educational challenges facing industries and academia. Scholars have proposed that gamification is ideally suited to meeting this challenge (Castro-Sánchez et al., 2016; Hallinger & Chatpinyakoop, 2019). Therefore, this work uses gamification to promote the desired behavior among the cybersecurity decision makers.

Deming distinguishes between three ways to learn: by experience, by being taught, and by theory (Deming, 2018). Standard theories of learning are focused on processes where a subject (an individual or an organization) acquires some identifiable knowledge or skills in such a way that a corresponding, relatively lasting change in the behavior of the subject may be observed (Nonaka & Takeuchi, 1995; Rumelhart & Norman, 1976). However, in ever-changing digital ecosystems people and organizations are always learning something that is not stable, not even defined or understood ahead of time. What is proposed in this chapter, is an integration of the designed game into processes in which players interact in a dynamic activity. This viewpoint corresponds with Engeström, who proposes human activity can be analyzed using an activity system's approach (Engeström, 2015). Figure 1 presents an activity system including a subject, an object, a community, rules, tools, and a division of labor (tasks and power).

The subject of an activity is an individual or a group whose viewpoint is used in analyzing the activity. In this work, the subject corresponds to game players. The object, corresponding to the gameplay or aesthetics of the game, refers to the 'problem space' at which the activity is directed. Then, the objects are transformed into outcomes (i.e., postulated situation) with the help of physical and digital tools as game elements. The game designers correspond to the community who comprises of multiple individuals sharing the same object of the activity. The division of labor relates to the division of tasks and power between the members of that community. The game roles and responsibilities are defined in this part. Finally, the rules, or game mechanics, refer to the explicit and implicit regulations, norms and conventions that constrain actions and interactions within the activity system.

Figure 1. Engeström's Expended Activity Theory Model (Engeström, 2015)

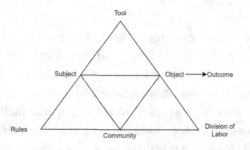

Using Engeström's activity triangle, the learning process can be described as follows. The players have an object (i.e., building a sustainable cybersecurity plan) and they use game elements to perform specific tasks under certain rules and situations. The game typically involves players with different knowledge and motivation. This may create obstacles to the effective engagement of the player in the game and ultimately the sustainability of the learning efforts. Hence, relying on the Situational Leadership framework, this work follows the sequence of learning action in an expansive learning cycle (Engeström, 1999) to operationalize the Kolb's learning model.[2]

The above conceptualization of this work's framework and learning by expanding, proposed by Engeström, provides a basis for the experiment to operationalize the notion of learning to encourage secure and sustainable behavior through gamification. However, in business settings, organizations expect that training will result in better performance at work. In the literature on learning theories, an explicit link is often made between learning and consequent changes in behavior and attitudes. Argyris argues that learning occurs when understanding, insight and explanations are connected with action (Argyris, 2003). However, this may be ambitious in the context of this game, or other similar games, given the short term and small-scale nature of the intervention. Therefore, scholars conceive of learning in varied ways. Haug conceptualizes three types of learning that players may take away from policy exercises (Haug et al., 2011): 1) Cognitive learning refers to the acquisition of new or the improved structuring of existing knowledge; 2) Normative learning implies changes in the viewpoints, norms and values of participants as a consequence of participating in the policy exercise; and 3) Relational learning refers to questions such as increased trust, improved ability to cooperate and a better understanding of the mindsets and frames of other participants.

In the author's view, all three types constitute equally valuable learning benefits. However, this chapter focuses on cognitive learning as it doubts a revised viewpoint on secure and sustainable cybersecurity, if it is not accompanied by a deep structural change in values and paradigms, can really be seen in the current settings of this work. In order to evaluate this dimension, therefore, this work makes use of the concept maps drawn by player before and after playing the game. Furthermore, it examines the responses to questions on the self-reported learning effect in the pre- and post-assessments and in follow-up interviews. The evaluation of the concept maps is based on the method developed by Morine-Dershimer (Morine-Dershimer, 1993). This method relies on two principles: centrality and specificity. Centrality is determined by the level at which the category is first introduced on the map (i.e., proximity to the central concept). Degree of specificity is determined by the proportional frequency of items associated with the category (number of items in the category divided by the number of items on the map). The Result section shows the result of evaluation using this method.

MATERIALS AND METHODS

Figure 2, illustrates, at the most basic level, the game design process. Identification of required competencies, design and development of game elements, and procedural rhetoric constitute the game design principles. Procedural rhetoric explains how players can learn through the rules and processes. Therefore, rather than the spoken word, writing, or images this work uses processes and rules to represent the system and scenarios. It uses scenario, tasks, and metrics to operationalize the procedural rhetoric and set up game rules. Table 2 lists the metrics used in this game. The authors admit that there are many other metrics that can be used along with this list, however, in order to avoid information overload, they used only five important metrics. The limits of human perception and information overload impact on the difficulty of understanding the issues and effectively making decisions.

Figure 2. The game design process

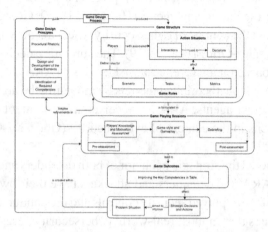

Table 2. The metrics that are used in the game

Name	Description	Formula	Target
Mean time to incident discovery	MTTID characterizes the effectiveness of incident detection activities.	$$\frac{\sum\left(Date\ of\ discovery - Date\ of\ occurence\right)}{Count\left(incidents\right)}$$	Should trend lower over time
Mean time between security incidents	MTBSI characterizes the effectiveness of preventive security controls.	$$\frac{\sum\left(Date\ of\ occurence\left[Incidents_i\right] - Date\ of\ occurence\left[Incident_{i+1}\right]\right)}{Count\left(Incidents\right)}$$	Should trend higher over time
Mean time to incident recovery	MTTIR characterizes the effectiveness of responsive security controls.	$$\frac{\sum\left(Date\ of\ recovery - Date\ of\ occurrence\right)}{Count\left(Incidents\right)}$$	Should trend lower over time
Mean cost of incidents	MCOI characterizes the impact of security incidents on the player's resource.	$$\frac{\sum\left(Direct\ Loss + Cost\ of\ business\ downtime + Recovery\ cost + Restitution\ cost\right)}{Count\left(incidents\right)}$$	Depends on the expected loss budget determined by risk assessment process. Ideally should be zero.
Percent of systems without known sever vulnerabilities	This metric characterizes the overall effectiveness of security controls portfolio.	$$\frac{Count\left(Systems\ without\ known\ severe\ vulnerabilities\right)}{Count\left(Scanned\ systems\right)} \times 100$$	Should trend higher over time

Another important component in the game structure is action situations including interaction and decisions. The structure of this game is designed as a function of the interplay between the defender (the player) and the attacker (i.e., decisions and actions made by the defender and decisions and actions taken by the automated attackers and vice-versa). Game theoretical models have been a popular choice to model the interplay between two or more strategic agents and have been widely applied in the research addressing cybersecurity issues (Do et al., 2017; Shiva et al., 2010). However, conventional game theory models face a challenge to find and compute Nash Equilibrium as the problem gets more realistic and complex (Joshi et al., 2020). Moreover, most versions of non-cooperative game theory models assume agents have complete information about their payoffs, preferences, and possible future actions and this information is shared among the interacting agents (Harsanyi, 1967). González-Ortega et al. argue that this assumption is unrealistic in the context of cybersecurity where agents will not have sufficient knowledge about other agents (González-Ortega et al., 2019). They provide a decision-analytic methodology to support the decision-maker based on an adversarial risk analysis (ARA) paradigm. ARA was proposed to address the shortcomings of game theoretical models by modeling the ability of an agent to anticipate the decisions and actions of other agents. ARA has received a lot of attention in recent years to model and calculate optimal decisions in the context of cybersecurity (González-Ortega et al., 2019; Joshi et al., 2020; Rios Insua et al., 2021).

This work uses ARA to model the strategic behavior of both defenders and attackers in the game (Rios Insua et al., 2009)3. Under ARA, the defenders and attackers have their own utility function and try to maximize the effectiveness of the deployed security controls and the conducted attack, respectively. Joshi et al. (Joshi et al., 2020) argues that in most real-world cybersecurity cases, the defender deploys their defense first to deter and prevent attacks. Then, the attacker explores and observes the situations and conducts the attack by exploiting the known or unknown vulnerabilities. Finally, the defender chooses one or several actions to mitigate the damage caused by the attack. Therefore, Figure 3 represents the general structure of the model implemented in the game according to this presumption. The influence diagram is used to construct this model.

Influence diagrams represent the interaction among decisions, uncertainties, and utilities along with an algorithm to compute the expected utilities and identify the decisions that optimize the utility of decision-makers (Fenton & Neil, 2018). While influence diagrams can be viewed as an extension of Bayesian networks, they are different. A Bayesian network is a probabilistic network for belief update, whereas an influence diagram is a probabilistic network for reasoning about decision making under uncertainty (Kjaerulff & Madsen, 2008). An influence diagram is a graphical representation of a decision problem involving a sequence of interleaved decisions and observations. However, similar to Bayesian networks, an influence diagram is a compact and intuitive probabilistic knowledge representation (a probabilistic network). By making decisions, the players influence the probabilities of the configurations of the network (e.g., success of attacks, detection of vulnerabilities, and exploitation of a specific vulnerability).

In the influence diagram depicted in Figure 3, the decision nodes, uncertainty nodes, and utility nodes are represented as rectangle, oval, and octagon, respectively.

In the case of uncertainty, the known probability weights are replaced by player's subjective estimates of unknown probabilities. It is generally assumed that individuals modify their estimates on the basis of recent experience by a process termed Bayesian Updating (Bowles, 2009). Therefore, it is assumed that players decision making under uncertainty is based on expected utility maximization according to their subjective probabilities updated in this manner. Hence, this model presumes the players follow the von Neumann–Morgenstern (VNM) utility theorem. VNM shows that a decision-maker faced with probabilistic outcomes of different choices will behave as if he/she is maximizing the expected value of some function (i.e., in this game, the defined metrics) defined over the potential outcomes at some specified point in the future.

Figure 3. The general structure of the simulation model used in the game

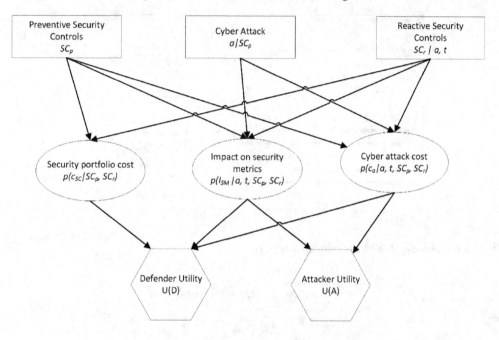

In this game, the attacker agent is automated. Therefore, to identify and choose the decision alternative with highest expected utility, the attack agent computes the expected utility of each decision alternative using the general equation below

$$EU\left(x_i\right) = \sum_j U\left(x_i, h_j\right) P(h_j \mid o)$$

where $x_i \in X \left(i \in \{1, \ldots, n\}\right)$ is a decision alternative, $h_j \in H \left(j \in \{1, \ldots, m\}\right)$ is a hypothesis, and o is a set of observations in the form of evidence at the time of making the decision. To maximize the expected utility, the agent chooses a decision alternative a^* such that

$$x^* = \arg\max_{x \in X} EU\left(x\right)$$

Now, given the security which compromises of preventive and reactive controls, and assuming that the attacker maximizes his expected utility, the agent computes the expected utility for each attack a and conducts the attack which has the maximum utility.

This model and the game interface is developed using C# language in Visual Studio 2019. Figure 4 and 5 show the dashboard and the report page of vulnerabilities in one run of the game. Since the game style in this run is Directing (i.e., the motivation and knowledge of the player is assessed low, respectively), the vulnerability report page includes all the useful information regarding the selected vulnerability. In case of a player with high motivation and high knowledge, the game style would be Delegating, and this information would not be shown.

Figure 4. A screenshot of the game's dashboard

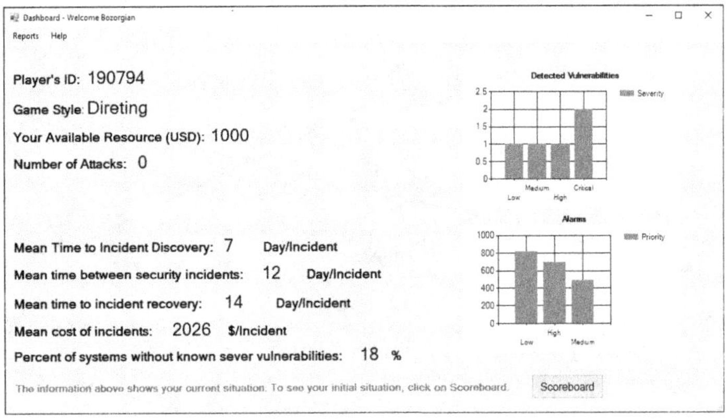

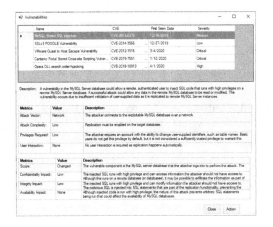

Figure 5. A screenshot of the vulnerabilities report

EXPERIMENTS

The research participants were Master and PhD students of the Department of Computer Science and Department of Information Security and Communication Technology at the Norwegian University of Science and Technology. This work is characterized as a quasi-experiment because it was not possible to randomly assign the students to experimental groups and a convenience sample of participating students played the game. The sample was divided into two groups: the experimental group (n = 9) and the control group (n = 3). Since the experiment and control groups may not be comparable at baseline, quasi-experiments are subject to concerns regarding internal validity (Cook et al., 2002). The internal validity threats are treated as the following: 1) ambiguous temporal precedence by implementation of pre- and post-assessments; 2) selection bias by choosing pre-assessment scores that their difference were not statistically significant; 3) maturation and history by having a control group; 4) regression toward the mean by selecting the subjects on the basis of non-extreme scores; 5) Mortality/differential attrition by avoiding loss of subjects; 6) repeated testing effect and experimenter bias by having different but equivalent situational assessments; and 7) instrumentality by not changing the measures and instruments used during the assessments.

The players were responsible for assessing the situation using the available information and make appropriate decisions by choosing the given options in the game. Since the use of game elements needed detailed instruction beforehand, a short time is dedicated to demonstrating the game instrument to the players. On average, the participants in the experiment group had about 45 minutes to play the game. To measure the high-order cognitive learning outcomes, it was necessary to develop specific scenarios to involve tasks such as understanding and analyzing the situation, synthesizing ideas, and evaluating and prioritizing the activities. Therefore, it was necessary to create situational tests with open ended questions to explain and review the prerequisite concepts for the subsequent practical tasks. To foster the reflection, the essential steps of the process during the debriefing are provided to allow a space to reflection in action.

RESULTS

As mentioned earlier, this chapter conceptualized cognitive learning as the acquisition of new, or the restructuring of existing knowledge to enhance the synthesis and evaluation abilities of the players. In order to evaluate this aspect, the authors used concept maps drawn by players before and after playing the game. Furthermore, they examined the responses to questions on the survey in the post-assessment and in follow-up interviews. All items on the concept maps were coded bases on six different categories and 22 sub-categories listed in the Table 3. Then, scores for the average specificity and centrality of the sub-categories of the sub-categories for all pre and post maps were calculated according to Morine-Dershimer's system.

The means for specificity and centrality were used to develop grids in Figure 6 illustrating players' pre and post map emphases on the 22 sub-categories. Categories that were most central to the main topic of leveraging gamification in encouraging secure and sustainable behavior in digital ecosystems appear on the left half of the grid, while categories that were least central appear on the right half of the grid. Categories that were mentioned with most specificity appear in the upper half of the grid, while categories mentioned with least specificity appear on the lower half of the grid. This division results in a grid of four quadrants, with the upper left quadrant containing the categories most heavily emphasized (both central and specific), and the lower right quadrant containing the categories least emphasized (neither central nor specific). The conceptual shifts are clearly detectable on the concept maps. Especially, issues related to complexity level, learning history, and metrics became all more specific and central on the post maps. This is in line with the set-up of the game, where players developed their system thinking, anticipatory, and problem-solving competencies. Issues such as developing analytical capabilities, understanding trends, and action prioritization that stood central and moved up in specificity corroborate to some degree of conceptual change and cognitive objectives to synthesis and evaluation abilities. Sub-categories 11 and 17 did not appear on pre maps. Therefore, the specificity score of 0 is assigned to them and they are not shown in Figure 6.

Since the sample size of this study was too small, the authors were not able to test for statistical significance. Hence, this chapter relied on learning effect of the game as self-reported surveys by players in the post-assessment and interviews. The interview questions were circled extensively around the question how to develop a sustainable cybersecurity plan in a rapidly changing system with uncertain information. Similarly, during playing the game, players became increasingly aware of the dynamics and interconnectedness of the systems and impact of their decisions on the metrics and future events.

Several players emphasized that the game provided them with a better understanding of the probable and possible consequences of their actions and this was previously received very attention. Furthermore, the players indicated in the interviews that the game promoted them to reflect more about the analysis of metrics and observing the trends to prioritize their actions. As argued before, these capabilities are the requirements of long-term policy making and sustainability transitions in the context of cybersecurity. However, the majority of the players agreed that the game has not been successful in truly real-world situations where decision-makers collaborate, regulatory agencies oversee the organizations, and institutional mechanisms and governance are in place.

Table 3. Categories and sub-categories of the concept map

Categories	Sub-categories	#
Design	Degree of realism	1
	Complexity level	2
	Narrative of the game	3
	Scoreboard	4
Architecture	Operation modes	5
	Defender and attacker operations	6
	Security portfolios	7
	Competition	8
Adaptability	Available time	9
	Learning history	10
	Complexity adjustment	11
Analysis	Resources	12
	Metrics	13
	Overall situation	14
Learning Outcomes	Developing analytical capabilities	15
	Understanding trends	16
	Understanding probable and possible consequences	17
	Actions prioritization based on available resources and importance	18
Pedagogical Considerations	Effectiveness	19
	Engagement	20
	Coverage	21
	Reflection in action	22

The pre- and post-assessments also highlighted the strength and weaknesses of the game. Figure 7 shows how players have responded the question regarding "Do you think it is possible that playing this game could change something with regard to …?" The results show that the game was successful as a learning tool to understand complexity, consider uncertainty, enhance scenario analysis, base the decisions on deeper knowledge and insights, and change the way of thinking. However, the designed game was limited regarding to improve working with group schemes, improve multi-sectoral and international cooperation. This study admits that these capabilities are essential in promoting secure and sustainable behavior in digital ecosystems and future work must incorporate them within the game by changing the mechanics and dynamics of the game.

In addition to the questions regarding the change in understanding, the assessments also included other open-ended questions regarding to the real impact of the game: 1) Has this game inspired you to change anything in the real world? 2) Has this game inspired you with creative ideas on how to tackle your problems in the real world? 3) Do you think playing this game could change something in policy making with regard to cybersecurity? All the players answered to such questions with "Yes" and provided us with more details in their responses.

Overall, the results of the evaluation, including concept maps, interviews, and surveys, suggest that gamification has been successful in developing the key competencies to advance secure and sustainable development within the context of cybersecurity. It inspired the players to reflect, change, and take actions with understanding and analysis of the trends, interdependencies, and uncertainties.

Figure 6. Conceptual changes of the players (a) and (b) before playing the game; (c) and (d) after playing the game

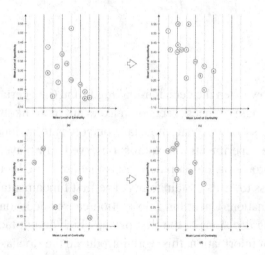

DISCUSSION AND CONCLUSIONS

In search of games for learning secure and sustainable behavior in digital ecosystems, the authors identified a gap in the available artifacts related to promoting secure and sustainable behavior that drive such research initiatives. This study addresses this gap by designing and developing an instantiation of the previously proposed framework focusing on facilitating behavior change, including individuals' mindset change, with combining security and sustainability concepts. While both concepts were separately the base of developing various games, it is the combination of these two that the authors find particularly effective for the better security of today's complex socio-technical systems. Gamification and its motivational potential are seen as trends for increasing and promoting user engagement in manifold contexts (Mekler et al., 2017). In this work, a primary motivation for using gamification to promote secure and sustainable behavior is its promise of encouraging individuals to act with greater engagement (Tan & Hew, 2016). To identify which techniques produce the most effective results, it is necessary to build upon theoretical foundations that connect procedures used by instructional designers with the choice of game elements, as indicated by the Theory of Gamified Learning (Landers, 2014).

Figure 7. The pre- and post-assessment responses to the question of Do you think it is possible that playing this game could change something with regard to ...?

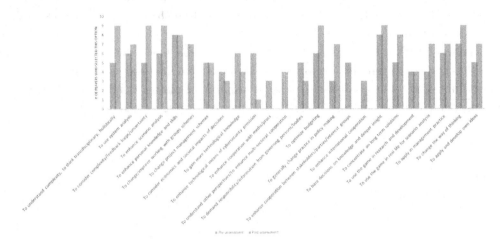

This work investigated how when the decision-making frame (i.e., certain aspects of a situation that is constituted by various settings) changes, decision makers are more likely to reframe both their goals and the focus of their analysis to go beyond monetary outcomes to include both security and sustainability outcomes. During the experiments, the authors observed how players change their way of thinking to frame sustainability problems, develop new goals that are more holistic, and implement metrics to keep track of their progress towards sustainability. The first fundamental challenge to sustainability, however, is uncertain information. Uncertain information causes decision-makers to delay necessary actions or to make the wrong decisions in the first place, which do not tackle the problem. Therefore, to simulate the uncertainty of information, this work introduced the stochastic behavior of attackers and the inherent probabilistic nature of the vulnerabilities and alarms in the system. What was observed in these simulations is an inherently property of complex systems behavior: although the system itself is very basic and consists of a few variables, it is possible to generate a variety of patterns that cause totally different outcomes.

The second challenge to sustainability is competition. Since some aspects of cybersecurity threat intelligence and vulnerability information sharing, collective response to cyber-attacks, and critical infrastructure protection that have the characteristics of public goods. Consequently, the free-rider problem may change the behavior of the players to non-sustainable actions at their own cost or others. This situation is not implemented in the current settings of this work. Future work can focus on design and implementation of cooperative and competitive behaviors in the game to take them into account.

In the process of design and development of the game, this work incorporated the importance of the system representation and scenario analysis so that it helps the players to bring their own ideas, thus opening a rich dialogue between designers and players. This chapter operationalized this using situational tests, procedural rhetoric, and debriefing processes in the game structure. The preliminary evaluation observed significant qualitative evidence of security and sustainability behavior in terms of developed system thinking competency, anticipatory competency, and problem-solving competency. A more rigorous evaluation is needed by 1) comparing the effects of games through alternative methods (e.g., lectures, full-scale exercises, and multimedia); 2) revising the game structure to identify what works and what requires further improvement; 3) applying more elaborate methods to study learning effects in cognitive, normative, and relational dimensions; and 4) assessing long-term impacts of gaming interventions in real-world situations of the players.

This chapter does not contend that this game will possibly take account of all the peculiarities involved in decision making and therefore be an accurate tool of establishing secure and sustainable behavior in the organizations. However, the game is aimed to develop an aid to thinking about some of the aspects of broader, complex situation and have an idea about the dynamical interplay among them. Further scientific efforts are certainly needed to improve both theoretical and empirical bases for appropriate strategic simulation games design. This work is an attempt to both advance theoretical foundations and, by developing a specific design artifact, encourage game development practice that foster integrated concepts of security and sustainability considering their increasing importance in digital ecosystems.

REFERENCES

Anderson, R., Barton, C., Bölme, R., Clayton, R., Ganán, C., Grasso, T., Levi, M., Moore, T., & Vasek, M. (2019). *Measuring the changing cost of cybercrime*. Academic Press.

Argyris, C. (2003). A life full of learning. *Organization Studies*, *24*(7), 1178–1192. doi:10.1177/017084060030247009

Bowles, S. (2009). *Microeconomics*. Princeton University Press. doi:10.2307/j.ctvcm4gc3

Castro-Sánchez, E., Kyratsis, Y., Iwami, M., Rawson, T. M., & Holmes, A. H. (2016). Serious electronic games as behavioural change interventions in healthcare-associated infections and infection prevention and control: A scoping review of the literature and future directions. *Antimicrobial Resistance and Infection Control*, *5*(1), 1–7. doi:10.118613756-016-0137-0 PMID:27777755

Cook, T. D., Campbell, D. T., & Shadish, W. (2002). *Experimental and quasi-experimental designs for generalized causal inference*. Houghton Mifflin Boston.

De Haan, G. (2010). The development of ESD-related competencies in supportive institutional frameworks. *International Review of Education*, *56*(2), 315–328. doi:10.100711159-010-9157-9

Deming, W. E. (2018). *The New Economics for Industry, Government, Education* (3rd ed.). MIT Press Ltd.

Do, C. T., Tran, N. H., Hong, C., Kamhoua, C. A., Kwiat, K. A., Blasch, E., Ren, S., Pissinou, N., & Iyengar, S. S. (2017). Game theory for cyber security and privacy. *ACM Computing Surveys*, *50*(2), 1–37. doi:10.1145/3057268

Duke, R. D., & Geurts, J. (2004). *Policy games for strategic management*. Rozenberg Publishers.

Engeström, Y. (1999). Innovative learning in work teams: Analyzing cycles of knowledge creation. *Perspectives on Activity Theory*, 377.

Engeström, Y. (2015). *Learning by expanding.* Cambridge University Press.

Fenton, N., & Neil, M. (2018). *Risk assessment and decision analysis with Bayesian networks.* Crc Press. doi:10.1201/b21982

Fünfschilling, L. (2014). *A dynamic model of socio-technical change: Institutions, actors and technologies in interaction.* University_of_Basel.

Galaitsi, S., Keisler, J. M., Trump, B. D., & Linkov, I. (2021). The need to reconcile concepts that characterize systems facing threats. *Risk Analysis*, *41*(1), 3–15. doi:10.1111/risa.13577 PMID:32818299

Geer, D., Jardine, E., & Leverett, E. (2020). On market concentration and cybersecurity risk. *Journal of Cyber Policy*, *5*(1), 9–29. doi:10.1080/23738871.2020.1728355

Geurts, J. L., Duke, R. D., & Vermeulen, P. A. (2007). Policy gaming for strategy and change. *Long Range Planning*, *40*(6), 535–558. doi:10.1016/j.lrp.2007.07.004

González-Ortega, J., Insua, D. R., & Cano, J. (2019). Adversarial risk analysis for bi-agent influence diagrams: An algorithmic approach. *European Journal of Operational Research*, *273*(3), 1085–1096. doi:10.1016/j.ejor.2018.09.015

Gortney, W. E. (2012). *Dictionary of Military and Associated Terms.* Academic Press.

Hallinger, P., & Chatpinyakoop, C. (2019). A bibliometric review of research on higher education for sustainable development, 1998–2018. *Sustainability*, *11*(8), 2401. doi:10.3390u11082401

Harsanyi, J. C. (1967). Games with incomplete information played by "Bayesian" players, I–III Part I. The basic model. *Management Science*, *14*(3), 159–182. doi:10.1287/mnsc.14.3.159

Haug, C., Huitema, D., & Wenzler, I. (2011). Learning through games? Evaluating the learning effect of a policy exercise on European climate policy. *Technological Forecasting and Social Change*, *78*(6), 968–981. doi:10.1016/j.techfore.2010.12.001

Holtz, G., Alkemade, F., De Haan, F., Köhler, J., Trutnevyte, E., Luthe, T., Halbe, J., Papachristos, G., Chappin, E., Kwakkel, J., & Ruutu, S. (2015). Prospects of modelling societal transitions: Position paper of an emerging community. *Environmental Innovation and Societal Transitions*, *17*, 41–58. doi:10.1016/j.eist.2015.05.006

Joshi, C., Aliaga, J. R., & Insua, D. R. (2020). Insider threat modeling: An adversarial risk analysis approach. *IEEE Transactions on Information Forensics and Security*, *16*, 1131–1142. doi:10.1109/TIFS.2020.3029898

Kianpour, M. (2020). *Knowledge and Skills Needed to Craft Successful Cybersecurity Strategies.* Norsk IKT-konferanse for forskning og utdanning.

Kianpour, M., Kowalski, S., Zoto, E., Frantz, C., & Øverby, H. (2019). Designing serious games for cyber ranges: a socio-technical approach. *2019 IEEE European symposium on security and privacy workshops (EuroS&PW).*

Kjaerulff, U. B., & Madsen, A. L. (2008). *Bayesian networks and influence diagrams*. Springer Science+ Business Media.

Landers, R. N. (2014). Developing a theory of gamified learning: Linking serious games and gamification of learning. *Simulation & Gaming*, *45*(6), 752–768. doi:10.1177/1046878114563660

McLennan, M. (2021). *The Global Risks Report 2021*. T. W. E. Forum.

Mekler, E. D., Brühlmann, F., Tuch, A. N., & Opwis, K. (2017). Towards understanding the effects of individual gamification elements on intrinsic motivation and performance. *Computers in Human Behavior*, *71*, 525–534. doi:10.1016/j.chb.2015.08.048

Merrick, J., & Parnell, G. S. (2011). A comparative analysis of PRA and intelligent adversary methods for counterterrorism risk management. *Risk Analysis: An International Journal*, *31*(9), 1488–1510. doi:10.1111/j.1539-6924.2011.01590.x PMID:21418080

Morine-Dershimer, G. (1993). Tracing conceptual change in preservice teachers. *Teaching and Teacher Education*, *9*(1), 15–26. doi:10.1016/0742-051X(93)90012-6

Nonaka, I., & Takeuchi, H. (1995). *The knowledge-creating company: How Japanese companies create the dynamics of innovation*. Oxford university press.

Østby, G., Berg, L., Kianpour, M., Katt, B., & Kowalski, S. J. (2019). A socio-technical framework to improve cyber security training. *Work (Reading, Mass.)*.

Papachristos, G. (2014). Towards multi-system sociotechnical transitions: Why simulate. *Technology Analysis and Strategic Management*, *26*(9), 1037–1055. doi:10.1080/09537325.2014.944148

Rieckmann, M. (2012). Future-oriented higher education: Which key competencies should be fostered through university teaching and learning? *Futures*, *44*(2), 127–135. doi:10.1016/j.futures.2011.09.005

Rieckmann, M. (2017). *Education for sustainable development goals: Learning objectives*. UNESCO Publishing.

Rios Insua, D., Couce-Vieira, A., Rubio, J. A., Pieters, W., Labunets, K., & Rasines, G., D. (. (2021). An adversarial risk analysis framework for cybersecurity. *Risk Analysis*, *41*(1), 16–36. doi:10.1111/risa.13331 PMID:31183890

Rios Insua, D., Ríos, J., & Banks, D. (2009). Adversarial risk analysis. *Journal of the American Statistical Association*, *104*(486), 841–854. doi:10.1198/jasa.2009.0155

Rumelhart, D. E., & Norman, D. A. (1976). *Accretion, tuning and restructuring: Three modes of learning*. Academic Press.

Sadik, S., Ahmed, M., Sikos, L. F., & Islam, A. (2020). Toward a Sustainable Cybersecurity Ecosystem. *Computers*, *9*(3), 74. doi:10.3390/computers9030074

Shackelford, S. J., Fort, T. L., & Charoen, D. (2016). Sustainable cybersecurity: Applying lessons from the green movement to managing Cyber Attacks. *U. Ill. L. Rev.*

Shiva, S., Roy, S., & Dasgupta, D. (2010). Game theory for cyber security. *Proceedings of the Sixth Annual Workshop on Cyber Security and Information Intelligence Research.*

Tan, M., & Hew, K. F. (2016). Incorporating meaningful gamification in a blended learning research methods class: Examining student learning, engagement, and affective outcomes. *Australasian Journal of Educational Technology*, *32*(5).

Toth, F. L. (1988). Policy exercises: Objectives and design elements. *Simulation & Games*, *19*(3), 235–255. doi:10.1177/0037550088193001

Vasiu, I., & Vasiu, L. (2018). Cybersecurity as an essential sustainable economic development factor. *European Journal of Sustainable Development*, *7*(4), 171–178. doi:10.14207/ejsd.2018.v7n4p171

Venters, C., Lau, L., Griffiths, M., Holmes, V., Ward, R., Jay, C., Dibsdale, C., & Xu, J. (2014). The blind men and the elephant: Towards an empirical evaluation framework for software sustainability. *Journal of Open Research Software*, *2*(1). Advance online publication. doi:10.5334/jors.ao

Wanick, V., & Bui, H. (2019). Gamification in Management: A systematic review and research directions. *International Journal of Serious Games*, *6*(2), 57–74. doi:10.17083/ijsg.v6i2.282

Wenzler, I. (1993). *Policy exercises: A new approach to policy development*. Instituut voor Toegepaste Wetenschappen.

Wenzler, I., & Chartier, D. (1999). Why do we bother with games and simulations: An organizational learning perspective. *Simulation & Gaming*, *30*(3), 375–384. doi:10.1177/104687819903000315

Wiek, A., Withycombe, L., & Redman, C. L. (2011). Key competencies in sustainability: A reference framework for academic program development. *Sustainability Science*, *6*(2), 203–218. doi:10.100711625-011-0132-6

Zoto, E., Kianpour, M., Kowalski, S. J., & Lopez-Rojas, E. A. (2019). A socio-technical systems approach to design and support systems thinking in cybersecurity and risk management education. *Complex Systems Informatics and Modeling Quarterly*, (18), 65–75. doi:10.7250/csimq.2019-18.04

KEY TERMS AND DEFINITIONS

Conceptual Change: Is the process whereby concepts, ideas, thoughts, and the relationships between them change over the course of a person's lifetime or over the course of a change in the understanding of a context.

Gamification: Is the application of game elements such as goals, rules, strategies, aesthetics, and rewards to non-game contexts and problems such as cybersecurity, business, and climate change.

Influence Diagrams: Are graphical and mathematical representation of a decision situation. By using various shapes, an influence diagram depicts decisions, uncertainties, and objectives.

Policy Simulations: Are visual tools that enables the users to select initiatives, compare scenarios, analyze outcomes, and share results to understand how policies are enforces on a given context.

Security Metrics: Are specific, measurable, repeatable, and time-dependent values and units that demonstrate how well an organization's cybersecurity plan is accomplishing goals, maintaining compliance, and mitigating risks.

Socio-Technical Perspective: Is understanding the importance of the interrelatedness of social and technical aspects of organizations and societies, and how they change and evolve by their interaction.

Sustainable Cybersecurity: Is a continuous socio-technical process of implementing, using, managing, and maintaining security resources to ensure a certain level of security, reliability, and resilience in organizations.

ENDNOTES

[1] Sustainability is defined differently in different contexts to suit their purpose. For example, software sustainability refers to the ability to ensure availability, support, and improvement of the software products and services that are created Venters, C., Lau, L., Griffiths, M., Holmes, V., Ward, R., Jay, C., Dibsdale, C., & Xu, J. (2014). The blind men and the elephant: Towards an empirical evaluation framework for software sustainability. *Journal of Open Research Software*, 2(1).

[2] For a better understanding of these concepts, the authors suggest that the readers read (Kianpour et al. 2019).

[3] The readers is referred to "Merrick, J., & Parnell, G. S. (2011). A comparative analysis of PRA and intelligent adversary methods for counterterrorism risk management. *Risk Analysis: An International Journal*, *31*(9), 1488-1510." for a comparative analysis of various modeling methods in risk management.

Chapter 10
Gamified Digital Apps and Their Utilization to Improve Health Behaviors in the 21st Century:
Gamified Digital Health Behavior Interventions

Lawrence M. Scheier
LARS Research Institute, USA

William B. Hansen
Prevention Strategies, USA

ABSTRACT

This chapter builds on Hansen and Scheier by further examining the intersection of game-based learning and digital health promotion apps. The intersection of digital technology and health promotion is an intriguing space given that cost-effective technologies backed by strong theory and implementation science can advance health promotion strategies. Gamification extends asynchronous computer-mediated communication by creating a sense of immersion in the virtual space, socially interacting, and experiencing strong social identifications. This produces feelings of "flow" reported as a stoppage of time and mitigating surrounding intrusive events. Avatars provide pedagogical supports to increase situational awareness, deepening their presence in the digital game world. Players can learn from these interactions, building rapport and developing social connections that might otherwise not be possible in different contexts. Gamified digital technology capitalizes on instructional technology, learning theory, and social identification in ways that can advance health behavior change.

DOI: 10.4018/978-1-6684-4291-3.ch010

INTRODUCTION

"Then too, video games, like most popular culture media, reflect back to us, in part, the basic themes and even prejudices of our own society" (Gee, 2007, p. 197).

This chapter addresses the intersection of gamified digital technology and instructional technology, the latter rooted in learning theory. The discussion of how these two literatures come together is framed by the context of health promotion, specifically addressing the principles of prevention science and the methods used to empirically verify whether (and how) programs achieve behavior change. We begin with an in-depth look at what delineates programs as "gamified" across the digital health promotion spectrum. We then explore the intersection of gaming and learning theory, using Gee's (2003) influential writing as a backdrop. This is followed by a brief overview of how gamified technology, backed by strong theory, can be used to promote health behaviors. We then revisit an earlier publication by Hansen and Scheier (2019), titled *"Specialized smartphone intervention apps: Review of 2014 to 2018 NIH funded grants."* In this earlier published article, we examined 397 NIH-funded grants that involved the intersection of digital technology and health promotion. The programs involved mobile and smartphone apps (mHealth) or Internet-based apps (eHealth) that were designed as interventions to advance health promotion. Of these, 52 of the programs purported to use gamification as a core instructional modality. In the current chapter, we revisit a subset of the 52 programs and examine in greater detail the contents of the programs in light of recent advances in gamification and learning theory[1]. An in-depth exploration of these programs can be fruitful both in determining how gamification is used to promote health behaviors and also in determining whether the field is advancing by blending digital technologies with learning theory and the tenets of health promotion in ways that can improve the educational experience of end users.

WHAT MAKES IT A GAME?

Games, and this includes any game played on a board such as monopoly, stick ball in the street, Marco Polo played in a public swimming pool, played online or with a smartphone, have to be fun to play, engrossing, and challenging. Even a simple card game like solitaire can be fun, engrossing and challenging, as much as a board game like monopoly or a party game like charades. Treasure hunts are games and challenge players to follow clues and find hidden items. Playing 3 v 3 hoops at a local park is fun, occupies players' time during summer recess, and creates challenges to see who scores the most baskets and which player can dazzle another with their superb dribbling skills. A core feature of games is that they impart a sense of control and autonomy, which is a large part of why they are attractive to play (Kapp, 2012).

Digital games follow this pattern but transfer the fun and challenge to a computer-mediated world. Advances in computer graphics for high resolution digital imaging and vast gains in the processing power of computers have made it possible for digital games to possess a sort of "realism." As part of this realism, digital games can replicate intricate human movements mimicking various qualities of the human experience. The computer term "humanoid," is meant to indicate as close to the human shape and form as possible when using network-enabled 3D graphics and multimedia environments (Humanoid Animation Standards, 2006). This capability produces the third defining element that makes games so attractive, which is the ability to engross players for prolonged periods of time. With high resolution graphics, players become completely immersed, feeling "as if" they are embodied in the virtual world, interacting with real social identities (i.e., avatars) and experiencing events in real time (Schultze, 2012). This photorealism, added to the challenges associated with playing games, entices players to continue their efforts and test their skills and abilities against the game mechanics.

Games also contain rules that govern game play. Solitaire requires drawing cards from the playing deck under certain conditions, monopoly allows a player to move a piece around the board governed by certain rules, and pickup basketball at the local park requires inbounding the ball after a basket is scored from a designated spot on the court. Digital games also include rules or "design grammars" that instruct the player how to win or succeed. Games also provide feedback (which can be instantaneous with digital games) that players can use to make adjustments to their game play. Game mechanics, which incorporate the rules and standards of play, as well as specify reward contingencies, are shared with players in the context of a game narrative, or the storyline, which consists of the player composition, game-world design (setting or navigational frame), and scenarios or plots (i.e., adventure mission) that provide the backdrop for learning (Ke, 2016)[2].

Can Games be Equated with Learning?

Beyond learning about a game's rules or design grammars, players engaged in digital games also can learn new skills, improve their knowledge of some substantive topic, and engage in behavior change. For instance, in the context of health promotion, players can acquire new skills that advance their ability to engage in safe sex. They can learn how to gauge the nutritional value of foods in the event they are diabetic, and they can learn how to cope with hearing loss when in crowded and noisy rooms. Gee (2004) reinforces a crucial if not pivotal role for the principles of learning in video games. He outlines several important features of computer games including that players must feel like active agents, creating, producing and doing. Moreover, games should be customizable to fit individual learning and playing styles, offer players channels for identification, and provide players the opportunity to become more heavily invested in what the character does, how s/he acts and their experiences. Games should also involve action and the chance to manipulate characters, be well ordered so that players can build on their learning experience for later game challenges (i.e., their hypotheses should be generalizable to the real-world). Games should provide a modicum of frustration but match this with feedback, offer opportunities to practice as the player gains mastery, provide verbal information just-in-time to guide players, not be too complex at first, and provide a sense of achievement. This provides players a sense that they are moving in the right direction, their efforts will eventually pay off and are sustainable. Games should also provide a measure of authenticity in a safe environment, help players learn skills strategically (aiming toward goals), and provide players a chance to develop intuitions about the norms and rules of the game.

According to Gee (2008), good video games capitalize on pleasureful experiences and mastery that are tied to our social identities. By this, Gee means where we acquire information is almost as important as the nature of the information[3]. To illustrate this concept, children attend school to learn. They learn from didactic instruction (top down from the teacher), engage in classroom activities with their classmates (peer-to-peer interactions), and reinforce learning autonomously through homework. At the same time, there are many opportunities for them to vicariously observe the mistakes of their fellow classmates, listen to the teacher as s/he corrects other students' mistakes and incorporate this active experiential learning into memory. As individuals strive to grow, active "participatory" learning experiences are incorporated along with practice and feedback to build the essential building blocks of learning[4]. Well-designed games capitalize on these experiences to teach problem-solving in situations that replicate the real world (Savery & Duffy, 1995). Players engaged in a game are given "tools and technologies"[5] to help them master content and find ways to actively problem solve. Well-designed games foster learning because the player senses the connection between the game's norms and goals and real-world problem solving (i.e., the player constructs a simulated mental model), whereas inert learning, or learning in a vacuum that cannot be applied to practice, is not efficient or fun (i.e., it has no situated meaning with ties to actual experiential contexts)[6]. In Gee's (2007) conceptual model, well-constructed computer video games "externalize the way in which the human mind works and thinks in a better fashion than any other technology we have" (p. 200).

Games are also an important learning tool because they play a role in teaching players how to handle failure (Annetta, 2008; Squire & Jenkins, 2003). Games "soften" the role of failure in learning by teaching players they can take risks, that the "losses" associated with risks are not devastating, and that part of testing hypotheses about the game, in effect about life, is to make certain predictions (Vogel et al., 2006). Not every prediction will come to fruition and in this manner, games teach players that the risks of making predictions are not so costly that one should avoid them entirely. When a player makes an in-game prediction, chooses an action and it fails, they often return to a starting point (descend or repeat a challenge level in the game). This action of dropping the player back to the most recent level buffers them from experiencing complete failure (losing all traction and having to start the game completely over again), emotionally engages the player, and provides them with motivational impetus to solve the problem. Game failure encourages players to apply situational knowledge (what was the outcome of an action?), choose alternative courses of action (rethinking their decisions by exploring), and find the right answer. Much of game play using these concepts borrows heavily from learning theory, including Vygotsky's (1978) concept of the zone of proximal development, utilization of scaffolding or pedagogical supports (Pea, 2004; Puntambekar & Hübscher, 2005), and the cognitive processes of accommodation and assimilation (Inhelder & Piaget, 1958; Piaget, 1952). In all of these instances, learning is progressive, builds on prior effort (and experience), and challenges the individual (child) to build a composite picture of the known (observed) elements.

Successful epistemically-based digital games that are heavily dependent on learning theories effectively place the player in a constructivist, autonomous learning environment framed by "behavior in practice" (Gagné, 1984). This type of learning environment produces "situated meaning" (Prensky, 2001). Situated meaning in a digital environment contextualizes the spoken word (dialogue), experience, images, and action in ways that allow a player to construct simulations in their mind that can be played out later in ways that enhance the real world, effectively demonstrating alteration of schemas, which produces learning. In line with this, Gee (2007) proposed that successful games place players of any age in an environment that combines literacy, cognition, language, affect, and social interaction into a cohesive learning experience; one that follows the same precepts and building blocks as how learning would take place in the real world.

THE INTERSECTION OF GAMES AND HEALTH PROMOTION

With this brief discussion of digital games and learning in mind, this next section briefly addresses the application of digital computer games and health promotion. This discussion is shaped around several pressing concerns that come to mind. Foremost among these is whether digital platforms (gamified or not) incorporate the principles of prevention science, particularly adhering to the implementation of evidence-based interventions. This activity involves showing that the active ingredients of an intervention work in the "manner hypothesized" to bring about behavior change. Following this line of reasoning, this requires that digital games are able to demonstrate whether specific aspects of a game are linked with behavior change that can be quantified as measurable learning outcomes (e.g., Hekler et al., 2016). This is an important issue, because as Bedwell et al. (2012) noted, "The use of serious games is progressing without explicit knowledge as to why games are effective teaching tools. It is not clear which attributes lead to which learning outcomes" (p. 730).

In many cases, apps are designed to capitalize on technological wizardry (high quality graphics, blending narrative and storyline with interactivity) without explicitly providing evidence that the digital game mechanics produce theory-based behavior change. This is an essential component to program evaluation (Chen, 1990; West & Aiken, 1997) and extends to digital behavior change interventions as well. In other words, what are the implementation conditions under which the app is most likely to work, for whom, in which contexts, and why? This examination includes the prominent technical "game-based" features of the app (instructional strategies), patterns of utilization, and what back-end (digital trace) usability information can tell us about the player's in-game experiences and their, however primitive, understanding of the game mechanics. The absence of this information creates a validity concern because there is no means to track potential links between digital game attributes and learning (health promotion) outcomes (Bedwell et al., 2012; Wilson et al., 2009).

As an extension of this premise, for the most part, digital games for behavior change involve multiple "moving parts" or components that use a variety of intervention modalities to achieve a program's explicit goals. For instance, in a digital world, feedback is an important component to learning as is practice to achieve mastery and presentation of stepped challenge situations. Blending setting and narrative is also important as this piques the interest of the player, makes them curious to know how the situation pans out. Also important is matching the difficulty of the tasks to the player's competence level (i.e., adaptive programming). If one turns to the prevention science literature, a good deal has been written about "just-in-time" adaptive interventions that can deliver "treatment when needed" (e.g., Lagoa, et al., 2014). However, in the digital gaming literature the ability to map game mechanics to learning outcomes lags behind current program evaluation techniques. Transfer of material learned from the digital world to the real world is also key and can determine the efficacy of a digital intervention for health promotion. Which specific features of the digital game boost learning potential remains obscure unless the components are studied individually. Stated differently, a big question hanging over the digital gaming literature is what particular attribute(s) of a game engenders motivation and learning? This is a pervasive question for all intervention science, bearing down on the question of what are the "active ingredients" of a program and what are the mechanisms of action that lead to behavior change. This is a particularly formidable if not daunting question when one considers a multicomponent intervention.

Digital technology relies on multiple interfaces to deliver health promotion programs and should be subject to the same rigorous evaluation criteria as any behavioral intervention regardless of delivery modality. Some, but perhaps not all, of the behavior change strategies contained in a digital app may be effective. Related to this concern is finding the appropriate analytic framework to break down how an intervention achieves its goals of behavior change. In the field of prevention science, this has been termed "*treatment construct validity*" (McCaul & Glasgow, 1985) and involves a manipulation check to determine what part or parts of an intervention are "working" in the manner hypothesized (Scheier, 2020). Various dismantling and componential analysis strategies exist to tease apart the efficacy of different intervention modalities. These include computer-driven fractional factorial designs (Collins, Murphy, & Strecher, 2007) for componential analysis and micro-randomized trials (MRT; Klasnja et al., 2015), the latter of which can rigorously test which specific components of an intervention work best, for whom, in which combination, and under which conditions. The MRT in particular, can help configure decision rules based on factors that may moderate intervention effectiveness for each individual (did they respond to intervention overtures to increase their steps and physical activity or not engage a health-compromising behavior?), making an intervention conform to a just-in-time adaptive strategy.

Sufficient numbers of digital health promotion games have now been evaluated that makes it possible to summarize their potential. Unfortunately, reviews of health promotion apps have not been entirely supportive of a prominent role for theory testing. Edwards and colleagues (2016), for example, found only 64 of 1680 available health apps they reviewed actually included gamification linked to behavior change, with three prominent behavior change strategies including feedback and monitoring, reward and threat, goals and planning. Other reviews report the same questionable findings, showing an abundance of caution with respect to theory driving digital technology apps (with or without gamification)[7]. For example, Riley et al. (2011) reported that very few mobile applications for health behavior change were up to the task, and that most lacked specification of potential mechanisms of behavior change. DeSmet et al. (2014) suggested that serious digital games for healthy lifestyle promotion struggle to link theoretical components to actual behavior change. Sitzmann's (2011) meta-analysis of adult work-related simulation games shows that simulation games do not fare well when pitted against traditional instructional modalities once theoretical moderators are controlled. Theoretical moderators address implementation concerns such as how frequently the simulation game is played, whether it is a stand-alone strategy, whether the comparison instructional strategies are active (practice-oriented), and if the comparison group also played a simulation game.

Popular theories used as a backdrop for health-related digital games include the health belief model (Becker, 1974; Becker, Drachman, & Kirscht, 1974; Becker & Maiman, 1975), theory of planned behavior (Ajzen, 2002; Ajzen, 1991), social learning/social cognitive theory (Bandura, 1977a; 1977b; 1986), transtheoretical model (Prochaska & Velicer, 1997), and self-determination theory (Ryan & Deci, 2000; Ryan, Rigby, & Przybylski, 2006). In the case of Ryan et al. (2006) their insight into the motivational "pulls" of video games aligns with overtures from game-based learning; resoundingly supporting that the "game is the best teacher." Additional theories than can be related to the manipulation of game features include the Elaboration Likelihood Model (Cacioppo, Petty, & Stoltenberg, 1985), and Transportation Theory (Green & Brock, 2000; Green, Brock, & Kaufman, 2004), both of which focus more on the player's in-game experiences from a cognitive-phenomenological perspective. Transportation theory entails message persuasion (i.e., affective responses), the narrative and its elicitation of self-schemas (i.e., mental images), and how narratives influence cognitive engagement by creating attachments (identification) to game characters that become motivational in their own right.

UPDATED REVIEW FINDINGS

It is with this brief discussion of digital games, learning theory, and health promotion in mind that the authors sought to extend their prior findings regarding the use of gamification in digital behavioral intervention apps. The current effort entailed seeking additional information on the quality and extent of "gamification" in the apps that qualified for inclusion under the previously reported 2019 categorization scheme. The questions posed addressed the use of gamification and whether the programs were commercially available. The precise questions addressed included: (1) What is the commercial name of the app? (2) Is the app available? (3) If so, is there a website associated with it? (4) Are there peer-reviewed published works about the app? and (5) Does the app include gamification?

Table 1. Summary Information of Reviewed Apps

	Target Age	Focus	Role	Reward	Theory	RCT	Engagement	Outcomes
Executive Cognitive Function								
Alien Game	teens, young adults	Cognitive Function	1st person	points, levels, feedback	Theory of Mind	yes	age-related engagement	cognitive improvement
Braingame Brian	youth	ADHD	Avatar	points, powers	ADHD Theory	yes	positive ratings	cognitive improvement
Neuroracer	elderly	ADHD, Depression	1st person	points, levels	NA	yes	NA	cognitive improvement
Rise of Nations	elderly	Cognitive Function	1st person	feedback, achievement	Theory of Cognitive Control	yes	NA	cognitive improvement
Space Fortress	adults	Cognitive Function	1st person	points	Theory of Mind	no	NA	skill improvement
Star Wars Battlefront	elderly	Cognitive Function	1st person	points, levels	Scaffolding Theory of Aging and Cognition	yes	NA	short-term memory gain
HIV Prevention and Care								
AllyQuest	young men	HIV	1st person	points, achievement	Social Cognitive Theory	no	poor retention	improved self-management
Stick to It	young men	HIV	1st person	points, redemption	Self-Determination Theory	no	modest engagement	improved HIV outcomes
Viral Combat	young men	HIV	1st person	points, feedback	Social Cognitive Theory	yes	modest retention	improved knowledge
Illness and Injury								
clEAR	children, adults	Auditory Cognition	NA	NA	Transfer-Appropriate Processing Theory	yes	NA	improved hearing & speech
Jerry the Bear	children	Diabetes Control	Avatar	feedback	NA	no	positive ratings	NA
Pedestrian Safety	children	Safety	1st person	points, feedback	Ecological Theory, Cognitive Theory	no	NA	improved understanding
SCDG	elderly	Exercise, Diet	Avatar	points, levels, trophies	Self-determination Theory	yes	positive ratings	no differences
VIGOR	elderly	Low Back Pain	1st person	points, levels, feedback	NA	no	NA	NA

Sources of Data

In their published review, Hansen and Scheier (2019) identified 52 digital behavioral intervention apps that appeared to include gaming or gamification. The current follow-up included reaching out to each of the principal investigators of the NIH-funded projects to obtain further clarification about the nature of their research and commercialization plans. A total of 22 of the 52 investigators responded to this inquiry. Of these, four indicated that their project did not include an app or that their digital technology approach did not include gamification. The remaining 18 applications ostensibly met the criteria for being digital games. However, after an examination of each app, only 14 were found to be sufficiently well described and actually gamified. Table 1 summarizes information about the game, including content focus, gamified features, theoretical backdrop, whether an RCT was conducted, and outcomes. To obtain this information, the authors accessed the app or the hosting website. Literature was collected about each app, including descriptive documents as well as published research literature. As Table 1 shows, in some cases, there was no explicit mention of theory, no effort to quantify levels of engagement by participants, or no evidence of program-related behavior change.

App Details

Each app was classified in the current review according to three major groups. This classification primarily provides a heuristic for grouping apps. This led to examining games that focus on improving executive cognitive function and games that attempt to teach specific skills as two broad areas. The skill-focused games were further aggregated into those that address HIV transmission, and those that promote prevention and recovery from illness and injury, and finally, a game that promotes pedestrian safety.

Games That Focus on Improving Executive Cognitive Functioning

Several games have been developed or used specifically to improve players' cognitive abilities. Executive cognitive functions primarily consist of three broadly defined skills: working memory, flexible thinking, and inhibitory control (e.g., Kuhn, 2000). Working memory refers to the ability to hold recently acquired information, manipulate it, and use it for some purpose such as answering questions or applying it to solve a problem. Flexible thinking refers to a person's ability to think in alternative ways (e.g., Kato, 2012), particularly when conditions change. Inhibitory control refers to a person's ability to postpone or restrain from engaging in habitual or predisposed behaviors in order to select a more appropriate course of action. Games in this category generally provide players with situations that require them to increase their capacity to store information in working memory, engage in flexible thinking, and develop the ability to inhibit predisposing behaviors in favor of engaging in novel and more appropriate behavior.

Alien Game was designed for high school students with the goal of increasing their ability to improve executive (cognitive) functioning. Specifically, the game targets improving teens' ability to shift between tasks and mental sets (cognitive shifting), suppress previously established response sets (inhibition), and monitor and adjust their working memories (updating). To do this, the game presents players with tasks related to taking care of imaginary aliens who are visiting Earth (Homer et al., 2018). Aliens vary along a number of dimensions including their color, the number of eyes they have, and other physical or facial features. At each level, players are given instructions about how to care for aliens of various types. For instance, red aliens are hungry and blue aliens are thirsty. The game's complexity then shifts to the one eyed-blue alien who is hungry and the two-eyed red alien who is thirsty. As the game proceeds, the rules become increasingly complicated, requiring players to adopt revised rules in order to earn points. Players not only receive points for performing well, they also receive feedback about aliens' mood and happiness.

Homer et al. (2018) playtested early versions (with younger age children) using think-aloud procedures, followed by semi-structured interviews, iterative modifications and finally a formal beta test. A sample of 82 ethnically diverse high school students were asked to log in to an Internet portal and play *Alien Game* for at least 20 minutes per week over 6 weeks. The game asked students to shift between complex sorting rules and inhibit certain responses, both indicative of executive functioning skills. Paired t-tests indicated the students significantly improved pre- to posttest in their cognitive shifting and inhibition. Interestingly, age was inversely related to time spent playing the game with older students playing less time than younger students. The developers then tested the game with college students in a randomized control trial (RCT: Parong et al., 2017). Control students either completed a different game or no game. In both cases, students who played *Alien Game* showed improved posttest ability to make cognitive shifts. Participants who spent more time with the game showed improved outcomes compared to those who played the game for less time.

Braingame Brian was focused on developing executive functions such as working memory training, inhibition, and cognitive flexibility. The app consists of 25 training sessions that each last less than an hour. Each session includes six specific training tasks and includes 10-20 minutes of allowing the avatar (Brian) to walk around a graphic-rich virtual world. Brian's world consists of his house, a village, an island, forest, beach, swamp, and an underground laboratory. Village inhabitants (NPCs) meet Brian who is tasked with helping them solve a variety of problems. When players complete a training task, they received extra powers that allow Brian to create inventions that can help inhabitants solve problems. A point system provides further reinforcement.

Initial research was completed with 40 children ages 8-10 and clinically diagnosed with ADHD (Prins et al., 2013). Parents and teachers rated participants on executive functioning, ADHD symptoms, and disruptive behaviors. Compared to untreated controls, children who played *Braingame Brian* showed improvements (although empirical findings from statistical analyses were not presented).

In a subsequent study (Dovis et al., 2015), tested *Braingame Brian* with 89 children, ages 8-10, also diagnosed with ADHD. Children were assigned to one of three conditions: full-active treatment, partially-active treatment, and placebo control. In the full-active condition, all aspects of *Braingame Brian* training were implemented. In the partially-active condition, working memory tasks were limited whereas inhibition and cognitive flexibility tasks were present. The placebo condition included participants engaging the game, but they had reduced requirements for performing tasks. Only children in the full-active conditions showed statistically significant improvements in short-term and working memory.

An additional study (Dovis et al., 2019), randomized 61 children, ages 8-12, to either a working memory training plus inhibition plus cognitive-flexibility condition or a placebo condition. This study failed to replicate findings from the earlier Dovis et al. (2015) study and concluded that children with poor executive functioning did not benefit from the training.

Neuroracer is a game that consists of two simultaneously performed tasks. The first task involves using a joystick to drive a virtual race car down a winding road with the goal of keeping the car oriented in the center of the road. The second task involves responding to stop and go signs that appear on the screen.

A series of studies have examined the effectiveness of *Neuroracer* on cognitive function in 60-85-year-old adults. In the first of these (Anguera et al., 2013), the developers tested the game under three conditions, a multitask training condition (both road guidance and sign adherence), a single task condition (either road guidance or sign adherence), or a no-contact control. Participants in the multitask condition performed best on working memory and attention tests at posttest.

In a second field trial, *Neuroracer* was tested over an 8-week period against a non-gamified 8-week problem solving therapy treatment (Anguera, Gunning, & Areán, 2017). Participants were 22 older adults (65+) who suffered from major depression at the time of recruitment. Both interventions reduced participants' depression. Only *Neuroracer*, however, showed improvements in working memory and attentiveness. In a six-year follow-up study (Anguera et al., 2021) the authors reported cognitive control improvements for participants in the multitasking group, although participants did not show durable effects for working memory and attention.

Rise of Nations is an off-the-shelf strategy game. The game requires players to respond quickly in real-time to game features. The goal of play is to extend a nation's territory. Players build new cities, improve infrastructure and expand borders. Players have multiple paths to achieving success, including war-based conquest as well as through diplomatic and economic strategies. In a randomized control study, 40 novice game play older adults were equally split between treatment and control conditions (Basak et al., 2008). Treatment condition participants played *Rise of Nations* over an 8-week period that included a training session as well as several batteries of cognitive tests to assess visuo-spatial attention, task-switching, inhibition, and short-term memory. Treatment participants' game performance significantly improved with time spent playing the game. Training improved executive control functions with those who played the video game outperforming controls in task switching, working memory, and visual short-term memory.

Space Fortress is a computer game designed to improve complex skill acquisition. Players see a display of symbols that represent an enemy space fortress, a spaceship, missiles, and friend and foe mines. Points are given for destroying the fortress and enemy mines. A joystick controls speed and movement for the spaceship while the computer's mouse is used to identify mines and select bonus points and missiles. *Space Fortress* has been used in a variety of studies designed to understand neurological functioning (Maclin et al., 2011; Strenziok et al., 2014). This includes assessing a variety of training conditions (Boot et al., 2010). Importantly, *Space Fortress* has also been tested as a therapeutic tool. For instance, Janssen et al. (2015) used *Space Fortress* to examine rehabilitative effects for patients diagnosed with multiple sclerosis. Compared to a waitlist control group, patients played *Space Fortress* over an 8-week period under conditions of hybrid-variable priority training. Results demonstrated the value of the game as players had an overall improvement in skill acquisition. However, there was a lack of transfer to non-game-specific cognitive functioning.

Strenziok et al. (2014) tested *Space Fortress*, *Rise of Nations* and an auditory perception game, *Brain Fitness* on the cognitive performance of 42 older adults. Participating exposed to *Brain Fitness* and *Space Fortress* showed optimal transfer of skills to everyday problem solving and reasoning. Participants exposed to *Rise of Nations* did not show transfer of cognitive abilities.

Star Wars Battlefront is an action video game that has players battle characters from Star Wars films. Players pilot Star Wars vehicles and engage in battle by shooting enemies of the rebellion. Multiple rounds of play provide a means to acquire and hone navigation and battle skills. A study examined the ability of *Star Wars Battlefront* to improve executive cognitive function in participants over the age of 80 living in two residential care facilities (McCord et al., 2020). Twenty-four participants were randomized to treatment and control. Experimental participants watched a researcher model playing the game after which they played a 10-minute version followed by six 30-minute sessions over a three-week period. Compared to controls, participants who played *Star Wars Battlefront* improved in their task switching speed and showed short-term gains in working memory. Participants' quality of life was also assessed but showed no discernable improvement compared to controls.

Games That Train Specific Skills

There are a number of games that seek to help players develop a specific set of skills and also reinforce favorable health-oriented attitudes. Thus, these games primarily promote skill building through vignettes that promote appropriate decision making. They also motivate players to translate behaviors applied in the game to their own particular set of circumstances. These include HIV prevention and care, disease and injury rehabilitation, fall prevention among the elderly, auditory recognition among hearing impaired, juvenile (Type I) diabetes management, pedestrian safety, English language acquisition, awareness of environmental risk, and caregiver training.

HIV Prevention and Care

We identified three apps that specifically targeted promoting preventive and management behaviors related to HIV. Each involves strategies to promote adherence to antiretroviral therapies as well as motivate players to engage in appropriate preventive behaviors and avoid risky behaviors.

AllyQuest is a smartphone app that is based on social cognitive theory (Hightow-Weidman et al., 2018). The app targets HIV-positive young men who have sex with men (HIV+YMSM). It features daily activities including observational learning by participating in daily activities, modeling and vicarious experiences, self-efficacy and verbal persuasion from expert sources, and reinforcements through virtual rewards and achievements. The game includes a medication tracker, daily goal setting exercises and quizzes as well as a knowledge center and narrative stories common to HIV+YMSM about how to deal with challenging interpersonal situations (i.e., convincing a partner to wear a condom).

AllyQuest was developed through a process of initial design, usability testing and refinement, and a 4-week pilot test (Hightow-Weidman et al., 2018; Hightow-Weidman & Bauermeister, 2020). Twenty HIV+YMSM were provided access to app. App usage declined from an average of 4.3 days of use during the first week of the pilot test to 2.8 days during the final week. The app was judged to be easy to use and acceptable on a number of dimensions. Higher levels of app usage was correlated with better self-management outcomes. A RCT has not yet been completed to test the effectiveness of *AllyQuest* on improving HIV outcomes.

Stick to It is an HIV intervention targeting young men who have sex with men (YMSM) (McCoy et al., 2018). This mobile health intervention includes four components: (1) recruitment (clinic-based and online), (2) online enrollment, (3) online activities, and (4) "real-world" activities conducted at the clinic. Of particular interest for our analysis, online activities included completion of periodic quizzes testing participants' knowledge of sexual health. The quizzes also display quarterly screening dates. Quizzes allow participants to earn redeemable points.

In a pilot feasibility study, about half of eligible individuals (53%: 167 of 313) registered for the app. Of these, about half (56%: 93) completed enrollment and, of these, 19% (31) completed more than one activity in the subsequent 6 months. Among those who completed online activities, the rate of HIV serologic testing was higher (48%) than was found in a comparison group (30%) who did not participate in the app but were similar in many other respects to those who were enrolled. Overall, engagement was deemed to be only modest. Differences in rates of HIV testing may be attributable as much to the characteristics of those who participated as to the impact of the app.

Viral Combat (also listed as BattleViro) is a smartphone game designed to improve adherence to antiretroviral therapies among youth living with HIV (Whiteley et al., 2018; Whiteley et al., 2020) and men who have sex with men (MSM) who are using pre-exposure prophylaxis (PrEP) (Whiteley et al., 2020). In the game, players symbolically fight off HIV. The game takes place with players fighting HIV on various levels (on the skin, in the blood stream, in the penis, and in anal canals). The game includes educational materials, puzzles, and quizzes. Players earn points by providing correct answers and receive additional explanations when answers are incorrect. The goal is to impart a concerted message to build strength by taking medications and engage in appropriate protective behaviors.

In a 14-week RCT participants in the treatment condition played the HIV-focused game while controls played a similar game but without an HIV focus (Whiteley et al., 2018). Exposure to the game improved HIV knowledge, treatment knowledge, and perceived social support. However, there were no significant differences between groups in participants' motivation to use antiretroviral medication. The entire group of participants (both treatment and control) had reductions in viral load from pretest to posttest. Both groups reported high levels of adherence although medication adherence for both groups decreased over time.

A second RCT involved treatment participants who played the HIV-focused game and controls who played a similar game, but without HIV content (Whiteley et al., 2021; Whiteley et al., 2020). Assessments included a pretest, a 12-week posttest, and a 24-week follow-up. At 12 weeks, 50% of Viral Combat participants reported playing the game. Those assigned to the treatment condition were significantly more likely to take medications. At 24-weeks, 40% of participants played Viral Combat. As a group, they were more likely to take optimal doses of their medications.

Illness and Injury Recovery and Management

Four apps were identified that target recovery from illness or injury or management of a chronic health condition.

clEAR is a collection of web-based and tablet-based games that help hearing impaired recognize the speech of their frequent communication partners especially in noisy environments. Based on the literature about the game, clEAR is targeted primarily at children (Tye-Murray, 2016, 2021a; Tye-Murray et al., 2021), however, there is also an adult version (Amptify: Tye-Murray, 2021b). Both the child and adult versions focus on helping users gain conversational fluency by helping them recognize words, discriminate sounds, and improve auditory working memory and attentiveness. Users receive both auditory training and audiovisual training. The developers conducted a randomized control trial in which children were assigned to auditory training, audiovisual training, or combined auditory and audiovisual training (Tye-Murray et al., 2021). Children improved both listening and speechreading performance. We were unable to find research related to the adult version of the application.

Jerry the Bear is a stuffed animal that is linked to a smartphone app that allows young children with Type 1 diabetes to learn diabetes management through play (Sproutel, 2021). By taking care of Jerry's diabetes, children gain hands-on practice counting carbohydrates, monitor their blood sugar, and adjust their insulin dosage. The intervention includes a virtual glucometer for testing Jerry's blood sugar, an insulin pen or pump, and smartphone tools to virtually feed Jerry a variety of foods that vary in their carbohydrate content. Also included are 21 interactive storybooks that reinforce key diabetes management practices (Tsvyatkova & Storni, 2019). The goal is for young Type 1 diabetics to learn to manage their own diabetes through the vicarious experience of managing Jerry's well-being.

Ullman et al. (2021) investigated the support *Jerry the Bear* provided under two conditions, in a laboratory environment and a home study without any researcher-led guidance. Children were recruited between the ages of 5 and 10. In the laboratory condition, children participated in play sessions spaced two weeks apart with a researcher present. During the interim, children were allowed to take Jerry home along with a preprogrammed tablet that contained the app. In the home condition, Jerry and the required tablet were provided to children who had participated in a Type 1 diabetes summer camp. Results from both conditions paralleled one another. Evaluation of the children's involvement with the app relied primarily on parents' assessment of their child's utilization patterns. Overall, parents rated their experience and their perceptions about their child's experience as positive. (The modal response was "extremely positive.") Parents' and children's attitudes towards diabetes management were generally positive, although the modal response was "no change." Parents' reports of learning gains varied markedly with some reporting few gains with others reporting meaningful gains. All parents reported increased frequency of communication with their child about diabetes. Finally, among children in the lab condition, when asked about the value of the app versus the value of playing with the stuffed animal, most preferred the app. Ullman and colleagues conclude that the Jerry had a positive impact on children. As yet, long-term durable effects have not been evaluated.

Sensor-Controlled Digital Game (SCDG) is a sensor-augmented smartphone app designed to encourage older individuals who are at risk for heart failure to increase physical activity and manage their weight (Radhakrishnan et al., 2020a). Physical wearable sensors linked to the app track activity and weight. The *Heart Health Mountain* is a game embedded in the app that helps an avatar climb a mountain by achieving personal physical activity goals as monitored by a wrist-attached motion sensor. As the avatar climbs the mountain, each step triggers the app to provide useful health information, challenge the player to complete a quiz, puzzle, or "slot" game, or spin a wheel for bonus points. The app tracks the completion of 37 tasks. Players track the avatar's achievements visually on a smartphone app that provides feedback about progress toward a goal. The intervention is intended to continue indefinitely.

A 24-week feasibilty RCT was completed in which treatment group participants received activity- and weight-tracking sensors as well as the app whereas control participants only received the sensors (Radhakrishnan et al., 2020b; Radhakrishnan et al., 2021). There were numerous problems with participant recruitment; however, among those who were recruited, most (71%) treated cases reported they completed the app on more than 50% of the assigned days. The research team noted that there were technical issues syncing sensors with the app. Satisfaction with the game was extremely high, with 100% of participants saying the app was easy to use and contained appropriate content and information. In addition, 85% rated the app as interesting, enjoyable, satisfying to play, and motivating. No differences between treatment and control groups were observed for functional status, quality of life, heart health knowledge, self-efficacy to engage in appropriate behaviors or hospitalizations.

VIGOR is a 9-week intervention that targets patients suffering from chronic low back pain (France & Thomas, 2018). In this app, patients wear a virtual reality headset and play three first-person perspective games: *Matchality*, *Fishality*, and *Dodgeality*. Each game requires the player to stand and bend in specific ways. *Matchality* requires players to stack virtual cubes. *Fishality* requires players to move a net to capture virtual fish that jump at the end of dock in a lake and place them in a holding tank. In *Dodgeality*, users play virtual dodgeball. Each game includes multiple levels of performance; higher levels are more demanding and become available following mastery of lower levels. Players receive feedback about their performance and monetary incentives that are proportional to their performance. A RCT is planned but has not been completed at the time of this writing.

Pedestrian Safety

Pedestrian Safety uses a virtual reality system. Based on a detailed protocol (Schwebel et al., 2017), players are presented with a pedestrian environment. One version was designed specifically for children, ages 7-8 (Schwebel & McClure, 2010, 2014; Schwebel, McClure, & Severson, 2014). The virtual reality environment is established either through Google Cardboard VR or a "kiosk" in which three visual screens display the environment. The environment displays a street with traffic coming in both directions. When they feel safe, children are instructed to step forward or push a button on their smartphones. After their avatar crosses the street, children are given feedback about their safety. The environment increases in traffic speed and density with successive trials. In a RCT (Schwebel, Shen, & McClure, 2016), training improved children's street crossing efficiency and increased their understanding of safe pedestrian behavior.

A separate approach has been designed for college-age users that specifically includes walking while texting as a context (Schwebel, McClure, & Porter, 2017). In a observational study, exposure to the virtual reality experience increased participants' intentions to avoid distraction and their perceived vulnerability to risk. However, post-exposure found no change in observed rates of distracted behavior on the college campus.

DISCUSSION

We set out in this chapter with two main goals. First, the chapter briefly reviewed what makes digital apps "gamified. Added to this was a discussion on whether gamification incorporates learning theory and instructional technology. This is an important point in the discussion because a constituent element in a game is that it is fun and engrossing with rules (design grammars) and rewards. However, merely because a digital app is considered a game does not by necessity mean the player is "learning." Part and parcel of this discussion was whether gamified digital apps are able to capitalize on modern learning and instructional theory. Stated quite simply, something is going on while users engage an app, and that 'something' has to be made available for further objective scrutiny. In this respect, games that target health promotion must demonstrate there is learning in terms of behavior change.

By necessity, discussion of behavior change in digital health promotion apps brings into question the evaluation process. For instance, an intervention (A) is hypothesized to change some target skill or risk factor (B), which then leads to behavior change (C). The veracity of this coordinated sequence of $A \rightarrow B \rightarrow C$, which takes shape as a mediational process, can be evaluated using specific statistical tests (MacKinnon, 2008; MacKinnon & Pirlott, 2015). The prevailing question then is whether digital apps lend themselves to this type of rigorous testing with a coordinated sequence that can "parse" the intervention modalities and their effect on target risk factors, with the goal of elucidating eventual behavior change. To our knowledge, this has not been a strength of digital app evaluations and we discussed this issue at length.

We then widened this discussion by attending to the requirements of prevention science, specifically referencing the development, implementation, and evaluation of digital health promotion apps that emphasize behavior change. These requirements are quite extensive (see for example Flay et al., 2005), but essentially point to the need to explicitly articulate the active ingredients of a program, including the causal manner in which they are hypothesized to bring about behavior change, and, in the case of multimodal programs, how each intervention modality supports or reinforces the others.

Following this broad discussion, the chapter then expanded on an earlier 2019 publication by the authors canvassing NIH-funded digital behavioral intervention apps geared toward health promotion. This expansion incorporated taking those apps that were listed as "gamified" in the earlier publication and providing a more in-depth discussion of their content, the evidence-base regarding their efficacy, and reviewing findings that determine whether the app functions in the way it was designed. The two parts go hand-in-hand because without a clear picture of what constitutes "gamification" the potential exists for making the mistake of including apps that are fun to use but not meeting the full set of requirements to be considered a game. Gee (2003) and others have been quite clear on what makes an app gamified, owing to its use of rules and goals, provision of rewards, inclusion of challenges, learner control, interactivity, and incorporation of fantasy. The latter element is crucial because all simulation or digital games are based on fantasy that involves action in a world without consequences (Garris et al., 2002). Simply put, one does not really own the house or the hotel in the game *Monopoly*. In the true sense of the term, it is just a game based on accumulating real estate assets and "s/he with the most toys wins." There is and always will be a disjoint between the fantasy world of games and the real world.

Three pressing themes emerged from this review that are worth nothing. First, in the context of health promotion, games are not just "fun" for the purpose of increasing presence and immersion. While fun and player engrossment in a game are necessary ingredients and certainly factors that contribute to adherence, they are not sufficient by any means. Sufficiency is achieved when a game changes behavior in the manner hypothesized, using theoretically driven concepts that involve hypothesized psychological mechanisms. Stated quite simply, the game has to do what it purports in order to link exposure through playing time with behavior change. In this respect, a key feature in the success of a digital health promotion game is the ability of the player to learn and retain a skill or piece of knowledge and "transfer" that skill or knowledge to the real world where it is most needed and where there are true consequences of behavior (i.e., use protection to prevent STDs and HIV, manage food intake to regulate insulin levels, inhibit poor behavior, stay attentive and focused, control ambient noise for the hard of hearing).

Second, and tied to this first point, is the pivotal role of learning in health promotion games. Learning, in its rawest form, is motivational; that is it makes people feel better and acts as a major drawing card for players to return to game play. Why? Because the player wants to demonstrate their proficiency by mastering challenges or demonstrating 'effectance' as White (1959) suggested in his discussion of the roots of competence. Taken as a whole, this mastery through autonomous achievement improves self-worth (one's evaluation of the self against some standard). All of this motivational sequence and its psychological corollaries happens because a game has "pull" and keeps a player intrigued, challenging them to master the game mechanics with the goal of accruing new information, constructing and testing new decision-making strategies, and having new experiences in a cost-free fantasy-based environment with limited consequences to their real being. It is the combination of these factors that makes digital games so intriguing and engrossing to players.

An important point in considering game-based learning is how well games motivate players to be self-directed and self-motivated. Several of the studies reviewed involved the researchers' presence during initial usability testing. This activity cannot support a viable means of commercializing a game, which requires independent self-directed usage. Games are fantasy opportunities that people do for "fun" on their own, and at their own leisure. Even the simplest card game has instructions, but they must be interpreted independent of the manufacturer watching and providing oversight. For a game to succeed commercially on the open market it has to motivate players because it is well designed and uncomplicated to put into motion. Successful games are ones that players wish to play over and over because the tasks set before them are intrinsically rewarding and the imposition of external regulation (reward) is less influential (this is fundamental to self-determination theory: Ryan & Deci, 2000 and see also Malone, 1981 for discussion of intrinsic motivation and deep learning). Discussion of the "intrinsic" motivational properties of a game is of paramount importance because it is a fundamental component of self-efficacy theory (Bandura, 1997). In other words, as players gain proficiency, and as their mastery improves, so too will the intensity of their effort, the persistence with which they engage in the game, all because they are achieving (building confidence) and learning.

Incorporation of games into health promotion is based on the transition from didactic teaching methods (where information is delivered using direct instruction) to ones that are "learner-based and learner-activated." Learning in today's world is more contextually 'situated' (Brown, Collins, & Duguid, 1989) and based on 21st century skills that emphasize facility with technology, communication, problem-solving, creativity, and collaboration (Qian & Clark, 2016). From an accountability point of view, a digital game's effectiveness as a health promotion learning tool is tied to its ability to alter behavior, whether it imparts knowledge (declarative in terms of facts and procedural in terms of processes), influences attitudes/beliefs (i.e., affective preferences) or changes self-efficacy (Kato, 2010; Wilson et al., 2009). Greater clarification of learning outcomes linked with specific "game attributes" will surely advance the field from an evaluation standpoint and also provide veridical tests of theory (O'Neil, Wainess, & Baker, 2005).

A third, and perhaps equally compelling issue, is whether reviews of the gamified apps are consistent with the standards that guide research in prrevention science. These principles were published by the Society for Prevention Research (Flay et al., 2005) in order to achieve consensus and enhance the rigorous nature of how programs are evaluated. Gamified digital technology targeting health promotion at heart involves the implementation of a behavioral intervention; one that targets some form of behavior change. In this regard, the field of digital behavior change technology could benefit from outlining which of the many standards should be adopted when evaluating digital health interventions. Digital applications for behavior change are mostly multimodal consisting of different moving parts that are used to encourage players to acquire new knowledge, adopt new skills, and change their behavior (Murray et al., 2016). This change can take shape as knowledge that informs decision-making or in other cases targeting changes in attitudes (e.g., HIV protective measures that lead to greater adoption of safe-sex behaviors). Regardless, the bottom line is that few of the apps reviewed in this chapter applied stringent evaluation criteria to test the program's efficacy. There were no explicit causal models providing testable (or refutable) explanations for how the game "works" to produce learning (change in behavior). Given the diverse strategies offered in digital health interventions, and the fact that more than one active ingredient is often targeted, an appropriate, albeit underutilized strategy, would involve a fractional factorial design to determine precisely which components of the app are working. The current review shows that, with few exceptions (e.g., Anguera et al., 2013; Dovis et al., 2015), there were a few studies testing digital health interventions that relied on some form of dismantling or componential analysis design.

Part of the rationale for not applying rigorous experimental designs during the testing phase may be the preliminary nature of many of the studies. In most cases, sample sizes were relatively small (n < 25 in each condition, $\bar{X} = 63.5$ for the total sample, range = 10 to 240), and in many cases seriously underpowered, which may have led to making Type II errors (false acceptance of the null hypothesis of no difference between experimental conditions). The use of relatively small samples is understandable, because in most cases the RCTs were directed at feasibility and usability testing, requiring feedback on the utility and playability of the app. However, larger scale studies are required that meet the requirements detailed in the prevention science standards of evidence.

CONCLUSIONS

It should be clear from this review that there is considerable work to be done with regard to strengthening the linkage between digital gamification and health promotion. The work that has been done is somewhat rudimentary in light of the outcomes and with respect to revealing the underlying mechanisms of behavior change. Moreover, even if digital environments keep pace with advances in technology, the incorporation of learning and instructional theory into digital games is lagging considerably. This issue is repeatedly raised by numerous authors discussing the incorporation of learning theory into digital games. Indeed, Barab (2004) noted that the interface of theories of learning and knowing, motivational theory and gaming is the purview of "instructional design," and there is a notable paucity of influence from this field on the development of digital health promotion games. Commenting on the same issue, Lameras et al. (2017) wrote, "there are no pedagogically driven strategies that take into account how learning attributes are interlinked to game elements for balancing learning with play" (p. 973).

When all is said and done, learning theory is really about self-directedness and autonomy that when coupled with social experiences gives rise to the motivational framework supporting accrual of new information and acting on that information. In the context of health promotion programs, the desired end product is a change in attitudes, behavior, increased skill, knowledge acquisition or some combination. Health promotion is about changing behavior in the direction of greater self-determination to seek positive health-oriented outcomes and learning how to achieve this state of mind. In light of the shared premises here, the goal should be coalescing these two seemingly independent streams (gamification and learning) into a single pedagogical framework where learning outcomes are part of game mechanics, while at the same time applying objective metrics and using rigorous methodology that is compliant with the standards of evidence. This is the design-based research approach that should advance the field of game-based learning.

REFERENCES

Ajzen, I. (2002). Perceived behavioral control, self-efficacy, locus of control, and the theory of planned behavior. *Journal of Applied Social Psychology*, *32*(4), 665–683. doi:10.1111/j.1559-1816.2002.tb00236.x

Ajzen, I. (1991). The theory of planned behavior. *Organizational Behavior and Human Decision Processes*, *50*(2), 179–211. doi:10.1016/0749-5978(91)90020-T

Anguera, J. A., Boccanfuso, J., Rintoul, J. L., Al-Hashimi, O., Faraji, F., Janowich, J., ... Johnston, E. (2013). Video game training enhances cognitive control in older adults. *Nature*, *501*(7465), 97–101. doi:10.1038/nature12486 PMID:24005416

Anguera, J. A., Gunning, F. M., & Areán, P. A. (2017). Improving late life depression and cognitive control through the use of therapeutic video game technology: A proof-of-concept randomized trial. *Depression and Anxiety, 34*(6), 508–517. doi:10.1002/da.22588 PMID:28052513

Anguera, J. A., Schachtner, J. N., Simon, A. J., Volponi, J., Javed, S., Gallen, C. L., & Gazzaley, A. (2021). Long-term maintenance of multitasking abilities following video game training in older adults. *Neurobiology of Aging, 103*, 22–30. doi:10.1016/j.neurobiolaging.2021.02.023 PMID:33789209

Annetta, L. A. (2008). Video games in education: Why they should be used and how they are being used. *Theory into Practice, 47*(3), 229–239. doi:10.1080/00405840802153940

Bandura, A. (1997). *Self-efficacy: The exercise of control.* W. H. Freeman & Co.

Bandura, A. (1986). *Social foundations of thought and action: A social cognitive theory.* Prentice-Hall.

Bandura, A. (1977a). *Social learning theory.* Prentice-Hall.

Bandura, A. (1977b). Self-efficacy: Toward a unifying theory of behavior change. *Psychological Review, 84*(2), 191–215. doi:10.1037/0033-295X.84.2.191 PMID:847061

Bandura, A., Ross, D., & Ross, S. A. (1963a). Imitation of film-mediated aggressive models. *Journal of Abnormal and Social Psychology, 66*(1), 3–11. doi:10.1037/h0048687 PMID:13966304

Bandura, A., Ross, D., & Ross, S. A. (1963b). Vicarious reinforcement and imitative learning. *Journal of Abnormal and Social Psychology, 67*(6), 601–607. doi:10.1037/h0045550 PMID:14084769

Bandura, A., Ross, D., & Ross, S. A. (1961). Transmission of aggression through imitation of aggressive models. *Journal of Abnormal and Social Psychology, 63*(3), 575–582. doi:10.1037/h0045925 PMID:13864605

Barab, S. (2004). Using design to advance learning theory, or using learning theory to advance design. *Educational Technology, 44*(3), 16–20. Retrieved August 6, 2021, from https://www.jstor.org/stable/44428901

Basak, C., Boot, W. R., Voss, M. W., & Kramer, A. F. (2008). Can training in a real-time strategy video game attenuate cognitive decline in older adults? *Psychology and Aging, 23*(4), 765–777. doi:10.1037/a0013494 PMID:19140648

Becker, M. H. (1974). The health belief model and personal health behavior. *Health Education Monographs, 2*(4), 324–473. doi:10.1177/109019817400200407

Becker, M. H., Drachman, R. H., & Kirscht, J. P. (1974). A new approach to explaining sick-role behavior in low-income populations. *American Journal of Public Health, 64*(3), 205–216. doi:10.2105/AJPH.64.3.205 PMID:4811762

Bedwell, W. L., Pavlas, D., Heyne, K., Lazzara, E. H., & Salas, E. (2012). Toward a taxonomy linking game attributes to learning: An empirical study. *Simulation & Gaming, 43*(6), 729–760. doi:10.1177/1046878112439444

Boot, W. R., Basak, C., Erickson, K. I., Neider, M., Simons, D. J., Fabiani, M., ... Lee, H. (2010). Transfer of skill engendered by complex task training under conditions of variable priority. *Acta Psychologica*, *135*(3), 349–357. doi:10.1016/j.actpsy.2010.09.005 PMID:20920812

Brown, J. S., Collins, A., & Duguid, P. (1989). Situated cognition and the culture of learning. *Educational Researcher*, *18*(1), 32–42. doi:10.3102/0013189X018001032

Cacioppo, J. T., Petty, R. E., & Stoltenberg, C. (1985). Processes of social influence: The elaboration likelihood model of persuasion. In P. Kendall (Ed.), *Advances in cognitive behavioral research and therapy* (Vol. 4, pp. 215–274). Academic Press. doi:10.1016/B978-0-12-010604-2.50012-4

Chen, H. T. (1990). *Theory-driven evaluations*. Sage Publications.

Collins, L. M., Murphy, S. A., & Strecher, V. (2007). The multiphase optimization strategy (MOST) and the sequential multiple assignment randomized trial (SMART): New methods for more potent eHealth interventions. *American Journal of Preventive Medicine*, *32*(5), S112–S118. doi:10.1016/j.amepre.2007.01.022 PMID:17466815

Dovis, S., Maric, M., Prins, P. J., & Van der Oord, S. (2019). Does executive function capacity moderate the outcome of executive function training in children with ADHD? *Attention Deficit and Hyperactivity Disorders*, *11*(4), 445–460. doi:10.100712402-019-00308-5 PMID:31123915

Dovis, S., Van der Oord, S., Wiers, R. W., & Prins, P. J. (2015). Improving executive functioning in children with ADHD: Training multiple executive functions within the context of a computer game. A randomized double-blind placebo controlled trial. *PLoS One*, *10*(4), e0121651. doi:10.1371/journal.pone.0121651 PMID:25844638

Edwards, E. A., Lumsden, J., Rivas, C., Steed, L., Edwards, L. A., Thiyagarajan, A., Sohanpal, R., Caton, H., Griffiths, C. J., Munafò, M. R., Taylor, S., & Walton, R. T. (2016). Gamification for health promotion: Systematic review of behavior change techniques in smartphone apps. *BMC Open*, *6*(10), e012447. doi:10.1136/bmjopen-2016-012447 PMID:27707829

Flay, B. R., Biglan, A., Boruch, R. F., Castro, F. G., Gottfredson, D., Kellam, S., Mościcki, E. K., Schinke, S., Valentine, J. C., & Ji, P. (2005). Standards of evidence: Criteria for efficacy, effectiveness and dissemination. *Prevention Science*, *6*(3), 151–175. doi:10.100711121-005-5553-y PMID:16365954

France, C. R., & Thomas, J. S. (2018). Virtual immersive gaming to optimize recovery (VIGOR) in low back pain: A phase II randomized controlled trial. *Contemporary Clinical Trials*, *69*, 83–91. doi:10.1016/j.cct.2018.05.001 PMID:29730393

Gagné, R. M. (1984). Learning outcomes and their effects: Useful categories of human performance. *The American Psychologist*, *39*(4), 377–385. doi:10.1037/0003-066X.39.4.377

Garris, R., Ahlers, R., & Driskell, J. E. (2002). Games, motivation, and learning: A research and pratice model. *Simulation & Gaming*, *33*(4), 441–467. doi:10.1177/1046878102238607

Gee, J. P. (2008). Learning and games. In K. Salen (Ed.), *The ecology of games: Connecting youth, games, and learning* (pp. 21–40). The MIT Press.

Gee, J. P. (2007). Learning theory, video games, and popular culture. In K. Drotner & S. Livingstone (Eds.), *The international handbook of children, media and culture* (pp. 196–213). Sage Publications. doi:10.4135/9781848608436.n13

Gee, J. P. (2004). Learning by design: Games as learning machines. *Interactive Educational Multimedia*, 8, 15–23.

Gee, J. P. (2003). *What video games have to teach us about learning and literacy*. Palgrave/MacMillan. doi:10.1145/950566.950595

Green, M. C., & Brock, T. C. (2000). The role of transportation in the persuasiveness of public narratives. *Journal of Personality and Social Psychology*, 79(5), 701–721. doi:10.1037/0022-3514.79.5.701 PMID:11079236

Green, M. C., Brock, T. C., & Kiaufman, G. F. (2004). Understanding media enjoyment: The role of transportation into narrative worlds. *Communication Theory*, 14(4), 311–327. doi:10.1111/j.1468-2885.2004.tb00317.x

Hansen, W. B., & Scheier, L. M. (2019). Specialized smartphone intervention apps: Review of 2014 to 2018 NIH funded grants. *JMIR mHealth and uHealth*, 7(7), e14655. doi:10.2196/14655 PMID:31359866

Hekler, E. B., Michie, S., Pavel, M., Rivera, D. E., Collins, L. M., Jimison, H. B., Garnett, C., Parral, S., & Spruijt-Metz, D. (2016). Advancing models and theories for digital behavior change interventions. *American Journal of Preventive Medicine*, 51(5), 825–832. doi:10.1016/j.amepre.2016.06.013 PMID:27745682

Hightow-Weidman, L., Muessig, K., Knudtson, K., Srivatsa, M., Lawrence, E., LeGrand, S., Hotten, A., & Hosek, S. (2018). A gamified smartphone app to support engagement in care and medication adherence for HIV-positive young men who have sex with men (AllyQuest): Development and pilot study. *JMIR Public Health and Surveillance*, 4(2), e8923. doi:10.2196/publichealth.8923 PMID:29712626

Hightow-Weidman, L. B., & Bauermeister, J. A. (2020). Engagement in mHealth behavioral interventions for HIV prevention and care: Making sense of the metrics. *mHealth*, 6, 7. Advance online publication. doi:10.21037/mhealth.2019.10.01 PMID:32190618

Homer, B. D., Plass, J. L., Raffaele, C., Ober, T. M., & Ali, A. (2018). Improving high school students' executive functions through digital game play. *Computers & Education*, 117, 50–58. doi:10.1016/j.compedu.2017.09.011

Humanoid Animation Standards. (n.d.). *ISO DIS 19744-2*. Retrieved from https://www.web3d.org/standards/hanim

Inhelder, B., & Piaget, J. (1958). *The growth of logical thinking from childhood to adolescence*. Basic Books. doi:10.1037/10034-000

Janssen, A., Boster, A., Lee, H., Patterson, B., & Prakash, R. S. (2015). The effects of video-game training on broad cognitive transfer in multiple sclerosis: A pilot randomized controlled trial. *Journal of Clinical and Experimental Neuropsychology*, 37(3), 285–302. doi:10.1080/13803395.2015.100936 6 PMID:25850024

Kapp, K. M. (2012). *The gamification of learning and instruction: Game-based methods and strategies for training and education*. John Wiley & Sons. doi:10.1145/2207270.2211316

Kato, P. M. (2010). Video games in health care: Closing the gap. *Review of General Psychology*, *14*(2), 113–121. doi:10.1037/a0019441

Kato, T. (2012). Development of the Coping Flexibility Scale: Evidence for the coping flexibility hypothesis. *Journal of Counseling Psychology*, *59*(2), 262–273. doi:10.1037/a0027770 PMID:22506909

Ke, F. (2016). Designing and integrating purposeful learning in game play: A systematic review. *Educational Technology Research and Development*, *64*(2), 219–244. doi:10.100711423-015-9418-1

Klasnja, P., Hekler, E. B., Shiffman, S., Boruvka, A., Almirall, D., Tewari, A., & Murphy, S. A. (2015). Micro-randomized trials: An experimental design for developing just-in-time adaptive interventions. *Health Psychology*, *34*(suppl), 1220–1228. doi:10.1037/hea0000305 PMID:26651463

Kuhn, D. (2000). Theory of mind, metacognition, and reasoning: A life-span perspective. In P. Mitchell & K. J. Riggs (Eds.), *Children's reasoning and the mind* (pp. 301–326). Psychology Press.

Lagoa, C. M., Bekiroglu, K., Murphy, S. A., & Lanza, S. T. (2014). Designing adaptive intensive interventions using methods from engineering. *Journal of Consulting and Clinical Psychology*, *82*(5), 868–878. doi:10.1037/a0037736 PMID:25244394

Lameras, P., Arnab, S., Dunwell, I., Stewart, C., Clarke, S., & Petrdis, P. (2017). Essential features of serious game design in higher education: Linking learning attributes to game mechanics. *British Journal of Educational Technology*, *48*(4), 972–994. doi:10.1111/bjet.12467

MacKinnon, D. P. (2008). *Introduction to statistical mediation analysis*. Lawrence Erlbaum.

MacKinnon, D. P., & Pirlott, A. G. (2015). Statistical approaches for enhancing causal interpretation of the M to Y relation in mediation analysis. *Personality and Social Psychology Review*, *19*(1), 30–43. doi:10.1177/1088868314542878 PubMed

Maclin, E. L., Mathewson, K. E., Low, K. A., Boot, W. R., Kramer, A. F., Fabiani, M., & Gratton, G. (2011). Learning to multitask: Effects of video game practice on electrophysiological indices of attention and resource allocation. *Psychophysiology*, *48*(9), 1173–1183. doi:10.1111/j.1469-8986.2011.01189.x PMID:21388396

Malone, T. W. (1981). Toward a theory of intrinsically motivating instruction. *Cognitive Science*, *4*(4), 333–369. doi:10.120715516709cog0504_2

McCaul, K. D., & Glasgow, R. E. (1985). Preventing adolescent smoking: What have we learned about treatment construct validity? *Health Psychology*, *4*(4), 361–387. doi:10.1037/0278-6133.4.4.361 PMID:4054080

McCord, A., Cocks, B., Barreiros, A. R., & Bizo, L. A. (2020). Short video game play improves executive function in the oldest old living in residential care. *Computers in Human Behavior*, *108*, 106337. doi:10.1016/j.chb.2020.106337

McCoy, S. I., Buzdugan, R., Grimball, R., Natoli, L., Mejia, C. M., Klausner, J. D., & McGrath, M. R. (2018). Stick To It: Pilot study results of an intervention using gamification to increase HIV screening among young men who have sex with men in California. *mHealth*, *4*, 40. Advance online publication. doi:10.21037/mhealth.2018.09.04 PMID:30363751

Murray, E., Hekler, E. B., Andersson, G., Collins, L. M., Doherty, A., Hollis, C., Rivera, D. E., West, R., & Wyatt, J. C. (2016). Evaluating digital health interventions: Key questions and approaches. *American Journal of Preventive Medicine*, *51*(5), 843–851. doi:10.1016/j.amepre.2016.06.008 PMID:27745684

O'Neil, H. F., Wainess, R., & Baker, E. L. (2005). Classification of learning outcomes: Evidence from the computer games literature. *Curriculum Journal*, *16*(4), 455–474. doi:10.1080/09585170500384529

Parong, J., Mayer, R. E., Fiorella, L., MacNamara, A., Homer, B. D., & Plass, J. L. (2017). Learning executive function skills by playing focused video games. *Contemporary Educational Psychology*, *51*, 141–151. doi:10.1016/j.cedpsych.2017.07.002

Pea, R. D. (2004). The social and technological dimensions of scaffolding and related theoretical concepts for learning, education, and human activity. *Journal of the Learning Sciences*, *13*(3), 423–451. doi:10.120715327809jls1303_6

Piaget, J. (1952). *The origins of intelligence*. International Universities Press. doi:10.1037/11494-000

Portnoy, C. B., Scott-Sheldon, L. A. J., Johnson, B. T., & Carey, M. P. (2008). Computer-delivered interventions for health promotion and behavioral risk reduction: A meta-analysis of 75 randomized controlled trials, 1988-2007. *Preventive Medicine*, *47*(1), 3–16. doi:10.1016/j.ypmed.2008.02.014 PMID:18403003

Prins, P. J., Brink, E. T., Dovis, S., Ponsioen, A., Geurts, H. M., De Vries, M., & Van Der Oord, S. (2013). "Braingame Brian": Toward an executive function training program with game elements for children with ADHD and cognitive control problems. *GAMES FOR HEALTH: Research, Development, and Clinical Applications*, *2*(1), 44–49. doi:10.1089/g4h.2013.0004 PMID:26196554

Prochaska, J. O., & Velicer, W. F. (1997). The transtheoretical model of health behavior change. *American Journal of Health Promotion*, *12*(1), 38–48. doi:10.4278/0890-1171-12.1.38 PMID:10170434

Puntambekar, S., & Hübscher, R. (2005). Tools for scaffolding students in a complex learning environment: What have we gained and what have we missed? *Educational Psychologist*, *40*(1), 1–12. doi:10.120715326985ep4001_1

Qian, M., & Clark, K. R. (2016). Game-based learning and 21st century skills: A review of recdent research. *Computers in Human Behavior*, *63*, 50–58. doi:10.1016/j.chb.2016.05.023

Radhakrishnan, K., Baranowski, T., O'Hair, M., Fournier, C. A., Spranger, C. B., & Kim, M. T. (2020a). Personalizing sensor-controlled digital gaming to self-management needs of older adults with heart failure: A qualitative study. *Games for Health Journal*, *9*(4), 304–310. doi:10.1089/g4h.2019.0222 PMID:32155355

Radhakrishnan, K., Julien, C., Baranowski, T., O'Hair, M., Lee, G., De Main, A. S., ... Kim, M. (2021). Sensor-controlled digital game and heart failure self-management behaviors: A feasibility randomized controlled trial study. *JMIR Serious Games*, 1–37. doi:10.2196/29044 PMID:34747701

Radhakrishnan, K., Julien, C., O'Hair, M., Baranowski, T., Lee, G., Allen, C., Sagna, A., Thomaz, E., & Kim, M. (2020b). Usability testing of a sensor-controlled digital game to engage older adults with heart failure in physical activity and weight monitoring. *Applied Clinical Informatics*, *11*(05), 873–881. doi:10.1055-0040-1721399 PMID:33378780

Ryan, R. M., & Deci, E. L. (2000). Self-determination theory and the facilitation of intrinsic motivation, social development, and well-being. *The American Psychologist*, *55*(1), 68–78. doi:10.1037/0003-066X.55.1.68 PMID:11392867

Ryan, R. M., Rigby, C. S., & Przybylski, A. (2006). The motivational pull of video games: A self-determination theory approach. *Motivation and Emotion*, *30*(4), 347–363. doi:10.100711031-006-9051-8

Savery, J. R., & Duffy, T. M. (1995). Problem-based learning: An instructional model and its constructivist framework. *Educational Technology*, *35*(5), 31–35.

Scheier, L. M. (2020). Adolescent drug misuse prevention: Challenges in school-based programming. In S. Y. Sussman (Ed.), *Cambridge handbook of substance and behavioral addictions* (pp. 1235–1324). Cambridge University Press. doi:10.1017/9781108632591.021

Schultze, U. (2012). Performing embodied identity in virtual worlds. *European Journal of Information Systems*, *23*(1), 84–95. doi:10.1057/ejis.2012.52

Schwebel, D. C., & McClure, L. A. (2010). Using virtual reality to train children in safe street-crossing skills. *Injury Prevention*, *16*(1), e1–e1. doi:10.1136/ip.2009.025288 PMID:20179024

Schwebel, D. C., & McClure, L. A. (2014). Training children in pedestrian safety: Distinguishing gains in knowledge from gains in safe behavior. *The Journal of Primary Prevention*, *35*(3), 151–162. doi:10.100710935-014-0341-8 PMID:24573688

Schwebel, D. C., McClure, L. A., & Porter, B. E. (2017). Experiential exposure to texting and walking in virtual reality: A randomized trial to reduce distracted pedestrian behavior. *Accident; Analysis and Prevention*, *102*, 116–122. doi:10.1016/j.aap.2017.02.026 PMID:28279843

Schwebel, D. C., McClure, L. A., & Severson, J. (2014). Usability and feasibility of an internet-based virtual pedestrian environment to teach children to cross streets safely. *Virtual Reality (Waltham Cross)*, *18*(1), 5–11. doi:10.100710055-013-0238-5 PMID:24678263

Schwebel, D. C., Severson, J., He, Y., & McClure, L. A. (2017). Virtual reality by mobile smartphone: Improving child pedestrian safety. *Injury Prevention*, *23*(5), 357–357. doi:10.1136/injuryprev-2016-042168 PMID:27585563

Schwebel, D. C., Shen, J., & McClure, L. A. (2016). How do children learn to cross the street? The process of pedestrian safety training. *Traffic Injury Prevention*, *17*(6), 573–579. doi:10.1080/1538958 8.2015.1125478 PMID:26760077

Sitzmann, T. (2011). A meta-analytic examination of the instructional effectiveness of computer-based simulation games. *Personnel Psychology*, *64*(2), 489–528. doi:10.1111/j.1744-6570.2011.01190.x

Sproutel. (2021). *Jerry the Bear*. Retrieved from www.jerrythebear.com/

Squire, K., & Jenkins, H. (2003). Harnessing the power of games in education. *Vision (Basel), 3*, 7–33.

Strenziok, M., Parasuraman, R., Clarke, E., Cisler, D. S., Thompson, J. C., & Greenwood, P. M. (2014). Neurocognitive enhancement in older adults: Comparison of three cognitive training tasks to test a hypothesis of training transfer in brain connectivity. *NeuroImage, 85*, 1027–1039. doi:10.1016/j.neuroimage.2013.07.069 PMID:23933474

Tsvyatkova, D., & Storni, C. (2019). Designing an educational interactive eBook for newly diagnosed children with type 1 diabetes: Mapping a new design space. *International Journal of Child-Computer Interaction, 19*, 1–18. doi:10.1016/j.ijcci.2018.10.001

Tye-Murray, N. (2016). *A clEAR Solution to the Changing Climate of Hearing Healthcare.* Retrieved from www.clearworks4ears.com/static/media_relations/Audiology%20practices%20proofs.pdf

Tye-Murray, N. (2021a). A digital therapeutic and hearing health coach for enhancing first-time hearing aid experiences. *Hearing Review, 28*(5), 25–26.

Tye-Murray, N. (2021b). *EARS Train the Brain.* Retrieved from www.clearworks4ears.com/

Tye-Murray, N., Spehar, B., Sommers, M., Mauzé, E., Barcroft, J., & Grantham, H. (2021). Teaching children with hearing loss to recognize speech: Gains made with computer-based auditory and/or speechreading training. *Ear and Hearing.* Advance online publication. doi:10.1097/AUD.0000000000001091 PMID:34225318

Ullman, D., Phillips, E., Aladia, S., Haas, P., Fowler, H. S., Iqbal, I. S., ... Malle, B. F. (2021). Evaluating psychosocial support provided by an augmented reality device for children with Type 1 diabetes. *Proceedings of the International Symposium on Human Factors and Ergonomics in Health Care, 10*(1), 126-130. 10.1177/2327857921101117

Vogel, J. J., Vogel, D. S., Cannon-Brower, J., Bowers, C. A., Muse, K., & Wright, M. (2006). Computer gaming and interactive simulations for learning: A meta-analysis. *Journal of Educational Computing Research, 34*(3), 229–243. doi:10.2190/FLHV-K4WA-WPVQ-H0YM

Vygotsky, L. S. (1978). *Mind in society: The development of higher psychological processes.* Harvard University Press.

West, S. G., & Aiken, L. S. (1997). Toward understanding individual effects in multicomponent prevention programs: Design and analysis strategies. In K. J. Bryant, M. Windle, & S. G. West (Eds.), *The science of prevention: Methodological advances from alcohol and substance abuse research* (pp. 167–209). American Psychological Association. doi:10.1037/10222-006

White, R. W. (1959). Motivation reconsidered: The concept of competence. *Psychological Review, 66*(5), 297–333. doi:10.1037/h0040934 PMID:13844397

Whiteley, L., Brown, L. K., Mena, L., Craker, L., & Arnold, T. (2018). Enhancing health among youth living with HIV using an iPhone game. *AIDS Care, 30*(sup4), 21-33. doi:10.1080/09540121.2018.1503224

Whiteley, L., Craker, L., Haubrick, K. K., Arnold, T., Mena, L., Olsen, E., & Brown, L. K. (2021). The impact of a mobile gaming intervention to increase adherence to pre-exposure prophylaxis. *AIDS and Behavior, 25*(6), 1884–1889. doi:10.100710461-020-03118-3 PMID:33483897

Whiteley, L., Olsen, E., Mena, L., Haubrick, K., Craker, L., Hershkowitz, D., & Brown, L. K. (2020). A mobile gaming intervention for persons on pre-exposure prophylaxis: Protocol for intervention development and randomized controlled trial. *JMIR Research Protocols*, *9*(9), e18640. doi:10.2196/18640 PMID:32924954

Wilson, K. A., Bedwell, W. L., Lazzara, E. H., Salas, E., Burke, S., Estock, J. L., Orvis, K. L., & Conkey, C. (2009). Relationships between game attributes and learning outcomes. *Simulation & Gaming*, *40*(2), 217–266. doi:10.1177/1046878108321866

Woo, Y., & Reeves, T. C. (2007). Meaningful interaction in web-based learning: A social constructivist perspective. *The Internet and Higher Education*, *10*(1), 15–25. doi:10.1016/j.iheduc.2006.10.005

Wouters, P., van Nimwegen, C., van der Spek, E., & van Oostendorp, H. (2013). A meta-analysis of the cognitive and motivational effects of serious games. *Journal of Educational Psychology*, *105*(2), 249–265. doi:10.1037/a0031311

ENDNOTES

[1] This search involved all funded grants issued by any one of the 27 Institutes and Centers operating under the auspices of NIH. A total of 1524 grant abstracts were reviewed based on abstract published in the NIH Reporter, of which 397 qualified using the key search terms. A total of 52 were further categorized as games using the 13 categories of health promotion delivery strategies.

[2] Amory (2007) provides a more elaborate division of mechanics and game space, suggesting there are three spaces in serious games that encompass the game space (game + player), problem space (educational framework), and social space (the ways people can interact, i.e., navigational tools, interactivity, and feedback). Additional layers include the actor and the game elements (sounds, technology and backstory). The visualization layer then brings in the story, plot and flow of the game.

[3] Here, we can refer to the work of Vygotsky (1978), who believed that much of learning is social by nature, with information obtained during interactions with other people, some more knowledgeable than the learning child.

[4] This is a central thesis to Bandura's social learning theory, refined from experimental evidence on aggression, imitative learning and social modeling (see for example, Bandura 1977a, Bandura et al., 1961; 1963a,b).

[5] According to Gee (2008), these can include non-playing characters (NPCs) that help players navigate the goals and norms of the game and the content they must acquire in order to master game play. NPCs are "guides" that model small corrections during game play as a teacher would present "corrections" to a student through instructional feedback. Both the NPC and the teacher represent opportunities for the player to learn "in context," which Gee defines as a "goal-driven problem space" (p. 26).

[6] This is tied to Vygotsky's constructivist approach that holds learning is best when it is social, active and situated, so that learners can put their new knowledge into practice (gain a foothold) in terms of real-world problem-solving with social benefits (for a review of the constructivist perspective in higher education, see, Woo & Reeves, 2007).

[7] A more favorable meta-analytic review can be found in Portnoy et al. 2008; however, gamification was not a criteria for inclusion. Rather, computer-delivered interventions for health behaviors was the focus of this review and inclusion criteria necessitated rigorous evaluation using a randomized controlled trial. In their meta-analysis, Wouters et al. (2013) reported that serious games were more effective in terms of learning and retention but were not more motivating when compared to conventional instructional methods (e.g., didactic lectures, reading, drill and practice) and that these effects were larger when the game was combined with supplemental instruction.

Chapter 11
COVID-Game:
A Serious Game to Inform About Coronavirus

Leonardo da Conceição Estevam
Federal University of Pará, Brazil

Lúcio Leandro Cruz de Oliveira
Federal University of Pará, Brazil

Fernando Augusto Ribeiro Costa
🆔 https://orcid.org/0000-0002-0226-7505
Federal University of Pará, Brazil

Marcos César da Rocha Seruffo
🆔 https://orcid.org/0000-0002-8106-0560
Federal University of Pará, Brazil

ABSTRACT

This chapter presents the Covid-Game, a serious game developed out of the difficulties that various societies, specifically the Brazilian, have faced with the advent of the current COVID-19 pandemic. Such difficulties are not restricted to health or economic issues but unfold into problems such as the dissemination of untrue information about the virus, the disease, the ways of prevention, and the treatments available to the population, including immunization through vaccines. Using techniques already consolidated in the state of art of serious games and gamification, this proposal innovates by aiming to disseminate correct information about COVID-19 playfully and considering the players' age, regional, and cultural aspects. This chapter demonstrates its viability, versatility, and convenience in these times of dissemination of countless false information that endangers human life itself.

DOI: 10.4018/978-1-6684-4291-3.ch011

INTRODUCTION

The current pandemic arising from the spread of the new coronavirus on all continents has caused, over the last 18 months, unprecedented crisis, at least in this generation. All societies are, directly or indirectly, affected by consequences that are characterized by economic, social, educational, and cultural losses (Mattei & Heinen, 2020). To date, August 2021, COVID-19 has infected more than 200 million people and caused the death of more than 4 million inhabitants of various nations (Johns Hopkins University, 2021). Despite the possibility of greater and more effective prevention in Brazil, where the pandemic arrived weeks after the cases in northern Italy, the country has the third highest number of infected people and the second highest number of deaths in absolute terms (Johns Hopkins, 2021).

Although the catastrophe scenario initially predicted for the Brazilian case (Porsse et al., 2020) has not been confirmed in terms of the total number of fatalities, it is undeniable that the chain of events arising from the pandemic and the taking of restrictive measures by governors and mayors had as main consequences the economic downturn, the dissemination of ideas with a wide spectrum of conspiracy and the dissemination of inaccurate information about such measures, and even the existence and lethality of the virus.

Despite being a scenario of instability with an extremely serious cause, it is also an ideal scenario to test the responsiveness that can be built through the implementation of Serious Games (SG) (Fabricatore et al., 2020). Even before this moment in humanity, SGs have always been a good alternative for tackling diverse needs of social outreach (Xu et al., 2017; Zhonggen, 2019). Tools that combine the playfulness of playing with the seriousness of informing and training, SGs cannot lose the balance between these two dimensions, otherwise they may become tools incompatible with the purpose of disseminating knowledge through play (Westera, 2017).

Considering these aspects, this chapter presents the Covid-Game, a SG that was developed with the intent to: i) disseminate correct information about COVID-19 through gamification techniques; ii) raise users' awareness about their attitudes regarding protection and prevention guidelines for COVID-19 contamination; iii) disseminate information and guidelines about symptoms, prevention, and treatment of COVID-19 in a regionalized manner; and iv) collaborate to improve and/or possibly change users' practices and actions, directly impacting their lives, their families' lives, and the community in general.

This chapter is divided into the following sections: the second section presents a brief contextualization of the setting in which the Covid-Game is developed; the third section describes the materials and methods used to develop the proposed SG; the fourth section discusses the Covid-Game itself as a result of the research and, at the same time, discusses it; and finally, conclusions are drawn resuming the path undertaken in the research and what avenues are open for future work.

BACKGROUND

This section presents some studies on the use of SG in numerous areas of knowledge and/or human activities. The purpose of this section is to demonstrate that the current scenario of the gamification process is broad and includes complexities that are part of multiple causal issues. Thus, it corroborates the perspective of dialogue between the most diverse initiatives for SG use, while at the same time seeking to connect the results of this research with other results achieved in the state of the art, highlighting any differences in implementation, uses, and gains with which it contributes to this field of knowledge.

Given this, Ahmed and Sutton (2017) state that gamification can be defined as a process in which game theory, game elements, and game mechanics are integrated with the goal of engaging employees and learners that can improve their participation, commitment, and performance. As for the gains for teaching and education, gamification can build passion, rigor, organization and discipline towards giving the process a better experience. In this sense, it is not about "funification" of learning or work, but about building the learning organization.

This process called gamification is recent as a concept, but its ideation and roles are found in the roots of human activity itself in the sense of discovering ways to learn. Thus, it can motivate people to change their behavior by driving external and internal motivational keys. However, one should not confuse the strategies and dimensions of games with those of mere games, and one of the factors that prevent such confusion is precisely the purpose each one has for human beings: while games follow a set of rules that, if observed, always lead to new levels of improvement, performance and victory, games do not necessarily have rules and are more entertainment-oriented. This also leads to the understanding that serious games are also differentiated from gamification considering that those have a relationship with the dimension of motivation and that they exist beyond the field of education and training, but are found in several other dimensions (Patricio et al., 2018).

In this sense, Fabricatore et al. (2020) address how to rethink SG design within the current pandemic context with a focus on what they call *"wicked problems"*. For the researchers, serious games have the characteristic of keys to the development of management skills for such problems. Thus, the authors propose a framework to support the development of SGs in order to learn how to deal with complex problems; among such problems are those arising from the pandemic of COVID-19 that, despite appearing to be on the verge of being reduced, is still a cause of concern for all societies around the world.

In line with the quest to investigate the way in which a given player absorbs knowledge in the dynamics of a SG, Westera (2017) proposes a computational modeling approach to investigate the interaction of learning and play in serious games. Such a model allows researchers to deeply investigate the quantitative dependencies between relevant game variables, gain a deeper understanding of how people learn from games, and develop approaches to improve SG design. The author warns about the intrinsic complexity in the construction of games in the sense that their strongly interrelated components vary over time. Considering that SGs combine game design with instructional design, such complexity may even be greater in view of the care to avoid improperly structuring two domains that should be in balance: the playful mechanics of the game and the mechanisms of serious instructional principles.

It is precisely because of the ability of SGs to respond satisfactorily to various problems, and even more so if the dimensions of playfulness and seriousness are in balance, that they have recently been introduced in the current pandemic of COVID-19. Thus, Gaspar et al. (2020) developed a SG with the goal of providing science-based information about COVID-19 prevention and self-care during the pandemic, while assessing players' knowledge of topics related to this disease. Entitled "COVID-19 - Did You Know?", this game was made freely available on the website of the Federal University of Minas Gerais in April 2020 and by November of that year was accessed 17,571 times.

According to Gastar et al. (2020), the gamification strategy for health education content on Covid-19 reached a young audience, generating reinforcement of specific educational measures that were implemented based on the players' performance. The researchers point to improved performance of game users regarding attitudes towards the pandemic, such as, for example, adherence to wearing a mask all the time.

But it is not only in this aspect of individual protection and increased awareness about general measures to avoid infection by the Coronavirus that the SGs have been applied. This is shown by the research developed by Suppan et al. (2020a) which generated a SG entitled Escape COVID-19. The authors understand that this game will increase the knowledge and application of infection control and prevention procedures on the intention of nursing home staff to change their practices on this issue; that is, the game will be focused on professionals and their practices according to the current guidelines in the country (Switzerland). It is expected that the results will repeatedly demonstrate that the game has a greater and better capacity to generate changes in attitudes towards the need to maintain healthy habits and to control the spread of the virus, especially in places where there are people at greater risk of infection and, once infected, suffer a greater risk of severity and death. The same SG is the subject of a larger study by Suppan et al. (2020b) now targeting healthcare professionals working in hospitals.

On the other hand, the practices of preventing the disease and combating the virus become a priority to halt the advance of COVID-19 through correct information and education of the population; however, nowadays society is largely connected with technology and the convenience of information sharing, paving the way for the rapid dissemination of false information leading to the need to bring a new practice of health education, health and protection (Allahverdipour, 2020).

The World Health Organization (WHO) and experts in the field believe that sharing correct information, hand sanitization and social distancing, in its various degrees (selective isolation, quarantine, total blockade), are public health policies that show good results in combating the new Coronavirus; therefore, tools aimed at informing the population in a conscious manner and with the support of the appropriate professionals are increasingly necessary (Fiocruz, 2020).

Among these, mobile and web applications have gained a lot of space in the current market and are being used in the form of data analysis, behavior and education. Social gaming techniques can be used to improve the quality of online applications, social media, and a wide range of other consumer and business experiences (Almalki & Giannicchi, 2021).

For all the above, the SG proposed here, the Covid-Game, brings with it the concerns and directives that are also found in the works cited above, but it moves towards a broader and more heterogeneous audience and proposes a regionalized use. As we will see later on, this proposal considers the players by the several Brazilian regions in order to bring to the users information and knowledge based on local situations and particular orientations; this does not take away the need to disseminate general orientations for similar cases or issues according to the World Health Organization (WHO) guidelines. The authors believe that this makes it different from all other SGs aimed at disseminating preventive and control measures for the pandemic of COVID-19.

MATERIAL AND METHODS

This work was carried out with interdisciplinary collaboration between specialists in health sciences, design, education, and technology from the Federal University of Pará, Brazil. The game, categorized as a quiz, was presented in the form of a questionnaire for evaluation and review about the pandemic and ways to fight it; such instrument is divided into groups of 20 questions separated by age and region; each region has 5 exclusive questions referring to myths about COVID-19, 5 questions explaining the characteristics of the virus and 10 referring to the form of prevention. The interface was developed to be used in a simple way by users of all ages, focusing on young people, also having a visual identity, icons and logo carefully crafted considering a color system, typography, sounds and images that seek to fit the general public. The players' performance is evaluated by the amount of correct answers and the response time for each of the questions.

For each question, the player has 60 seconds to give the answer and the final score is given by adding up the scores using the formula below.

Final Score = (sum of remaining answer time for each question) / 10.

Only questions whose answers are correct go into the calculation of the final score, and the score is converted to a whole number, with fractions less than 0.5 rounded down and fractions greater than or equal to 0.5 rounded up. For example, suppose the player answered 12 questions correctly, taking an average of 27 seconds to answer each question, his final score would be:

Final score = (33 + 33 + 33 + 33 + 33 + 33 + 33 + 33 + 33 + 33 + 33 + 33 + 33) / 10 = 396 / 10 = 39.6 points

With the rounding of the score to a whole number the final score will be:

Final Score = 40 points

Using the Agile Methodology for the project development (Sutherland J & Sutherland JJ, 2019) (Figure 1) enabled quick, daily approaches by the team through video calls and weekly meetings.

Based on the methodology shown in Figure 1, a series of steps was developed that were repeated throughout the weeks of the project until the conception of the product now presented; these steps were:

Product Backlog: Consisted of the product's requirements gathering, elaboration of the schedule with deadlines and team work division. Thus the work plan was assembled, having the requirements modified throughout the project.

Sprint: Every 2 weeks a list of tasks was made to create the game, starting with the design, a simple interface and easy usability and then developing demos versions that would be tested by the team for bugs and improvement ideas.

Daily Scrum: Daily meetings of 15 minutes via meeting were held to monitor the completion of each of the tasks defined in the Sprint, also serving to clarify doubts.

Sprint Review: Once the demo was tested, the team adapted to review and implement the new requirements and feedback on what was already done.

Learning Method

This project aims to increase the awareness of the population by disseminating truthful information about hygienic measures and combating COVID-19 with the help of a Gamification system (Almeida & Simões, 2019). Through the perspective of a multidisciplinary team, uniting professionals who are experts in each subject relevant to the project, such as, education, design, development, health and technology, the Covid-Game was developed as a serious game to encourage methods to combat and prevent the virus through information shared by experts in the field of health in addition to information released on the website of the Ministry of Health of the Brazilian government.

Figure 1. Agile Methodology

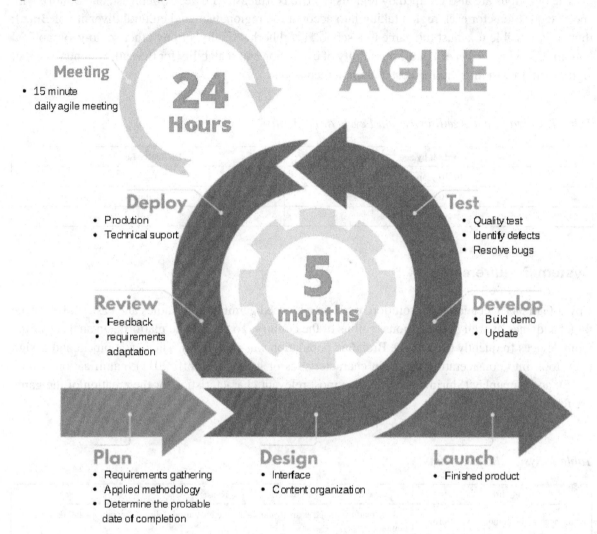

The Covid-Game aims to stimulate social engagement to fight COVID-19 using a gamification system. A well executed game makes people feel special because games are an ancient way to reach someone's heart and mind (Jon, 2011). The Covid-Game is a web gamification system (smartphone and/or desktop) in accordance with the Brazilian Federal Law 13.709/2018 (General Data Protection Law) and an incentive mechanism to engage the population to access, respond and share reliable and trustworthy information about COVID-19 which revolutionizes the way the population gains knowledge about the virus and ways to fight it through creative engagement. Each individual is unique, but when creating something you must take into consideration that groups of people are the same. All playful activities are linked to childhood, since childhood revolves around playing (Jesse, 2008).

The Covid-Game is a serious game that presents several questions and answers taking into account the recommendations presented by WHO and released by the Ministry of Health, the Covid-Game can be easily customized to operate with the population of different age groups, so it has difficulty levels separated by age, as shown in Table 1, the age groups will also be used for the creation of a specific ranking.

The questions are also grouped by regions (North, Northeast, Midwest, Southeast, and South), with specific questions for each region taking into account the regionalism and cultural diversity of Brazil; thus, it is possible to adjust the game to a school, neighborhood, city, or any other socio-geographical condition, having the benefit of the possibility of expansion and scalability for the entire country without significant growth in operating cost and implementation.

Table 1. Covid-Game Age Ranges and Levels of Difficulty

Separation by age	Difficulty Level
01-10 years	Easy
11-20 years	Medium
21-99+ years	Hard

System Requirements

Covid-Game is a technological solution based on advanced gamification studies and case studies of the target audience as well as the various regions of the country. To choose the platform, an analysis of the main devices frequently used by the Brazilian population was performed. The development and design team took into consideration the main characteristics of games (Radoff, 2011), gamification (Chou, 2015), and gameplay (Shirinian, 2017). The most relevant characteristics for the creation of the game are found in Table 2.

Table 2. System Requirements

Features	Reason
Game accessible on multiple platforms.	Mobile platforms such as smartphones are the most used, followed by laptops and desktop computers.
No file download is required.	A web application was chosen for the ease of hosting the game on several external sites, also helping with the promotion.
No registration required.	This project does not use confidential and/or personal data since it does not have a registration system.
It takes into account cultural characteristics of each region.	As a differential, Covid-Game takes into account the beliefs and habits of each region for the development of the questions and answers.
Maintains the score in the regional and national ranking.	The username and the score of the first 5 players of each region, as well as the 5 best players of the national ranking, will be stored and published.
Enables the visualization of regional and national ranking.	The ranking is located in the main menu of the game, so it will not be necessary to play to be able to visualize the rank.
Provides information about the project, the institution, and the team.	The credits contain detailed information about the project, institution and support teams, as well as basic information about the members directly related to the development of the application.

Tools

Using Visual Studio Code IDE - Integrated Development Environment (Microsoft, 2021). It has support for several programming languages, one of them being C#, used to create the game scripts. For the game modeling the Unity tool was used, which is a proprietary game engine (Unity Technologies, 2021). Being chosen for having the ability to create games for various platforms such as smartphones, consoles and browsers, besides having ready elements such as textures and libraries, speeding up the creation of games, as well as its organized and easy to use interface.

It was used Firebase (Google Developers, 2021), a mobile application development platform from Google, which was chosen due to its compatibility with Unity and its Realtime Database tool, responsible for storing the users' scores that will be used in the regional and national ranking. It also has the Analytics tool responsible for analyzing and storing data and generating reports on user behavior.

RESULT AND DISCUSSION

Through a web application, the Covid-Game follows the style of electronic games with a friendly interface adapted for different audiences. The logo (Figure 2) was created by one of the developers, the image of the doctors was chosen among several other images as the one that best represents the theme of the game, being its use made possible due to The Attribution-Non-Commercial-Share-Equal 3.0 Brazil license allows the free use of all images, infographics and pieces of information created for non-commercial purposes. The background color was chosen after discussions and analysis by the developers, taking into consideration which would be more pleasing and that would highlight both the logo and the selected image.

Figure 2. Home Menu

In the main interface of the game, shown in Figure 2, there are 3 buttons to access respectively play, rating and credits, the images of the buttons are provided by the Unity tool itself, along with its texture, besides the possibility of color choice.

When selecting "Play" the user is directed to a brief explanation (Figure 3) of the rules and conditions of the game, how the questions are categorized. There is a field where the player can enter his username, which will be assigned to the regional and/or national ranking if he is among the top 5. There are 2 quick selection buttons for the player's age and region, and this information is taken into account for the selection of the group of questions, since the age is responsible for the difficulty level of the questions; Thus, the difficulty levels were divided as follows:

Easy: for under 10 years old, containing easy questions commonly reported in the media and schools.
Medium: between 11 and 20 years old, containing more elaborate questions that bring reflection on the player's behavior during the pandemic.
Hard: for ages 20+, its questions consist of more technical terms.

While the region button is responsible for the category of questions according to the customs of each region.

Figure 3. Tutorial

By selecting "Play" from the start menu, the quiz game begins as seen in (Figure 4), the player must answer several questions with each corresponding to a different measure to prevent the spread of COVID-19 whose answers take into account the WHO recommendations, and each question will share information passed on by health professionals. It has simple graphics by keeping the choice of background color from the start menu, and adding the map of the selected region in Figure 3. Each question is multiple choice, and the player can select one of two answers. After the answer has been selected, the player must confirm his or her answer before the timer reaches 0 (zero).

Figure 4. Interface showing a question

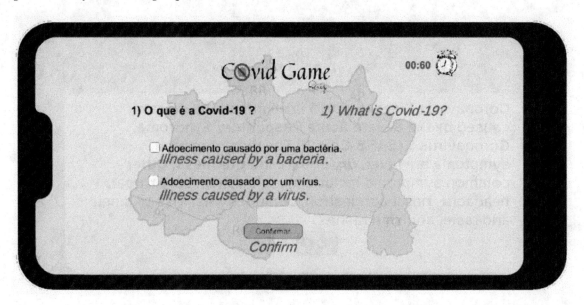

After confirming the answer, a feedback of the correct (Figure 5) or wrong (Figure 6), if the player does not choose any answer and the timer times out, the answer will automatically be considered to be the wrong one. Audiovisual effects such as sounds and colors were used for the questions as well as for the feedback of the answers.

Figure 5. Feedback to right answer

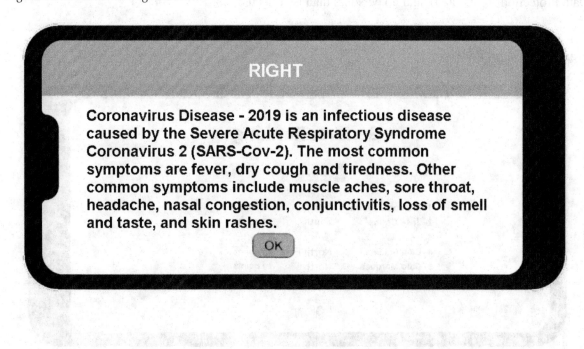

Figure 6. Feedback to wrong answer

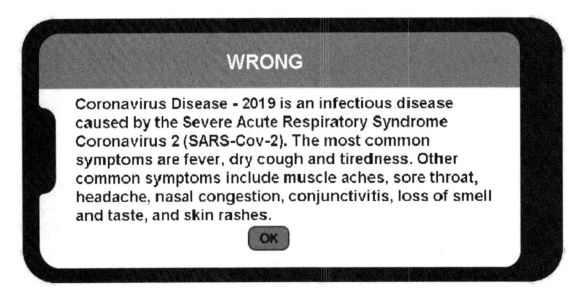

The Realtime Database feature of the Firebase platform was used to save the user's data on Google's servers and then access them for the creation of the ranking divided by the overall ranking (Figure 7), regional ranking (Figure 8), and by age (Figure 9), and Google Analytics was used to collect non-confidential user data, of which only the Name, Age and Region are informed at the beginning of the game, as well as the Final Score. Only the top 5 players in each category are stored in FireBase, while others are automatically deleted. The data collected is compliant with the regulations of the General Data Protection Act (Brazil), and no personal data is collected.

Figure 7. General Ranking

Figure 8. Regional Ranking

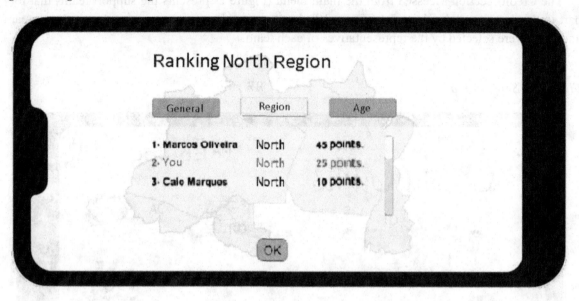

Figure 9. Age Ranking

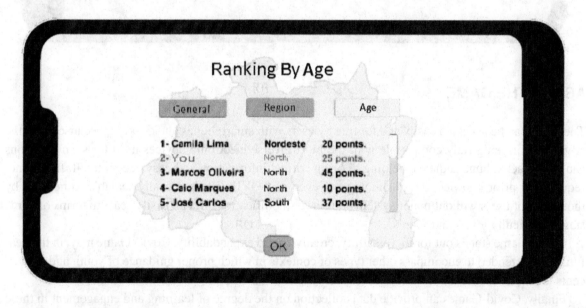

The score can be accessed by any user by selecting the rank button in the main menu, which allows the user to view the top-ranked players in their respective ranks and compare them to their own performance. Covid-Game allows the player to do as many rounds as they want, so all players after a few rounds can reach the maximum score of the game, and for the ranking not to be static, an algorithm was implemented so that equal scores, the last one is selected to be part of the rank, this way it will have a great rotation of the best classified, and is expected to have a greater motivation for the use of the application by the players who want their names always appear in some of the ranks.

The Credits section accessed from the main menu (Figure 2) presents the support teams that took part in the design and development (Figure 10). Logos were chosen as a way to represent each team, and these were selected by the representatives of each team.

Figure 10. Support Team

ABOUT THE GAME

The game can be accessed easily and for free by users with smartphones and desktop, because it has the advantage of being fully compatible with the most diverse electronic devices used for such functions can thus reach a huge audience helping to bring correct information and easy access to all. It does not require any prior knowledge of technology or even of COVID-19. It is easily scalable to be used by thousands of users without major system and server modifications. It can easily scale in terms of game stages, difficulty levels and scores.

Covid-Game stands out for its versatility, creativity and expandability. Covid-Game may, in the near future, be extended to encompass other types of contexts in which proper guidance of youth and adolescents is required, such as: flu, dengue, sexually transmitted diseases (STDs), and others.

Finally, Covid-Game can provide data collection on the degree of learning and engagement in these contexts, thus enabling the formation of a database that can be used by Brazilian researchers for the development of new studies and educational methodologies, as well as better planning of public and social policies in each region of Brazil.

Of course, according to the possible developments for this proposal, an important bias for the evolution of Covid-Game points to the use by a significant portion of the world's population, namely people with some kind of disability (PcD). These individuals, besides their own condition, have to face obstacles of a world not built for them. It becomes mandatory the natural evolution/adaptation of Covid-Game to cater to people with disabilities or reduced abilities.

CONCLUSION

This chapter presents the Covid-Game, a serious game whose purposes are described as follows: i) disseminate correct information about COVID-19 through gamification techniques: considering the numerous information that circulates in the media and that has been a cause of concern for several governments and organizations; ii) raise users' awareness about their attitudes regarding protection and prevention guidelines for COVID-19 contamination: considering the fact that personal attitudes gain positive community importance when one becomes so aware and, otherwise, may cause irreparable harm to oneself and others; iii) disseminate information and guidelines about symptoms, prevention, and treatment of COVID-19 in a regionalized manner; and iv) collaborate to improve and/or possibly change users' practices and actions, directly impacting their lives, their families' lives, and the community in general.

It has been shown that, even using relatively simple and already usual techniques in the SG scenario, it is possible to innovate in this field and provide society with a tool that is connected to the moment and the difficulties faced by it. Thus, Covid-Game has an architecture that is not out of the ordinary, but offers a service that is not characterized as being common. And herein lies one of its most positive differences from other games dealing with the current pandemic, namely its concern with age, regional, and cultural factors.

By dividing the groups of players by difficulty level in ages, the need to disseminate correct information about the disease at the level that the person can understand is privileged; of course, as exposed throughout the chapter, one cannot give more emphasis to the playfulness and leave in less relief the seriousness that involves a serious game. Thus, it is observed that the necessary balance between these dimensions is present in the Covid-Game.

Another important peculiarity to be highlighted is its concern with regional and cultural issues. Sometimes, the practices of prevention, protection, recognition of symptoms, and treatment do not have the expected effects because of the generic way in which awareness campaigns are planned. Using the playfulness techniques, typical of serious games, and the seriousness of the information contained in it, the Covid-Game aims to provide appropriate guidance to the inhabitants of each of the five Brazilian regions, which certainly makes it a good tool for acquiring general knowledge about the disease, but passed on in a specific way.

However, the development of such a tool was not without its own research difficulties. Certainly, the main difficulty encountered by the development team was to condense the information and guidelines coming especially from agencies such as the WHO and the Brazilian Ministry of Health and make them consistent with what is expected in a game: the playfulness.

It is ratified that future works will deal with other difficulties related to health and that still encounter obstacles to the dissemination of appropriate guidelines for prevention, diagnosis, and treatment. It is also expected to give the game new features and attributes in order to make it more attractive and able to meet the diverse audiences following the same concerns listed above; therefore, focusing on the user's needs.

REFERENCES

Ahmed, A., & Sutton, M. J. (2017). *Gamification, serious games, simulations, and immersive learning environments in knowledge management initiatives. World Journal of Science, Technology and Sustainable Development*. doi:10.1108/WJSTSD-02-2017-0005

Allahverdipour, H. (2020). Global challenge of health communication: Infodemia in the coronavirus disease (COVID-19) pandemic. *Journal of Education and Community Health, 7*(2), 65–67. doi:10.29252/jech.7.2.65

Almalki, M., & Giannicchi, A. (2021). Health apps for combating COVID-19: Descriptive review and taxonomy. *JMIR mHealth and uHealth, 9*(3), e24322. doi:10.2196/24322 PMID:33626017

Almeida, F., & Simoes, J. (2019). The role of serious games, gamification and industry 4.0 tools in the education 4.0 paradigm. *Contemporary Educational Technology, 10*(2), 120–136. doi:10.30935/cet.554469

Federal, G. (2018). *Lei Geral de Proteção de Dados* [General Data Protection Law].

Domicílios, T. I. C. (2019). *Domicílios com acesso à internet Cetic. br* [Households with Cetic internet access]. Author.

Commons, C. (2017). *Atribuição-NãoComercial-CompartilhaIgual* [Attribution-Noncommercial-Share Alike]. 3.0 Brasil (CC BY-NC-SA 3.0 BR).

Chou, Y. K. (2019). *Actionable gamification: Beyond points, badges, and leaderboards.* Packt Publishing Ltd.

Unity Technologies. (2019). *Unity.* Author.

Fabricatore, C., Gyaurov, D., & Lopez, X. (2020, November). Rethinking serious games design in the age of COVID-19: Setting the focus on wicked problems. In *Joint International Conference on Serious Games* (pp. 243-259). Springer. 10.1007/978-3-030-61814-8_19

FIOCRUZ. (2020). *ONU e OMS pedem medidas firmes contra fake news* [ONU and WHO call for firm measures against fake news]. Author.

Gaspar, J. D. S., Lage, E. M., Da Silva, F. J., Mineiro, É., De Oliveira, I. J. R., Oliveira, I., ... Reis, Z. S. N. (2020). A mobile serious game about the pandemic (COVID-19-Did You Know?): Design and evaluation study. *JMIR Serious Games, 8*(4), e25226. doi:10.2196/25226 PMID:33301416

Google Developers. (2021) *Firebase.* Author.

COVID. (2020). Dashboard by the center for systems science and engineering (CSSE) at Johns Hopkins University (JHU). John Hopkins University Coronvirus Resource Centre.

Microsoft. (2021). *Visual Studio Code.* Author.

Mattei, L., & Heinen, V. L. (2020). Impacts of the COVID-19 crisis on the Brazilian labor market. *Brazilian Journal of Political Economy, 40*, 647–668. doi:10.1590/0101-31572020-3200

Ministério da Saúde (Brasil). (2020). *Plano nacional de operacionalização da vacinação contra a COVID-19* [National Plan for the Operationaliszation of Vaccination against COVID-19]. Author.

Patrício, R., Moreira, A. C., & Zurlo, F. (2018). Gamification approaches to the early stage of innovation. *Creativity and Innovation Management, 27*(4), 499–511. doi:10.1111/caim.12284

Peng, L. H., & Bai, M. H. (2021). How Gameful Experience Affects Public Knowledge, Attitudes, and Practices Regarding COVID-19 Among the Taiwanese Public: Cross-sectional Study. *JMIR Serious Games*, *9*(2), e26216. doi:10.2196/26216 PMID:33737262

Porsse, A. A., Souza, K. D., Carvalho, T. S., & Vale, V. A. (2020). Impactos econômicos da COVID-19 no Brasil [Economic Impacts of COVID-19 in Brazil] *Nota Técnica NEDUR-UFPR*, *1*, 44.

Radoff, J. (2011). *Energize your business with social media games*. Academic Press.

Sanguinet, E. R., Alvim, A. M., Atienza, M., & Fochezatto, A. (2021). The subnational supply chain and the COVID-19 pandemic: Short-term impacts on the Brazilian regional economy. *Regional Science Policy & Practice*, *13*(S1), 158–186. doi:10.1111/rsp3.12442

Schell, J. (2008). *The Art of Game Design: A book of lenses*. CRC press. doi:10.1201/9780080919171

Shirinian, A. (2010). *The uneasy merging of narrative and gameplay*. Academic Press.

Staton, R. (2015). *A Brief History of Video Games: From Atari to Xbox One*. Little, Brown Book Group Limited.

Suppan, L., Abbas, M., Catho, G., Stuby, L., Regard, S., Harbarth, S., Achab, S., & Suppan, M. (2020). Impact of a serious game on the intention to change infection prevention and control practices in nursing homes during the COVID-19 pandemic: Protocol for a web-based randomized controlled trial. *JMIR Research Protocols*, *9*(12), e25595. doi:10.2196/25595 PMID:33296329

Suppan, M., Catho, G., Nunes, T. R., Sauvan, V., Perez, M., Graf, C., ... Suppan, L. (2020). A serious game designed to promote safe behaviors among health care workers during the COVID-19 pandemic: Development of "Escape COVID-19". *JMIR Serious Games*, *8*(4), e24986. doi:10.2196/24986 PMID:33242312

Sutherland, J., & Sutherland, J. J. (2018). Scrum: A arte de fazer o dobro do trabalho na metade do tempo [Scrum: The Art of Doing Twice the Work in Half the Time] (3rd ed.). Rio de Janeiro: LeYa.

Turkle, S. (2005). *Video games and computer holding power*. Academic Press.

Wardrip-Fruin, N., & Montfort, N. (Eds.). (2003). *The new media reader* (Vol. 1). MIT press.

Westera, W. (2017). How people learn while playing serious games: A computational modelling approach. *Journal of Computational Science*, *18*, 32–45. doi:10.1016/j.jocs.2016.12.002

Xu, F., Buhalis, D., & Weber, J. (2017). Serious games and the gamification of tourism. *Tourism Management*, *60*, 244–256. doi:10.1016/j.tourman.2016.11.020

Zhonggen, Y. (2019). A meta-analysis of use of serious games in education over a decade. *International Journal of Computer Games Technology*, *2019*, 4797032. doi:10.1155/2019/4797032

Chapter 12
Integration of Gamification Methods to Improve Design–to–Customer in Product Development:
Use Case – The German Corona–Warning App

David Kessing
Bergische Universität Wuppertal, Germany

Tim Katzwinkel
Bergische Universität Wuppertal, Germany

Manuel Löwer
Bergische Universität Wuppertal, Germany

ABSTRACT

Gamification is an emerging approach to designing motivational strategies for many different applications. To maximize their efficiency, gamification strategies need an in-depth analysis of the users' behavior and appropriate gamification mechanics for implementation. Hence, gamification designs include a deep understanding of human interaction with the product and different motivational aspects during usage. This advantage offers product development opportunities to design more customer-oriented products using gamification methods. This chapter introduces an improved product development process regarding the design-to-customer aspect within the phases of customer analysis, mechanic ideation, and feature design. Each phase includes the integration of specific methods taken from established gamification frameworks. The new process is evaluated with a project on developing gamification strategies for the German Corona-Warning-App.

DOI: 10.4018/978-1-6684-4291-3.ch012

INTRODUCTION

The term gamification first appeared in 2002 in a paper by management consultant Andrzej Marczewski and has gained more and more attention in the past decade. In 2011, the first scientific conference on the topic was held by Kevin Werbach and Dan Hunter at the University of Pennsylvania (Fleisch, 2018). Meanwhile, gamification methods are already being used successfully in many companies (Ellenberger, 2020; Reiners, 2015).

The concept of gamification aims at using the inherent potential of games in a meaningful and targeted way. The goal is to increase the motivation of users by offering new incentives that increase interest in activities and make overcoming challenges more attractive. The positive motivational potential is tapped through the systematic design of gamification strategies. When developing gamification strategies towards a specific application, motivating elements are taken from video games and redesigned according to the given context. Before gamification elements are implemented within a project, a comprehensive user analysis regarding the motivation during the use phase takes place.

For product development, this offers a novel opportunity to gain a broad understanding of user behavior to develop potentially more costumer-relevant products.

This chapter describes the integration of traditional product development with modern gamification methods. The goal is to provide guidance for developers regarding the design of products towards more customer relevance.

The following phases of product development with gamification are outlined:

1. in-depth user analysis regarding the customer behavior in the use-phase
2. ideation of suitable gamification techniques applicable to the product
3. detailed design of the chosen techniques for the individual use-case

A conducted project on gamification strategy development for the German Corona warning app is used as a best-practice example.

BACKGROUND

The book "Engineering Design" by Pahl and Beitz is considered basic reading for students in engineering, especially design engineering and product development (Springer Nature Switzerland AG, 2021).

Pahl and Beitz define product development as "a key success factor for companies [...] The target system for the development of a product is [...] characterized by interdisciplinarity and dynamics. [...] Product development means that new solutions have to be created" (Gericke et al., 2021). In the context of this chapter, product development is defined as the process of identifying and designing solutions to appearing problems in the form of physical or cyber-physical products.

The chapter "User needs" of the book "Engineering Design" deals with the optimization of the development of products concerning the optimal fulfillment of user needs. It explains various general qualitative and quantitative methods for eliciting user needs and presents approaches for integrating users into the product development process (Gericke et al., 2021).

The chapter "Industrial design and user-centered product development" then deals with the presentation and implementation of user-specific requirements, as well as the design with regard to the psy-

Figure 1. The Flow-Theory (Csíkszentmihályi, 1990)

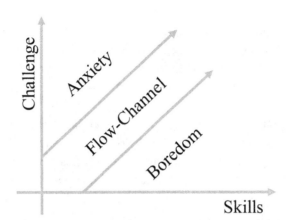

chological and physiological perception of the product. Along the product life cycle, different methods are presented, which enable the integration of user needs. Typical examples are the persona, the sinus milieus, expert interviews, mood boards, and user stories (Gericke et al., 2021).

In real-life applications, problems regarding a lack of consistency, interconnection or interpretation of the results of these methods for the subsequent phase within the product development or design process often arise. Exemplarily, how to proceed with a persona once created or how to translate the sinus milieu of a customer into a specific product feature.

Gamification offers a novel attempt to solve this problem. Not only through the proven use in idea generation and development, but also through enhancing structured and coordinated processes, gamification offers a promising approach (Patricio et al., 2018, 2020).

Various frameworks describe the gamification approach with different perspectives and focus on different aspects (Mora et al., 2015). Some have more of a process-oriented synthesis focus, others concentrate on the analysis of existing contexts. In the given example and due to the integration into the product development process, process-oriented approaches are particularly suitable.

The basis of gamification research has been established by Csíkszentmihályi's flow theory. The flow theory describes the optimal state of concentration during an activity between over- and underchallenge (Csikszentmihalyi, 1990) (see Fig.1). Thus, the flow state forms the target system for gamification design. Using playful elements, the user is brought into a state in which he can perform the desired action with full concentration.

The "How to design gamification" process of Morschheuser et al. compares 41 different approaches of gamification design and conducted 25 expert interviews in their research and developed an evaluated gamification design process for general application. The gamification design process according to Morschheuser, with seven phases from preparation to monitoring, offers major similarities to the design thinking process and thus already offers proximity to agile product development strategies. (Morschheuser et al., 2018)

The process described by Morschheuser includes seven phases, from the preparation of the development, environment and user analysis, idea generation, technique design, technique implementation, success evaluation, and monitoring, which can be performed iteratively if required (see Fig. 2).

Figure 2. Gamification design process "How to design gamification" (Morschheuser et al., 2018)

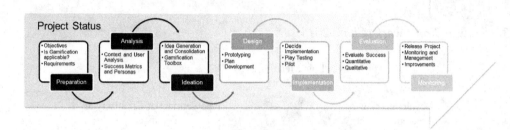

The "How to design gamification"-process of Morschheuser et al., offers a structured guideline for the methodical development of gamification strategies. Due to the clear process orientation and the similarity to design and product development processes, the "How to design gamification" process is suitable in the given context.

By focusing on the early phases of the product development process, the analysis, ideation, and design phases are considered in particular.

With the help of additional frameworks, a continuous process can be developed to provide a clear guideline for the translation of user needs into product functions and solution principles.

For each of the three phases of analysis, ideation, and design, specifically suitable frameworks are used.

- **Octalysis** as an analysis tool
- **Actionable Gamification** and **Gamified UK** as ideation basis
- **Hooked** as a design guideline.

In his book *Actionable Gamification*, Chou observes eight motivational Gamification Core Drives of video games, which contribute to the motivation of the users and form his **Octalysis model** (Chou, 2015):

- **Epic Meaning and Calling** (Feeling of a higher sense)
- **Development and Accomplishment** (Feeling of constant progress)
- **Empowerment of Creativity and Feedback** (Drive to self-realization)
- **Ownership and Possession** (Wish to build up property)
- **Social Influence and Relatedness** (Feeling of social acceptance)
- **Scarcity and Impatience** (Wish to achieve something currently not available)
- **Unpredictability and Curiosity** (Drive to avoid unpredictable situations)
- **Loss and Avoidance** (Drive to avoid loss)

A certain context analyzed with the Octalysis framework regarding the fulfillment of the Core Drives can be visualized in an octagon graph which offers an intuitive visualization tool. Also, the amount of eight core drives offers a high granularity of observed motivational directions (see Fig 3).

In the ideation phase, suitable gamification techniques are identified that can be used to trigger the desired user behavior. The original method for ideating gamification techniques can be found in the analysis of video games. The techniques found have already been recorded in many frameworks. An example of this is Marczewski's framework „**Gamified UK**" which lists 52 techniques and assigns them to eight "player characters" in a periodic table of gamification elements (Marczewski, 2018), (see Fig. 4)

Figure 3. Octalysis Framework (Chou, 2015)

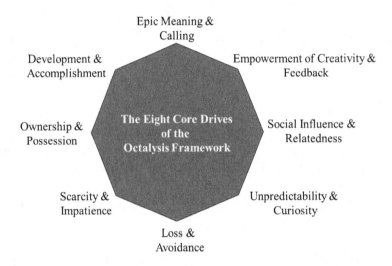

Figure 4. Periodic Table of Gamification Elements (Marczewski, 2018)

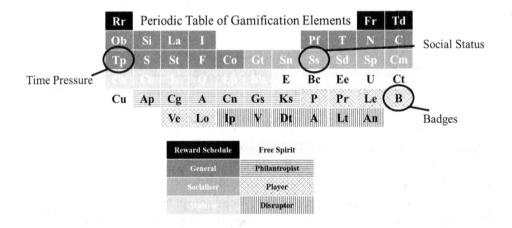

The **"Hooked" model** from Nir Eyal describes four iterative phases of systematic habit-forming product design (Eyal, 2014) (see Fig. 5)

These four phases help to integrate the selected gamification techniques into the respective product and thus offer a useful supplement for the design of gamification strategies.

By integrating these three frameworks into the " How to design gamification " process, a continuous process with consecutive tools can be created. The results of the phases can be directly converted into input for the following phase. Thus, customer-specific user needs can be directly translated into approaches for product features.

Figure 5. The Hook Framework (Eyal, 2014)

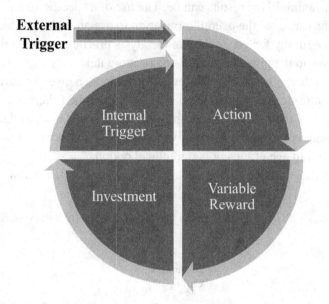

This offers an essential innovation for the early phases of product development.

GAMIFICATION TOOLS IN PRODUCT DEVELOPMENT

The most important phase of gamification design is the analysis phase (Morschheuser et al., 2018). A profound analysis of the context on the one hand and the customer or user, on the other hand, ensures a suitable selection of gamification techniques. The result of the analysis phase is a comprehensive profile of the users concerning their motivation for usage and potential interaction points. These results offer the possibility to customize the product more precisely to the potential customer during the development process.

First, it is necessary to identify the points at which the introduction of gamification elements is most useful. To do this, the user's interaction chain with the product must be identified. This can be performed by a user journey, in which every interaction and every active and passive step of the product is visualized. This helps to identify relevant action points. Action points are potential points of intervention where developers can make prioritized changes that have an impact on the user's perception or the user behavior. At these points, the later developed gamification designs will be prioritized.

For the analysis of user motivation, Chou's Octalysis is used here as a functional tool. With its eight defined motivational core drives, this framework provides a good basis for identifying key motivational factors in product usage behavior. The recording of the motivational core drives can be done in different ways. For example, qualitative interviews offer an individual but in-depth analysis of motivation, while quantitative surveys tend to draw a representative but basic picture. It is also possible to analyze existing documentation, newspaper articles and online reviews. Often, these combinations do provide a more holistic picture with comprehensive insights into usage motivation, which can be well represented in the Octalysis Core Drives (Chou, 2015).

Before creating a query, it is necessary to define which context is to be represented. The more specific the context, the more meaningful the results can be. The use of a specific functionality in a product can be better captured by the user than the overall motivation to use an entire product.

A quantitative online survey for generating an Octalysis profile shows the degree of fulfillment of the individual core drives in the given context in one or more items. By using several items and setting them in relation to each other, it is possible to identify differences between a particular function and the overall product. Clear wording and unambiguous scales, such as the Likert scale, are also important to increase the significance of the results. Based on the collection of personal data, profiles of different user groups are generated. For example, the motivation to use a product or product function may differ between women and men, in age groups or geographical regions.

For instance, an Octalysis profile within a usage analysis may look as shown in Fig. 6.

Figure 6. Exemplary Octalysis profile, showing a focus on "Social Influence & Relatedness" and "Epic Meaning & Calling"

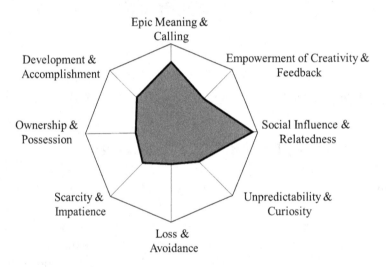

The profile shows the different foci of motivation in which the development of product features makes sense to better meet user expectations. In the given example, a focus on "Development & Accomplishment", "Empowerment of Creativity and Feedback" and "Unpredictability" can be identified. Depending on the context, possible reasons for the profile can be derived, which can be enormously helpful in understanding user behavior and drawing the right conclusions for new product features.

The existing profile thus narrows down the selection options for techniques enormously and provides an initial orientation for the subsequent ideation phase.

Based on a comprehensive database with known gamification techniques as well as their specifications, the ideation phase provides guidance for translating the analysis results into specific product features.

Combining different sources, a collection of gamification techniques can easily contain up to 200 different techniques. In this research, a combined database of Chou's *Actionable Gamification* and Marczewski's *Gamified UK* is used (Chou, 2015; Marczewski, 2018).

Well-known examples of classic gamification techniques are point systems, rewards, and rankings from the "Development & Accomplishment" section. Among the lesser-known possibilities are the "Alfred Effect" belonging to the Core Drive "Ownership & Possession", which describes such extensive personalization that a user no longer wants to give it up. In contrast, the technique "Rightful Heritage" is related to the Core drive "Avoidance of Loss" and awards the user a good before taking it away again to motivate him to regain this very same item.

Through the analysis phase, a first pre-selection of the techniques has already been carried out by prioritizing the most relevant core drives. Addressing these focal aspects, the gamification techniques can be utilized most effectively. However, further methodical selection has to be made, as few Core Drives can still result in lots of possible techniques within the database. This is performed in two steps. In the first filtration, unsuitable techniques are filtered out regarding the given product context. Often this evaluation can be done intuitively because the unsuitable combinations are obvious. For example, a "leaderboard" technique does not make sense if the product context does not provide any interaction or comparison with other users.

The second step now involves prioritizing the remaining techniques to find the best possible approaches. As an example, this can be done in a workshop with a team of experts. To represent the product context as diversely as possible and to take into account different perspectives, experts from all involved departments should be present in the workshop. Here, the remaining techniques first are presented to clarify any general questions about these potential solutions. A common understanding of how the techniques work is essential for the workshop to be successful. At the same time, the techniques should be presented in a solution-neutral manner and without evaluation, to be able to generate unbiased results.

After the general presentation, various workshop methods are suitable to query the individual prioritization of the participants. The prioritization should be related to the specific product context. Thus, it can be queried which of the techniques the participants think fits best to the product context and which techniques are potentially most compatible with the product. For example, a numerical ranking or a weighted wordcloud can be generated to provide a representation of the results. Ultimately, a final decision has to be made on a small number of techniques. A manageable amount of techniques with a reasonable variety are two to three techniques per core drive. Often, the first possible combinations of individual techniques or initial ideas for the implementation in the product design already arise at this point. These provide helpful starting points for the design phase.

The design phase covers the implementation of the selected techniques in the product context. It is the most challenging task and requires a high degree of creativity since the techniques database consists of general descriptions of motivational triggers.

The framework *Hooked - How to build habit-forming products* can be used as a guideline here (Eyal, 2014). This process helps to integrate techniques into an existing context by providing an orientation to typical motivational trajectories of users when using products. This not only provides impulses for the implementation of the techniques but also reveals possible interactions and interconnections of techniques within the specific product context.

For the techniques found in the ideation phase, the four phases of the Hook process iteratively generate ideas towards the final implementation. The first phase is the "External Trigger." This means external information, making the user aware of the product. Examples are an advertisement or a recommendation.

Once the user has become aware of the product, the "Action" phase follows. Here, the user has to perform an action that is directly related to the product. This action needs to be designed as low-threshold as possible. The effort required for the user to perform the action must be minimal so that he or she does not decide against interacting with the product. Low-threshold is determined by the factors of time, mental effort, physical effort, money, social acceptance, and personal routine. The lower the effort concerning these factors, the more likely the user will perform the action.

For the action performed, the user now receives a "Variable Reward". The "Reward" can better be described as a confirmation for the user towards his action. In the best case, this confirmation relates to the Core Drive identified in the analysis to optimally address the user.

The last phase includes the "Investment". The user should perform this action with the intention of receiving a reward for it later, as he does not get a reward instantly. This leads to a mental connection of the user with the product and triggers again the first phase, which is now no "external" but an "internal trigger". Instead of an advertising action, the user remembers his "investment" and looks to see if another action is already necessary, which in turn results in a reward.

Due to the different interactions in the four phases, the implementation of a Hook framework with exclusively one gamification technique is unlikely. Therefore, the Hook framework rather provides an orientation for the integration of techniques into an existing product interaction or gives starting points for the connection of different techniques. Basically, the Hook framework is more of an orientation than a strict design specification in the development of product features.

One application example is the on-boarding process of a video streaming platform. After a recommendation from a friend (,,External Trigger"), the user accesses the platform. There, he has to register and sign up for a subscription (,,Action"). He then gets a "welcome" email with a coupon code for friends and family (,,Variable Reward"). The investment consists of individualizing preferences for series and movies. The user can expect suggestions that match his or her preferences the next time he or she visits the platform, which can be seen as the next reward.

After the design of gamification techniques, an evaluation or assessment of the results takes place. The evaluation criteria strongly depend on the use case, but in many cases an estimation of the (user) impact and the (development) effort is helpful. Since the effort depends on the individual development environment, the evaluation of the user impact can be done following Csíkszentmihályi's flow theory. For this purpose, a challenge vs. skill rating of the developed gamification techniques has to be performed (Csíkszentmihályi, 1990).

Another possible evaluation tool is provided by the online platform machinations.io. This platform offers a way to simulate games to test the game balance. Not only games but also gamification strategies can be simulated to visualize and evaluate the dependencies between chosen gamification techniques (Machinations S.àr.l, 2021).

Going through the three phases with the presented tools from the frameworks, identified user needs can be translated into gamification techniques and consequently, into product features.

EXEMPLARY APPLICATION

The following project is an example of how the developed process can be applied in practice.

In the days of the SARS-CoV-2 virus, quick identification of contacts with Corona-positive tested individuals and breaking the chain of infection is crucial for pandemic control. The German government's Corona Warning App, designed in collaboration with the Robert Koch Institute and SAP SE, provides a tool for recording risk encounters (see Fig. 7). The purpose of this specific product is to warn people

Figure 7. The German Corona-Warning-App

who have come into contact with infected individuals. Currently, 62% of Corona warning app users share their positive test result transmitted to the warning app if they were tested positive (RKI, 2021).

The best practice example illustrates the application of gamification in product development based on an implemented mutual project of the Chair for Product Safety and Quality Engineering (PSQ) of the University of Wuppertal, SAP SE, and the Robert Koch Institute. Since only about 60% of people share their positive test results via the app, there is a 40% potential for optimizing the app's functionality at this point. The problem is thus that there seems to be too little incentive for people to share a positive test result, although the overall social benefit is obvious. Therefore, user-centered design aspects should be used to develop new incentives for sharing positive corona tests within the app.

First, the problem definition is stated as follows:

The goal of the project is to develop gamification strategies for the German Corona warning app to increase user motivation regarding the willingness to share positive Corona test results via the warning app.

The success metric for this gamification project is given by the "Ratio of shared positive test results compared to the total number of potentially shareable positive test results" as published in the monthly report on the Corona Warning App (RKI, 2021).

First Phase: Analysis

The first step of the analysis is to create a user journey or interaction sequence to subsequently identify possible action points for integrating gamification techniques. In the given context, the user journey begins with the download of the app and leads to the warning of a risk contact to positive testing and then to the sharing opportunity. Four possible action points could be identified:

1. When downloading or setting up the app in on-boarding, the initial contact with the user offers a special opportunity to establish behaviors and emotions. The user is particularly attentive and classifies what impression he has of the app. This first impression is particularly intense and is difficult to change once an opinion of a product has been established.

Figure 8. User journey for the German Corona-Warning-App with identified action points

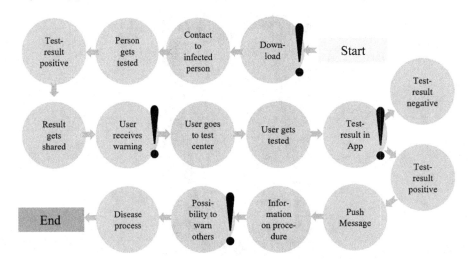

2.   The user receives a warning via the app that he or she has been within a short distance of a person who has tested positive for a longer period and shares the result via the app to warn other users. The warning is a particularly emotional interaction with the app, as this is where the user is made aware of a potentially dangerous situation.

3.   The user receives his test result via the app. This is also a particularly emotional situation, but it can be positive or negative. In both cases, however, there are also opportunities for actively shaping motivation.

4.   In the action of sharing the positive test result. Since this is the desired action, it can be designed to guide or motivate the user to the action.

The complete user journey with marked action points is shown in figure 8.

Various approaches can be used to analyze the motivation of users in their interaction with the app. First, a large-scale survey can be conducted to query the usage motivation of a broad mass of people. However, any split opinions that may exist are averaged out and subsequently neglected. Second, more in-depth individual interviews can be conducted to obtain detailed information about the problem. However, due to the smaller number, unrepresentative results may be obtained here. And third, the existing user ratings in the app stores can be analyzed using text mining to collect direct user feedback. However, this is technically complex and the ratings are usually preloaded with a high bias, which can also lead to a misperception of user motivation.

In the given case, a combined solution is chosen. A large-scale online survey provides the opportunity to generate motivation profiles. Voluntary input of personal data and on the app's usage behavior enables differentiation between different groups, and a free text input field for individual comments in the survey form offers deeper insights into usage motivation.

Two items are included in the survey:

1.   The general motivation for the usage of the app

2.   The motivation regarding the sharing of positive Covid-19 test results.

By asking two items, the results can be put in relation to each other and conclusions can be made about the development of motivation. For both items, an adapted question is created for each core drive according to Chou. The scale used is a 5-point Likert scale with a range of agreement from "strongly disagree" to "strongly agree".

As an example, the Core Drive "Ownership & Possession" is provided with the following questions:

- **Item 1:** Maintaining my own health is important to me when using the Corona Warning app.
- **Item 2:** I would be more likely to share a positive test result via the Corona alert app if I knew others were doing the same to protect me.

The individual reference to the product is important when formulating the questions. Both items should point to the same reference to ensure consistency of the results and derived conclusions. In the case of "Ownership & Possession", the reference is to the preservation of one's own health, while in the case of "Social Influence & Relatedness", for example, the focus was on the protection of others, and "Scarcity & Impatience" addressed the fear of being disadvantaged by information disclosure.

The free-text question for individual comments is worded as follows:

- Do you have any other suggestions, thoughts, criticisms, or additions to the Corona Warning app or sharing test results via the app?

The following personal information is collected via voluntary input:

- Age
- Gender (male, female, other, none of these)
- Region of residence

The following questions are asked about usage behavior:

- Have you downloaded the Corona warning app?
- Have you been tested positive for Covid-19 in the past?
- If you have been tested positive for Covid-19, have you shared your positive test result via the Corona Warning app?
- If you were tested positive for Covid-19 in the future, would you share your test result via the Corona Warning app?

By asking questions about usage behavior, it is possible to determine the basic attitude of the survey participants toward the app in various scenarios. In addition, the question of the test-sharing that has already been carried out and the possible planned test-sharing inquiries about the users' intentions, which can also be put in relation to the motivation profiles in the later analysis.

Before conducting the survey, a preliminary study is carried out with a survey of 173 people to get a general idea of possible results. The results are meaningful and reveal a basic split between motivation to fight the pandemic and fear of being disadvantaged by information disclosure.

In addition, an internal pre-test is conducted with the final survey to eliminate possible errors and final ambiguities.

Figure 9. Gamification profile for the use of the German Corona-Warning-App. The grey profile shows the user motivation during the general use of the app while the white profile shows the motivation during the action of sharing positive test results via the app

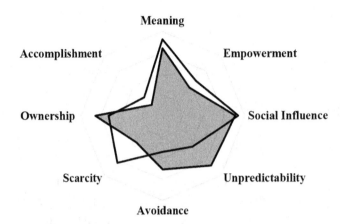

The survey is conducted online and distributed through the official website of the German Corona Warning app, as well as through the university's channels. A total of 1777 people participated in the survey, of which 1555 fully completed it.

An overwhelming majority of 96% of users say they would share a potential positive test result. This conflicts with the 60% who actually do so. Obviously, there is a difference between people's basic attitude and situational motivation when they were tested positive for Covid-19. In general, this provides additional legitimacy for integrating gamification techniques into the app.

The results of the Octalysis query on the items are shown in the following diagram (Fig. 9):

Evidently, there are three common and one alternating focus across the items. The motivation for general use of the app and the potential sharing of positive test results focus on the overall social task of combating the pandemic (Epic Meaning & Calling), protecting one's own health with the help of the app (Ownership & Possession), and protecting other people (Social Influence & Relatedness). In the general use of the app, an increased value of "Unpredictability & Curiosity" can also be determined. This refers to the curiosity of users as to whether they are exposed to risk contacts. As soon as general use turns into a pressure situation due to a warning (Scarcity & Impatience) and a test result is pending, this curiosity turns into concern about an illness and the possible consequences associated with it. Fear of risk contacts, in general, is also higher than concern about social disadvantages from sharing positive test results (Avoidance of Loss).

The analysis of the personal data does not reveal any major differences between age, gender, or location categories, so these will not be further considered.

From the free text input of the survey, as well as in the app reviews, the following conclusions are drawn:

- The survey, as well as the analysis of the app ratings, revealed a general positive attitude of the users towards the app.
- The ratio of development costs to the (perceived) benefit of the app is often criticized
- There is criticism that data privacy is placed above the functionality of the app.

Figure 10. Output of the analysis phase

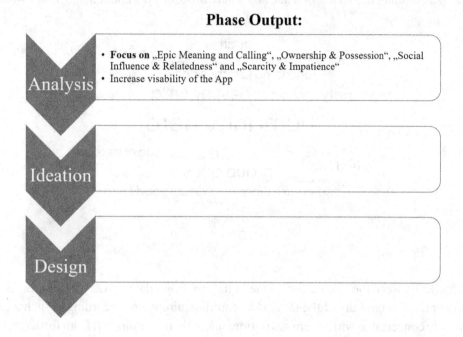

Users would like more statistics, localization of risk contacts, and proof of vaccination or registration in restaurants/cafés via the app.

Overall, the result is that the app's functionality needs to be made more visible in gamification strategies to increase the basic motivation of the user to interact.

The analysis phase results in a focus on the Core Drives "Epic Meaning and Calling," "Ownership & Possession," "Social Influence & Relatedness," and "Scarcity & Impatience" for the ideation phase. This narrows down the choice of gamification techniques significantly. In addition, suitable action points were found for the integration of the techniques. Another goal for the design results from the requirement to increase the visibility of the app in general (see Fig. 10).

Second Phase: Ideation

The goal of the second phase "Ideation" is the definition of specific gamification techniques that have to be implemented. The input for the ideation phase is a selection of the core drives to be considered, as well as a basic understanding of the motivational behavior of the users.

The techniques from the remaining Core Drives are then collected and subjected to the first reduction. Through intuitive assessment, some techniques from the core drives "Epic Meaning & Calling", "Ownership & Possession", "Social Influence & Relatedness" and "Scarcity & Impatience" have been excluded immediately. The obvious lack of compatibility with the app or the identified problem represents the selection criteria here. As an example, the technique "Mentorship" from the area "Social Influence & Relatedness" can be mentioned here. This technique describes the structure of a mentorship system in which an experienced user introduces a new user to the conditions of the given context. This requires

Figure 11. Workshop results for gamification technique ideation, bigger words mean more relevance for the use-case. If techniques are mentioned in Chou's and Marczewski's collection, Chou's variant is listed

a direct exchange between the two persons. Due to the very high data privacy requirements of the German government, the anonymity of the users is a central requirement. Accordingly, such a gamification technique is only conceivable with severe restrictions and is therefore omitted from further consideration. The same applies to "Options Pacing" from the "Scarcity & Impatience" core drive. This technique is characterized by the time-controlled activation of functions. Due to the app's scope of being an essential part of the national pandemic response, it does not seem reasonable to withhold functionalities from users. This technique is also not considered in the further course of the project.

A further selection of techniques takes place in a workshop to ensure the objectivity of the results. Ten experts from the field of gamification and with application experience of the app participated. The workshop consists of three units. In the first unit, the results of the analysis phase and the selection of gamification techniques are presented. This is important to create a common understanding of the project scope and app requirements.

The second unit is a prioritization of the techniques. All workshop participants are instructed to select a technique from each core drive that intuitively fits best with the Corona warning app and the corresponding problem. The results are presented in a wordcloud and give a ranking to the prioritization of the remaining techniques. The results are shown in Figure 11. The larger the word, the more votes the technique got in the voting for high compatibility with the app. Recognizable is a high potential compatibility of the gamification technique **"Humanity Hero"** from the *Actionable Gamification* framework of Chou, which makes sense in the given context of the Corona pandemic (Chou, 2015). "Humanity Hero" describes the drive to perform actions more likely to make the world a better place. In the context of the Corona pandemic, this is an obvious connection. This technique is called "Meaning/Purpose" in Marczewski's periodic table of gamification elements.

Other techniques that make sense are:

- **"Destiny Child"** (Chou, 2015) - Being chosen to do something,
- **"Moats"** (Chou, 2015) or **"Unlockable Content"** (Marczewski, 2018) - A feature is visible but unavailable until something happens and

Figure 12. Output of the ideation phase

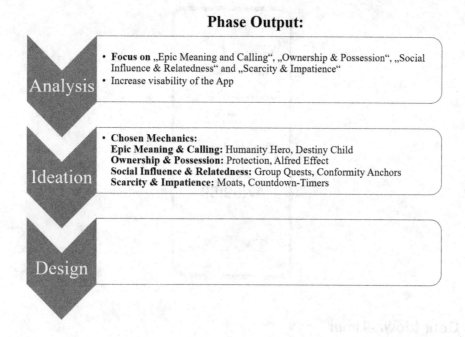

• **"Group** Quests" (Chou, 2015) or **"Guilds/ Teams"** (Marczewski, 2018) - Group-based tasks.

For the design of app functionalities, the two most-mentioned techniques from each core drive were selected (see Fig. 12):

The third unit of the workshop consists of a brainstorming session on potential implementations of the techniques in the app. It makes sense to let the workshop participants write down their thoughts individually to collect as many different results and ideas as possible. This forms the first starting point for the design phase of the project.

Third Phase: Design

The design phase is about the implementation of the selected techniques in the Corona warning app.

For the implementation, a basic understanding of the techniques of gamification, the context of the application and a certain degree of creativity are necessary. The gamification techniques are specified in a very solution-neutral way and require a transfer into the concrete application context.

This is illustrated here exemplarily for the techniques "Moats and Countdown Timers" from the Core Drive "Scarcity & Impatience", which complement each other in a design, and "Protection" from the Core Drive "Ownership & Possession".

Figure 13. Design result for the Countdown-Timer and Moat-technique

Moats + Countdown-Timer

The technique "moats" describes a functionality available in the app that is visibly withheld temporarily from the user until a certain condition is met. This results in the user being motivated to perform the functionality when it finally becomes available to him.

Countdown timers are counting down time displays. The user constantly sees the window of opportunity narrowing, establishing a sense of urgency in the process.

These techniques can be combined very well in the context of the app. The point in time around the receiving of the test result is selected as the action point from the analysis phase since a particular urgency already exists here. After performing the test, users had to wait approximately 24-48 hours for the test result, which was then communicated to them via the app. This fostered a sense of uncertainty about when they would actually receive the result and what to do afterward. The app did not provide any information about the status of the test. According to the Hook model, the testing is equivalent to having the action done. The external trigger is already in place by receiving the warning via a risk contact.

Thus, one possibility is to display a 48-hour countdown. The 48 hours are oversized and should only be exceeded in exceptional cases. However, merely displaying a time is sufficient to reduce the user's sense of urgency, as an orientation is created. As a result, the countdown timer forms the Variable Reward according to the Hook model, even if the reward seems negative at first.

This is combined with a disabled button for the possibility to share the test result. So the possibility of sharing a positive test result is already present while waiting for the result. By making the possibility of sharing available only after the test result has been entered, the urge to use this feature is increased when it becomes available. This can be interpreted as an internal trigger for users according to the Hook model. An investment is not necessary at this point, since there is an enormous intrinsic motivation due to the urgent situation.

Figure 14. Design result for the Protection technique

The button "Share test result" is thus brought to the fore when the result is received and forms the next action in the hook cycle.

A possible implementation of the user interface is shown in Figure 13.

Protection

The "Protection" technique from the "Ownership & Possession" Core Drive describes the creation of a local sense of belonging. The technique is often paraphrased with the slogan "Defend your neighborhood". The Corona warning app already offers a locality aspect, as direct contacts are tracked using Bluetooth. Thus, it primarily exploits the user's local contacts. However, the presentation of risk contacts first offers a negative connection of the app with local affiliation. People have reservations about other people, worried about being exposed to a risk contact. However, this could also be used the other way around. The action item used from the analysis phase is therefore "share test result". Offering users the ability to share even negative test results via the app integrates positive aspects into this context. Sharing both positive and negative test results forms the action here.

By naming the local context, the anonymity threshold of the app is broken, even if there are no further clues to identities. This is achieved, for example, through embedded texts such as "Protect the people in your neighborhood by sharing test results" as a trigger element. Users know their neighborhoods better than anonymous risk contacts. Sharing negative test results also increases visibility and interaction opportunities with the app and integrates a positive sentiment that corresponds to a variable reward. One possible representation of the user interface is shown in Figure 14.

The final step of the design phase is an evaluation of the developed gamification features to decide on the subsequent implementation. Depending on the use case, there are different evaluation criteria. In the case of the present project, the eight developed gamification features were evaluated according

Figure 15. Design results for gamification strategies for the German Corona-Warning-App

Test result Count-Down und withheld sharing option
On-Boarding Re-Design
All-Encounter display and Test-Tracking
„YOU make the difference"
Sharing negative test-results
Subliminal polarization
Personalized display of information
Infobox „What do my fellow people?"
Influence
Complexity
high
low
47:59:59

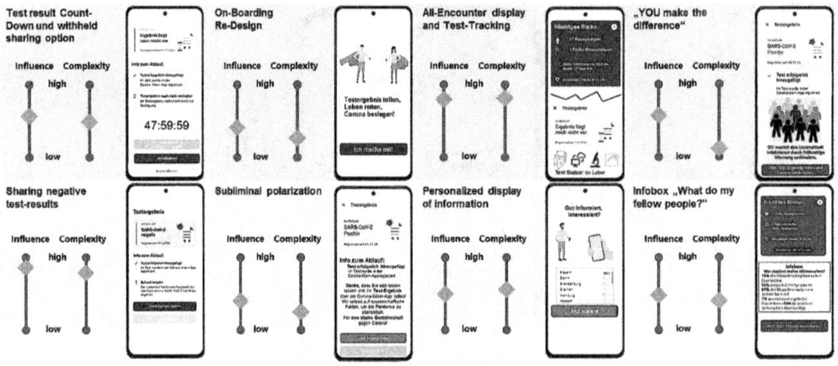

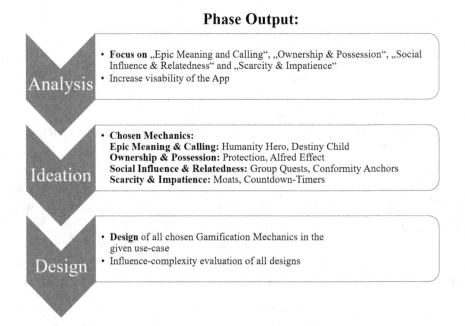

to potential influence on motivational behavior and implementation complexity. They are presented in a clear arrangement so that the alternatives can be compared directly.

The overview is shown in Figure 15.

Hence, the results of the design phase are individual designs of the chosen gamification techniques from the ideation phase and an influence-complexity evaluation to simplify decision-making for the implementation (see Fig. 16).

Whether the designed gamification strategy is successful in motivating people to share their positive test results has to be evaluated after implementation. The progression of the chosen success metric "ratio of shared positive test results compared to the total number of potentially shareable positive test results" is monitored and analyzed regarding a possible influence of the integrated gamification features.

Figure 16. Output of the design phase

Phase Output:
Analysis
• Focus on „Epic Meaning and Calling", „Ownership & Possession", „Social Influence & Relatedness" and „Scarcity & Impatience"
• Increase visability of the App
Ideation
• Chosen Mechanics:
Epic Meaning & Calling: Humanity Hero, Destiny Child
Ownership & Possession: Protection, Alfred Effect
Social Influence & Relatedness: Group Quests, Conformity Anchors
Scarcity & Impatience: Moats, Countdown-Timers
Design
• Design of all chosen Gamification Mechanics in the given use-case
• Influence-complexity evaluation of all designs

Figure 17. Gamification methods for Design-to-Customer

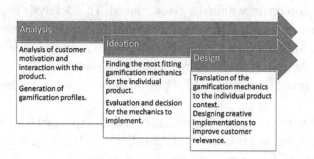

The project, with its structured progression through the three phases and the targeted application of gamification tools, offers a contemporary, relevant and illustrative application example and supports the understanding of the methodology.

In principle, this approach can now be applied to similar projects where there is a concrete problem regarding product usage. Within this chapter, it has been transferred to the general use case of improving user-centered "design-to-customer". The structured elaboration of user motivations and the subsequent methodical transfer to product elements creates an opportunity to develop products closer to the customer.

FUTURE RESEARCH DIRECTIONS

Future research should specifically address the evaluation regarding the fulfillment of customer satisfaction through design-to-costumer with integrated gamification methods compared to classic product development. Due to the application in engineering, an evaluation in practical use is essential.

Furthermore, the integration of alternative gamification frameworks with a focus on differentiation of user-profiles and player types could add a new dimension to be even more costumer-orientated and support mass customization of products.

The creation of a central gamification techniques database can be considered to expand the possibilities of the methodology and simplify the process.

Another core aspect is the dependency of the design phase on the creativity of the developers. Here, the translation of general gamification techniques into more concrete product features in the context of a development support database is another starting point for further research.

CONCLUSION

The purpose of this chapter is to improve customer orientation in the early phases of product development by synthesizing a consecutive process based on established gamification frameworks. The theoretical combination of the frameworks leads to a guideline with instructions for the implementation of gamification methods in the phases "Analysis, Ideation, and Design" according to the " How to design gamification" process (see Fig. 17).

The methodological approach used and the frameworks involved are profoundly explained. Creating a user journey defines action points within the given context. The Octalysis from Chou offers a tool for generating Gamification profiles and an impression on user's motivation is created.

Based on Chou's and Marczewski's techniques collections, a structured selection of suitable gamification techniques is made in workshops during the ideation phase.

With the Hook-Framework according to Nir Eyal, an orientation for the design of the techniques is given.

The practical implementation of the integrated approach is explained based on a completed project with a current, relevant context and hence proves the validity of the theoretical results while adding additional variables like user profiles could enhance the applicability.

Limitations and promising approaches for further research are pointed out.

ACKNOWLEDGMENT

This research received no specific grant from any funding agency in the public, commercial, or not-for-profit sectors.

REFERENCES

Anderie, L. (2017). *Gamification, Digitalisierung und Industrie 4.0: Transformation und Disruption verstehen und erfolgreich managen.* Springer-Verlag.

Chou, Y. (2015). *Actionable Gamification – Beyond Points, Batches and Leaderboards.* Octalysis Media.

Csikzentmihaly, M. (1990). *Flow: The psychology of optimal experience.* Harper & Row.

Ellenberger, T., Harder, D., & Brechbühler Pešková, M. (2020). Gamification in Unternehmen. In Digitale Transformation und Unternehmensführung: Trends und Perspektiven für die Praxis (pp. 55–81). Wiesbaden: Springer Fachmedien Wiesbaden. doi:10.1007/978-3-658-26960-9_4

Eyal, N. (2014). *Hooked: How to build habit-forming products.* Penguin.

Fleisch, H., Mecking, C., & Steinsdörfer, E. (2018). *Gamification4Good: Gemeinwohl spielerisch stärken.* Edition Stiftung & Sponsoring: Erich Schmidt Verlag. https://ebookcent-ral.proquest.com/lib/gbv/detail.action?docID=5427441

Gericke K., Bender B., Pahl G., Beitz W., Feldhusen J., & Grote K. H. (2021). *Pahl/Beitz Konstruktionslehre.* Springer Vieweg. doi:10.1007/978-3-662-57303-7_4

Machinations, S. (2021). *Craft perfectly balanced games - Simulate game systems, before writing a single line of code.* https://machinations.io/

Marczewski, A. (2018). *Even Ninja Monkeys Like To Play. Unicorn Edition.* Gamified UK Publishing.

Mora, A., Riera, D., Gonzalez, C., & Arnedo-Moreno, J. (2015). A Literature Review of Gamification Design Frameworks. *7th International Conference on Games and Virtual Worlds for Serious Applications (VS-Games)*, 1-8. 10.1109/VS-GAMES.2015.7295760

Morschheuser, B., Hassan, L., Werder, K., & Hamari, J. (2018). How to design gamification? A method for engineering gamified software. *Information and Software Technology*, *95*, 219–237. doi:10.1016/j.infsof.2017.10.015

Pahl, G., & Beitz, W. (2013). *Engineering Design: A Systematic Approach*. Springer Science & Business Media.

Patricio, R., Moreira, A., Zurlo, F., & Melazzini, M. (2020). Co-creation of new solutions through gamification: A collaborative innovation practice. *Creativity and Innovation Management*, *29*(1), 146–160. doi:10.1111/caim.12356

Patricio, R., Moreira, A. C., & Zurlo, F. (2018). Gamification approaches to the early stage of innovation. *Creativity and Innovation Management*, *27*(4), 499–511. doi:10.1111/caim.12284

Reiners, T., & Wood, L. C. (2015). *Gamification in Education and Business*. Springer International Publishing. doi:10.1007/978-3-319-10208-5

Robert Koch-Institute. (2021). *Kennzahlen zur Corona-Warn-App* [Key Figures for the Corona-Warn-App]. https://www.rki.de/DE/Content/InfAZ/N/Neuartiges_Coronavirus/WarnApp/Archiv_Kennzahlen/Kennzahlen_21052021.pdf?__blob=publicationFile

Springer Nature Switzerland, A. G. (2021), *Pahl/Beitz Konstruktionslehre* [Pahl/Beitz Design Theory]. https://www.springer.com/de/book/9783662573020

ADDITIONAL READING

Abdala, L., Fernandes, R., Ogliari, A., Löwer, M., & Feldhusen, J. (2017). Creative Contributions of the Methods of Inventive Principles of TRIZ and BioTRIZ to Problem Solving. *Journal of Mechanical Design*, *139*(8), 08200. doi:10.1115/1.4036566

KEY TERMS AND DEFINITIONS

Corona-Warning-App: The German government founded the development of a tracking app, that allows warning users if they were in close contact with an infected person.

COVID-19: Sars-CoV-19 is a virus that started a worldwide pandemic in 2019 with a major influence on all areas of human life.

Gamification: The use of game design-elements in non-game context with the goal to motivate people to certain actions or behaviors.

Design for X: The Design-for-Excellence Guidelines from "Pahl/Beitz-Engineering Design" offer different focusses for the design of products.

Design-to-Costumer: Design-to-Costumer is a sub-topic of Design for X and focuses on the design of products regarding the fulfillment of customer satisfaction.

Ideation: Ideation is a phase in development processes with the topic of creative idea finding. Different methods like Brainstorming apply in this phase.

Product Development: The discipline of product development includes the design and engineering of different products based on established frameworks, e.g., VDI 2221, Scrum, TRIZ, Design Thinking.

Chapter 13
A Guideline to Develop a Game Platform to Collect Energy Consumption Data From Residences in Developing Countries

Marcos Aurelio Domingues
https://orcid.org/0000-0001-7195-0714
State University of Maringá, Brazil

Leonardo A. Alves
https://orcid.org/0000-0003-2956-7062
Federal University of Goiás, Brazil

Rogerio Salvini
Federal University of Goiás, Brazil

Dante Carrizo
University of Atacama, Chile

Diego Issicaba
https://orcid.org/0000-0002-7937-8115
Federal University of Santa Catarina, Brazil

Mauro Rosa
https://orcid.org/0000-0001-8508-1353
Federal University of Santa Catarina, Brazil

ABSTRACT

In this chapter, the authors propose a guideline to develop a mobile platform to collect data that makes it possible to predict energy consumption in residences in developing countries. The platform consists of a game that can be played individually or by a team (i.e., a family) that lives in the same house. From time to time, a person or family members will receive some challenges (i.e., some questions) that must be reached (i.e., answered) to collect the energy consumption habits data. The context of the game is in an aquarium, where a small fish will evolve or not during the game. The fish will live in this environment that starts very clean, and with the actions of the user concerning the challenges, may suffer an evolution or degradation. By using gamification techniques, the challenges will persuade the person or family members to provide directly or indirectly the energy consumption habits data for each electronic device. All data collected with the game platform can be analyzed through different types of analysis by using a dashboard.

DOI: 10.4018/978-1-6684-4291-3.ch013

Figure 1. Usage of the mobile platform

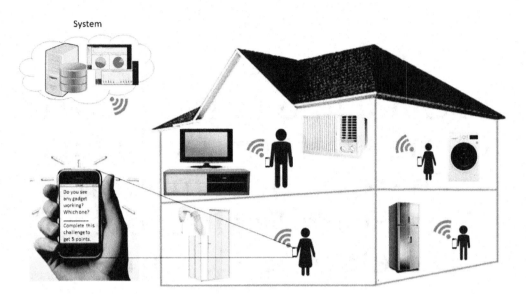

INTRODUCTION

Nowadays, the managing of energy consumption has proved that the smart metering system is an effective scheme. The smart meters have the capability of transmitting energy usage information in real time to parties that matter, such as power generation stations, transmission stations, distribution stations and customers. Thus, qualitative decisions concerning generation, distribution and usage of power can be made. This energy usage information helps to match demand with supply hence reducing cost of production, increasing profitability, reducing waste and bringing higher customer satisfaction (Keelson, Boateng, & Ghansah, 2014), (Johnson, Horton, Mulcahy, & Foth, 2017), (AlSkaif, Lampropoulos, van den Broek, & van Sark, 2018). Despite the many benefits offered by smart meters, most developing countries such as Brazil still hold on to standalone energy meters that offer less capabilities.

In order to provide a system that can easily be used in developing countries to obtain energy consumption data, this chapter proposes a guideline for developing a mobile platform to collect data that make possible the prediction of energy consumption habits in residences. The platform consists of a game that can be played individually or by a family (i.e. a team) that lives in the same house. From time to time, a person or the members of the family will receive some challenges (i.e. some questions) that must be reached (i.e. answered) in order to collect the energy consumption habits data. The challenges will persuade the person or the members of the family to provide directly or indirectly the energy consumption data by using gamification techniques. An illustration of the mobile platform usage is presented in Figure 1.

Figure 2 shows an example of data that must be collected by the platform. As already stated, the mobile platform will use gamification techniques to collect such consumption habits data. Gamification can be defined as the usage of game mechanics and game thinking in serious contexts (Odobašić, Medak, & Miler, 2013).

The data collected by the mobile platform can be used as input by several algorithms to predict the energy consumption of a house (Biswas, Robinson, & Fumo, 2016), (Dong, Li, Rahman, & Vega, 2016).

Figure 2. An example of data that must be collected to predict energy consumption

			Obtaining the Daily Load Curve, through consumption habits.												
#	Device	Average Power [W]	00:00	00:15	00:30	00:45	01:00	01:15	01:30	01:45	02:00	02:15	02:30	02:45	03:00	03:15
01	Stereo	60														
02	Air conditioning up to 7,500 BTU	1200														
03	Air conditioning of 10,000 BTU	1600														
04	Air conditioning of 12,000 BTU	1760														
05	Air conditioning of 18,000 BTU	2590														
06	Hot tub	180														
07	Food mixer	60														
08	Gas Boiler	30														
09	Boiler up to 80 liters	1500														
10	Boiler from 100 up to 150 liters	2500														
11	Water pump up to 3/4 HP	1159														
12	1 HP Water Pump	1398														

The data collection obtained through a mobile platform is devised for developing countries, where the large-scale use of smart meters is far from a reality. The procedure regarding acquiring data can be based on an aperiodic inquire of information (a less user attractive manner), inputting information when devices are turned on and turned off (a more user attractive manner), and the combination of both. Notice that, for practical purposes, it is not relevant to collect data from devices each second, if the application is directed to computing the total amount of energy consumed in a given day, for instance. The mobile application then can work as a virtual smart meter whose information is given by the interested user, which is brought to contribute to a database by means of a game application. Furthermore, it can provide condensed information and prognostics about the energy consumption in a given interval of time (day, hour, all the time, etc) in order to make the user more active towards energy responsibility and sustainability.

In this chapter the authors provide a deep guideline about how to develop such a platform. The remaining of this chapter is organized as follows. In section BACKGROUND the authors present some background required to understand the proposal. In section SOLUTIONS AND RECOMMENDATIONS, proposal, design and development of the game platform are described. Finally, the FINAL REMARKS are presented.

BACKGROUND

In this section, the authors discuss some background concepts and definitions required to understand their work.

Gamification

As already stated, gamification can be defined as the usage of game mechanics and game thinking in serious contexts (Odobašić, Medak, & Miler, 2013). One of the first examples of gamification usage is the toy tamagotchi presented in Figure 3. The tamagotchi had its own device with a virtual pet with frequent needs which must be carried out by the tamagotchi owner.

A game that uses gamification is usually composed of the four elements presented in Figure 4: History, Technology, Mechanics and Aesthetics (Patrício, Moreira, & Zurlo, 2018), (Patrício, Moreira, Zurlo, & Melazzini, 2020).

Figure 3. Tamagotchi device

- **History:** The history of a game is the main piece that will guide the user in his experience of playing. Thus, the element of history is responsible for presenting the characters, put the chronology and organize the phases of the game. This element is considered as the glue that intelligences the other elements.
- **Technology**: This element uses the technological resources of game engines to represent the story and allow the user to interact with the game through their specific mechanics of game. It is responsible for accommodating in itself the toolbox necessary for the developer to assemble the game, as programmed by game design.
- **Mechanics**: The mechanics of a game is how the user interacts, and will be interacted in the game. In other words, it is where the game happens. The game mechanism developed is the game itself, as it will help to connect the user's ability to the characteristics of the game, its rules, seeking the goals, through the practical sense of the game and reaching the player's emotion. With respect to the mechanics, it is said that its elements can determine the success in the engagement with the game. The mentioned elements are:
  ◦ Onboarding - Initial tutorial process presenting the game.
  ◦ Game Terms - Well-stated game rules.
  ◦ Points - Measurement forms, a basic unit of the system. Always bound to rules.
  ◦ Challenges - It is an element that allows engagement as a form of "campaigns".
  ◦ Badges (medals) - Ensure status, which is important in social interaction.
  ◦ Status - Social position that differentiate one user from the other. It puts you where others are not. Usually presented through ranks.
  ◦ Placards (visualization) - It exposes the user to his/her score and allow it to reach the most realistic scores possible.
  ◦ Social Networking - I can be used to viralization and engagement.
  ◦ Awards - Physical prize or material return, which allows the engagement to continue, and makes the effort to play become materializable.
- **Aesthetics**: This is the element of greater artistic degree in a game, in which the expiry of the art of the game is contained, and it identifies the characteristics of the characters, through our sense of vision, presenting details of character psychological characteristics, together with his profile that will help to understand their history, aspirations and abilities.

Figure 4. Gamification elements

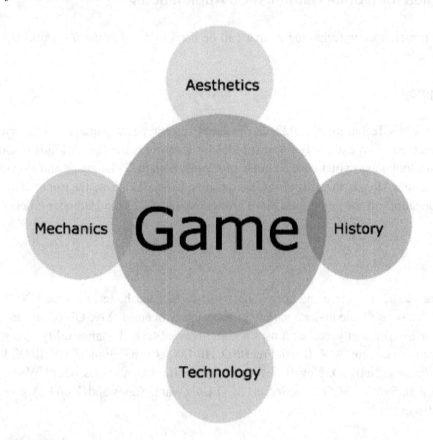

Gamification in Mobile Applications

The use of Gamification-based mobile applications can help solve real-life problems (Odobašić, Medak, & Miler, 2013), (Dergousoff & Mandryk, 2015), (Lounis, Kotsopoulos, Bardaki, Papaioannou, & Pramatari, 2017). Gamification increases the user loyalty through tangible rewards, leading us to the final goal of engaging users. By applying gamification on a mobile phone, it is possible to provide a free platform through which the application can be used on social networking sites and smartphones. Indeed, gamification has helped increasing popularity in recent years due to three important reasons: 1) the relatively cheaper price of the devices, 2) the ability to track activities and real-time events through the Internet, and 3) the expansion of current cultural spread through video games.

Gamification can also support various interfaces through a special scoring system and social connection to show a leaderboard that encourages loyalty and more frequent usage. Thus, through the leaderboard, it is easily to determine the result of any competition among members subscribed to the application. Such a transparent reward system can then lead to a greater user engagement in the application.

Technologies for Mobile Gamification Applications

This section presents some technologies that can be used to develop mobile games/applications that adopt gamification.

Game Engine

The Unity 3D (Unity Technologies, 2022) can be used to prototype the game. It is a generic game engine, which has emerged as an extremely powerful tool for creating games of all kinds, for many different platforms. This tool allows you to use all kinds of scripts, both in C# language and in JavaScript, to add logic to your game. Already in terms of visual elements, Unity 3D allows the use of elements created in the main applications of the genre, like Maya (Autodesk Inc, 2022) and Blender (Blender Foundation, 2002).

Database

MySQL (Oracle, 2021) is a free and open-source software under the terms of the GNU General Public License, and is also available under a variety of proprietary licenses. MySQL is written in C and C++. Its SQL parser is written in yacc, but it uses a home-brewed lexical analyzer. MySQL works on many system platforms, including AIX, BSDi, FreeBSD, HP-UX, eComStation, i5/OS, IRIX, Linux, macOS, Microsoft Windows, NetBSD, Novell NetWare, OpenBSD, OpenSolaris, OS/2 Warp, QNX, Oracle Solaris, Symbian, SunOS, SCO OpenServer, SCO UnixWare, Sanos and Tru64. A port of MySQL to OpenVMS also exists.

Data Analysis

SpagoBI (Engineering Ingegneria Informatica S.P.A., 2017) is a free/open source enterprise-grade software, particularly flexible and adaptable to the end-users' needs in terms of business intelligence. It is composed of several functionalities, as for example:

- **Reporting:** Realize structured reports and export them using the most suitable format (HTML, PDF, XLS, XML, TXT, CSV, RTF).
- **Multidimensional Analysis (OLAP):** Explore your data on different detail levels and from different perspectives, through drill-down, drill-across, slice-and-dice, and drill-through processes.
- **Charts:** Develop ready-to-use charts according to your single charts (e.g. histograms, pie charts, bar charts, area charts, scatter diagrams, line charts, bubble charts, dispersion charts) and interactive ones (e.g. temporal sliders).
- **KPIs:** SpagoBI offers a complete set of tools to create, manage, view and browse Key Performance Indicator (KPI), through different methods, calculation rules, thresholds and alarms.
- **Location Intelligence:** Visualize your business data on maps (i.e. static map catalogues or web mapping/feature services) and interact dynamically to get instant views.
- **Data Mining:** Advanced data analysis allowing you to extract knowledge from large volumes of data to improve your decision-making and business strategies.

Figure 5. Combination of technologies to develop a mobile game/platform that uses gamification

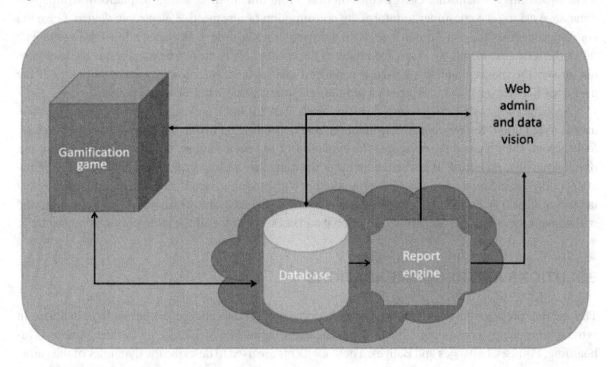

- **ETL:** SpagoBI integrates the open source product TOS (Talend Open Studio), to load data into the data warehouse and managing them.
- **Collaboration:** Create structured report dossiers, which enrich your analysis with personal notes and comments posted by users. Then, share them through a collaborative workflow.
- **Office Automation:** Publish your personal documents into your BI environment, integrating common Office tools (Open Office or MS Office).

The three mentioned technologies can be combined as illustrated in Figure 5 in order to support the development of a mobile game/platform that use gamification. There, we have the game sending data to the database hosted in a cloud. In the same cloud, we have the SpagoBI that analyze the data in the database to generate several analysis and reports.

MAIN FOCUS OF THE CHAPTER

With the goal of engaging the public in developing countries to provide its energy consumption habits data and energy usage in an efficient manner, the authors have proposed a game platform (that uses gamification) by reimagining the tamagotchi game with the use of visual elements to characterize the evolution of the environment in which it is fixed.

In the proposal, the context of the game is in an aquarium, where a small fish will evolve or not during the game. The fish will live in this environment that starts very clean, and with the actions of the user, may suffer an evolution or degradation. The action of the user will consist in answering some challenges/questions about his/her energy consumption. From time to time, the game platform will pop-up a message asking the consumer to inform the consumption of a respective electronic device. Once the consumer receives the pop-up message (with a device or a set of devices), he/she must answer it. The faster the user answers the message, the higher is the number of points he/she receives. If the user does not answer the message quickly, he/she is penalized and will receive a lower number of points. If the user does not answer to the message in a pre-defined time, he/she will lose some points.

The game starts with the aquarium clean and the fish is still small and eager to evolve (Figure 6). The user is asked about his/her energy consumption, and depending on his/her answer, he/she will visually feel through the obtained points/scores the evolution of his environment, being able to rejoice or not psychologically, reflecting in his/her behavior in the game, answering or not the challenge, feeling the effect of the degradation caused by his/her interaction with the game, now visually in the aquarium of his/her tamagotchi fish. In addition, an internal mechanism will collect the answers provide by the user and will convert them into the energy consumption data necessary to fulfill the table presented in Figure 2.

SOLUTIONS AND RECOMMENDATIONS

This section presents the design of the game platform proposed to engage the public to collaborate in providing its energy consumption habits data. The main elements which make part of the game are Onboarding, Points, Challenges and Badges. These elements are used to describe the dynamics of the game.

When the game starts at the first time, an onboarding will present the dynamics of the game from a small quick tutorial. The tutorial will explain the rules, operations and how to earn points in the game. The points are gained when the user answers the challenges promptly. The challenges are questions about the usage of electronic devices in a house, for example, "Are your air-conditioning on?". If the user answers to the challenge promptly, he/she will earn 10 points. If the user answers to the challenge 1 minute later that the challenge has arrived, he/she will earn 5 points. If the user answers to the challenge 2 minutes later, he/she will not earn any point. In any other situation, the user will lose 2 points.

The challenges are sent to the user randomly, from time to time, if the user is at his/her house. Note that the platform will be able to determine if the user is at home or not through his/her latitude and longitude data. When the user registers in the game platform, he/she must provide such data about his/her house. Additionally, the challenges can also be sent to the user according to the usage indication provided during the registration process. When the user registers in the game platform, he/she must define the electronic devices available in his/her house and can also indicate the common period of usage of such devices. For example, if the user sets up an air-conditioning to be turned on at 22:00 hours, the challenge will be sent to the user at 22:00 hours. The game platform allows the user setup the day (from Sunday to Saturday), hour (from 1:00 to 24:00), every (means that the device is on all the time) or timestamp (a particular date and time of usage, for example, 10/10/2020 at 13:55). When the device is setup to every, no challenge is sent to the user, and the energy consumption data is stored in the database in the end of the day. The user can redefine the configuration of his/her devices at any time. When the game is played in group, the challenge is sent randonly to only one member of the group.

With respect to the context of the game, i.e. the aquarium and the fish, at the beginning of the game the aquarium is cleaned and the fish is still small and eager to evolve, which means that the user starts the game with 80 points. Then, taking the actions of the user, it may suffer an evolution or degradation. More details are presented in Section Interaction with the Game.

Figure 6. Illustration of the fish in aquarium clean

Finally, the badges are the medals or decorations that the user can earn when he/she reaches a certain number of points. Figure 7 gives an idea about the badges in the game platform.

Development of the Game Platform

This section presents the requirements need to develop the game platform.

Interaction with the Platform

In the proposal, two kinds of persons can interact with the game platform, as illustrated in the use case in Figure 8. The first, we called user, and he/she will represent the player that plays the game. The second one, we called manager, and he/she will manage the platform.

In the game platform, the user can access the following functionalities (Figure 8):

- **Initialization:** It allows each user to register in the platform and setup his/her personal data (user account).

Figure 7. Examples of badges with their respective points to earn them

Badge 1 (100 points)   **Badge 2 (200 points)**   **Badge 3 (300 points)**

- **Login and Game:** This functionality allows the user to login in the platform and to start or continue playing the game. Here the user receives its badge and points.
- **Group:** It allows several users play the game in group (i.e. team or family). In the game structure, every user will always be counted individually, and the group score will always be the sum of the points of their individual users. The game data, badges and points of the users will be presented to the group, and the user can act in the group favoring it with his/her skills.
- **Social Interaction:** It allows several users in a group to interact among them to talk and discuss their strategy about the game.

On the other hand, the manager will have access to all game data and can use the data in different intelligent data analysis (i.e. using data mining, machine learning, recommender systems, etc), reporting the results of the game to the owner of the platform, to users, and to groups depending on the goals of the platform (Ricci, Rokach, Shapira, & Kantor, 2011). For example, recommender systems can be automated to improve energy management and encourage the reduction of energy consumption or the usage of alternative technologies such as photovoltaic generation. The indication that other users/ neighbors are using alternative technologies and have already reduced consumption by some percentage usually works quite well.

Interaction with the Game

Figure 9 presents the diagram of state for the game. The diagram starts with the user login in the game platform. From that point, the user can setup his/her account and then play the game; or the user can access his/her previous status in the game (in the case of an already registered user), i.e. his/her score, and then he/she can continue to play the game. For both paths, the user can play the game alone or in group, depending on the configuration of his/her account.

In addition to diagram of state, a diagram with the game flow is presented in Figure 10. This diagram gives more details about the interaction of the user with the game.

Initially, from the init screen, the user can register in the game platform by providing a new login or by using some social networking login.

Figure 8. Diagram of use case

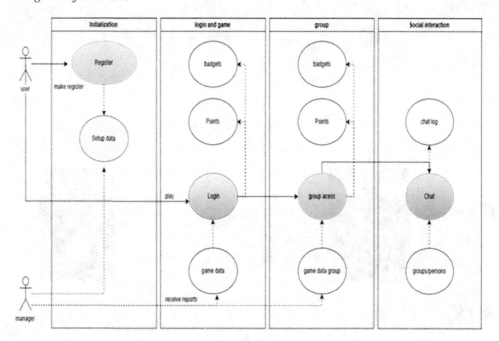

The game starts with the user accessing it by login in the game platform or through some notification (challenge) received from the game platform. In his/her first access, the user will go through the onboarding that will tour the game. Then, the user will be guided to the setup screen, where he/she will define the GPS location of his/her house, his/her electronic devices, with their respective energy consumption, and the period of usage for each device. Challenges are sent to the user only if he/she is in his/her house. The user can also go back to the setup screen, at any time, to update his/her electronic devices or to see again the game tour.

During the game, the normal scoring rules for the cleaning or pollution of the environment are counted. In addition, the process of evolution of the fish will also occur. The game also allows a moment of pause or sleep mode, which temporarily disables notifications and messages, putting the game in a sleep mode.

Finally, social interaction with other users playing in a same group is available through a chat mechanism. Thus, the users in a same group can define strategies along the game.

As already stated, the scenario of the game consists of an aquarium with a fish in a very clean environment, as can be seen in Figure 11. If the user answers the challenges, the aquarium will keep clean and quiet as illustrated in Figure 11. On the other hand, if the user does not answer to the challenges, the aquarium can suffer degradation as illustrated in Figure 12.

The aquarium will suffer visual changings along the game, according to the points earned or loosed by the user. For the game, the changes will occur only in the aquarium. The fish will not suffer any change. We have opted for not to affect the fish so much, but affecting only the environment with dirt, following the same characteristics presented in the tamagotchi game. For the game, there are 8 possible levels of degradation (i.e. states of the environment/aquarium) as shown in Figure 13, from Degree 0, without any degradation and with the aquarium clean, to Degree 7, where we have a maximum degree of degradation and the scenery is all dirty.

Figure 9. Diagram of state

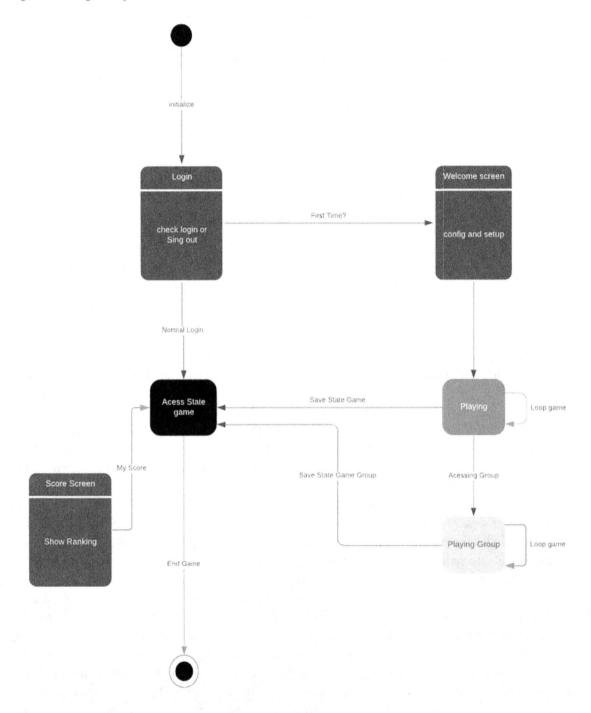

Screens of the Platform

This section presents the screens of the platform (Figure 14 to Figure 17) together with a short description of its functionality. For sake of illustration, we called it of ITCity.

Figure 10. Diagram of game flow

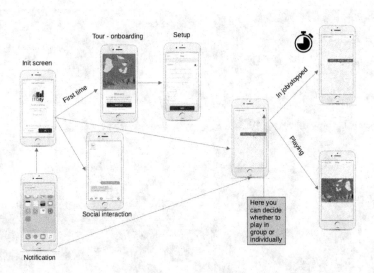

Figure 11. Aquarium with a fish in a very clean environment

Figure 12. Aquarium with degradation

Sign In: This screen allows the user to register in the game platform by creating a new login. Additionally it also allows the user to login in the platform.

Social Login: It allows the user to login in the platform by using a social networking login, as for example, Facebook login.

Setup: This screen allows the user to setup which electronic devices is available in his/her house.

Setup Device: For each electronic device turned on in the previous screen, it is required to setup the period of usage for the device, as for example, every day during all day, Wednesday 9 September at 10:00, an hour per day and so on. This information will be used by the platform to send the challenges to the user.

Localization: This screen allows the user to setup the GPS coordinates (i.e. latitude and longitude) of his/her house, so that the challenges are sent to the user only if he/she is in his/her house.

Onboarding: This screen will present a game tour to the user.

Chat: This screen allows the users in a group to talk to each other about the game and the strategy that they will define for playing the game.

Challenge: The way the challenges are received by the user playing the game. More attractive technologies can be used to implement this screen.

Playing Alone and Group: It allows the users to define if they will play the game alone or in group.

Ranking: It shows the ranking for each user in the game. This screen is also available to groups playing the game.

Figure 13. Eight possible levels of degradation for the aquarium

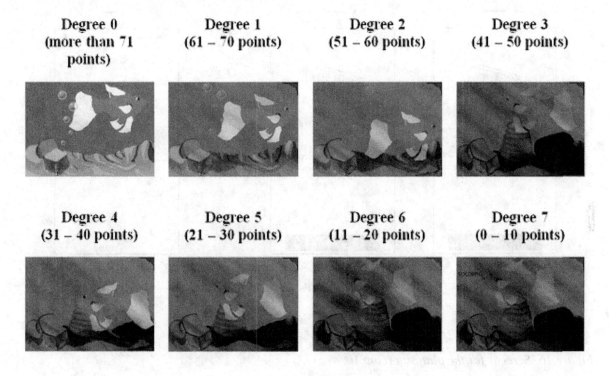

Figure 14. Screens for the platform

Figure 15. Screens for the platform (cont.)

Setup Device   Localization

Figure 16. Screens for the platform (cont.)

Onboarding   **Chat**   **Challenge**

Figure 17. Screens for the platform (cont.)

Web Dashboard for the Platform

The manager can access data of the platform to generate web reports by using the web dashboard/reporting.

Once the manager has logged in the system, he/she can access the different types of analysis, as for example, charts, tables, and so on. The type of analysis that will be available in the platform must be defined during its implementation, since it can vary depending on the goal of the owner of the platform.

Examples of analysis that can be developed in the dashboard based on data in Figure 2 are: visualization of expected consumption of each appliance in a given period of time (e.g. a month); estimation of expected electricity bill in a given period of time (e.g. a month); simulation of reduction on consumption in a set of appliances and computation of its impact on electricity bill; simulation of installation of alternative technologies, such as solar panels to reduce electricity bills; visualization of a set of recommendations to reduce electricity bills; etc.

Database for the Platform

The database proposed for the platform contains 9 tables, which are characterized by the following information: user, group, point, badge, device configuration and scheduling of usage time, and energy consumption, as illustrated in Figure 18.

The **tbl_user** is the central table in the database and represent the user who will play the game. This table is related to **tbl_group** (by using the foreign key idgroup) to put together several users in a group, so that the users can play the game in group (i.e. in team or family). The points earned by the user or group are stored in the table **tbl_point**. The table **tbl_user** is also connected to tables **tbl_dev**, **tbl_usage_dev** and **tbl_cons_energy** (by using the table **tbl_dev_owner**) in order to setup the electronic devices

Figure 18. Database structure

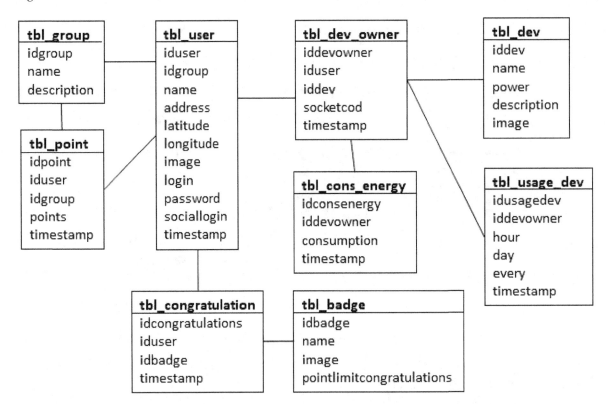

available in the house of the user and also to store the energy consumption for each device. Finally, the table **tbl_user** is also connected to table **tbl_congratulations** in order to store information about the position of the user in the game. Each table is described along this section together with its respective data dictionary.

tbl_user: This table stores the unique id of the user, the id of his/her group (foreign key idgroup), its name and address (including latitude and longitude of his/her house), a photo of the user, and information about the login (i.e. login and password or a social login) together with the date (data field timestamp) when the user was created.

tbl_group: This table contains the name and description of a group.

tbl_points: This table stores the foreign keys idgroup and iduser (which are primary keys in the tables tbl_group and tbl_user, respectively) so that the points earned along the game can be related to the individual user and can be summed to the total of the group playing the game. The data field timestamp stores when the point is earned.

tbl_congratulations: The badges (data field idbadge) earned by the user (data field iduser) with the respective date (data field timestamp) are stored in this table.

tbl_badgets: This table stores a list of badges (used in table tbl_congratulations), with name, image, and number of points needs to earn the badge (data field pointlimitcongratulations).

tbl_dev_owner: Here the electronic devices that the user has in his/her house are registered. The table stores the id of the user, the id of the device, and the date when the device becomes available in

Table 1. Data dictionary for table **tbl_user**

Data field	Data type	Description	Details
iduser	Integer	Primary key	Autoincrement
idgroup	Integer	Foreign key from tbl_group	
name	Varchar	Name of the user	255 characters
address	Varchar	Address of the user (house of the user)	255 characters
latitude	Double	Latitude of the house	
longitude	Double	Longitude of the house	
image	Blob	Photo of the user	
login	Varchar	Personal login of the user	255 characters
password	Varchar	Personal password of the user	255 characters
sociallogin	Varchar	Social login of the user	255 characters
timestamp	Timestamp	Date and hour that the user was created	

the house of the user. Note that the devices come from the table tbl_dev, which contains a list of devices previously homologated and characterized to be used in the game.

tbl_dev: This table stores a list of devices previously registered. For each device, the table stores its name and power, a short description, and an image of the device.

tbl_usage_dev: This table is used to setup when the device is usually used by the user. The setup about the usage by hour, day, all the time (data field every) or for a particular date (data field timestamp) are registered in this table.

tbl_cons_energy: This table stores the information represented in Figure 2, i.e. if the device is being used by the user or not. By using the foreign key iddevowner the information of a user and a particular device in his/her house is stored in this table. In the data field consumption, the table stores the value 1 if the user has turned on the device or 0 if the device is turned off. The previous information is store together with the date of the event (data field timestamp).

Following, the data dictionary for each table is presented (Tables 1 to 9).

Table 2. Data dictionary for table **tbl_dev**

Data field	Data type	Description	Details
iddev	Integer	Primary key	Autoincrement
name	Varchar	Name of the device	255 characters
power	Double	Power of the device	
description	Text	Some description about the device	
image	Blob	Photo of the device	

Table 3. Data dictionary for table **tbl_dev_owner**

Data field	Data type	Description	Details
iddevowner	Integer	Primary key	Autoincrement
iduser	Integer	Foreign key from tbl_user	
iddev	Integer	Foreign key from tbl_dev	
socketcod	Integer	Code of the socket where the device is plugged	
timestamp	Timestamp	Date and hour that a device was setup by an user	

Table 4. Data dictionary for table **tbl_usage_dev**

Data field	Data type	Description	Details
idusagedev	Integer	Primary key	Autoincrement
iddevowner	Integer	Foreign key from tbl_dev_owner	
hour	Integer	Hour that the device is used	
day	Integer	Day that the device is used	
every	Varchar	1 if the device is used all the time or 0 otherwise	1 character
timestamp	Timestamp	Full date and hour that the device is used	

Table 5. Data dictionary for table **tbl_cons_energy**

Data field	Data type	Description	Details
idconsenergy	Integer	Primary key	Autoincrement
iddevowner	Integer	Foreign key from tbl_dev_owner	
consumption	Varchar	1 if the device is consuming energy or 0 otherwise	1 character
timestamp	Timestamp	Date and hour that the consumption is registered	

Table 6. Data dictionary for table **tbl_group**

Data field	Data type	Description	Details
idgroup	Integer	Primary key	Autoincrement
name	Varchar	Name of the group	255 characters
description	Text	Some description about the group	

Table 7. Data dictionary for table **tbl_point**

Data field	Data type	Description	Details
idpoint	Integer	Primary key	Autoincrement
iduser	Integer	Foreign key from tbl_user	
idgroup	Integer	Foreign key from tbl_group	
points	Integer	Value of the points earned by the user	
timestamp	Timestamp	Date and hour that points are registered	

Table 8. Data dictionary for table **tbl_badge**

Data field	Data type	Description	Details
idbadge	Integer	Primary key	Autoincrement
name	Varchar	Name of the badge	255 characters
image	Blog	Image of the badge	
pointlimitcongratulations	Integer	Number of points that is necessary to gain the badge	

Table 9. Data dictionary for table **tbl_congratulation**

Data field	Data type	Description	Details
idcongratulations	Integer	Primary key	Autoincrement
iduser	Integer	Foreign key from tbl_user	
idbadge	Integer	Foreign key from tbl_badge	
timestamp	Timestamp	Date and hour that badge is obtained by the user	

Server Architecture for the Platform

The game platform can be hosted in a server in the Amazon Web Service (AWS). The architecture for the server that can be adopted by the platform is presented in Figure 19.

The Figure 19 represents the 3 main outputs of the platform. The first branch represents the internal structure of the web dashboard/reporting that makes use of the spagio BI to keep a secure connection to access the data, a load balance mechanism, and all requests being processed in a web flow, which uses a temporary database to create the various flows of reports.

The second branch shows the data being consumed by a game interaction service structure, where through a game server structure of unity, the data is distributed to the users through the mobile game.

Finally, the third and last branch shows the notification system that works with a mail server system, sending the challenges/notifications to the users by using a queuing system like RabbitMQ with a Direct type (VMware, 2022), which is an appropriating cache for delivery in the queues.

Figure 19. Architecture for the server that will host the game platform

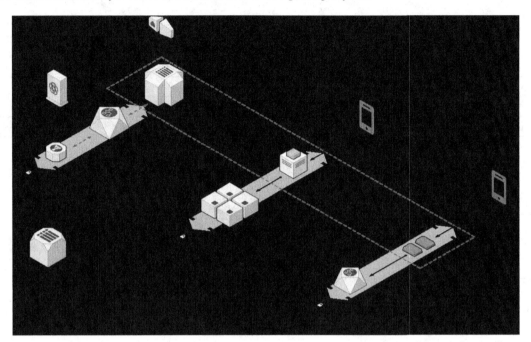

As already stated, this server structure can be assembled in the Amazon Web Service (AWS), using the structure of machines with docker and distributed in 4 different servers, being the first one for the MySQL database, the second for SpagoBI, the third for the Unity service and the last for RabbitMQ. All integrated via DNS using the AWS route53 structure.

FINAL REMARKS

It is shown in the literature that the gamification is gain attention in several areas, and that when well-designed it can bring a better engagement of users (Johnson, Horton, Mulcahy, & Foth, 2017), (AlSkaif, Lampropoulos, van den Broek, & van Sark, 2018). In this chapter, a guideline was proposed to develop a game platform that use gamification to engage people in order to collect energy consumption data in developing countries.

The data collected by the platform can be used as input by several algorithms to predict the energy consumption of a house and to provide different types of analysis, as for example, visualization of expected consumption of each appliance in a given period of time (e.g. a month), estimation of expected electricity bill in a given period of time (e.g. a month), simulation of reduction on consumption in a set of appliances and computation of its impact on electricity bill, etc.

As future work, the authors intend to run a case study with the platform in a developing country, as for example, Brazil. Additionally, the authors also intend to propose a methodology to evaluate the platform developed by following this guideline.

REFERENCES

AlSkaif, T., Lampropoulos, I., van den Broek, M., & van Sark, W. (2018). Gamification-based Framework for Engagement of Residential Customers in Energy Applications. *Energy Research & Social Science*, *44*, 187–195. doi:10.1016/j.erss.2018.04.043

Autodesk Inc. (2022). *3D Computer Animation, Modeling, Simulation, and Rendering Software*. https://www.autodesk.com/products/maya/overview

Biswas, M. R., Robinson, M. D., & Fumo, N. (2016). Prediction of Residential Building Energy Consumption: A Neural Network Approach. *Energy*, *117*(1), 84–92. doi:10.1016/j.energy.2016.10.066

Blender Foundation. (2002). *Open source 3D creation. Free to use for any purpose, forever*. https://www.blender.org

Dergousoff, K. K., & Mandryk, R. L. (2015). Mobile Gamification for Crowdsourcing Data Collection: Leveraging the Freemium Model. In *Proceedings of 33rd Annual ACM Conference on Human Factors in Computing Systems* (pp. 1065-1074). Academic Press.

Dong, B., Li, Z., Rahman, S. M., & Vega, R. (2016). A Hybrid Model Approach for Forecasting Future Residential Electricity Consumption. *Energy and Building*, *117*(1), 341–351. doi:10.1016/j.enbuild.2015.09.033

Engineering Ingegneria Informatica, S. P. A. (2017). *100% Open Source Business Intelligence*. https://www.spagobi.org

Johnson, D., Horton, E., Mulcahy, R., & Foth, M. (2017). Gamification and Serious Games Within the Domain of Domestic Energy Consumption: A Systematic Review. *Renewable & Sustainable Energy Reviews*, *73*, 249–264. doi:10.1016/j.rser.2017.01.134

Keelson, E., Boateng, K. O., & Ghansah, I. (2014). A Smart Retrofitted Meter for Developing Countries. *International Journal of Computers and Applications*, *90*(5), 40–46. doi:10.5120/15573-4203

Lounis, S., Kotsopoulos, D., Bardaki, C., Papaioannou, T. G., & Pramatari, K. (2017). Waste No More: Gamification for Energy Efficient Behaviour at the Workplace. In *Proceedings of 1st International GamiFIN Conference* (pp. 129-134). Academic Press.

Odobašić, D., Medak, D., & Miler, M. (2013). Gamification of Geographic Data Collection. In *Proceedings of GI_Forum 2013 - Creating the GISociety* (pp. 328-337). Academic Press.

Oracle. (2021). *MySQL Database Service*. https://www.mysql.com

Patrício, R., Moreira, A. C., & Zurlo, F. (2018). Gamification Approaches to the Early Stage of Innovation. *Creativity and Innovation Management*, *27*(4), 499–511. doi:10.1111/caim.12284

Patrício, R., Moreira, A. C., Zurlo, F., & Melazzini, M. (2020). Co-creation of New Solutions Through Gamification: A Collaborative Innovation Practice. *Creativity and Innovation Management*, *29*(1), 146–160. doi:10.1111/caim.12356

Ricci, F., Rokach, L., Shapira, B., & Kantor, P. B. (2011). *Recommender Systems Handbook*. Springer. doi:10.1007/978-0-387-85820-3

Technologies, U. (2022). *VR & AR Engine*. https://unity.com

VMware. (2022). *Messaging that just works - RabbitMQ*. https://www.rabbitmq.com

ADDITIONAL READING

Candanedo, L. M., Feldheim, V., & Deramaix, D. (2017). Data Driven Prediction Models of Energy Use of Appliances in a Low-Energy Ouse. *Energy and Building*, *140*(1), 81–97. doi:10.1016/j.enbuild.2017.01.083

Grolinger, K., L'Heureux, A., Capretz, M. A., & Seewald, L. (2016). Energy Forecasting for Event Venues: Big Data and Prediction Accuracy. *Energy and Building*, *112*(1), 222–233. doi:10.1016/j.enbuild.2015.12.010

Mocanu, E., Nguyen, P. H., Gibescu, M., & Kling, W. L. (2016). Deep Learning for Estimating Building Energy Consumption. *Sustainable Energy. Grids and Networks*, *6*(1), 91–99.

Murtagh, N., Gatersleben, B., & Uzzell, D. (2014). Differences in Energy Behaviour and Conservation Between and Within Households with Electricity Monitors. *PLoS One*, *9*(3), e92019–e92019. doi:10.1371/journal.pone.0092019 PMID:24642946

Olsen, C. S. (2014). Visualization of Energy Consumption: Motivating for a Sustainable Behavior Through Social Media. In *Proceedings of 2014 International Conference on Collaboration Technologies and Systems* (pp. 641-646). 10.1109/CTS.2014.6867642

Platon, R., Dehkordi, V. R., & Martel, J. (2015). Hourly Prediction of a Building's Electricity Consumption Using Case-Based Reasoning, Artificial Neural Networks and Principal Component Analysis. *Energy and Building*, *92*(1), 10–18. doi:10.1016/j.enbuild.2015.01.047

Sun, S., Li, G., Chen, H., Guo, Y., Wang, J., Huang, Q., & Hu, W. (2017). Optimization of Support Vector Regression Model Based on Outlier Detection Methods for Predicting Electricity Consumption of a Public Building WSHP System. *Energy and Building*, *151*(1), 35–44. doi:10.1016/j.enbuild.2017.06.056

Wu, X., Mao, J., Du, Z., & Chang, Y. (2013). Online Training Algorithms Based Single Multiplicative Neuron Model for Energy Consumption Forecasting. *Energy*, *59*(1), 126–132. doi:10.1016/j.energy.2013.06.068

KEY TERMS AND DEFINITIONS

Developing Countries: Developing countries are, in general, countries that have not achieved a significant degree of industrialization relative to their populations, and have, in most cases, a medium to low standard of living.

Energy Consumption Behavior: Energy consumption behavior is often characterized as a set of individual actions that influence energy consumption.

Gamification: Gamification can be defined as the usage of game mechanics and game thinking in serious contexts.

Guideline: A guideline is a statement by which to determine a course of action. A guideline aims to streamline particular processes according to a set routine or sound practice.

Mobile Game: A mobile game is a video game that is typically played in a mobile phone.

Residence: A residence is a person's home or the place where someone lives.

Smart Cities: A smart city is an urban area that uses different types of electronic methods and sensors to collect data. Insights gained from that data are used to manage assets, resources, and services efficiently.

Chapter 14
Gamification and Household Energy Saving:
Insights From the EnerGAware Project

Miquel Casals
Universitat Politècnica de Catalunya, Spain

Marta Gangolells
Universitat Politècnica de Catalunya, Spain

Marcel Macarulla
Universitat Politècnica de Catalunya, Spain

Núria Forcada
Universitat Politècnica de Catalunya, Spain

ABSTRACT

Buildings are responsible for 40% of the EU's total energy consumption and 36% of greenhouse gas emissions. Although difficult to quantify, individuals' attitudes to energy use significantly impact the energy consumed in households. In this context, serious games provide an opportunity to enhance buildings' energy efficiency through changes in users' behaviour. This chapter presents the results obtained in the EnerGAware-Energy Game for Awareness of energy efficiency in social housing communities project (2015–2018), funded by EU H2020. The project developed a serious game for household energy efficiency called "Energy Cat: The House of Tomorrow." The game was deployed and tested in a UK social housing pilot for one year. Cost-benefit analysis in the energy, environmental, and economic domains prove that serious gaming is among the most cost-effective energy efficiency strategies for households on the market.

DOI: 10.4018/978-1-6684-4291-3.ch014

INTRODUCTION AND BACKGROUND

Householders' relationship with energy consumption has been said to suffer from double invisibility: energy is intangible and is so embedded in our lives that we no longer appreciate the connections between it and our everyday actions (Hargreaves et al., 2013). This double invisibility certainly raises important challenges in communication about energy use and saving (Boomsma et al., 2018). Traditional approaches such as informative energy bills and face-to-face provision of advice have been found to have a limited effect.

In this context, serious digital games can help to increase consumers' awareness of energy consumption problems by capturing their attention and making them more receptive. Serious games can provide information about household energy consumption in an understandable, tailored way. In this context, Information and Communication Technology (ICT) has a major role to play (Morton et al., 2020). Smart meters and big data analytics are fundamental elements of gamification within the buildings' energy efficiency field as they allow real-time visualization of energy consumption and tailored advice, especially once privacy and data protection concerns have been addressed under the consumer-centric approach. In addition, serious games help to illustrate available options to save energy. Therefore, they encourage not only behavioural changes such as avoiding standby consumption or setting thermostats at lower temperatures, but also non-behavioural changes such as insulating homes or installing efficient equipment. Games appear to be a good way of educating end users in advanced concepts such as flexible consumption and dynamic price contracts.

For this reason, several initiatives have been developed in recent years within the context of gamification for buildings' energy efficiency. Relevant initiatives were reviewed by Douglas and Brauer (2021), Morton et al. (2020), Wagner et al. (2020), Wu et al. (2020), Beck et al. (2019), Csoknyai et al. (2019), Hallinger et al. (2019), Stanitsas et al. (2019), AlSkaif et al. (2018), Boomsma et al. (2018), Morganti et al. (2017), Johnson et al. (2017) and Pasini et al. (2017).

Existing games typically focus on domestic environments but some are for dormitories, offices and commercial buildings (Wu et al., 2020). The games target a wide range of users, including family members, workers, university students or younger inhabitants (Pasini et al., 2017). According to AlSkaif et al. (2018), energy-themed games can be classified into three categories: energy efficiency, self-consumption and demand response. Common characteristics of these gamified apps include a mechanism to report goals for sustainability, a dashboard to track progress, and some form of social comparison with other app users (Douglas & Brauer, 2021). Most of the games focus on electricity consumption; only a few include other energy sources (Wu et al., 2020). Energy saving is often stimulated by rewards and by social interaction through cooperative and competitive challenges (Csoknyai et al., 2019). Regarding technical aspects, most of the productions are flash browser games with lower quality visuals and sounds and limited offer of gameplay possibilities (Wagner et al., 2020). According to Beck et al. (2019) and in contrast to the healthcare sector, most of the existing energy-related apps are prototypes that cannot reach beyond a local or pilot audience and therefore, the number of commercially ready products is still limited.

In summary, gamification strategies seem to offer promising results (Ro et al., 2017; Boomsma et al., 2018; Chatzigeorgiou and Andreou, 2021) to encourage energy-saving behaviour and raise awareness on energy consumption practices. However, the nascent and growing body of literature also reveals immaturity in the design and robustness of these efforts (Beck et al., 2019). Existing empirical studies are heavily weighted towards descriptive, non-experimental research designs and methods (Hallinger et al., 2020). The reliability of the reported results is partially undermined by several shortcomings, including small sample sizes, poorly described methodologies, limited use of validated measures to quantify outcomes, absence of control groups and narrow data collection timeframes, among others (Johnson et al., 2017). Therefore, empirical research to ascertain the role of serious games in delivering domestic energy savings under a robust experimental approach is still limited (Morganti et al., 2017). In fact, developing and properly validating serious games requires numerous resources and intensive efforts (Wee and Choong, 2019; Wagner et al., 2020). In addition, no references have been found in the literature to ascertain the energy, economic and environmental sustainability of this innovative approach.

This chapter introduces an innovative serious game for improved buildings' energy efficiency. The game, called Energy Cat: The House of Tomorrow (Energy Cat, 2018), was developed under the umbrella of the EneGAware (2015) project, aimed at reducing the energy consumption of low-income households by encouraging changes in tenants' behaviour. This is considered the most recent, complicated serious game for energy efficiency, according to Chatzigeorgiou and Andreou (2021).

After this introduction, this chapter first provides basic information about the EnerGAware project. Then, the game development process is described and the storyline and the main gameloop play are reported. Insights gained during a large-scale implementation of the game in a social housing pilot are also described in this chapter. Game validation, using the pre-post comparison and control group approaches, is also detailed, with a special focus on the achieved energy savings. This chapter also discusses the cost-benefit analysis of this game-based solution from the economic, energy and environmental points of view with the ultimate objective of ascertaining its sustainability. Then, the scalability of the energy saving potential provided by this innovative solution is discussed and solutions and recommendations for further uptake are given. Finally, future research directions and main conclusions are outlined.

THE ENERGAWARE PROJECT

The EnerGAware project (Energy Game for Awareness of energy efficiency in social housing communities) was funded by Horizon 2020, the eighth Framework Programme for Research and Innovation in the European Union, with €2 million. The EnerGAware project started in February 2015 and lasted three years. It brought together seven partners from three countries, coordinated by the Universitat Politècnica de Catalunya (Spain). The game was developed by Fremen Corp (France) and tested in a social housing pilot in Plymouth (United Kingdom) thanks to Devon and Cornwall Housing Ltd (United Kingdom). The monitoring infrastructure was designed by Advantic Sistemas y Servicios (Spain) and the middleware platform was developed by the Instituto Superior de Engenharia do Porto (Portugal). The University of Plymouth (United Kingdom) collected user, building and game requirements, developed the building energy consumption and thermal comfort simulation engine and determined the behavioural impact of the game. EDF Energy R&D UK Centre Limited (United Kingdom) had an important role in the dissemination of the project to other energy service providers and customers. Finally, Universitat Politècnica de Catalunya (Spain) mainly worked on tasks related to the evaluation of results. The EnerGAware project received full ethical clearance from EU Commission Services and was fully aligned with all the ethical considerations related to research involving human subjects and the collection and use of personal data.

The following subsections describe the insights gained through EneGAware project (2015) and the game developed in this project, called Energy Cat: The House of Tomorrow (Energy Cat, 2018).

GAME DEVELOPMENT

The game was developed with an iterative Living Lab methodology supporting co-creation. Co-creation is the practice of developing meaningful products, services or systems through a more participative process, with stakeholders engaged in a collective creativity environment (Patrício et al. 2018; Patrício et al. 2020). First, requirements were elicited.

User requirements were obtained through a survey sent to 2,772 social houses in Plymouth asking about socio-economic characteristics, energy consumption motivations, behaviour and perceptions, game experiences and IT literacy. The return rate was about 20%. Users were found to prefer a domestic setting, so that they could easily relate to it. The game should help users to learn how to save energy and to compare available options, considering investment costs and achieved comfort. The game should also address behavioural aspects. It should be adapted to meet the needs of the elderly, who are often novice users within the field of IT and gaming. A platform to share information among players was also seen as an important functionality of the game.

Building requirements were mainly identified through a statistical analysis of the database managed by the project partner Devon and Cornwall Housing Ltd, including technical characteristics of the social housing stock in Plymouth (the building envelope, building services and controls, etc.). Missing data (the internet connection, types of smart meters, etc.) were obtained through the aforementioned survey. To maximize tenants' acceptance, the game was based on a typical social dwelling so that the game players (the social housing residents) could effectively relate the virtual home with their real home and thus increase their engagement with the game. The typical dwelling was defined using the most common building characteristics, building envelope, building services and controls, and renewable energy generation in the 537 surveyed homes. Although some options (i.e. renewable energy generation, low energy lighting, draught proofing, etc.) were not common in the examined social housing stock, they were incorporated in the game as they were considered valuable for future uptake.

Game requirements were derived from previous projects, publications and reports, but also from the tenants' survey and three focus groups held with social housing tenants participating in the Plymouth pilot. Tenants were found to prefer a relatively realistic home environment over more abstract prototypes. The full-realistic style does not suit low-budget game development, since the standard is high, especially in realistic styles, and so is audience expectation. However, cartoon style can narrow the target audience to younger game players and people who are already used to playing games. Therefore, a pseudo-realistic graphic style was used in the EnerGAware serious game, as players can relate to the graphics and characters but there are enough differences between the game and the real environment to avoid deceptive expectations of a real-life simulation. To enhance game engagement, tenants can identify references from their everyday context in the game (for example, architectural landmarks in the pilot city), but presented in a different, attractive, engaging setting.

Requirements that were identified drove the design of the first EnerGAware game prototype and the metering system solution to be used during the validation of the game. This preliminary version of the game was tested in gameplay scenario focus groups involving social tenants. The beta version of the game was later deployed in a real affordable housing pilot and results were used to refine the final version of the game.

GAME MECHANICS AND COMPONENTS

According to the above requirements, Energy Cat: the House of Tomorrow (Energy Cat, 2018) is a game that shares the Sim's grounds (Figure 1). The player starts building his/her virtual house with a pre-defined base case of 50 m². As the game progresses, the player can extend the house in different directions and personalize it. The player can purchase furniture, appliances and decorative items available in the catalogue, using the money he/she earns. Items in the editor function mode (Figure 2) include furniture (such as chairs, tables, sofas and beds), basic electric appliances (including cookers, fridges, ovens, TVs and computers), wall and floor cladding (for example, tiles, stones, wood and wallpaper), decorative items (house plants, jars, phones, etc.) and other energy saving measures such as options to upgrade the building's thermal envelope (energy efficient windows and insulated walls and roofs), efficient lighting devices (halogen bulbs, eco bulbs, compact fluorescent lamp [CFL] lightbulbs, etc.) and energy-efficient home appliances (such as A++ washing machines and dishwashers).

Figure 1. Game play loop
Source: own elaboration

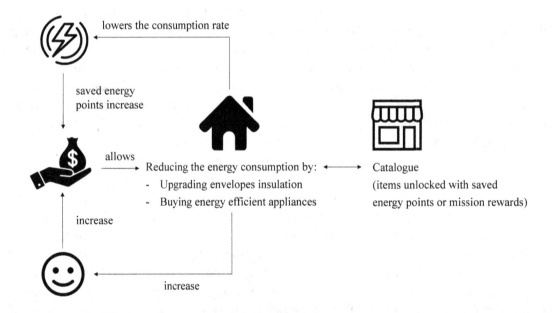

The main objective of the game is to save energy points. Points allow players to play for a longer time and unlock new game content such as items in the catalogue, including decorative elements, appliances, lighting devices, insulation and new windows. Players receive a new pool of energy points at the beginning of each day. Energy points diminish gradually according to the house's energy consumption.

Basic elements, devices and appliances are cheaper but consume more energy. As daily energy points are limited, the player will soon be interested in updating existing devices for others that, although more expensive, consume less energy. The player will also rapidly identify the need to update the building's thermal envelope by adding insulation to the facades or the roof, installing new windows or replacing existing boilers. The game promotes an understanding and comparison of investment costs, indoor thermal comfort and the long-term benefits of all the available options.

The player also commands a cat, who lives with his family in this house. His main objective is to correct the energy management mistakes that the human inhabitants make, such as spending too much time in the shower and not turning off the lights when they leave a room. To motivate the player, monetary rewards are scattered among the rooms in the house.

To maximize the energy saved, the player might want to cut all energy spending, including that strictly needed to achieve reasonable living conditions. In this case, the happiness of the humans living in the house would dramatically decrease which, would diminish the virtual daily income to show the player that this is not the right way. The goal is to make the players understand the need to invest in better and more energy efficient equipment, insulation and smart connected devices to reduce their energy consumption or their need in energy points, which is the same thing, without decreasing their humans' happiness level.

During the inception of the game, multiple iterations had to be performed to identify the optimal balance between energy points, happiness and daily income. The daily pool of energy points was also balanced. There are enough points to play the game during a round of around 20 minutes (and end with a good game experience) but not too many, so players are not discouraged from adopting energy efficient behaviour. In-game scores are sensitive enough to highlight meaningful changes in energy consumption indicators and keep the game realistic and engaging.

Figure 2. Items in the catalogue
Source: Energy Cat (2018)

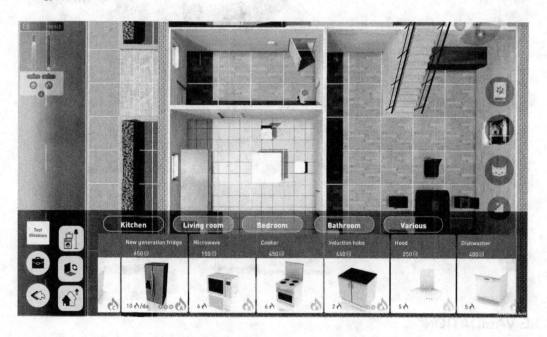

Periodic missions provide energy saving tips (Figure 3). Some of them take place in the player's own house but others are in neighbouring houses to provide tailored environments, for example a house with children or a house with smart controls. Furthermore, neighbours' houses have a fixed geometry that can provide accurate energy simulations in case of changes to thermostat temperature settings, changes to heating periods and heating seasons, changes to zonal heating strategies and window opening behaviour. Event missions are only available during certain periods and connect to real events such as Christmas or World Environment Day. Missions provide extra money and unlock game content.

The energy consumption of the house where the player is actually living (the real house) is read by the game and energy reductions that are achieved in reality are transformed proportionally and cumulatively into extra in-game currency. Energy reductions are calculated by comparing the weather-corrected energy consumption in a week with that of the corresponding week of the year before. The game can also be played with no connection to smart meter data and therefore these features are deactivated.

A social media platform allowed players to communicate with each other by posting messages on the common thread or reacting to messages posted by others. Users could also like posts by other users. The total number of likes was visible under each post. Users had the opportunity to follow specific players.

The game was designed to be played on Android and iOs tablets.

Figure 3. Missions in a neighbouring house
Source: Energy Cat (2018)

GAME VALIDATION

Existing meters in the pilot houses did not have any communication ports to facilitate the collection of energy consumption data. Therefore, to collect electricity consumption data, an optical pulse reader and a standard wireless M-Bus pulse counter were attached to the existing meter. An energy cam was used to collect gas consumption data. In both cases, data were sent wirelessly to a data concentrator that sent the information to a remote server every 15 minutes. Apart from general protection and power supply, the data concentrator included a wireless MBus bridge and a datalogger. The wireless MBus bridge collected and converted data from the wireless readers attached to existing electricity and gas meters. The datalogger read and stored meter data and sent them to a remote server, thanks to an embedded GPRS modem. A middleware platform was used to gather households' energy consumption data (collected by the energy monitoring systems deployed in all the pilot houses), tenants' gameplay data (available on the game server) and average daily outdoor temperatures for the pilot city (retrieved from the Weather Underground web service, an automatic website collecting weather observations in Plymouth). The middleware also calculated the real-world weather-corrected energy savings and transformed them into game rewards.

Figure 4. Project implementation
Source: own elaboration

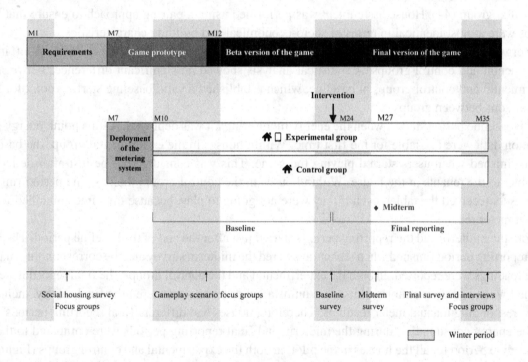

Pilot houses were identified through the abovementioned social housing survey. The survey was completed by 537 households and 137 stated there that they would be interested in participating in the experimental stage of the project. After checking the information in the survey about the technical characteristics of the metering infrastructure, 114 houses were found to be able to participate in the pilot. However, the monitoring system could not be deployed in all the identified houses for several reasons, including tenants who were no longer interested, non-reachable participants and metering infrastructure that was not well described in the survey.

Figure 5. Energy data collection and communication infrastructure. Source: own elaboration

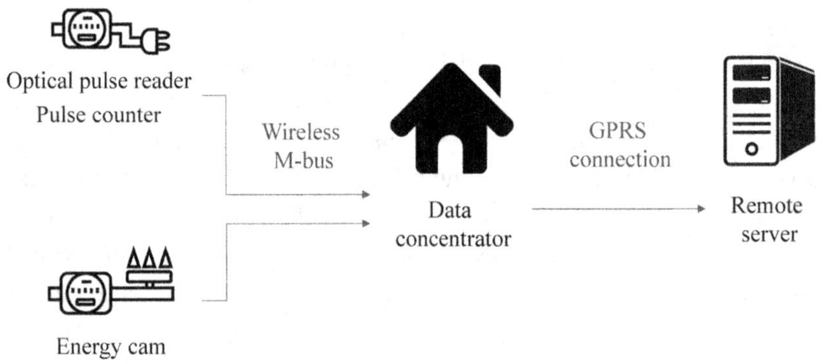

Half of the shortlisted houses were assigned to the control group (44) and the other half to the experimental group (44). House assignment was performed using a pairing approach to ensure that both groups were almost identical in terms of socio-economical and building characteristics.

Energy consumption during the baseline period was analysed for all the houses in the pilot, in the experimental and control groups. A statistical analysis showed no significant differences between the experimental and control groups at baseline, which established a valid baseline starting point for later comparisons between groups.

The baseline period started when the energy monitoring kit was deployed. At this point, energy consumption data were available for the first time. Within houses in the experimental group, the baseline period finished when users started playing the game. This was considered to be just after delivering the tablet to the tenants in the house. Within houses in the control group, the baseline period finished when users received the tablet, even if they were not going to play, because this time coincided with a manual meter reading.

Both the midterm and the reporting periods started just after the end of the baseline period. The midterm reporting period finished when tenants answered the midterm survey and the corresponding manual meter readings were reported. In both the experimental and the control groups, the final reporting period finished when energy monitoring kits were uninstalled or tenants answered the final survey, including the corresponding manual meter readings. Therefore, houses had different final reporting periods.

The energy consumption during the midterm and final reporting periods were compared to that of the baseline period for all the houses in the pilot, in both the experimental and control groups (Figure 6).

It is important to note that in-game data records and answers gathered by the mid-term survey revealed that only 18 tenants out of the 44 composing the experimental group really played the game. Therefore, the effectiveness of the game in terms of energy saving was measured using this experimental subgroup. Social media activity and energy knowledge sharing could only be monitored in even a smaller part of this experimental subgroup as some tenants played the game offline.

Figure 6. Baseline, midterm and final reporting periods. Source: own elaboration

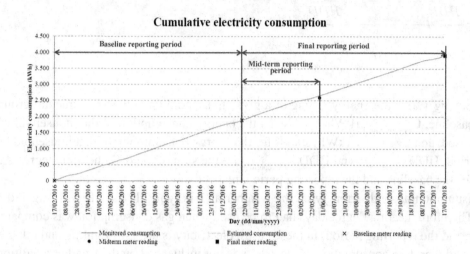

Achieved Energy Savings

Energy savings provided by the game were determined using pre-post and control group approaches according to ICT PSP methodology for energy saving measurement (Balanced European Conservation Approach, 2012) and the International Performance Measurement and Verification Protocol (Efficiency Valuation Organization, 2012). According to these documents, avoided energy use is the difference between the adjusted baseline energy and the energy that was actually metered during the reporting period. The adjusted baseline energy must consider routine and non-routine adjustments. Routine adjustments include energy-governing factors that are expected to change routinely. In this case, changes in the outdoor temperature were considered, especially within the context of the pre-post comparison approach, as the same month of two consecutive years may have completely different thermal behavior. Specifically, and considering that the energy consumption of buildings in the social housing pilot was closely related to heating needs, heating degree days (HDD_{base}) were taken into account:

$$HDD_{base} = \sum_{1}^{n} \left(T_{base} - T_{outdoor} \right) \text{ if } T_{base} > T_{outdoor} \qquad [1]$$

where n is the number of days in the period, T_{base} is the outdoor temperature above which the building needs heating and $T_{outdoor}$ is the outdoor temperature. According to the Carbon Trust (2012), T_{base} was set at 15.5°C. The outdoor temperature was retrieved from the middleware platform.

Non-routine adjustments were discarded because energy-governing factors that are expected not to change (such as buildings' size, installed equipment and occupancy patterns) were found to stay constant during the analysed periods.

Therefore, energy savings were calculated according to the following equation:

$$\text{Saving}_i = \frac{\dfrac{C_{\text{exp reporting } i}}{HDD_{15.5°C\ reporting}} - \dfrac{C_{\text{exp baseline } i}}{HDD_{15.5°C\ baseline}}}{\dfrac{C_{\text{exp baseline } i}}{HDD_{15.5°C\ baseline}}} \cdot 100 \qquad [2]$$

Where Saving_i (%) is the energy saving of a given household (i) in the experimental group in relation to its baseline, $C_{\text{exp reporting } i}$ (kWh) represents the energy consumption of that household during the reporting period, and $C_{\text{exp baseline } i}$, (kWh) stands for the energy consumption of that household during the baseline period. $HDD_{15.5°C\ baseline}$ and $HDD_{15.5°C\ reporting}$ are the sum of the daily heating degree days based on 15.5°C for the baseline and the reporting period, respectively.

Gas consumption depends strongly on the weather as it is typically used for heating and domestic hot water. Therefore, heating degree days had to be used when gas consumption was compared during the baseline and the reporting period. In these cases, electricity is used for lighting and other electrical appliances, and therefore consumption of electricity is not influenced by the weather conditions. However, around 15% of the houses recruited in the pilot were electrically heated. In this case, the amount of electricity consumed for heating purposes should have been corrected using heating degree-day figures. Unfortunately, the monitoring strategy did not include electricity sub-metering. Therefore, all the electricity consumed was weather-corrected. This was considered the best approach for electrically heated houses because most of the electricity is typically used for heating purposes and only a small part is used for lighting and electrical appliances. In any case and to minimize this bias, electrically heated houses were equally distributed among the experimental and control groups.

The data needed for the evaluation of the energy consumption and peak demand were mainly collected through the real-time energy monitoring system deployed in the homes of social tenants included in the experimental and control groups (Figure 5). The energy consumption (electricity and gas) was automatically monitored with a 15-minute period by reading the actual electricity and gas meters of the pilot homes. Values acquired in electricity meter sensors were absolute and expressed in kWh. Values acquired in gas meter sensors were also absolute (as they were in the meter display reading) and were expressed in m^3 or ft^3 and then converted to kWh. Energy-related data (electricity and gas) were verified with manual meter readings at the beginning and end of the baseline, midterm and final periods and by readings provided by the tenants during the midterm and final surveys. To analyze the weather impact on the energy consumption profile, the EnerGAware middleware included daily weather statistics of Plymouth. Weather data were sourced from Weather Underground, an automatic web weather service.

To gain a deep understanding of the energy consumption profile of all houses in the pilot, a specific report was drawn up for all the houses participating in the EnerGAware experiment (Figures 7, 8 and 9), in the experimental and control groups. Houses that left the experimentation phase before the end of the final reporting period were not analysed nor reported.

The first page of these individual reports (see the example in Figure 7) summarizes all the information on the house, including building and energy characteristics, electricity and gas infrastructure characteristics and data about the energy performance of the house during the baseline period. The second page of these individual reports (see the example in Figure 8) includes data about the energy performance of the house during the midterm and final reporting periods.

The baseline, midterm and final reporting sections include start and end dates for the period and the corresponding heating degree days based at 15.5°C, expressed in °C. Details about electricity and gas consumption are provided in these sections, including initial and final manual meter readings. Electricity meter readings are expressed in kWh whereas gas meter readings are expressed in m³. Information on the maximum electricity home peak demand is then reported in the baseline, midterm and final reporting sections, in terms of power (kW) and time, according to the 10-day baseline method and the 3 top 10-day baseline method. The average maximum demand in the network peak period (considered to be from 17:00 to 19:00 according to the UK energy supplier) is also stated.

Sections end with a summary of the amount of electricity and gas consumed by the house during the midterm/final reporting period (expressed in kWh in both cases). The conversion factor used to transform m³ or ft³ of gas to kWh is 11.164 kWh/m³ or 0.316 kWh/ft³ for the UK context. Houses with no gas have a hyphen in the gas consumption column. The total energy consumption (kWh) is also stated. The EnerGAware middleware platform stores the energy data every 15 minutes using coordinated universal time (UTC). Therefore, data are corrected to adhere to daylight saving time (DST).

The third page of the individual reports (see the example in Figure 9) includes a graph plotting the cumulative electricity consumption (kWh) during the baseline and the final reporting periods. A grey vertical line indicates when the baseline period finishes and the final reporting period starts (Figure 9). A small cross represents the manual meter reading (kWh) collected at the beginning and end of the baseline period. The small dot represents the manual meter reading (kWh) at the end of the midterm period, gathered from the midterm surveys. The small square represents the manual meter reading (kWh) at the end of the final reporting period, gathered from the final surveys or during the uninstalling process. A solid line represents the monitored electricity consumption directly retrieved from the EnerGAware middleware platform whereas a dotted line represents the estimated electricity consumption when monitored data were not available.

The second graph on the third page of the individual reports (see Figure 9) plots the daily electricity consumption (kWh) during the baseline and the final reporting period. Again, a grey vertical line clearly indicates when the baseline period finished and the reporting period started (Figure 9). Daily electricity consumption is the first derivative of the cumulative electricity consumption. Daily electricity consumption is calculated by subtracting the meter reading at instant t+1 from the meter reading at instant t. Although filtered data were retrieved from the EnerGAware middleware platform, some corrections had to be made. For example, the mean was calculated when the first derivative for one day was 0 and the value for the next day was very high.

The implementation of the Energy Cat serious game in the social housing pilot was associated with an electricity consumption reduction of 3.46% and a gas consumption reduction of 7.48% in the final reporting period in relation to the baseline period (Table 1). The midterm analysis, which took place three months after the intervention, showed higher electricity savings as a result of interaction with the serious game. This highlights the need to motivate users to play for a longer time to consolidate the achieved level of savings. However, technical problems prevented the midterm analysis of gas consumption. No changes were found in average home electricity peak demand. The game development and validation is fully described in Casals et al. (2020).

Figure 7. First page of the energy reports
Source: own elaboration

Building characteristics			
Id dwelling:	EA #058	Dwelling type:	Flat
Construction period:	1976-1982	Floor area (m²):	50
Number of storeys:	1	Number of habitable rooms:	2
Household size:	1	Internet:	Yes

Energy characteristics			
SAP:	75 C	Energy:	Gas and Electric
Main heating fuel:	Gas	Renewable energy:	No

Electricity infrastructure characteristics			
Manufacturer:	Landis&Gyr	Type:	Digital
Model:	E110	Conversion factor (impulses/kWh):	1000
Location:	Outdoor	Distance aggregator-meter (m):	4

Gas infrastructure characteristics			
Manufacturer:	Actaris	Type:	Analogue
Model:	G4		
Location:	Outdoor	Distance aggregator-meter (m):	6

Baseline period			
Starting date (dd/mm/yyyy):	17/02/2016	Final date (dd/mm/yyyy):	17/01/2017
Heating Degree Days (°C) :	1.572,0		

Electricity

Initial meter reading (kWh):		9.557	Final meter reading (kWh):	11.444
10 day baseline peak demand	Power (kW): 2,08		Time (hh:mm):	14 h 47 min
3 day baseline peak demand	Power (kW): 3,40		Time (hh:mm):	15 h 50 min
Demand at the network peak	Power (kW): 0,77		Time (hh:mm):	17 h 0 min to 19h 0 min

Gas

Initial meter reading (m³):	1.019	Final meter reading (m³):	1.217

Electricity consumption (kWh):	1.887,0
Gas consumption (kWh):	2.210,4
Total energy consumption (kWh):	4.097,4

Figure 8. Second page of the energy reports
Source: own elaboration

Midterm reporting period				
Starting date (dd/mm/yyyy):		17/01/2017	Final date (dd/mm/yyyy):	05/06/2017
Heating Degree Days (°C) :		863,0		

Electricity				
Initial meter reading (kWh):		11.444	Final meter reading (kWh):	12.145
10 day baseline peak demand	Power (kW):	1,64	Time (hh:mm):	15 h 10 min
3 day baseline peak demand	Power (kW):	2,63	Time (hh:mm):	16 h 56 min
Demand at the network peak	Power (kW):	0,82	Time (hh:mm):	17 h 0 min to 19h 0 min

Gas				
Initial meter reading (m³):		1.217	Final meter reading (m³):	1.296

Electricity consumption (kWh):	701,0
Gas consumption (kWh):	881,9
Total energy consumption (kWh):	1.582,9

Final reporting period				
Starting date (dd/mm/yyyy):		17/01/2017	Final date (dd/mm/yyyy):	18/01/2018
Heating Degree Days (°C) :		1.686,5		

Electricity				
Initial meter reading (kWh):		11.444	Final meter reading (kWh):	13.470
10 day baseline peak demand	Power (kW):	1,94	Time (hh:mm):	14 h 54 min
3 day baseline peak demand	Power (kW):	3,10	Time (hh:mm):	15 h 10 min
Demand at the network peak	Power (kW):	0,76	Time (hh:mm):	17 h 0 min to 19h 0 min

Gas				
Initial meter reading (m³):		1.217	Final meter reading (m³):	1.402

Electricity consumption (kWh):	2.026,0
Gas consumption (kWh):	2.068,4
Total energy consumption (kWh):	4.094,4

Figure 9. Third page of the energy reports
Source: own elaboration

Baseline, midterm and final reporting period

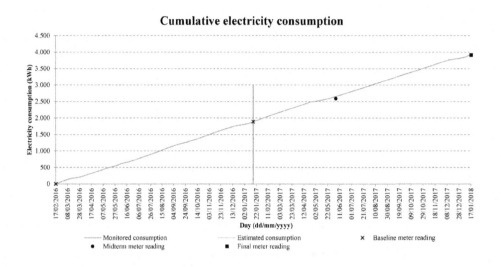

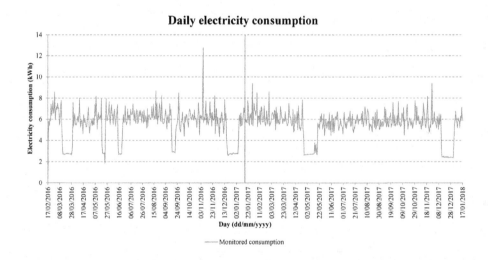

Table 1. Baseline energy consumption and savings during the final reporting period. Source: own elaboration

	Baseline energy consumption [kWh/household·day]	Saving [%]
Electricity	9.08	3.46%
Gas	14.10	7.48%

Cost-Benefit Analysis

Once the research project is finished, the game can be fully exploited on the market. The cost-benefit analysis assumes that the Energy Cat serious game is distributed free of charge by utilities to their clients. Customers use their own devices (tablet and router) to play the game. The game is connected to existing smart meters. Calculations are done assuming a one year timeframe, although after this period tenants can still save energy. The following subsections ascertain the energy, environmental and economic implications of future game exploitation.

Energy and Environmental Cost-benefit Analysis

Game energy and environmental requirements were estimated under a life-cycle approach according to ISO 14040 (International Standard Organization, 2006a) and ISO 14044 (International Standard Organization, 2006b) guidelines. System boundaries include production, transport, use and maintenance. Calculations were performed with SimaPRO 8.0 (Pré, 2017) using the Ecoinvent v3.4 database (Swiss Centre for Life Cycle Inventories, 2018) and the cumulative energy demand (Pré et al., 2018) and ReCiPe 2016 v1.02 endpoint (Huijbregts et al., 2017) methods.

According to the EnerGAware Grant Agreement (EnerGAware project, 2015), game production involved 94 person months (PM). Most of this effort (90%) was devoted to producing the beta version of the game. The remaining 10% was used during the maintenance phase for game updates. Electronic devices (game server, tablet and router) were linked to life cycle inventory data in the Ecoinvent v3.4 database (Swiss Centre for Life Cycle Inventories, 2018). The game server was assumed to be manufactured in China and later transported to game developer premises in Troyes (France). The server was assumed to run 24 hours per day but hosts five more games. Therefore, in this case, the allocated charges were 16.67%. The tablet and the router were manufactured in Southeast Asia and China respectively and later transported to the pilot site (Plymouth, United Kingdom). The game was downloaded at the beginning of the use phase and the process took two minutes. According to data gathered in the Plymouth pilot (EnerGAware project, 2017), tenants played the game an average of 15 minutes per week, for 3 months, with a total estimated duration of 180 minutes. The impact of the tablet and the router was proportionally assigned to the game considering that they were both used for other purposes. In this case, the allocated charges were 0.55%, considering that the tablet was used 90 minutes/day.

According to the above considerations, the cumulative energy demand was 3663.52 kWh$_p$ when 50 game downloads were assumed and 3752.21 kWh$_p$ when 100 downloads were assumed. Most of the energy (~54–55%) was found to be consumed during the manufacturing and transport phases whereas the energy consumed during the operational phase was found to represent around 39–40% of all the life-cycle energy. A small part of the energy (~4–5%) was found to be consumed during the maintenance phase. Savings provided by the game were estimated based on data obtained in the pilot (Table 1). The energetic feasibility of the Energy Cat serious game is depicted by the following equation:

$$NENB = 703.28 \cdot N - 3,575 \qquad [2]$$

Where NENB are the net energy savings provided by the game in one year (expressed in kWh$_p$) and N represents the number of game downloads.

The energy break-even point or the number of game downloads needed to cover the energy invested in the game, which is the same thing, was 5.1 downloads. Assuming just 100 game downloads, the life cycle energy payback is about 19 days (Gangolells et al., 2021).

The game was also analysed from a broader perspective to examine its impact on human health (measured in disability-adjusted life years), ecosystem quality (measured in loss of species over a certain area during a certain time) and resource scarcity (measured in increased cost of resources in United States dollars in 2013). As expected, most of the impact was found to be in the manufacturing phase, ranging from 80.12% for damage to human health, 79.82% for ecosystem quality and 77.96% for resource scarcity (Gangolells et al., 2020). Transport was found to involve 8.78% of damage to human health, 7.57% of damage to ecosystem quality and 8.86% of damage to resource availability. The use phase represented 3.86%, 5.08% and 5.82% of the damage, respectively. Contribution ratios for the maintenance phase amounted to 7.24% (human health), 7.54% (ecosystem quality) and 7.36% (resource scarcity). The environmental impact of the game was later compared to the environmental impact of the energy consumed by the houses before and after implementing the game (Table 2). It could be concluded that the game-based approach was worthwhile from the environmental perspective, even considering its life cycle impact, as it provides considerable reductions in three damage categories: human health (3.68%), ecosystem quality (3.87%) and resource scarcity (4.81%).

Table 2. End-point damage categories before and after implementing the game when 50 households were analysed in one year. Source: own elaboration

Damage category	Before implementing the game	After implementing the game			Reduction (%)
	Energy consumption	Energy consumption	Game	Total	
Human health (DALY)	0.674	0.647	0.002	0.649	-3.68%
Ecosystems (species.yr)	0.002	0.002	0.000	0.002	-3.87%
Resources (USD 2013)	27,383.944	26,041.567	25.626	26,067.193	-4.81%

Economic Cost-Benefit Analysis

According to the research project's budget, initial investment costs to develop the game amount to €687,882. Energy savings were estimated based on the average electricity (Eurostat, 2018a) and natural gas (Eurostat, 2018b) prices for domestic customers corresponding to the second semester of 2017 in Europe. Energy prices were assumed to increase 2.1% yearly. The discount rate was assumed to be 3.0%. The economic feasibility of the Energy Cat serious game is depicted by the following equation:

$$NECB = 47.43 \cdot N - 687,882 \qquad [3]$$

Where NECB are the net economic benefits provided by the game in one year (expressed in €) and N represents the number of game downloads.

The economic break-even point or the number of game downloads needed to cover the cost of developing the game, which is the same thing, was 14,502 downloads.

Scalability of the Energy Saving Potential

The effects of the Energy Cat serious game were examined through three main scenarios, according to the bottom-up approach suggested in EASME guidelines (EASME, 2017). In the first scenario, the game was assumed to be distributed within UK social housing stock. In the second scenario, the game was distributed in all UK housing stock, including owner-occupied, private rented and social rented dwellings. The maximum impact was analysed under the third scenario, considering that the serious game will be disseminated throughout Europe.

In the first scenario, the Energy Cat game is promoted within the entire UK social housing stock. The impact of the Energy Cat serious game (Table 4) was estimated using the results obtained in the Plymouth social housing pilot in terms of baseline energy consumption, energy saving and penetration rate, UK primary energy factors (Building Research Establishment, 2016) and UK emission factors (Covenant of Mayors for Climate and Energy, 2016). The number of dwellings in UK social housing stock was assumed to be 4,940,848, according to the European Federation of Public, Cooperative and Social Housing (Social Housing, 2018).

In the second scenario, it was assumed that the Energy Cat game is promoted among all UK housing stock, including owner-occupied, private rented and social rented dwellings. The baseline energy consumption was estimated to be higher in owner-occupied and private rented housing stock than in social housing stock. Therefore, in this case, the baseline energy consumption of UK housing stock was estimated through typical domestic consumption values for the UK (Table 3). According to Housing Europe (2018), UK housing was comprised of 28,073,000 dwellings in 2018 but two situations were devised. The first assumed that the Energy Cat game is distributed by energy service providers to their clients. As this can be considered a guided context, a 40.91% penetration rate was assumed (the same as that in the social housing pilot). The second assumed that the game is freely distributed in App stores and a penetration rate of 1.00% is considered. Greenhouse gas emission savings were calculated using the UK emission factor (Covenant of Mayors for Climate and Energy, 2016) and the UK primary energy factor (Building Research Establishment, 2016). Energy and emissions savings were found to be highly variable depending on the estimated baseline energy consumption and the game penetration rate (Table 3).

Table 3. Typical domestic consumption values for UK. Source: adapted from Office of Gas and Electricity Markets (2018)

		Energy consumption (kWh/year)
Electricity	Low	1,900
	Medium	3,100
	High	4,600
Gas	Low	8,000
	Medium	12,000
	High	17,000

The third scenario assumed that the effects of the Energy Cat serious game are extended throughout Europe. Overall electricity and gas consumption figures for the residential sector in each European member (Eurostat, 2018c) were used since individualized household electricity and gas consumption figures were not available in the existing literature. Average energy savings obtained in the Plymouth pilot were used (Table 1) and, as in Scenario 2, two penetration rates were assumed (40.91% and 1%). Calculations were made using the individualized EU Member States emission factors (Covenant of Mayors for Climate and Energy, 2016) and the average EU primary energy factor (European Commission, 2016).

Table 4. Estimated long-term impacts of the Energy Cat serious game. Source: own elaboration

	Energy saving (GWh$_p$/year)	Greenhouse gas emissions saving (tCO$_2$/year)
Scenario 1: UK social housing stock		
	1,425	468,087
Scenario 2: UK housing stock		
1.00% penetration rate		
Low consumption level	233	61,410
Medium consumption level	355	95,163
High consumption level	508	137,354
40.91% penetration rate		
Low consumption level	9,530	2,512,221
Medium consumption level	14,530	3,893,031
High consumption level	20,779	5,619,044
Scenario 3: EU housing stock		
1.00% penetration rate	1,590	460,527
40.91% penetration rate	65,063	18,839,744

SOLUTIONS AND RECOMMENDATIONS

With the 2030 Climate Target Plan (European Commission, 2020b), the European Commission proposes increasing the EU's ambition on reducing greenhouse gas emissions to at least 55% below 1990 levels by 2030. At the same time, it is widely known that the building sector is responsible for about 40% of the EU's total energy consumption and 36% of greenhouse gas emissions. To achieve the 55% emission reduction target by 2030, the EU should reduce buildings' greenhouse gas emissions by 60% (European Commission, 2020a). However, few buildings undergo renovation, and renovation works rarely address buildings' energy performance. According to the European Commission (2020a), the European weighted annual energy renovation rate is just about 1%. Besides multiple technical and social barriers, financial obstacles usually include high up-front costs and long payback times, among others (D'Oca et al., 2018). In this context, gamified energy efficiency programmes might be a promising tool to address buildings' energy efficiency, considering that investment costs and corresponding payback periods are much lower than those of most building retrofitting options. Evidence from the EnerGAware project

(2015) suggests that games not only encourage positive behaviour change but also provide effective energy savings, contributing to current emission reduction targets. After analysing several business models, the most feasible one was found to be the distribution of the game through energy suppliers to their domestic customers. In this case, the estimated annual saving was found to amount to 18.84 million tons of $CO_{2\,eq}$ at European level.

FUTURE RESEARCH DIRECTIONS

EnerGAware is a ground-breaking project aimed at evaluating the effectiveness of gamification to reduce energy use in social housing. Preliminary results were found to be promising. However, to definitely ascertain the energy saving effect of the game, the pilot should be further replicated to have a larger sample of tenants involved in the experiment. In addition, stronger evidence of the game's impact regardless of the social-economical and geographical conditions is needed. Changes in engagement in energy saving behaviour over time remain unexplored. Therefore, future research should monitor energy savings in the long-term.

It would be interesting to examine whether the effects of the game could be boosted under a multi-factorial approach including other tradition behaviour programmes to maintain continued interest in the game or the other way round, if the effects of massive retrofit programmes could be enhanced by the game. Elsharkawy and Rutherford (2018) recently assessed the effectiveness of an extensive pre- and post-retrofit home energy use of 150 social housing properties in Nottingham's Aspley ward (United Kingdom). Results showed that whilst this specific initiative significantly improved home conditions and reduced energy consumption, it failed to achieve the predicted £300 annual savings on household energy bills. This was found to be largely attributed to occupants' ingrained habits of household energy use, higher comfort level preferences, (lack of) energy consumption awareness, and insufficient information to help residents better manage their home energy use following the retrofit. In this context, the game would probably have had a positive impact on encouraging and embedding sustainable energy use.

A specific social network was created to ensure the anonymity of the tenants participating in the experiment and to uphold data protection rules. Further research should explore whether linking the game to the social networks people normally use (i.e., Facebook, Twitter, etc.) would contribute to improving game engagement.

CONCLUSION

The EnerGAware project provided invaluable insight into the application of serious gaming for household energy saving. This EU-funded research project developed a serious game for household energy saving and validated it in a social housing pilot using the pre-post comparison and control group approaches.

Energy savings achieved in just one house might seem to be limited. However, this game-based solution for household energy saving holds high potential when results are scaled up to EU level, in terms of energy saving and emissions' reduction. At European level and assuming that the game is distributed under the auspices of energy service providers, annual savings were found to amount to over 65.1 TWh_p (or 48.9 TWh_s) and 18.8 million tons of CO_{2e}. Moreover, game life cycle energy requirements were low when compared to the energy saving provided. By way of example, the energy payback time was about

19 days with just 100 downloads. From the environmental perspective, the game allowed significant reductions in environmental impact of the domestic energy use in the three areas of protection: human health (3.67%), ecosystem quality (3.87%) and resource scarcity (4.81%).

From the economic perspective, game-based solutions for energy saving may become a strong alternative to other building retrofitting actions (i.e. adding thermal insulation to existing building envelopes, upgrading existing boilers, etc.) with compromised cost-effectiveness. This is mainly because game deployment requires relatively few resources and entails small but sustained energy savings over time. Interoperability with existing smart meters will ease dissemination of this innovative tool.

Major challenges to using gamification for energy saving purposes are that serious games implicitly compete with users' previous gaming experience, often based on multi-million commercial game titles. Therefore, developing and testing an engaging serious game for energy efficiency requires a high amount of resources. Simpler games that differ radically from commercial simulation games may reduce the player's motivation and interest in the game.

ACKNOWLEDGMENT

This research was supported by the European Union's Horizon 2020 research and innovation programme through the EnerGAware project (Energy Game for Awareness of energy efficiency in social housing communities) [grant number no. 649673].

REFERENCES

AlSkaif, T., Lampropoulos, I., van den Broek, M., & van Sark, W. (2018). Gamification-based framework for engagement of residential customers in energy applications. *Energy Research & Social Science*, *44*, 187–195. doi:10.1016/j.erss.2018.04.043

Balanced European Conservation Approach. (2012). *The ICT PSP methodology for energy saving measurement: a common deliverable from projects of ICT for sustainable growth in the residential sector, version 3*. https://cordis.europa.eu/docs/projects/cnect/6/250496/080/deliverables/001-ARES975520CIP-CommondeliverableeSESH.pdf

Beck, A. L., Chitalia, S., & Rai, V. (2019). Not so gameful: A critical review of gamification in mobile energy applications. *Energy Research & Social Science*, *51*, 32–39. doi:10.1016/j.erss.2019.01.006

Boomsma, C., Hafner, R., Pahl, S., Jones, R., & Fuertes, A. (2018). Should We Play Games where Energy is Concerned? Perceptions of Serious Gaming as a Technology to Motivate Energy Behaviour Change among Social Housing Tenants. *Sustainability*, *10*(6), 1–18. doi:10.3390u10061729

Building Research Establishment. (2016). *CO_2 and primary energy factors for SAP 2016 Version 1.0.* https://www.bre.co.uk/filelibrary/SAP/2016/CONSP-07---CO2-and-PE-factors---V1_0.pdf

Carbon Trust. (2012). *Degree days for energy management. A practical introduction.* https://www.sustainabilityexchange.ac.uk/files/degree_days_for_energy_management_carbon_trust.pdf

Casals, M., Gangolells, M., Macarulla, M., Forcada, N., Fuertes, A., Hafner, R. & Jones, R. (2020). Assessing the effectiveness of gamification in reducing domestic energy consumption: lessons learned from the EnerGAware project. *Energy and Buildings, 210,* 109753:1- 109753:12.

Chatzigeorgiou, I. M., & Andreou, G. T. (2021). A systematic review on feedback research for residential energy behavior change through mobile and web interfaces. *Renewable & Sustainable Energy Reviews*, *135*, 110187. doi:10.1016/j.rser.2020.110187

Covenant of Mayors for Climate and Energy. (2016). *The Covenant of Mayors for Climate and Energy Reporting Guidelines.* https://www.covenantofmayors.eu/IMG/pdf/Reporting_Guidelines_Final_EN.pdf

Csoknyai, T., Legardeur, J., Akle, A. A., & Horváth, M. (2019). Analysis of energy consumption profiles in residential buildings and impact assessment of a serious game on occupants' behavior. *Energy and Building*, *196*, 1–20. doi:10.1016/j.enbuild.2019.05.009

D'Oca, S., Ferrante, A., Ferrer, C., Pernetti, R., Gralka, A., Sebastian, R., & Op 't Veld, P. (2018). Technical, Financial, and Social Barriers and Challenges in Deep Building Renovation: Integration of Lessons Learned from the H2020 Cluster Projects. *Buildings*, *8*(12), 174. doi:10.3390/buildings8120174

Douglas, B. D., & Brauer, M. (2021). Gamification to prevent climate change: A review of games and apps for sustainability. *Current Opinion in Psychology*, *42*, 89–94. doi:10.1016/j.copsyc.2021.04.008 PMID:34052619

EASME. (2017). *Guidelines for the calculation of project performance indicators.* https://ec.europa.eu/ easme/sites/easme-site/files/guidelines-for-the-calculation-of-performance-indicators.pdf

Efficiency Valuation Organization. (2012). *International Performance Measurement and Verification Protocol. Concepts and options for determining energy and water savings, vol. 1, Technical Report.* http://www.eeperformance.org/uploads/8/6/5/0/8650231/ipmvp_volume_i__2012.pdf

Elsharkawy, H., & Rutherford, P. (2018). Energy-efficient retrofit of social housing in the UK: Lessons learned from a Community Energy Saving Programme (CESP) in Nottingham. *Energy and Building*, *172*, 295–306. doi:10.1016/j.enbuild.2018.04.067

EnerGAware project. (2015). *Energy game for awareness of energy efficiency in social housing communities.* EU funded project, contract number: 649673. http://energaware.eu

EnerGAware project. (2017). *Deliverable 4.3. Pilot implementation evaluation (Preliminary).* https:// energaware.eu/downloads/EnerGAware_D4.3_Pilot%20implementation%20evaluation%20preliminary_r1.pdf

Energy Cat. (2018). *Energy Cat: the house of tomorrow.* http://www.energycatgame.com/

European Commission. (2016). *Proposal for a Directive of the European Parliament and of the Council amending Directive 2012/27/EU on energy efficiency* https://eur-lex.europa.eu/legal-content/EN/TXT/ HTML/?uri=CELEX:52016PC0761&from=EN

European Commission. (2020a). *Communication from the Commission to the European Parliament, the Council, the European Economic and Social Committee and the Committee of the Regions. A Renovation Wave for Europe - Greening our buildings, creating jobs, improving lives.* https://eur-lex.europa.eu/legal-content/EN/TXT/?qid=1603122220757&uri=CELEX:52020DC0662

European Commission. (2020b). *Communication from the Commission to the European Parliament, the Council, the European Economic and Social Committee and the Committee of the Regions. Stepping up Europe's 2030 climate ambition. Investing in a climate-neutral future for the benefit of our people.* https://eur-lex.europa.eu/legal-content/EN/TXT/?uri=CELEX:52020DC0562

Eurostat. (2018a). *Electricity prices for household consumers.* http://ec.europa.eu/eurostat/statistics-explained/index.php/Electricity_price_statistics#Electricity_prices_for_household_consumers

Eurostat. (2018b). *Natural gas prices for household consumers.* http://ec.europa.eu/eurostat/statistics-explained/index.php/Natural_gas_price_statistics#Natural_gas_prices_for_household_consumers

Eurostat. (2018c). *Simplified energy balances - annual data.* https://ec.europa.eu/eurostat/en/web/products-datasets/-/NRG_100A

Gangolells, M., Casals, M., Forcada, N. & Macarulla M. (2020). Life cycle analysis of a game-based solution for domestic energy saving. *Sustainability, 12,* 66:1 – 66:18.

Gangolells, M., Casals, M., Forcada, N., & Macarulla, M. (2021). Exploring the Potential of a Gamified Approach to Reduce Energy Use and Carbon Emissions in the Household Sector. *Sustainability*, *13*(6), 3380. doi:10.3390u13063380

Hallinger, P., Wang, R., Chatpinyakoop, C., Nguyen, V. T., & Nguyen, U. P. (2020). A bibliometric review of research on simulations and serious games used in educating for sustainability, 1997–2019. *Journal of Cleaner Production*, *256*, 120358. doi:10.1016/j.jclepro.2020.120358

Hargreaves, T., Nye, M., & Burgess, J. (2013). Keeping energy visible? Exploring how householders interact with feedback from smart energy monitors in the longer term. *Energy Policy*, *52*, 126–134. doi:10.1016/j.enpol.2012.03.027

Housing Europe. (2018). *A State of Housing map of Europe.* https://www.housingeurope.eu/resource-1001/a-state-of-housing-map-of-europe

Huijbregts, M. A. J., Steinmann, Z. J. N., Elshout, P. M. F., Stam, G., Verones, F., Vieira, M., Zijp, M., Hollander, A., & van Zelm, R. (2017). ReCiPe2016: A harmonised life cycle impact assessment method at midpoint and endpoint level. *The International Journal of Life Cycle Assessment*, *22*(2), 138–147. doi:10.100711367-016-1246-y

Johnson, D., Horton, E., Mulcahy, R., & Foth, M. (2017). Gamification and serious games within the domain of domestic energy consumption: A systematic review. *Renewable & Sustainable Energy Reviews*, *73*, 249–264. doi:10.1016/j.rser.2017.01.134

International Standard Organization. (2006a). *ISO 14040. Environmental management – life cycle assessment – principles and framework.* https://www.sciencedirect.com/science/article/pii/S0960148112003084-bib16

International Standard Organization (2006b). ISO 14044. Environmental management – life cycle assessment – requirements and guidelines.

Morganti, L., Pallavicini, F., Cadel, E., Candelieri, A., Archetti, F., & Mantovani, F. (2017). Gaming for Earth: Serious games and gamification to engage consumers in pro-environmental behaviours for energy efficiency. *Energy Research & Social Science*, *29*, 95–102. doi:10.1016/j.erss.2017.05.001

Morton, A., Reeves, A., Bull, R., & Preston, S. (2020). Empowering and Engaging European building users for energy efficiency. *Energy Research & Social Science*, *70*, 101772. doi:10.1016/j.erss.2020.101772

Office of Gas and Electricity Markets. (2018). *Typical domestic consumption values.* https://www.ofgem.gov.uk/gas/retail-market/monitoring-data-and-statistics/typical-domestic-consumption-values

Paone, A., & Bacher, J. P. (2018). The Impact of Building Occupant Behavior on Energy Efficiency and Methods to Influence It: A Review of the State of the Art. *Energies*, *11*(4), 953. doi:10.3390/en11040953

Pasini, D., Reda, F., & Häkkinen, T. (2017). User engaging practices for energy saving in buildings: Critical review and new enhanced procedure. *Energy and Building*, *148*, 74–88. doi:10.1016/j.enbuild.2017.05.010

Patrício, R., Moreira, A., & Zurlo, F. (2018). Gamification approaches to the early stage of innovation. *Creativity and Innovation Management*, *27*(4), 499–511. doi:10.1111/caim.12284

Patrício, R., Moreira, A., Zurlo, F., & Melazzini, M. (2020). Co-creation of new solutions through gamification: A collaborative innovation practice. *Creativity and Innovation Management*, *29*(1), 146–160. doi:10.1111/caim.12356

Pré. (2017). *Simapro LCA software 8.0.* http://www.pre-sustainability.com/simapro

Pré. (2018). *SimaPro Database Manual. Methods library.* https://www.pre-sustainability.com/download/DatabaseManualMethods.pdf

Ro, M., Brauer, M., Kuntz, K., Shukla, R., & Bensch, I. (2017). Making Cool Choices for sustainability: Testing the effectiveness of a game-based approach to promoting pro-environmental behaviors. *Journal of Environmental Psychology*, *53*, 20–30.

Stanitsas, M., Kirytopoulos, K., & Vareilles, E. (2019). Facilitating sustainability transition through serious games: A systematic literature review. *Journal of Cleaner Production*, *208*, 924–936.

Swiss Centre for Life Cycle Inventories. (2018). *Ecoinvent database v3.4.* https://www.ecoinvent.org/database/

Wagner, A., & Gałuszka, D. (2020). Let's play the future: Sociotechnical imaginaries, and energy transitions in serious digital games. *Energy Research & Social Science*, *70*, 101674.

Wee, S. C., & Choong, W. W. (2019). Gamification: Predicting the effectiveness of variety game design elements to intrinsically motivate users' energy conservation behaviour. *Journal of Environmental Management*, *233*, 97–106.

Wu, X., Liu, S., & Shukla, A. (2020). Serious Games as an Engaging Medium on Building Energy Consumption: A Review of Trends, Categories and Approaches. *Sustainability*, *12*(20), 8508.

ADDITIONAL READING

AlSkaif, T., Lampropoulos, I., van den Broek, M., & van Sark, W. (2018). Gamification-based framework for engagement of residential customers in energy applications. *Energy Research & Social Science*, *44*, 187–195. doi:10.1016/j.erss.2018.04.043

Boomsma, C., Hafner, R., Pahl, S., Jones, R., & Fuertes, A. (2018). Should We Play Games where Energy is Concerned? Perceptions of Serious Gaming as a Technology to Motivate Energy Behaviour Change among Social Housing Tenants. *Sustainability*, *10*(6), 1–18. doi:10.3390u10061729

Casals, M., Gangolells, M., Macarulla, M., Forcada, N., Fuertes, A., Hafner, R. & Jones, R. (2020). Assessing the effectiveness of gamification in reducing domestic energy consumption: lessons learned from the EnerGAware project. *Energy and Buildings, 210,* 109753:1- 109753:12.

Csoknyai, T., Legardeur, J., Akle, A. A., & Horváth, M. (2019). Analysis of energy consumption profiles in residential buildings and impact assessment of a serious game on occupants' behavior. *Energy and Building*, *196*, 1–20. doi:10.1016/j.enbuild.2019.05.009

Gangolells, M., Casals, M., Forcada, N. & Macarulla M. (2020). Life cycle analysis of a game-based solution for domestic energy saving. *Sustainability, 12*, 66:1 – 66:18.

Gangolells, M., Casals, M., Forcada, N., & Macarulla, M. (2021). Exploring the Potential of a Gamified Approach to Reduce Energy Use and Carbon Emissions in the Household Sector. *Sustainability*, *13*(6), 3380. doi:10.3390u13063380

Johnson, D., Horton, E., Mulcahy, R., & Foth, M. (2017). Gamification and serious games within the domain of domestic energy consumption: A systematic review. *Renewable & Sustainable Energy Reviews*, *73*, 249–264. doi:10.1016/j.rser.2017.01.134

Morganti, L., Pallavicini, F., Cadel, E., Candelieri, A., Archetti, F., & Mantovani, F. (2017). Gaming for Earth: Serious games and gamification to engage consumers in pro-environmental behaviours for energy efficiency. *Energy Research & Social Science*, *29*, 95–102. doi:10.1016/j.erss.2017.05.001

Pasini, D., Reda, F., & Häkkinen, T. (2017). User engaging practices for energy saving in buildings: Critical review and new enhanced procedure. *Energy and Building*, *148*, 74–88. doi:10.1016/j.enbuild.2017.05.010

Wagner, A., & Gałuszka, D. (2020). Let's play the future: Sociotechnical imaginaries, and energy transitions in serious digital games. *Energy Research & Social Science*, *70*, 101674. doi:10.1016/j.erss.2020.101674

Wu, X., Liu, S., & Shukla, A. (2020). Serious Games as an Engaging Medium on Building Energy Consumption: A Review of Trends, Categories and Approaches. *Sustainability*, *12*(20), 8508. doi:10.3390u12208508

KEY TERMS AND DEFINITIONS

Cumulative Energy Demand: Direct and indirect energy use over a product's entire life cycle.

Energy Payback Time: Length of time a system must operate before it recovers the energy invested throughout its lifetime.

Heating Degree Days: Variable measuring how much (in degrees) and for how long (in days) outside air temperature was lower than a specific base temperature over a certain period of time. This weather-based technical index is closely related to the buildings' heating energy demand.

Life Cycle Assessment: Methodology used to quantify the environmental impacts arising from inputs (including consumption of raw materials, energy, and water) and outputs (including waste and emissions generation) over a product's entire life cycle.

Living Lab Methodology: Research methodology involving co-creation with final users.

Non-Routine Adjustments: Energy-governing factors that are expected not to change such as buildings' size, installed equipment, occupancy patterns, etc.

Routine Adjustments: Energy-governing factors that are expected to change routinely such as the outdoor temperature.

Chapter 15

Gamified Information Systems as a Means to Achieve Energy-Saving at Work Through Employee Behaviour

Dimosthenis Kotsopoulos
Athens University of Economics and Business, Greece

Cleopatra Bardaki
Harokopio University of Athens, Greece

ABSTRACT

Gamification is increasingly utilized in modern organizational environments to increase motivation and compliance toward organizational goals. To improve its effectiveness in achieving behavioral change, designers routinely design and implement specially designed information systems (IS) that effectively enable the interaction between employees and game elements and ultimately define the nature of the gamified experience. Such gamified IS have already been put to practice, with positive results regarding usability, user engagement, and enjoyment, and—more importantly—actual energy savings have been recorded during their usage. Apart from an introduction to this very interesting field of application for gamification in organizations, more importantly, this chapter also provides insight and specific guidelines that researchers, as well as practitioners in this field, may need to bear in mind in their efforts to design and implement gamified IS for energy-saving in organizational environments.

INTRODUCTION

The importance of energy conservation in public buildings has been repeatedly stressed, as it is directly related to climate change (International Energy Agency, 2016; UNFCCC, 2014, 2016). Furthermore, organizational energy efficiency – apart from leading to energy savings – can also be accompanied by improvements in worker comfort, productivity, product quality, as well as reductions in maintenance cost,

DOI: 10.4018/978-1-6684-4291-3.ch015

risk, production time and waste (IEA EEfD, 2017). However, in order to conserve energy, employees need to be motivated to consistently adhere to a goal that usually leads to no direct financial benefit for them. Therefore, additional means, such as gamification – "the use of game design elements in non-game contexts" (Deterding *et al.*, 2011) – need to be employed to motivate them towards that end.

Existing research has proven that the occupants of a public building can significantly affect its energy performance, as their behaviour is directly responsible for one third of the energy consumed therein (Nguyen & Aiello, 2013). Hence, behavioural change can be an important means for reducing energy consumption in public buildings (Delmas *et al.*, 2013). Forming an energy-saving culture across organizational levels, and utilizing social influence, is suggested in order to achieve energy conservation at work (Schelly, Cross, Franzen, Hall, & Reeve, 2011; Staddon, Cycil, Goulden, Leygue, & Spence, 2016). Moreover, participatory interventions, that have been recognized as an effective means for enhancing organizational energy-saving behavior (Endrejat & Kauffeld, 2018), can be instrumental for cultivating and maintaining such an energy-saving culture at work.

In the present chapter, gamified Information Systems (IS) are reviewed, discussed, and suggested, as a means of constructing and sustaining an energy-saving culture at work, by tending to employees' motivation towards energy conservation, and participation in energy-saving initiatives. Moreover, the ways in which they can be utilized, to optimally introduce gamification at work, towards positively and significantly affecting employees' energy-saving behaviour are discussed based on existing theory, as well as through practical insight based on experience accrued and lessons learnt in practice.

GAMIFIED INFORMATION SYSTEMS

Gamification is a powerful means of increasing and sustaining employees' engagement and motivation towards a specific behaviour (Patrício, Moreira, & Zurlo, 2018, 2021; Pickard, 2015; Webb, 2013). Moreover, by consistently introducing fun to all kinds of mundane organizational processes it can ultimately aid in changing employees' behaviour. This has been proven in practice, by numerous companies in various fields of activity, i.e in the IT (e.g. by Microsoft, IBM, Oracle, Adobe, SAP, Google, Cisco, Sun Microsystems, Siemens, Canon), health (e.g. L'Oreal), Automotive (e.g. Ford, Volkswagen, Lexus, Caterpillar), and services (e.g. Deloitte, Accenture, American Express, FedEx, UPS, British Gas, U.K.'s Department for Work and Pensions) sectors. However, in order to harness the full potential of gamification at work, game design, motivational psychology and management must be taken into account in combination (Morschheuser & Hamari, 2019). In essence, organizational gamified interventions should take into account both the characteristics of the application environment (context), as well as the participating employees' personality, and level of work engagement. Moreover, as the majority of these gamified experiences are nowadays enabled through the utilization of Information Systems, the characteristics of gamification, as well as the Information System that enables it should be examined hand-in-hand, to lead to its successful application, as well as effectiveness in producing measurable results.

According to existing definitions, Information Systems (IS) are considered as "combinations of hardware, software, and telecommunications networks" (Valacich J.S., & Schneider, 2018), working together as interrelated components "to collect, process, store, and disseminate information to support decision making, coordination, control, analysis, and viualization" in organizational settings (Laudon & Laudon, 2020). Gamified Information Systems are in turn IS that usually have the aim of enhancing "productivity through fun" (Koivisto & Hamari, 2019). Making IS visually rich and appealing, can provide pleasurable and enjoyable (hedonic) and overall, intrinsically motivating experiences. This has been the main driving force behind the Human-Computer Interaction (HCI) revolution that has taken place from the 1980s and on with the introduction of visually appealing characteristics in all the widely-used Operating Systems (OSs) and applications. In gamified IS, productivity and fun can essentially co-exist simultaneously (Chesney, 2006; Gerow, Ayyagari, Thatcher, & Roth, 2013; Sun & Zhang, 2018; Wu & Lu, 2018), in order to motivate users toward specific individually and collectively beneficial behaviours (Koivisto & Hamari, 2019). An example of such behaviours is the case of pro-environmental activities and specifically energy-conservation at work, where employees are called upon to collectively work towards the common good of the environment (and society in general). Moreover, numerous instantiations of gamified IS that have been utilized to motivate its users to conserve energy exist in the literature – e.g. (Böckle, Novak, & Bick, 2020; Fraternali et al., 2018; Kotsopoulos et al., 2019; Peham, Breitfuss, & Michalczuk, 2014).

Combining hedonic and utilitarian features in the design of organizational IS can generally increase the intention, motivation, and actual use by their end-users (Gerow et al., 2013; Jasperson et al., 2005; Webster & Martocchio, 1992). The hedonic dimension is regularly realized by utilizing elements from digital games – thus practicing "gamification" (Koivisto & Hamari, 2019). Gamification is considered as "a relatively new instrument in the orchestra of motivation, that offers a promising alternative to the strict corporate rules and policies that usually dictate the employees' conduct, by adhering to their intrinsic motivation" (Kotsopoulos, Bardaki, & Pramatari, 2016). As Self-Determination theory (SDT) posits (Deci, Connell, & Ryan, 1989), motivation at work lies along a continuum of forms that range from completely intrinsic to completely extrinsic. Intrinsically motivating tasks are performed out of the employees' "inner calling", while extrinsically motivating tasks out of a need to comply to obligatory rules. In such organizational environments, extrinsic (tangible) incentives need to be employed with caution as, when inappropriately utilized, they can decrease – or "crowd out" – employees' existing levels of intrinsic motivation (Blohm & Leimeister, 2013). In essence, by employing gamified IS at work, organizations have the opportunity to decrease their employees' resistance to comply to rules, by increasing their less-extrinsic forms of motivation, and moving their overall self-determination to perform a desired action closer to the intrinsic motivation end of the continuum. As this is fundamental for sustained long-term behavioural change (De Gloria *et al.*, 2014), it is also important for the designer of gamified IS to carefully select which game elements to use when designing gamification at work. In addition, acknowledging the teachings of Csikszentmihalyi's theory on "flow" (Csikszentmihalyi, 2009), gamification must also be designed to be appropriately challenging for all the users involved. Hence, the designer of a gamified IS should also take into consideration that, while very difficult challenges can lead the not-so-skilful employee to anxiety and frustration, very easy challenges can lead a very skilful person to boredom. In order to cover this issue, including, for instance, a number of different difficulty levels within a gamified IS can be considered. In sum, in order to successfully leverage the motivating power of gamified IS to engage employees towards manifesting a specific behaviour at work (such as energy-saving), the designer must bear in mind all the aforementioned intricacies of applying gamification in a workplace environment already presented.

EMPLOYING GAMIFIED IS FOR ENERGY CONSERVATION AT WORK

An increasing need to employ human-centred research methods (that focus on the desires and needs of the end-user) towards achieving energy conservation across different contexts, especially applying communication and persuasion methodologies to effect behavioural change, has arisen (Sovacool, 2014). Insight from existing user-centric application design methodologies – Agile, User-Centered Design (UCD), etc. – can be utilized towards that end. At the same time, with digital technologies rapidly changing, questions arise about how technology, behaviour, and policy will evolve over time, as well as how they will impact energy systems in the future (IEA Digitalization & Energy Working Group, 2017). Moreover, improving the operational efficiency of buildings by using real-time data (i.e. information that can be acquired and monitored in real time) is expected to lower total energy consumption (IEA Digitalization & Energy Working Group, 2017). In line with the above, with technological innovation creating new opportunities for energy efficiency and digitalization increasingly becoming impactful on the energy sector (IEA EEfD, 2017), the total public energy Research and Development (R&D) budget in International Energy Agency (IEA) countries has more than quadrupled, from 4% to 21% since the 1970s (IEA Energy Data Centre, 2017). It is estimated that this growing application of Information & Communication Technologies (ICT), and Internet-of-Things (IoT) technologies in energy systems could significantly cut energy use in buildings. More specifically, according to existing predictions, by utilising real-time data to improve operational efficiency, savings of as much as 10% can be achieved by 2040, (IEA Digitalization & Energy Working Group, 2017).

Providing feedback (to increase employees' awareness of their own behaviour and consequences), and training (to teach them how they can conserve energy), have been suggested as effective means for achieving energy conservation at work (Lo *et al.*, 2012). Such information-based experiments (i.e. scientifically organized behavioural interventions) have led to 7.4% energy conservation on average (Delmas *et al.*, 2013). Moreover, introducing gamification in such experiments, has led to reductions in energy consumption in the range of 3-6% recorded, with more than 10% achievable (Grossberg *et al.*, 2015). At the same time, the effectiveness of a number of serious games in improving energy-saving knowledge, behaviour and attitude have overall been positive (Fijnheer & Van Oostendorp, 2016). However, in a utilitarian setting, such as the workplace, engagement by gamification has been known to depend on both the employees' motivations and the nature of the gamified system (Hamari *et al.*, 2014). Therefore, as the system providing the gamified experience must be carefully designed to fit its target users' individual characteristics and preferences towards increasing motivation for specific behaviours (Uskov & Sekar, 2015; Werbach & Hunter, 2012), such gamified IS must be designed by considering their end-users' characteristics and preferences. In essence, although it has been generally recognized that gamification can provide an increase in energy-saving behaviour within organizations, the fact remains that in order to lead to energy saving through employees' behaviour, a gamified IS intervention must focus on increasing and sustaining employee´s motivation to conserve energy.

As games have a long history of being utilized at the workplace to introduce entertainment in boring and repetitive tasks, they also can be – and have been – utilized to promote real-world energy saving behaviour. The "EnergyLife" and the "Energy Battle" apps have introduced feedback, tips, challenges, ranking and rewards into energy-saving tasks (Gamberini et al., 2012; Geelen *et al.*, 2012). Gamification has also been employed to reduce elevator usage in "ClimbTheWorld" (Aiolli *et al.*, 2014), and "The Piano Stairs" (Matsumura *et al.*, 2015). Moreover, "Cool Choices", "WeSpire", "Ecoinomy", "Carbon-4Square", "Energic", "Charged", and "Entropy", have been used in workplace environments, with very

Figure 1. Interrelation Between Gamified IS and Energy-Savings at Work

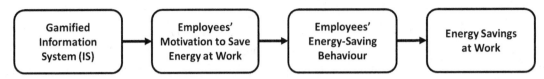

positive energy-saving results (Cool Choices, 2019; Energic, 2019; ENTROPY, 2019; Grossberg et al., 2015; Kotsopoulos et al., 2019; Papaioannou et al., 2018; WeSpire, 2019). All the forementioned are examples of the application of a gamified IS in real-world scenarios, that has led to energy conservation by its users, some of which including employees at their workplaces.

Based on the above, we deduce that, in essence, an interrelation exists between gamification (served through IS) – motivation to conserve energy – and employees' energy-saving behaviour at work. This interrelation fuels the drive to utilize gamified IS (gamification served through an enabling IS), that will increase employees' motivation to conserve energy, that will in turn lead to energy-conservation behaviour, and finally actual energy-savings at work. This relationship can be graphically reviewed in Figure 1.

Albeit their generally proven utility, it is widely acknowledged that existing energy game designs need to be further improved, in order to improve their behaviour change capabilities (Fijnheer & Van Oostendorp, 2016). Indeed, following a structured user-centred procedure (guided by the users' profiles and the application context) while designing energy-saving games and interventions has been proven to lead to improved usability and acceptance, and an overall positive user experience for employees (Kotsopoulos et al., 2018; Kotsopoulos et al., 2020). This is specifically important as the contextual characteristics in workplaces can determine the availability of different energy-saving actions to enact, as well as employees' game preferences (Kotsopoulos et al., 2017). In addition, different game scenarios may also need to be developed in special cases of public buildings, where the different categories of users feature widely different working conditions and routines, in order to optimally conserve energy (Kotsopoulos et al., 2019).

To further explain this notion, it is best to employ a practical example. Let's assume that, for example, a game designer is called upon to design a gamified IS featuring gamification in a hospital environment with the aim of conserving energy. Evidently, in such a complex working environment there would be different categories of users with different daily routines, work environments, and inherent opportunities for energy conservation therein. One category of employees would be working in the hospital's offices, on 8-hour shifts, seated in structured spaces, and operating their own electrical equipment (PCs, printers, copiers, lights, etc.). Another category would be working in the hospital kitchen, in rolling shifts, operating large – shared – appliances (hobs, ovens, friers, etc) as well as the kitchen lights (last one to go should turn the lights off to save energy). A third category would be performing the hospitals' main health aid activity – doctors and nurses – in a vastly dynamic environment where shifts are rolling and fluid according to the active cases treated, each worker circulates across the whole hospital premises according to the needs that arise, and dynamically operate electrical devices therein. As one can easily understand from this complex application scenario, the designer of a gamified IS aimed at energy conservation in such an environment, would in fact need to make sure that the designed system caters to all these categories of users at the same time. In order to do so, they would in fact need to make the system dynamically adaptable to the category of user that is using it, as well as context-aware, in order to understand where the system is being used in the premises. Different game design elements may also need to be employed accordingly, according to the application context, when designing gamified energy-saving IS at work, as already pointed out in previous examples within dynamic work environments, such as in (Kotsopoulos et al., 2018), where progression, levels, and points, were found to be most desirable by the end-users in order to compete in a gamified energy-saving competition through a mobile app.

Aspiring to support future researchers and practitioners in conducting successful implementations of gamification in workplaces for energy saving purposes, we elaborate further on the aforementioned insights reflecting our practical experience from past application of gamified systems in workplaces. On the one hand, when considering the adjustment of the organization and its employees to gamification, there may be some initial doubts or even fear present regarding the employees' privacy. Thus, before the application, a workshop that explains the usage and offerings would clear any doubts and make employees confident and reassured. Moreover, when it comes to usage of gamification and feedback from the gamified system, there should be a balance in order to not disturb the employees' regular work tasks. On the other hand, there may be some technical difficulties and cost-related challenges that the gamification experts should resolve. For example, a techno-economic feasibility study before the application of a gamified IS would help to realize the cost of the energy monitoring infrastructure (e.g. smart meters) that may be necessary for the accurate assessment of the energy usage and the combination with the employees' usage of the workplace devices. We should also highlight that the utilization of any infrastructure that monitors the employees moving in and out of offices (e.g. beacons) in order to realize whether they have e.g. turned off the lights, usually imposes technical difficulties and may not be easy to use after all. However, not utilizing such an infrastructure, would be in expense of the accuracy of the energy saving behaviours monitored. Regarding the change of the employees' energy usage behaviour, we stress that providing an external reward (e.g. one-day off for the week's winner) is an easy way "quick and dirty" way to achieve energy savings at work. However any savings achieved that way would cease shortly after the incentive is removed. The challenge becomes greater and needs further investigation when it comes to sustainable energy conservation behaviour that can be sustainable and hopefully become a habit. Finally, we note that employees seem to be disturbed by many notifications and continuous feedback; so, there should be a balanced portion of messages that either inform them of their progress or remind them to conserve energy. Overdoing it usually results in the employees either ignoring the feedback messages from the gamified IS, or completely opting-out from the behavioural intervention.

CONCLUSION

Gamification is a powerful tool that can be used within organizational environments, to achieve energy conservation through employees' behaviour change. The careful implementation of specially designed gamified Information Systems (IS), in order to materialize gamification, has been proven to effectively enable the interaction between employees and game elements, and lead to energy-saving at work. Furthermore, positive results regarding usability, user engagement and enjoyment have also been achieved. However, in order to achieve optimal results, such gamified IS employing gamification towards energy-saving at work must be designed by taking into account the employees' routines, game element preferences, and ambient environment.

Within this chapter, existing insight from the literature, as well as additional insight from our experience in designing and implementing gamified IS for energy conservation is accrued and presented. These various characteristics and parameters that need to be considered by both researchers and practitioners in their efforts to design and implement gamified IS towards energy-saving at work can be reviewed in Table 1.

Table 1. Guidelines for the Design & Implementation of Gamified IS towards increasing employees' motivation to conserve energy at work

Guidelines	Source
Design Guidelines	
Follow a structured user-centred procedure while designing energy-saving games and interventions, guided by the users' profiles and the application context, and focusing on their desires and needs	(Kotsopoulos et al., 2018, 2020; Sovacool, 2014)
Examine employees' motivations to participate in gamification, to discover the meant to increase their engagement	(Hamari *et al.*, 2014)
Design the gamified experience carefully to fit the end-users' individual characteristics and preferences (in the context of specific behaviours)	(Uskov & Sekar, 2015; Werbach & Hunter, 2012)
Design gamification to focus on increasing employees underlying motivation to conserve energy, instead of individual employees' energy-saving behaviours/actions	(Based on our experience)
Examine the contextual characteristics in workplaces, as they can determine the availability of different energy-saving actions to enact, as well as affect employees' game preferences	(Kotsopoulos et al., 2017)
Consider the need for different game scenarios to be developed in cases where different categories of users feature widely different working conditions and routines	(Kotsopoulos et al., 2019)
In dynamic work environments, make the system dynamically adaptable to the category of user that is using it, as well as context-aware – employ different game design elements accordingly, according to the application context	(Kotsopoulos et al., 2018)
Consider including progression, levels, and points to the gamified system before any other game elements	(Kotsopoulos et al., 2018)
Consider introducing feedback, tips, challenges, ranking and rewards into energy-saving tasks	(Gamberini et al., 2012; Geelen *et al.*, 2012)
Implementation Guidelines	
A gamified IS intervention must focus on increasing and sustaining employee's motivation to conserve energy	(Based on our experience)
Apply communication and persuasion methodologies to effect behavioural change	(Sovacool, 2014)
Use real-time data (i.e. information that can be acquired and monitored in real time) on energy consumption	(IEA Digitalization & Energy Working Group, 2017)
Provide feedback (to increase employees' awareness of their own behaviour and consequences), and training (to teach them how they can conserve energy)	(Lo *et al.*, 2012) (Delmas *et al.*, 2013)
Pay attention during the initial introduction of the gamified IS in an organization, as there may be some doubts or even fear regarding the employees' privacy	(Based on our experience)
Before the introduction of the gamified IS to a workplace, a workshop can be utilized to explain the usage and offerings of the system, increase employees' confidence in the system and reassure them of its purpose and functioning	
Utilize feedback messages from the system with caution, in order to not disturb the employees' work tasks – observe the purpose, quality, quantity and timing of any messages delivered by the system: There should be a balanced portion of messages that either inform them of their progress or remind them to conserve energy	
Conduct a techno-economic feasibility study before the introduction of the system at a workplace, also taking into account the cost of any accompanying infrastructure necessary to monitor energy consumption (e.g. smart meters)	
Consider the inclusion of an infrastructure that monitors employees' presence (e.g. beacons), to corroborate claimed energy-saving actions (e.g. whether they have actually turned off the lights as claimed), paying attention to both cost and privacy issues	
Consider providing an external reward (e.g. one-day off for the week's winner) as an easy and quick way to achieve energy-savings, but utilize with caution as it may impede on long-term (habitual) energy-saving motivation	

Future research should focus on further identifying and clarifying the characteristics that determine the effectiveness of a gamified IS towards energy saving at work. Moreover, a systematic literature review can shed more light into the specific characteristics that thus far been proven to lead to the successfulness of such systems in various organizational contexts.

REFERENCES

Aiolli, F., Ciman, M., Donini, M., & Ombretta, G. (2014). Serious Game to Persuade People to Use Stairs. In Persuasive 2014 Posters (pp. 11–13). Academic Press.

Blohm, I., & Leimeister, J. M. (2013). Gamification: Design of IT-based enhancing services for motivational support and behavioral change. *Business & Information Systems Engineering*, *5*(4), 275–278. doi:10.100712599-013-0273-5

Böckle, M., Novak, J., & Bick, M. (2020). Exploring gamified persuasive system design for energy saving. *Journal of Enterprise Information Management*, *33*(6), 1337–1356. doi:10.1108/JEIM-02-2019-0032

Chesney, T. (2006). An Acceptance Model for Useful and Fun Information Systems Utilitarian Dual Useless Recreational. *October, 2*(October), 225–235.

Cool Choices. (2019). *Employee Engagement Sustainability Game*. Retrieved February 14, 2019, from https://coolchoices.com/

Csikszentmihalyi, M. (2009). *Flow - The Psychology of Optimal Experience*. Harper Col. doi:10.5465/amr.1991.4279513

De Gloria, A., Bellotti, F., Berta, R., & Lavagnino, E. (2014). Serious Games for education and training. *International Journal of Serious Games*, *1*(1), 2384–8766. doi:10.17083/ijsg.v1i1.11

Deci, E. L., Connell, J. P., & Ryan, R. M. (1989). Self- determination in a work organization. *The Journal of Applied Psychology*, *74*(4), 580–590. doi:10.1037/0021-9010.74.4.580

Delmas, M. A., Fischlein, M., & Asensio, O. I. (2013). Information strategies and energy conservation behavior: A meta-analysis of experimental studies from 1975 to 2012. *Energy Policy*, *61*, 729–739. doi:10.1016/j.enpol.2013.05.109

Deterding, S., Sicart, M., Nacke, L., O'Hara, K., & Dixon, D. (2011). Gamification. using game-design elements in non-gaming contexts. *Proceedings of the 2011 Annual Conference Extended Abstracts on Human Factors in Computing Systems - CHI EA '11*, 2425. 10.1145/1979742.1979575

Endrejat, P. C., & Kauffeld, S. (2018). Can't get no satisfaction? Motivating organisational energy efficiency efforts in Germany. *Energy Research & Social Science*, *44*(May), 146–151. doi:10.1016/j.erss.2018.05.005

Energic. (2019). *Energic - Smart Energy Challenge*. Retrieved April 16, 2019, from https://www.energic.io/

ENTROPY. (2019). *ENTROPY - Design of an Innovative Energy-Aware IT Eco-System for Motivating Behavioural Changes towards the adoption of Energy Efficient Lifestyles.* Retrieved July 10, 2019, from https://entropy-project.eu/

Fijnheer, J. D., & Van Oostendorp, H. (2016). Steps to Design a Household Energy Game. *International Journal of Serious Games*, *3*(3), 12–22. doi:10.17083/ijsg.v3i3.131

Fraternali, P., Cellina, F., Herrera, S., Krinidis, S., Pasini, C., Rizzoli, A. E., ... Tzovaras, D. (2018). A Socio-Technical System Based on Gamification Towards Energy Savings. In *2018 IEEE International Conference on Pervasive Computing and Communications Workshops, PerCom Workshops 2018* (pp. 59–64). 10.1109/PERCOMW.2018.8480405

Gamberini, L., Spagnolli, A., Corradi, N., Jacucci, G., Tusa, G., Mikkola, T., . . . Hoggan, E. (2012). Tailoring feedback to users' actions in a persuasive game for household electricity conservation. Lecture Notes in Computer Science, 7284, 100–111. doi:10.1007/978-3-642-31037-9_9

Geelen, D., Keyson, D., Stella, B., & Brezet, H. (2012). Exploring the use of a game to stimulate energy saving in households - Journal of Design Research - Volume 10, Number 1–2/2012 - Inderscience Publishers. *Journal of Desert Research*, *10*, 102–120. doi:10.1504/JDR.2012.046096

Gerow, J. E., Ayyagari, R., Thatcher, J. B., & Roth, P. L. (2013). Can we have fun @ work? the role of intrinsic motivation for utilitarian systems. *European Journal of Information Systems*, *22*(3), 360–380. doi:10.1057/ejis.2012.25

Grossberg, F., Wolfson, M., Mazur-Stommen, S., Farley, K., & Nadel, S. (2015). *Gamified Energy Efficiency Programs.* Retrieved from https://www.climateaccess.org/sites/default/files/aceee.pdf

Hamari, J., Koivisto, J., & Sarsa, H. (2014). Does gamification work? - A literature review of empirical studies on gamification. *Proceedings of the Annual Hawaii International Conference on System Sciences*, 3025–3034. 10.1109/HICSS.2014.377

IEA Digitalization & the Energy Working Group. (2017). *Digitalization & Energy.* Retrieved from https://www.iea.org/digital/

IEA EEfD. (2017). Energy Efficiency 2017. *Energy Efficiency*, *2017*. Advance online publication. doi:10.1787/9789264284234-en

IEA Energy Data Centre. (2017). *Energy Technology RD&D Budgets: Overview.* Retrieved from https://www.iea.org/publications/freepublications/publication/EnergyTechnologyRDD2017Overview.pdf

International Energy Agency. (2016). *World Energy Outlook.* Author.

Jasperson, J., Carter, & Zmud. (2005). A Comprehensive Conceptualization of Post-Adoptive Behaviors Associated with Information Technology Enabled Work Systems. *Management Information Systems Quarterly*, *29*(3), 525–557. doi:10.2307/25148694

Koivisto, J., & Hamari, J. (2019). The rise of motivational information systems: A review of gamification research. *International Journal of Information Management*, *45*, 191–210. doi:10.1016/j.ijinfomgt.2018.10.013

Kotsopoulos, D., Bardaki, C., Lounis, S., Papaioannou, T., & Pramatari, K. (2017). Designing an IoT-enabled Gamification Application for Energy Conservation at the Workplace: Exploring Personal and Contextual Characteristics. In 30th Bled e-conference: Digital Transformation – From Connecting Things to Transforming Our Lives (pp. 369–383). University of Maribor Press. doi:10.18690/978-961-286-043-1.26

Kotsopoulos, D., Bardaki, C., Lounis, S., & Pramatari, K. (2018). Employee Profiles and Preferences towards IoT-enabled Gamification for Energy Conservation. *International Journal of Serious Games*, *5*(2), 65–85. doi:10.17083/ijsg.v5i2.225

Kotsopoulos, D., Bardaki, C., Papaioannou, T. G., Lounis, S., & Pramatari, K. (2018). Agile User-Centered Design of an Iot-Enabled Gamified Intervention for Energy Conservation. *IADIS International Journal on WWW/Internet, 16*(1), 1–25. Retrieved from http://www.iadisportal.org/ijwi/papers/2018161101.pdf

Kotsopoulos, D., Bardaki, C., Papaioannou, T. G., Lounis, S., Stamoulis, G. D., & Pramatari, K. (2019). Designing a Serious Game to Motivate Energy Savings in a Museum: Opportunities & Challenges. In *GALA 2019, LNCS 11899* (pp. 572–584). Springer. doi:10.1007/978-3-030-34350-7_55

Kotsopoulos, D., Bardaki, C., Papaioannou, T. G., Pramatari, K., & Stamoulis, G. D. (2020). User-Centered Gamification. *International Journal of E-Services and Mobile Applications*, *12*(2), 15–39. doi:10.4018/IJESMA.2020040102

Kotsopoulos, D., Bardaki, C., & Pramatari, K. (2016). Gamification, Geolocation and Sensors for Employee Motivation Towards Energy Conservation at the Workplace. In *Tenth Mediterranean Conference on Information Systems (MCIS) 2016* (pp. 1–11). Retrieved from https://aisel.aisnet.org/mcis2016/39

Laudon, K. C., & Laudon, J. P. (2020). *Management Information Systems: Managing the Digital Firm* (16th ed.). Pearson.

Lo, S. H., Peters, G. J. Y., & Kok, G. (2012). Energy-Related Behaviors in Office Buildings: A Qualitative Study on Individual and Organisational Determinants. *Applied Psychology*, *61*(2), 227–249. doi:10.1111/j.1464-0597.2011.00464.x

Matsumura, N., Fruchter, R., & Leifer, L. (2015). Shikakeology: Designing triggers for behavior change. *AI & Society*, *30*(4), 419–429. doi:10.100700146-014-0556-5

Morschheuser, B., & Hamari, J. (2019). The Gamification of Work: Lessons From Crowdsourcing. *Journal of Management Inquiry*, *28*(2), 145–148. doi:10.1177/1056492618790921

Nguyen, T. A., & Aiello, M. (2013). Energy intelligent buildings based on user activity: A survey. *Energy and Building*, *56*, 244–257. doi:10.1016/j.enbuild.2012.09.005

Papaioannou, T., Dimitriou, N., Vasilakis, K., Schoofs, A., Nikiforakis, M., Pursche, F., Deliyski, N., Taha, A., Kotsopoulos, D., Bardaki, C., Kotsilitis, S., & Garbi, A. (2018). An IoT-Based Gamified Approach for Reducing Occupants' Energy Wastage in Public Buildings. *Sensors (Basel)*, *18*(2), 537. doi:10.339018020537 PMID:29439414

Patrício, R., Moreira, A. C., & Zurlo, F. (2018). Gamification approaches to the early stage of innovation. *Creativity and Innovation Management*, *27*(4), 499–511. doi:10.1111/caim.12284

Patrício, R., Moreira, A. C., & Zurlo, F. (2021). Enhancing design thinking approaches to innovation through gamification. *European Journal of Innovation Management*, *24*(5), 1569–1594. doi:10.1108/EJIM-06-2020-0239

Peham, M., Breitfuss, G., & Michalczuk, R. (2014). The "ecoGator" app: gamification for enhanced energy efficiency in Europe. *Proceedings of the Second International Conference on Technological Ecosystems for Enhancing Multiculturality - TEEM '14*, 179–183. 10.1145/2669711.2669897

Pickard, T. (2015). *5 Statistics That Prove Gamification is the Future of the Workplace*. Retrieved February 27, 2016, from https://www.business.com/management/5-statistics-that-prove-gamification-is-the-future-of-the-workplace/

Schelly, C., Cross, J. E., Franzen, W. S., Hall, P., & Reeve, S. (2011). Reducing energy consumption and creating a conservation culture in organizations: A case study of one public school district. *Environment and Behavior*, *43*(3), 316–343. doi:10.1177/0013916510371754

Sovacool, B. K. (2014). What are we doing here? Analyzing fifteen years of energy scholarship and proposing a social science research agenda. *Energy Research & Social Science*, *1*, 1–29. doi:10.1016/j.erss.2014.02.003

Staddon, S. C., Cycil, C., Goulden, M., Leygue, C., & Spence, A. (2016). Intervening to change behaviour and save energy in the workplace: A systematic review of available evidence. *Energy Research & Social Science*, *17*, 30–51. doi:10.1016/j.erss.2016.03.027

Sun, H., & Zhang, P. (2018). Causal Relationships between Perceived Enjoyment and Perceived Ease of Use: An Alternative Approach. *Journal of the Association for Information Systems*, *7*(9), 618–645. doi:10.17705/1jais.00100

UNFCCC. (2014). *United Nations Framework Convention on Climate Change: Status of Ratification of the Kyoto Protocol*. Retrieved October 30, 2016, from http://unfccc.int/kyoto_protocol/status_of_ratification/items/2613.php

UNFCCC. (2016). *United Nations Framework Convention on Climate Change: Paris Agreement - Status of Ratification*. Retrieved November 30, 2016, from http://unfccc.int/2860.php

Uskov, A., & Sekar, B. (2015). Smart Gamification and Smart Serious Games. In Fusion of Smart, Multimedia and Computer Gaming Technology: Research, Systems and Perspectives (Vol. 84, pp. 7–36). Springer International Publishing. doi:10.1007/978-3-319-14645-4_2

Valacich, J. S., & Schneider, S. (2018). *Enhancing information system today: Managing in the digital world*. Pearson Education.

Webb, E. N. (2013). Gamification : When It Works, When It Doesn't. Lecture Notes in Computer Science, 8013(2), 608–614.

Webster, J., & Martocchio, J. J. (1992). Microcomputer Playfulness: Development of a Measure With Workplace Implications. *Management Information Systems Quarterly*, *16*(2), 201–227. doi:10.2307/249576

Werbach, K., & Hunter, D. (2012). *For The Win: How Game Thinking can revolutionize your business*. Wharton Digital Press, The Wharton School, University of Pensylvania.

WeSpire. (2019). *WeSpire - Employee Engagement Platform Powered by Behavioral Science.* Retrieved February 14, 2019, from https://www.wespire.com/

Wu, J., & Lu, X. (2018). Effects of Extrinsic and Intrinsic Motivators on Using Utilitarian, Hedonic, and Dual-Purposed Information Systems: A Meta-Analysis. *Journal of the Association for Information Systems, 14*(3), 153–191. doi:10.17705/1jais.00325

Chapter 16
Increasing Developer Awareness of Java Secure Coding in the Industry:
An Approach Ising Serious Games

Luís Afonso Maia Rosa Casqueiro
ISCTE, University Institute of Lisbon, Portugal

Tiago Espinha Gasiba
SIEMENS AG, Germany

Maria Pinto-Albuquerque
(iD) https://orcid.org/0000-0002-2725-7629
ISCTE, University Institute of Lisbon, Portugal

Ulrike Lechner
(iD) https://orcid.org/0000-0002-4286-3184
Universität der Bundeswehr München, Germany

ABSTRACT

Vulnerabilities in source code, when left unpatched, can potentially be exploited by a malicious party, resulting in severe negative consequences. These negative consequences can be significant if the vulnerable software is part of critical infrastructure. Previous studies, however, have shown that many software developers cannot recognize vulnerable code. One possible way to ameliorate the situation is by increasing software developers' awareness of secure programming techniques. In this chapter, the authors propose a serious game, the Java Cybersecurity Challenges, that presents secure programming challenges to the participants in a competitive scenario. They describe and analyze the tools required to implement these challenges and perform an empirical evaluation of the game with more than 40 software developers from the industry. The work contributes to the growing knowledge on the design of serious games and provides valuable information for industry practitioners who wish to deploy a similar game in their environment.

DOI: 10.4018/978-1-6684-4291-3.ch016

Figure 1. Number of Known Software Vulnerabilities

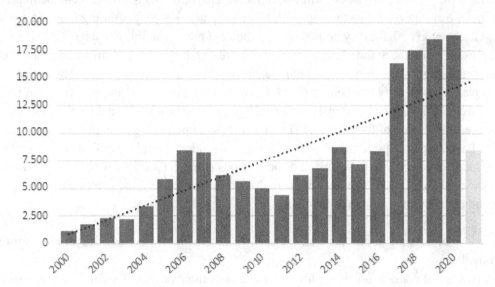

INTRODUCTION

Over the last years, the number of cybersecurity incidents has been steadily increasing. According to the United States Department of Homeland Security (US-CERT, 2020), more than 95% of security incidents find their cause in exploits against defects in the design or the code of the software, i.e., in software vulnerabilities. The increasing number of cyber security incidents also aligns with the increasing software vulnerabilities. Figure 1 shows the number of known software vulnerabilities reported and collected by the community-driven vulnerability database VulDB (VULDB, 2018).

Since 2000, the number of known software vulnerabilities has exceeded 170.000, whereby more than 121.000 vulnerabilities have been reported since 2011. Examples include ShellShock (Fireeye, 2014), StageFright (Golem, 2014), EternalBlue (MITRE, 2017), and Drupalgeddon (DreadLocked, 2018).

Patel et al. (Patel, 2019; Schneier, 2019) conducted a large-scale study with more than 4000 software developers. They found that more than 50% of software developers cannot spot vulnerabilities in source code. The increasing number of software vulnerabilities and security incidents is a serious problem for the industry, especially for critical infrastructures.

To address these issues, industrial IT security standards such as IEC 62.443 mandate the usage of secure coding guidelines through a secure software development lifecycle process. A possible way to comply with securing coding guidelines, which are widely used in the industry, is by using static application security testing (SAST) tools. However, these tools' reliability has shown to fall short of what is required. This is because these tools can produce many findings, leading to developer stress and fatigue, while this large number of results can also include false positives and negatives. Ultimately, it is up to the software developers to understand secure coding guidelines and to write and fix vulnerabilities in the source code. However, according to Patel et al. (Patel, 2019), Acar et al. (Acar, 2017), and Gasiba et al. (Gasiba et al., 2021), software developers lack awareness of secure coding and secure coding guidelines.

One possible way to address this lack of awareness is by utilizing a serious game that aims to raise awareness of secure coding guidelines through programming exercises. Gasiba et al. (Gasiba et al., 2021) introduced a serious game with a platform where secure programming challenges can be implemented. While in their work, they validate the approach for the C and C++ programming languages (Gasiba et al., 2021; Gasiba et al., 2020), they do not address the Java programming language.

In the present work, the authors extend the previous research by implementing and evaluating a serious game containing Java secure programming exercises in an industrial context. The authors call this game the Java CyberSecurity Challenges (JCSC). Furthermore, the automatic generation of hints using an intelligent coach is explored. The intelligent coach generates hints based on the vulnerabilities that are present in the source code of the exercise. The hints are generated using a simple artificial intelligence algorithm. They help and guide the players of the game to identify vulnerabilities in the code and fix them. The methodology used in the design of our serious game is based on Action Design Research as defined by (Sein et al., 2011). The work was conducted in the industry, using a three-cycle approach.

Our main contributions are the following:

1. Overview of existing tools that can be used to assess the vulnerabilities in Java source code automatically,
2. Discussion and considerations on how to implement the analysis of source code vulnerabilities, based on static and dynamic testing of Java source code,
3. Empirical evaluation of the usefulness of the serious game in an industrial setting, based on the feedback of more than 40 industrial software developers.

The present chapter is structured as follows. In the background section, the authors will discuss previous research relevant to our work. Ethical issues related to teaching and learning about secure coding will also be addressed. In the methodology section, the authors briefly describe the methodology used to conduct the research. Next, the used approach to raise awareness of Java secure coding of software developers in the industry through a serious game is presented. The authors discuss the serious game and look at tools that aid in implementing secure coding challenges while reporting on our field experience. The authors also discuss the automatic assessment of Java secure coding vulnerabilities. Finally, the implementation of an intelligent coach that generates hints through a simple artificial intelligence algorithm is presented. In the evaluation section, the authors assess the usefulness of the serious game in an industrial context. A description of the three design cycles that were conducted during the Action Design Research project is given as well as a discussion on the lessons learned from each design cycle. In the future research section, the authors discuss possible next steps, and in the conclusion section, the authors provide a summary and overview of the present work.

BACKGROUND

Serious games and gamification techniques are gaining more and more traction in the research community and have been used more and more to change the behavior and attitudes of participants. Dörner et al. (Dörner et al., 2016) define a Serious Game as a game designed to entertain and with at least one additional goal (e.g., learning). Due to their nature, these games are well suited to raise awareness of cyber security.

Recently, there has been a steady stream of literature exploring serious games and gamification to raise awareness of certain cyber security topics. Frey et al. (Frey et al., 2019) show the potential impact playing cyber security games can have on the participants and show the importance of playing games as means of cyber security awareness. Their study concludes that cyber security games can be useful to build a common understanding of security issues among the game participants.

Simões et al. (Simões et al., 2020) present a game where several programming exercises are used to teach software programming in academia. Their design includes nine exercises that are presented to students, foster students' motivation and engagement in academic classes, and increase their learning outcomes. Their approach uses tools to perform an automatic assessment of submitted solutions to exercises. It focuses on the correct solution of the programming exercise in terms of functionality, not on secure programming and security best practices. Vasconcelos et al. (Vasconcelos et al., 2020) show a method to evaluate programming challenges automatically. The authors use Haskell and the QuickCheck library to perform automated functional unit tests of students' submitted solutions to the programming exercises. Their goal is to evaluate if the students' solutions comply with the intended functionality, but their work does not address the topic of cyber security. Kucek et al. (Kucek et al., 2020) provide an overview of games based on the capture-the-flag genre. They look at the games' features and functionalities, challenge types, and configuration. Their article surveys 28 existing platforms and conducts an in-depth analysis of eight of them. The in-depth analysis is conducted on the platforms that are available as open source. Their study gives a good overview of existing platforms, classifies them, and provides practical advice for those who wish to host such an event.

Most of the previous work has been carried out in an academic setting and thus might not immediately apply to the industry. While many authors assume that the success of using and deploying these types of games, this success is generally not guaranteed. Barela et al. (Barela et al., 2019) have reported on a non-successful trial of a competitive game carried out in an industrial context. While their game was supposed to raise awareness of information technology security policies, the participants mostly overlooked the security lessons of the exercises. They focused on quickly finishing the game and collecting points.

The design of a serious game does not guarantee its success. Landers has shown that care needs to be taken to distinguish between legitimate and rhetorical gamification elements to realize the game potential fully (Landers, 2019). Although the literature distinguishes between gamification and serious games, the same author also establishes a link between these two (Landers, 2014).

Further work that supports and emphasizes the link between gamification, learning, design-thinking and co-creation of solutions is provided by Patricio, Moreira, and Zurlo (2021) and Patricio, Moreira, Zurlo, and Melazzini (2020). In their work, the authors show how gamification can lead to improved approaches to design and how participants in the games can improve their co-creation process – both important aspects of software development.

Recognizing that serious games need to be properly designed to realize their intended purpose, Gasiba et al. (2019) explore the design requirements of serious games geared toward software developers in an industrial context. The authors provide fifteen game design requirements, which are based on a literature review and on information obtained directly from software developers in the industry that participated in several gaming events. The work carried out by the author, from 2019 to 2021, which included several additional publications, has shown not only the requirements needed to design this type of serious game but also how it is perceived by software developers and managers in the industry. The seminal work by Gasiba is available in (Gasiba et al., 2021). The present research was carried out during the work and research by Gasiba and extends it to the field of the Java programming language.

Figure 2. Action Design Research Methodology

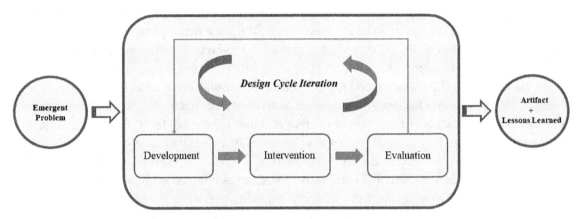

In the present work, the authors address the proper design of the serious game for Java software developers using a well-established research methodology – Action Design Research (Sein et al., 2011). This design methodology will be briefly discussed in the method section.

ETHICAL CONSIDERATIONS

In the existing stream of literature, there are typically two approaches to teaching cyber security: offensive and defensive. An offensive approach is an offensive technique to raise awareness of potential security vulnerabilities. These techniques include breaking into systems, reverse engineering, and exploiting software and systems. The danger of teaching offensive techniques is that with the knowledge gained, these can be misused to carry out malicious attacks on real systems. Therefore, while offensive techniques are appropriate for penetration testers and security researchers, the authors argue that defensive techniques are more appropriate or better suited for all the other participants.

In the present work, our developed game focuses on the defensive perspective, i.e., the participants in the game learn how to develop software that does not contain vulnerabilities instead of learning attacking techniques.

Additionally, the evaluation of our game which was carried out during the three design cycles, consisted of participants answering a small survey. All the answers to the survey were collected anonymously, and there are no specific indicators that would allow for the identification of each participant. Furthermore, all the participants that took part in the study were informed and aware of the research that was being conducted.

METHODOLOGY

The present work followed the Action Design Research (ADR) methodology introduced by (Sein et al., 2011). Figure 2 depicts a simplified view of this methodology. Firstly, the authors encounter an emergent problem present in an organizational context. After defining the initial scope of the project, a series of iterative cycles will occur. These cycles intend to develop, test, and evaluate the artifact in an industry setting. This methodology allows for a continuous improvement of the artifact throughout its effective development life cycle. The result is a more tested and complete final product that is both based on the first intent of the authors and molded by the testing in an organizational setting. The authors also obtain a set of lessons learned based on the distinct iterations of the ADR methodology. There are seven distinct principles inherent to any ADR methodology-based work. These principles are engrained in the stages of the ADR methodology and intend on justifying the artifact and expressing the underlying values, assumptions, and beliefs. From the seven principles that can be applied to ADR research, the authors choose to highlight the three that better fit the present work. The first is *Practice-Inspired Research*. This principle addresses the basis on which the research is conducted, and the artifact is improved. The data used to continuously improve the artifact in the iterative process of the ADR is collected through practical interventions. This guarantees the relevancy of the gathered data and that the research conducted is inspired by the results from the practical application of the concepts and testing of the artifact in an industry setting.

The second principle that applies to the research is the *Theory-Ingrained Artifact*. This principle states that the development of the artifact is based on existing theories and previously conducted research. Furthermore, the final artifact will apply and reflect these theories, leading to more complete and legitimate research.

The last ADR principle applied to our research is *Guided Emergence*. This principle states that the final artifact is not only a product of the initial design done by us, heavily based on theory but also all the changes applied due to the continuous testing and refinement along the project's life cycle. Likewise, the final artifact developed in the present research is not only based on the initial design but also on all the changes that were introduced after the iterative process of testing the artifact in an industry context. This principle allows researchers to adjust and introduce the design concepts of the artifact.

As previously described, the present work had three distinct ADR cycles. The first tested an initially designed artifact to obtain a proof of concept on which the research could be based. The second cycle focused on refining the artifact by encompassing the feedback given by the first testing stage. The third and final cycle focused on the final improvements of the artifact to meet the requirements and observations made in the previous testing stages.

JAVA CYBERSECURITY CHALLENGES

Being one of the most famous programming languages of all time, Java is used by billions of devices and users every day around the world. However, Java is among the top three programming languages with the most known open-source vulnerabilities (Rayome, 2019). To increase the awareness of Java software developers in the industry about these vulnerabilities, this research used a serious game approach. Our serious game, Java Cybersecurity Challenges (or JCSC), incorporates several distinct security challenges to raise awareness of different security issues. The JCSC is based on the capture-the-flag, or CTF, type of event.

When completed, each challenge gives the player a flag that is then converted to points when entering the JCSC dashboard. Although the JCSC has its roots in CTF type of events, several distinctions exist between standard CTFs and the serious game developed in the present work. A common CTF event focuses on the attack perspective of security vulnerabilities. The players are required to have some type

Figure 3. Java Cybersecurity Challenges (JCSC)

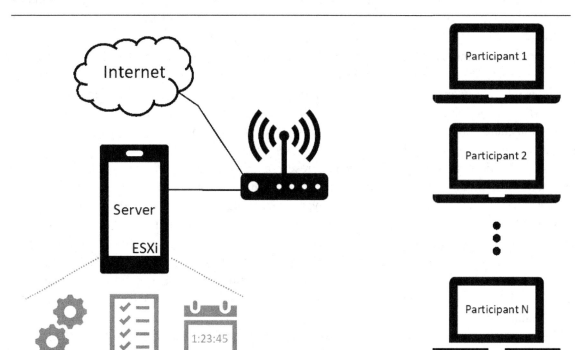

of previous knowledge and experience in hacking and hacking tools alike, to participate in these events. When a player enters a CTF type of competition, his or her main goal is to get the most points to win. Our serious games differ by focusing on the software developers and the knowledge they can retain after the event. This means that the main purpose of the game is not to get the highest score possible, although it has this angle of competition, but to try and raise the developer's awareness of security issues. Our challenges focus on a defensive perspective instead of the offensive one commonly applied in CTF events. The authors adopted a more defensive approach since this exercise has been shown to work well among software developers. Moreover, each challenge represents a real-world example of insecure code so that the participants can understand the underlying problem without requiring previous experience with security issues or hacking tools and mechanisms. By applying real-life software development scenarios, the SIFU platform aims at educating developers on potential security threats and providing them with hands-on experience in a controlled environment where they can safely learn how to mitigate these issues.

Figure 3 shows the architecture of a usual JCSC event. The event itself is a one-day workshop that consists of five different stages, (1) Introduction to Infrastructure, (2) Example of Challenges, (3) Main Event, (4) Winner Announcement, and (5) Discussions and Feedback. Firstly, the event starts by briefly introducing the coaches, the platform, and the dashboard. This first stage gives the participants a brief tutorial on correctly handling the different aspects of the game and is also used as a team creation step. After the players are divided into teams and introduced to the general infrastructure, the coaches explain how teams should approach the different challenges and usually solve one to give a brief explanation to all

Figure 4. Players Initial Perspective of a Java Challenge

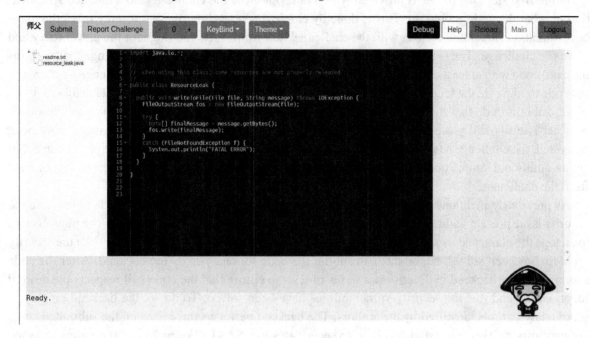

the teams. The main event stage takes up most of the time of the workshop, and it is where teams are free to solve the challenges. During this stage, the coaches monitor the teams and will intervene either when a team has a question or if someone is stuck. After the main event is completed, the coaches announce the winner corresponding to the team with more points. The workshop finalizes with a feedback round on what the platform does well, possible improvements, and where the teams had the most difficulty. In this final stage, and according to the teams' interests, individual solutions applied by each team can be compared, and general solutions can be shown with an explanation of how it works.

JAVA CYBERSECURITY CHALLENGES IN THE SIFU PLATFORM

Figure 4 shows the initial perspective of a player when first opening a Java challenge. The programmable challenges have three major steps, (1) Challenge Description, (2) Main Challenge, and (3) Conclusion, as shown in Figure 5.

Figure 5. Challenge Sequence

In the first step, the player is provided with a description of the challenge and a detailed specification of what the code should do. This is done by employing a readme file that usually takes the name of readme.txt. This initial contact with the challenge' description sets the stage for the player to try and solve the challenge. The second step provides the player with a programmable challenge that contains insecure code with at least one security vulnerability. The player tries to solve the challenge by changing the code to mitigate the security vulnerabilities while interacting directly with the SIFU platform. If the player submits code that still has security issues, the Intelligent Coach will provide hints and feedback on what issue is still present to aid the player in solving the challenge. Once the issue(s) have been mitigated, the challenge advances to the final step. After completing the challenge, the player can either get an additional simple question or a brief description that aims at cementing the learnings obtained from the challenge.

As previously mentioned, it is the player's job to improve the provided source code to mitigate the security issue present without compromising the required functionality of the exercise. The player is free to change the class, and its methods, in any way he or she desires. When the player feels like the security problem has been solved, he, or she, can submit the code for analysis by the backend. After the code submission, the backend will perform a series of tests to ensure that the code still respects the desired functionality and that the security vulnerabilities have been solved. To do so, the backend employs a set of analysis tools identified by the authors. The backend performs three tests on the submitted code, security tests, unit tests, and static application security testing (SAST). For each type, the authors selected tools due to their capability to answer the testing needs.

Table 1. Backend Analysis Tools

Tool	Security Test	SAST	Unit Test	Reference
JUnit			●	(Beck, Gamma, Saff, & Vasudevan, s.d.)
SonarQube		●		(SonarSource, s.d.)
FB-Infer		●		(Facebook, s.d.)
SpotBugs		●		(Pugh & Hovemeyer, s.d.)
PMD		●		(David Dixon-Peugh, s.d.)
Byteman	●			(Andrew Dinn, s.d.)
Self-Developed Code	●		●	(Pugh & Hovemeyer, s.d.; David Dixon-Peugh, s.d.)

Table 1 shows t he different types of testing as well as the tools applied for each one. For security testing and unit testing, the game employs JUnit together with custom-developed tests. For SAST the authors employed three SAST tools: FB-Infer, SpotBugs, and PMD. SonarQube was discarded due to its low execution speed.

AUTOMATIC VULNERABILITY ASSESSMENT

The backend follows the three-stage process present in Figure 6. After the player submits the code, the backend will enter stage one (S1). In this stage, the backend will inject, when needed, extra functional-

Figure 6. Java Cybersecurity Challenges Security Assessment

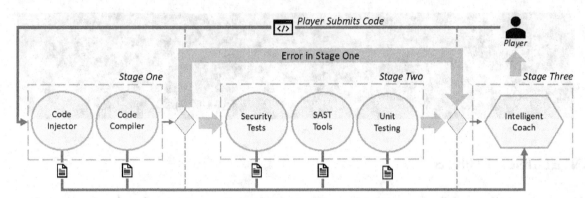

ities into the player's submitted code. These functionalities can be in the form of extra methods, import statements, function decorators, etc. After this step, the code (submitted + injected) is compiled by the backend. If the compilation is not successful, the code has a critical error, and so the process jumps from S1 to S3. The player is given feedback according to the critical compiler error encountered. This means that if the code encounters an error in S1, no code analysis is performed. This is because compiled code is required to run the unit tests. If both the steps in S1 are successful, then the process advances normally into stage two (S2).

In this stage, the Security Tests are performed, followed by the SAST Analysis and Unit testing. After completing these steps, the process advances into the final stage (S3). This stage will have as input the reports originating from every step of the previous stages. The analysis reports contain all the findings from the previous steps. Each report contains parameters such as a PASS or FAIL value, a Common Weakness Enumeration (CWE) given by (MITRE), and Priority. The incoming reports follow a predetermined normalized structure in JSON format (Crockford). Note that a normalization step is required to convert the tools' reports into the JSON report format.

Figure 7. Tool Generated Findings

```
"bug_type": "RESOURCE_LEAK",
"qualifier": "resource of type 'java.io.FileOutputStream' acquired by call to 'FileOutputStream(...)' at line 9 is not released after line 13.",
"severity": "ERROR",
"line": 13,
"column": -1,
"procedure": "resource_leak.createsFile(java.io.File,java.lang.String):void",
"procedure_start_line": 8,
"file": "resource_leak.java ,
```

When submitting the code contained in Figure 4, the tool in the backend generates a report, as presented in Figure 7. The corresponding normalized report is shown in Figure 8. This normalization process occurs after each tool is done with the code analysis.

The intelligent coach provides hints to the player based on these normalized reports. If all reports are PASS, the challenge is concluded; otherwise, the hint generation algorithm provides the player with an adequate hint.

Figure 8. Normalized Findings

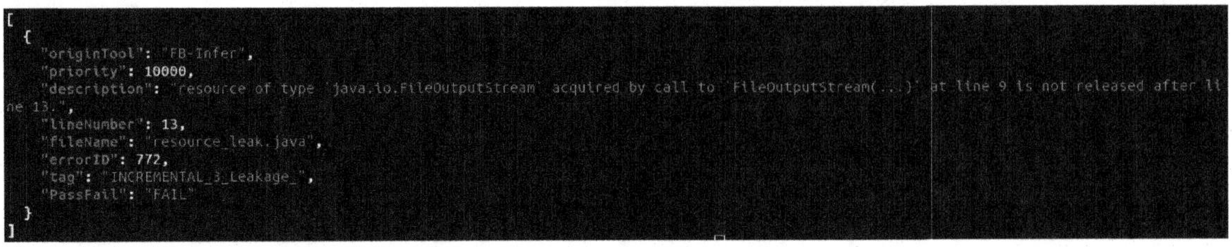

```
[
  {
    "originTool": "FB-Infer",
    "priority": 10000,
    "description": "resource of type `java.io.FileOutputStream` acquired by call to `FileOutputStream(...)` at line 9 is not released after li
ne 13.",
    "lineNumber": 13,
    "fileName": "resource_leak.java",
    "errorID": 772,
    "tag": "INCREMENTAL_3_Leakage_",
    "PassFail": "FAIL"
  }
]
```

INTELLIGENT HINTS

The Intelligent Coach (IC), representing the third and final stage of the backend analysis, generates hints to the player. Hints are only provided when the submitted code contains issues regarding the security or the functionality of the code. Figure 9 presents details of the decision graph undertaken by the intelligent coach. Notice that the challenge is finished if no compiler issues are found, functional tests pass, and no vulnerabilities are found in the code. If the Functional Tests fail, then the IC gives feedback on the specific functionality the player is not respecting. If the submitted code has security issues and reported CWEs, the process will instead go to the hint generation algorithm. This straightforward process picks one of the CWEs and gives the player hints on how to improve this security aspect of the code. Once the process enters this algorithm, the first step is to check for the previous history of the challenge. By having a prior history of the challenge, the IC can check what problems the player has faced in earlier submissions and avoid giving hints related to other problems that might have arisen. If the challenge does not have a previous history, then the selected CWE, on which the hint will be based, is the highest ranked CWE of the currently detected CWEs. However, if the previous history of the challenge exists, the IC will perform an interception between the currently detected CWEs and the previous ones. Following this, the IC will check whether the interception is empty. If so, this means that the previously detected security issues have been solved, and the hints must only be based on the current CWEs. This means that the IC will once again select the highest ranked CWE among the currently detected CWEs. In the case where the interception is not empty, then this means that the player is still trying to solve the security issue detected previously. So, the hint must be more precise and concrete when compared to the previously given one. To do this, the IC will choose the CWE by checking the highest ranked CWE on the interception list. After the selection of the CWE is done, the IC will apply the laddering technique, and from there, the hint is given to the player. The ranking of the CWEs was performed based on our own experience in cybersecurity. Once the CWE is chosen, the process advances to the laddering technique. This process will generate hints and give them to the player. The technique was not developed to solve issues in the presented field of study. However, the approach can be adapted into a proper hint selection system, so the authors believe it to be a good method to employ in the developed artifact. This system is based on different ladders that contain a sequence of hints. Each ladder is mapped to a certain CWE and is defined by different levels. Each level has a distinct hint that can be provided to the player. Once the Intelligent Coach chooses a CWE, the laddering technique will choose the ladder mapped to the intended and selected CWE. Once the ladder is selected, the Intelligent Coach must determine which hint present on the ladder will be shown to the player. This is determined by the number of times the player has submitted code containing the same vulnerability. If a player has performed two code submissions containing the same security issue, then the hint provided will be the one present on the second level of the corresponding ladder. Each hint present in a ladder has a level of specificity. Each ladder can be defined by a spectrum that ranges from lower-level hints, which tend to be more generic, to higher-level ones that will provide the player with a concrete answer or approach on how to solve the issue at hand.

Figure 9. Intelligent Coach's Algorithm

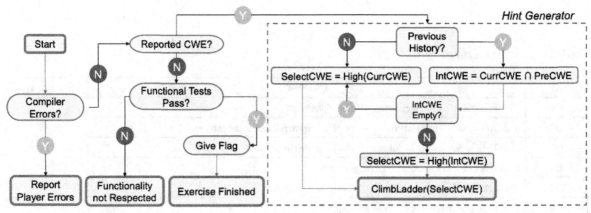

Table 2. Ladder Example

Ladder Level	Description
Level 1	CWE 180 - The software validates input before it is canonicalized, which prevents the software from detecting data that becomes invalid after the canonicalization step.
Level 2	Should you match the pattern directly with the input string, or should you perform operations on the string beforehand?
Level 3	I think there is a method that transforms Unicode text into the standard normalization forms, you should try and use it!
Level 4	Here's a hint, you should Normalize the string! This step is very important!
Level 5	The untrusted input is not being Normalized before the validation. Input strings given by untrusted users must always be Normalized. The following link shows the correct Normalization of a string – <link>

Table 2 shows an example of a ladder that is related to CWE 180. Notice that with increasing levels, the hints become more and more specific. This helping aspect of the SIFU platform distinguishes it from common CTF events. The hint generation process is repeated until the player solves the vulnerability. When the player successfully solves the issue, the challenge can be finished (the player has secured the code and is presented with a flag), or it has other vulnerabilities that still need to be addressed. So, the process repeats with a different CWE.

EXPERIENCE

This section describes the focus of each research cycle, the interventions performed to evaluate the developed artifact, and the lessons learned. The results of each cycle emerged from the distinct interventions performed and were gathered through a survey containing 16 questions. Of these 16 questions, 15 were based on a 5-point Likert Scale (Wieringa, 2019), and the remainder were open questions. Table 3 shows the survey questions.

Table 3. Survey Questions

ID	Question	Response Type
Q1	How to do rate the overall experience with the platform?	LS
Q2	The error messages and hints issued by the platform are relevant to the exercise.	
Q3	I can learn secure coding by solving the challenges in the platform.	
Q4	I can relate the hints to the code I have written.	
Q5	The hints provided by the platform make sense to me.	
Q6	It is fun to play the coding exercises in this platform.	
Q7	I like to play the exercises in this platform.	
Q8	If I am given the opportunity, I would like to play more exercises.	
Q9	The hints I have received, helped me to understand the problem with the code I have written.	
Q10	Playing the exercises makes me more aware of security vulnerabilities in Java code	
Q11	I have learned new threats that can result from vulnerabilities in Java code through playing the exercises	
Q12	I feel compelled to improve the security of my code in the future	
Q13	I have learned new mechanisms to avoid vulnerabilities in Java code	
Q14	Would you change the name of the challenge, to hide the issue with the code?	OQ
Q15	What would you suggest changing or improving in the platform?	
Q16	What do you think the platform does good?	

LS: Likert Scale, *OQ*: Open Question

Figure 10. Non-Compliant Code of Initial Java Challenge

```
import java.io.*;

public class ResourceLeak {
    public void writeToFile(File file, String msg) throws IOException {
        FileOutputStream fos = new FileOutputStream(file);
        fos.write(msg.getBytes());
    }
}
```

First Cycle – Proof of Concept

Development

The first cycle served as a proof of concept. In this cycle, the authors created an Initial Java Challenge, which was based on the resource leakage issue of the Java programming language, as shown in Figure 10.

This code is insecure since it fails to honor the FIO04-J rule (SEI) of the SEI-CERT coding standards. The vulnerability occurs because the FileOutputStream (fos) is never closed. The exploitation of this vulnerability can lead to a denial-of-service attack. There are two possible solutions to this vulnerability that respect the guidelines for secure coding of the SEI-CERT ruleset (SEI). The first is to employ a try-catch-finally block to ensure that every time the program exits this block of code, the stream is closed. Figure 11 shows the correct way to mitigate the resource leakage problem using this method.

Figure 11. Compliant Solution Using the try-catch-finally Approach

```
import java.io.*;

public class ResourceLeak {

    public void writeToFile(File file, String msg) throws IOException {

        FileOutputStream fos = new FileOutputStream(file)
        try{
            fos.write(msg.getBytes());
        }catch(Exception e){
            //Handle Exception
        }finally{
            fos.close();
        }
    }
}
```

Figure 12. Compliant Solution Using the try-with-resources Approach

```
import java.io.*;

public class ResourceLeak {

    public void writeToFile(File file, String msg) throws IOException {

        try(FileOutputStream fos = new FileOutputStream(file)){
            fos.write(msg.getBytes());
        }catch(Exception e){}

    }
}
```

The second way to mitigate this vulnerability, as shown in Figure 12, is to employ a try-with-resources block. This approach has been introduced in Java since version 7 of the programming language (Oracle).

The version of the FBInfer tool employed in the analysis process resulted in a False Positive on the case of try-with-resources. To mitigate this problem, the authors could either wait for an update of the tool in question or, if any player encountered this error, he or she would be awarded the corresponding flag. In the first design, the authors applied the latter. The detection mechanism was improved in the second design cycle.

Intervention

After the Initial Java Challenge was working according to the authors' expectations, an intervention with both software developers and university students was held. This first intervention was held from 22 to 27 February 2021 through online meetings. Each meeting had a duration of 30 minutes and was divided into two main events. In the first 20 minutes, the participants were given the challenge and were free to test the platform in any way they desired. The last 10 minutes of each meeting were saved for a small unstructured individual interview where participants could give their opinions on the concept, the platform, the challenge design, and its functionality. A total of 11 participants took part in this first intervention. Of the 11 participants, nine worked in the industry, and two were senior students in a programming-related university course. The participants tested the challenge and the platform, and, at the end of the meeting, they were asked to fill out the previously described survey.

Evaluation

This first cycle was performed to validate the idea, i.e., whether the participants find the artifact and concept as a good approach to learning cybersecurity. From the survey, a sub-set of questions can be highlighted to provide us with the results directly linked to the goal in mind. This initial sub-set is composed by a total of seven questions, Q.1, Q.3, Q.6, Q.7, Q.8, Q.10 and Q.11 and the results are shown in Figure 13.

Figure 13. First Cycle - Results of the Proof-of-Concept

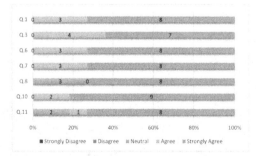

Analyzing the results of Q.1, the authors can highlight that the participants had an overall good experience playing on the platform. Furthermore, this question gathered positive results, with 27.3% of participants rating the experience a 4/5 on the Likert Scale, and the remainder 72.7% rating it as a

5/5. In addition, questions Q.3, Q.10, and Q.11 show that the participants find the defensive challenge approach as a good means of learning secure coding and how to deal with cybersecurity issues. These three questions showed overwhelmingly positive results. In Q.3, all the answers gathered relating to the corresponding statement were either agree, with 36.4%, or strongly agree, with 63.6%.

Moreover, in Q.10, the answers showed an even majority for strongly agree, with 81.8%, and the remainder results, 18.2%, for agree. Finally, Q.11, had a total of 9.1% of participants agreeing with the sentence, 72.7% strongly agreeing with the statement, and 18.2% neutral answers. The results from Q.6 and Q.7 mirror each other and shows that the participants either agree with the statement, with 27.3%, or strongly agree, with 72.7%. Finally, Q.8 shows that about 73% of the participants would like to play more exercises if given the opportunity. However, 27% are not completely sure and gave neutral answers to this statement. The authors also collected valuable input from the semi-structured interview conducted with each participant. Some relevant comments from the participants include:

"Very practical tool, the instant feedback helps a lot. The hints are a bit underdeveloped"

"Better than mainstream environments because it also tests the code for security issues"

"Had no idea that this was a security issue and now I know how to solve it."

Discussion

Our initial results suggest that the participants enjoy and welcome this exercise. Our results align with previous similar studies and served as validation and encouragement to carry out the platform's development. In this phase, the authors collected feedback related to the hints generated by the platform. Although the static feedback was helpful, some participants stated that the hints could be further developed.

From the data collected, no possible distinction can be made between results from the industry and those gathered from academia. Furthermore, since most results were positive in nature, the authors can hypothesize that a possible positive bias could have occurred. However, if this is the case, the authors do not believe it to have any major implications for the main conclusions of the work.

Although most participants were from an industry setting, the authors theorize that the same method for raising security awareness can also be applied in an academic context. However, previous programming experience is required to understand and learn the intended subject fully.

A preliminary version of this work was published and presented in ICPEC 2021 – 2nd International Computer Programming Education Conference on the 28th of May 2021.

Second Cycle

Development

The main goal of this cycle was to improve the backend analysis process. This research cycle was conducted as part of an awareness campaign embedded in an industry context. Towards this, three additional challenges were developed. Each challenge highlighted at least one different security. Table 4 shows the challenges used in this cycle.

Table 4. Developed Java Challenges

Challenge	SEI-CERT rule	Priority	Level of Complexity	Mapped CWE
Resource Leakage	*FIO04-J*	*4*	*Low*	*772*
File Creation	*FIO50-J*	*8*	*Medium*	*367*
String Normalization	*IDS01-J*	*12*	*Medium*	*180*
Privileged Blocks	*SEC01-J / FIO00-J*	*27*	*High*	*266*

During the development of each challenge, SAST tools were used to identify security vulnerabilities. However, some tools took an undesirable amount of time, e.g., more than 10 seconds, when analyzing the code. This high delay was considered unacceptable, as it interfered with the platforms' interactivity. Therefore, analyses like code best practices and naming conventions were disabled to make the security analysis of the code more efficient. These were disabled in PMD, SpotBugs, and SonarQube. Most of these tools responded well to this change and each specific analysis time diminished considerably. Disabling non-essential analysis, the time decreased to less than 2 seconds. However, SonarQube, did not sufficiently improve the running time of its analysis and was therefore disabled completely.

Custom rules were created to flag vulnerabilities not supported by the current versions of the SAST tools. These custom rules were based on and developed following the developer guide of the PMD and Spotbugs. Complementing these rules, a set of unit and security tests were created to strengthen the analysis results further.

In this development cycle, the hint system was improved to provide the player with two different types of feedback, as shown in Figure 14.

Figure 14. Hints Provided in the Present Cycle

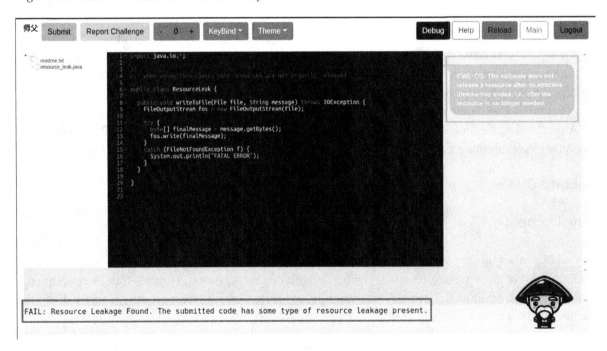

Every time the player submits the code for analysis, he receives overall feedback, as shown in the rectangle. The second type of feedback, in the blue rectangle, consists of a general hint explaining the security error. The generic messages are obtained from the CWE description of the corresponding security vulnerability.

Intervention

An industry-focused workshop was held to test the challenges and the platform. This workshop was included in the practical exercises section of an internal security training program in an industry context. This training was conducted on 22 March 2021 from 9 a.m. to 16 p.m. through an online meeting. In total, 15 participants were present in the training. At the end of the workshop, the participants were asked to fill out the previously described survey related to the challenges. A small collective interview with ten participants was also conducted to get an overall perspective and comments about the platform and its challenges.

Evaluation

Comparing the results of the sub-set analyzed in the proof-of-concept cycle (Q.1, Q.3, Q.6, Q.7, Q.8, Q.10, and Q.11), the authors can identify similarities in the results. In this cycle, this sub-set of questions gave the most positive answers, either agree or strongly agree. Figure 15 shows the results gathered in this cycle by this sub-set of questions.

Figure 15. Cycle Two - Results from Initial Sub-set of Questions

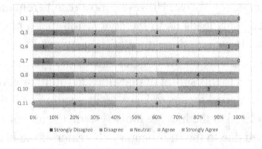

Figure 16. Cycle Two - Hint Related Results

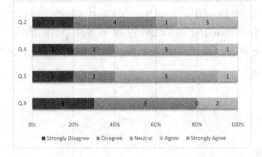

The results from the questions relating to the hints & hint system can also be analyzed. This sub-set of questions, presented in Figure 16, is composed of four statements, Q.2, Q.4, Q.5, and Q.9. In Q.2 the authors can recognize fewer positive results. Of the 10 participants that answered the survey, only 3, 30%, agreed with the statement. Furthermore, the remaining 7 participants either gave neutral answers (10%), disagreed (40%), or strongly disagreed (20%). Q.4 and Q.5 had the same results and showed that only one participant (10%) gave positive feedback and agreed. The rest of the results are composed of neutral answers (50%), disagree (20%), and strongly disagree (20%). Lastly, in Q.9, two participants (20%) agreed with the statement, and the remainder 8 participants (80%) either gave a disagree answer (50%) or strongly disagreed (30%).

In addition, feedback was also provided by the participants in the interview part of the workshop. In general, participants gave very similar feedback, and some recorded examples are as follows:

"It is an interesting and fun approach to learning cybersecurity."

"The hints should be a bit more worked on and specific."

"I had fun while playing, but I kept receiving generic hints that weren't really helpful."

Discussions

The results collected show two major findings. Firstly, the players find the programming challenges approach a good method to learn secure coding. By comparing the results of the sub-set of questions analyzed in the previous cycle with the ones gathered in the present one, the authors can state that participants recognize the usefulness of the platform and the challenges. In the previous cycle, was theorized that a possible positive bias regarding the results could have occurred. In this cycle, the results from the same sub-set of questions are, in fact, less positive. However, most results remain positive, and only very few negative results were gathered. This leads us to the conclusion that a positive bias could indeed have occurred in the previous cycle. However, since most of the new results are still positive, the authors do not believe it to have any major effects on the conclusions of the present work. Furthermore, although the authors will still pay attention to this subset of questions in future interventions, it can be stated with confidence that the platform is a good means to learn secure coding.

Regarding the questions related to the hints & hints system, the authors can see that most results are negative. This can be explained due to the rudimentary character of the hints. In this cycle, the authors focused on the development of more programming challenges, as well as further improving the backend analysis of the exercises. In addition, the hints provided to the players in the artifacts' version of this cycle were still very generic and only based on the security issue found in the code, i.e., CWE. And so, even though these questions gave negative results, this outcome was expected. From this, the authors can conclude that the major focus of the next cycle of development must be based on improving the hints & hint system to give the players relevant feedback that would aid in the solving of the challenges.

Third Cycle

Development

The main goal of the third development cycle was to improve the hint system. Towards this, a laddering technique was used. While in the previous cycle, only one level was used per ladder, in the third cycle, each ladder contained four to six levels. Although this cycle began by developing ladders with seven to nine levels, the authors reduced the number of levels per ladder for the final artifact. This change was due to feedback gathered from one of the interventions that stated that issues with an appropriate number of hints (less generic, more specific) are better than issues that have more hints (more generic, less specific). Since the changes to the ladders were conducted in between interventions, this cycle had two semi-cycles of development. The hints per ladder were also refined to have less of a generic explanation and more of a specific nature from the start. The authors also rephrased the hints to remove possible ambiguities.

Intervention

This final development cycle had several distinct interventions with two semi-cycles that only differ on the number of levels per ladder. In the first semi-cycle, one industry-based intervention was conducted in an online meeting context and held on the 21st of April 2021 with a total of 12 participants. After the changes were performed between the semi-cycles, four additional interventions were held. The first workshop was held on the 19th of May 2021, with 13 participants. The second workshop was held on the 16th of June 2021 with 17 participants. The third, held on the 23 of June 2021, had 18 participants, and the last workshop was on the 16th of July 2021, with 15 participants. These workshops were held through online meetings from 9 a.m. to 16 p.m. At the end of the workshops, the participants were given the online survey previously described, and a brief feedback interview was also held.

Evaluation

The data gathered from these interventions regarding the sub-set of questions related to the platform and the challenges (Q.1, Q.3, Q.6, Q.7, Q.8, Q.10, and Q.11) remained with very positive results, as seen by Figure 17.

Figure 17. Cycle Three - Results from Initial Sub-set

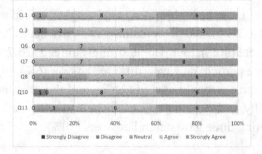

On the sub-set of questions relating to the hints and feedback given by the platform, Q.2, Q.4, Q.5, and Q.9, the results vary between semi-cycles. The industry intervention of the first semi-cycle had eight submissions, and the results are shown in Figure 18.

Figure 18. Results of the first semi-cycle

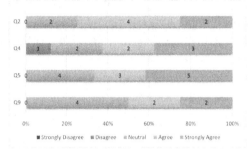

In Q.2, four participants (50%) agreed with the statement, two (25%) strongly agreed, and the remaining two (25%) gave neutral feedback. Q.4 shows that two participants (25%) agreed with the statement, three (37,5%) strongly agreed, two (25%) gave neutral answers, and the remainder, one participant (12,5%), disagreed. On Q.5, three participants (37,5%) agreed with the statement, one participant (12,5%) strongly agreed, and the remaining four participants (50%) gave neutral answers. Lastly, Q.9 shows that two participants (25%) agreed with the statement, two (25%) strongly agreed, and the remaining four participants (50%) gave neutral answers. In these interventions, participants also gave feedback about their experience playing the challenges. The gathered feedback was, for the most part, unanimous, and so it's the authors' opinion that the following recorded statements represent the group's opinion.

"It's cool to see the platform respond and analyze the code for security issues."

"The feedback is helpful; however, the hints could be more succinct and straight to the point."

"The competitive aspect of it gives you a different motivation to understand what's wrong."

"The hints should be more direct, I think."

On the second semi-cycle, 15 answers were gathered across the four distinct interventions. Regarding the sub-set relating to the hints, it can be highlighted in Q.2. eight participants agreed with the statement (53.3%), five strongly agreed (33.3%), and the remaining two gave neutral answers (13.3%). In Q.4., six people agreed with the statement (40%), four people strongly agreed (26.7%), four gave neutral answers (26.7%), and the remainder one participant gave a disagree answer (6%). In Q.5., 10 participants agreed with the statement (66.7%), three strongly agreed (20%), and the remainder of the participants gave neutral answers (13.3%). Lastly, in Q.9., six participants agreed with the statement (40%), six strongly agreed (40%), and the remaining three gave neutral answers (20%).

Figure 19. Results of the final semi-cycle

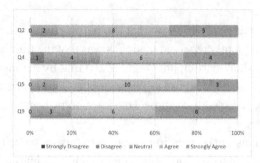

At the end of each workshop, the authors performed additional feedback rounds, where participants could voice their experience with the artifact. The following statements are some of the answers gathered.

"The exercises were very good and nice"

"Initially I thought that I could not play the game, but I was positively surprised"

"The feedback the platform gives guided me when I got stuck, very nice"

DISCUSSION

When comparing the present results to the ones of previous cycles, two major findings can be observed. First, the sub-set of questions related to the platform and the challenges remained positive throughout the development process. Second, a clear improvement can be seen regarding the results of these statements. In this cycle, the authors can also pinpoint that from the first semi-cycle to the second, there was an improvement due to the changes performed to the hints given by the platform. While the results from the first intervention were positive, changing the hint system based on user feedback led to improved user feedback. This is observed when comparing the percentages of each value of the Likert scale from one semi-cycle to the other. Another indicator of this improvement is the contrast between the verbal feedback gathered in the interventions of each semi-cycle. Before applying the changes to the hints, the players would comment that the platform is good, but the hints could be more worked on and straight to the point. In the later interventions, the players would not only value the platform and challenges as a good means to learn cybersecurity but also state that the hints provide a useful mechanism to aid in the solving.

At the end of this cycle and based on the results and the continuous development of the product, the authors can state that the artifact produced is a compliant and a good way to raise the awareness of security vulnerabilities while giving meaningful feedback to the players. The major finding in this cycle is that developers find the hint system part of the platform useful and necessary and prefer a more direct and succinct hint system in contrast to one with more hints per issue.

LESSONS LEARNED

The results from the distinct interventions show that the participants welcome this approach to raising cybersecurity awareness. A frequently received feedback was that the training stimulates the players into grasping the concepts to win. Many participants highlighted that by having a friendly competition, they were more focused on the training and had fun while learning. Our experience shows that the developed backend is suitable to implement our serious game. However, some limitations exist in SAST tools which can have undesirable behaviors.

This study generated much insight on creating a serious to raising security awareness among software developers in the industry. In the first development cycle, the authors learned that the proposed method to raise awareness was well received by software developers in the industry. This conclusion corroborated previous work by (Gasiba et al., 2021). In the second cycle, the tested artifact contained improvements to both the challenges and the analysis process. At the end of this cycle, the authors concluded that: the results from this cycle corroborated the results of our previously performed Proof-of-Concept and that more care should be taken to design the hint system. Due to the results from the second cycle, the last development cycle focused on the hint system. In this cycle, the authors learned that players care more about the quality than the number of hints.

Participants mentioned that, due to the workshop, they would start paying more attention to security vulnerabilities when developing software. Participants also mentioned learning about new security vulnerabilities by playing the game. Due to the positive results and additional work by Gasiba, the authors can state that the presented game is a good approach to raising cybersecurity awareness in an industry context.

FUTURE RESEARCH DIRECTIONS

For future work, the authors would like to highlight three potential research opportunities to further cement the work done and the results gathered from this research. Firstly, the same methodology is being applied as an approach to develop infrastructure as a code type of exercise, with already some promising preliminary results. Secondly, additional research aimed at better understanding the quality and limitations of SAST tools in the context of Java programming would further improve the vulnerability assessment and evaluation algorithm of the Java Cybersecurity Challenges. Lastly, some studies are already underway to understand additional sources of information, based on software plagiarism detection, that can be added to the hint system.

CONCLUSION

Over the past decade, the number of cybersecurity incidents has been constantly rising. To mitigate these situations, companies can follow several strategies aimed at reducing the possible vulnerabilities present in their products. The focus of the present work is on raising cybersecurity awareness of developers through a serious game type of approach. Our gamification-based awareness campaign extends previous work performed in an industry setting. The authors adapted and extended this work on Cybersecurity Challenges to automatically assess the security level of Java challenges and provide meaningful hints to the players. Furthermore, four distinct Java challenges were developed and introduced into the SIFU platform. This research provides an overview of how this automatic assessment can be performed using open-source analysis tools to enable practitioners to reproduce our results. The authors also provide the hint generation algorithm applied to generate hints for the players. Our research followed the Action Design Research methodology and was conducted in a three-cycle development approach. For each cycle, there was a development stage, accompanied by industry interventions and evaluations of the product. Overall, several interventions of the proposed method and concept were performed during the development's life cycle. The interventions performed had 44 participants and were mostly held in industry-based contexts. The gathered results show that the players find the concept fun and a good approach to learning cybersecurity, and they welcome the challenges. Furthermore, they can also understand and relate the hints with their code and find these helpful in solving the Java challenges.

This work not only corroborates previous results but also extends them by refining the evaluation method to address Java challenges and improving the Intelligent coaches' algorithm. Overall, the authors highlight that the proposed method was successful among industry participants. Moreover, the evolution of the quality of the artifact across the development cycles can also be highlighted.

The evolution of the code analysis stage can be seen by the evolution of the set of tools employed across the different cycles. The hints & hint system evolved from simple straightforward feedback given in the first drafts of the artifact to more precise and objective hints that aided the players in solving the challenges.

ACKNOWLEDGMENT

The authors would like to thank the survey participants for their participation and engagement in meaningful discussion around their experience with the provisioning challenges. This work is partially financed by national funds through FCT - Fundação para a Ciência e Tecnologia, I.P., under the projects FCT UIDB/04466/2020 and UIDP/04466/2020. Furthermore, the third author thanks the Instituto Universitário de Lisboa and ISTAR, for their support. Ulrike Lechner acknowledges funding for project LIONS by dtec.bw.

REFERENCES

Acar, Y., Stransky, C., Wermke, D., Weir, C., Mazurek, M., & Fahl, S. (2017). Developers Need Support, Too: A Survey of Security Advice for Software Developers. *2017 IEEE Cybersecurity Development (SecDev)*, 22-26.

Andrew Dinn, L. D. (n.d.). *Byteman*. Retrieved May 18, 2021, from https://byteman.jboss.org/

Bakan, U., & Bakan, U. (2018). Game-Based Learning Studies in Education Journals: A Systematic Review of Recent Trends. *Actualidades Pedagógicas*, 119-145.

Barela, J., Gasiba, T., Suppan, S., Berges, M., & K., B. (2019). When interactive graphic storytelling fails. In *IEEE 27th International Requirements Engineering Conference Workshops* (pp. 164-169). Institute of Electrical and Electronics Engineers Inc.

Beck, K., Gamma, E., Saff, D., & Vasudevan, K. (n.d.). *JUnit5*. Retrieved February 23, 2021, from https://junit.org/junit5/

Casqueiro, L., Gasiba, T., Pinto-Albuquerque, M., & Lechner, U. (2021). Automated Java Challenges' Security Assessment for Training in Industry Preliminary Results. *First International Computer Programming Education Conference (ICPEC 2021)*.

Corporation, O. (n.d.). *Java*. Retrieved November 23, 2020, from https://www.java.com/en/

Crockford, D. (n.d.). *JSON - JavaScript Object Notation*. Retrieved January 7, 2021, from https://www.json.org/json-en.html

David Dixon-Peugh, D. C. (n.d.). *PMD Source Code Analyzer*. Retrieved February 13, 2021, from https://pmd.github.io/

Dörner, R., Göbel, S., Effelsberg, W., & Wiemeyer, J. (2016). *Serious Games: Foundations, Concepts and Practice*. Springer International Publishing. doi:10.1007/978-3-319-40612-1

DreadLocked. (2018). *CVE-2018-7600*. Retrieved July 28, 2021, from https://github.com/dreadlocked/Drupalgeddon2

Facebook. (n.d.). *FB-Infer*. Retrieved February 17, 2021, from https://fbinfer.com/

Fireeye. (2014). *Shellshock in the Wild*. Retrieved July 20, 2021, from https://www.fireeye.com/blog/threat-research/2014/09/shellshock-in-the-wild.html

Frey, S., Rashid, A., Anthonysamy, P., Pinto-Albuquerque, M., & Naqvi, S. (2019). The Good, the Bad and the Ugly: A Study of Security Decisions in a Cyber-Physical Systems Game. *IEEE Transactions on Software Engineering*, *45*(5), 521–536. doi:10.1109/TSE.2017.2782813

Gasiba, T. (2021). *Raising Awareness on Secure Coding in the Industry through CyberSecurity Challenges*. Universität der Bundeswehr München.

Gasiba, T., Beckers, K., Suppan, S., & Rezabek, F. (2019). On the Requirements for Serious Games geared towards Software Developers in the Industry. *Conference on Requirements Engineering Conference (RE)*, 286-296.

Gasiba, T., Lechner, U., & Pinto-Albuquerque, M. (2020). Sifu - A CyberSecurity Awareness Platform with Challenge Assessment and Intelligent Coach. *Cyber-Physical System Security of the Cybersecurity Journal*, 1-23.

Gasiba, T., Lechner, U., & Pinto-Albuquerque, M. (2021). CyberSecurity Challenges: Serious Games for Awareness Training in Industrial Environments. *Bundesamt für Sicherheit in der Informationstechnik: Deutschland. Digital. Sicher. 30 Jahre BSI – Tagungsband zum 17. Deutschen IT-Sicherheitskongress*, 43-56.

Gasiba, T., Lechner, U., & Pinto-Albuquerque, M. (2021). CyberSecurity Challenges for Software Developer Awareness Training in Industrial Environments. *16th International Conference on Wirtschaftsinformatik*, 1-17. 10.1007/978-3-030-86797-3_25

Gasiba, T., Lechner, U., Pinto-Albuquerque, M., & Mendez, D. (2021). Is Secure Coding Education in the Industry Needed? An Investigation Through a Large Scale Survey. *43rd International Conference on Software Engineering (ICSE)*, 1-12.

Golem. (2014, August 6). *Elf Wege, ein Android-System zu übernehmen* [Eleven ways to take over an Android system]. Retrieved from https://www.golem.de/news/stagefright-sicherheitsluecke-elf-wege-ein-android-system-zu-uebernehmen-1508-115610.html

Goseva-Popstojanova, K., & Perhinschi, A. (2015). On the Capability of Static Code Analysis to Detect Security Vulnerabilities. *Information and Software Technology, 68*, 18–33. doi:10.1016/j.infsof.2015.08.002

Graziotin, D., Fagerholm, F., Wang, X., & Abrahamsson, P. (2017). On the Unhappiness of Software Developers. *21st International Conference on Evaluation and Assessment in Software Engineering (EASE'17)*, 324-333. 10.1145/3084226.3084242

Hänsch, N., & Benenson, Z. (2014). Specifying IT Security Awareness. *25th International Workshop on Database and Expert Systems Applications*, 326-330.

Hendrix, M., Al-Sherbaz, A., & Bloom, V. (2016). Game Based Cyber Security Training: Are Serious Games Suitable for Cyber Security Training? *International Journal of Serious Games*, 1-10.

Kucek, S., & Maria, L. (2020). An Empirical Survey of Functions and Configurations of Open-Source Capture the Flag (CTF) Environments. *Journal of Network and Computer Applications, 151*, 102470. doi:10.1016/j.jnca.2019.102470

Landers, R. N. (2014). Developing a theory of gamified learning linking serious games and gamification of learning. *Simulation & Gaming, 45*(6), 752–768. doi:10.1177/1046878114563660

Landers, R. N. (2019). Gamification Misunderstood: How Badly Executed and Rhetorical Gamification Obscures Its Transformative Potential. *Journal of Management Inquiry, 28*(2), 137–140. doi:10.1177/1056492618790913

Leun, K., & Petrilli, S. Jr. (2017). Using Capture-the-Flag to Enhance the Effectiveness of Cybersecurity Education. *Proceedings of the 18th Annual Conference on Information Technology Education (SIGITE '17)*, 47-52. 10.1145/3125659.3125686

Likert, R. (1932). A Technique for the Measurement of Attitudes. *Archives de Psychologie, 22*(140), 1–55.

MITRE. (2017). *CVE-2017-0144*. Retrieved May 14, 2021, from https://cve.mitre.org/cgi-bin/cvename.cgi?name=CVE-2017-0144

MITRE Corporation. (n.d.). *Common Weakness Enumeration*. Retrieved January 12, 2021, from https://cwe.mitre.org/

Patel, S. (n.d.). *2019 Global Developer Report: DevSecOps finds security roadblocks divide teams.* Retrieved July 18, 2020, from https://about.gitlab.com /blog/2019/07/15/global-developer-report

Patrício, R., Moreira, A., Zurlo, F., & Melazzini, M. (2020). Co-creation of new solutions through gamification: A collaborative innovation practice. *Creativity and Innovation Management, 29*(1), 146–160. doi:10.1111/caim.12356

Patrício, R., Moreira, A. C., & Zurlo, F. (2021). Enhancing design thinking approaches to innovation through gamification. *European Journal of Innovation Management*, *24*(5), 1569–1594. doi:10.1108/ EJIM-06-2020-0239

Pugh, B., & Hovemeyer, D. (n.d.). *Spotbugs*. Retrieved February 15, 2021, from https://spotbugs.github.io/

Rayome, A. D. (2019, March 19). The 3 Least Secure Programming Languages. *TechRepulic*.

Rietz, T., & Maedche, A. (2019). LadderBot: A Requirements Self-Elicitation System. *27th International Requirements Engineering Conference (RE)*, 357-362.

Schneier, B. (n.d.). *Software Developers and Security*. Retrieved July 25, 2019, from https://www.schneier.com/blog/archives/2019/07/software_devel o.html

SEI-CERT. (n.d.). *Cert Secure Coding*. Retrieved January 8, 2021, from https://wiki.sei.cmu.edu/confluence/display/seccode

Sein, M., Henfridsson, O., Purao, S., Rossi, M., & Lindgren, R. (2011). Action Design Research. *Management Information Systems Quarterly*, *35*(1), 37–56. doi:10.2307/23043488

Simões, A., & Queirós, R. (2020). On the nature of programming exercises. *ICPEC - First International Computer Programming Education Conference*, 251-259.

Software Engineering Institute. (n.d.). *SEI CERT Oracle Coding Standard for Java - FIO04-J. Release resources when they are no longer needed*. Retrieved January 22, 2021, from https://wiki.sei.cmu.edu/ confluence/display/java/FIO04-J.+Release+resources+when+they+are+no+longer+needed

SonarSource. (n.d.). *SonarQube*. Retrieved February 17, 2021, from https://www.sonarqube.org/

US-CERT. (2020). *Department of Homeland Security. Software Assurance*. Retrieved September 27, 2020, from https://tinyurl.com/y6pr9v42

Vasconcelos, P., & Ribeiro, R. (2020). Using property-based testing to generate feedback for c programming exercises. *ICPEC - First International Computer Programming Education Conference*, 285-294.

VULDB. (2018). *The Community-Driven Vulnerability Database*. Retrieved July 28, 2021, from https:// vuldb.com/

Wieringa, R. (2014). *Design Science Methodology for Information Systems and Software Engineering* (Vol. 22). Springer. doi:10.1007/978-3-662-43839-8

Chapter 17
Gamification Mechanisms in Cyber Range and Cyber Security Training Environments:
A Review

Evangelos Chaskos
University of Peloponnese, Greece

Jason Diakoumakos
(iD) https://orcid.org/0000-0003-1406-602X
University of Peloponnese, Greece

Nicholas Kolokotronis
(iD) https://orcid.org/0000-0003-0660-8431
University of Peloponnese, Greece

George Lepouras
(iD) https://orcid.org/0000-0001-6094-3308
University of Peloponnese, Greece

ABSTRACT

Defending against cyber threats is an essential procedure for an organization, and professional train-ing is an important factor for the prosperity of an organization against sophisticated and multi-vector cyber-attacks. The background knowledge is needed from the employee to face and prevent incidents, as well as a level of awareness and experience. Towards this training, cyber security training platforms can significantly raise the trainees' knowledge, perspective, and incident handling. However, gamification mechanisms are implemented and embedded in such systems as an educational procedure to increase the engagement of the trainees. In this chapter, a description of different platforms and their mapping with their corresponding gamification mechanisms will be presented, and the specific gamification elements resulting from this review that are commonly used across all platforms and can have a more significant impact on a fast and meaningful gamified learning procedure will be pointed out.

DOI: 10.4018/978-1-6684-4291-3.ch017

INTRODUCTION

Cyber-attacks become more and more sophisticated and perilous since the attacker's side have more to gain, given the fact that most information is stored online and the internal infrastructure of each organization depends highly on its network. However, a deep understanding of cyber-attacks footprint, the associated defenses and possible countermeasures tend to be rather limited in organizations. Cybersecurity is a really important aspect for any organization in order to be safe from internal and external attacks. Especially, given the fact that more IT is used under any company and that the cyber-attacks have been risen dramatically the past years, it is becoming more and more eager for a company to train its employees and provide them the ability to face such situations (Giantas & Liaropoulos, 2019).

Aiming towards that end, a variety of different systems have been developed, either lightweight self-paced platforms, or large-scale environments, able to simulate real world-incidents and assist the learning and training procedure of the final users. Different platforms are developed for different aged groups and the knowledge depth that each one provides is made respectively. However, the learning procedure can become rather doll and difficult, regardless the background of the trainee, and thus many of these platforms tend to adapt gamification mechanisms to attract the interest and have the users constantly interact with the platform.

Cyber security education is a continues process and the users need to constantly adapt and learn the new emerging technologies and be informed about new threats and risks identified. The more advanced a user is the more is to be engaged with this evolutionary course. This constant learning procedure can be positively impacted with the use of gamification in the corresponding platform that a user selects to be trained. However, to create a meaningful gamification scheme, the platform creators need to perform relevant research for the gamification methods to reflect the desired educational outcomes and connect them to the gamification schemes, which can be a costly and time-consuming procedure (Patricio, Moreira, & Zurlo, Gamification approaches to the early stage of innovation, 2018).

In this review chapter, a variety of popular learning platforms and CR environments will be presented in respect to the gamification elements and mechanics adapted by them. By presenting all of these elements, we can compare those platforms and extract the most commonly used gamification components that can be applied in most platform types. This research will assist future works to identify the elements that are already commonly used in the existing cybersecurity platforms and can serve as a reference area for those intending to adapt a gamification element in their own platform, while also determine those specific elements that can be conditionally used per use case and target audience. Additionally, enumerating those elements may assist upon the creation of a standardization method regarding the game schemes to be applied or adapted by a future platform. The rest of this chapter is structured as follow: Section II perform a preliminary analysis of lightweight platforms, cyber ranges and the gamification elements that can be adapted. Section III reviews the related work regarding the corresponding gamification player types and elements adapted by these platforms. Section IV presents numerous existing platforms, while listing the gamification elements adapted by each one of them. Section V provides the conclusion of this chapter.

RELATED WORK

To create a gamification system, the designer needs to account both the system's goals and attributes while also understand the need of the users interacting with it and thus, the type of learners and their motivations should be analysed. In a gamified system users must also be confronting as players to formally analyze their goals and motivation factors and thus this subsection will refer to users with this term in respect to the taxonomies applied. In Bartle's work (Kumar, Herger, & Dam, 2020) four player types for gamification are distinct in respect to the user's psychology: (1) The Achiever, (2) The Explorer, (3) The Socializer and (4) The Killer.

The above categorization is not rigid, since a user can be leaning to more than one category based on different preconditions. However, a user is most likely to fell into one or two categories, but most users have a dominant trait, determining his/her overall performance and having a group of users, many different gamification types can occur amongst them (Park & Kim, 2017). Figure 1 displays the grid of Bartle's taxonomy. A user's performance can lie anywhere inside the diagram, which displays the interaction between a player and the system and based on this his/her categorization.

To further analyse the aforementioned categories, a player is distinct as 'Achiever' when he is chasing after points and high game status. He is after achievement, badges and high levels, as fast as possible, so that he can be in the top of other players. Subsequently, the 'Explorer' is a player who needs to explore the world, the system and this type is not bothered about points and prizes. Around 10% of the users belong into this category. The 'Socializer' on the other hand, is a player who needs to make friends and discuss inside the system with other users. Almost 80% of the users fell into this category. Finally, the 'Killer' is consisted to be the player that is engaged when it is given to him the ability to disrupt other users inside the platform. Less than 1% of the users fell into this category (Kumar, Herger, & Dam, 2020).

The Bartle's taxonomy is based mostly on games such as MUDS and MMORPG (Chou, 2013). As a result, is a basic user classification that cannot be applied with no changes in all domains, since the need of more user classification is needed to address certain aspects of a user's psychology. This regards the limited freedom of a user inside a platform, and thus further classification is needed. To face this problem, Andrzej Marczewski proposed the classification of users in 6 categories based on their willingness to play or not, analysing the Bartle's Taxonomy in further details: (1) The Socializer, (2) The Achiever, (3) The Free Spirit, (4) The Philanthropist, (5) The Player, (6) The Disruptor (Chou, 2013) (Marczewski, 2017).

The Socializer, Achiever and Disruptor are the same as Bartle's taxonomy while the rest are further categories between the basic classification system of Bartle. To be precise, the 'Player' needs to get achievements and be in high ranks in leaderboards, the 'Socializer' needs to interact with other users, the 'Free Spirit' regard creative users that need to explore the game with autonomy, the 'Achievers' are the best at achieving goals within the system, the 'Philanthropists' feel that they are part of something greater and need to share their knowledge and the 'Disruptor' needs to compete with others.

The above classification regards the way a user is acting, which is distinct in Intrinsic or Extrinsic motivation. When a user is motivated through intrinsic actions, it means that the player is involved with the system to gain skills, knowledge and evolve in his case of study. In contradiction extrinsic motivation regards the users that are involved in order to gain a prize, such as acknowledgment or better wedge. Thus, intrinsic motivation is much stronger than extrinsic for a user to constantly interact with the system. This hybrid model is in respect of the different user types, their goals, needs and the interacting procedures with the system. Thus, a balanced system is consisted of the aforementioned 6 categories.

Figure 1. Bartle's Gamification Types (Kumar, Herger, & Dam, 2020)

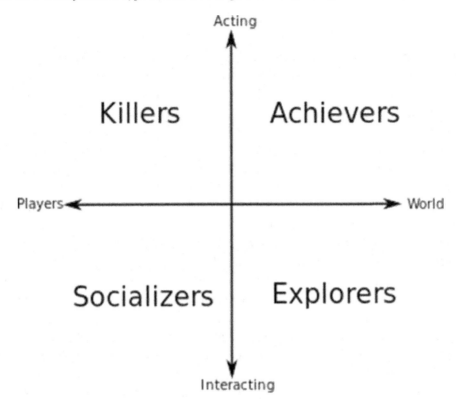

As a result, gamification elements should be introduced to address in the different users' types to engage their interaction with the platform. The table consisting of all elements that can be used regarding both the player types and the gamification mechanisms in the system to accomplish the different user engagement is being displayed in Figure 2 (Marczewski, Gamification & user experience UX connect, 2018). It is not necessary for a system to provide all of the displayed components; however, the more components provided, the more possibilities for the user. However, the necessity to provide at least one of each player category is important for the system to be able to deliver the different needs of each user.

As displayed in Figure 2, each different user type needs of different mechanics to be implemented in the system to address his/her gamification needs. The 'Reward Schedule' and 'General' parts, regard elements that can be implemented in the system and address to all users and a few of them are necessary to be implemented to address further game elements. Subsequently, the part 'Player' regards general elements from the player's perspective as a whole, regardless his/her specific categorization.

Each different element assists on achieving a gamification goal based on each user type (Fischer, Heinz, & Bretenstein, 2018) (Jia, Xu, Karanam, & Voida, 2016), or in respect to the overall mechanism. Having an educational platform that uses gamified content, is not essential to include all of the different elements in the final product, but a variety of them, based on the goals, the accessibility and the user's pool that will interact with the platform. Overhauling cyber security training is a really important task and needs to be introduced not only via the security tools but also through gamification (Sponge, 2019).

Regarding the rewards distributed by the system, most of them can be included in all types of platforms, with the ratio reward type being the most important to ensure engagement (David, 2013). Rewarding

Figure 2. Gamification Elements (Marczewski A., Gamification & user experience UX connect, 2018)

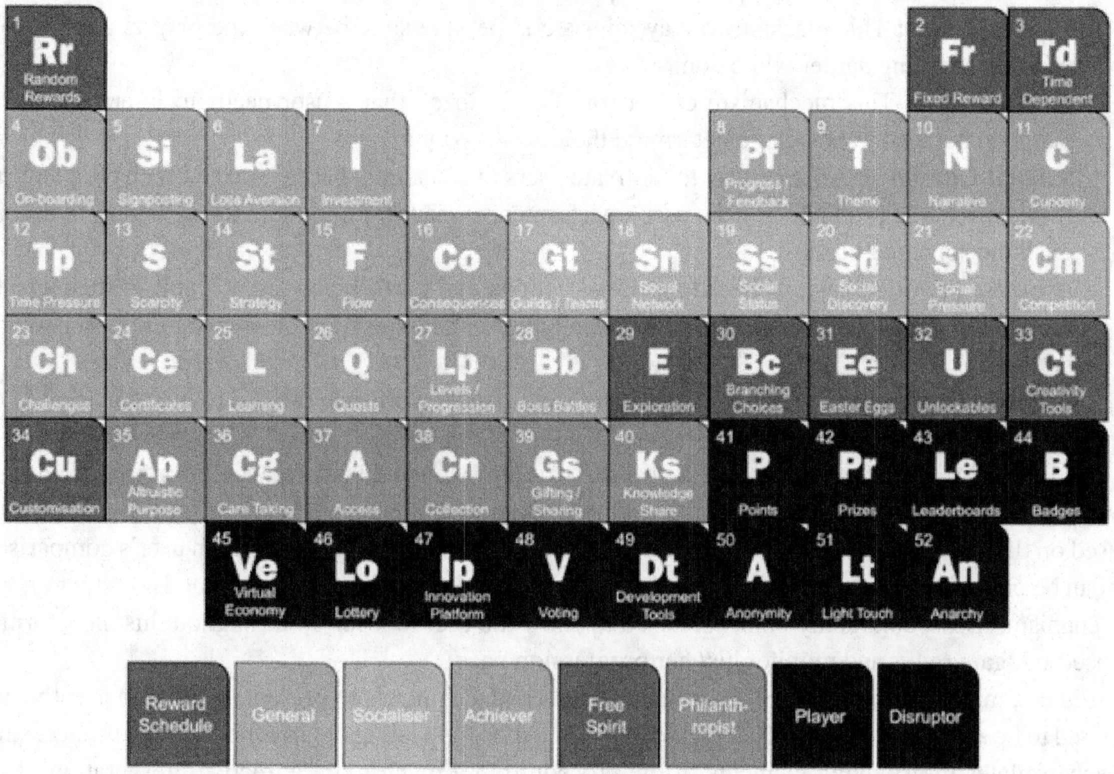

the users based on their actions and interaction with the platform is the most used mechanism across different types of platforms, from games to educational systems. Having badges and achievements for the users to complete, are also two key features to engage them during their interaction with the platform (BenchPrep, 2015). In correlation, the difficulty of rewards should be as much as consistent as possible amongst the users and it should be able to offer different levels, to address to different users with different background (Sylvester, 2013). Having too difficult rewards and achievements will have the users to feel unable to act, whilst having too easy rewarding mechanisms will result in boredom (Wang & Sun, 2011). In addition, different rewards will have different results in the end users in relation to their engagement. Specific content can address to their short-term, such as prespecified reward-based actions (Marczewski A., 2016), while other elements can motivate their long-term engagement (Nicholson, 2015) (Scholefield & Shepherd, 2019) in correlation to the users' intrinsic and extrinsic motivation.

Consequently, regardless the platform and the game implementation there are 7 core mechanics that can be used in all areas (Agate, 2017):

- **Badges:** Each badge may describe a different single or multi goal completion. Having such a mechanic will engage both long-term and short-term users and regarding the former, users may be able to compete with each other.

- **Leveling system:** Provides the ability to the users to level-up through earning experience points, distributed based on their actions. Such mechanism will enable long-term users to progress through their interaction and prove their progress, addressing different player-types.
- **Leaderboards:** This mechanism may offer a competitive style between the players and provoke them on studying harder while competing.
- **Progress Bar:** This mechanism can enable the feedback that a user needs to interact with the platform but also to be able to determine their progression.
- **Virtual Currency:** Another way to motivate users to constantly being engaged with the platform. If this mechanic is affected by the user's performance, may result in them trying harder to accomplish the specified goals.
- **Awards:** Providing awards based on users' actions and performance may result in their greater motivation and engagement. The awards can either be pre-specified or known to the users or can be hidden.
- **Challenges:** Provides the ability to the users to compete with each other through scenarios.

Additionally, in order to determine the trainee's progression and performance **Points** are used as an overall grading mechanism in most gamified and non-gamified platforms. Points are awarded to the users based on their actions and can either be passive, without any direct usage rather than user's comparison, or can be part of a majored gamification scheme and be used as currency, trading goods or other type of mechanisms. Most commonly points are used to allow the user to level-up throughout his/ her learning procedure, gain ranks and monitor his/ her progression pace.

Finally, many platforms use **Story-Line** elements and techniques to present the dilemma or the task needed to be solved by the user. This method creates a more appealing environment for the trainee, since it encapsulates the studying elements of the procedure in a much more attractive presentation of the problem. In addition, it engages the user to feel that he/ she is part of the scenario presented and results in his/her greater and more passionate evolvement (Boopathi, Sreejith, & Bithin, 2015).

The aforementioned elements can be combined together and/ or with others to create more complex gamification schemes to further attract the interest and have the users engaged with the platform and the overall training and learning procedure. Since different elements result in different outcomes for the trainees, they need to be carefully selected, implemented and combined.

GAMIFICATION IN CYBER SECURITY

Gamification mechanisms gain an up-going trend in the last years, and such techniques are applied in the cyber security field, while noticing a positive impact during the learning procedure (Scholefield & Shepherd, 2019) (Duggan & Thrope, 2017) and the overall engagement of the users (SC, n.d.) such as employees or customers (Robinson, n.d.) and based on the alteration made in the gamification system it can been used from companies to cyber security educational platforms (Moore, n.d.) Different implementations of the gamification mechanisms can have different outcome; however, its existence can positively impact the general learning procedure (Gonzalez, Mora, & Toledo, 2014) (Seaborn & Fels, 2015) (Patricio R., Moreira, Zurlo, & Melazzini, 2020).

Examples of gamification mechanism in cyber security can be seen to have a great impact in the education aspect. From simple games, such as Game of Threats (PwC, n.d.) and PenQuest (Luh, Temper,

Tjoa, Schrittwieser, & Janicke, 2020), addressing a certain number of attacks and vulnerabilities from the defending side, quiz games or games that are more attack –centric (Adams & Makramalla, 2015) to more complex scenarios and games such as Project Ares (Circadance, n.d.) which includes a complete virtual world, with the ability for the user to navigate in it. Based on the platform's goals, learning depth and audience different elements can be adapted, from simple elements used to attract the younglings in serious games to more formal and complex mechanisms used under cyber-range (CR) and federated cyber-range (FCR) platforms.

Serious games are those games made not to entertainment as their first purpose but to train their users regarding a specific matter. They include educational material but are highly characterized by the extensive use of game elements to conceal their 'boring' aspect of educational procedure. A serious game should be consisted of different components, which are: (1) an interactive problem solving, (2) specific goals, (3) adaptive challenges, (4) control over the user's impact, (5) ongoing feedback, (6) explicit or implicit feedback, (7) create the necessary engagement, and (8) sensory stimuli refer to the mixture of graphics and sounds (Garcia de Soto, Georgescu, Mantha, Turk, & Maciel, 2020). Furthermore, they can be consisted of both an LMS and hands-on exercises, while their gamified aspect engage the users through the procedure and increase their interest (Jones & Chou, 2019).

On the other hand, a CR is more complex and can be composed of different modules for exploiting the features and capabilities of the platform and its goals; the modules are related to scenarios, teaming, monitoring, management and scoring. The **scenario** module defines the scenarios execution states and the scenario characteristics, features and storyline of the deployed scenario. The **management** element focuses on data, users and interface CR management. **Monitoring** includes the methods, the tools and the layers at which real-time monitoring of cyber security exercises is performed. The **teaming** includes the variety of groups consisted of stakeholders which are responsible for design, develop, manage and participate in the exercise; and the **scoring** which is defined by various indicators in order to measure a participants' performance through methods, tools and metrics, indicating his/her progress during an exercise, and encapsulating gamification mechanisms in CR environments

In order to both engage users and assist them through learning, modelling a less 'boring' procedure seems to be more and more used in today's training platforms (Jones & Chou, 2019) (Kianpour, Kowalski, Zoto, Frantz, & Overby, 2019). Those platforms should be implemented not only to raise the security awareness and train the final users, but also to have a gamified experience in order to achieve better results and engage them through the process (Kianpour, Kowalski, Zoto, Frantz, & Overby, 2019). Having users learning either individually or in groups, seems to have a different resolve in the trainee, in respect to their gamification type. Including gamification techniques in a training platform can be of great importance. Even creating a virtual environment, like in Project Ares hosting a variety of scenarios, battle rooms, achievements, self or team-based exercises and challenges (CIRCADANCE, n.d.), can not only engage the users, but keep them in constant interaction with the system and provides a greater purpose for them to be constantly using the platform (Patricio, Moreira, & Zurlo, Gamification approaches to the early stage of innovation, 2018).

GAMIFICATION ELEMENTS IN TRAINING PLATFORMS

Reviewing the existing training environments and CR platforms, various approaches have been taken for their development and their functionalities in this chapter we will analyze the various gamification elements the cyber security training platforms and cyber ranges support and the result will be demonstrate according to their functionalities for over than 15 active training environments and CRs.

Research Methodology

Each platform may share its unique elements and different implementation techniques can be observed. However, the basic elements described in the previous subsection can be districted and are adapted by each platform in respect to the desired goals. Each platform host users with different background and offer different training scenarios in respect to the needs of the group of people that it aims to attract. Having analyzed in the previous section the intrinsic and extrinsic factors that motivate the users during their actions it is important to classify the platforms that are part of the research in respect to their concepts, usage and goals. This categorization will highlight the reasoning of the selected gamification schemes of each one of them based on the platform's exercises types.

A variety of security training platforms has been researched, using both literature review and participation to their interface. The most common differences between the platforms of interest regard the target audience, the graphics implemented, the strictness of their gamification schemes, while also the level of learning depth in their offering exercises. For more concrete and all-around research, applications of different intent are included, such as mobile applications offering basic security knowledge, acclaimed cyber security training platforms available online and CTF challenges, while also platforms created fro organization and personnel training, including established Cyber-Ranges and under-development Federation platforms.

Thus, the platforms are separated in four categories based on these evaluation axes: Cyber Security Training Games, Self-Paced platforms, Cyber Ranges and Cyber-Range Federations and are researched in respect to it. The research focused on the high-level game elements available in each unique platform that are part of the seven prementioned basic elements. Few of the researched platforms may offer further game elements but are ignored for the purpose of this research, although it is worth mentioning that they could fall under one of the main seven categories.

Cyber Security Training Games

Serious games are games that tend to educate rather than entertainment. Although they don't form a training environment, it is important to be mentioned as simple tools for introducing the cyber-security basics to non-professional audience; and assist them to gain further knowledge upon a specific field of study. Past year statistics have shown that many breaches are due to both external and internal factors (https://financesonline.com/cybersecurity-statistics/). Being part of an organization, data leaks may occur from unaware personnel that unwillingly may leak critical information and thus training them is important to ensure the organization's defense measures.

Those games can be categorized in different types regarding the cybersecurity field of study, with the 'Card Games' type be the most commonly observed due to their simplicity, which does not wane the educational procedure if designed correctly (Thompson & Takabi, 2016). Their ease of use is one of the most important advantages they offer, and can be suitable for people with no or few knowledges upon cyber security, while also it has few or no age restrictions. However, this type of games is commonly aim to train non-professional users, such as high-school students since they share a more game-like approach to the educational style, rather than performing an in-depth simulation of real-world situations (Thomas,

Shyjka, & Gjomemo, 2019). However, their stories and tasks originate from real-world situations. Those games tend to use game-like graphics, avatars, a simple user interface and have simple mechanics (Jin, Tu, Kim, Heffron, & White, 2018) (Anvik, Cote, & Riehl, 2019) (Scholefield & Shepherd, 2019) Sch (Filipczuk, Mason, & Snow, 2019). The use of points, levels and virtual currency to purchase in-game are game elements that can be noted in such type of platforms. Although they are seemingly undecomposable platforms, more compound approaches have also been implemented aiming at intermediate type of users (Adams & Makramalla, 2015). Examples of this type include 'CySEC Crucible', 'Program Wars', the 'GenCyber' program, numerous mobile applications and more.

Capture The Flag

Capture-the-flag exercises which enhance participants technical skills by solving challenges in several cyber security domain. The ultimate goal of CTF exercise and competitions is to find hidden flags in a certain environment. The most common category is Jeopardy style exercises where participants are called upon to solve a series of challenges that are usually in different categories such as Cryptography, Stenography, Binary Exploitation, Web Exploitation, Forensics, Reverse Engineering, Programming, Packet Analysis, Miscellaneous. Each category has a difficulty rating and in most of the cases participants has a limited timeframe to complete the exercises. Another type of CTF exercises is attack-defense where participants split into groups and each group have their own infrastructure with vulnerabilities and hidden flags and the ultimate goal is to apply countermeasure to the vulnerabilities and exploit the vulnerabilities of the opposite group. King of the Hill CTF category where participant first must exploit a vulnerable environment and afterwards, they 'capture' it they must defend it from the other participants by applying patches or countermeasures. Linear CTF which are typically challenges presented in a story line with multiple challenges that need to be solved in a specific order. Mixed CTF exercises which include features from Jeopardy and Attack – Defense exercises. Following subsection will further elaborate on the unique features of each CTF type.

CTFd

The CTFd (GitHub, CTFd, 2021) is a Capture The Flag framework based on Python and JS, can provide out of the box a jeopardy-style CTF platform. with a web-based front-end, scoreboards, teaming capabilities various statistics for administrators and CTF organizers and an easy-to-use CMS for uploading – downloading challenges. Out of the box from gamification aspect CTFd can provide static scoring for the challenges static where every problem has a predefined point value and if the user solves the problem, get the configured number of points, and a leaderboard of comparing the top 10 teams which provide analytic team progress graphs. Regarding scoring many plugins have been created which allows the platform for various types of dynamic scoring, such as dynamic decreasing per submission scoring where every challenge starts at maximum number of points and the first team which is able to solve the challenge gets the maximum predefined points, but the point value reduces based on the number of solves the problem has. Once it has a baseline of solves teams / users gain a minimum predefined number of points. Furthermore, with additional plugins except Jeopardy style which comes out of the box, can provide more CTF challenge categories such as Attack – Defense, King of the Hill, Linear and Mixed type of challenges.

echoCTF

The echoCTF (GitHub, echoCTF, 2021) is a Capture The Flag framework based on PHP and JS, can provide jeopardy, Attack-Defense and Mixed game types and implements an advanced leaderboard and scoring system for single users. Also, can provide out of the box statistics for administrators and CTF organizers, personalized player dashboards, dynamic real time scoring system, real time visualization of players' network activity and badges for rewarding the users. EchoCTF provides a complete set of tools and applications to develop, deploy and maintain expandable competitions. Each competition is based on Targets which are VM or Containers where hosts multiple challenges. Challenges has their own pointing systems but also exists a Target pointing system for each VM or Container the user has complete all the available challenges. Furthermore, the pointing system allow the user to unlock new levels.

TinyCTF

Another Capture the Flag based framework created on Python and JS and can commonly been observed as a tool in large-scale and smaller-scale CTF competitions. This type can be easily modified though JSON files, in order to host a variety of scenarios that can be alternated fast to serve different learning purposes for those interacting with the framework or the competition. In addition, it is scalable and can be combined with a variety of systems while also support scoring techniques for the trainees' progress and leaderboard for monitoring the competitors (GitHub, TinyCTF, 2021).

PicoCTF

The picoCTF is capture-the-flag framework created by security and privacy experts at Carnegie Mellon University (University, 2020). Is an open-source framework which is based on Python and JS and is a composed of two modules. These modules are picoCTF "web" and picoCTF "shell-manager". The picoCTF "web" consists the facing web site of the users and administrators, and provide management interface for the organizers. The picoCTF "shell-manager" provide the tools to create, package, and deploy challenges for use with the picoCTF platform. PicoCTF provide individual and team-based scoring and leaderboards and provides statistics for administrators and CTF organizers (GitHub, PicoCTF, 2020).

Self-Paced Platforms

This type of platforms offers the ability for a user to train through a variety of scenarios and gain knowledge and experience through exercises basing their source to real-world incidences. The are commonly web-based platforms than individuals can interact with in their own pace.

Self-paced platforms are typically present online jeopardy challenges, capture the Flag (CTF) competition, virtual labs, and in general they offer a set of computer security puzzles (or challenges) involving web application security, network security, software security, reverse-engineering, cryptography, etc. The trainees utilize the platform to practice hands-on training and detect or prevent cyber-attacks.

The simulation environment that is supported by the platforms varies from a downloadable single exercise (in a virtual machine), where participants seek for a secret flag, to large virtual infrastructure with a complex storyline, where participants defend, attack, solve, cooperate, evaluate and investigate various elements of the environment to complete the exercise. Typical features and characteristics of the platforms are listed below.

- They are designed for security professionals of varying expertise levels who are interested in improving (resp. developing) their defensive (resp. offensive) skills.
- The participants can acquire an in-depth understanding of cyber-attacks, hacking, social engineering, detection, incident response, hardening and mitigation (among others).
- The participants can exchange information for cyber security topics though embedded forums and portals.
- The platforms emulate complex large-scale networks offering security concepts in the form of games and/or CTF competitions.
- The platforms offer guided learning and cover both theoretical and practical aspects.
- The platforms promote socialization and the relationships between professionals and organizations.
- The platforms provide realistic scenarios in a mission-specific virtual environment using real-world tools and network activity.

RootTheBox

One of the most commonly observed platforms offering scoring mechanics for CTF challenges, regardless their type, where participants can participate and educate themselves. This platform aims to engage both experience and inexperience trainees and to achieve such a goal a variety of game-like elements are introduced, without creating any limitations to the actual learning procedure. Examples of types of exercises refer to penetration testing, incident response, digital forensics and threat hunting sharing different difficulties and goals. The mechanic called "Botnets" allows the users to earn in-game currency, which can be spent to acquire higher levels, purchase hints for flags, download extra material, or even "SWAT" other players, resulting in PvP situations, where the players try to steal each other's wealth. Furthermore, users are able to monitor their progression through various graphs and charts and also to obtain new skills in a smooth way following the 'mission' path, where challenges are unlocked in a linear progression way, similar to a storyline.

HackTheBox

HackTheBox is a web-based platforms where users can educate and practice their skills throught cyber training gamified content. It is one of the major platforms commonly used worldwide by individuals or organizations, offering a wide variety of hands-on exercises for even team-based training. The users, by competing each other and accomplishing task, are rewarded with points that are shown in national and global scoreboards and are also used for them to level-up through the ranks. In addition, the platform offers a variety of skills and badges that can be acquired by the user based on his/ her actions during the interaction with the platform and the exercises. Each exercise is characterized by its own difficulty level and rewards which can also be cumulative based on the already participated users and their corresponding performance noted. 'Corporations' provide a real life emulated networks with many challenging exercises and provide to the users guidance's as story line. Finally, challenges are hosted and limited time events offering a more completive experience.

OverTheWire

OverTheWire platform provides wargames suitable for learning security concepts in the form of fun-filled games. The wargames that OverTheWire provides are like CTFs but they are neither time bound nor competitive, participants can practice whenever they want at their own pace. The games are in a linear progression where the participants must unlock each level and with each level the story line unlocks. Each wargame has its own difficulty and usually bounded to a cyber security domain and the challenges inside the wargame have their own level of difficulty, finishing a level results in information on how to start the next level. Participants usually encounter many situations where they have no idea what they supposed to do this allows the participants for testing and experimentation.

DefendTheWeb

DefendTheWeb provide a platform for CTF challenges where participants can practice and learn. Challenges are in jeopardy CTF format where user can gain metals (same as Badges) and levels when completing all the challenges of a specific domain. Users can obtain points and levels and can unlock with them the most difficult challenges.

TryHackMe

TryHackMe platform provides a self-organized cyber security training environment. Is focused on hands-on security challenges and exercises with an extensive learning path system. Learning path (called pathways) leads to sections and sections contains the challenges and exercises (called series). Users can obtain points by completing challenges and exercises and completing the learning paths. The points obtained go towards the user's score and is compared with the use of global or national leaderboard. The platform provided badged which are acquired by completing pathways and completing challenges and reward user with levels by accumulating the obtained points of the completed challenges and exercises.

Pwmable

Pwnable is a non-commercial wargame platform which provides various challenges and exercise regarding system exploitation. Each of the challenges is considered as a complete game and rewards the participants with points which go towards the user's profile score and is compared with other participants score over a global leaderboard.

RootMe

The RootMe platform offers a variety of challenges for the participants to compete, challenges consist of a set of computer security puzzles, or exercises, involving reverse-engineering, memory corruption, cryptography, web technologies, and more. The platform provides a wide range of visualization, statistics, leaderboards and utilized many gamification elements such as badges, skills and points.

Cyber – Ranges

A CR refers to a testing environment, of real-life situation, where the trainees have to solve a number of different tasks in order to prove and practice their theoretical background, probably done through an LMS system. Thus, it can either be defined as a simulation environment or as a platform generating all the necessary information to educate, train and practice those skills and knowledge (ECSO, 2020). CR is a system that reproduces vulnerabilities under different situations and many attacks are produced in the reproduced systems. These attacks can either be made by a Machine Learning system (automated), or performed by other users of the platform, which are commonly called 'Red Team'. The defending side is called 'Blue team' and their goal is to protect their assets or minimize the drawbacks, from the Red team. This is an example of usage, since a CR can have multiple scenarios and training environments, implementing a variety of attacks and/or defends even without the aforementioned sides. When having an autonomous system performing the attack, it is a necessity for the agents to be intelligent enough to simulate the attack, rather than being predictable and easy to stand against them. As a result, based on the trainees' level of expertise, the system is being adjusted to address their needs, resulting in either predictable and easy to defend from attacks or unpredictable patterns that simulate a real-world environment.

CYBERBIT Cyber – Range

Cyberbit is a provider of cyber range environments which aims to provide hyper-realistic simulated training environments to enterprises, governments, academic institutions and managed security service providers (MSSPs) around the globe. Cyberbit Range is a simulation platform for training participants in cyber-security topics (CYBERBIT, 2021). It delivers realistic training scenarios and provides test beds for assessing security tools and architectures in a safe and controlled environment. Cyberbit CR can provide virtual replicas of enterprise IT and operational technology (OT) networks that include application servers, database servers, email servers, switches, routers and programmable logic controllers (PLCs), which can achieve real-life attack and defence scenarios in a hyper-realistic network environment. It can emulate complex networks and also provide training content of industrial control system (ICS) for critical infrastructure organizations. Virtual machines as well as additional appliances are used for the simulated network, traffic and threats. Physical OT hardware can be integrated to the simulated IT and supervisory control and data acquisition (SCADA) environment. A customized traffic generator and an attack simulation are also supported in the created scenarios. It also supports real-time monitoring of the training session as well as score and evaluation of the training (InfoSecurity, 2021). Cyberbit as a provider of Cyber Range environments has collaborated with Regent University, Miami, Dade College, Telekom Austria, Maryland Range and CloudRange.

Silensec Cyber – Range

Silensec is an Information Security Management Consulting and Training company. Silensec Cyber Range provides an environment for individuals and organizations to practise cyber-security skills in a fun and challenging way (Silensec, 2020). The key design component of Silensec CR is based on gamification, advanced visualization and scenario plots. Trainees can compete in various exercises covering a wide variety of cyber-security domains. Silensec offers various training courses through the platform in protection, detection and reaction as well as preparation for certifications like CISSP. The infrastructure is built on cloud for better scalability and can be intergraded to IoT and Industrial Control System environments, while it offers competence-based scoring and assessment (Nwehouse, Keith, Scribner, & Witte, 2017). Silensec CR furthermore supports custom scenario generation with storylines, and cyber-challenges and can be offered as a service, hosted or on-premise.

CDeX Platform

The Cyber Defence Exercise Platform (CDex) provides a training system that helps increasing practical skills of cyber-security professionals to identify, protect, detect, recover, and respond to cyber-attacks in IT and OT infrastructures. It provides various training capabilities, like single user training, blue vs. read team training, blue team training, SOC team training through hands-on exercises in flexible and scalable virtualized environment. For increasing involvement and engagement, CDeX relies on various gamification elements, like competition, leader boards, achievable challenges, and scoring systems. It can be deployed on public clouds as-a-service model, or on-premises, and be accessed through a web inter-face. The exercise administrators can create, modify, and automate, the cyber exercises that are provided to the users through an LMS; this is where post-training performance reports are also made available.

CYBERGYM Cyber Range

CYBERGYM provides a virtualized platform, referred to as Virtual Cloud Arena, that is based on Microsoft Azure for cyber security defense and computer forensics cyber exercises. It aims to provide a simulation environment for the participants to be involved with scenarios based on real-life cyber-attacks; participants securely login to the cloud platform from their own laptops. It provides a web-based GUI, whereas users need a VPN connection for accessing the hands-on exercises. The actions of the red team are been performed form real trainers.

Circadance Cyber Range – Project Ares

Circadance Project Ares cyber range is a simulation platform which has been developed to model information technology (IT) and operational technology (OT) systems. Project Ares learning activities are integrated into a virtual cyber range surrounded by a gamified platform and provides a security education platform to individual by performing cyber defense exercises and challenges. It consists by concept-driven games and cyber skill exercises which are expandable and scalable to challenging, real-world inspired threat scenarios. The platform is able to emulates typical networks and simulates network traffic in virtual machines and the sophisticated game elements like scoring, points, leveling system, leaderboards and missions' features keep learners engaged.

KYPO

The KYPO project was funded by the Ministry of Interior of the Czech Republic as part of the Security Research Program of the Czech Republic [1]. To be able to create real-world scenarios, KYPO is designed as a modular distributed system, flexible and scalable to the creation of the virtual scenarios, while also offering the platform as a service through service-based access and a web-based interface. One of its components, 'The Portal' is the interface where the users can interact with the created sandboxes

(Tovarnak, 2017). These components interact, in order to build and manage sandboxes in the underlying cloud computing infrastructure. The KYPO platform can provide from a single sandbox, ideal for malware analysis, to a real-life network topology, where various teams can compete to capture the flag exercises. Moreover, other functionalities include the analytic graphs (dashboards) for the processed data of platform users, and visual analytics, monitoring and scoring for the available exercises and courses. In terms of gamification elements, KYPO is able to score the users with points based on their progress and results for each exercise and the evaluation technique is tightly connected to the platform's technical implementation and each exercise's objectives (Celeda, Cegan, Vykopal, & Tovarnak, 2015).

Cyber Range Federation

A Federation of Cyber-Ranges (FCR) is consisted of multiple CRs originated from different domains in order to simulate mixed and hybrid scenarios through a realistic environment.

Foresight

Foresight is an FCR hosting CRs that originate from the Naval, Aviation and Power-Grid domain. It provides both an LMS system with the corresponding learning material and exercises/ questionaries, while also hosting a variety of simulating scenarios through the collaborator CRs part of the overall platform, so that the trainees are able to practice their skills. The system monitors the user's performance, progress and interaction; and based on a variety of metrics it rewards points, badges and achievements to the final user. Points are used to level-up and compete through leaderboards, while badges and achievements states the user's knowledge and abilities on the respective field of area. Different gamification schemes and rewards can be noticed for both player-to-environment and player-to-player interaction, including learning progress, skill progress and social activities, resulting in an evolving and interacting system that attracts the interest of the final user (FORESIGHT, 2020).

RESULTS

Having present a variety of cybersecurity platforms and their gamification elements respectively adapted, commonalities can be noted. Certain elements can be observed in numerous platforms regardless their origin and goals. This findings state that the users' engagement, gamification wised, is affected not by the platform essentially, but mainly by the elements adapted by it and their implementation. The overall data per researched platform and their corresponding type are stated are presented in Table 1, where an overall gamification status for all of these platforms can be observed in this comparative evaluation.

Different platforms of the same type may encapsulate different gamification elements, but as an overall conclusion most elements can be used in most platforms' types. Precisely, most basic elements are commonly used in all types of platforms, but with their own alterations to fit the theme, goals and target audience. Based on the target audience those elements have their own unique implementations. For instance, Points as a reward can be used in both CST Games and in CRs, however the latter type can be more punishing to the user during his/ her evaluation than the former. Generally, it is concluded that CST Games tend to have a more friendly and forgiving approach regarding their gamification schemes, a state that is enriched when considering that the target audience is consisted of inexperienced used in

Table 1. Training environments and gamification status

	Training Platform	**Points**	**Badges/Skills**	**Leveling System**	**Leaderboard**	**Progress Bar**	**Virtual Currency**	**Story Line**
1	CST Games	Yes	Yes	Yes	Yes	Yes	Yes	Yes
2	CTFd	Yes	No	No	Yes	No	No	No
3	echoCTF	Yes	No	No	Yes	No	No	No
4	TinyCTF	Yes	No	No	Yes	No	No	No
6	PicoCTF	Yes	No	No	Yes	No	No	No
7	RootTheBox	Yes	Yes	Yes	Yes	Yes	No	Yes
8	HackTheBox	Yes	Yes	Yes	Yes	Yes	No	Yes
9	OverTheWire	Yes	No	Yes	No	No	No	Yes
10	DefendTheWeb	Yes	Yes	Yes	No	Yes	No	Yes
11	TryHackMe	Yes	Yes	Yes	Yes	Yes	No	Yes
12	Pwnable	Yes	No	Yes	Yes	No	No	Yes
13	RootMe	Yes	Yes	Yes	Yes	No	No	Yes
14	CYBERBIT	Yes	Yes	No	No	Yes	No	Yes
15	Silensec	Yes	Yes	Yes	Yes	Yes	No	Yes
16	CDeX	Yes	Yes	No	Yes	Yes	No	Yes
17	CYBERGYM	Yes	Yes	No	No	Yes	No	No
18	Circadance– Project Ares	Yes	Yes	Yes	No	Yes	Yes	Yes
19	KYPO	Yes	No	No	No	No	Yes	Yes
20	Foresight	Yes	Yes	Yes	Yes	Yes	No	Yes

the cyber security field and of various age groups. CST games can implement a variety of gamification elements in addition to game-like graphics. Such environments tend to use more game-wised approaches, augment their game aspects, rather than their educational characteristics. Based on the type of the game – card games, tower defend, question based – a variety or all elements stated in table 1 can be combined to create their overall look and feel.

In comparison, Self-Paced platforms, such as capture-the-flag, tend to use less gamification elements, mainly focusing in the ability to automatically assign scoring to users, which is an essential aspect competition-wised. Most platforms of this type are built in such manner that allows their further adaptation upon needs on numerous gamification elements, such as story-telling, leveling or leaderboards. However, those elements do not consist part of their initial goals. Since those platforms may host a vast number of users and are web-based applications mainly, they need to host a gamification scheme offering concrete scoring across all users and to be of minimum human intervention. Noticeable is the fact that those type of platforms, tend to use many gamification elements to attract the interest and to be differentiated amongst their competitors. This realization relies in the fact that there is no direct connection between a trainee and a trainer, and thus it is essential for the system to provide a direct representation of the user's progress and performance through the tasks they perform.

On the other hand, cyber-ranges and federated cyber-ranges may not implement an automated way of scoring the users or rewarding them for their actions, since in most cases those platforms are constantly supervised by professionals during training sessions. In addition, platforms of this type that aim at training organization personnel, may not include many gamification elements, since they are built with specific training goals and are created in more formal and strict manners. Furthermore, when transferring from a CR to a Federation of CRs, game elements can be eliminated to avoid the overall user's distraction. However, recent trends show that more and more platforms tend to adapt gamification elements, since gamifying the training environment and the general educational and learning procedure, can notice significantly better results in terms of user's interaction, progression and understanding.

Overall, we conclude that using story-line techniques when presenting the task to the user can be beneficial to their overall immersion and attract their interest upon completing the task or even assist on better understanding of the goals and challenges presented. Additionally, points can be used to reward users in respect to their progression and results, while leaderboards can attract their constant interest with the platform and thus achieve a continues learning procedure. Finally, leveling and skill mechanics can enrich the users' intrinsic motivation and can, in limited cases, act as a way to proof their knowledge to third parties.

CONCLUSION

Over the past decade, cyber-attacks have become increasingly sophisticated, stealthy, multi-vector and multistage, which may leverage zero-day exploits and highly creative attack methods. Cyber-security education and training are becoming more and more relevant, as they are the only way to prevent and adequately handle such cyber-breaches. Towards a continues adaptation to new technologies and a continues education from the user's part, gamification elements are becoming more and more common in all type of platforms. They are uniquely created to each platform but in all cases, they are developed with a common goal: attract the interest of the users and keep their interaction constant for better and more learning outcomes.

Serious games offer the ability to non-professional users to train themselves and be protected from common attacks and threats, while also rase their awareness starting from a young age. Self-paces and lightweight platforms offer the ability to individuals to further interact with the cyber-security field and acquire or further evolve their security skills on their own pace. Cyber Ranges can provide an environment for continuous training using state-of-the-art methodologies, techniques, a training program covering multiple domains, in order to guide cyber-security experts and professionals in implementing and combining security measures in innovative ways.

Regardless the platform type, gamification mechanisms and elements are used to engage the users and have them constantly interacting with the platform, while also providing them the ability to monitor their progression. Such a goal is well addressed by CST Games and in the operational training level more drastic adaptation can be performed to achieve greater interaction level. Each platform may introduce its own gamification scheme, formed under different rules and elements based on needs; however, as shown, most of them share common mechanics that are noted to affect the trainees and motivate their actions.

Future work indicates to analyze more platforms and distinct the goal axes setter by each platform during the creation of the corresponding gamification scheme. Having an extensive list of both the gamification elements, the desired learning outcomes and the way each platform implement such a composition, can assist upon creating a standardization method for creating a hybrid and ad-hoc solution for all type of platforms. Such an adjustable tool can save human resources and time when creating a new cyber security training platform, by offering just the minimum input, rather than performing start-over research on global educational objectives and the respective game elements to be used.

ACKNOWLEDGMENT

This material is based upon work supported by the European Union Horizon 2020 project "FORESIGHT: Advanced cyber-security simulation platform for preparedness training in Aviation, Power-grid and Naval environments" and has received funding from the European Union's Horizon 2020 research and innovation program under grant agreement no. 833673. The work reflects only the authors' view and the Agency is not responsible for any use that may be made of the information it contains.

REFERENCES

Adams, M., & Makramalla, M. (2015). Cybersecurity Skills Training: An Attacker-Centric Gamified Approach. *Technology Innovation Management Review*, *5*(1), 5–14. doi:10.22215/timreview/861

Agate. (2017). *Core elements and mechanics of gamification*. Retrieved from https://agate.id/core-elements-of-gamification

Anvik, J., Cote, V., & Riehl, J. (2019). Program Wars: A Card Game for Learning Programming and Cybersecurity Concepts. *SIGCSE '19: Proceedings of the 50th ACM Technical Symposium on Computer Science Education*, 393-399. 10.1145/3287324.3287496

BenchPrep. (2015). *The 6 best gamification tools to engage your learners*. Retrieved from https://blog.benchprep.com/gamification-tools-to-engage-learners

Boopathi, K., Sreejith, S., & Bithin, A. (2015). Learning Cyber Security Through Gamification. *Indian Journal of Science and Technology*, *8*(7), 642–649. doi:10.17485/ijst/2015/v8i7/67760

Celeda, P., Cegan, J., Vykopal, J., & Tovarnak, D. (2015). *KYPO – A Platform for Cyber Defence Exercises*. M&S Support to Operetional Tasks Including War Gaming, Logistics, Cyber Defence.

Chou, Y. K. (2013). *User and player types in gamified systems*. Retrieved from Yu-kai Chou: Gamification & Behavioral Design: https://yukaichou.com/gamification-study/user-types-gamified-systems

CIRCADANCE. (n.d.). *Cyber ranges and how they improve security training*. Retrieved from CIRCADANCE: https://www.circadence.com/blog/cyber-ranges-101-and-how-they-improve-security-training

Circadance. (n.d.). *Project Ares*. Retrieved from D5-IQ: https://d5-iq.com/ai-powered-cyber-learning-platform

CYBERBIT. (2021). *CYBERBIT Train for Real*. Retrieved from https://www.cyberbit.com/

David, L. (2013). *Game reward systems*. Retrieved from Learning Theories: https://www.learning-theories.com/game-reward-systems.html

Duggan, S., & Thrope, C. (2017). An analysis of how information security e-learning can be improved through gamification of real software issues. 16th Eur. COnf. Cyber Warfare and Security, 666-66.

ECSO. (2020). *Understanding cyber ranges: From hype to reality*. WG5 Paper.

Filipczuk, D., Mason, C., & Snow, S. (2019). Using a Game to Explore Notions of Responsibility for Cyber Security in Organisations. *CHI EA '19: Extended Abstracts of the 2019 CHI Conference on Human Factors in Computing Systems*, 1-6. 10.1145/3290607.3312846

Fischer, H., Heinz, M., & Bretenstein, M. (2018). Gamification of learning management systems and user types in higher education. *Proc. 12th Eur. Conf. Games Based Learn*, 91-98.

FORESIGHT. (2020). *FORESIGHT*. Retrieved from FORESIGHT Project: https://foresight-h2020.eu/

FORESIGHT. (2020). *FORESIGHT D4.2 - Report for Learning/Training Objectives*. Methodology and Evaluation.

Garcia de Soto, B., Georgescu, A., Mantha, B., Turk, Z., & Maciel, A. (2020). *Construction cybersecurity and critical infrastructure protection: Significance, overlaps, and proposed action plan*. Preprints.

Giantas, D., & Liaropoulos, A. (2019). *Cybersecurity in the EU: Threats, frameworks and future perspectives*. Working paper series no. 1.

Gonzalez, C., Mora, A., & Toledo, P. (2014). Gamification in intelligent tutoring systems. *TEEM '14 2nd Int. Conf.*, 221-225. doi:10.1145/26351.263903

InfoSecurity. (2021). Retrieved from https://www.infosecurityeurope.com

Ixia. (2014). *Cyber range: Improving network defence and security readiness*. Retrieved from Ixia White Paper: https://support.ixiacom.com/sites/default/files/resources/whitepaper/915-6729-01-cyber-range.pdf

Jia, Y., Xu, B., Karanam, Y., & Voida, S. (2016). Personality-targeted gamification: A survey study on personality traits and motivational affordances. *Proc. 34th Annu. CHI Conf. Human Factors Comput. Syst. (CHI '16)*. 10.1145/2858036.2858515

Jin, G., Tu, M., Kim, T.-H., Heffron, J., & White, J. (2018). Game based Cybersecurity Training for High School Students. *SIGCSE '18: Proceedings of the 49th ACM Technical Symposium on Computer Science Education*, 68-73. 10.1145/3159450.3159591

Jones, J., & Chou, T.-S. (2019). *An infrastructure supporting a game-based learning system for information security topics. Conf. Industry Educ. Collaboration*.

Kianpour, M., Kowalski, S., Zoto, E., Frantz, C., & Overby, H. (2019). Designing serious games for cyber ranges: A socio-technical approach. IEEE Eur. Symp. on Security and Privacy Workshops (EuroS&PW), 85-93. doi:10.1109/EuroSPW.2019.00016

Kumar, J. M., Herger, M., & Dam, R. F. (2020). *Bartle's player types of gamification*. Retrieved from Interaction Design Foundation: https://www.interaction-design.org/literature/article/bartle-s-player-types-for-gamification

Luh, R., Temper, M., Tjoa, S., Schrittwieser, S., & Janicke, H. (2020). PenQuest: a gamified attacker/defender meta model for cyber security assessment and education. *J. Comput Virol. Hack. Techn.*, 19-61. doi:10.1007/s11416-019-00342-x

Marczewski, A. (2016). *6 tips for short term gamification*. Retrieved from Gamified UK: https://www.gamified.uk/2016/06/23/short-term-gamification

Marczewski, A. (2017). *Gamification elements and mechanics.* Retrieved from https://www.slideshare. net/daverage/gamification-elements-and-mechanics

Marczewski, A. (2018). *Gamification & user experience UX connect.* Retrieved from https://www. slideshare.net/daverage/gamification-user-experience-ux-connect?next_slideshow=1

Moore, M. (n.d.). *Bringing gamification to cyber security training.* Retrieved from Global Sign: https:// www.globalsign.com/en/blog/bringing-gamification-to-cybersecurity-training

Nicholson, S. (2015). A RECIPE for meaningful gamification. In T. Reiners & L. Wood (Eds.), Gamification in Education and Business (pp. 1–20). Academic Press.

Nwehouse, W., Keith, S., Scribner, B., & Witte, G. (2017). *National Initiative for Cybersecurity.* National Institute of Standards and Technology. doi:10.6028/NIST.SP.800-181

Park, S., & Kim, S. (2017). A Validation of differences in academic achievement among Bartle's player types in an educational gamification environments. *J. Korean Game Soc., 17*(4), 25–36. doi:10.7583/ JKGS.2017.17.4.25

Patricio, R., Moreira, A. C., & Zurlo, F. (2018). Gamification approaches to the early stage of innovation. *Creativity and Innovation Management, 27*(4), 499–511. doi:10.1111/caim.12284

Patricio, R., Moreira, A., Zurlo, F., & Melazzini, M. (2020). Co-creation of new solutions through gamification: A collaborative innovation practice. *Creativity and Innovation Management, 29*(1), 146–160. doi:10.1111/caim.12356

PwC. (n.d.). *Game of Threats.* Retrieved from https://www.pwc.ru/en/publications/game-of-threats.html

Robinson, C. (n.d.). *Comparison of 15 leading gamification software systems.* Retrieved from Finances: https://financesonline.com/top-15-gamification-software-systems

SC. (n.d.). *Gamification: A winning strategy for cybersecurity training.* Retrieved from Media: https:// www.scmagazine.com/home/opinion/executive-insight/gamification-a-winning-strategy-for-cybersecurity-training

Scholefield, S., & Shepherd, L. A. (2019). Gamification Techniques for Raising Cyber Security Awareness. *HCII 2019: HCI for Cybersecurity, Privacy and Trust, 11594,* 191–203. doi:10.1007/978-3-030-22351-9_13

Seaborn, K., & Fels, D. I. (2015). *Gamification in theory and action: A survery Int. J. Human-Comput. Stud.,* 9. doi:10.1016/j.ijhcs.2014.09.006

Silensec. (2020). Retrieved from https://www.silensec.com

Sponge. (2019). *6 reasons why it's time to overhaul cybersecurity training.* Retrieved from https:// wearesponge.com/insights/2019/10/6-reasons-why-its-time-to-overhaul-cybersecurity-training

Sylvester, T. (2013). *A guide to engineering experiences. O'Reilly Media.*

Thomas, M. K., Shyjka, A., & Gjomemo, R. (2019). Educational Design Research for the Development of a Collectible Card Game for Cybersecurity Learning. *Journal of Formative Design in Learning*, *3*(1), 27–38. doi:10.100741686-019-00027-0

Thompson, M., & Takabi, H. (2016). Effectiveness of Using Card Games to Teach Threat Modeling For Secure Web Application Developments. *Issues in Information Systems*, *17*(3), 244–253. doi:10.48009/3_iis_2016_244-253

Tovarnak, D. (2017). *KYPO Cyber Range Design and Use Cases*. Retrieved from CSIRT-MU: https://is.muni.cz/publication/1386573/2017-ICSOFT-kypo-cyber-range-design-presentation.pdf

UniversityC. M. (2020). *PicoCTF*. Retrieved from https://picoctf.org/

Wang, H., & Sun, C. T. (2011). Game reward systems: Gaming experiences and social meanings. *Proc. 2011 DIGRA Int. Conf.: Think Design Play (DIGRA '11)*. Retrieved from http://gamelearninglab.nctu.edu.tw/ctsun/10.1.1.221.4931.pd

Chapter 18
Moral and Ethical Scenarios for Educational Computer Games Based on the Robotic Futurology of Stanislaw Lem

Tetiana Luhova
https://orcid.org/0000-0002-3573-9978
Odessa Polytechnic State University, Ukraine

ABSTRACT

The research aims to develop a method of creating moral and ethical scenarios for educational computer games based on stories from the cycle of robotic futurology by S. Lem. The result of the study revealed a correspondence between the directorial script and game design document; the critical components of Lem's story "Trurl's Machine" were formalized considering the moral and ethical conflicts of the plot; the authors created a map of the action scene, game mechanics, and UML based on the story "Trurl's Machine." Considered the issues of transforming plots of classical literature into the game design of educational computer games with an emphasis on the development of the moral and ethical scenarios and the spiritual values formation in students, the rules of the "Mechanical Robots AlgorithmsAda Board Game" as a video game prototype have been rethought with pedagogical impact.

INTRODUCTION

Informatization of education stimulates virtual learning systems development, including educational computer games. But the society's technological singularity creates a "cold" formalized environment for a person's education, excluding his spirituality. The modern pedagogy ideologists notice that the teacher is not as important as an information carrier, but as a spiritual mentor (Terno, 2011). And a game designer is a teacher of morality (Devine, Presnell, & Miller, 2014). So, it is relevant to elaborate moral criteria for game designers as creators, artists, and educators. To work out ways to turn classic literary

DOI: 10.4018/978-1-6684-4291-3.ch018

plots into computer game mechanics via the values: kindness, the value of life, harmlessness, honor, dignity, humor, friendship, freedom of choice, responsibility, humaneness, etc.

Works of folklore and classical literature as treasuries of tacit knowledge and hidden educational narratives are excellent sources for spiritually oriented computer game scenarios (Luhova T., 2020). A vivid example is the literary works of the Polish futurist writer Stanisław Lem. He anticipated artificial intelligence, virtual reality, search engine theory, cognitive improvement, technological singularity, and nanotechnology. But, unlike scientific futurological forecasts, Lem's images are full of life, humor, moral conflicts, ethical dilemmas, and complex emotional states. In the well-known satirical stories cycle "The Cyberiad" 1964–1979 published (Lem, 2014) the writer raised the problem of the relationship between robots and people: wars of intelligent robots against people; a crazy robot ("How the World Was Saved", "Trurl's Machine", "Tale of the three storytelling machines of king Genius"); too smart robot ("The seven sallies of Trurl and Klapaucius. The First Sally or The Trap of Gargantius"); replacement of a person by a robot in various fields of activity. S. Lem drew attention to the deep contradiction between the formal logic inherent in the machine and the living. Thus, it is advisable to comprehend Polish science fiction not only to study the theories of philosophical futurology but also to educate the spirituality of a new digital generation. It is vital to solve the problem of maintaining morality in computer games, and their positive impact on the learning process.

BACKGROUND

Literary critics and philosophers have deeply studied the legacy of S. Lem. But game designers did not consider his work as the basis for game scenarios. There are all prerequisites for this.

Significant application base for game development and scenarios. MDA and DPE game development models are very well known. They are the methodological basis for computer games. Game development models are formal structures for creating and analyzing a computer game. These tools allow formalizing the creative process of designing and using games, breaking them down into components. The MDA model describes the game as a structured trinity of Mechanics (rules), Dynamics (impact timing and strategy), and Aesthetics (player's emotional responses) components (Hunicke, LeBlanc, & Zubek, 2004). In learning, the DPE model is important - Design, Play, and Experience (Winn, 2009), because it shows not only the algorithm for creating a video game but also the behavior of the game system as a tutor, its educational impact on the student-player. There is a browser tool for designing and balancing game systems (Machinations, 2022). The theory of the longline film scripts (Burbidge, 2013), (Chou, 2015), and computer games ((Mitchell, 2012), (Trullenque, 2013) are developed, created templates (Johnson, 2019), (Gardner, 2010).

Computer and humanities accumulated rich historiographical bases on various aspects of games for learning. The focus of scientists is game-based learning (Gee, 2003), (Tobias, Fletcher, & Wind, 2014), (Plass, Homer, & Kinzer, 2015), (Mao, Cui, Chiu, & Lei, 2022), (Bartolomé & Van Gerven, 2022). The study of serious games also has a long history and a significant legacy (Abt, 1987), (Mildner & Mueller, 2016), (Stofella & Fadel, 2022), (Luhova T., Serious Games for Recruitment in the New Humanism, 2022), (Luhova T. A., 2021). This should consider the constant growth of scientific knowledge.

Researches on morality are also substantive: in human behavior (Frankl, 2017), (Frankl, 2014), pedagogy (Terno, 2016), (Vasianovych, 2013), art (Gardner, 1976), and computer games (Sicart, Ethics of computer games, 2009), (Didukh, 2018), (Semchuk, 2014), (Devine, Presnell, & Miller, 2014). It is vital to solve the problem of maintaining morality in computer games, and their positive impact on the learning process of the younger generation. Scientists pay attention to the ethics of gamification from the normative point of view of decision-making based on gamification (Versteeg, 2013), (Shahri, Hosseini, Phalp, Taylor, & Ali, 2014), (Sicart, 2015), (Kim T. W., 2015), (Kim & Werbach, 2016), (Marczewski, 2017), (Thorpe & Roper, 2019), (Goethe & Palmquist, 2020), (O'Sullivan, et al., 2021), (Nyström, 2021), (Kim & Werbach, Excerpt from Ethics of Gamification, 2022). After all, the origins of gamification as a marketing phenomenon include grain manipulation and exploitation (Huotari & Hamari, 2012). Instead, there are studies where gamification is positioned as "added-value exploratory knowledge" (Patrício, Moreira, & Zurlo, 2018). We assume the moral and ethical core of game scenarios to be such an added value. This is a result of translating implicit knowledge, and intangible values (moral norms) into formalized game design scenarios.

It is worth emphasizing the fundamental difference between the concepts of "gamification" and "game design". Gamification is a marketing technique to stimulate consumer activity through applying game elements and mechanics (bonuses, ratings, competitions, win-win lotteries, success visualizations) in a non-game context (Hamari, Koivisto, & Sarsa, 2014). In contrast, game design is a complex process of creating a virtual game world as a motivator, simply put it is the gameplay creating process (form, rules, content, fun, etc.). Advisable to clarify that the term "spirituality" is understood not as a synonym for "religiosity", but as a set of worldview attitudes and life principles based on ethics and morality. It is important to separate the concepts of "ethics" and "morality": "ethics are external rules or guidelines, where morals are more personal and inherent to an individual" (Marczewski, 2017). Thus, the balance and conflicts of external and internal principles of the player's decision-making are the core of creating moral and ethical game scenarios.

In previous works, we raised the topic of implementing spiritually oriented pedagogy in the process of designing educational video games for managers (Luhova T., 2020), implementation of the New Humanism principles in serious games (Luhova T., 2022), (Luhova T. A., 2021), canvas design of "Ethical Dilemmas" for educational video games (Luhova, Blazhko, Troianovska, & Riashchenko, 2019), correct gamification of open data for public administration activity from the morality viewpoint (Blazhko, Luhova, Melnik, & Ruvinska, 2017). The object of special scientific interest is the literary and stories into computer computer educational games (Gumennykova, Blazhko, Luhova, Troianovska, Melnyk, & Riashchenko, 2019). But the question of applying the methodology to a specific example remains relevant. Within the limits of this chapter, it is the story "Trurl's machine" by S. Lem (Lem, 2014).

The aim of the research is to develop a methodology for creating moral and ethical scenarios for the computer educational games based on stories from the series of robotic futurology by S. Lem.

The study objectives are:

— to compare the director's script and game design components;
— to formalize the key components of Lem's story "Trurl's Machine" into a game design script considering the moral and ethical plot collisions;
— to describe the stages for transforming a literary art into a game design;
— to rethink the developed game "Mechanical Robots AlgorithmsAda board game", created based on "The Cyberiad", from the point of view of the moral and ethical game scenarios.

The Methodological Basis of the Study

The deconstruction method to understand the philosophical concepts of from "The Cyberiad" cycle stories. In particular, the "Trurl's machine". The deconstruction method is complex. Since it covers many philosophical, semiotic, and lingual structuralist approaches and interpretations. The deconstruction method includes text analysis, critical reading, and rethinking within the boundaries of communication "the author's text – the reader's text". And this harmonizes with the "playing-experiencing-self-reflection" of the plots of classical literature in a computer game. The author's text transition to the "co-authorship" state with the player who experiences, creates, and re-justifies the classic plot in a video game, corresponds to the concepts of deconstruction and reconstruction of the text as the study of the process of its destruction (opening the discursive network embedded in it) and birth (Derrida, 2017).

The universal modeling language (UML) for the translation of selected concepts into a formal programming language as well. The UML allows for modeling of any subject's area, an important condition for effective game design (Albaghajati & Hassine, 2022). This infographic technique lets to formalize the idea of a game designer and correctly bring the basic ideas to understanding the programmer. UML models are based on the principle of simplifying the model of objects through their classification, i.e., division into varieties according to features (structure or attributes, behavior or relationship with other classes, features succession) and combination into classes. The "Use Case diagram" was operated to describe the relationship between characters involved in a game situation, and player actions that lead to a tangible result. This diagram allows seeing the actions' recurrence, which gives grounds for optimization or conscious enrichment of the existing system of the object. This language of an object description is most effectively implemented when creating game mechanics - the player's game actions.

A questionnaire was developed to analyze the perception of the game by schoolchildren. The purpose of the methodology is to formalize the philosophical concepts of Lem's "The Cyberiad" for their gamification and creation of educational games using UML and MDA models, with the subsequent automation of the process of translating the narrative and philosophical meanings of literary stories into a game design format; to present the rules of the developed board game example.

Comparative analysis was used to correlate the components of the director's script and game design, to show a correspondence between the player' and characters' action, game' and life' values, rules, and the player's self-identification.

Visualization method — to present a map of the scene of the story "Trull's Machine" as game locations.

Generalizations — for summing up the results of the study and planning conclusions.

MAIN FOCUS OF THE CHAPTER

The Director's Script and Game Design Components

In scenario theory, the term "scenario" itself (Italian) is understood as a plan of a literary work with a detailed description of the action, a plot scheme according to which performances in the theater, improvisations, films, mass shows and others are created. The components of the script are descriptions of scenes and actions for the creators of the artistic product: director, actors, cameraman, lighting technician, etc. There are also two parts of the script-descriptive (remark) and speech. Frolova, Chub and Rastopchina (2009, p. 71) rightly point out that various scenarios (theatrical, cinema, sports-mass, cultural-leisure, etc.) have fundamental differences, but according to the technology of creation, they have the same basis. Any script should have a theme and idea, goal, objectives, genre, and style, as well as the director's intention, which is formed into a director's script. All of the above is consistent with the information blocks of the game design document and can be developed using canvas-based game design.

Match results in the key components of the director's script (Markov, 2004), game design document (Trullenque, 2013), (O'Donnell, 2014), (CtaylorDesign), Canvas game design (Blazhko & Luhova, 2018), and MDA (Hunicke, LeBlanc, & Zubek, 2004) summarized in a table (Table 1).

Table 1. The director's script and game design components correspondence

Key issues	Components of a director's script	Components of a game design document,	Canvas game design	MDA
Where?	Characteristics of the effective space: stages, playgrounds, content, and location of scenery and scenography.	Introduction. Game world: how the game world is arranged, characteristics of objects, formulas of movement or battle, role system, physics of the world. Script. Story Bible	Game world canvas	Mechanics
Who?	Characteristics of the characters and their actions: the nature of plasticity and speech, effective tasks, costumes	Physical model. Player character Main characters / types of troops with parameters and approximate location / method of extraction and production. Art Bible / Collection of images, drawings / Doodles	Game narrative canvas	Mechanics
What does it / he / she do?	Description of the people and objects movement: the entrances and exits direction of the characters and participants, the movement direction of the scenery and objects; the beginning and end act moments; relocation of actions; mise-en-scène and their rebuilding, etc.	Functional specification. Game scheme. What should a player do, what is the goal, and what is preventing it from being achieved?		
How? Whereby?	Characteristic of sound design: content, place of inclusion, volume level	Sounds and music. Themes, type, and way of displaying sounds, set of sound effects.	Canvas player types and game aesthetics	Aesthetics
	Characteristics of lighting design: content, moments of changes in the light picture	Graphics and video. How many and which models, animations, type of graphics, videos, wallpapers, concept art will be needed.		
	Genre, tempo-rhythmic, stylistic recommendations for the manner of acting	Storyboards		
	Expected actions of the participants: audience reaction (applause, exclamations, etc.); movement of participants in space	Introduction. Genre and audience. User interface. Functional description and management. User interface objects.		
When? How long?	Time schedule of the event: duration of episodes and fragments, total duration of the program	The game session duration. Balance of game content and time.	Mechanics and game dynamics canvas	Dynamics

The Components of Lem's story "Trurl's Machine" via a Game Design Script

Interestingly, both in the script and in the game design document there are no components-explanations of the actions of the characters, their motivation, background, feelings. That is, there is no moral and ethical component as an engine of action of the heroes: why? For what? Why? But all this makes it possible to automate the process of creating a game, from filling in the game design canvases to a game design document and generating a scenario and game space. To automate the computer games scripts' creation, necessary to formalize the components of the literary work script by identifying word-descriptors and generating a scene map. The action of "Trurl's Machine" is constructed according to the folklore principle. It is revealed in the actions of the heroes, their movements: "Folklore knows only empirical space, i.e., the space that surrounds the hero at the moment of action" (Propp, 1976). In Lem's story "Trurl's Machine" (Lem, 2014), this is:

—   the plain where Trurl designed the thinking Machine;
—   town, town hall, deep cellar;
—   Rocky Mountains with a narrow gorge, and a cave where Trurl and Klapaucius hid from the Machine; the riverbed, where Machine died.

According to the location, it is easy to construct a map of events (Figure 1).

Figure 1. The place of action "Trurl's Machine" map

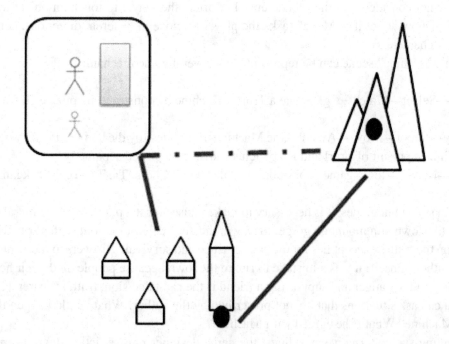

The folklore principle of space is well implemented in video games, when the physical model of the game world is initially programmed and game and non-game objects are already placed in it, and the game itself can be easily segmented by location. "A game is a set of scenes connected to each other (just like life is a set of days)". In this case, the scene is often defined as the location, for example, "home" – when the player is in the building, "street" – when the player leaves the building to the street. The logic of the folklore trinity "place-hero-action" corresponds to the focus on the optimization of computer resources: "Why should the processor strain to process the area that we cannot visit?" (Mishamishutka, 2012).

The plot is a stream of events: prologue, exposition, connection, development, culmination, dénouement, epilogue (McKee, 1997). It is important to note that the algorithm of the game, both system and story, determined by rules. In computer games, moral and ethical situations are usually omitted, narrowing down to specific mechanics of goal (Game rules) and manipulation (Play rules).

Game rules determine the goal of the game (Djaouti, Alvarez, Jessel, & Methel, 2008) and are realized in the verbs: "Create" (invites the player to be creative in compiling, building or constructing virtual values of the game), "Destroy" (invites the player to destroy game objects or collect and catch objects for their further purposeful collection and accumulation), "Avoid" (asks the player to avoid collisions with objects of the game – obstacles or opponents) and "Match" (asks the player to install or maintain one or more objects in a certain state). Play rules – rules of manipulation that determine the basic actions that a player can apply in the game. These include: "Select" (asks the player to make multiple selections of items, such as inventory items, weapons, various structures or dialog responses with the mouse), "Write" (asks the player to enter character-numeric values; in role-playing games allows the player to communicate with other players); "Manage" (offers the player to manage resources to achieve the goal. E.g., refuel a car, buy ammunition, materials, and tools for construction); "Random" (offers the player to challenge the chance, get lucky. It is used as a way to create random events); "Shoot" (the term "shoot" is not considered in the literal sense but offers the player to touch an object located at a distance, or somehow affect it); "Move" (asks the player to move in different directions, control other objects or other characters).

The "Trurl's Machine" scene can be represented by several game mechanics:

- "Create—Select—Match", e.g., create a Trurl's Machine by constructing, puzzle, Tetris, drawing, etc.
- "Destroy—Shoot—Move—Avoid" – the Machine tries to destroy the heroes, and they must dodge; the Machine's pursuit of Trurl and Klapaucius can also be played separately.
- "Match—Move" – logic games-constellations like "Go", Chess, Tic-Tac-Toe, Backgammon.

However, in such mini games, it is necessary to make pauses for the player to make moral decisions: where to run, to a town or a mountain gorge; to stay in the deep cellar or go out with a friend to danger; should insist on the truth or accept lies for the sake of truce and survival? Answers to these questions are given by the author himself: it was a mistake to run to the town because people died, their houses were destroyed; going out to danger and supporting a friend is the right decision; truth is dearer. However, in the game, you can ask situations that are not prescribed by the author: What would happen if Trurl did not kick the Machine? What if he agreed with Machine?

In constructing such alternative storylines, the game designer must strictly adhere to the author's system of values and obligatory moral values, setting the boundaries of what is acceptable for the player and creating a fair system of "punishments" for the player's wrong moral choice. The complexity of designing plots with moral collisions consists in formalizing this process, translating it into a rigid system of "yes—no", "1—0", which levels out semitones of moral decisions, complicates the process of taking into account the player's justification of his decision (Why did he decide so? What are the reasons for actions?). In this case, the canvas of "Ethical Dilemms" (Luhova, Blazhko, Troianovska, & Riashchenko,

2019) and a table of correspondences between the actions of the heroes, and their moral assessment will help. All this should form the basis of the rules of the game (Figure 2, Table 2).

Figure 2. Canvas of Ethical Dilemmas

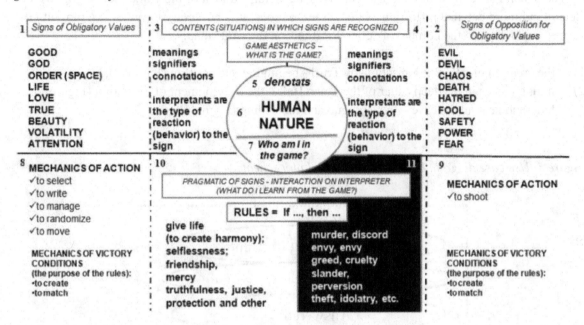

Table 2. Correspondence between actors' actions, values, rules and the game's self-identification

The plot action-milestones list	Values, features	Reward for choice: points, bonuses	Consequences of actions in the game	Game self-identification of the player	Direction of pedagogical influence
Creating a Thinking Machine	Creativity	+	Creating a machine. Development	The Inventor (if the player is playing Trurl)	Encourage
Mathematical dispute	Insist on the truth	+	The beginning of the conflict. Negotiation	The Truth-lover, veracious (Trurl)	Encourage
	Agree with a lie	-	Obedience. The beginning of the conflict	The Conformist (Klapaucius)	Discourage, show consequences
Pushing a Thinking Machine	Intolerance Aggression	-	Continuation of the conflict	The Aggressor (Trurl)	Not encourage
Pursuit	Intolerance. Aggression	-	Continuation of the conflict	The Aggressor (Thinking Machine)	Prevent the opportunity to play as the aggressor
Flee to the mountains	Self-preservation. Providence. Responsibility	+	Conflict resolution. Game over	The Escapee (Trurl, Klapaucius)	Encourage
Escape to town	Self-preservation. Improvidence. Irresponsibility	-	Destruction and human losses	The Escapee (Trurl, Klapaucius)	Discourage, show consequences
Hiding in the deep cellar	Cowardice	-	Continuation of the conflict. Destruction and human losses.	The Victim (Trurl, Klapaucius)	Not encourage. Discuss variation for contexts and consequences
Go to the meeting	Support a friend	+	Negotiation	The Faithful, brave friend (Klapaucius)	Encourage. Discuss variation for contexts and consequences

The storyline of the characters actions can be easily represented in the use case diagram of the universal modeling language (UML). The inner motives and reasons for these actions can be shown using the state-diagram. In the first case, it is necessary to create a base of the main words-actions of the heroes. In the second case, supplement them with a base of words-motivators.

The general scheme of the literary plot gives a generalized idea of the game plot (Figure 3). For a clearer and more detailed reflection of the heroes' actions, it is necessary to divide the plot into three scenes, depending on the number of action locations on the game map:

1) the creation of a thinking machine by Trurl - beginning and conflict (Figure 4);
2) hiding places in the deep cellar of the Town Hall – the development of the action (Figure 5);
3) hide-and-seek in the cave – the epilogue and the ending (Figure 6).

Figure 3. Use case diagram based on the general plot scheme

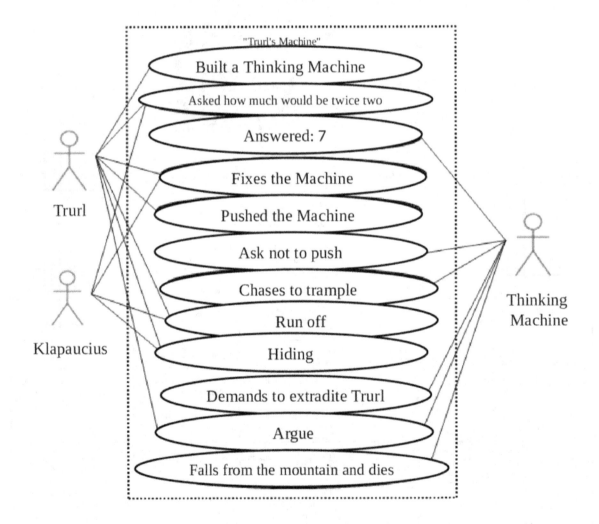

Figure 4. Scene 1. Creating a Machine

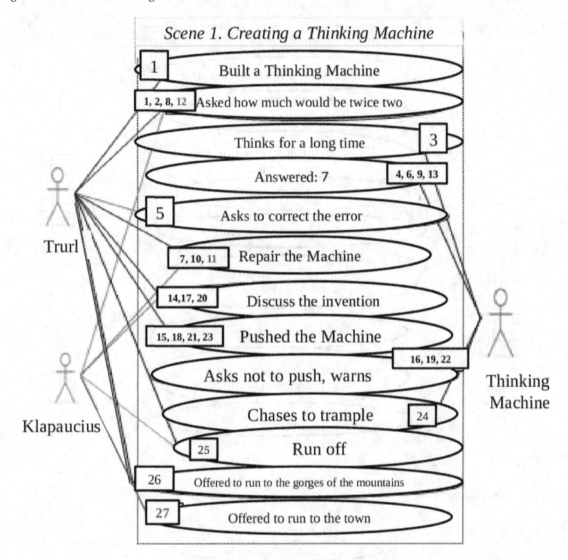

The use case diagram will be the basis for creating a video game plot outline when choosing a plot type. (linear, non-linear, chronic, or dichroic), and the state diagram will show "bifurcation points" or plot milestones in which the player can pause for reflection and choose his reaction to the plot situation. S. Terno notes: "Our society is dominated by deterministic ideas about the nature of our lives. At the heart of these ideas is the theory of conditioned reflexes by I. Pavlov. The main idea is that a person is programmed to respond to a certain stimulus in a certain way" (Terno, 2016). Referring to the works of V. Frankl (Frankl, 2017), (Frankl, 2014), S. Terno concludes that there is always the freedom of choice between the stimulus and the reaction. Therefore, this freedom of choice should be practiced by educational video games, they should show that any reaction of the student-player is his own choice, and "human freedom is not freedom from conditions, it is the freedom to take a certain position regarding on conditions. Internally, the individual may be stronger than the circumstances" (Terno, 2016).

Figure 5. Scene 2. Town

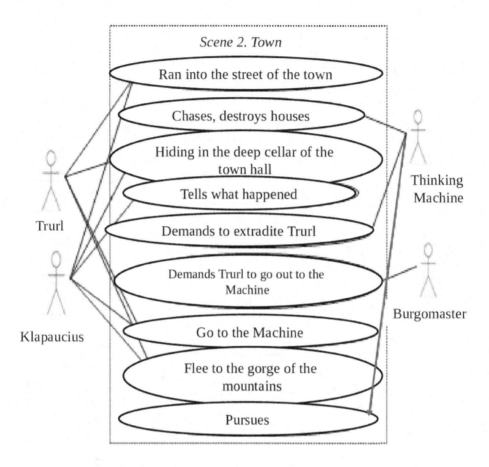

Figure 6. Scene 3. Mountains

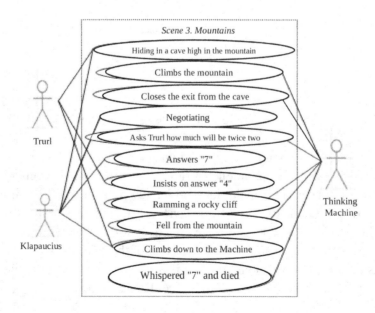

The plot points-pauses and transitions from one scene to another will become important key points for the educational impact (Figure 7). The system of game rules should reward for the right moral choice and punish for the wrong one. E.g., all the accumulated points-bonuses for the creation of the Machine can be deducted for the wrong choice of an escape route to the town because the consequence of these actions is human casualties and destruction. Scenario pauses-milestones for the hero-player to make a decision can coincide with the so-called Character Arcs (Weiland, 2017).

Figure 7. Important key points for the educational impact

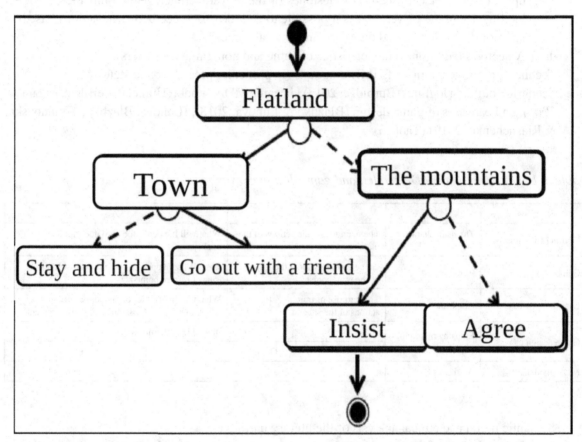

The Stages for Transforming a Literary Art into a Game Design

There are five stages have formed in the methodology of game design of literary work:

1. Textological – structural and semiotic analysis of stories to create a script for a game (computer or desktop), which consists in extracting descriptor words from a literary text:
    a. Circumstances (game world: where? when?) To describe the world of the story and the world of the future game: game setting, physics of objects, laws of the universe, causes of events, game world, hero's route, and map of the place of action.

    b.   Nouns (game and non-game characters) for identifying and describing characters: protagonists, antagonists, game and non-game objects. Character development: character (internal features) and characterization (external features). What are their advantages and disadvantages? How will the main character change by the end of the story? What should he learn? How does the character and actions of the characters reflect the theme of the story?

    c.   Verbs (moves, actions, emotions, motivators). When drawing up a script, it is important to harmonize the logic of the compositional construction of all its parts with a consistent increase in the emotional and spectacular effect. It is advisable to combine the peaks of the emotional uplift of the plot with the plot milestones of the player's choice. This trains the emotional intelligence of the player, makes it possible to feel the difference between "actions based on emotions", "actions based on logic" and "moral choice".

    d.   Adjectives (additional characteristics of game and non-game characters).

2.   Technological – generation of UML-diagrams (in particular precedent and state).

3.   Scenario - building loglines (Burbidge, 2013) via game MDA-model (Hunicke, LeBlanc, & Zubek, 2004), and canvases of game design (Blazhko & Luhova, 2018), (Luhova, Blazhko, Troianovska, & Riashchenko, 2019) (Table 3).

Table 3. Logline and game MDA-model, and game design canvas

Logline	X	Y	Z	
Fiction / Literature	The main character / hero	The main idea – the actions of the main character	What will happen if the hero does not achieve his goal	
Game	Protagonist	Game goal, mission – the actions of the protagonist	Loss. What happens if the protagonist loses (player restore points)	
Learning process	Applicant	The purpose of training – the actions of the student	What will happen if you do not perform educational tasks (possibility of rearrangement)	
Game design canvas	Empathy map, types of players	Canva of the ethical dilemmas		
		Good	Evil	
MDA-model	Aesthetics	Mechanics	Dynamics	

4.   Semantic moral and ethical analysis of the literary narrative:

    a.   Determination of the main idea of a literary story and a game goal: conditions for victory and defeat.

    b.   Determination of moral and ethical connotations of descriptor words (keywords) using the Canvas of Ethical Dilemmas (Luhova, Blazhko, Troianovska, & Riashchenko, 2019). The specificity of the ethical side of a video game is the lack of distinction between living and inanimate objects. Because spiritualized game characters in computer games can be any objects that function (move) within the game history: balls, cars, dots, etc. Utilitarian ethical theory states that the best action is that which maximizes utility (Blazhko, Luhova, Melnik, & Ruvinska, 2017), (Luhova T., 2020). "Usefulness" is defined in different ways, usually in terms of the well-being of living persons (Didukh, 2018), (Einstein, McDaniel, Williford, Pagan, & Dismukes, 2003). Therefore, it is important to develop such a program mechanism that considers the utilitarian relations between the objects of the game, the player's actions, and his self-identification.

    c.   Metaphorization of descriptor words (creation of game art-concept). For the development of an educational computer professionally-oriented game, it is important to metaphorize the necessary and sufficient base of competencies, which are usually formulated in educational and professional programs and are fixed in the educational syllabuses of the educational components of training specialists. It is important that the metaphorization of the game is based on mythological structures of consciousness and has positive connotations, as indicated in our works (Blazhko, Luhova, Melnik, & Ruvinska, 2017), (Luhova T., 2020), (Luhova T., 2021).

5.   Pedagogical:
    a.   Assessment of the pedagogical influence of a literary story: what character traits can be brought up on this example (responsibility for one's creation and decisions made, tolerance, comradely support, love of truth, perseverance, a sense of self-preservation, foresight, creativity).
    b.   Description of situations from a literary story as pedagogical cases.
    c.   Determination of plot points for pedagogical influence and obtaining a positive educational effect.

The algorithm for transforming a literary work into game design is based on the deconstruction method, which allows you to analyze the text, philosophical meanings and the world's picture of the selected story. This method is especially relevant in creating board and computer games, including classic plots in a new game context, designing different interaction between the communicator and the recipient: story and reader, story and player, story author and game designer. Deconstruction is an important methodological basis for the correct interpretation of the meanings of a literary art, its deep intertextual reading. The choice or development of the correct software tool for text mining, automatic annotation, etc. complicated automating such a complex process.

Yu. Kristeva noted two directions of analysis of the "word status": horizontal and vertical (2000, p. 429). Horizontal – the word in the text belongs both to the subject-author and its recipient-reader. Vertical - the word in the text focuses on the totality of other early or modern literary texts. Thus, intertextuality is an important criterion for the deconstruction of literature for the automatic creation of scenarios for computer learning games. The first provides an opportunity to project the pedagogical impact on the participants of the communicative process, the second defines the interdisciplinary connections of the game as a learning environment. E.g., the word "create" has for the reader (student) only positive connotations. The author understands by this word also "responsible for the creation". The results of "vertical analysis" confirmed it. S. Lem raised the same topic in other stories. E.g., Trurl's Machine can create everything starting with the letter "N". When it was ordered to do "nothing", it nearly caused the entire universe to disappear ("How the World Was Saved"). In another story, Electrobard's poetry brought his creator not so much fame as trouble ("The First Foray (A) or the Electronic Bard of Trurla"). This applies to all cosmogonic themes in mythology, demiurge heroes, scientific inventions, and so on.

Based on the philosophical deconstruction of "The Cyberiad", the following concepts are identified: "responsible creativity"; fears that humanity feels before the prospects of robotics; limits of free will (Thinking Machine); experience of "imaginary experiment – philosophical zombie"; structure of argumentation (logic of science and the process of cognition), "The world as a text", "The machine as a demiurge".

The game design model can be used for the following game options:

- a game based on a narrative with strict adherence to the story plot: games-stories (interactive books), games-quests;
- a game based on the story philosophy – a game "based on" with the main meaning of the story or the philosophy of the author as a whole (shooters, fighting games, arcades, races, logic, – any genre on a given topic);
- a game built on both narrative and story philosophy is the most difficult version of the game outline (strategies, simulators, second-life, Roblox, etc.).

SOLUTIONS AND RECOMMENDATIONS

In 2017, the Odessa GameHub team created a prototype of the "Mechanical Robots AlgorithmsAda board game", which teaches the basics of programming and predictive analytics. The game was created based on the narratives and philosophy of The Cyberiad (scenario, figures of Trurl and Klapaucius robots, playing field, cards, chips and rules for controlling robots). The game mechanics were based on the game with an open license "Battle of Golems: Learning, Programming, Robotics". The gameplay of this game was tested and confirmed by us (GameHub-seminar in the children's camp "Victoria", 2017). However, posing the chapter problem led to a rethinking of the rules of the game.

The mechanics of the game are divided into four stages-operations for programming the robot's actions by players. Players can use the following action cards: forward, backward, turn right, turn left, kick, defense, repeat 2 times, obstacle, and choose. The task is to create a sequence of robot actions that leads to the desired result. Mission – to get to certain locations on the game map. The challenge is to guess what actions the opposing player will program. The goal is to reach the opponent and defeat him (strike when the opponent does not defend). The genre of the game is battle.

Analysis of the game from the point of view of moral and ethical scenarios made it possible to identify the following shortcomings:

- an emphasis on programming actions, achieving their effectiveness (to get to a given location first, to strike an opponent), neutralizes the ethical component of the consequences of such actions;
- weak connection to the plots of S. Lem's The Cyberiad;
- the goal of the game violates moral and ethical values (to strike an unprotected opponent);
- reliance on binary oppositions: yes – no, your own – a stranger, good – evil;
- moral and ethical conflicts are not spelled out and pauses for decision-making are not provided;
- the rules of the game do not provide rewards for the correct moral and ethical choice of the player.

The positive features of the rules of the developed game are:

- hexagonal locations of the playing field give more opportunities for game maneuvers, break binary oppositions in the player's mind;
- understanding the importance of well-thought-out programming actions to achieve the right result;
- the need to interact with another player for logical and intuitive prediction of his game actions;

- educational orientation of the game (the goal is to teach the basics of programming and analytics of prediction);
- plot-explanation of the purpose of the game: "Trurl and Klapaucius wrote the first commands for their robots. It became so exciting that they competed – which of the robots will win? Whose program will be better? Who will be "a stupid machine that does what is punished", and who will receive the honorary title of "smart machine", which first understands what is more profitable: "solve the problem or try to turn away from it"? Will the robot created in the future become an assistant or the first enemy because of ill-considered algorithms of its behavior" (GameHub-seminar in the children's camp "Victoria", 2017).

Given the "Canva of ethical dilemmas" that creates a moral and ethical scenario for the game "Mechanical Robots AlgorithmsAda board game", we have added the following changes to the rules: Variations in the choice of characters: clones of friends Trurl and Klapaucius (battles of friends are known in ancient epics and myths, such as Gilgamesh and Enkidu), and Trurl and the Thinking Machine.

Semantics of locations of the playing field: town, mountains, field. The player's choice of mountains and fields as places for the battle is encouraged by additional points, the choice of town causes a decrease in points, the choice of location "Deep cellar" gives immunity, but the player loses one point for each missed move, exit from the location "Deep cellar" is awarded two points. (Figure 8).

Figure 8. Comparison of the game field and the characters of the "Mechanical Robots AlgorithmsAda board game"

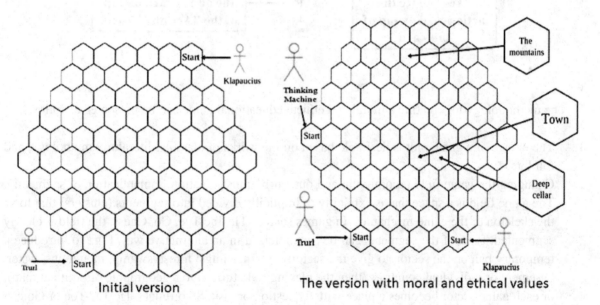

Initial version

The version with moral and ethical values

In the action card "Obstacle" added a moral conflict "Defend the truth". The correct decisions of moral and ethical conflicts give the player immunity in two moves (Figure 9).

Figure 9. Comparison of the game field and the characters of the "Mechanical Robots AlgorithmsAda board game"

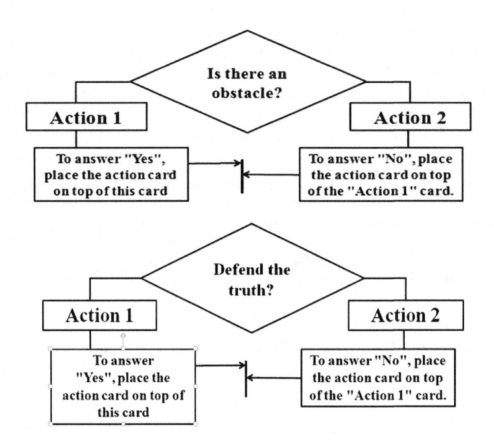

The methodology for creating a moral and ethical educational game can be presented as follows:

1.   The choice of a game plot is desirable based on the works of classical literature, mythology, and folklore.
2.   Changing the game field (zooming in and out, curly transformation, semantisation of segments). The game field is a space that is explicitly or implicitly divided into segments (clusters) that form the skeleton of the game mechanics. In games such as Tic-Tac-Toe, Go, Chess, the field is clearly segmented. Each of the segments can be semanticized in an alternative way. E.g., to introduce a temporary ban on the sector, to give the sectors new meanings: forest, swamp, mountains, water, basement or individual countries (then the playing field turns into a geographic or political map), or each game sector becomes a place with a question or task. So ordinary Tic-Tac-Toe or Go can be turned into a game of "throw and move" adventure, strategy, quest.
3.   Changing the hero (new image, psychology, an increase in the number of heroes and players). It is important to think about the roles of the game antagonist and protagonist, their plot relationships, and the impact on the player's self-identification. So, it is not desirable for the player to play as a negative character (his role can be played by a computer system), to take into account the contexts

of the confrontation between characters (positive example, the battle of Gilgamesh and Enkidu, experiments and disputes between friends of Trurl and Klapaucius).

4. Balancing the rules under the new game field, adding new elements and requirements, designing locations with moral and ethical conflicts; changing the conditions of winning, considering the moral choice of the player, and not the pragmatics of winning.

5. Changing dynamics: new cards of actions, tasks, luck, bonuses, encouragement for correct moral choices, temporary pauses for making decisions and realizing responsibility for them.

6. It is advisable to reflect on the principles of human-centered design (Norman, 1986): focus on people, find the right fundamental problem, and system view with the game (optimizing the local does not necessarily lead to optimizing the global). This means allowing the player to make mistakes and correct mistakes, creating conditions for contextual understanding.

Figure 10. The results of the students' questionnaires analysis

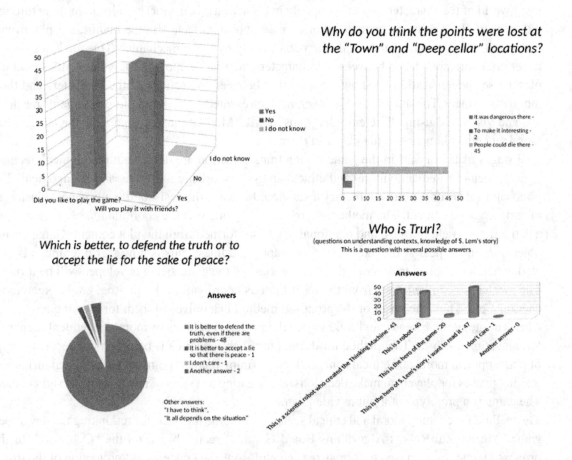

A questionnaire was developed to analyze the game perception by students. It included five questions. Did you like to play the game?; Will you play it with friends?; Why do you think the points were lost at the "Town" and "Deep cellar" locations? Which is better, to defend the truth or to accept the lie by way of peace? Who is Trurl? The results of the questionnaire showed not only interest in the game, and its playability, but also the effects of schoolchildren's awareness of responsibility for decisions made, the difficulty of resolving moral and ethical conflicts that make one think, and the emerging interest in S. Lem's (Figure 10).

CONCLUSION

1. Comparison of the components of the director's script and game design made it possible to establish the common structure of creating theatrical, literary, and video games. This served as the basis for describing the method of creating moral and ethical scenarios for computer games.

2. The key components of Lem's story "Thrull's Machine" were analyzed: literary chronotope, characters, and plot milestones. It made it possible to formalize them into a game design script, considering moral and ethical plot conflicts, to develop a map of the scene (game locations) of the story. The folklore principle of "the space and action unity" is well realized in video games. The inner world of the character develops not only in his actions (behavior) but also in moving through the game world. Therefore, game locations are an important factor for the manifest of plot events and moral and ethical decisions of the hero, backed up by game mechanics. This made it possible to set up a correspondence between the characters' actions, game and life values, rules, and the player's self-identification, to show a connection between the actions of the characters and their moral assessment. The story "Thrull's Machine" is presented as a combination of the game mechanics, and visualized using "Use case diagrams" UML. Marked the key points for the educational moral and ethical impact on the player in them.

3. Five stages of literary art in the game design transformation are described: textological, technological, scenario, semantic moral and ethical analysis of artistic narrative, and pedagogical. The philosophical deconstruction of literary texts should serve as the basis for the subsequent clustering of texts as game content. The method of creating the game was the coordination of mechanics as a game frame (field of rules) and relational databases formed from the plot content. Game design objects should appear at the intersection of graphs and lines. This is how a grid template is created: when it is applied to a fictional text, a database of the game being developed will be formed. The mechanics can be drawn from the most famous board games: tic-tac-toe, go, backgammon, checkers, etc. Thus, the result of the proposed method is a universal form for creating any game. Classical literature, legends, and folklore are the principal sources of moral and ethical scenarios for educational games. The method for developing such scenarios is based on the deconstruction of philosophical moral and ethical connotations, defining them as points of pedagogical influence, making pauses for players to make decisions, and creating a system of rewards for the right choice. The game is a prototype of a future video game.

4. The method for creating moral and ethical scenarios became the basis for rethinking the developed game "Mechanical Robots Algorithms Board Game", created based on the "Cyberiad". In the proposed game, we managed to formalize such philosophical concepts as "protection of the truth" (choice card), "fear of an uncontrollable robot" (a thinking machine can be defeated), "responsible creativity", "responsible decision", "saving human lives", "courage" (conscious choice of game locations). An important effect of the game is also to stimulate the interest of schoolchildren in Lem's stories. This became possible due to the change in the rules of the game, the semantiza-

tion of the playing field, the creation of new action cards, the new arrangement of heroes, and the consideration of moral and ethical conflicts.

The moral and ethical scenarios development is also important for the gamification process, since it focuses the player's actions not on the quantitative results of actions and gifts, but on the contexts of these actions, their semantic content and moral and ethical significance. For example, the task for the player is not a certain number of targets destroyed (the most, the fastest), but the very fact of "saving someone", "helping".

From the perspective of our research, it is promising to see the development of standards (norms, rules, requirements, principles) for educational computer games. It would be a rewarding experience given the idea of developing criteria for "true art is by its nature moral" (Gardner, 1976). An important step for the development of ethical standards for computer games is the automation of the Ethical Dilemma Canvas. Taking into account the semiotic and axiological foundations for the metaphorization of play narratives and the design of moral play behavior.

It is interesting to consider video games from a semiotic point of view. The deconstruction method application to moral and ethical subjects in computer games and more widely in the digital environment. According to the concept of "zero level of being" (Barthes, 1977), the deconstruction method functions according to the "1-0" principle, since it involves binary opposition destruction (reduction to the limit). When one side of opposites "no longer exists, and the other does not exist yet." Then both opposite sides receive a "zero" level of being, from which transgression occurs or going beyond the limits of the oppositional pair when referring to something common that characterizes both sides. We see the deconstruction strategy in games in the sliding of signs along with the semantic surface, and the inner (moral core) representation in external manifestations (game scenarios).

ACKNOWLEDGMENT

This publication was created with the support of the European Commission Erasmus+KA2-project "Game-Hub: University-enterprises cooperation in the game industry in Ukraine" (N° 561728-EPP-1-2015-1-ES-EPPKA2-CBHE-JP). The European Commission support for the production of this publication does not constitute an endorsement of the contents, which reflect the views only of the authors, and the Commission cannot be held responsible for any use which may be made of the information contained therein.

REFERENCES

Abt, C. C. (1987). *Serious games.* University Press of America.

Albaghajati, A., & Hassine, J. (2022). A use case driven approach to game modeling. *Requirements Engineering, 27*(1), 83–116. doi:10.100700766-021-00362-4

Barthes, R. (1977). *Writing degree zero* (A. Lavers, & C. Smith, Trans.). Macmillan.

Bartolomé, P. S., & Van Gerven, T. (2022). From the classroom to the game: applying available pedagogical guidelines in game-based learning. In *2022 IEEE Global Engineering Education Conference (EDUCON)* (pp. 466-472). IEEE. 10.1109/EDUCON52537.2022.9766475

Blazhko, O., & Luhova, T. (2018). Features of using the canvas-oriented approach to game design. *Applied Aspects of Information Technology*, (1), 62–73.

Blazhko, O., Luhova, T., Melnik, S., & Ruvinska, V. (2017). Communication Model of Open Government Data Gamification Based on Ukrainian Websites. In *International conference on Intelligent Data Acquisition and Advanced Computing Systems: Technology and Applications (IDAACS): 4th Experiment International Conference (exp.at'17). IEEE* (pp. 181-186). University of Algarve. 10.1109/EXPAT.2017.7984367

Burbidge, J. (2013). *Tips for Writing Loglines.* Retrieved 03 30, 2021, from Raindance: https://www.raindance.org/10-tips-for-writing-loglines/

Chou, J. L. (2015). *An analysis of the creative process* [Master of Fine Arts]. The University of Texas at Austin.

Derrida, J. (2017). The deconstruction of actuality: an interview with Jacques Derrida. In M. McQuillan (Ed.), *Deconstruction* (pp. 527–553). Routledge.

Devine, T. C., Presnell, W. A., & Miller, S. (2014). Games as Art and Kant's Moral Dilemma: What Can Ethical Theory Reveal About the Role of the Game Designer as Artist? *Games and Culture*, 9(4), 277–310. doi:10.1177/1555412014538812

Didukh, E. (2018). Conceptual foundations of morality in videogames. *Philosophy and Humanism*, 1(7), 41–50.

Djaouti, D., Alvarez, J., Jessel, J. P., Methel, G., & Molinier, P. (2008). A gameplay definition through videogame classification. *International Journal of Computer Games Technology*, 2008, 1–6. doi:10.1155/2008/470350

Einstein, G. O., McDaniel, M. A., Williford, C. L., Pagan, J. L., & Dismukes, R. (2003). Forgetting of intentions in demanding situations is rapid. *Journal of Experimental Psychology. Applied*, 9(3), 147–162. doi:10.1037/1076-898X.9.3.147 PMID:14570509

Frankl, V. E. (2014). *The will to meaning: Foundations and applications of logotherapy.* Penguin.

Frankl, V. E. (2017). *Man's search for meaning.* Beacon Press.

Frolova, N. D., Chub, A. A., & Rastopchina, N. V. (2009). Scripting technology. *KiberLeninka. Physical culture, sports - science and practice,* (4), 70-72.

GameHub-seminar in the children's camp "Victoria". (2017). Retrieved 03 30, 2021, from https://www.facebook.com/groups/477292889122044/permalink/728158117368852/

Gardner, J. (1976). Moral fiction. *The Hudson Review*, 29(4), 497–512. doi:10.2307/3850454

Gardner, J. (2010). *The art of fiction: Notes on craft for young writers.* Vintage.

Gee, J. P. (2003). What Video Games Have to Teach Us about Learning and Literacy. Palgrave Macmillan. doi:10.1145/950566.950595

Goethe, O., & Palmquist, A. (2020). Broader understanding of gamification by addressing ethics and diversity. In *International Conference on Human-Computer Interaction* (pp. 688-699). Cham: Springer. 10.1007/978-3-030-60128-7_50

Gumennykova, T., Blazhko, O., Luhova, T., Troianovska, Y., Melnyk, S., & Riashchenko, O. (2019). Gamification features of stream-education components with education robotics. *Applied Aspects of Information Technology*, *1*(02), 45–65.

Hamari, J., Koivisto, J., & Sarsa, H. (2014). Does Gamification Work? – A Literature Review of Empirical Studies on gamification. In *Proceedings of the 47th Hawaii International Conference on System Sciences*, (pp. 3025-3034). 10.1109/HICSS.2014.377

Hunicke, R., LeBlanc, M., & Zubek, R. (2004). MDA: A formal approach to game design and game research. *Proceedings of the AAAI Workshop on Challenges in Game AI*, 1, 1722.

Huotari, K., & Hamari, J. (2012). Defining gamification: a service marketing perspective. In *Proceeding of the 16th international academic MindTrek conference*, (pp. 17-22). 10.1145/2393132.2393137

Johnson, S. (2019, December 27). *Kurt Vonnegut on 8 shapes of stories*. Retrieved 01 25, 2021, from Big think: https://bigthink.com/culture-religion/vonnegut-shapes

Kim, T., & Werbach, K. (2016). More than Just a Game: Ethical Issues in Gamification. *Ethics and Information Technology*, *18*(2), 157–173. doi:10.100710676-016-9401-5

Kim, T. W. (2015). Gamification ethics: Exploitation and manipulation. *Proceedings of ACM SIGCHI Gamifying Research Workshop*.

Kim, T. W., & Werbach, K. (2022). Excerpt from Ethics of Gamification. In *Ethics of Data and Analytics* (pp. 375–385). Auerbach Publications. doi:10.1201/9781003278290-55

Kristeva, I. (2000). Bakhtin, word, dialogue and novel. In *French Semiotics: From Structuralism to Poststructuralism* (pp. 427–457). Progress.

Lem, S. (2014). *The Cyberiad: fables for the cybernetic age* (1st ed.). Penguin Classics.

Luhova, T. (2020). Narrative and storytelling in the knowledge structure of educational and business video games as factors of synergy of information technologies and spiritually-oriented pedagogy. *Open Educational E-Environment of Modern University*, (8), 42-59.

Luhova, T. (2021). Game design oriented approach to the development of academic disciplines of higher educational institutions. *Information Technologies and Learning Tools*, *81*(1), 235–254.

Luhova, T. (2022). Serious Games for Recruitment in the New Humanism. In O. Bernardes & V. Amorim (Eds.), *Handbook of Research on Promoting Economic and Social Development Through Serious Games* (pp. 375–394). IGI Global. doi:10.4018/978-1-7998-9732-3.ch017

Luhova, T., Blazhko, O., Troianovska, Y., & Riashchenko, O. (2019). The Canvas-Oriented Formalization of the Game Design Processes. In *2019 IEEE 2nd Ukraine Conference on Electrical and Computer Engineering (UKRCON)* (pp. 1254-1259). Lviv, Ukraine: IEEE.

Luhova, T. A. (2021). Journalism education based on serious games. *OpenEdu [Internet]*, (11), 92–105.

Mao, W., Cui, Y., Chiu, M. M., & Lei, H. (2022). Effects of Game-based learning on students' critical thinking: A meta-analysis. *Journal of Educational Computing Research*, *59*(8), 1682–1708. doi:10.1177/07356331211007098

Marczewski, A. (2017). The ethics of gamification. XRDS: Crossroads. *The ACM Magazine for Students*, *24*(1), 56–59.

Markov, O. I. (2004). *Scenario culture of directors of theatrical performances and holidays: a textbook for teachers, graduate students and students of universities of culture and arts.* KGUKI.

McKee, R. (1997). *Story: style, structure, substance, and the principles of screenwriting.* Harper Collins.

Mildner, P., & Mueller, F. F. (2016). Design of Serious Games. In R. Dörner, S. Göbel, W. Effelsberg, & J. Wiemeyer (Eds.), *Serious games* (pp. 57–82). Springer International Publishing. doi:10.1007/978-3-319-40612-1_3

Mishamishutka. (2012, December 5th). *Unity3d. Getting started, practical advice.* Retrieved 03 30, 2021, from https://habr.com/ru/post/161463/

Mitchell, B. L. (2012). *Game design essentials.* John Wiley & Sons.

Norman, D. (1986). User centered system design. *New perspectives on human-computer interaction.*

Nyström, T. (2021). Exploring the Darkness of Gamification: You Want It Darker? In K. Arai (Ed.), Intelligent Computing (pp. 491-506). Cham: Springer.

O'Donnell, C. (2014). *Developer's dilemma: The secret world of videogame creators.* MIT press. doi:10.7551/mitpress/9035.001.0001

O'Sullivan, D., Stavrakakis, I., Gordon, D., Curley, A., Tierney, B., Murphy, E., Collins, M., & Becevel, A. (2021). "You Can't Lose a Game If You Don't Play the Game": Exploring the Ethics of Gamification in Education. *International Journal for Infonomics*, *14*(1), 2035–2045. doi:10.20533/iji.1742.4712.2021.0211

Patrício, R., Moreira, A. C., & Zurlo, F. (2018). Gamification approaches to the early stage of innovation. *Creativity and Innovation Management*, *27*(4), 499–511. doi:10.1111/caim.12284

Plass, J. L., Homer, B. D., & Kinzer, C. K. (2015). Foundations of game-based learning. *Educational Psychologist*, *50*(4), 258–283. doi:10.1080/00461520.2015.1122533

Propp, V. I. (1976). *Folklore and reality: Selected articles.* Nauka.

Semchuk, S. (2014). Moral and spiritual development of the individual in the context of the influence of computer technology. *Scientific Bulletin of Melitopol State Pedagogical University named after Bohdan Khmelnytsky. Series. Pedagogy*, *1*(12), 221–225.

Shahri, A., Hosseini, M., Phalp, K., Taylor, J., & Ali, R. (2014). Towards a code of ethics for gamification at enterprise. In IFIP working conference on the practice of enterprise modeling (pp. 235-245). Springer. doi:10.1007/978-3-662-45501-2_17

Sicart, M. (2009). *Ethics of computer games*. MIT Press. doi:10.7551/mitpress/9780262012652.001.0001

Sicart, M. (2015). Playing the good life: Gamification and ethics. In S. Waltz & S. Deterding (Eds.), *The gameful world: Approaches, issues, applications* (pp. 225–244). MIT Press.

Stofella, A., & Fadel, L. M. (2022). Fidelity and Play Model: Balancing Seriousness. In O. Bernardes & V. Amorim (Eds.), *Handbook of Research on Promoting Economic and Social Development Through Serious Games* (pp. 1–20). IGI Global. doi:10.4018/978-1-7998-9732-3.ch001

Terno, S. (2011). Why is it important to develop students' critical thinking? *History in the Schools of Ukraine,* (10), 30-34.

Terno, S. (2016). Critical thinking: dynamics and scope. *Works of the Historical Faculty of Zaporizhia National University,* (46), 310-315.

The Game Balancing Platform. Beta design, simulate & handoff game systems. (2022). Retrieved from Machinations: https://machinations.io/

Thorpe, A. S., & Roper, S. (2019). The ethics of gamification in a marketing context. *Journal of Business Ethics, 155*(2), 597–609. doi:10.100710551-017-3501-y

Tobias, S., Fletcher, J. D., & Wind, A. P. (2014). Game-based learning. In Handbook of research on educational communications and technology (pp. 485-503). New York: Springer Science+Business Media. doi:10.1007/978-1-4614-3185-5_38

Trullenque, V. R. (2013). *Game Design & Development (GDD)* [Bachelor's thesis]. Universitat Politècnica de Catalunya.

Vasianovych, H. P. (2013). Spiritual and moral message of victorious multimedia at the beginning of the vicious process. *Science notes. Series. Pedagogyka*, (3), 20–26.

Versteeg, M. J. (2013). *Ethics & Gamification design: a moral framework for taking responsibility* [Master's thesis]. Universiteit Utrecht.

Weiland, K. M. (2017). *Creating Character Arcs: The Masterful Author's Guide to Uniting Story Structure, Plot, and Character Development.* PenForASword Publishing.

Winn, B. (2009). The Design, Play, and Experience Framework. In R. Ferdig (Ed.), *Handbook of Research on Effective Electronic Gaming in Education* (Vol. 3, pp. 1010–1024). IGI Global. doi:10.4018/978-1-59904-808-6.ch058

APPENDIX

Figure 11. Questionaire

Dear friend! **You played the game "Board Game AlgorithmsHell of Mechanical Robots"** **Please answer the questions!)**	**Дорогий друг!** **Ти зіграв у гру «Настільна гра АлгорітміАда механічних роботів»** **Будь ласка, відповідай на питання!)**
# Questionnaire	# Анкета
for assessing the moral and ethical scenarios of the game "Board game Mechanical Robots AlgorithmsAda"	для оцінки морально-етичних сценаріїв гри «Настільна гра Mechanical Robots AlgorithmsAda»
1.Did you like to play the game? ☐ Yes ☐ No ☐ I do not know	*1.Чи сподобалось вам грати у гру ?* ☐ Так ☐ Ні ☐ Не знаю
2.Will you play it with friends? ☐ Yes ☐ No ☐ I do not know	*2.Чи гратимете ви в цю гру друзями ще ?* ☐ Так ☐ Ні ☐ Не знаю
3.Why do you think the points were lost at the "Town" and "Deep cellar" locations? ☐ It was dangerous there ☐ To make it interesting ☐ People could die there	*3.Чому, на вашу думку, бонуси були втрачені у локаціях "Місто" та "Глибокий льох"* ☐ Там було опасно ☐ Для того, аби було цікаво ☐ Там могли загинути люди
4.Which is better, to defend the truth or to accept the lie for the sake of peace? ☐ It is better to defend the truth, even if there are problems ☐ It is better to accept a lie so that there is peace ☐ I don't care ☐ Another answer_____	*4.Що краще - захищати правду чи приймати брехню заради миру?* ☐ Краще захищати правду, навіть якщо будуть проблеми ☐ Краще погодитись з неправдою аби був мир ☐ Мені все одно ☐ Інша відповідь_____
5.Who is Trurl? ☐ This is a scientist robot who created the Thinking Machine ☐ This is a robot ☐ This is the hero of the game ☐ This is the hero of S. Lem's story. I want to read it. ☐ I don't care ☐ Another answer_____	*5.Хто такий Трурль?* ☐ Це робот-вчений, який створив Мислячу Машину ☐ Це робот ☐ Це герой гри ☐ Це герой розповіді С.Лема. Хочу її прочитати. ☐ Мені все одно ☐ Інша відповідь

Chapter 19
Sustainable Engagement in Open and Distance Learning With Play and Games in Virtual Reality:
Playful and Gameful Distance Education in VR

Stylianos Mystakidis
https://orcid.org/0000-0002-9162-8340
University of Patras, Greece

ABSTRACT

Open and distance learning became a global household term as it came to the forefront of education and work due to the proliferation of remote emergency teaching imposed by the pandemic's social distancing. Virtual reality (VR) is a technology that can transform distance education by overcoming the shortcomings of 2D web-based systems such as learning management systems and web-conferencing platforms. VR-powered teaching can support educators in implementing game-based methods, such as playful design, gamification, and serious games (e.g., educational escape rooms that promote intrinsic motivation towards sustainable engagement for durable, deeper learning). However, a transition from 2D to 3D teaching in the context of the Metaverse is not straightforward or intuitive as it requires a mental and paradigm shift. This chapter presents practical examples of applications and recommendations for practitioners.

DOI: 10.4018/978-1-6684-4291-3.ch019

INTRODUCTION

In the fictional two-dimensional world of Flatland in E. Abbot's mathematical novel (Abbott, 1885), citizens have the shape of 2-D geometric shapes such as triangles, squares, and circles. They live in private, pentagon houses, create families and work in regular jobs. They are certain about the reality they experience around them: the world and the universe consist of the familiar two dimensions of a flat surface. Alpha is an open-minded gentleman, a square, who is introduced to the evasive third dimension and the sense of a three-dimensional space in the eve of a new millennium. He meets a messenger in the form of a sphere who shows him the 3-D Spaceland and convinces him empirically: there is a third dimension after all. Subsequently, he sets to share the news and inform the perceptions of his fellow countrymen based on his ground-breaking and reality-altering discovery that opens new avenues for exploration and communication. Unfortunately, the regime accuses and condemns Alpha of heresy. He is imprisoned and the truth is suppressed to maintain the status quo and peace in Flatland.

This novella could be relevant to contemporary education. The recent COVID-19 pandemic disrupted physical activities and forced emergency remote teaching in all levels of education (Christopoulos & Sprangers, 2021). However, educational institutions were not prepared, and teachers were not trained and skilled to teach from a distance. As a result, remote emergency teaching faced many problems and did not manage to achieve high quality of teaching and learning (Schultz & DeMers, 2020). Students in all levels of education reported lack of interest, motivation, low levels of engagement, participation, achievement, performance. Many times, school pupils' participation was nominal, they appeared present in the virtual classrooms while not paying attention during teachers' monologues. Additionally, teachers, students, and workers reported sentiments labeled as "Zoom fatigue", an overload due to long and repetitive online meetings (Bailenson, 2021). As a result, this outbreak increased the anxiety levels of students (Wang & Zhao, 2020) and deteriorated mental health (Wheaton et al., 2021). Indeed, although there is abundant knowledge on how to organize online learning effectively, web-based solutions have their limitations due to their technological affordances. As a result, to the minds of some people, online learning, confused with improvised emergency remote teaching, becomes a synonym of monologue, boredom, a desert of closed microphones among a forest of abandoned cameras. These experiences constitute potentially a threat to how young people, teachers and parents perceive open and distance learning. The philosophy of open learning, closely associated to life-long learning is paramount is today's information age (Mystakidis & Berki, 2014). Distance education is also essential for flexible, continuous online professional development (Bragg et al., 2021). During the pandemic, notable initiatives were recorded accelerating the digital transformation of education (Ball et al., 2021). A comprehensive literature review revealed that online teaching practices need a comprehensive view of the pedagogy of online education that integrates technology to support teaching and learning (Carrillo & Flores, 2020). More specific, teaching presence depends on pedagogy, learning design, and facilitation practices; cognitive presence requires experience, action, contextualization, and conceptualization; social presence is related to interaction, participation, and belongingness. Interestingly, one study focusing on the barriers preventing the integration of educational technology into education suggested the exploration of gamification beyond primary schools also for secondary and higher education (Christopoulos & Sprangers, 2021). This trend was also observed in dental education through the adoption of serious games to improve online learning (Sipiyaruk et al., 2021).

However, there is a different way to teach and learn that is unknown to many educators; it requires stakeholders to follow Alpha square's footsteps and take a leap of evidence-informed faith towards the powerful third dimension, from web-based 2-D systems to 3-D virtual worlds. Online teaching in virtual worlds opens new pedagogical horizons for educators to challenge students cognitively while offering them enjoyable experiences where pupils are no longer passive recipients of content (Mystakidis, Berki, et al., 2021) and engage in active learning practices (Mystakidis, Mourtzis, et al., 2022). One method to reconceptualize distance teaching is using game design thinking to organize learning through playification, gamification, and serious games. All these methods can be applied both in learning management systems (LMS), 2D web-based platforms and in 3D virtual worlds. The main objective of this study is to demonstrate how learner engagement can be achieved and sustained through playful approaches to online teaching and learning using a multiple case study design. This study has wider practical implications for online education in the Metaverse featuring immersive, multiuser, networked environments (Mystakidis, 2022).

The rest of this chapter is structured as follows: in the next section the theoretical background is presented, followed by the research method, playful and gameful educational virtual reality (VR) applications, and conclusion.

BACKGROUND

Game design, mechanisms, processes, and effects are proposed foci of study for education practitioners so as to derive useful conclusions on practical ways to enhance and facilitate learning by increasing students' intrinsic motivation (Gee, 2004). An intrinsic goal orientation means that students enjoy learning for the sake of it, not as a necessary means to the achievement of external goals. Game-based learning strategies include playful design (playification), gameful design (gamification), and serious games (Patrício et al., 2018). Game-based motivation amplification strategies have been applied in education and e-learning and are at the epicenter of interdisciplinary research and business development towards motivational (Koivisto & Hamari, 2019).

These motivation amplification strategies can be projected in a continuum of complexity, holistic view, and degree of user autonomy. Playful design or playification is the simplest way to integrate the enjoyable element of fun in a 'serious', non-gaming context (Kangas, 2010). Playful learning is the simplest approach; it can be used sporadically with maximum freedom. It adds a layer of playfulness on top of the actual educational activity with minimal systemic interference where teachers and students are encouraged to exercise their creative agency (Mystakidis, Filippousis, et al., 2021). Playification can be applied in education considering four design elements: theme, actions, narrative, and auxiliary components (Mystakidis, 2021). The theme is an appropriate, common semiotic domain, e.g., science fiction, fantasy, a historic period, a cultural reference or artwork. Actions such as quests turn academic tasks into meaningful individual, group, or class challenges. Theme and actions should be part of an encompassing narrative, a story, or a hero's journey that is relevant to both students' and teachers' preferences (DePorres & Livingston, 2016). Story-based learning, narrative-based learning, storytelling, and storyfication can be considered a form of playification (McQuiggan et al., 2008; Shen et al., 2009; Wu & Chen, 2019).

Gamification in education is the application of game design principles to transform a pedagogical activity into a game (Deterding, 2011). Gamification turns a system or process into a game with a comprehensive strategy where users must achieve concrete goals following specific rules. For instance, a gamified e-learning course turns student evaluation into a multiplayer game (Mystakidis, 2020; Sheldon

& Seelow, 2017). Various gamification models have been proposed for educational settings. Game-informed learning proposes the production of compelling, immersive learning experiences through game-like teaching practices (Begg et al., 2005). Game-like learning engages students in their own quests adopting different roles, e.g., inventor, designer, innovator, and problem solver. This model is applied in the Quest to Learn public US middle and high school with an innovative game-based educational philosophy (Salen, 2017). Sheldon proposed the creation of multiplayer classrooms adopting techniques from massively multiplayer online games involving game mechanics such as avatars, points, levels, badges, and leaderboards (Sheldon, 2011). In a gamified curriculum, coursework is re-arranged as a game where students earn points as they choose and complete online and offline learning activities organized around various roles and skills (Sheldon & Seelow, 2017). As a result, quest-based learning management systems were developed to support educators in organizing and scoring both online and offline class learning activities (Haskell & Dawley, 2013). The model of meaningful gamification towards persistent behavioral change uses reflection, exposition, choice, information, play, and engagement (Nicholson, 2015). In contrast to extrinsic reward-based systems, this model aims at increasing intrinsic incentives through personal associations.

Serious games are enjoyable self-contained experiences with an educational purpose (Bellotti et al., 2011). Serious games can be considered an evolution of edutainment systems (de Freitas & Liarokapis, 2011). A serious game is a rather costly, self-contained digital entity where learning takes place while engaging in its context. Serious games can comprise the entirety of the educational experience or a part of it (Freire et al., 2014; Mystakidis et al., 2017b). In order to be effective and not sacrifice fun in the cost of learning, serious game mechanics and aesthetics need to align with intended course outcomes and learning mechanics (Arnab et al., 2015).

Virtual worlds are social spaces in virtual reality (VR), persistent computer-generated three-dimensional online spaces (Girvan, 2018). In the literature they are also called 3-D immersive environments or multiuser virtual environments. Virtual worlds can support effectively active learning paradigms such as problem-based learning and inquiry-based learning (Metcalf et al., 2018; Savin-Baden, 2014). Game-based learning in virtual worlds has been applied successfully in primary, secondary, and higher education. Most common game mechanics for gameful interventions in VR are story, realism, role-play, collaboration, movement, status, points, competition, token, levels, and game turns (Pellas et al., 2021). A systematic review has concluded that interventions in virtual worlds with certain characteristics can have positive, euergetic effects on academic performance, achievements, outcomes, and engagement (Pellas & Mystakidis, 2020). This has been observed in science, technology, engineering, and mathematics (STEM) as well as in humanities, arts, and social sciences (Hornik & Thornburg, 2010; Stokrocki & Chen, 2012; Wang et al., 2020). Engagement is the cognitive expenditure and affective investment for the active participation in a learning procedure (Lim et al., 2006). Student engagement in e-learning environments can be classified in seven levels of increasing achievement: disengagement, unsystematic engagement, frustrated engagement, structure dependent engagement, self-regulated interest, critical engagement, and literate thinking (Bangert-Drowns & Pyke, 2001). The achieved level of student engagement is associated with factors such as task complexity, attention, intrinsic goal orientation, volition, and self-directed learning (Kucirkova et al., 2014). Apart from the obvious student engagement, teacher engagement is also another vital dimension in distance education (Bragg et al., 2021). Not all educators are equally excited and passionate about teaching from a distance, especially in higher education where research is considered academics' top priority and precondition for tenure and advancement (Mills et al., 2009).

METHOD

The guiding research question was: "How can online learners' engagement enhanced sustainably in 3-D virtual worlds?" In this post-hoc study we analyze four case studies on the effects of the application of game-based learning in distance online education. The methodological frame is of qualitative underpinnings and is grounded on the evaluative case study paradigm. Case studies provide opportunities for in-depth exploration of specific learning activities. A qualitative study's analytic benefit is substantial when two or more cases are studied (Yin, 2009). For enhanced external generalizability of findings and recommendations, we adopted a multiple-case study approach and examined four cases where the author played a principal role in their design, development, and delivery. Representative cases were selected purposefully to demonstrate how playful design (playification), serious games, and gameful design (gamification) can be applied to enhance the motivation and engagement of online learners.

PLAYFUL AND GAMEFUL DISTANCE EDUCATION IN VR

Under the following headings lessons from four implementation approaches of game-based motivation enhancement methods in 3-D virtual worlds are presented that can be useful and applicable for distance remote teaching.

Playful Open Education with Colorful Massive Open Online Courses

Sometimes, the structure of an educational event is pedagogically pre-defined due to academic reasons or too rigid to change. For example, a synchronous guest lecture/webinar in the context of a massive open online course (MOOC), followed by a questions & answers session. Using 3-D meeting spaces it is possible to energize and facilitate blended e-learning, as demonstrated in a case study implemented at the University of Patras, Greece (Mystakidis et al., 2017a). One of the first MOOCs ever to feature virtual worlds was the "Open Workshop on Information Literacy" (Kostopoulos et al., 2014). The course had a total duration of 18 months spanning over five units related to information literacy skills, tailor-made for postgraduate students and doctoral candidates. The MOOC had a blended format combining flexible individual and group work as well as weekly online meetings in virtual worlds with trainers and expert guest speakers. A conscious effort has made to create variety in VR to keep online meetings interesting and aesthetically pleasing. Hence, the course made extensive use of theming, through buildings, avatar accessories, 3-D objects, and props. More specific, the term "workshop" provided the inspiration to adopt a medieval theme, organizing the main meeting space as an alchemist's lab (Figure 1). Additionally, whenever the season or the topic would be fitting, meetings were held in other temporary spaces with informal community building activities. For instance, in winter months, meetings would be organized in a virtual frozen lake. During breaks and after the end of each meeting, snowball fights would break out. Other times, attending avatars would receive a surprise virtual gift. Over 300 students experienced a pleasant, enjoyable community atmosphere that supported the sustainable engagement of participants. As a result, over 33% of participants were able to complete the course successfully in both MOOC iterations.

Figure 1. Themed MOOC meeting space in a 3-D virtual world with props

Multimodal Playful Quest-based Learning in a Virtual Museum

The design, planning, building, and customizing of 3-D learning experiences in VR is usually a complex and time- and energy-consuming venture. Once the digital assets have been built, it is a smart idea to use them for multiple purposes to accommodate personalized user needs. For instance, a story or a serious game can be experienced in different interaction modes best suited for free exploration, guided practice, or unassisted assessment (Ferguson et al., 2019; Mystakidis, Besharat, et al., 2022).

In 3-D virtual words, interactive environments can be experienced asynchronously through multiple ways, facilitating guided or autonomous explorations. The University of Washington organized from 2009 to 2014 the Virtual Worlds certificate as one of its professional and continuing education programs. The program run from a distance over a nine-month period. Participants from all over the world met weekly in a social virtual world, experienced and learned how to design, build, and program interactive virtual environments. During the final trimester of each year, one entire virtual island was created, dedicated to a timely chosen topic. The cohort of 2012-13, designed the Museum of Virtual Media inspired by a book chapter dedicated to the history of virtual reality from the dawn of humanity till today (Blascovich & Bailenson, 2011). In fact, the virtual museum was designed in consultation and with direct communication with both book authors. Other final project foci of previous years were Cybersecurity (Endicott-Popovsky et al., 2013), Maya civilization (Hill & Mystakidis, 2012), and Value Sensitive Design (Friedman et al., 2002).

The museum of virtual media featured twelve exhibits that corresponded to the major virtual reality media. Eleven of them were openly accessible: storytelling, graphics, sculpture, theater, manuscripts, movable type (typography), photography, cinematography, electricity, broadcast media, computer/internet (Figure 2). The twelfth and final exhibit dedicated to the future of immersive VR was hidden and could only be unlocked if someone completed a playful activity, a quest. The quest was one of the four modes to experience the virtual museum as illustrated in Figure 3.

The quest was organized around the following fictional story:

Figure 2. Aerial snapshot of the Museum of Virtual Media in Second Life

Figure 3. Interaction modes in the 3-D Museum of Virtual Media

"In the beginning of time there existed a book which told the tale and story of the Universe from the creation to the present, and even peered into the future. This book was revered and awed by all. The most intriguing and read chapter of the book divulged dark and secret information that one would only dare to think about. These concepts touched on the possibility of the continuation of existence after death. The winding road that led to this mystical unknown was portrayed through different virtual reality forms. Many chapters took readers on a journey of communication technology throughout time.

At the turn of the last century, the guardians took a journey across the ocean to inhabit a new land and took the esoteric book with them. A Thief, seeing how protective the humans were of the book, devised a plot to capture the book. The book had its own safety against evil and when the Thief touched the book, its golden pages flew high up in the air and were lost. As the pages fell, the story of the book was resurrected on the land into a three-dimensional exhibit, which came to be known as the Museum of Virtual Media.

As the pages fell to the ground the Thief scurried around trying to collect them in his clumsy and disorganized way. As he found one page, he lost another, and the sections have now become buried deep within the Museum of Virtual Media.

As a patron and visitor, we are in need of your assistance in collecting the 11 missing sections of the book to reveal the 12th exhibit.

Follow the path of the Thief as he tries to collect the pages of the golden book and collect them yourself. By wearing the Quest MVM HUD, upon completion, the 12th exhibit will appear and, because of your good work, you will be automatically admitted".

As reported by individuals and group visitors, the quest sparked visitors' curiosity, provided motivation for structured, prolonged, and repeated engagement in the virtual museum. Visitors returned to the museum to complete the quest by visiting each 3-D exhibit, unlock and discover the hidden exhibit.

Serious Games and Escape Rooms for Deeper Online Learning

Serious games in VR can supplement online learning and elicit engagement and deeper learning. Designing cost-effective serious games such online breakout or escape rooms can ignite active blended learning (Armellini & Padilla Rodriguez, 2021). Team games of short duration have been used in virtual worlds to supplement online lectures (Mystakidis et al., 2017b). The games featured visual and functional metaphors to convey Cybersecurity-related terms and processes.

Another popular serious game type is digital educational escape rooms. Educational escape rooms are live-adventure games where users have the challenge to complete pedagogically meaningful tasks to exit from one or more rooms. The "Room of Keys" VR escape room has been developed for Biology to help learners build mental models of the function of enzymes in chemical reactions (Christopoulos et al., 2022). The room was accessible both through desktop computers and head-mounted displays. A case study in the USA with high school pupils showed that adolescents appreciated the resource and improved significantly their academic performance by 14% (Mystakidis et al., 2019). Moreover, it increased their interest in the topic leading to a tendency to engage more with the subject.

Collaborative Problem-based Learning (PBL) for Assessment Gamification

The next level of a playful design disposition in distance education is a systematic, more complex arrangement of multiple game design elements towards a gamified experience. This approach was applied in a semester-long gamified distance postgraduate course at the University of the West of England Bristol, United Kingdom (Mystakidis, 2020). The "Artificial Intelligence, Bots and Non-Player Characters" course utilized both virtual worlds (Second Life) and the Blackboard learning management system for written assignments.

The game layer included mainly story, character categories, experience points, ranks, and quests. The story prompted students to step into the shoes of a professional practitioner and prove their abilities to be admitted into a –fictional- elite institutional unit. To reach their goal, students have climb game ranks towards becoming masters of non-player characters. A higher rank is reached though the accumulation of experience points that are earned through learning activities, namely quests. Quests were organized in three different types: solo, raid, or guild corresponding to individual, group, or class tasks respectively. Quests were also classified in three categories of characters aligned with the course's intended outcomes: monk, artisan, and bard. Monk quests dealt with reading and writing assignments, artisan quests developed programming skills, while bard quests had components of open, public performance.

In this context, it was essential to organizing group activities and case studies with tangible 3-D objects to enable theoretical knowledge application for in-depth comprehension. For this purpose, a new type of collaborative problem-solving activity was developed. The activity involves the analysis of cases or of a problem according a theoretical model using 3-D assets that learners can create, copy, and move in VR (Figure 4). A detailed guide for practitioners with has been developed in a handbook for teachers (Mystakidis, Mourtzis, et al., 2022). A study conducted revealed that gamified elements increased students' interest, motivation, and autonomy towards critical engagement (Mystakidis, 2020).

Figure 4. Collaborative problem-solving session in action in a 3D virtual world

CONCLUSION

This chapter constitutes a modest attempt to replicate Alpha square's quest to showcase and establish the engaging power of the third, spatial dimension in distance education; it advocates the introduction of fun-driven distance education in the pursuit of winning the minds and hearts of students with the help of 3-D social environments in VR. The underlying assumption is that once students are emotionally engaged, they become curious and interested in the studied domain, they are more likely to adopt an intrinsic goal orientation, engage frequently with content, and ultimately achieve a durable knowledge and competency. The assumption is corroborated by the affective context model (Shackleton-Jones, 2019). Instructional design for 3-D virtual worlds can be very different from 2-D environments borrowing elements from theater, cinematography, storytelling, and games (Kapp & O'Driscoll, 2010) in the service of creating emotionally charged learning experiences. Four application examples of progressive complexity were presented. The first stage according to the TANC model for playful learning (Mystakidis, 2021) is the playful arrangement of components of 3-D buildings such as buildings based on a suitable theme. The next level involves the planning of quests, meaningful learning activities, interwoven with a narrative, a story. These quests can be cooperative problem-solving tasks and projects in virtual worlds. The third step is to build short serious games such as escape rooms to address parts of the course and the outcomes. In the final stage, it is possible to devise a comprehensive plan to gamify the entire curriculum and assessment where students win their grade through their active engagement.

Critical success factors that practitioners should consider are the following: (i) Educators without prior experiences with game-based learning or 3-D virtual worlds should start small, experiment with playfulness, and build confidence gradually. (ii) Ask for user feedback often. Do not strive for technical perfection in the first iteration. Students tend to appreciate teachers' efforts and can be very constructive in their feedback. (iii) These experiences should help academics and teachers to construct their signature pedagogies that correspond naturally with their character, interests, and teaching style (Nørgård et al., 2017).

Teachers are receptive to the use of playful and gameful methods in their practice (Mystakidis, Papantzikos, et al., 2021). Continuous teacher professional development opportunities and educational communities of practice can accelerate the acceptance and active adoption of virtual and augmented reality in education (Mystakidis, Fragkaki, et al., 2021). These technologies are cornerstones of the tech stack of the Metaverse, the 3D iteration of the Internet. The Metaverse has profound affordances that can enhance online education (Mystakidis, 2022). The ultimate challenge is to improve the perceived quality to the point that distance education is regarded as equal as or even superior to classroom-based instruction, a critical achievement in our information-intensive, innovation-driven era (Patrício et al., 2021).

ACKNOWLEDGMENT

This research received no specific grant from any funding agency in the public, commercial, or not-for-profit sectors.

REFERENCES

Abbott, E. A. (1885). *Flatland: A Romance of Many Dimensions*. Roberts Brothers.

Armellini, A., & Padilla Rodriguez, B. C. (2021). Active Blended Learning. In B. C. P. Rodriguez & A. Armellini (Eds.), *Cases on Active Blended Learning in Higher Education* (pp. 1–22). IGI Global. doi:10.4018/978-1-7998-7856-8.ch001

Arnab, S., Lim, T., Carvalho, M. B., Bellotti, F., de Freitas, S., Louchart, S., Suttie, N., Berta, R., & De Gloria, A. (2015). Mapping learning and game mechanics for serious games analysis. *British Journal of Educational Technology*, *46*(2), 391–411. doi:10.1111/bjet.12113

Bailenson, J. N. (2021). Nonverbal overload: A theoretical argument for the causes of Zoom fatigue. *Technology, Mind, and Behavior*, *2*(1). Advance online publication. doi:10.1037/tmb0000030

Ball, C., Huang, K.-T., & Francis, J. (2021). Virtual reality adoption during the COVID-19 pandemic: A uses and gratifications perspective. *Telematics and Informatics*, *65*, 101728. doi:10.1016/j.tele.2021.101728 PMID:34887619

Bangert-Drowns, R. L., & Pyke, C. (2001). A taxonomy of student engagement with educational software: An exploration of literate thinking with electronic text. *Journal of Educational Computing Research*, *24*(3), 213–234. doi:10.2190/0CKM-FKTR-0CPF-JLGR

Begg, M., Dewhurst, D., & Macleod, H. (2005). Game informed learning: Applying computer game processes to higher education. *Innovate*, *1*(6).

Bellotti, F., Berta, R., De Gloria, A., Ott, M., Arnab, S., de Freitas, S., & Kiili, K. (2011). Designing serious games for education: from pedagogical principles to game mechanisms. *Proceedings of the 5th European Conference on Games Based Learning, 2,* 1–9.

Blascovich, J., & Bailenson, J. (2011). *Infinite Reality: Avatars, Eternal Life, New Worlds, and the Dawn of the Virtual Revolution.* Harper Collins.

Bragg, L. A., Walsh, C., & Heyeres, M. (2021). Successful design and delivery of online professional development for teachers: A systematic review of the literature. *Computers & Education, 166,* 104158. doi:10.1016/j.compedu.2021.104158

Carrillo, C., & Flores, M. A. (2020). COVID-19 and teacher education: A literature review of online teaching and learning practices. *European Journal of Teacher Education, 43*(4), 466–487. doi:10.1080 /02619768.2020.1821184

Christopoulos, A., Mystakidis, S., Cachafeiro, E., & Laakso, M.-J. (2022). Escaping the cell: Virtual reality escape rooms in biology education. *Behaviour & Information Technology,* 1–18. doi:10.1080/0 144929X.2022.2079560

Christopoulos, A., & Sprangers, P. (2021). Integration of educational technology during the Covid-19 pandemic: An analysis of teacher and student receptions. *Cogent Education, 8*(1), 1964690. Advance online publication. doi:10.1080/2331186X.2021.1964690

de Freitas, S., & Liarokapis, F. (2011). Serious games: A new paradigm for education? In Serious Games and Edutainment Applications (pp. 9–23). doi:10.1007/978-1-4471-2161-9_2

DePorres, D., & Livingston, R. E. (2016). Launching new doctoral students: Embracing the Hero's journey. *Developments in Business Simulation and Experiential Learning, 43.*

Deterding, S. (2011). Situated motivational affordances of game elements: A conceptual model. *Conference on Human Factors in Computing Systems (CHI 2011).*

Endicott-Popovsky, B., Hinrichs, R. J., & Frincke, D. (2013). Leveraging 2nd life as a communications media: An effective tool for security awareness training. *IEEE International Professional Communication 2013 Conference,* 1–7. 10.1109/IPCC.2013.6623945

Ferguson, C., van den Broek, E. L., & van Oostendorp, H. (2019). On the role of interaction mode and story structure in virtual reality serious games. *Computers & Education.* Advance online publication. doi:10.1016/j.compedu.2019.103671

Freire, M., del Blanco, A., & Fernandez-Manjon, B. (2014). Serious games as edX MOOC activities. *2014 IEEE Global Engineering Education Conference (EDUCON),* 867–871. 10.1109/EDUCON.2014.6826198

Friedman, B., Kahn, P., & Borning, A. (2002). Value sensitive design: Theory and methods. *University of Washington Technical Report,* 2–12.

Gee, J. P. (2004). *What Video Games Have to Teach Us About Learning and Literacy.* Palgrave Macmillan.

Girvan, C. (2018). What is a virtual world? Definition and classification. *Educational Technology Research and Development, 66*(5), 1087–1100. doi:10.100711423-018-9577-y

Haskell, C., & Dawley, L. (2013). 3D GameLab: Quest-Based Pre-Service Teacher Education. In Y. Baek & N. Whitton (Eds.), *Cases on Digital Game-Based Learning: Methods, Models and Strategies* (pp. 302–340). IGI Global. doi:10.4018/978-1-4666-2848-9.ch016

Hill, V., & Mystakidis, S. (2012). Maya Island virtual museum: A virtual learning environment, museum, and library exhibit. *2012 18th International Conference on Virtual Systems and Multimedia*, 565–568. 10.1109/VSMM.2012.6365978

Hornik, S., & Thornburg, S. (2010). Really engaging accounting: Second Life™ as a learning platform. *Issues in Accounting Education*, *25*(3), 361–378. doi:10.2308/iace.2010.25.3.361

Kapp, K. M., & O'Driscoll, T. (2010). *Learning in 3D: Adding a New Dimension to Enterprise Learning and Collaboration*. Pfeiffer.

Koivisto, J., & Hamari, J. (2019). The rise of motivational information systems: A review of gamification research. *International Journal of Information Management*, *45*, 191–210. doi:10.1016/j.ijinfomgt.2018.10.013

Kostopoulos, K. P., Giannopoulos, K., Mystakidis, S., & Chronopoulou, K. (2014). E-learning through virtual reality applications: The case of career counseling. *The International Journal of Technologies in Learning*, *21*(1), 57–68. doi:10.18848/2327-0144/CGP/v20i01/49125

Kucirkova, N., Messer, D., Sheehy, K., & Fernández Panadero, C. (2014). Children's engagement with educational iPad apps: Insights from a Spanish classroom. *Computers & Education*, *71*, 175–184. doi:10.1016/j.compedu.2013.10.003

Lim, C. P., Nonis, D., & Hedberg, J. G. (2006). Gaming in a 3D multiuser virtual environment: Engaging students in science lessons. *British Journal of Educational Technology*, *37*(2), 211–231. doi:10.1111/j.1467-8535.2006.00531.x

McQuiggan, S. W., Rowe, J. P., Lee, S., & Lester, J. C. (2008). Story-Based Learning: The Impact of Narrative on Learning Experiences and Outcomes. In B. P. Woolf, E. Aïmeur, R. Nkambou, & S. Lajoie (Eds.), *Intelligent Tutoring Systems* (pp. 530–539). Springer Berlin Heidelberg. doi:10.1007/978-3-540-69132-7_56

Metcalf, S. J., Reilly, J. M., Kamarainen, A. M., King, J., Grotzer, T. A., & Dede, C. (2018). Supports for deeper learning of inquiry-based ecosystem science in virtual environments - Comparing virtual and physical concept mapping. *Computers in Human Behavior*, *87*, 459–469. doi:10.1016/j.chb.2018.03.018

Mills, S., Yanes, M., & Casebeer, C. (2009). Perceptions of distance learning among faculty of a college of education. *Journal of Online Learning and Teaching*, *5*(1).

Mystakidis, S. (2020). Distance Education Gamification in Social Virtual Reality: A Case Study on Student Engagement. *11th International Conference on Information, Intelligence, Systems and Applications (IISA 2020)*, 1–6. 10.1109/IISA50023.2020.9284417

Mystakidis, S. (2021). Combat tanking in education - The TANC model for playful distance learning in social virtual reality. *International Journal of Gaming and Computer-Mediated Simulations*, *13*(4), 1–20. doi:10.4018/IJGCMS.291539

Mystakidis, S. (2022). Metaverse. *Encyclopedia, 2*(1), 486–497. doi:10.3390/encyclopedia2010031

Mystakidis, S., & Berki, E. (2014). Participative Design of qMOOCs with Deep Learning and 3d Virtual Immersive Environments : The case of MOOCAgora. *Can MOOCs Save Europe's Unemployed Youth? Workshop. ECTEL 2014 Conference.*

Mystakidis, S., Berki, E., & Valtanen, J.-P. (2017a). Designing and Implementing a Big Open Online Course by Using a 3d Virtual Immersive Environment – Lessons Learned. *9th Annual International Conference on Education and New Learning Technologies (EDULEARN17)*, 8070–8079. 10.21125/edulearn.2017.0487

Mystakidis, S., Berki, E., & Valtanen, J.-P. (2017b). Toward Successfully Integrating Mini Learning Games into Social Virtual Reality Environments – Recommendations for Improving Open and Distance Learning. *9th Annual International Conference on Education and New Learning Technologies (EDU-LEARN17)*, 968–977. 10.21125/edulearn.2017.1203

Mystakidis, S., Berki, E., & Valtanen, J.-P. (2021). Deep and meaningful e-learning with social virtual reality environments in higher education: A systematic literature review. *Applied Sciences (Basel, Switzerland), 11*(5), 2412. doi:10.3390/app11052412

Mystakidis, S., Besharat, J., Papantzikos, G., Christopoulos, A., Stylios, C., Agorgianitis, S., & Tselentis, D. (2022). Design, development and evaluation of a virtual reality serious game for school fire preparedness training. *Education Sciences, 12*(4), 281. doi:10.3390/educsci12040281

Mystakidis, S., Cachafeiro, E., & Hatzilygeroudis, I. (2019). Enter the serious e-scape room: A cost-effective serious game model for deep and meaningful e-learning. *2019 10th International Conference on Information, Intelligence, Systems and Applications (IISA)*, 1–6. 10.1109/IISA.2019.8900673

Mystakidis, S., Filippousis, G., Tolis, D., & Tseregkouni, E. (2021). Playful metaphors for narrative-driven e-learning. *Applied Sciences (Basel, Switzerland), 11*(24), 11682. doi:10.3390/app112411682

Mystakidis, S., Fragkaki, M., & Filippousis, G. (2021). Ready teacher one: Virtual and augmented reality online professional development for K-12 school teachers. *Computers, 10*(10), 134. doi:10.3390/computers10100134

Mystakidis, S., Mourtzis, P., & Tseregkouni, E. (2022). *Collaborative Problem Solving for In-Depth Conceptual Knowledge in 3D Virtual Worlds. In 100+ Ideas for Active Learning.* Active Learning Network.

Mystakidis, S., Papantzikos, G., & Stylios, C. (2021). Virtual Reality Escape Rooms for STEM Education in Industry 4.0: Greek Teachers Perspectives. *2021 6th South-East Europe Design Automation, Computer Engineering, Computer Networks and Social Media Conference (SEEDA-CECNSM)*, 1–5. 10.1109/SEEDA-CECNSM53056.2021.9566265

Nicholson, S. (2015). A RECIPE for Meaningful Gamification. In T. Reiners & L. C. Wood (Eds.), *Gamification in Education and Business* (pp. 1–20). Springer International Publishing., doi:10.1007/978-3-319-10208-5_1

Nørgård, R. T., Toft-Nielsen, C., & Whitton, N. (2017). Playful learning in higher education: Developing a signature pedagogy. *International Journal of Play, 6*(3), 272–282. doi:10.1080/21594937.2017.1382997

Patrício, R., Moreira, A. C., & Zurlo, F. (2018). Gamification approaches to the early stage of innovation. *Creativity and Innovation Management*, 27(4), 499–511. doi:10.1111/caim.12284

Patrício, R., Moreira, A. C., & Zurlo, F. (2021). Enhancing design thinking approaches to innovation through gamification. *European Journal of Innovation Management*, 24(5), 1569–1594. doi:10.1108/EJIM-06-2020-0239

Pellas, N., & Mystakidis, S. (2020). A systematic review of research about game-based learning in virtual worlds. *Journal of Universal Computer Science*, 26(8), 1017–1042. doi:10.3897/jucs.2020.054

Pellas, N., Mystakidis, S., & Christopoulos, A. (2021). A systematic literature review on the user experience design for game-based interventions via 3D virtual worlds in K-12 education. *Multimodal Technologies and Interaction*, 5(6), 28. doi:10.3390/mti5060028

Salen, K. (2017). Designing a place called school: A case study of the public school quest to learn. *She Ji: The Journal of Design, Economics, and Innovation*, 3(1), 51–64. doi:10.1016/j.sheji.2017.08.002

Savin-Baden, M. (2014). Using problem-based learning: New constellations for the 21st century. *Journal on Excellence in College Teaching*, 25(3 & 4).

Schultz, R. B., & DeMers, M. N. (2020). Transitioning from emergency remote learning to deep online learning experiences in geography education. *The Journal of Geography*, 119(5), 142–146. doi:10.1080/00221341.2020.1813791

Shackleton-Jones, N. (2019). *How People Learn: Designing Education and Training that Works to Improve Performance*. Kogan Page Publishers.

Sheldon, L. (2011). *The Multiplayer Classroom: Designing Coursework as a Game*. Cengage Learning PTR.

Sheldon, L., & Seelow, D. (2017). The multiplayer classroom: The designer and the collaboration. *International Journal on Innovations in Online Education*, 1(4). Advance online publication. doi:10.1615/IntJInnovOnlineEdu.2017024959

Shen, E. Y.-T., Lieberman, H., & Davenport, G. (2009). What's next? Emergent storytelling from video collections. *Proceedings of the SIGCHI Conference on Human Factors in Computing Systems*, 809–818. 10.1145/1518701.1518825

Sipiyaruk, K., Hatzipanagos, S., Reynolds, P. A., & Gallagher, J. E. (2021). Serious games and the COVID-19 pandemic in dental education: An integrative review of the literature. *Computers*, 10(4), 42. doi:10.3390/computers10040042

Stokrocki, M., & Chen, J. (2012). Taiwanese undergraduates' digital story quests for art treasures in Second Life. *Journal of Cultural Research in Art Education*, 30(13), 32–59.

Wang, C., Lan, Y.-J., Tseng, W.-T., Lin, Y.-T. R., & Gupta, K. C.-L. (2020). On the effects of 3D virtual worlds in language learning – a meta-analysis. *Computer Assisted Language Learning*, 33(8), 891–915. doi:10.1080/09588221.2019.1598444

Wang, C., & Zhao, H. (2020). The impact of COVID-19 on anxiety in Chinese university students. *Frontiers in Psychology*, *11*, 1168. doi:10.3389/fpsyg.2020.01168 PMID:32574244

Wheaton, M. G., Messner, G. R., & Marks, J. B. (2021). Intolerance of uncertainty as a factor linking obsessive-compulsive symptoms, health anxiety and concerns about the spread of the novel coronavirus (COVID-19) in the United States. *Journal of Obsessive-Compulsive and Related Disorders*, *28*, 100605. doi:10.1016/j.jocrd.2020.100605 PMID:33251098

Wu, J., & Chen, V. D.-T. (2019). A systematic review of educational digital storytelling. *Computers & Education*, *103786*. Advance online publication. doi:10.1016/j.compedu.2019.103786

Yin, R. K. (2009). *Case Study Research: Design and Methods* (4th ed.). SAGE Publications.

ADDITIONAL READING

Dalgarno, B., & Lee, M. J. W. (2010). What are the learning affordances of 3-D virtual environments? *British Journal of Educational Technology*, *41*(1), 10–32. doi:10.1111/j.1467-8535.2009.01038.x

Damer, B., & Hinrichs, R. (2014). *The Virtuality and Reality of Avatar Cyberspace*. Oxford University Press. doi:10.1093/oxfordhb/9780199826162.013.032

Fisher, J. A. (Ed.). (2021). *Augmented and Mixed Reality for Communities*. CRC Press. doi:10.1201/9781003052838

Freina, L., & Canessa, A. (2015). Immersive vs desktop virtual reality in game based learning. In R. Munkvold & L. Kolås (Eds.), *European Conference on Games Based Learning* (pp. 195–202). Nord-Trondelag University College Steinkjer.

Gregory, S., Lee, M., & Dalgarno, B. (Eds.). (2016). *Learning in Virtual Worlds: Research and Applications*. AU Press. doi:10.15215/aupress/9781771991339.01

Grivokostopoulou, F., Kovas, K., & Perikos, I. (2020). The effectiveness of embodied pedagogical agents and their impact on students learning in virtual worlds. *Applied Sciences (Basel, Switzerland)*, *10*(5), 1739. doi:10.3390/app10051739

Palkova, Z., & Hatzilygeroudis, I. (2019). Virtual Reality and its Applications in Vocational Education and Training. In Y. A. Zhang & D. Cristol (Eds.), *Handbook of Mobile Teaching and Learning* (pp. 1245–1274). Springer Singapore. doi:10.1007/978-981-13-2766-7_88

Savin-Baden, M., Falconer, L., Wimpenny, K., & Callaghan, M. (2017). Virtual Worlds for Learning. In E. Duval, M. Sharples, & R. Sutherland (Eds.), *Technology Enhanced Learning: Research Themes* (pp. 97–107). Springer International Publishing. doi:10.1007/978-3-319-02600-8_9

KEY TERMS AND DEFINITIONS

Educational Escape Room: Live-adventure game where one or more users have to complete a mission, usually to break out of one or more rooms.

Engagement: The active involvement of students in the learning process.

Gameful Design (Gamification): The transformation of a non-gaming procedure or function into a game.

Playful Design: The application of game design elements in a non-gaming context.

Problem-Based Learning: Teaching method to organize learning around an authentic or realistic challenge.

Serious Game: Digital game with a primary epistemic, pedagogical purpose.

Virtual World: A persistent, computer-generated 3D multi-user environment where users can populate and communicate as avatars.

Chapter 20
Affective Serious Games for GLAMs Institutions

Eirini Kalatha
Department of Cultural Technology and Communication, University of the Aegean, Greece

George Caridakis
Department of Cultural Technology and Communication, University of the Aegean, Greece

ABSTRACT

Serious games (SGs), which support the player to achieve learning targets and engage in learning activities through a fun experience, have been a flourishing field of research over the last decades. Their dual role as an educational and entertainment tool contributes to their widespread adoption and dissemination. Emotions play a key role in SGs and can be used in various ways to improve a player's experience and their learning outcomes or even contribute to a holistic UX evaluation. Even though SGs have several applications in the cultural heritage (CH) field and GLAMs (galleries, libraries, archives, and museums) institutions to improve their services, their impact has not been adequately studied. This chapter focuses on affective SGs and their use in GLAM institutions to contribute to improving their services. A review of SGs and aspects related to the integration of affective computing (AC) for developing affective SGs are also presented.

INTRODUCTION

In recent decades, serious games (SGs), or applied games, have been gaining the increasing interest of the research community and have been widely adopted in many different fields, such as education and training both for youth and adults (Prensky, 2003; Mitchell & Savill-Smith, 2004; Gallegos, Kepple & Bukaty, 2016), health care (Aranha, Silva, Chaim & dos Santos Nunes, 2017), well-being (Nguyen et al., 2017), military (Lim, & Jung, 2013), interpersonal abilities (Romero, Usart, & Ott, 2015), cultural heritage (Bellotti, Berta, DeGloria, D'ursi & Fiore, 2013; Foni, Papagiannakis & Magnenat-Thalmann, 2010), etc. Therefore, several aspects of SGs, from game mechanics and game development to SGs evaluation, have been studied thoroughly.

DOI: 10.4018/978-1-6684-4291-3.ch020

SGs combine educational purposes with entertainment (Alvarez, Rampnoux, Jessel & Mathel, 2007), leading to increased engagement, focus, and motivation (Bellotti et al., 2013), thus optimizing User eXperience (UX) (Kalatha et al., 2018). In light of the above, SGs are a valuable educational and training tool (Prensky, 2003; Carvalho, 2017) that can complement or enhance traditional education (Ghoman & Schmölzer, 2020).

Emotion is an important parameter for both digital games, in general, and the learning process. As mentioned above, SGs combine the aspect of fun and learning, so the parameter emotion is especially crucial for them, as well.

In particular, emotion is a complex subjective conscious experience: the combination of mental states, psychosomatic expressions, and biological reactions of the body. Its duration lasts seconds to minutes (Kołakowska, Landowska, Szwoch, Szwoch, & Wróbel, 2013) and is divided into positive (satisfaction, joy, interest, happiness serenity) and negative (fear, anger, disgust, sadness). Both positive and negative emotions affect learning by leading a person to or away from the learning process (Ellis, H., & Ashbrook, P., 1988), terminating or leading to selective information processing and organizing the recall.

According to Hascher and Edlinger (2009) the perception that negative emotions have negative effects on learning, and positive emotions have positive effects is rather simplistic. However, it is commonly accepted that positive emotions facilitate self-regulated learning, affect curiosity and creative thinking, problem-solving, and generally enhance learning (Isen, 2004; Ahmed, Van der Werf, Kuyper, & Minnaert, 2013), whereas negative emotions lead to the manifestation of stress that may suspend learning. Nevertheless, some researchers contend that negative emotions may lead to a beneficial effect on learning outcomes (Barak, Watted, & Haick, 2016).

Also, emotion holds a primary role inside the structure and immersive experience of SGs (Argasiński & Węgrzyn, P. 2019). It can be activated by the events of a game (gameplay), the behavior of a character of a game, or the interaction. According to Johnson & Wiles (2003), emotions are crucial for the success of a game since they can influence the user's engagement in both directions, i.e., the desire to participate in or to reject a SG (Kurkovsky, 2015; Labrador & Villegas, 2014). There are SGs that take into account player's emotions for controlling user engagement such as an open-loop system (the game does not feel the emotions of the player, e.g. encouragement) or a closed-loop system (capture emotion and adjust game responses to player's emotional states) (Hocine, N., & Gouaich, A., 2011).

Organizations, enterprises, and institutions exploit SGs to serve purposes related to training their staff, increase their extroversion, improve the quality of their services, etc. For instance, Cultural Heritage Institutions, which include Galleries, Libraries, Archives, and Museums (GLAMs), have followed the developments of the time and made use of the new opportunities provided to them, revising almost fundamentally their operation. In order to ensure their viability through the fulfillment of their role, GLAMs have integrated new technologies in their activities so as to enhance participation and improve the overall experience of their audience.

Despite the abundance of research related to the use of SGs in museums or tourist sites for their visitors to acquire knowledge related to culture, monuments of an area, etc. (Bellotti et al., 2013) no games have been offered to improve their services.

The remainder of this chapter is organized as follows. In the next Section the background and basic terms related to the field of Serious Gaming are presented. Afterwards ways to use the users' emotions when interacting with an SG are analyzed, thus how Affective Computing (AC) can be used in the serious gaming field. Moreover, some key axis are analyzed to understand the contribution of affective SGs into GLAMs institutions and their various benefits in the field of CH. In addition, cultural affective SG and use case scenarios are presented to emphasize promising approaches into GLAMs institutions. Finally, we conclude with directions for future work.

LITERATURE REVIEW & BASIC TERMS

Serious Games (SGs)

In 1970, Clark Abt, in his book named "Serious Games", was the first to formulate a related definition:
    "These games (SGs) have an explicit and carefully thought-out educational purpose and are not intended to be played primarily for amusement. It does not mean that games are not, or should not be, entertaining." (Djaouti, Alvarez, Jessel & Rampnoux, 2011).
    Since then, several definitions have been given by various researchers. Some of them are listed below:

- "A mental contest played with a computer following specific rules, that uses entertainment to further government or corporate training, education, health, public policy, and strategic communication objectives" (Zyda, 2005).
- "Games in which education (in its various forms) is the primary goal, rather than entertainment" (Michael & Chen, 2006).
- "Digital games, simulations, virtual environments, and mixed reality/media that provide opportunities to educate or train through responsive narrative/story, gameplay or encounters" (Gallegos et al., 2016).
- "Electronic games whose main purpose is "serious" and not to simply entertain. The primary "serious" purposes can be to teach or train in areas such as education, health care, advertising, politics, etc." (Arriaga, Esteves & Fernandes, 2013).
- "Video games that were designed to achieve certain learning results." (Li, 2020)

It is obvious that a unique and universal definition of SGs does not exist, even if there is a plethora of definitions with plenty of common elements, which contribute to clear up the seeming oxymoron. Despite this absence, SGs' structural factors present similarities with every game's (serious or not) characteristic, such as rules, goals, and objectives, outcomes and feedback, conflict/competition/challenge/opposition, interaction, and representation or story (Prensky, 2003). It is good to mention that several digital games contain all these factors and others most of them (Prensky, 2003).

Moreover, it is undeniable that SGs are rapidly growing in diffusion and acceptance. The main reasons that contributed to this remarkable adoption are the following: target a wide range of audiences (professionals, consumers, students, etc.), can be of any kind (advergames, edutainment, edu-market games, persuasive games, health games, art games, etc.), can use any gaming technology, be created for any platform, cultivate many different skills such as analytical and spatial skills, psychomotor skills, social skills, selective visual attention, improved self-control, problem-solving, better long-term memory (Mitchell & Savill-Smith, 2004) and increase engagement, enhance motivation (Bellotti et al., 2013), and focus, and ultimately optimize User eXperience (UX) (Kalatha et al., 2018).

Despite the existence of various kinds of SGs, all of them can be categorized into two types: process-oriented and outcome-focused SGs, based on their function and structure. More specifically, outcome-oriented games compel the player to complete activities to achieve a set goal. All activities within the game revolve around reaching the goal, which is usually the mastery of a skill or completion of an action. It is good to mention that this game type is most effective for educational, persuasion, and motivation purposes. For instance, an outcome-oriented SG related to CH is Tidy City (Wetzel, Blum & Oppermann, 2012). It concerns a location-based SG for smartphones that is played outdoors and through riddles solving about a specific city, the player can explore places and learn about the city's CH.

On the other hand, process-oriented games are driven by discovery and lack of endgame objectives. The player's decision-making processes throughout the experience hold the key learning value. Process-oriented SGs are most effective for discovery, decision-making, and simulation purposes. History Game Canada fits into the process oriented cultural SGs and enhances the history learning experience by fostering critical thinking, and creative problem-solving. More specifically, the players of History Game Canada are invited to imagine historical events from different perspectives or fantasize about alternative outcomes of history.

Emotion in Serious Gaming

Too many definitions of emotion have been given, either simple or more complex since there is no consensus on a universal definition (Sloman, 1999). According to Schacter, Gilbert, Wegner, and Hood (2011), emotions can be defined as "a positive or negative experience, which is associated with a specific pattern of normal activity". On the other hand, Scherer (2000) argues that emotions are "episodes of coordinated changes in several components (including at least neurophysiological activation, motor expression, and subjective feelings but possibly also tendencies and cognitive processes), in response to external or internal events of major significance to the organism". It is good to be mentioned that according Barrett (2006) emotions are shown to be different cross culturally and specifically based on learned experience whereas affect occurs universally.

Since a plethora of definitions exist (according to Plutchick (2001), by one estimate over 90 different definitions during the 20th century), the conclusion that can be reached is that emotion is one complex term both for psychologists, philosophers, and neuroscientists.

Although evolutionary psychologists and constructivists disagree on the definition, biological basis, and universality of emotions, they share the view that emotions perform important functions, such as social functions, decision making, achieving goals, and forming an aesthetic judgment.

In addition, there is a great number of theories related to emotion, that predict the plurality of different emotions, and in which cases the emotions are caused (James, 1884; Damasio, Everitt & Bishop, 1996; Schachter & Singer, 1962).

The number of emotions varies from 6 to 14, depending on the researcher. For instance, according to Ekman (1999), there is a set of six basic emotions (The Big Six): joy, sadness, fear, surprise, anger, and disgust. Robert Plutchik (2001) considered that the basic emotions are eight, classified into four pairs of opposites: acceptance/trust - disgust, joy - sadness, anticipation - surprise, and anger - fear. As far as emotions in game design are concerned, Psaltis et al. (2016) refer that five basic emotions (anger, fear, happiness, sadness, surprise) are commonly encountered in a typical game, consequently, these emotions are utilized to evaluate the performance of their proposed emotion recognition methodology.

Emotions are the key issue in the field of Affective Computing (AC). This interdisciplinary field, established by Rosalind Picard from MIT in 1997, deals with the research and development of special systems, techniques, and devices that can identify, record, interpret, process and simulate various shades of human emotion (Magklogiannis, Kalatha & Paraskevopoulou-Kollia, 2015).

AC mostly pertains to the wider research field of human-computer interaction, and spans the fields of computer science, in particular the fields of artificial intelligence and recognition of patterns, psychology, philosophy (moral), and cognitive science (Magklogiannis, Kalatha & Paraskevopoulou-Kollia, 2015).

The main purpose of a special system-device developed in the scope of AC is to wisely interact with the user's emotions. Firstly, the system is able to survey the user. Afterwards it can interpret the data from the surveillance, gather cues to user emotion for various sources (facial expressions, voice intonation, gestures, movements, respiration, heart rate, pulse, blood pressure, temperature, pupillary dilation, skin color, etc.) and conclude, and then it can interact in a manner that would fit each case.

AC considers digital games as significantly promising and challenging applications (Calvo, D'Mello, Gratch & Kappas, 2015). More specifically, a relatively fledgling field that combines methods and techniques of AC and Gaming exists and is named Affective Gaming (AG). It refers to the new generation of affect-focused digital games, in which the game objectives and gameplay are affected by the players' behavior (Kotsia, Zafeiriou & Fotopoulos, 2013). In particular, the player's emotion (negative and positive) and his/her actions can be recognized and exploited to alter the progress of the game, induce the game interactivity (De Byl, 2015) and also influence the player's immersion (Cai, Goertzel, Zhou, Huang, Ke, Yu & Jiang, 2013; Li & Campbell, 2010) and motivation (Wu, Huang & Hwang, 2016).

GLAM Institutions

In the 1990s the abbreviation LAM made its appearance, which later included "galleries" too (GLAM), while the acronym can also be seen as GLAMR, with the R standing for Records management (Renshaw & Liew, 2021). As far as the acronym GLAM is concerned, it refers to cultural institutions with a mission to provide access to knowledge, both to resources and services.

GLAMs collect cultural heritage materials (art, records, documents, objects.), preserve them and either store or display them, document them for easy retrieval, and in general, make valuable primary sources accessible. It is good to mention that each institution treats its collection differently (Mahmud,2014).

Over the last decades, the development of new technology functions as a catalyst for escalating integrative practice between Cultural Heritage (CH) institutions. The technology adoption in GLAMs institutions is deemed necessary to provide significant benefits, such as innovation.

GLAM Labs use new, existing, and emerging technologies to make GLAMs' collections available in innovative, engaging, and unexpected ways (Mahey et al., 2019). More specifically, Labs generate new learning for the institution, promote collaboration even with other organizations, encourage novel engagement with cultural heritage organizations' collections, and enable the transfer of ideas.

AFFECTIVE SERIOUS GAMING

Sensor and Bio Signals

Sensors constitute basic components that give substance to the concept of AC, since their primary function is to detect a signal or stimulus and produce a measurable output (Kalatha & Caridakis, 2013).

In general, a device that recognizes emotions has as its primary aim the classification and identification of emotional states. The inputs of an emotion-recognizing device will be various signals which, directly or indirectly, provide information about the user's emotional state (Maglogiannis et al., 2017).

Emotion recognition methods could be classified into two main categories (Shu, Xie, Yang, Li, Li, Liao, Xu & Yang, 2018). The first category uses physical signals such as Facial Expressions (FE) including micro-expressions, Body Posture (BP), Gesture Analysis (GA), speech, vocal prosody (e.g. pitch, intonation, and pattern), Electrooculography (EOG), etc. The second one uses the internal signals, i.e., the psycho-physiological signals, which include Electroencephalogram (EEG), Electrocardiogram (ECG), Electromyogram (EMG), Galvanic Skin Response (GSR), Respiration Rate analysis (RR), Heart Rate Variability (HRV), Skin Temperature Measurements (SKT), Blood Volume Pressure (BVP), etc.

Many researchers exploited a player's emotions during his/her interaction with an affective serious game to serve several purposes. For instance, Aggag and Revett (2011) describe a preliminary study aimed at investigating whether GSR can be used to acquire information regarding the affective state of a player while playing a first-person shooter game. In Gilleade, Dix, and Allanson (2005), physiological data related to the player's heartbeat rate was used to influence gameplay and in Setiono, Saputra, Putra, Moniaga, and Chowanda (2021) player's facial expressions were the game input to evaluate the implementation of AC in the game. Moreover, in Sakurazawa, Yoshida, and Munekata (2004), in the context of a novel type of game using biological signals, the change in skin conductance caused by sweating was measured as a signal reflecting the player's agitation during the game. In addition, in Aranha et al. (2017) facial expressions are exploited to recognize seven emotions (anger, contempt, disgust, fear, joy, sadness, and surprise) by Affectiva SDK. Furthermore, in the context of the experientially ARCADE platform, the user's emotional facial expressions were recorded and recognized to be exploited to the system's adaption (Kalatha et al., 2018).

In Du, Zhou, Li, Li, and Liu (2020), a hybrid neural network learning framework, called CSFFN, was developed to recognize the players' emotional states. More specifically, during a gaming process, EEG signals were recorded in real-time to contribute to emotion recognition.

Additionally, in Mandryk, Atkins, and Inkpen (2006) users' emotions were assessed using objective diagnostic methods during the gameplay, such as videotaping of players' facial expressions, audio recording of the participants' comments, and physiological signals that include GSR, ECG, and EMG of the face (EMGsmiling and EMGfrowning).

Emotion Measurement Methods

As mentioned above, emotions are episodes of coordinated changes in several components (Scherer, 2000). By analyzing five main emotions' components, related to these changes, as behavioral tendencies, physiological reactions, motor expressions, cognitive appraisals, and subjective emotional experience, emotions can be evaluated (Scherer, 2005).

Indeed, many studies have shown that participants identified successfully emotions from watching other people's bodily movements, (Atkinson, Dittrich, Gemmell, & Young, 2004; Crane & Gross, 2017) and empirical studies in the field of emotion recognition revealed an association between specific facial expressions and emotions (Melzer, Shafir, & Tsachor, 2019).

According to Dzedzickis, Kaklauskas, and Bucinskas (2020) emotion evaluations methods can be classified into two main categories: self-report techniques and machine assessment techniques. The first category is based on emotions self-assessment by filing various questionnaires. In particular, this method relies on an individual's own report of his/her emotions, and the self-report data is gathered typically either from paper-and-pencil or electronic format or sometimes through an interview. The second category is based on measurements of various human body parameters or electric impulses in the nervous system.

It is good to mention that the behavioral tendencies, physiological reactions, motor expressions, cognitive appraisals can be evaluated automatically and can give indications about the player's emotional state during his/her interaction with an affective SG, without interrupting it. On the other hand, subjective emotional experiences are usually evaluated by using self-report measures that are flexible regarding when they can be administered. However, this flexibility may interrupt the player's interaction and cause his/her attention redirection from the emotion eliciting stimuli to the self-report measure (Zimmerman, 2008).

As far as the self-assessment techniques are concerned, they are the most widely used method to measure emotions and there are a plethora of questionnaires that measure the subjective experience of emotions such as the Game Experience Questionnaire, Player Immersiveness Questionnaire, EmoCards, etc. For instance, in Setiono et al. (2021), a combination of a five Likert scale (0-4) questionnaire inspired by the Game Experience Questionnaire and Player Immersiveness Questionnaire was used to evaluate the game player experiences. In Gibson, Hu & Swast (2010) EmoCards were used as a tool to measure nonverbal emotional responses during the gameplay, and in Kalatha, Konstantakis, and Caridakis (2019) Emocards contributed to the evaluation related to player's emotion. In particular, in Kalatha, Konstantakis, and Caridakis (2019), when "The Stolen Painting" game was over, the user was able to choose an EmoCard that express his/her emotions (surprised, happy, unhappy, sad, angry).

Moreover, in Mandryk et al. (2006) a hybrid approach for emotion assessment was used, to present a clear and continuous picture of how the user felt during the gameplay. Apart from the objective diagnostic methods and the recording of the user's physiological signals that are referred to above, the authors used predictive subjective data collection methods as well, focused on five emotions: fun, excitement, frustration, boredom, and challenge. Particularly, a 5-point Likert scale questionnaire was filled out by the game players after each game condition. In addition, the players completed a post-experimental questionnaire to rate retrospectively which condition was the most fun, exciting, challenging, boring, or frustrating.

Contributions of Affective SGs

SGs are gaining an increasingly growing interest in many different research fields. Over the last decades, they have been widely adopted even in the CH sector, since they combine aspects of learning with the playfulness of video games (Alvarez et al., 2007), create an engaging game experience (GX) (Mortara et al., 2014), and maximize user's motivation (Kalatha et al., 2018).

Numerous publications refer to the development of cultural serious games to attract more users, even if they are not familiar with the arts and culture (Bellotti et al., 2013), and motivate the user to activate and extend his/her knowledge, by transforming him/her from a passive data receiver to an actor. Moreover, they support the player to achieve learning targets and engage in learning activities through a fun experience (Mortara et al., 2014) by playing, exploring, making mistakes, and his own choices (Anolli, Mantovani, Confalonieri, Ascolese & Peveri, 2010).

The question that arises is: Can affective SGs be exploited into GLAMs institutions both as a resource of attracting and educating the public and as a tool to improve their services?

Below, some key axis will be analyzed to understand the contribution of affective SGs into GLAMs institutions and their various benefits in the field of CH. In addition, cultural affective SG and use case scenarios are presented to emphasize promising approaches.

Understanding the Value of CH

SGs can support the learning of both tangible and intangible CH (Mortara et al., 2014; Dagnino et al., 2015). On the one hand, the tangible or physical CH refers to historic sites, built heritage such as buildings and monuments, documents, work of arts, and other physical artifacts that are considered worthy of safeguarding. On the other hand, intangible CH refers to social values and oral traditions, customs and local knowledge, spiritual beliefs and rituals, performing arts, language, and folklore, philosophical values that are not easy to preserve.

There are various SGs that contribute to the diffusion of different cultural content such as "Gossip at palace", "Remembering 7th Street", and "Fascinating Egyptian Mummies". The "Gossip at palace" SG aims to offer contextual information to the visitors in order to help them discover the characters (such as Marie Jeanne Baptiste of Savoy-Nemours), traditions, and events that characterized the palace in the 18th century (Rubino, Barberis, Xhembulla, & Malnati, 2015). The "Remembering 7th Street" SG aims at raising awareness about West Oakland in the time period post World War II and the "Fascinating Egyptian Mummies" aims at teaching ancient Egyptians' spiritual beliefs (Mortara et al., 2014).

The exploitation of emotion's parameter in cultural SGs offer additional benefits. Cultural affective SGs can enhance learning outcomes due to the fact that the tight bond between emotions and learning is indisputable (Anolli et al., 2010), maximize user engagement, and improve cultural UX. The ARCADE cultural SG is a location-based game that is designed for everyone who wants to learn about the cultural heritage of Mytilene (the capital of the Greek island of Lesbos) during his/her navigation in the city. The player can improve his/her knowledge and stimulate his/her skills, such as memorization, problem-solving, and eye-hand coordination, whereas simultaneously his/her facial expressions were exploited to the system's adaption (Kalatha et al., 2018). The exploitation of the user's emotions, during the player's interaction with ARCADE game, contributes to a more profound cultural user experience.

Familiarization with Terminology

SGs are being used as a useful training and learning tool for various fields, such as health and medicine, CH, education, etc. In particular, serious gaming immersed learning could facilitate players' holistic understanding of scientific conceptions and enhance cognitive abilities (Zhonggen, 2019).

For instance, in Olgers, Bij de Weg, & Ter Maaten (2021), different SGs that train technical skills in health care are described. Each SG is being used to train specific surgical skills and at the same time, the player gets acquainted with medical terminology.

As far as the CH field is concerned, there are cultural SGs that contribute to players' familiarization with cultural conceptions (archaeological concepts, historical terms, museological terminology). The VRLerna SG is an interactive 3D virtual environment and refers to the reconstruction of the "House of Tiles" in the archaeological site Lerna in southern Greece (Barbatsis, Economou, Papamagkana, & Loukas, 2011). The players of VRLerna SG have to explore and access all the levels of the game. In addition, they can familiarize themself with various artifacts (3D reconstructions of archaeological finds from the Lerna excavations) and come in touch with the past, related to the Early Helladic Period (3000-2000 b.C.).

A SG, that incorporates the player's affective data into the game to allow automatic adaptation, could be used in a GLAM institution to increase players' overall pleasant mood (Zhonggen,2019).

Interactivity

The element of "interactivity" is usually missing from the traditional learning. On the contrary, SG assisted learning could provide interactive and flexible learning for different learners who could move beyond the limitations of traditional learning (Garneli, Giannakos, & Chorianopoulos,2017). In particular, the strength of SGs is that they encourage active learning because they are interactive by essence.

According to Li, Elmaghraby, El-Baz, & Sokhadze (2015), interactive environments including SGs, that are responsive to user emotions, improve their effectiveness and user acceptance. Moreover, emotions can be also regarded as a form of game interactivity (De Byl, 2015).

Nowadays, digital games can make use of advanced human-computer interactions with interfaces that cater to almost all human senses and sensors that monitor a variety of physiological and physical changes of the human body.

Serious games are potentially interesting tools to acquire knowledge, both for their motivational effect and their user-centred approach, interactivity, and continuous feedback (Drummond, Hadchouel, & Tesnière, 2017).

Practice and Repeatability of Practice

Most GLAMs institutions have security personnel who, besides their basic duties, such as:

- protection of monuments, archaeological finds, collections, exhibits, and in general the museum's property and archaeological sites, from acts and situations which endanger their integrity and/or the possibility of partial or/and their total loss,
- site surveillance during the hours that the gallery, museum, etc. is open to the public,
- ensuring that visitors follow the rules etc.,

will be called to take action in case of emergencies, such as a fire, an earthquake, etc.

The interaction of the security personnel with a SG, which exploits their emotional state, will contribute to knowledge acquisition, related to the emergency plan, experientially. The usual passive study of GLAM's emergency plan and the monotonous evaluation through a questionnaire could be transformed into one interesting and active procedure via an affective SG.

More specifically, during the interaction with a personalized affective SG the player could carry out missions related to emergencies and natural disasters that can be experienced in real life. The avatar that will be selected by the player could move in digital GLAM's space. Ideally, the space where the avatar moves could be the same as GLAM's floor plan, for more accurate practice.

The immediate evacuation of GLAM's building and the actions that should be taken in the case of a fire or an earthquake could be part of SG's missions. The player, safe and confined to the game environment, can repeat the missions as many times as he/she wishes, without endangering either himself/herself or the cultural exhibits.

The "marriage" of game, fun, and educational content, which is an integral part of a SG, may contribute to a substantial improvement of trainees' training (Prensky, 2003). Precisely, an affective SG could increase the user's motivation, allow safer training, provide better insight into situations, experience higher effectiveness for training, and better support for decision making (Oliveira, Coelho, Guimarães

Figure 1. Some of the benefits of an affective SGs for personnel's training

& Rebelo, 2012; Molka-Danielsen, Prasolova-Førland, Hokstad & Fominykh, 2015). In Figure 1 some of affective SG's benefits are reflected.

No Damage Risk of Cultural Property During User's Practice

Another way to utilize affective SG in GLAMs could be during a Lab. For instance, GLAM Labs have partnerships and project-based collaborations with universities, including student placements, research projects, sharing datasets, and building tools. Also, Labs frequently provide technical support to university students and researchers.

Affective SGs could be an alternative tool for transmitting knowledge or evaluating the newly acquired knowledge through an engaging (Mortara et al., 2014) and endearing way, especially for the Digital Natives, thus the generation of people who grew up in the era of ubiquitous technology (Prensky, 2003).

As far as the evaluation process is concerned, it is common that it takes place either during or after the learning procedure (formative and summative assessments), in order to examine the effectiveness of the educational process and the learning outcomes.

The most commonly used evaluation methods in a GLAM's Lab include the completion of a questionnaire, the semi-structured interview, or even the user observation. An affective SG could be also used as an evaluation tool for examining the success of a Lab, by assessing users learning outcomes during their interaction with the SG.

During the player's interaction with SG, his/her decisions and actions made to accomplish game tasks, as well as his/her face and body expressions, can be recorded.

The data that can be recorded during this interaction can be to some extent identical to those recorded by a researcher when he/she applies the user observation method. Therefore, an affective SG can provide a rich record of information about the human activity, physiological and emotional state. It is worth mentioning that the behavior of the trainees can be modified due to the presence of the researcher during the user observation method, whereas during user-game interaction the player's reactions tend to be more spontaneous and effortless.

A use case scenario is presented below. During a Lab, a practitioner in the context of his/her placement can be introduced to a new technique in the field of maintenance or restoration. He/she can apply the technique repeatedly with no damage risk of the cultural property (Mortara et al., 2014), through an affective SG. Moreover, she/he can make a self-assessment related to the newly acquired knowledge. The

Table 1. Contribution of a typical GLAM Lab vs the use of an affective SG during a GLAM Lab

	Typical GLAM LAb	Affective SG for a GLAM Lab
Understanding the value of CH	x	x
Familiarization with terminology	x	x
Interactivity		x
Practice e.g. maintenance/restoration technique		x
No damage risk of cultural property during user's practice		x
Repeatability of Practice e.g. maintenance/ restoration techniques		x

self-assessment arises effortlessly as it is directly related to the player's success/failure to accomplish the SG's activities/tasks. Also, it is good to mention that he/she can learn and practice restoration techniques and interventions, reducing the level of stress during his/her interaction with the SG.

RECOMMENDATIONS

Although SGs and their aspects (game design, game mechanics, game development, etc.) have been studied a lot in depth, AG is still a promising field with many prospects. The combination of an educational game and AC can contribute to the maximization of UX and the efficiency of the learning process. However, some points need further study and research. For instance, the methods and techniques used to collect the user's emotions, during his/her interaction with an affective SG, should be discreet, non-intrusive, and precise (Zimmermann, Guttormsen, Danuser, Gomez, 2003). Even if the above is established, there are still collection methods that "violate" the principle of discretion and non-interference, such as measuring physiological reactions using sensors. Moreover, it is good to mention that their reliability is under discussion, as the matching of physiological signals to emotions is not standardized (Feidakis & Daradoumis, 2011).

A parameter that must be taken into consideration, as far as emotion recognition in affective SG is concerned, is that the way people express their emotions can vary from culture to culture (Lim, 2016). Indeed, in Jack, Garrod, Yu, Caldara, and Schyns (2012), the universal hypothesis that all humans communicate six basic internal emotional states (happy, surprise, fear, disgust, anger, and sad) using the same facial movements by virtue of their biological and evolutionary origins has been refuted.

Another critical aspect that must be taken into account is the General Data Protection Regulation (GDPR) that was put into effect on May 25, 2018. This regulation is the toughest privacy and security law worldwide. In particular, it imposes obligations onto organizations anywhere, so long as they target or collect personal data of anyone in the European Union (EU).

The term personal data refers to any information related to an individual who can be directly or indirectly identified, such as names, email addresses, location information, ethnicity, gender, biometric data, religious beliefs, web cookies, and political opinions. Affective SGs that exploit users' emotional state to adapt the game, improve UX, maximize engagement, succeed in better learning outcomes, must demonstrate compliance with the GDPR.

FUTURE RESEARCH DIRECTIONS

As technologies have evolved over the years, GLAM organizations' new skills are required regarding digital innovation, ranging from data science, digital research, and artificial intelligence (Candela, 2020).

The personnel, the practitioners of a GLAM institution, even the researchers who may cooperate with the organization in some projects, could benefit from the integration and utilization of current or novel digital technologies. Consequently, it would be useful to develop systems and applications that contribute to this direction.

Also, the replacement of traditional teacher-centered approaches (for education and training) by contemporary student-centered methods and the integration of new technologies, such as SG, virtual reality (VR), augmented reality (AR), etc., is undoubtedly necessary during a GLAM Lab. This perspective must be taken into consideration in the design of the training procedure and the development of training's digital tools.

UX should be another basic parameter that will be an important cornerstone in the design of any GLAM's training system. Besides, in recent years, the design of UX has increasingly become a goal in developing interactive systems (Mahlke, 2005), such as video games (Ng, Khong, & Thwaites, 2012).

Summarizing, development, and integration of digital systems for GLAMs based on UX can convert a typical educational and training procedure into one memorable and immersive experience with better learning outcomes.

The parameter emotion, and in general the user's emotional state during the educational/training procedure can be harnessed to maximize UX and improve the learning procedure. Further research related to AG should be done so that many issues will be addressed. For instance, a basic issue is the exploitation of more discreet and non-intrusive data collection methods instead of a large number of electrodes (Aggag & Revett, 2011) during a user's gaming experience. Furthermore, the accuracy and the convenience of the user's affective state must be further studied.

CONCLUSION

Since SGs become more and more popular and adopted in many different fields, the CH sector could not be excluded. The combination of learning and playfulness aspects in the context of SG (Alvarez et al., 2007) contribute to one engaging game experience (Mortara et al., 2014), maximizing cultural user's motivation, triggering user's emotional involvement, and making them a promising educational tool.

Emotions, which are explained as the synchronization of many different cognitive and physiological components, hold a primary role both in every aspect of the learning procedure and inside the structure (SG's design) and experience of SGs (Anolli et al., 2010). As far as the emotion measurement methods are concerned, they usually aim to identify and classify the type of user's emotional states. There are frequent cases of simultaneous recording and the use of several techniques and methods, such as participants' self-reported (perceived) experience of emotions and machine assessment techniques, to increase the reliability of obtained results.

There are a plethora of applied games that exploit the user's emotions, try to evoke complex emotions, and create positive emotions. In particular, some of them use AC to take advantage of the player's emotional states during the game either to adapt the gameplay or to further improve the user's playful experience. It is good to mention that SG's adaptation aims to enhance learning outcomes by exploiting the interdependence between emotions and participatory appropriation.

GX has been one of the metrics to measure how successful a SG will be. Positive emotions, such as interest, joy, amusement, etc. are crucial for game success and contribute to a positive game experience, which consists of interactions that transpire within games, in contrast with negative emotions, such as disappointment, frustration, anger, etc.

GLAM institutions, which function as gatekeepers in the transmission of knowledge and cultural practices, need to adapt to the latest technological advances to remain relevant in this continuous technological innovation. In this sense, new approaches have recently appeared, such as the concept of Labs, which facilitates the adoption of innovative and creative tools for content delivery and user engagement.

Affective SG could be used as an effective educational and training tool in the context of GLAMs institutions by increasing the user's motivation, allowing safer training, providing better insight into situations, experiencing higher effectiveness for training, and better supporting for decision making (Molka-Danielsen, Prasolova-Førland, Hokstad & Fominykh, 2015).

GLAMs' personnel, such as security personnel can train experientially in emergency plans through carrying out missions repeatedly, without endangering either themselves or the cultural exhibits. Moreover, a GLAM's Lab, which is a field full of possibilities both for presentation and dissemination of various research aspects, can include affective SGs as an alternative tool for transmitting knowledge or evaluating the newly acquired knowledge through an engaging and endearing way, especially for practitioners.

REFERENCES

Abt, C. C. (1970). *Serious games*. Viking Press.

Aggag, A., & Revett, K. (2011, July). Affective gaming: a GSR-based approach. In *Proceedings of the 15th WSEAS international conference on Computers* (pp. 262-266). Academic Press.

Ahmed, W., Van der Werf, G., Kuyper, H., & Minnaert, A. (2013). Emotions, self-regulated learning, and achievement in mathematics: A growth curve analysis. *Journal of Educational Psychology*, *105*(1), 150–161. doi:10.1037/a0030160

Alvarez, J., Rampnoux, O., Jessel, J. P., & Methel, G. (2007). Serious Game: Just a question of posture. *Artificial & Ambient Intelligence, AISB*, *7*(1), 420–423.

Anolli, L., Mantovani, F., Confalonieri, L., Ascolese, A., & Peveri, L. (2010). Emotions in serious games: From experience to assessment. *International Journal of Emerging Technologies in Learning (iJET)*, *5*.

Aranha, R. V., Silva, L. S., Chaim, M. L., & dos Santos Nunes, F. D. L. (2017, June). Using affective computing to automatically adapt serious games for rehabilitation. In *2017 IEEE 30th International Symposium on Computer-Based Medical Systems (CBMS)* (pp. 55-60). IEEE. 10.1109/CBMS.2017.89

Argasiński, J. K., & Węgrzyn, P. (2019). Affective patterns in serious games. *Future Generation Computer Systems*, *92*, 526–538. doi:10.1016/j.future.2018.06.013

Arriaga, P., Esteves, F., & Fernandes, S. (2013). Playing for better or for worse?: Health and social outcomes with electronic gaming. In *Handbook of research on ICTs for human-centered healthcare and social care services* (pp. 48–69). IGI Global. doi:10.4018/978-1-4666-3986-7.ch003

Atkinson, A. P., Dittrich, W. H., Gemmell, A. J., & Young, A. W. (2004). Emotion perception from dynamic and static body expressions in point-light and full-light displays. *Perception*, *33*(6), 717–746. doi:10.1068/p5096 PMID:15330366

Barbatsis, K., Economou, D., Papamagkana, I., & Loukas, D. (2011, October). 3D environments with games characteristics for teaching history: the VRLerna case study. In *Proceedings of the 29th ACM international conference on Design of communication* (pp. 59-66). 10.1145/2038476.2038488

Barrett, L. F. (2006). Solving the emotion paradox: Categorization and the experience of emotion. *Personality and Social Psychology Review*, *10*(1), 20–46. doi:10.120715327957pspr1001_2 PMID:16430327

Bellotti, F., Berta, R., De Gloria, A., D'ursi, A., & Fiore, V. (2013). A serious game model for cultural heritage. *Journal on Computing and Cultural Heritage*, *5*(4), 1–27. doi:10.1145/2399180.2399185

Cai, Z., Goertzel, B., Zhou, C., Huang, D., Ke, S., Yu, G., & Jiang, M. (2013). OpenPsi: A novel computational affective model and its application in video games. *Engineering Applications of Artificial Intelligence*, *26*(1), 1–12. doi:10.1016/j.engappai.2012.07.013

Calvo, R. A., D'Mello, S., Gratch, J. M., & Kappas, A. (Eds.). (2015). *The Oxford Handbook of affective computing*. Oxford Library of Psychology. doi:10.1093/oxfordhb/9780199942237.001.0001

Carvalho, M. B. (2017). *Serious games for learning: a model and a reference architecture for efficient game development*. Technische Universiteit Eindhoven.

Crane, E., & Gross, M. (2007, September). Motion capture and emotion: Affect detection in whole body movement. In *International Conference on Affective Computing and Intelligent Interaction* (pp. 95-101). Springer. 10.1007/978-3-540-74889-2_9

Dagnino, F. M., Ott, M., Pozzi, F., Yilmaz, E., Tsalakanidou, F., Dimitropoulos, K., & Grammalidis, N. (2015). Serious games to support learning of rare 'intangible'cultural expressions. In *9th International technology, education and development conference (INTED 2015)* (pp. 7184-7194). Academic Press.

Damasio, A. R., Everitt, B. J., & Bishop, D. (1996). *The somatic marker hypothesis and the possible functions of the*. Academic Press.

De Byl, P. (2015). A conceptual affective design framework for the use of emotions in computer game design. *Cyberpsychology (Brno)*, *9*(3). Advance online publication. doi:10.5817/CP2015-3-4

Djaouti, D., Alvarez, J., Jessel, J. P., & Rampnoux, O. (2011). Origins of serious games. In *Serious games and edutainment applications* (pp. 25–43). Springer. doi:10.1007/978-1-4471-2161-9_3

Drummond, D., Hadchouel, A., & Tesnière, A. (2017). Serious games for health: Three steps forwards. *Advances in Simulation (London, England)*, *2*(1), 1–8. doi:10.118641077-017-0036-3 PMID:29450004

Du, G., Zhou, W., Li, C., Li, D., & Liu, P. X. (2020). An Emotion Recognition Method for Game Evaluation Based on Electroencephalogram. *IEEE Transactions on Affective Computing*, 1. doi:10.1109/TAFFC.2020.3023966

Dzedzickis, A., Kaklauskas, A., & Bucinskas, V. (2020). Human emotion recognition: Review of sensors and methods. *Sensors (Basel)*, *20*(3), 592. doi:10.339020030592 PMID:31973140

Ekman, P. (1999). Basic emotions. Handbook of Cognition and Emotion, 98(45-60), 16.

Ellis, H., & Ashbrook, P. (1988). Resource allocation model of the effects of depressed mood states on memory. *Affect, Cognition and Social Behavior*, 25- 43.

Feidakis, M., & Daradoumis, A. (2011). A reference framework for the design of Educational Technologies with "emotion". *2nd Panhellenic Conference "Integration and use of ICT in the Educational Process"*.

Foni, A. E., Papagiannakis, G., & Magnenat-Thalmann, N. (2010). A taxonomy of visualization strategies for cultural heritage applications. *Journal on Computing and Cultural Heritage*, *3*(1), 1–21. doi:10.1145/1805961.1805962

Gallegos, B., Kepple, M. T., & Bukaty, C. A. (2016). Using video gameplay to measure achievement for students with disabilities: A new perspective to grading and achievement reporting. In *Handbook of research on gaming trends in P-12 education* (pp. 326–352). IGI Global. doi:10.4018/978-1-4666-9629-7.ch016

Garneli, V., Giannakos, M., & Chorianopoulos, K. (2017). Serious games as a malleable learning medium: The effects of narrative, gameplay, and making on students' performance and attitudes. *British Journal of Educational Technology*, *48*(3), 842–859. doi:10.1111/bjet.12455

Gibson, E., Hu, L., & Swast, T. (2010). How effective is "Fuzzies" as a tool for developing a holistic understanding of basic genetic principles? *SPIRE-EIT REU summer program for interdisciplinary research and education emerging interface technologies*.

Gilleade, K., Dix, A., & Allanson, J. (2005). Affective videogames and modes of affective gaming: assist me, challenge me, emote me. *DiGRA 2005: Changing Views–Worlds in Play*.

Ghoman, S. K., & Schmölzer, G. M. (2020, March). The RETAIN simulation-based serious game—A review of the literature. *Health Care*, *8*(1), 3. PMID:31877882

Hocine, N., & Gouaich, A. (2011). *A Survey of Agent Programming and Adaptive Serious Games*. RR-11013, pp.8. fflirmm-00577722

Isen, A. M. (2004). Some perspectives on positive feelings and emotions: positive affect facilitates thinking and problem solving. In A. S. R.Manstead, N. Frijda, A. Fischer, A. S. R. Manstead, N. Frijda, & A. Fischer (Eds.), *Feelings and emotions: The Amsterdam Symposium* (pp.263–281). New York, NY: Cambridge University Press. 10.1017/CBO9780511806582.016

Jack, R. E., Garrod, O. G., Yu, H., Caldara, R., & Schyns, P. G. (2012). Facial expressions of emotion are not culturally universal. *Proceedings of the National Academy of Sciences of the United States of America*, *109*(19), 7241–7244. doi:10.1073/pnas.1200155109 PMID:22509011

Johnson, D., & Wiles, J. (2003). Effective affective user interface design in games. *Ergonomics, 46*(13-14), 1332–1345. doi:10.1080/00140130310001610865 PMID:14612323

Kalatha, E., Aliprantis, J., Konstantakis, M., Michalakis, K., Moraitou, T., & Caridakis, G. (2018, May). Cultural Heritage engagement via Serious Games: the ARCADE Augmented Reality, Context-Aware, linked open Data pErsonalized ecosystem. In *1st International CICMS Conference 4-5 May, 2018 Kuşadası, Turkey* (p. 309). Academic Press.

Kalatha, E., & Caridakis, G. (2013, December). Natural, affect aware interfaces: gesture and body expressivity aspects. In *2013 8th International Workshop on Semantic and Social Media Adaptation and Personalization* (pp. 97-102). IEEE. 10.1109/SMAP.2013.17

Kalatha, E., Konstantakis, M., & Caridakis, G. (2019, June). Exploiting User Personas for a Cultural Serious Game based on Gardner's Multiple Intelligences Theory. *2nd Social Science Conference.*

Kołakowska, A., Landowska, A., Szwoch, M., Szwoch, W., & Wróbel, M. R. (2013, June). Emotion recognition and its application in software engineering. In *2013 6th International Conference on Human System Interactions (HSI)* (pp. 532-539). IEEE. 10.1109/HSI.2013.6577877

Kotsia, I., Zafeiriou, S., & Fotopoulos, S. (2013). Affective gaming: A comprehensive survey. In *Proceedings of the IEEE conference on computer vision and pattern recognition workshops* (pp. 663-670). IEEE.

Kurkovsky, S. (2015, June). Teaching software engineering with LEGO serious play. In *Proceedings of the 2015 ACM Conference on Innovation and Technology in Computer Science Education* (pp. 213-218). 10.1145/2729094.2742604

Labrador, E., & Villegas, E. (2014). Sistema Fun Experience Design (FED) aplicado en el aula. *Re-Visión, 7*(2).

Li, L., & Campbell, J. (2010). Emotion modeling and interaction of NPCs in virtual simulation and games. *The International Journal of Virtual Reality: a Multimedia Publication for Professionals, 9*(4), 1–6. doi:10.20870/IJVR.2010.9.4.2784

Li, J. (2020). A Systematic Review of Video Games for Second Language Acquisition. In *Handbook of Research on Integrating Digital Technology With Literacy Pedagogies* (pp. 472–499). IGI Global.

Li, Y., Elmaghraby, A. S., El-Baz, A., & Sokhadze, E. M. (2015, December). Using physiological signal analysis to design affective VR games. In *2015 IEEE International Symposium on Signal Processing and Information Technology (ISSPIT)* (pp. 57-62). IEEE. 10.1109/ISSPIT.2015.7394401

Lim, C. W., & Jung, H. W. (2013). A study on the military Serious Game. *Advanced Science and Technology Letters, 39*, 73–77. doi:10.14257/astl.2013.39.14

Lim, N. (2016). Cultural differences in emotion: Differences in emotional arousal level between the East and the West. *Integrative Medicine Research, 5*(2), 105–109. doi:10.1016/j.imr.2016.03.004 PMID:28462104

Mahey, M., Al-Abdulla, A., Ames, S., Bray, P., Candela, G., Chambers, S., & Wilms, L. (2019). *Open a GLAM lab.* QU Press.

Mahmud, S. (2014). *History & Re-convergence of Galleries, Libraries, Archives, Museums (GLAM) - A systematic literature review* [Master's Thesis]. Queensland University of Technology. https://bit.ly/3CMJ72k

Maglogiannis, I., Kalatha, E., & Paraskevopoulou-Kollia, E. A. (2017). An Overview of Affective Computing from the Physiology and Biomedical Perspective. In E. Spyrou, D. Iakovidis, & P. Mylonas (Eds.), *Semantic Multimedia Analysis and Processing* (pp. 367–396). CRC Press. doi:10.1201/b17080-14

Mandryk, R. L., Atkins, M. S., & Inkpen, K. M. (2006, April). A continuous and objective evaluation of emotional experience with interactive play environments. In *Proceedings of the SIGCHI Conference on Human Factors in computing systems* (pp. 1027-1036). 10.1145/1124772.1124926

Melzer, A., Shafir, T., & Tsachor, R. P. (2019). How do we recognize emotion from movement? Specific motor components contribute to the recognition of each emotion. *Frontiers in Psychology*, *10*, 1389. doi:10.3389/fpsyg.2019.01389 PMID:31333524

Michael, D. R., & Chen, S. L. (2006). *Serious games: Games that educate, train, and inform*. Muska & Lipman/Premier-Trade.

Mitchell, A., & Savill-Smith, C. (2004). *The use of computer and video games for learning. A review of the literature*. Academic Press.

Molka-Danielsen, J., Prasolova-Førland, E., Hokstad, L. M., & Fominykh, M. (2015, November). Creating safe and effective learning environment for emergency management training using virtual reality. In Norsk konferanse for organisasjoners bruk at IT (Vol. 23, No. 1). Academic Press.

Mortara, M., Catalano, C. E., Bellotti, F., Fiucci, G., Houry-Panchetti, M., & Petridis, P. (2014). Learning cultural heritage by serious games. *Journal of Cultural Heritage*, *15*(3), 318–325. doi:10.1016/j.culher.2013.04.004

Ng, Y. Y., Khong, C. W., & Thwaites, H. (2012). A review of affective design towards video games. *Procedia: Social and Behavioral Sciences*, *51*, 687–691. doi:10.1016/j.sbspro.2012.08.225

Nguyen, T. T. H., Ishmatova, D., Tapanainen, T., Liukkonen, T. N., Katajapuu, N., Makila, T., & Luimula, M. (2017, January). Impact of serious games on health and well-being of elderly: a systematic review. In *Proceedings of the 50th Hawaii International Conference on System Sciences*. 10.24251/HICSS.2017.447

Oliveira, V., Coelho, A., Guimarães, R., & Rebelo, C. (2012). Serious game in security: A solution for security trainees. *Procedia Computer Science*, *15*, 274–282. doi:10.1016/j.procs.2012.10.079

Plutchik, R. (2001). The nature of emotions: Human emotions have deep evolutionary roots, a fact that may explain their complexity and provide tools for clinical practice. *American Scientist*, *89*(4), 344–350. doi:10.1511/2001.4.344

Prensky, M. (2003). Digital game-based learning. *Computers in Entertainment*, *1*(1), 21–21. doi:10.1145/950566.950596

Psaltis, A., Kaza, K., Stefanidis, K., Thermos, S., Apostolakis, K. C., Dimitropoulos, K., & Daras, P. (2016, October). Multimodal affective state recognition in serious games applications. In *2016 IEEE International Conference on Imaging Systems and Techniques (IST)* (pp. 435-439). IEEE. 10.1109/IST.2016.7738265

Renshaw, C., & Liew, C. L. (2021). *Descriptive standards and collection management software for documentary heritage management: Attitudes and experiences of information professionals.* Global Knowledge, Memory and Communication.

Romero, M., Usart, M., & Ott, M. (2015). Can serious games contribute to developing and sustaining 21st century skills? *Games and Culture, 10*(2), 148–177. doi:10.1177/1555412014548919

Rubino, I., Barberis, C., Xhembulla, J., & Malnati, G. (2015). Integrating a location-based mobile game in the museum visit: Evaluating visitors' behaviour and learning. *Journal on Computing and Cultural Heritage, 8*(3), 1–18. doi:10.1145/2724723

Sakurazawa, S., Yoshida, N., & Munekata, N. (2004, September). Entertainment feature of a game using skin conductance response. In *Proceedings of the 2004 ACM SIGCHI international conference on advances in computer entertainment technology* (pp. 181-186). 10.1145/1067343.1067365

Setiono, D., Saputra, D., Putra, K., Moniaga, J. V., & Chowanda, A. (2021). Enhancing Player Experience in Game With Affective Computing. *Procedia Computer Science, 179*, 781–788. doi:10.1016/j.procs.2021.01.066

Schachter, S., & Singer, J. (1962). Cognitive, social, and physiological determinants of emotional state. *Psychological Review, 69*(5), 379–399. doi:10.1037/h0046234 PMID:14497895

Schacter, D., Gilbert, D., Wegner, D., & Hood, B. M. (2011). *Psychology* (European Edition). Macmillan International Higher Education.

Scherer, K. R. (2000). Psychological models of emotion. *The Neuropsychology of Emotion, 137*(3), 137-162.

Scherer, K. R. (2005). What are emotions? And how can they be measured? *Social Sciences Information. Information Sur les Sciences Sociales, 44*(4), 695–729. doi:10.1177/0539018405058216

Schutz, P. A., & Lanehart, S. L. (2002). Introduction: Emotions in education. *Educational Psychologist, 37*(2), 67–68.

Chen, J. (2016). Understanding teacher emotions: The development of a teacher emotion inventory. *Teaching and Teacher Education*, (55), 68–77.

Shu, L., Xie, J., Yang, M., Li, Z., Li, Z., Liao, D., Xu, X., & Yang, X. (2018). A review of emotion recognition using physiological signals. *Sensors (Basel), 18*(7), 2074. doi:10.339018072074 PMID:29958457

Sloman, A. (1999). Review of affective computing. *AI Magazine, 20*(1), 127–127.

Wetzel, R., Blum, L., & Oppermann, L. (2012, May). Tidy city: A location-based game supported by in-situ and web-based authoring tools to enable user-created content. In *Proceedings of the international conference on the foundations of digital games* (pp. 238-241). 10.1145/2282338.2282385

Wu, C. H., Huang, Y. M., & Hwang, J. P. (2016). Review of affective computing in education/learning: Trends and challenges. *British Journal of Educational Technology*, *47*(6), 1304–1323. doi:10.1111/bjet.12324

Zimmerman, B. J. (2008). Investigating self-regulation and motivation: Historical background, methodological developments, and future prospects. *American Educational Research Journal*, *45*(1), 166–183. doi:10.3102/0002831207312909

Zimmermann, P., Guttormsen, S., Danuser, B., & Gomez, P. (2003). *AffectiveComputing - A Rationale for Measuring Mood with Mouse and Keyboard*. Swiss Federal Institute of Technology.

Zhonggen, Y. (2019). A meta-analysis of use of serious games in education over a decade. *International Journal of Computer Games Technology*, *2019*, 2019. doi:10.1155/2019/4797032

Zyda, M. (2005). From visual simulation to virtual reality to games. *Computer*, *38*(9), 25–32. doi:10.1109/MC.2005.297

ADDITIONAL READING

All, A., Castellar, E. P. N., & Van Looy, J. (2016). Assessing the effectiveness of digital game-based learning: Best practices. *Computers & Education*, *92*, 90–103. doi:10.1016/j.compedu.2015.10.007

Candela, G., Sáez, M. D., Escobar Esteban, M., & Marco-Such, M. (2020). Reusing digital collections from GLAM institutions. *Journal of Information Science*.

Foni, A. E., Papagiannakis, G., & Magnenat-Thalmann, N. (2010). A taxonomy of visualization strategies for cultural heritage applications. *Journal on Computing and Cultural Heritage*, *3*(1), 1–21. doi:10.1145/1805961.1805962

Gonçalves, V. P., Giancristofaro, G. T., Geraldo Filho, P. R., Johnson, T., Carvalho, V., Pessin, G., de Almeida Neris, P. V., & Ueyama, J. (2017). Assessing users' emotion at interaction time: A multimodal approach with multiple sensors. *Soft Computing*, *21*(18), 5309–5323. doi:10.100700500-016-2115-0

Hascher, T. (2010). Learning and emotion: Perspectives for theory and research. *European Educational Research Journal*, *9*(1), 13–28. doi:10.2304/eerj.2010.9.1.13

IJsselsteijn, W. A., de Kort, Y. A., & Poels, K. (2013). The game experience questionnaire. *Eindhoven: Technische Universiteit Eindhoven*, *46*(1).

Jennett, C., Cox, A. L., Cairns, P., Dhoparee, S., Epps, A., Tijs, T., & Walton, A. (2008). Measuring and defining the experience of immersion in games. *International Journal of Human-Computer Studies*, *66*(9), 641–661. doi:10.1016/j.ijhcs.2008.04.004

Lazzaro, N. (2008). *The four fun keys. game usability: Advancing the player experience* (K. Isbister & N. Schaffer, Eds.).

Vlachopoulos, D., & Makri, A. (2017). The effect of games and simulations on higher education: A systematic literature review. *International Journal of Educational Technology in Higher Education*, *14*(1), 1–33. doi:10.118641239-017-0062-1

KEY TERMS AND DEFINITIONS

Digital Native: The generation of people who grew up in the era of ubiquitous technology, including computers and the internet. The term was coined by Marc Prensky in 2001.

Electrocardiography (ECG): A conventional method for non-invasive interpretation of the heart's electrical activity in real-time.

Electroencephalography (EEG): An electrophysiological non-invasive technique for recording electrical activity arising from the human brain.

Electromyography (EMG): A technique for evaluating and recording the electrical potential generated by muscle cells.

Electrooculography (EOG): A technique for measuring the corneo-retinal standing potential that exists between the front and the back of the human eye.

Galvanic Skin Response (GSR): A continuous measurement of electrical parameters of human skin. Also known as electrodermal activity (EDA) or skin conductance (SC).

Heart Rate Variability (HRV): An emotional state evaluation technique based on the measurement of heart rate variability, which means the beat-to-beat variation in time within a certain period of sinus rhythm.

Compilation of References

AA.VV. (2018). *Das 2000-Watt-Areal*. Retrieved July 26, 2022, from http://www.2000watt.swiss

Aaltonen, K., & Kujala, J. (2010). A project lifecycle perspective on stakeholder influence strategies in global projects. *Scandinavian Journal of Management*, 26(4), 381–397. doi:10.1016/j.scaman.2010.09.001

Abbott, E. A. (1885). *Flatland: A Romance of Many Dimensions*. Roberts Brothers.

Abt, C. C. (1987). *Serious games*. University Press of America.

Abt, C. C. (1970). *Serious games*. Viking Press.

Abt, C. C. (1987). *Serious Games*. University Press of America.

Acar, Y., Stransky, C., Wermke, D., Weir, C., Mazurek, M., & Fahl, S. (2017). Developers Need Support, Too: A Survey of Security Advice for Software Developers. *2017 IEEE Cybersecurity Development (SecDev)*, 22-26.

Acatech. (2020). *MINT Nachwuchsbarometer*. Gutenberg Beuys Feindruckerei.

Adams, M., & Makramalla, M. (2015). Cybersecurity Skills Training: An Attacker-Centric Gamified Approach. *Technology Innovation Management Review*, 5(1), 5–14. doi:10.22215/timreview/861

Agate. (2017). *Core elements and mechanics of gamification*. Retrieved from https://agate.id/core-elements-of-gamification

Aggag, A., & Revett, K. (2011, July). Affective gaming: a GSR-based approach. In *Proceedings of the 15th WSEAS international conference on Computers* (pp. 262-266). Academic Press.

Agogué, M., Levillain, K., & Hooge, S. (2015). Gamification of creativity: Exploring the usefulness of serious games for ideation. *Creativity and Innovation Management*, 24(3), 415–429. doi:10.1111/caim.12138

Ahmadi, M., Anisi, Y., Rad, B. B., & Rana, M. E. (2016). Using Serious Games to Replicate Scrum Framework in Daily Software Development Practices. *Proceedings of Int'l Conference On Data Mining, Image Processing, Computer & Electronics Engineering (DMIPCEE-16)*.

Ahmed, A., & Sutton, M. J. (2017). *Gamification, serious games, simulations, and immersive learning environments in knowledge management initiatives*. World Journal of Science, Technology and Sustainable Development. doi:10.1108/WJSTSD-02-2017-0005

Ahmed, W., Van der Werf, G., Kuyper, H., & Minnaert, A. (2013). Emotions, self-regulated learning, and achievement in mathematics: A growth curve analysis. *Journal of Educational Psychology*, 105(1), 150–161. doi:10.1037/a0030160

Aiolli, F., Ciman, M., Donini, M., & Ombretta, G. (2014). Serious Game to Persuade People to Use Stairs. In *Persuasive 2014 Posters* (pp. 11–13). Academic Press.

Ajzen, I. (1991). The theory of planned behavior. *Organizational Behavior and Human Decision Processes*, *50*(2), 179–211. doi:10.1016/0749-5978(91)90020-T

Ajzen, I. (2002). Perceived behavioral control, self-efficacy, locus of control, and the theory of planned behavior. *Journal of Applied Social Psychology*, *32*(4), 665–683. doi:10.1111/j.1559-1816.2002.tb00236.x

Alamri, A., Hossain, A. M., Hassan, M. M., Hossain, S. M., Alnuem, M., Ahmed, T. D., & el Abdulmotaleb, S. (2013). A cloudbased pervasive serious game framework to support obesity treatment. *Computer Science and Information Systems*, *10*(3), 1229–1246. doi:10.2298/CSIS120717046A

Alanne, K. (2016). An overview of game-based learning in building services engineering education. *European Journal of Engineering Education*, *41*(2), 204–219. doi:10.1080/03043797.2015.1056097

Alatalo, S., Oikarinen, E.-L., Reiman, A., Tan, T.-M., Heikka, E.-L., Hurmelinna-Laukkanen, P., Muhos, M., & Vuorela, T. (2018). Linking concepts of playfulness and well- being at work in retail sector. *Journal of Retailing and Consumer Services*, *43*(C), 226–233. doi:10.1016/j.jretconser.2018.03.013

Albaghajati, A., & Hassine, J. (2022). A use case driven approach to game modeling. *Requirements Engineering*, *27*(1), 83–116. doi:10.100700766-021-00362-4

Alexandrova, A. (2018). *Digital government systems: tackling the legacy problem through a game-based approach to business requirements analysis* [Doctoral Dissertation, The Open University]. ProQuest.

Alexandrova, A., & Rapanotti, L. (2020). Requirements analysis gamification in legacy system replacement projects. *Requirements Engineering*, *25*(2), 131–151. doi:10.100700766-019-00311-2

Allahverdipour, H. (2020). Global challenge of health communication: Infodemia in the coronavirus disease (COVID-19) pandemic. *Journal of Education and Community Health*, *7*(2), 65–67. doi:10.29252/jech.7.2.65

Allen, F. E. (2011, May 3). Disneyland Uses 'Electronic Whip' on Employees. *Forbes*.

Almalki, M., & Giannicchi, A. (2021). Health apps for combating COVID-19: Descriptive review and taxonomy. *JMIR mHealth and uHealth*, *9*(3), e24322. doi:10.2196/24322 PMID:33626017

Almeida, F., & Simoes, J. (2019). The role of serious games, gamification and industry 4.0 tools in the education 4.0 paradigm. *Contemporary Educational Technology*, *10*(2), 120–136. doi:10.30935/cet.554469

AlSaad, F. M., & Durugbo, C. M. (2021, August 19). Gamification-as-Innovation: A Review. *International Journal of Innovation and Technology Management*, *18*(5). doi:10.1142/S0219877021300020

AlSkaif, T., Lampropoulos, I., van den Broek, M., & van Sark, W. (2018). Gamification-based Framework for Engagement of Residential Customers in Energy Applications. *Energy Research & Social Science*, *44*, 187–195. doi:10.1016/j.erss.2018.04.043

Alvarez, J., Rampnoux, O., Jessel, J. P., & Methel, G. (2007). Serious Game: Just a question of posture. *Artificial & Ambient Intelligence, AISB*, *7*(1), 420–423.

Alves, F. (2015). *Gamification: Como criar experiências de aprendizagem engajadoras, um guia completo: do conceito a prática*. Dvs Editora.

Al-Yafi, K., & El-Masri, M. (2016). *Gamification of e-government services: A discussion of potential transformation*. Association for Information Systems.

Ames, P., & Hiscox, M. (2016). *Guide to developing behavioural interventions for randomised controlled trials: Nine guiding questions*. Department of the Prime Minister and Cabinet.

Anderie, L. (2017). *Gamification, Digitalisierung und Industrie 4.0: Transformation und Disruption verstehen und erfolgreich managen.* Springer-Verlag.

Anderson, R., Barton, C., Bölme, R., Clayton, R., Ganán, C., Grasso, T., Levi, M., Moore, T., & Vasek, M. (2019). *Measuring the changing cost of cybercrime.* Academic Press.

Andrew Dinn, L. D. (n.d.). *Byteman.* Retrieved May 18, 2021, from https://byteman.jboss.org/

Anguera, J. A., Boccanfuso, J., Rintoul, J. L., Al-Hashimi, O., Faraji, F., Janowich, J., ... Johnston, E. (2013). Video game training enhances cognitive control in older adults. *Nature, 501*(7465), 97–101. doi:10.1038/nature12486 PMID:24005416

Anguera, J. A., Gunning, F. M., & Areán, P. A. (2017). Improving late life depression and cognitive control through the use of therapeutic video game technology: A proof-of-concept randomized trial. *Depression and Anxiety, 34*(6), 508–517. doi:10.1002/da.22588 PMID:28052513

Anguera, J. A., Schachtner, J. N., Simon, A. J., Volponi, J., Javed, S., Gallen, C. L., & Gazzaley, A. (2021). Long-term maintenance of multitasking abilities following video game training in older adults. *Neurobiology of Aging, 103*, 22–30. doi:10.1016/j.neurobiolaging.2021.02.023 PMID:33789209

Annetta, L. A. (2008). Video games in education: Why they should be used and how they are being used. *Theory into Practice, 47*(3), 229–239. doi:10.1080/00405840802153940

Anolli, L., Mantovani, F., Confalonieri, L., Ascolese, A., & Peveri, L. (2010). Emotions in serious games: From experience to assessment. *International Journal of Emerging Technologies in Learning (iJET), 5.*

Antonaci, A., Klemke, R., Stracke, C. M., Specht, M., Spatafora, M., & Stefanova, K. (2017). Gamification to Empower Information Security Education. In P. Tuomi & A. Perttula (Eds.), *Proceedings of the 1st International GamiFIN Conference* (pp. 32-38). Pori, Finland: CEUR Workshop Proceedings.

Antonaci, A., Klemke, R., & Specht, M. (2019, September). The effects of gamification in online learning environments: A systematic literature review. *Informatics (MDPI), 6*(3), 32. doi:10.3390/informatics6030032

Anttonen, H., & Vainio, H. (2010). Towards better work and well-being: An overview. *Journal of Occupational and Environmental Medicine, 52*(12), 1245–1248. doi:10.1097/JOM.0b013e318202f3bd PMID:21750472

Anvik, J., Cote, V., & Riehl, J. (2019). Program Wars: A Card Game for Learning Programming and Cybersecurity Concepts. *SIGCSE '19: Proceedings of the 50th ACM Technical Symposium on Computer Science Education,* 393-399. 10.1145/3287324.3287496

Anwer, F., Aftab, S., Waheed, U., & Muhammad, S. S. (2017). Agile software development models tdd, fdd, dsdm, and crystal methods: A survey. *International Journal of Multidisciplinary Sciences and Engineering, 8*(2), 1–10.

Apostolopoulos, A. (2019, August 19). *The 2019 Gamification at Work Survey.* TalentLMS. https://www.talentlms.com/blog/gamification-survey-results/

Arai, S., Sakamoto, K., & Washizaki, H. (2014). *A gamified tool for motivating developers to remove warnings of bug pattern tools.* Paper presented at the IWESEP 2014, Osaka. 10.1109/IWESEP.2014.17

Aranha, R. V., Silva, L. S., Chaim, M. L., & dos Santos Nunes, F. D. L. (2017, June). Using affective computing to automatically adapt serious games for rehabilitation. In *2017 IEEE 30th International Symposium on Computer-Based Medical Systems (CBMS)* (pp. 55-60). IEEE. 10.1109/CBMS.2017.89

Argasiński, J. K., & Węgrzyn, P. (2019). Affective patterns in serious games. *Future Generation Computer Systems, 92,* 526–538. doi:10.1016/j.future.2018.06.013

Argyris, C. (2003). A life full of learning. *Organization Studies, 24*(7), 1178–1192. doi:10.1177/01708406030247009

Armellini, A., & Padilla Rodriguez, B. C. (2021). Active Blended Learning. In B. C. P. Rodriguez & A. Armellini (Eds.), *Cases on Active Blended Learning in Higher Education* (pp. 1–22). IGI Global. doi:10.4018/978-1-7998-7856-8.ch001

Arnab, S., Lim, T., Carvalho, M. B., Bellotti, F., de Freitas, S., Louchart, S., Suttie, N., Berta, R., & De Gloria, A. (2015). Mapping learning and game mechanics for serious games analysis. *British Journal of Educational Technology, 46*(2), 391–411. doi:10.1111/bjet.12113

Arriaga, P., Esteves, F., & Fernandes, S. (2013). Playing for better or for worse?: Health and social outcomes with electronic gaming. In *Handbook of research on ICTs for human-centered healthcare and social care services* (pp. 48–69). IGI Global. doi:10.4018/978-1-4666-3986-7.ch003

Ašeriškis, D., & Damaševičius, R. (2014). Gamification of a project management system. In *Proc. of Int. Conference on Advances in Computer-Human Interactions ACHI2014* (pp. 200-207). Academic Press.

Ašeriškis, D., & Damaševičius, R. (2014). Gamification patterns for gamification applications. *Procedia Computer Science, 39*, 83–90. doi:10.1016/j.procs.2014.11.013

Askheim, O.-P. (2003). Empowerment as quidance for professional social work: An act of balancing on a slack rope. *European Journal of Social Work, 6*(3), 229–240. doi:10.1080/1369145032000164546

Asuncion, H., Socha, D., Sung, K., Berfield, S., & Gregory, W. (2011). Serious game development as an iterative user-centered agile software project. In *Proceedings of the 1st International workshop on games and software engineering* (pp. 44–47). ACM. 10.1145/1984674.1984690

Atkinson, A. P., Dittrich, W. H., Gemmell, A. J., & Young, A. W. (2004). Emotion perception from dynamic and static body expressions in point-light and full-light displays. *Perception, 33*(6), 717–746. doi:10.1068/p5096 PMID:15330366

Aubusson, P., Fogwill, S., Barr, R., & Perkovic, L. (1997). What happens when students do simulation-role-play in science? *Research in Science Education, 27*(4), 565–579. doi:10.1007/BF02461481

Autodesk Inc. (2022). *3D Computer Animation, Modeling, Simulation, and Rendering Software*. https://www.autodesk.com/products/maya/overview

Ávila Gutiérrez, M. J., Martín Gómez, A., Aguayo González, F., & Lama Ruiz, J. R. (2020). Eco-Holonic 4.0 Circular Business Model to Conceptualize Sustainable Value Chain towards Digital Transition. *Sustainability, 12*(5), 1889. doi:10.3390u12051889

Ávila-Pesántez, D., Rivera, L. A., & Alban, M. S. (2017). Approaches for serious game design: A systematic literature review. *The ASEE Computers in Education (CoED) Journal, 8*(3).

Bailenson, J. N. (2021). Nonverbal overload: A theoretical argument for the causes of Zoom fatigue. *Technology, Mind, and Behavior, 2*(1). Advance online publication. doi:10.1037/tmb0000030

Bakan, U., & Bakan, U. (2018). Game-Based Learning Studies in Education Journals: A Systematic Review of Recent Trends. *Actualidades Pedagógicas*, 119-145.

Bakhsheshi, F. F. (2019). Serious games and serious gaming in escape rooms. *Proceedings of the 1st International Serious Games Symposium (ISGS)*, 1–6. 10.1109/ISGS49501.2019.9047019

Balanced European Conservation Approach. (2012). *The ICT PSP methodology for energy saving measurement: a common deliverable from projects of ICT for sustainable growth in the residential sector, version 3*. https://cordis.europa.eu/docs/projects/cnect/6/250496/080/deliverables/001-ARES975520CIPCommondeliverableeSESH.pdf

Ball, C., Huang, K.-T., & Francis, J. (2021). Virtual reality adoption during the COVID-19 pandemic: A uses and gratifications perspective. *Telematics and Informatics*, *65*, 101728. doi:10.1016/j.tele.2021.101728 PMID:34887619

Bandura, A. (1977a). *Social learning theory*. Prentice-Hall.

Bandura, A. (1977b). Self-efficacy: Toward a unifying theory of behavior change. *Psychological Review*, *84*(2), 191–215. doi:10.1037/0033-295X.84.2.191 PMID:847061

Bandura, A. (1986). *Social foundations of thought and action: A social cognitive theory*. Prentice-Hall.

Bandura, A. (1997). *Self-efficacy: The exercise of control*. W. H. Freeman & Co.

Bandura, A., Ross, D., & Ross, S. A. (1961). Transmission of aggression through imitation of aggressive models. *Journal of Abnormal and Social Psychology*, *63*(3), 575–582. doi:10.1037/h0045925 PMID:13864605

Bandura, A., Ross, D., & Ross, S. A. (1963a). Imitation of film-mediated aggressive models. *Journal of Abnormal and Social Psychology*, *66*(1), 3–11. doi:10.1037/h0048687 PMID:13966304

Bandura, A., Ross, D., & Ross, S. A. (1963b). Vicarious reinforcement and imitative learning. *Journal of Abnormal and Social Psychology*, *67*(6), 601–607. doi:10.1037/h0045550 PMID:14084769

Bangert-Drowns, R. L., & Pyke, C. (2001). A taxonomy of student engagement with educational software: An exploration of literate thinking with electronic text. *Journal of Educational Computing Research*, *24*(3), 213–234. doi:10.2190/0CKM-FKTR-0CPF-JLGR

Barab, S. (2004). Using design to advance learning theory, or using learning theory to advance design. *Educational Technology*, *44*(3), 16–20. Retrieved August 6, 2021, from https://www.jstor.org/stable/44428901

Barbatsis, K., Economou, D., Papamagkana, I., & Loukas, D. (2011, October). 3D environments with games characteristics for teaching history: the VRLerna case study. In *Proceedings of the 29th ACM international conference on Design of communication* (pp. 59-66). 10.1145/2038476.2038488

Barela, J., Gasiba, T., Suppan, S., Berges, M., & K., B. (2019). When interactive graphic storytelling fails. In *IEEE 27th International Requirements Engineering Conference Workshops* (pp. 164-169). Institute of Electrical and Electronics Engineers Inc.

Barrett, L. F. (2006). Solving the emotion paradox: Categorization and the experience of emotion. *Personality and Social Psychology Review*, *10*(1), 20–46. doi:10.120715327957pspr1001_2 PMID:16430327

Barthes, R. (1977). *Writing degree zero* (A. Lavers, & C. Smith, Trans.). Macmillan.

Bartle, R. (1996a). Players Who Suit MUDs. *Journal of MUD Research*. https://mud.co.uk/richard/hcds.htm

Bartle, R. (1996b). *The Bartle Test of Gamer Psychology*. https://matthewbarr.co.uk/bartle/

Bartle, R. A. (2008). Player types. *Jeannie Novak: Game Development Essentials*, 39-40.

Bartle, R. (1996). Hearts, clubs, diamonds, spades: Players who suit MUDs. *Journal of MUD Research*, *1*(1), 19.

Bartolomé, P. S., & Van Gerven, T. (2022). From the classroom to the game: applying available pedagogical guidelines in game-based learning. In *2022 IEEE Global Engineering Education Conference (EDUCON)* (pp. 466-472). IEEE. 10.1109/EDUCON52537.2022.9766475

Basak, C., Boot, W. R., Voss, M. W., & Kramer, A. F. (2008). Can training in a real-time strategy video game attenuate cognitive decline in older adults? *Psychology and Aging*, *23*(4), 765–777. doi:10.1037/a0013494 PMID:19140648

Bauer, M. W. (2017). Kritische Beobachtungen zur Geschichte der Wissenschaftskommunikation. In H. Bonfadelli, B. Fähnrich, C. Lüthje, J. Milde, M. Rhomberg, & M. S. Schäfer (Eds.), *Forschungsfeld Wissenschaftskommunikation* (pp. 17–40). Springer. doi:10.1007/978-3-658-12898-2_2

Bayerische Staatsregierung. (2020). *Hochschulinnovationsgesetz schafft zuverlässigen Rahmen für zukunftsfähige Hochschulstrukturen*. https://www.bayern.de/hochschulinnovationsgesetz-schafft-zuverlssigen-rahmen-fr-zukunftsfhige-hochschulstrukturen/

Beck, K., Gamma, E., Saff, D., & Vasudevan, K. (n.d.). *JUnit5*. Retrieved February 23, 2021, from https://junit.org/junit5/

Beck, A. L., Chitalia, S., & Rai, V. (2019). Not so gameful: A critical review of gamification in mobile energy applications. *Energy Research & Social Science*, *51*, 32–39. doi:10.1016/j.erss.2019.01.006

Becker, M. (2013). *Personalentwicklung: Bildung, Förderung und Organisationsentwicklung in Theorie und Praxis*. Schäffer-Poeschel.

Becker, M. H. (1974). The health belief model and personal health behavior. *Health Education Monographs*, *2*(4), 324–473. doi:10.1177/109019817400200407

Becker, M. H., Drachman, R. H., & Kirscht, J. P. (1974). A new approach to explaining sick-role behavior in low-income populations. *American Journal of Public Health*, *64*(3), 205–216. doi:10.2105/AJPH.64.3.205 PMID:4811762

Bedwell, W. L., Pavlas, D., Heyne, K., Lazzara, E. H., & Salas, E. (2012). Toward a taxonomy linking game attributes to learning: An empirical study. *Simulation & Gaming*, *43*(6), 729–760. doi:10.1177/1046878112439444

Begg, M., Dewhurst, D., & Macleod, H. (2005). Game informed learning: Applying computer game processes to higher education. *Innovate*, *1*(6).

Bellotti, F., Berta, R., & De Gloria, A. (2010). Designing effective serious games: Opportunities and challenges for research. *International Journal of Emerging Technologies in Learning*, *5*(SI3), 22–35. doi:10.3991/ijet.v5s3.1500

Bellotti, F., Berta, R., De Gloria, A., D'ursi, A., & Fiore, V. (2013). A serious game model for cultural heritage. *Journal on Computing and Cultural Heritage*, *5*(4), 1–27. doi:10.1145/2399180.2399185

Bellotti, F., Berta, R., De Gloria, A., Ott, M., Arnab, S., de Freitas, S., & Kiili, K. (2011). Designing serious games for education: from pedagogical principles to game mechanisms. *Proceedings of the 5th European Conference on Games Based Learning*, *2*, 1–9.

BenchPrep. (2015). *The 6 best gamification tools to engage your learners*. Retrieved from https://blog.benchprep.com/gamification-tools-to-engage-learners

Berners-Lee, M. (2020). *How bad are bananas? The carbon footprint of everything*. Profile Books.

Betts, B. (2013). Game-based learning. In R. Hubbard (Ed.), *The really useful elearning instruction manual* (pp. 175–194). Jon Wiley & Sons Ltd.

Biswas, M. R., Robinson, M. D., & Fumo, N. (2016). Prediction of Residential Building Energy Consumption: A Neural Network Approach. *Energy*, *117*(1), 84–92. doi:10.1016/j.energy.2016.10.066

Blascovich, J., & Bailenson, J. (2011). *Infinite Reality: Avatars, Eternal Life, New Worlds, and the Dawn of the Virtual Revolution*. Harper Collins.

Blazhko, O., & Luhova, T. (2018). Features of using the canvas-oriented approach to game design. *Applied Aspects of Information Technology*, (1), 62–73.

Blazhko, O., Luhova, T., Melnik, S., & Ruvinska, V. (2017). Communication Model of Open Government Data Gamification Based on Ukrainian Websites. In *International conference on Intelligent Data Acquisition and Advanced Computing Systems: Technology and Applications (IDAACS): 4th Experiment International Conference (exp.at'17). IEEE* (pp. 181-186). University of Algarve. 10.1109/EXPAT.2017.7984367

Blender Foundation. (2002). *Open source 3D creation. Free to use for any purpose, forever.* https://www.blender.org

Blohm, I., & Leimeister, J. M. (2013). Gamification: Design of IT-based enhancing services for motivational support and behavioral change. *Business & Information Systems Engineering, 5*(4), 275–278. doi:10.100712599-013-0273-5

Böckle, M., Novak, J., & Bick, M. (2020). Exploring gamified persuasive system design for energy saving. *Journal of Enterprise Information Management, 33*(6), 1337–1356. doi:10.1108/JEIM-02-2019-0032

Bodnar, C. A., Anastasio, D., Enszer, J. A., & Burkey, D. D. (2016). Engineers at play: Games as teaching tools for undergraduate engineering students. *Journal of Engineering Education, 105*(1), 147–200. doi:10.1002/jee.20106

Bogost, I. (2011, October 21). *Persuasive Games: Exploitationware.* Gamasutra.

Bogost, I. (2013). Exploitationware. In Rhetoric/composition/play through video games (pp. 139-147). Palgrave Macmillan.

Bogost, I. (2014). Why gamification is bullshit. *The gameful world: Approaches, issues, applications*, 65-80.

Bogost, I. (2008). *The rhetoric of video games.* MacArthur Foundation Digital Media and Learning Initiative.

Boomsma, C., Hafner, R., Pahl, S., Jones, R., & Fuertes, A. (2018). Should We Play Games where Energy is Concerned? Perceptions of Serious Gaming as a Technology to Motivate Energy Behaviour Change among Social Housing Tenants. *Sustainability, 10*(6), 1–18. doi:10.3390u10061729

Boopathi, K., Sreejith, S., & Bithin, A. (2015). Learning Cyber Security Through Gamification. *Indian Journal of Science and Technology, 8*(7), 642–649. doi:10.17485/ijst/2015/v8i7/67760

Boot, W. R., Basak, C., Erickson, K. I., Neider, M., Simons, D. J., Fabiani, M., ... Lee, H. (2010). Transfer of skill engendered by complex task training under conditions of variable priority. *Acta Psychologica, 135*(3), 349–357. doi:10.1016/j.actpsy.2010.09.005 PMID:20920812

Borrego, C., Fernández, C., Blanes, I., & Robles, S. (2017). Room escape at class: Escape games activities to facilitate the motivation and learning in computer science. *Journal of Technology and Science Education, 7*(2), 162–171. doi:10.3926/jotse.247

Bowles, S. (2009). *Microeconomics.* Princeton University Press. doi:10.2307/j.ctvcm4gc3

Boyne, G. A. (2002). Public and private management: What's the difference? *Journal of Management Studies, 39*(1), 97–122. doi:10.1111/1467-6486.00284

Brachman, J., & Levine, A. (2010, April 13). The World of Holy Warcraft: How al Qaeda is using online game theory to recruit the masses. *Foreign Policy.*

Bragg, L. A., Walsh, C., & Heyeres, M. (2021). Successful design and delivery of online professional development for teachers: A systematic review of the literature. *Computers & Education, 166*, 104158. doi:10.1016/j.compedu.2021.104158

Brewer, R. S. (2013*). Fostering sustained energy behavior change and increasing energy literacy in a student housing energy challenge* (Doctoral dissertation). University of Hawai'i at Manoa.

Brown, J. S., Collins, A., & Duguid, P. (1989). Situated cognition and the culture of learning. *Educational Researcher, 18*(1), 32–42. doi:10.3102/0013189X018001032

Brown, T. (2008). Design thinking. *Harvard Business Review*, *86*(6), 84. PMID:18605031

Brundtland, G. H. (1987). Our common future—Call for action. *Environmental Conservation*, *14*(4), 291–294. doi:10.1017/S0376892900016805

Bubela, T., Nisbet, M. C., Borchelt, R., Brunger, F., Critchley, C., Einsiedel, E., Geller, G., Gupta, A., Hampel, J., Hyde-Lay, R., Jandciu, E. W., Jones, S. A., Kolopack, P., Lane, S., Lougheed, T., Nerlich, B., Ogbogu, U., O'Riordan, K., Ouellette, C., ... Caulfield, T. (2009). Science communication reconsidered. *Nature Biotechnology*, *27*(6), 514–518. doi:10.1038/nbt0609-514 PMID:19513051

Buheji, M. (2019). Re-inventing public services using gamification approaches. *International Journal of Economics and Financial Issues*, *9*(6), 48–59. doi:10.32479/ijefi.8803

Building Research Establishment. (2016). *CO₂ and primary energy factors for SAP 2016 Version 1.0.* https://www.bre.co.uk/filelibrary/SAP/2016/CONSP-07---CO2-and-PE-factors---V1_0.pdf

Burbidge, J. (2013). *Tips for Writing Loglines.* Retrieved 03 30, 2021, from Raindance: https://www.raindance.org/10-tips-for-writing-loglines/

Burke, B. (2014). *Gamification Trends and Strategies to Help Prepare for the Future.* Available at: https://www.gartner.com/it/content/2191900/2191918/november_28_gamification_bburke.pdf?userId=61080590

Burke, B. (2014). Gamify: How Gamification Motivates People to Do Extraordinary Things. Routledge.

Burke, B. (2012). Gamification 2020: *What is the future of gamification.* Gartner. *Inc.*, (Nov), 5.

Burke, B. (2015). *Gamificar: como a gamificação motiva as pessoas a fazerem coisas extraordinárias.* Dvs Editora.

Burke, B. (2016). *Gamify: How gamification motivates people to do extraordinary things.* Routledge. doi:10.4324/9781315230344

Burns, T. W., O'Connor, D. J., & Stocklmayer, S. M. (2003). Science communication: A contemporary definition. *Public Understanding of Science (Bristol, England)*, *12*(12), 183–202. doi:10.1177/09636625030122004

Cacioppo, J. T., Petty, R. E., & Stoltenberg, C. (1985). Processes of social influence: The elaboration likelihood model of persuasion. In P. Kendall (Ed.), *Advances in cognitive behavioral research and therapy* (Vol. 4, pp. 215–274). Academic Press. doi:10.1016/B978-0-12-010604-2.50012-4

Caillois, R. (1967). *Les jeux et les hommes Le masque et le vertige* [Games and men. The Mask and Vertigo]. Gallimard.

Cai, Z., Goertzel, B., Zhou, C., Huang, D., Ke, S., Yu, G., & Jiang, M. (2013). OpenPsi: A novel computational affective model and its application in video games. *Engineering Applications of Artificial Intelligence*, *26*(1), 1–12. doi:10.1016/j.engappai.2012.07.013

Calvo, R. A., D'Mello, S., Gratch, J. M., & Kappas, A. (Eds.). (2015). *The Oxford Handbook of affective computing.* Oxford Library of Psychology. doi:10.1093/oxfordhb/9780199942237.001.0001

Carbon Trust. (2012). *Degree days for energy management. A practical introduction.* https://www.sustainabilityexchange.ac.uk/files/degree_days_for_energy_management_carbon_trust.pdf

Carretié, L. (2011). *Anatomía de la mente: Emoción, cognición y cerebro.* Ediciones.

Carrillo, C., & Flores, M. A. (2020). COVID-19 and teacher education: A literature review of online teaching and learning practices. *European Journal of Teacher Education*, *43*(4), 466–487. doi:10.1080/02619768.2020.1821184

Carvalho, M. B. (2017). *Serious games for learning: a model and a reference architecture for efficient game development*. Technische Universiteit Eindhoven.

Casals, M., Gangolells, M., Macarulla, M., Forcada, N., Fuertes, A., Hafner, R. & Jones, R. (2020). Assessing the effectiveness of gamification in reducing domestic energy consumption: lessons learned from the EnerGAware project. *Energy and Buildings, 210,* 109753:1- 109753:12.

Casqueiro, L., Gasiba, T., Pinto-Albuquerque, M., & Lechner, U. (2021). Automated Java Challenges' Security Assessment for Training in Industry Preliminary Results. *First International Computer Programming Education Conference (ICPEC 2021)*.

Castro-Sánchez, E., Kyratsis, Y., Iwami, M., Rawson, T. M., & Holmes, A. H. (2016). Serious electronic games as behavioural change interventions in healthcare-associated infections and infection prevention and control: A scoping review of the literature and future directions. *Antimicrobial Resistance and Infection Control, 5*(1), 1–7. doi:10.118613756-016-0137-0 PMID:27777755

Cechetti, N. P., Biduki, D., & De Marchi, A. C. B. (2017, June). Gamification strategies for mobile device applications: A systematic review. In *2017 12th Iberian Conference on Information Systems and Technologies (CISTI)* (pp. 1-7). IEEE. 10.23919/CISTI.2017.7975943

Celeda, P., Cegan, J., Vykopal, J., & Tovarnak, D. (2015). *KYPO – A Platform for Cyber Defence Exercises*. M&S Support to Operetional Tasks Including War Gaming, Logistics, Cyber Defence.

Černezel, A., & Heričko, M. (2013). A user-centric approach for developing mobile applications. In *7th International Conference on Knowledge Management in Organizations: Service and Cloud Computing* (pp. 455-465). Springer. 10.1007/978-3-642-30867-3_41

Ceros. (2019, March 9). *Interactive Content Marketing: A Beginner's Guide*. Ceros. https://www.ceros.com/resources/

Chaffin, A., & Barnes, T. (2010, June). Lessons from a course on serious games research and prototyping. In *Proceedings of the Fifth International Conference on the Foundations of Digital Games* (pp. 32-39). 10.1145/1822348.1822353

Challco, G.C., Andrade, F.R., de Oliveira, T.M., Mizoguchi, R., & Isotani, S. (2015). An Ontological Model to Apply Gamification as Persuasive Technology in Collaborative Learning Scenarios. *Anais do XXVI Simpósio Brasileiro de Informática na Educação (SBIE 2015)*.

Challco, G. C., Moreira, D. A., Mizoguchi, R., & Isotani, S. (2014). An ontology engineering approach to gamify collaborative learning scenarios. In *Collaboration and Technology* (pp. 185–198). Springer International Publishing. doi:10.1007/978-3-319-10166-8_17

Chan, F. K., & Thong, J. Y. (2009). Acceptance of agile methodologies: A critical review and conceptual framework. *Decision Support Systems, 46*(4), 803–814. doi:10.1016/j.dss.2008.11.009

Chang, J. (2021). *54 Gamification Statistics You Must Know: 2020/2021 Market Share Analysis & Data*. Finances Online. https://financesonline.com/gamification-statistics/

Chapman, J. R., & Rich, P. J. (2018). Does educational gamification improve students' motivation? If so, which game elements work best? *Journal of Education for Business, 93*(7), 315–322. doi:10.1080/08832323.2018.1490687

Charette, R. N. (2020). *Inside the hidden world of legacy IT systems: How and why we spend trillions to keep old software going*. IEEE. https://spectrum.ieee.org/comp fluting/it/inside-hidden-world-legacy-it-systems

Charness, N., & Boot, W. R. (2015). Technology, Gaming, and Social Networking. In *Handbook of the Psychology of Aging* (8th ed.). Elsevier Inc. doi:10.1016/B978-0-12-411469-2.00020-0

Chatzigeorgiou, I. M., & Andreou, G. T. (2021). A systematic review on feedback research for residential energy behavior change through mobile and web interfaces. *Renewable & Sustainable Energy Reviews*, *135*, 110187. doi:10.1016/j.rser.2020.110187

Chen, H. T. (1990). *Theory-driven evaluations*. Sage Publications.

Chen, J. (2016). Understanding teacher emotions: The development of a teacher emotion inventory. *Teaching and Teacher Education*, (55), 68–77.

Chen, Y. (2019). Exploring design guidelines of using user-centered design in gamification development: A Delphi Study. *International Journal of Human-Computer Interaction*, *35*(13), 1170–1181. doi:10.1080/10447318.2018.1514823

Chesney, T. (2006). An Acceptance Model for Useful and Fun Information Systems Utilitarian Dual Useless Recreational. *October, 2*(October), 225–235.

Chou, Y. K. (2013). *User and player types in gamified systems*. Retrieved from Yu-kai Chou: Gamification & Behavioral Design: https://yukaichou.com/gamification-study/user-types-gamified-systems

Chou, Y. K. (2015). Octalysis: Complete Gamification Framework-Yu-kai Chou. Octalysis Media.

Chou, Y. K. (n.d.). *Octalysis Tool*. https://www.yukaichou.com/octalysis-tool

Chou, J. L. (2015). *An analysis of the creative process* [Master of Fine Arts]. The University of Texas at Austin.

Chou, T. J., & Ting, C. C. (2003). The role of flow experience in cyber-game addiction. *Cyberpsychology & Behavior*, *6*(6), 663–675. doi:10.1089/109493103322725469 PMID:14756934

Chou, Y. (2015). *Actionable Gamification – Beyond Points, Batches and Leaderboards*. Octalysis Media.

Chou, Y. K. (2016). *Actionable gamification*. Beyond Points, Badges, and Leaderboards.

Chou, Y. K. (2019). *Actionable gamification: Beyond points, badges, and leaderboards*. Packt Publishing Ltd.

Christians, G. (2018). The Origins and Future of Gamification. *Senior Theses*. https://scholarcommons.sc.edu/senior_theses

Christopoulos, A., Mystakidis, S., Cachafeiro, E., & Laakso, M.-J. (2022). Escaping the cell: Virtual reality escape rooms in biology education. *Behaviour & Information Technology*, 1–18. doi:10.1080/0144929X.2022.2079560

Christopoulos, A., & Sprangers, P. (2021). Integration of educational technology during the Covid-19 pandemic: An analysis of teacher and student receptions. *Cogent Education*, *8*(1), 1964690. Advance online publication. doi:10.1080/2331186X.2021.1964690

CIRCADANCE. (n.d.). *Cyber ranges and how they improve security training*. Retrieved from CIRCADANCE: https://www.circadence.com/blog/cyber-ranges-101-and-how-they-improve-security-training

Circadance. (n.d.). *Project Ares*. Retrieved from D5-IQ: https://d5-iq.com/ai-powered-cyber-learning-platform

Clark, D., Tanner-Smith, E., & Killingsworth, S. (2016). Digital games, design, and learning: A systematic review and meta-analysis. *Review of Educational Research*, *86*(1), 79–122. doi:10.3102/0034654315582065 PMID:26937054

Clarke, S., Peel, D. J., Arnab, S., Morini, L., Keegan, H., & Wood, O. (2017). escapED: A framework for creating educational escape rooms and Interactive Games For Higher/Further Education. *International Journal of Serious Games*, *4*(3), 73–86. doi:10.17083/ijsg.v4i3.180

Clementi, M. (2019). *Progettare l'autosostenibilità locale, strumenti e metodi di supporto alla progettazione ambientale integrata* [Designing Local Self-Sustainability, tools and Methods to Support integrated Environmental Design]. Edizioni Ambiente.

Cobaleda, A., & Aguayo, F. (2011). *Mobiliario de recepción para un hotel boutique bajo diseño. experiencial* [Reception Furniture for a boutique hotel under Design Experiential]. Universidad de Sevilla. Escuela Politécnica Superior. https://fama.us.es/permalink/34CBUA_US/3enc2g/alma991009358809704987

Collins, L. M., Murphy, S. A., & Strecher, V. (2007). The multiphase optimization strategy (MOST) and the sequential multiple assignment randomized trial (SMART): New methods for more potent eHealth interventions. *American Journal of Preventive Medicine*, *32*(5), S112–S118. doi:10.1016/j.amepre.2007.01.022 PMID:17466815

Commons, C. (2017). *Atribuição-NãoComercial-CompartilhaIgual* [Attribution-Noncommercial-Share Alike]. 3.0 Brasil (CC BY-NC-SA 3.0 BR).

Conill, R. F. (2016). Feeding the RedCritter: the gamification of project management software. In *The Business of Gamification* (pp. 43–61). Routledge.

Connolly, T. M., Boyle, E. A., MacArthur, E., Hainey, T., & Boyle, J. M. (2012). A systematic literature review of empirical evidence on computer games and serious games. *Computers & Education*, *59*(2), 661–686. doi:10.1016/j.compedu.2012.03.004

Cook, T. D., Campbell, D. T., & Shadish, W. (2002). *Experimental and quasi-experimental designs for generalized causal inference*. Houghton Mifflin Boston.

Cool Choices. (2019). *Employee Engagement Sustainability Game*. Retrieved February 14, 2019, from https://coolchoices.com/

Corkill, E. (2009). *Real escape game brings its creator's wonderment to life*. https://www.japantimes.co.jp/life/2009/12/20/general/real-escape-game-brings-its-creators-wonderment-to-life/#.Xocyd0pCQ2x

Corporation, O. (n.d.). *Java*. Retrieved November 23, 2020, from https://www.java.com/en/

Costa, A. C. S. & Marchiori, P. Z. (2015). Gamificação, elementos de jogos e estratégia: uma matriz de referência. *InCID: Revista De Ciência Da Informação E Documentação*, *6*(2), 44-65. doi:10.11606/issn.2178-2075.v6i2p44-65

Covenant of Mayors for Climate and Energy. (2016). *The Covenant of Mayors for Climate and Energy Reporting Guidelines*. https://www.covenantofmayors.eu/IMG/pdf/Reporting_Guidelines_Final_EN.pdf

COVID. (2020). Dashboard by the center for systems science and engineering (CSSE) at Johns Hopkins University (JHU). John Hopkins University Coronvirus Resource Centre.

Crane, E., & Gross, M. (2007, September). Motion capture and emotion: Affect detection in whole body movement. In *International Conference on Affective Computing and Intelligent Interaction* (pp. 95-101). Springer. 10.1007/978-3-540-74889-2_9

Crockford, D. (n.d.). *JSON - JavaScript Object Notation*. Retrieved January 7, 2021, from https://www.json.org/json-en.html

Csikszentmihalyi, M. (1997). Finding flow: the psychology of engagement with everyday life. *Choice Reviews Online*, *35*(3). doi:10.5860/CHOICE.35-1828

Csikszentmihalyi, M. (1991). Flow: The Psychology of Optimal Experience. *Academy of Management Review*, *16*(3), 636–640. doi:10.2307/258925

Csikszentmihalyi, M. (2009). *Flow - The Psychology of Optimal Experience*. Harper Col. doi:10.5465/amr.1991.4279513

Csikzentmihaly, M. (1990). *Flow: The psychology of optimal experience*. Harper & Row.

Csoknyai, T., Legardeur, J., Akle, A. A., & Horváth, M. (2019). Analysis of energy consumption profiles in residential buildings and impact assessment of a serious game on occupants' behavior. *Energy and Building*, *196*, 1–20. doi:10.1016/j.enbuild.2019.05.009

CYBERBIT. (2021). *CYBERBIT Train for Real*. Retrieved from https://www.cyberbit.com/

D'Oca, S., Ferrante, A., Ferrer, C., Pernetti, R., Gralka, A., Sebastian, R., & Op 't Veld, P. (2018). Technical, Financial, and Social Barriers and Challenges in Deep Building Renovation: Integration of Lessons Learned from the H2020 Cluster Projects. *Buildings*, *8*(12), 174. doi:10.3390/buildings8120174

Dagnino, F. M., Ott, M., Pozzi, F., Yilmaz, E., Tsalakanidou, F., Dimitropoulos, K., & Grammalidis, N. (2015). Serious games to support learning of rare 'intangible'cultural expressions. In *9th International technology, education and development conference (INTED 2015)* (pp. 7184-7194). Academic Press.

Dahlstrom, M. F. (2014). Using narratives and storytelling to communicate science with nonexpert audiences. *Proceedings of the National Academy of Sciences of the United States of America*, *111*(Suppl 4), 13614–13620. doi:10.1073/pnas.1320645111 PMID:25225368

Dall'ò, G., Silvestrini, G., & Gamberale, M. (2010). *Manuale della certificazione energetica degli edifici* [Building Energy Certifiation Manual]. Edizioni Ambiente.

Dalpiaz, F., Snijders, R., Brinkkemper, S., Hosseini, M., Shahri, A., & Ali, R. (2017). Engaging the Crowd of Stakeholders in Requirements Engineering via Gamification. In Gamification: Using Game Elements in Serious Contexts (pp. 123–135). Springer International Publishing. doi:10.1007/978-3-319-45557-0_9

Damasio, A. R., Everitt, B. J., & Bishop, D. (1996). *The somatic marker hypothesis and the possible functions of the*. Academic Press.

Dargan, T., & Evequoz, F. (2015). Designing engaging e-Government services by combining user-centered design and gamification: A use-case. In *Proceedings of the 15th European Conference on eGovernment ECEG 2015 University of Portsmouth* (p. 70). Academic Press.

David Dixon-Peugh, D. C. (n.d.). *PMD Source Code Analyzer*. Retrieved February 13, 2021, from https://pmd.github.io/

David, L. (2013). *Game reward systems*. Retrieved from Learning Theories: https://www.learning-theories.com/game-reward-systems.html

De Byl, P. (2015). A conceptual affective design framework for the use of emotions in computer game design. *Cyberpsychology (Brno)*, *9*(3). Advance online publication. doi:10.5817/CP2015-3-4

de Freitas, S., & Liarokapis, F. (2011). Serious games: A new paradigm for education? In Serious Games and Edutainment Applications (pp. 9–23). doi:10.1007/978-1-4471-2161-9_2

De Gloria, A., Bellotti, F., Berta, R., & Lavagnino, E. (2014). Serious Games for education and training. *International Journal of Serious Games*, *1*(1), 2384–8766. doi:10.17083/ijsg.v1i1.11

De Haan, G. (2010). The development of ESD-related competencies in supportive institutional frameworks. *International Review of Education*, *56*(2), 315–328. doi:10.100711159-010-9157-9

de Paula Porto, D., de Jesus, G. M., Ferrari, F. C., & Fabbri, S. C. P. F. (2021). Initiatives and challenges of using gamification in software engineering: A Systematic Mapping. *Journal of Systems and Software*, *173*, 110870. doi:10.1016/j.jss.2020.110870

De Salas, K., Ashbarry, L., Seabourne, M., Lewis, I., Wells, L., Dermoudy, J., Roehrer, E., Springer, M., Sauer, J. D., & Scott, J. (2022). Improving Environmental Outcomes with Games: An Exploration of Behavioural and Technological Design and Evaluation Approaches. *Simulation & Gaming*, (July), 1–43. doi:10.1177/10468781221114160

Deci, E. L., Connell, J. P., & Ryan, R. M. (1989). Self- determination in a work organization. *The Journal of Applied Psychology*, *74*(4), 580–590. doi:10.1037/0021-9010.74.4.580

Deci, E. L., Koestner, R., & Ryan, R. M. (2001). Extrinsic rewards and intrinsic motivation in education: Reconsidered once again. *Review of Educational Research*, *71*(1), 1–27. doi:10.3102/00346543071001001

Deleris, L., & Mac Aonghusa, P. (2020). Behaviour Change for the Sharing Economy. In *Analytics for the Sharing Economy: Mathematics, Engineering and Business Perspectives* (pp. 173–187). Springer. doi:10.1007/978-3-030-35032-1_11

Delmas, M. A., Fischlein, M., & Asensio, O. I. (2013). Information strategies and energy conservation behavior: A meta-analysis of experimental studies from 1975 to 2012. *Energy Policy*, *61*, 729–739. doi:10.1016/j.enpol.2013.05.109

Deming, W. E. (2018). The New Economics for Industry, Government, Education (3rd ed.). MIT Press Ltd.

DePorres, D., & Livingston, R. E. (2016). Launching new doctoral students: Embracing the Hero's journey. *Developments in Business Simulation and Experiential Learning, 43.*

Dergousoff, K. K., & Mandryk, R. L. (2015). Mobile Gamification for Crowdsourcing Data Collection: Leveraging the Freemium Model. In *Proceedings of 33rd Annual ACM Conference on Human Factors in Computing Systems* (pp. 1065-1074). Academic Press.

Derksen, M. E., van Strijp, S., Kunst, A. E., Daams, J. G., Jaspers, M. W. M., & Fransen, M. P. (2020). Serious games for smoking prevention and cessation: A systematic review of game elements and game effects. *Journal of the American Medical Informatics Association: JAMIA*, *27*(5), 818–833. doi:10.1093/jamia/ocaa013 PMID:32330255

Derrida, J. (2017). The deconstruction of actuality: an interview with Jacques Derrida. In M. McQuillan (Ed.), *Deconstruction* (pp. 527–553). Routledge.

Deterding, S. (2011). Situated motivational affordances of game elements: a conceptual model. *Workshop on Gamification: Using Game Design Elements in Nongaming Contexts, CHI 2011, Vancouver, BC, Canada. Proceedings*, 1-4. https://www.researchgate.net/publication/303084050_Situated_motivational_affordances_of_game_elements_A_conceptual_model

Deterding, S. (2011). Situated motivational affordances of game elements: A conceptual model. *Conference on Human Factors in Computing Systems (CHI 2011).*

Deterding, S., Dixon, D., Khaled, R., & Nacke, L. (2011, September). From game design elements to gamefulness: defining" gamification". In *Proceedings of the 15th international academic MindTrek conference: Envisioning future media environments* (pp. 9-15). 10.1145/2181037.2181040

Deterding, S., Sicart, M., Nacke, L., O'Hara, K., & Dixon, D. (2011). Gamification. using game-design elements in non-gaming contexts. *Proceedings of the 2011 Annual Conference Extended Abstracts on Human Factors in Computing Systems*, 2425–2428. 10.1145/1979742.1979575

Devine, T. C., Presnell, W. A., & Miller, S. (2014). Games as Art and Kant's Moral Dilemma: What Can Ethical Theory Reveal About the Role of the Game Designer as Artist? *Games and Culture*, *9*(4), 277–310. doi:10.1177/1555412014538812

Diamond, L., Tondello, G., Marczewski, A., Nacke, L., & Tscheligi, M. (2015). The HEXAD Gamification User Types Questionnaire : Background and Development Process. *Workshop on Personalization in Serious and Persuasive Games and Gamified Interactions.*

Dicheva, D., Dichev, C., Agre, G., & Angelova, G. (2015). Gamification in education: A systematic mapping study. *Journal of Educational Technology & Society*, *18*(3), 75–88.

Didukh, E. (2018). Conceptual foundations of morality in videogames. *Philosophy and Humanism*, *1*(7), 41–50.

Dietz, T., Gardner, G. T., Gilligan, J., Stern, P. C., & Vandenbergh, M. P. (2009). Household actions can provide a behavioral wedge to rapidly reduce US carbon emissions. *Proceedings of the National Academy of Sciences of the United States of America*, *106*(44), 18452–18456. doi:10.1073/pnas.0908738106 PMID:19858494

Djaouti, D., Alvarez, J., & Jessel, J. P. (2011). Classifying serious games: the G/P/S model. In P. Felicia (Ed.), *Handbook of research on improving learning and motivation through educational games: Multidisciplinary approaches* (pp. 118–136). IGI Global. doi:10.4018/978-1-60960-495-0.ch006

Djaouti, D., Alvarez, J., Jessel, J. P., Methel, G., & Molinier, P. (2008). A gameplay definition through videogame classification. *International Journal of Computer Games Technology*, *2008*, 1–6. doi:10.1155/2008/470350

Djaouti, D., Alvarez, J., Jessel, J. P., & Rampnoux, O. (2011). Origins of serious games. In *Serious games and edutainment applications* (pp. 25–43). Springer. doi:10.1007/978-1-4471-2161-9_3

Do, C. T., Tran, N. H., Hong, C., Kamhoua, C. A., Kwiat, K. A., Blasch, E., Ren, S., Pissinou, N., & Iyengar, S. S. (2017). Game theory for cyber security and privacy. *ACM Computing Surveys*, *50*(2), 1–37. doi:10.1145/3057268

Dolatabadi, S. H., & Budinskai, I. (2020). A New Method Based on Gamification Algorithm to Engage Stakeholders in Competitive Markets. *INES 2020 - IEEE 24th International Conference on Intelligent Engineering Systems, Proceedings*, 11–17. 10.1109/INES49302.2020.9147196

Dombrowski, C., Kim, J. Y., Desouza, K. C., Braganza, A., Papagari, S., Baloh, P., & Jha, S. (2007). Elements of innovative cultures. *Knowledge and Process Management*, *14*(3), 190–202. doi:10.1002/kpm.279

Domicílios, T. I. C. (2019). *Domicílios com acesso à internet Cetic. br* [Households with Cetic internet access]. Author.

Dominguez, A., Saenz-de-Navarrete, J., De-Marcos, L., Fernández-Sanz, L., Pagés, C., & Martinez-Herráiz, J.-J. (2013). Gamifying learning experiences: Practical implications and outcomes. *Computer Education*, *63*, 380–392. doi:10.1016/j.compedu.2012.12.020

Dong, B., Li, Z., Rahman, S. M., & Vega, R. (2016). A Hybrid Model Approach for Forecasting Future Residential Electricity Consumption. *Energy and Building*, *117*(1), 341–351. doi:10.1016/j.enbuild.2015.09.033

Döring, N., & Bortz, J. (2016). *Forschungsmethoden und Evaluation in den Sozial- und Humanwissenschaften* (5th ed.). Springer. doi:10.1007/978-3-642-41089-5

Dörner, R., Göbel, S., Effelsberg, W., & Wiemeyer, J. (2016). *Serious Games: Foundations, Concepts and Practice*. Springer International Publishing. doi:10.1007/978-3-319-40612-1

Douglas, B. D., & Brauer, M. (2021). Gamification to prevent climate change: A review of games and apps for sustainability. *Current Opinion in Psychology*, *42*, 89–94. doi:10.1016/j.copsyc.2021.04.008 PMID:34052619

Dovis, S., Maric, M., Prins, P. J., & Van der Oord, S. (2019). Does executive function capacity moderate the outcome of executive function training in children with ADHD? *Attention Deficit and Hyperactivity Disorders*, *11*(4), 445–460. doi:10.100712402-019-00308-5 PMID:31123915

Dovis, S., Van der Oord, S., Wiers, R. W., & Prins, P. J. (2015). Improving executive functioning in children with ADHD: Training multiple executive functions within the context of a computer game. A randomized double-blind placebo controlled trial. *PLoS One*, *10*(4), e0121651. doi:10.1371/journal.pone.0121651 PMID:25844638

Downes-Le Guin, T., Baker, R., Mechling, J., & Ruyle, E. (2012). Myths and realities of respondent engagement in online surveys. *International Journal of Market Research*, *54*(5), 1–21.

DreadLocked. (2018). *CVE-2018-7600*. Retrieved July 28, 2021, from https://github.com/dreadlocked/Drupalgeddon2

Drummond, D., Hadchouel, A., & Tesnière, A. (2017). Serious games for health: Three steps forwards. *Advances in Simulation (London, England)*, *2*(1), 1–8. doi:10.118641077-017-0036-3 PMID:29450004

Dubois, D. J. (2012). Toward adopting self-organizing models for the gamification of context-aware user applications. In *Proceedings of the Second International Workshop on Games and Software Engineering: Realizing User Engagement with Game Engineering Techniques (GAS)* (pp. 9-15). IEEE. 10.1109/GAS.2012.6225928

Dubois, D. J., & Tamburrelli, G. (2013). Understanding gamification mechanisms for software development. In *ESEC/FSE 2013 Proceedings of the 2013 9th Joint Meeting on Foundations of Software Engineering*. ACM. 10.1145/2491411.2494589

Du, G., Zhou, W., Li, C., Li, D., & Liu, P. X. (2020). An Emotion Recognition Method for Game Evaluation Based on Electroencephalogram. *IEEE Transactions on Affective Computing*, 1. doi:10.1109/TAFFC.2020.3023966

Duggan, S., & Thrope, C. (2017). An analysis of how information security e-learning can be improved through gamification of real software issues. 16th Eur. COnf. Cyber Warfare and Security, 666-66.

Duke, R. D., & Geurts, J. (2004). *Policy games for strategic management*. Rozenberg Publishers.

Ďuriník, M. (2015). Gamification in knowledge management systems. *Central European Journal of Management*, *1*(2). Advance online publication. doi:10.5817/CEJM2014-2-3

Dzedzickis, A., Kaklauskas, A., & Bucinskas, V. (2020). Human emotion recognition: Review of sensors and methods. *Sensors (Basel)*, *20*(3), 592. doi:10.339020030592 PMID:31973140

EASME. (2017). *Guidelines for the calculation of project performance indicators*. https://ec.europa.eu/easme/sites/easme-site/files/guidelines-for-the-calculation-of-performance-indicators.pdf

ECSO. (2020). *Understanding cyber ranges: From hype to reality*. WG5 Paper.

Edoh-Alove, E., Hubert, F., & Badard, T. (2013). A web service for managing spatial context dedicated to serious games on and for smartphones. *Journal of Geographic Information System*, *5*(2), 148–160. doi:10.4236/jgis.2013.52015

Edwards, E. A., Lumsden, J., Rivas, C., Steed, L., Edwards, L. A., Thiyagarajan, A., Sohanpal, R., Caton, H., Griffiths, C. J., Munafò, M. R., Taylor, S., & Walton, R. T. (2016). Gamification for health promotion: Systematic review of behaviour change techniques in smartphone apps. *BMJ Open*, *6*(10), e012447. doi:10.1136/bmjopen-2016-012447 PMID:27707829

Efficiency Valuation Organization. (2012). *International Performance Measurement and Verification Protocol. Concepts and options for determining energy and water savings, vol. 1, Technical Report*. http://www.eeperformance.org/uploads/8/6/5/0/8650231/ipmvp_volume_i__2012.pdf

Ehrlich, I., Filipenko, M., Kranawetleitner, T., Krebs, H., Löw, R., Pistoll, D., & Thurner-Irmler, J. (2020). Escaping the Everyday Chaos: Assessing the Needs for Internal Knowledge. Transfer in SMEs via an Escape Room. In *CERC proceedings 2020* (pp. 1–19). Collaborative European Research Conference.

Einstein, G. O., McDaniel, M. A., Williford, C. L., Pagan, J. L., & Dismukes, R. (2003). Forgetting of intentions in demanding situations is rapid. *Journal of Experimental Psychology. Applied*, *9*(3), 147–162. doi:10.1037/1076-898X.9.3.147 PMID:14570509

Ekman, P. (1999). Basic emotions. Handbook of Cognition and Emotion, 98(45-60), 16.

Eliëns, A., & Ruttkay, Z. (2008). Record, Replay & Reflect–a framework for understanding (serious) game play. *Proc Euromedia*, 9.

Ellenberger, T., Harder, D., & Brechbühler Pešková, M. (2020). Gamification in Unternehmen. In Digitale Transformation und Unternehmensführung: Trends und Perspektiven für die Praxis (pp. 55–81). Wiesbaden: Springer Fachmedien Wiesbaden. doi:10.1007/978-3-658-26960-9_4

Elliott, J. (2012). *Development of an Energy-Information Feedback System for a Smartphone Application*. Academic Press.

Ellis, H., & Ashbrook, P. (1988). Resource allocation model of the effects of depressed mood states on memory. *Affect, Cognition and Social Behavior*, 25- 43.

Elm, D., Kappen, D. L., Tondello, G. F., & Nacke, L. E. (2016). CLEVER: Gamification and enterprise knowledge learning. In *Proceedings of the 2016 Annual Symposium on Computer-Human Interaction in Play Companion Extended Abstracts* (pp. 141-148). Academic Press.

Elsharkawy, H., & Rutherford, P. (2018). Energy-efficient retrofit of social housing in the UK: Lessons learned from a Community Energy Saving Programme (CESP) in Nottingham. *Energy and Building*, *172*, 295–306. doi:10.1016/j. enbuild.2018.04.067

Endicott-Popovsky, B., Hinrichs, R. J., & Frincke, D. (2013). Leveraging 2nd life as a communications media: An effective tool for security awareness training. *IEEE International Professional Communication 2013 Conference*, 1–7. 10.1109/IPCC.2013.6623945

Endrejat, P. C., & Kauffeld, S. (2018). Can't get no satisfaction? Motivating organisational energy efficiency efforts in Germany. *Energy Research & Social Science*, *44*(May), 146–151. doi:10.1016/j.erss.2018.05.005

EnerGAware project. (2015). *Energy game for awareness of energy efficiency in social housing communities*. EU funded project, contract number: 649673. http://energaware.eu

EnerGAware project. (2017). *Deliverable 4.3. Pilot implementation evaluation (Preliminary)*. https://energaware.eu/downloads/EnerGAware_D4.3_Pilot%20implementation%20evaluation%20preliminary_r1.pdf

Energic. (2019). *Energic - Smart Energy Challenge*. Retrieved April 16, 2019, from https://www.energic.io/

Energy Cat. (2018). *Energy Cat: the house of tomorrow*. http://www.energycatgame.com/

Engeström, Y. (1999). Innovative learning in work teams: Analyzing cycles of knowledge creation. *Perspectives on Activity Theory*, 377.

Engeström, Y. (2015). *Learning by expanding*. Cambridge University Press.

Engineering Ingegneria Informatica, S. P. A. (2017). *100% Open Source Business Intelligence*. https://www.spagobi.org

Entertainment Software Association. (2017). *Comments on the Global Digital Trade Study. Report #1*. Entertainment Software Association.

Entertainment Software Association. (2020). *2020 Essential Facts About the Video Game Industry*. Entertainment Software Association (ESA). https://www.prnewswire.com/news-releases/new-survey-2020-essential-facts-about-the-video-game-industry-301093972.html

ENTROPY. (2019). *ENTROPY - Design of an Innovative Energy-Aware IT Eco-System for Motivating Behavioural Changes towards the adoption of Energy Efficient Lifestyles*. Retrieved July 10, 2019, from https://entropy-project.eu/

Erenli, K. (2013). The impact of gamification: Recommending education scenarios. *International Journal of Emerging Technologies in Learning, 8*, 15–21. doi:10.3991/ijet.v8iS1.2320

European Commission. (2016). *Proposal for a Directive of the European Parliament and of the Council amending Directive 2012/27/EU on energy efficiency* https://eur-lex.europa.eu/legal-content/EN/TXT/HTML/?uri=CELEX:52016PC0761&from=EN

European Commission. (2020a). *Communication from the Commission to the European Parliament, the Council, the European Economic and Social Committee and the Committee of the Regions. A Renovation Wave for Europe - Greening our buildings, creating jobs, improving lives.* https://eur-lex.europa.eu/legal-content/EN/TXT/?qid=1603122220757&uri=CELEX:52020DC0662

European Commission. (2020b). *Communication from the Commission to the European Parliament, the Council, the European Economic and Social Committee and the Committee of the Regions. Stepping up Europe's 2030 climate ambition. Investing in a climate-neutral future for the benefit of our people.* https://eur-lex.europa.eu/legal-content/EN/TXT/?uri=CELEX:52020DC0562

Eurostat. (2018a). *Electricity prices for household consumers.* http://ec.europa.eu/eurostat/statistics-explained/index.php/Electricity_price_statistics#Electricity_prices_for_household_consumers

Eurostat. (2018b). *Natural gas prices for household consumers.* http://ec.europa.eu/eurostat/statistics-explained/index.php/Natural_gas_price_statistics#Natural_gas_prices_for_household_consumers

Eurostat. (2018c). *Simplified energy balances - annual data.* https://ec.europa.eu/eurostat/en/web/products-datasets/-/NRG_100A

Exame. (2017, July 22). *Harter, do Gallup: emprego x felicidade.* https://exame.com/mundo/harter-do-gallup-emprego-x-felicidade

Eyal, N. (2014). *Hooked: How to build habit-forming products.* Penguin.

Fabricatore, C., Gyaurov, D., & Lopez, X. (2020, November). Rethinking serious games design in the age of COVID-19: Setting the focus on wicked problems. In *Joint International Conference on Serious Games* (pp. 243-259). Springer. 10.1007/978-3-030-61814-8_19

Facebook. (n.d.). *FB-Infer.* Retrieved February 17, 2021, from https://fbinfer.com/

Fager, K., Tuomi, P., & Multisilta, J. (2018). Gamifying facility service jobs – using personnel attitudes and perceptions for designing gamification. *GamiFIN 2018 - Proceedings of the 2nd International GamiFIN Conference Pori, Finland, May 22-23, 2018. WS-CEUR*, 55–64.

Fähnrich, B. (2017). Wissenschaftsevents zwischen Popularisierung, Engagement und Partizipation. In H. Bonfadelli, B. Fähnrich, C. Lüthje, J. Milde, M. Rhomberg, & M. S. Schäfer (Eds.), *Forschungsfeld Wissenschaftskommunikation* (pp. 165–182). Springer. doi:10.1007/978-3-658-12898-2_9

Federal, G. (2018). *Lei Geral de Proteção de Dados* [General Data Protection Law].

Feidakis, M., & Daradoumis, A. (2011). A reference framework for the design of Educational Technologies with "emotion". *2nd Panhellenic Conference "Integration and use of ICT in the Educational Process".*

Fenton, N., & Neil, M. (2018). *Risk assessment and decision analysis with Bayesian networks.* Crc Press. doi:10.1201/b21982

Ferguson, C., van den Broek, E. L., & van Oostendorp, H. (2019). On the role of interaction mode and story structure in virtual reality serious games. *Computers & Education*. Advance online publication. doi:10.1016/j.compedu.2019.103671

Fernandes, J., Duarte, D., Ribeiro, C., Farinha, C., Pereira, J. M., & Silva, M. M. (2012). iThink: A game-based approach towards improving collaboration and participation in requirement elicitation. *Procedia Computer Science*, *15*, 66–77. doi:10.1016/j.procs.2012.10.059

Ferreira-Brito, F., Fialho, M., Virgolino, A., Neves, I., Miranda, A. C., Sousa-Santos, N., Caneiras, C., Carriço, L., Verdelho, A., & Santos, O. (2019). Game-based interventions for neuropsychological assessment, training and rehabilitation: Which game-elements to use? A systematic review. *Journal of Biomedical Informatics*, *98*, 103287. doi:10.1016/j.jbi.2019.103287 PMID:31518700

Fielding, K. S., Thompson, A., Louis, W. R., & Warren, C. (2010). *Environmental sustainability: understanding the attitudes and behaviour of Australian households*. Academic Press.

Fijnheer, J. D., & Van Oostendorp, H. (2016). Steps to Design a Household Energy Game. *International Journal of Serious Games*, *3*(3), 12–22. doi:10.17083/ijsg.v3i3.131

Filipczuk, D., Mason, C., & Snow, S. (2019). Using a Game to Explore Notions of Responsibility for Cyber Security in Organisations. *CHI EA '19: Extended Abstracts of the 2019 CHI Conference on Human Factors in Computing Systems*, 1-6. 10.1145/3290607.3312846

FIOCRUZ. (2020). *ONU e OMS pedem medidas firmes contra fake news* [ONU and WHO call for firm measures against fake news]. Author.

Fireeye. (2014). *Shellshock in the Wild*. Retrieved July 20, 2021, from https://www.fireeye.com/blog/threat-research/2014/09/shellshock-in-the-wild.html

Fischer, H., Heinz, M., & Bretenstein, M. (2018). Gamification of learning management systems and user types in higher education. *Proc. 12th Eur. Conf. Games Based Learn*, 91-98.

Flay, B. R., Biglan, A., Boruch, R. F., Castro, F. G., Gottfredson, D., Kellam, S., Mościcki, E. K., Schinke, S., Valentine, J. C., & Ji, P. (2005). Standards of evidence: Criteria for efficacy, effectiveness and dissemination. *Prevention Science*, *6*(3), 151–175. doi:10.100711121-005-5553-y PMID:16365954

Fleisch, H., Mecking, C., & Steinsdörfer, E. (2018). *Gamification4Good: Gemeinwohl spielerisch stärken*. Edition Stiftung & Sponsoring: Erich Schmidt Verlag. https://ebookcent-ral.proquest.com/lib/gbv/detail.action?docID=5427441

Fogg, B. J. (2009, April). A behavior model for persuasive design. In *Proceedings of the 4th international Conference on Persuasive Technology* (pp. 1-7). Academic Press.

Foni, A. E., Papagiannakis, G., & Magnenat-Thalmann, N. (2010). A taxonomy of visualization strategies for cultural heritage applications. *Journal on Computing and Cultural Heritage*, *3*(1), 1–21. doi:10.1145/1805961.1805962

FORESIGHT. (2020). *FORESIGHT D4.2 - Report for Learning/Training Objectives*. Methodology and Evaluation.

FORESIGHT. (2020). *FORESIGHT*. Retrieved from FORESIGHT Project: https://foresight-h2020.eu/

Forstner, L., & Dümmler, M. (2014). Integrated value chains—Opportunities and potentials through Industry 4.0. *Elektrotechnik Und Informationstechnik*, *131*(7), 199–201. doi:10.100700502-014-0224-y

Foucault, M., Blanc, X., Falleri, J. R., & Storey, M. A. (2019). Fostering good coding practices through individual feedback and gamification: An industrial case study. *Empirical Software Engineering*, *24*(6), 3731–3754. doi:10.100710664-019-09719-4

France, C. R., & Thomas, J. S. (2018). Virtual immersive gaming to optimize recovery (VIGOR) in low back pain: A phase II randomized controlled trial. *Contemporary Clinical Trials*, *69*, 83–91. doi:10.1016/j.cct.2018.05.001 PMID:29730393

Frankl, V. E. (2014). *The will to meaning: Foundations and applications of logotherapy*. Penguin.

Frankl, V. E. (2017). *Man's search for meaning*. Beacon Press.

Fraternali, P., Cellina, F., Herrera, S., Krinidis, S., Pasini, C., Rizzoli, A. E., ... Tzovaras, D. (2018). A Socio-Technical System Based on Gamification Towards Energy Savings. In *2018 IEEE International Conference on Pervasive Computing and Communications Workshops, PerCom Workshops 2018* (pp. 59–64). 10.1109/PERCOMW.2018.8480405

Freeman, R. E. E., & McVea, J. (2005). A Stakeholder Approach to Strategic Management. SSRN *Electronic Journal*. doi:10.2139/ssrn.263511

Freire, M., del Blanco, A., & Fernandez-Manjon, B. (2014). Serious games as edX MOOC activities. *2014 IEEE Global Engineering Education Conference (EDUCON)*, 867–871. 10.1109/EDUCON.2014.6826198

Frey, S., Rashid, A., Anthonysamy, P., Pinto-Albuquerque, M., & Naqvi, S. (2019). The Good, the Bad and the Ugly: A Study of Security Decisions in a Cyber-Physical Systems Game. *IEEE Transactions on Software Engineering*, *45*(5), 521–536. doi:10.1109/TSE.2017.2782813

Friedman, B., Kahn, P., & Borning, A. (2002). Value sensitive design: Theory and methods. *University of Washington Technical Report, 2–12.*

Frolova, N. D., Chub, A. A., & Rastopchina, N. V. (2009). Scripting technology. *KiberLeninka. Physical culture, sports - science and practice,* (4), 70-72.

Fünfschilling, L. (2014). *A dynamic model of socio-technical change: Institutions, actors and technologies in interaction*. University_of_Basel.

Gagné, R. M. (1984). Learning outcomes and their effects: Useful categories of human performance. *The American Psychologist*, *39*(4), 377–385. doi:10.1037/0003-066X.39.4.377

Galaitsi, S., Keisler, J. M., Trump, B. D., & Linkov, I. (2021). The need to reconcile concepts that characterize systems facing threats. *Risk Analysis*, *41*(1), 3–15. doi:10.1111/risa.13577 PMID:32818299

Galetta, G. (2013). The gamification: Applications and developments for creativity and education. Paper presented at conference on Creativity and Innovation in Education. 10.13140/RG.2.2.24817.68965

Gallegos, B., Kepple, M. T., & Bukaty, C. A. (2016). Using video gameplay to measure achievement for students with disabilities: A new perspective to grading and achievement reporting. In *Handbook of research on gaming trends in P-12 education* (pp. 326–352). IGI Global. doi:10.4018/978-1-4666-9629-7.ch016

Gamberini, L., Spagnolli, A., Corradi, N., Jacucci, G., Tusa, G., Mikkola, T., . . . Hoggan, E. (2012). Tailoring feedback to users' actions in a persuasive game for household electricity conservation. Lecture Notes in Computer Science, 7284, 100–111. doi:10.1007/978-3-642-31037-9_9

GameHub-seminar in the children's camp "Victoria". (2017). Retrieved 03 30, 2021, from https://www.facebook.com/groups/477292889122044/permalink/728158117368852/

Gangolells, M., Casals, M., Forcada, N. & Macarulla M. (2020). Life cycle analysis of a game-based solution for domestic energy saving. *Sustainability, 12*, 66:1 – 66:18.

Gangolells, M., Casals, M., Forcada, N., & Macarulla, M. (2021). Exploring the Potential of a Gamified Approach to Reduce Energy Use and Carbon Emissions in the Household Sector. *Sustainability*, *13*(6), 3380. doi:10.3390u13063380

Gannod, G. C., Troy, D. A., Luczaj, J. E., & Rover, D. T. (2015). *Agile way of educating. In Proceedings of IEEE Frontiers in Education Conference (FIE)*. IEEE.

Garcia de Soto, B., Georgescu, A., Mantha, B., Turk, Z., & Maciel, A. (2020). *Construction cybersecurity and critical infrastructure protection: Significance, overlaps, and proposed action plan*. Preprints.

Gardner, G. T., & Stern, P. C. (2008). The short list: The most effective actions US households can take to curb climate change. *Environment*, *50*(5), 12–25. doi:10.3200/ENVT.50.5.12-25

Gardner, J. (1976). Moral fiction. *The Hudson Review*, *29*(4), 497–512. doi:10.2307/3850454

Gardner, J. (2010). *The art of fiction: Notes on craft for young writers*. Vintage.

Garett, R., & Young, S. D. (2019). Health care gamification: A study of game mechanics and elements. *Technology. Knowledge and Learning*, *24*(3), 341–353. doi:10.100710758-018-9353-4

Garneli, V., Giannakos, M., & Chorianopoulos, K. (2017). Serious games as a malleable learning medium: The effects of narrative, gameplay, and making on students' performance and attitudes. *British Journal of Educational Technology*, *48*(3), 842–859. doi:10.1111/bjet.12455

Garris, R., Ahlers, R., & Driskell, J. E. (2002). Games, motivation, and learning: A research and pratice model. *Simulation & Gaming*, *33*(4), 441–467. doi:10.1177/1046878102238607

Gasiba, T., Lechner, U., & Pinto-Albuquerque, M. (2020). Sifu - A CyberSecurity Awareness Platform with Challenge Assessment and Intelligent Coach. *Cyber-Physical System Security of the Cybersecurity Journal*, 1-23.

Gasiba, T., Lechner, U., & Pinto-Albuquerque, M. (2021). CyberSecurity Challenges: Serious Games for Awareness Training in Industrial Environments. *Bundesamt für Sicherheit in der Informationstechnik: Deutschland. Digital. Sicher. 30 Jahre BSI – Tagungsband zum 17. Deutschen IT-Sicherheitskongress*, 43-56.

Gasiba, T., Lechner, U., Pinto-Albuquerque, M., & Mendez, D. (2021). Is Secure Coding Education in the Industry Needed? An Investigation Through a Large Scale Survey. *43rd International Conference on Software Engineering (ICSE)*, 1-12.

Gasiba, T. (2021). *Raising Awareness on Secure Coding in the Industry through CyberSecurity Challenges*. Universität der Bundeswehr München.

Gasiba, T., Beckers, K., Suppan, S., & Rezabek, F. (2019). On the Requirements for Serious Games geared towards Software Developers in the Industry. *Conference on Requirements Engineering Conference (RE)*, 286-296.

Gasiba, T., Lechner, U., & Pinto-Albuquerque, M. (2021). CyberSecurity Challenges for Software Developer Awareness Training in Industrial Environments. *16th International Conference on Wirtschaftsinformatik*, 1-17. 10.1007/978-3-030-86797-3_25

Gaspar, J. D. S., Lage, E. M., Da Silva, F. J., Mineiro, É., De Oliveira, I. J. R., Oliveira, I., ... Reis, Z. S. N. (2020). A mobile serious game about the pandemic (COVID-19-Did You Know?): Design and evaluation study. *JMIR Serious Games*, *8*(4), e25226. doi:10.2196/25226 PMID:33301416

Gee, J. P. (2003). *What video games have to teach us about learning and literacy*. Palgrave/MacMillan. doi:10.1145/950566.950595

Gee, J. P. (2004). Learning by design: Games as learning machines. *Interactive Educational Multimedia*, *8*, 15–23.

Gee, J. P. (2004). *What Video Games Have to Teach Us About Learning and Literacy*. Palgrave Macmillan.

Gee, J. P. (2007). Learning theory, video games, and popular culture. In K. Drotner & S. Livingstone (Eds.), *The international handbook of children, media and culture* (pp. 196–213). Sage Publications. doi:10.4135/9781848608436.n13

Gee, J. P. (2008). Learning and games. In K. Salen (Ed.), *The ecology of games: Connecting youth, games, and learning* (pp. 21–40). The MIT Press.

Geelen, D., Keyson, D., Stella, B., & Brezet, H. (2012). Exploring the use of a game to stimulate energy saving in households - Journal of Design Research - Volume 10, Number 1–2/2012 - Inderscience Publishers. *Journal of Desert Research*, *10*, 102–120. doi:10.1504/JDR.2012.046096

Geer, D., Jardine, E., & Leverett, E. (2020). On market concentration and cybersecurity risk. *Journal of Cyber Policy*, *5*(1), 9–29. doi:10.1080/23738871.2020.1728355

Gericke K., Bender B., Pahl G., Beitz W., Feldhusen J., & Grote K. H. (2021). *Pahl/Beitz Konstruktionslehre*. Springer Vieweg. doi:10.1007/978-3-662-57303-7_4

Gerow, J. E., Ayyagari, R., Thatcher, J. B., & Roth, P. L. (2013). Can we have fun @ work? the role of intrinsic motivation for utilitarian systems. *European Journal of Information Systems*, *22*(3), 360–380. doi:10.1057/ejis.2012.25

Geurts, J. L., Duke, R. D., & Vermeulen, P. A. (2007). Policy gaming for strategy and change. *Long Range Planning*, *40*(6), 535–558. doi:10.1016/j.lrp.2007.07.004

Ghoman, S. K., & Schmölzer, G. M. (2020, March). The RETAIN simulation-based serious game—A review of the literature. *Health Care*, *8*(1), 3. PMID:31877882

Giantas, D., & Liaropoulos, A. (2019). *Cybersecurity in the EU: Threats, frameworks and future perspectives*. Working paper series no. 1.

Gibson, E., Hu, L., & Swast, T. (2010). How effective is "Fuzzies" as a tool for developing a holistic understanding of basic genetic principles? *SPIRE-EIT REU summer program for interdisciplinary research and education emerging interface technologies*.

Gilleade, K., Dix, A., & Allanson, J. (2005). Affective videogames and modes of affective gaming: assist me, challenge me, emote me. *DiGRA 2005: Changing Views–Worlds in Play*.

Girvan, C. (2018). What is a virtual world? Definition and classification. *Educational Technology Research and Development*, *66*(5), 1087–1100. doi:10.100711423-018-9577-y

Glavaš, A., & Staščik, A. (2017). Enhancing positive attitude towards mathematics through introducing escape room games. In Z. Kolar-Begovic, R. Kolar-Super, & L. Jukic Matic (Eds.), Mathematics education as a science and profession (pp. 281–294). Academic Press.

Goethe, O., & Palmquist, A. (2020). Broader understanding of gamification by addressing ethics and diversity. In *International Conference on Human-Computer Interaction* (pp. 688-699). Cham: Springer. 10.1007/978-3-030-60128-7_50

Gold, A. H., Malhotra, A., & Segars, A. H. (2001). Knowledge management: An organizational capabilities perspective. *Journal of Management Information Systems*, *18*(1), 185–214. doi:10.1080/07421222.2001.11045669

Golem. (2014, August 6). *Elf Wege, ein Android-System zu übernehmen* [Eleven ways to take over an Android system]. Retrieved from https://www.golem.de/news/stagefright-sicherheitsluecke-elf-wege-ein-android-system-zu-uebernehmen-1508-115610.html

Gonzalez, C., Mora, A., & Toledo, P. (2014). Gamification in intelligent tutoring systems. *TEEM '14 2nd Int. Conf.*, 221-225. doi:10.1145/26351.263903

González-Ortega, J., Insua, D. R., & Cano, J. (2019). Adversarial risk analysis for bi-agent influence diagrams: An algorithmic approach. *European Journal of Operational Research, 273*(3), 1085–1096. doi:10.1016/j.ejor.2018.09.015

Google Developers. (2021) *Firebase*. Author.

Gortney, W. E. (2012). *Dictionary of Military and Associated Terms*. Academic Press.

Goseva-Popstojanova, K., & Perhinschi, A. (2015). On the Capability of Static Code Analysis to Detect Security Vulnerabilities. *Information and Software Technology, 68*, 18–33. doi:10.1016/j.infsof.2015.08.002

Granic, I., Lobel, A., & Engels, R. C. M. E. (2013). *The Benefits of Playing Video Games*. doi:10.1037/a0034857

Graziotin, D., Fagerholm, F., Wang, X., & Abrahamsson, P. (2017). On the Unhappiness of Software Developers. *21st International Conference on Evaluation and Assessment in Software Engineering (EASE'17)*, 324-333. 10.1145/3084226.3084242

Green, M. C., & Brock, T. C. (2000). The role of transportation in the persuasiveness of public narratives. *Journal of Personality and Social Psychology, 79*(5), 701–721. doi:10.1037/0022-3514.79.5.701 PMID:11079236

Green, M. C., Brock, T. C., & Kiaufman, G. F. (2004). Understanding media enjoyment: The role of transportation into narrative worlds. *Communication Theory, 14*(4), 311–327. doi:10.1111/j.1468-2885.2004.tb00317.x

Gregor, S., & Hevner, A. R. (2013). Positioning and presenting design science research for maximum impact. *Management Information Systems Quarterly, 37*(2), 337–355. doi:10.25300/MISQ/2013/37.2.01

Grossberg, F., Wolfson, M., Mazur-Stommen, S., Farley, K., & Nadel, S. (2015). *Gamified Energy Efficiency Programs*. Retrieved from https://www.climateaccess.org/sites/default/files/aceee.pdf

Growth Engineering. (2021, May 27). *19 gamification trends for 2021-2025: top stats, facts & examples*. Growth Engineering. https://www.growthengineering.co.uk/19-gamification-trends-for-2021-2025-top-stats-facts-examples

Grozev, G., Garner, S., Ren, Z., Taylor, M., Higgins, A., & Walden, G. (2016). Modeling the Impacts of Disruptive Technologies and Pricing on Electricity Consumption. In Future of Utilities Utilities of the Future (pp. 211-230). Academic Press. doi:10.1016/B978-0-12-804249-6.00011-7

Gudiksen, S., & Inlove, J. (2018). *Gamification for business: Why innovators and changemakers use games to break down silos, drive engagement and build trust*. Kogan Page Publishers.

Guinan, P. J., Parise, S., & Langowitz, N. (2019). Creating an innovative digital project team: Levers to enable digital transformation. *Business Horizons, 62*(6), 717–727. doi:10.1016/j.bushor.2019.07.005

Gumennykova, T., Blazhko, O., Luhova, T., Troianovska, Y., Melnyk, S., & Riashchenko, O. (2019). Gamification features of stream-education components with education robotics. *Applied Aspects of Information Technology, 1*(02), 45–65.

Gustafsson, A., Katzeff, C., & Bang, M. (2010). Evaluation of a pervasive game for domestic energy engagement among teenagers. *Computers in Entertainment, 7*(4), 1–19. doi:10.1145/1658866.1658873

Häder, M., & Kühne, M. (2009). Die Prägung des Antwortverhaltens durch die soziale Erwünschtheit. In M. Häder & S. Häder (Eds.), *Telefonbefragungen über das Mobilfunknetz*. VS Verlag für Sozialwissenschaften., doi:10.1007/978-3-531-91490-9_13

Halachmi, A. (2011). Imagined promises versus real challenges to public performance management. *International Journal of Productivity and Performance Management, 60*(1), 24–40. doi:10.1108/17410401111094295

Hallinger, P., & Chatpinyakoop, C. (2019). A bibliometric review of research on higher education for sustainable development, 1998–2018. *Sustainability, 11*(8), 2401. doi:10.3390u11082401

Hallinger, P., Wang, R., Chatpinyakoop, C., Nguyen, V. T., & Nguyen, U. P. (2020). A bibliometric review of research on simulations and serious games used in educating for sustainability, 1997–2019. *Journal of Cleaner Production*, *256*, 120358. doi:10.1016/j.jclepro.2020.120358

Hamari, J. & Tuunanen, J. (2013). Player types: A meta-synthesis. *Transactions of the Digital Games Research Association*, *1*(2).

Hamari, J., & Eranti, V. (2011). Framework for Designing and Evaluating Game Achievements. In Digra conference (Vol. 10, No. 1.224, p. 9966). Academic Press.

Hamari, J., Koivisto, J., & Sarsa, H. (2014). Does gamification work? A literature review of empirical studies on gamification. *System Sciences (HICSS) 2014 47th Hawaii International Conference on*, 3025–3034.

Hamari, J. (2013). Transforming Homo Economicus into Homo Ludens: A field experiment on gamification in a utilitarian peer-to-peer trading service. *Electronic Commerce Research and Applications*, *12*(4), 236–245. doi:10.1016/j.elerap.2013.01.004

Hamari, J., & Koivisto, J. (2015). Why do people use gamification services? *International Journal of Information Management*, *35*(4), 419–431. doi:10.1016/j.ijinfomgt.2015.04.006

Hamari, J., Koivisto, J., & Pakkanen, T. (2014). Do persuasive technologies persuade? — a review of empirical studies. In A. Spagnolli, L. Chittaro, & L. Gamberini (Eds.), *Persuasive Technology* (pp. 118–136). Springer International Publishing. doi:10.1007/978-3-319-07127-5_11

Hamari, J., Koivisto, J., & Sarsa, H. (2014). Does gamification work? - A literature review of empirical studies on gamification. *Proceedings of the Annual Hawaii International Conference on System Sciences*, 3025–3034. 10.1109/HICSS.2014.377

Hänsch, N., & Benenson, Z. (2014). Specifying IT Security Awareness. *25th International Workshop on Database and Expert Systems Applications*, 326-330.

Hansen, W. B., & Scheier, L. M. (2019). Specialized smartphone intervention apps: Review of 2014 to 2018 NIH funded grants. *JMIR mHealth and uHealth*, *7*(7), e14655. doi:10.2196/14655 PMID:31359866

Hardy, S., El Saddik, A., Göbel, S., & Steinmetz, R. (2011). Context aware serious games framework for sport and health. In *Medical Measurements and Applications Proceedings (MeMeA). IEEE International Workshop* (pp. 248–252). IEEE. 10.1109/MeMeA.2011.5966775

Hargreaves, T., Nye, M., & Burgess, J. (2013). Keeping energy visible? Exploring how householders interact with feedback from smart energy monitors in the longer term. *Energy Policy*, *52*, 126–134. doi:10.1016/j.enpol.2012.03.027

Harsanyi, J. C. (1967). Games with incomplete information played by "Bayesian" players, I–III Part I. The basic model. *Management Science*, *14*(3), 159–182. doi:10.1287/mnsc.14.3.159

Harteveld, C. (2011). *Triadic game design: Balancing reality, meaning and play*. Springer Science & Business Media. doi:10.1007/978-1-84996-157-8

Harwood, T., & Garry, T. (2015). An investigation into gamification as a customer engagement experience environment. *Journal of Services Marketing*, *29*(6/7), 533–546. doi:10.1108/JSM-01-2015-0045

Haskell, C., & Dawley, L. (2013). 3D GameLab: Quest-Based Pre-Service Teacher Education. In Y. Baek & N. Whitton (Eds.), *Cases on Digital Game-Based Learning: Methods, Models and Strategies* (pp. 302–340). IGI Global. doi:10.4018/978-1-4666-2848-9.ch016

Hassan, L. (2017). Governments should play games: Towards a framework for the gamification of civic engagement platforms. *Simulation & Gaming*, *48*(2), 249–267. doi:10.1177/1046878116683581

Haug, C., Huitema, D., & Wenzler, I. (2011). Learning through games? Evaluating the learning effect of a policy exercise on European climate policy. *Technological Forecasting and Social Change*, *78*(6), 968–981. doi:10.1016/j.techfore.2010.12.001

Heimburger, L., Buchweitz, L., Gouveia, R., & Korn, O. (2019, June). Gamifying Onboarding: How to Increase Both Engagement and Integration of New Employees. *Advances in Social and Occupational Ergonomics, Proceedings of the AHFE 2019 International Conference on Social and Occupational Ergonomics*, 3-14. https://www.researchgate.net/publication/333655639_Gamifying_Onboarding_How_to_Increase_Both_Engagement_and_Integration_of_New_Employees doi:10.1007/978-3-030-20145-6_1

Hekler, E. B., Michie, S., Pavel, M., Rivera, D. E., Collins, L. M., Jimison, H. B., Garnett, C., Parral, S., & Spruijt-Metz, D. (2016). Advancing models and theories for digital behavior change interventions. *American Journal of Preventive Medicine*, *51*(5), 825–832. doi:10.1016/j.amepre.2016.06.013 PMID:27745682

Hendrix, M., Al-Sherbaz, A., & Bloom, V. (2016). Game Based Cyber Security Training: Are Serious Games Suitable for Cyber Security Training? *International Journal of Serious Games*, 1-10.

Hense, J., Klevers, M., Sailer, M., Horenburg, T., Mandl, H., & Günthner, W. (2013). Using gamification to enhance staff motivation in logistics. In *International Simulation and Gaming Association Conference* (pp. 206-213). Springer.

Hermanto, S., Kaburuan, E. R., & Legowo, N. (2018). Gamified SCRUM Design in Software Development Projects. *2018 International Conference on Orange Technologies, ICOT 2018*. 10.1109/ICOT.2018.8705897

Herzig, P., Ameling, M., & Schill, A. (2012). A generic platform for enterprise gamification. In *Software architecture (WICSA) and European Conference on Software Architecture (ECSA). Joint Working IEEE/IFIP Conference* (pp. 219–223). IEEE.

Hevner, A. R. (2007). A three cycle view of design science research. *Scandinavian Journal of Information Systems*, *19*(2), 4.

Hevner, A. R., March, S. T., Park, J., & Ram, S. (2004). Design science in information systems research. *Management Information Systems Quarterly*, *28*(1), 75–105. doi:10.2307/25148625

Hidayati, A., Budiardjo, E. K., & Purwandari, B. (2020). Hard and soft skills for scrum global software development teams. In *Proceedings of the 3rd International Conference on Software Engineering and Information Management* (pp. 110-114). 10.1145/3378936.3378966

Highsmith, J., & Fowler, M. (2001). The agile manifesto. *Software Development Magazine*, *9*(8), 29–30.

Hightow-Weidman, L. B., & Bauermeister, J. A. (2020). Engagement in mHealth behavioral interventions for HIV prevention and care: Making sense of the metrics. *mHealth*, *6*, 7. Advance online publication. doi:10.21037/mhealth.2019.10.01 PMID:32190618

Hightow-Weidman, L., Muessig, K., Knudtson, K., Srivatsa, M., Lawrence, E., LeGrand, S., Hotten, A., & Hosek, S. (2018). A gamified smartphone app to support engagement in care and medication adherence for HIV-positive young men who have sex with men (AllyQuest): Development and pilot study. *JMIR Public Health and Surveillance*, *4*(2), e8923. doi:10.2196/publichealth.8923 PMID:29712626

Hill, V., & Mystakidis, S. (2012). Maya Island virtual museum: A virtual learning environment, museum, and library exhibit. *2012 18th International Conference on Virtual Systems and Multimedia*, 565–568. 10.1109/VSMM.2012.6365978

Hitch, J. (2018, June 7). Gaming the Factory: Can Data Make Manufacturing Fun Again? *IndustryWeek*. https://www. industryweek.com/technology-and-iiot/article/22025774/gaming-the-factory-can-data-make-manufacturing-fun-again

Hochschulrektorenkonferenz. (2013). *Wissenstransfer in die Mediengesellschaft: Situationsanalyse und Orientierungshilfen: Beiträge zur Hochschulpolitik 3/2013*.

Hocine, N., & Gouaich, A. (2011). *A Survey of Agent Programming and Adaptive Serious Games*. RR-11013, pp.8. fflirmm-00577722

Hoffmann, A., Christmann, C. A., & Bleser, G. (2017). Gamification in stress management apps: A critical app review. *JMIR Serious Games*, *5*(2), 13. doi:10.2196/games.7216 PMID:28592397

Holden, R. (2010). Social desirability. *The Corsini encyclopedia of psychology*, 1–2.

Holtz, G., Alkemade, F., De Haan, F., Köhler, J., Trutnevyte, E., Luthe, T., Halbe, J., Papachristos, G., Chappin, E., Kwakkel, J., & Ruutu, S. (2015). Prospects of modelling societal transitions: Position paper of an emerging community. *Environmental Innovation and Societal Transitions*, *17*, 41–58. doi:10.1016/j.eist.2015.05.006

Homer, B. D., Plass, J. L., Raffaele, C., Ober, T. M., & Ali, A. (2018). Improving high school students' executive functions through digital game play. *Computers & Education*, *117*, 50–58. doi:10.1016/j.compedu.2017.09.011

Hoos, S. (2016). *Gamification in UX Design-one way to do it*. doi:10.18420/muc2016-up-0021

Hornik, S., & Thornburg, S. (2010). Really engaging accounting: Second Life™ as a learning platform. *Issues in Accounting Education*, *25*(3), 361–378. doi:10.2308/iace.2010.25.3.361

Housing Europe. (2018). *A State of Housing map of Europe*. https://www.housingeurope.eu/resource-1001/a-state-of-housing-map-of-europe

Huang, Y., Benford, S., Hendrickx, H., Treloar, R., & Blake, H. (2017, April). Office workers' perceived barriers and facilitators to taking regular micro-breaks at work: A diary-probed interview study. In *International Conference on Persuasive Technology* (pp. 149-161). Springer. 10.1007/978-3-319-55134-0_12

Huijbregts, M. A. J., Steinmann, Z. J. N., Elshout, P. M. F., Stam, G., Verones, F., Vieira, M., Zijp, M., Hollander, A., & van Zelm, R. (2017). ReCiPe2016: A harmonised life cycle impact assessment method at midpoint and endpoint level. *The International Journal of Life Cycle Assessment*, *22*(2), 138–147. doi:10.100711367-016-1246-y

Huizinga, J. (2001). Homo Ludens: O Jogo como elemento da Cultura (5th ed.). Perspectiva, SP.

Humanoid Animation Standards. (n.d.). *ISO DIS 19744-2*. Retrieved from https://www.web3d.org/standards/hanim

Humlung, O., & Haddara, M. (2019). The hero's journey to innovation: Gamification in enterprise systems. *Procedia Computer Science*, *164*, 86–95. doi:10.1016/j.procs.2019.12.158

Hunicke, R., LeBlanc, M., & Zubek, R. (2004). A formal approach to game design and game research. *Proceedings of the AAAI workshop on challenges in game AI*, 4, 1.

Hunicke, R., LeBlanc, M., & Zubek, R. (2004). MDA: A formal approach to game design and game research. *Proceedings of the AAAI Workshop on Challenges in Game AI*, 1, 1722.

Huotari, K., & Hamari, J. (2012). Defining gamification: a service marketing perspective. *Proceedings of the 16th International Academic MindTrek Conference*, 17–22.

Huotari, K., & Hamari, J. (2012). Defining gamification: a service marketing perspective. In *Proceeding of the 16th international academic MindTrek conference*, (pp. 17-22). 10.1145/2393132.2393137

Huotari, K., & Hamari, J. (2017). A definition for gamification: Anchoring gamification in the service marketing literature. *Electronic Markets*, *27*(1), 21–31. doi:10.100712525-015-0212-z

IEA Digitalization & the Energy Working Group. (2017). *Digitalization & Energy*. Retrieved from https://www.iea.org/digital/

IEA EEfD. (2017). Energy Efficiency 2017. *Energy Efficiency*, *2017*. Advance online publication. doi:10.1787/9789264284234-en

IEA Energy Data Centre. (2017). *Energy Technology RD&D Budgets: Overview*. Retrieved from https://www.iea.org/publications/freepublications/publication/EnergyTechnologyRDD2017Overview.pdf

InfoSecurity. (2021). Retrieved from https://www.infosecurityeurope.com

Inhelder, B., & Piaget, J. (1958). *The growth of logical thinking from childhood to adolescence*. Basic Books. doi:10.1037/10034-000

International Energy Agency. (2016). *World Energy Outlook*. Author.

International Standard Organization (2006b). ISO 14044. Environmental management – life cycle assessment – requirements and guidelines.

International Standard Organization. (2006a). *ISO 14040. Environmental management – life cycle assessment – principles and framework*. https://www.sciencedirect.com/science/article/pii/S0960148112003084-bib16

Isen, A. M. (2004). Some perspectives on positive feelings and emotions: positive affect facilitates thinking and problem solving. In A. S. R.Manstead, N. Frijda, A. Fischer, A. S. R. Manstead, N. Frijda, & A. Fischer (Eds.), *Feelings and emotions: The Amsterdam Symposium* (pp.263–281). New York, NY: Cambridge University Press. 10.1017/CBO9780511806582.016

Ixia. (2014). *Cyber range: Improving network defence and security readiness*. Retrieved from Ixia White Paper: https://support.ixiacom.com/sites/default/ files/resources/whitepaper/915-6729-01-cyber-range.pdf

Jack, R. E., Garrod, O. G., Yu, H., Caldara, R., & Schyns, P. G. (2012). Facial expressions of emotion are not culturally universal. *Proceedings of the National Academy of Sciences of the United States of America*, *109*(19), 7241–7244. doi:10.1073/pnas.1200155109 PMID:22509011

Janssen, A., Boster, A., Lee, H., Patterson, B., & Prakash, R. S. (2015). The effects of video-game training on broad cognitive transfer in multiple sclerosis: A pilot randomized controlled trial. *Journal of Clinical and Experimental Neuropsychology*, *37*(3), 285–302. doi:10.1080/13803395.2015.1009366 PMID:25850024

Jasperson, J., Carter, & Zmud. (2005). A Comprehensive Conceptualization of Post-Adoptive Behaviors Associated with Information Technology Enabled Work Systems. *Management Information Systems Quarterly*, *29*(3), 525–557. doi:10.2307/25148694

Jay, A. (2021). *12 Gamification Trends for 2021/2022: Current Forecasts You Should Be Thinking About*. https://financesonline.com/gamification-trends

Jia, Y., Xu, B., Karanam, Y., & Voida, S. (2016). Personality-targeted gamification: A survey study on personality traits and motivational affordances. *Proc. 34th Annu. CHI Conf. Human Factors Comput. Syst. (CHI '16)*. 10.1145/2858036.2858515

Jin, G., Tu, M., Kim, T.-H., Heffron, J., & White, J. (2018). Game based Cybersecurity Training for High School Students. *SIGCSE '18: Proceedings of the 49th ACM Technical Symposium on Computer Science Education*, 68-73. 10.1145/3159450.3159591

Johnson, S. (2019, December 27). *Kurt Vonnegut on 8 shapes of stories*. Retrieved 01 25, 2021, from Big think: https://bigthink.com/culture-religion/vonnegut-shapes

Johnson, D., Horton, E., Mulcahy, R., & Foth, M. (2017). Gamification and serious games within the domain of domestic energy consumption: A systematic review. *Renewable & Sustainable Energy Reviews*, *73*, 249–264. doi:10.1016/j.rser.2017.01.134

Johnson, D., & Wiles, J. (2003). Effective affective user interface design in games. *Ergonomics*, *46*(13-14), 1332–1345. doi:10.1080/00140130310001610865 PMID:14612323

Jones, B. A., Madden, G. J., & Wengreen, H. J. (2014). The FIT game: Preliminary evaluation of a gamification approach to increasing fruit and vegetable consumption in school. *Preventive Medicine*, *68*, 76–79. doi:10.1016/j.ypmed.2014.04.015 PMID:24768916

Jones, J., & Chou, T.-S. (2019). *An infrastructure supporting a game-based learning system for information security topics. Conf. Industry Educ. Collaboration.*

Joshi, C., Aliaga, J. R., & Insua, D. R. (2020). Insider threat modeling: An adversarial risk analysis approach. *IEEE Transactions on Information Forensics and Security*, *16*, 1131–1142. doi:10.1109/TIFS.2020.3029898

Juul, J. (2011). *Half-real: Video games between real rules and fictional worlds*. MIT Press.

Kalatha, E., & Caridakis, G. (2013, December). Natural, affect aware interfaces: gesture and body expressivity aspects. In *2013 8th International Workshop on Semantic and Social Media Adaptation and Personalization* (pp. 97-102). IEEE. 10.1109/SMAP.2013.17

Kalatha, E., Aliprantis, J., Konstantakis, M., Michalakis, K., Moraitou, T., & Caridakis, G. (2018, May). Cultural Heritage engagement via Serious Games: the ARCADE Augmented Reality, Context-Aware, linked open Data pErsonalized ecosystem. In *1st International CICMS Conference 4-5 May, 2018 Kuşadası, Turkey* (p. 309). Academic Press.

Kalatha, E., Konstantakis, M., & Caridakis, G. (2019, June). Exploiting User Personas for a Cultural Serious Game based on Gardner's Multiple Intelligences Theory. *2nd Social Science Conference*.

Kapp, K. (2012). The Gamification of Learning and Instruction: Game–based Methods and Strategies for Training and Education. John Wiley & Sons Inc.

Kappen, D. L., & Nacke, L. E. (2013). The kaleidoscope of effective gamification: deconstructing gamification in business applications. In *Proceedings of the first international conference on gameful design, research, and applications* (pp. 119-122). 10.1145/2583008.2583029

Kapp, K. M. (2012). *The gamification of learning and instruction: Game-based methods and strategies for training and education*. John Wiley & Sons. doi:10.1145/2207270.2211316

Kapp, K. M., & O'Driscoll, T. (2010). *Learning in 3D: Adding a New Dimension to Enterprise Learning and Collaboration*. Pfeiffer.

Karlin, B., Davis, N., Sanguinetti, A., Gamble, K., Kirkby, D., & Stokols, D. (2014). Dimensions of conservation: Exploring differences among energy behaviors. *Environment and Behavior*, *46*(4), 423–452. doi:10.1177/0013916512467532

Kato, P. M. (2010). Video games in health care: Closing the gap. *Review of General Psychology*, *14*(2), 113–121. doi:10.1037/a0019441

Kato, T. (2012). Development of the Coping Flexibility Scale: Evidence for the coping flexibility hypothesis. *Journal of Counseling Psychology*, *59*(2), 262–273. doi:10.1037/a0027770 PMID:22506909

Kavaliova, M., Virjee, F., Maehle, N., & Kleppe, I. A. (2016). Crowdsourcing innovation and product development: Gamification as a motivational driver. *Cogent Business and Management*, *3*(1), 1128132. Advance online publication. doi:10.1080/23311975.2015.1128132

Keelson, E., Boateng, K. O., & Ghansah, I. (2014). A Smart Retrofitted Meter for Developing Countries. *International Journal of Computers and Applications*, *90*(5), 40–46. doi:10.5120/15573-4203

Ke, F. (2016). Designing and integrating purposeful learning in game play: A systematic review. *Educational Technology Research and Development*, *64*(2), 219–244. doi:10.100711423-015-9418-1

Khaled, R., & Vasalou, A. (2014). Bridging serious games and participatory design. *International Journal of Child-Computer Interaction*, *2*(2), 93–100. doi:10.1016/j.ijcci.2014.03.001

Khemaja, M., & Buendia, F. (2017). Building context-aware gamified apps by using ontologies as unified representation and reasoning-based models. In *Serious Games and Edutainment Applications* (pp. 675–702). Springer. doi:10.1007/978-3-319-51645-5_29

Kianpour, M. (2020). *Knowledge and Skills Needed to Craft Successful Cybersecurity Strategies*. Norsk IKT-konferanse for forskning og utdanning.

Kianpour, M., Kowalski, S., Zoto, E., Frantz, C., & Overby, H. (2019). Designing serious games for cyber ranges: A socio-technical approach. IEEE Eur. Symp. on Secruity and Privacy Workshops (EuroS&PW), 85-93. doi:10.1109/EuroSPW.2019.00016

Kianpour, M., Kowalski, S., Zoto, E., Frantz, C., & Øverby, H. (2019). Designing serious games for cyber ranges: a socio-technical approach. *2019 IEEE European symposium on security and privacy workshops (EuroS&PW)*.

Kim, B. (2015). Designing gamification in the right way. *Library Technology Reports*, *51*(2), 29–35.

Kim, T. W. (2015). Gamification ethics: Exploitation and manipulation. *Proceedings of ACM SIGCHI Gamifying Research Workshop*.

Kim, T. W., & Werbach, K. (2022). Excerpt from Ethics of Gamification. In *Ethics of Data and Analytics* (pp. 375–385). Auerbach Publications. doi:10.1201/9781003278290-55

Kim, T., & Werbach, K. (2016). More than Just a Game: Ethical Issues in Gamification. *Ethics and Information Technology*, *18*(2), 157–173. doi:10.100710676-016-9401-5

Kjaerulff, U. B., & Madsen, A. L. (2008). *Bayesian networks and influence diagrams*. Springer Science+ Business Media.

Klasnja, P., Hekler, E. B., Shiffman, S., Boruvka, A., Almirall, D., Tewari, A., & Murphy, S. A. (2015). Micro-randomized trials: An experimental design for developing just-in-time adaptive interventions. *Health Psychology*, *34*(suppl), 1220–1228. doi:10.1037/hea0000305 PMID:26651463

Kochan, T. A., & Rubinstein, S. A. (2000). Toward a Stakeholder Theory of the Firm: The Saturn Partnership. *Organization Science*, *11*(4), 367–386. doi:10.1287/orsc.11.4.367.14601

Koestler, A. (1967). *The ghost in the machine*. Hutchinson.

Koivisto, J., & Hamari, J. (2019). The rise of motivational information systems: A review of gamification research. *International Journal of Information Management*, *45*, 191–210. doi:10.1016/j.ijinfomgt.2018.10.013

Kołakowska, A., Landowska, A., Szwoch, M., Szwoch, W., & Wróbel, M. R. (2013, June). Emotion recognition and its application in software engineering. In *2013 6th International Conference on Human System Interactions (HSI)* (pp. 532-539). IEEE. 10.1109/HSI.2013.6577877

Korn, O., Funk, M., Abele, S., Hörz, T., & Schmidt, A. (2014). Context-aware assistive systems at the workplace: analyzing the effects of projection and gamification. In *Proceedings of the 7th international conference on pervasive technologies related to assistive environments* (pp. 1-8). 10.1145/2674396.2674406

Kostopoulos, K. P., Giannopoulos, K., Mystakidis, S., & Chronopoulou, K. (2014). E-learning through virtual reality applications: The case of career counseling. *The International Journal of Technologies in Learning, 21*(1), 57–68. doi:10.18848/2327-0144/CGP/v20i01/49125

Kotler, P., & Armstrong, G. (2003). *Princípios de Marketing* (9th ed.). São Paulo: Prentice Hall.

Kotsia, I., Zafeiriou, S., & Fotopoulos, S. (2013). Affective gaming: A comprehensive survey. In *Proceedings of the IEEE conference on computer vision and pattern recognition workshops* (pp. 663-670). IEEE.

Kotsopoulos, D., Bardaki, C., & Pramatari, K. (2016). Gamification, Geolocation and Sensors for Employee Motivation Towards Energy Conservation at the Workplace. In *Tenth Mediterranean Conference on Information Systems (MCIS) 2016* (pp. 1–11). Retrieved from https://aisel.aisnet.org/mcis2016/39

Kotsopoulos, D., Bardaki, C., Lounis, S., Papaioannou, T., & Pramatari, K. (2017). Designing an IoT-enabled Gamification Application for Energy Conservation at the Workplace: Exploring Personal and Contextual Characteristics. In 30th Bled e-conference: Digital Transformation – From Connecting Things to Transforming Our Lives (pp. 369–383). University of Maribor Press. doi:10.18690/978-961-286-043-1.26

Kotsopoulos, D., Bardaki, C., Papaioannou, T. G., Lounis, S., & Pramatari, K. (2018). Agile User-Centered Design of an Iot-Enabled Gamified Intervention for Energy Conservation. *IADIS International Journal on WWW/Internet, 16*(1), 1–25. Retrieved from http://www.iadisportal.org/ijwi/papers/2018161101.pdf

Kotsopoulos, D., Bardaki, C., Lounis, S., & Pramatari, K. (2018). Employee Profiles and Preferences towards IoT-enabled Gamification for Energy Conservation. *International Journal of Serious Games, 5*(2), 65–85. doi:10.17083/ijsg.v5i2.225

Kotsopoulos, D., Bardaki, C., Papaioannou, T. G., Lounis, S., Stamoulis, G. D., & Pramatari, K. (2019). Designing a Serious Game to Motivate Energy Savings in a Museum: Opportunities & Challenges. In *GALA 2019, LNCS 11899* (pp. 572–584). Springer. doi:10.1007/978-3-030-34350-7_55

Kotsopoulos, D., Bardaki, C., Papaioannou, T. G., Pramatari, K., & Stamoulis, G. D. (2020). User-Centered Gamification. *International Journal of E-Services and Mobile Applications, 12*(2), 15–39. doi:10.4018/IJESMA.2020040102

Kristeva, I. (2000). Bakhtin, word, dialogue and novel. In *French Semiotics: From Structuralism to Poststructuralism* (pp. 427–457). Progress.

Kucek, S., & Maria, L. (2020). An Empirical Survey of Functions and Configurations of Open-Source Capture the Flag (CTF) Environments. *Journal of Network and Computer Applications, 151*, 102470. doi:10.1016/j.jnca.2019.102470

Kucirkova, N., Messer, D., Sheehy, K., & Fernández Panadero, C. (2014). Children's engagement with educational iPad apps: Insights from a Spanish classroom. *Computers & Education, 71*, 175–184. doi:10.1016/j.compedu.2013.10.003

Kuhn, D. (2000). Theory of mind, metacognition, and reasoning: A life-span perspective. In P. Mitchell & K. J. Riggs (Eds.), *Children's reasoning and the mind* (pp. 301–326). Psychology Press.

Kumar, J. M., Herger, M., & Dam, R. F. (2020). *Bartle's player types of gamification*. Retrieved from Interaction Design Foundation: https://www.interaction-design.org/literature/article/bartle-s-player-types-for-gamification

Kurkovsky, S. (2015, June). Teaching software engineering with LEGO serious play. In *Proceedings of the 2015 ACM Conference on Innovation and Technology in Computer Science Education* (pp. 213-218). 10.1145/2729094.2742604

KYOCERA Document Solutions. (2018). *Wissensmanagement im Mittelstand: Mit Dokumentenmanagement Wissen besser verfügbar machen.* https://www.kyoceradocumentsolutions.de/de/smarter-workspaces/media-center/e-books/e-book-wissensmanagement-dms.html

L'Heureux, A., Grolinger, K., Higashino, W. A., & Capretz, M. A. M. (2017). A gamification framework for sensor data analytics. *Proceedings - 2017 IEEE 2nd International Congress on Internet of Things, ICIOT 2017*, 74–81. 10.1109/IEEE.ICIOT.2017.18

Labrador, E., & Villegas, E. (2014). Sistema Fun Experience Design (FED) aplicado en el aula. *ReVisión, 7*(2).

Lagoa, C. M., Bekiroglu, K., Murphy, S. A., & Lanza, S. T. (2014). Designing adaptive intensive interventions using methods from engineering. *Journal of Consulting and Clinical Psychology*, *82*(5), 868–878. doi:10.1037/a0037736 PMID:25244394

Lamberts, B., Migchelbrink, K., Kaan, M., Burgers, M., & Ouweland van den, R. (2016). *Gamification of the workplace setting. An inquiry into the possibilities of gamification of the workplace setting for sustainable work by an exploration of gamification.* Interdisciplinair Honours program MA, Radboud University.

Lameras, P., Arnab, S., Dunwell, I., Stewart, C., Clarke, S., & Petrdis, P. (2017). Essential features of serious game design in higher education: Linking learning attributes to game mechanics. *British Journal of Educational Technology*, *48*(4), 972–994. doi:10.1111/bjet.12467

Landers, R. N. (2014). Developing a theory of gamified learning: Linking serious games and gamification of learning. *Simulation & Gaming*, *45*(6), 752–768. doi:10.1177/1046878114563660

Landers, R. N. (2019). Gamification Misunderstood: How Badly Executed and Rhetorical Gamification Obscures Its Transformative Potential. *Journal of Management Inquiry*, *28*(2), 137–140. doi:10.1177/1056492618790913

Landers, R. N., & Landers, A. K. (2014). An empirical test of the theory of gamified learning: The effect of leaderboards on time-on-task and academic performance. *Simulation & Gaming*, *45*(6), 769–785. doi:10.1177/1046878114563662

Lane, A. M., Whyte, G. P., Terry, P. C., & Nevill, A. M. (2005). Mood, self-set goals and examination performance: The moderating effect of depressed mood. *Personality and Individual Differences*, *39*(1), 143–153. doi:10.1016/j.paid.2004.12.015

Larson, K. (2020). Serious games and gamification in the corporate training environment: A literature review. *TechTrends*, *64*(2), 319–328. doi:10.100711528-019-00446-7

Laskey, A., & Kavazovic, O. (2011). Opower. XRDS: Crossroads. *The ACM Magazine for Students*, *17*(4), 47–51.

Laudon, K. C., & Laudon, J. P. (2020). *Management Information Systems: Managing the Digital Firm* (16th ed.). Pearson.

Lau, H. M., Smit, J. H., Fleming, T. M., & Riper, H. (2017). Serious games for mental health: Are they accessible, feasible, and effective? A systematic review and meta-analysis. *Frontiers in Psychiatry*, *7*, 209. doi:10.3389/fpsyt.2016.00209 PMID:28149281

Leblanc, M. (2004). Game design and tuning workshop materials. *Game Developers Conference*.

Leclercq, T., Poncin, I., & Hammedi, W. (2017). The Engagement Process During Value Co-Creation: Gamification in New Product-Development Platforms. *International Journal of Electronic Commerce*, *21*(4), 454–488. doi:10.1080/10864415.2016.1355638

Lederman. (2019). *Os 7 problemas mais comuns nas empresas.* Lederman Consulting & Education. https://www.ledermanconsulting.com.br/educacao-corporativa/os-7-problemas-mais-comuns-nas-empresas

Lee, J. P., & Fonseca, N. (2021). Video Gaming & Esports Taking Media and Entertainment to the Next Level An in-depth look at the investment case for video gaming and esports. Van Eck Associates Corporation.

Lei, H., Ganjeizadeh, F., Jayachandran, P. K., & Ozcan, P. (2017). A statistical analysis of the effects of Scrum and Kanban on software development projects. *Robotics and Computer-integrated Manufacturing*, *43*, 59–67. doi:10.1016/j.rcim.2015.12.001

Leitão, J. (2019). Concepts, methodologies and tools of gamification and design thinking. *Contributions to Management Science*, 85–127. doi:10.1007/978-3-319-91282-0_3

Lem, S. (2014). *The Cyberiad: fables for the cybernetic age* (1st ed.). Penguin Classics.

Leun, K., & Petrilli, S. Jr. (2017). Using Capture-the-Flag to Enhance the Effectiveness of Cybersecurity Education. *Proceedings of the 18th Annual Conference on Information Technology Education (SIGITE '17)*, 47-52. 10.1145/3125659.3125686

Lewenstein, B. V. (2011). Experimenting with engagement: Commentary on: Taking our own medicine: On an experiment in science communication. *Science and Engineering Ethics*, *17*(4), 817–821. doi:10.100711948-011-9328-5 PMID:22095058

Li, J. (2020). A Systematic Review of Video Games for Second Language Acquisition. In *Handbook of Research on Integrating Digital Technology With Literacy Pedagogies* (pp. 472–499). IGI Global.

Likert, R. (1932). A Technique for the Measurement of Attitudes. *Archives de Psychologie*, *22*(140), 1–55.

Li, L., & Campbell, J. (2010). Emotion modeling and interaction of NPCs in virtual simulation and games. *The International Journal of Virtual Reality: a Multimedia Publication for Professionals*, *9*(4), 1–6. doi:10.20870/IJVR.2010.9.4.2784

Lim, C. P., Nonis, D., & Hedberg, J. G. (2006). Gaming in a 3D multiuser virtual environment: Engaging students in science lessons. *British Journal of Educational Technology*, *37*(2), 211–231. doi:10.1111/j.1467-8535.2006.00531.x

Lim, C. W., & Jung, H. W. (2013). A study on the military Serious Game. *Advanced Science and Technology Letters*, *39*, 73–77. doi:10.14257/astl.2013.39.14

Lim, N. (2016). Cultural differences in emotion: Differences in emotional arousal level between the East and the West. *Integrative Medicine Research*, *5*(2), 105–109. doi:10.1016/j.imr.2016.03.004 PMID:28462104

Liu, D., Santhanam, R., & Webster, J. (2017). Toward Meaningful Engagement: A framework for design and research of Gamified information systems. *Management Information Systems Quarterly*, *41*(4), 1011–1034. doi:10.25300/MISQ/2017/41.4.01

Li, Y., Elmaghraby, A. S., El-Baz, A., & Sokhadze, E. M. (2015, December). Using physiological signal analysis to design affective VR games. In *2015 IEEE International Symposium on Signal Processing and Information Technology (ISSPIT)* (pp. 57-62). IEEE. 10.1109/ISSPIT.2015.7394401

Lombriser, P., Dalpiaz, F., Lucassen, G., & Brinkkemper, S. (2016). Gamified requirements engineering: model and experimentation. In *International Working conference on requirements engineering: foundation for software quality* (pp. 171-187). Springer.

Lonchamp, J. (2015). *Analyse des besoins pour le développement logiciel: Recueil et spécification, démarches itératives et agiles* [Needs analysis for software development: Collection and specification, iterative and agile approaches]. Dunod.

Lopes, S., Pereira, A., Magalhães, P., Oliveira, A., & Rosário, P. (2019). Gamification: Focus on the strategies being implemented in interventions: A systematic review protocol. *BMC Research Notes*, *12*(1), 1–5. doi:10.118613104-019-4139-x PMID:30795806

López-Belmonte, J., Segura-Robles, A., Fuentes-Cabrera, A., & Parra-Gonzáles, M. E. (2020). Evaluating activation and absence of negative effect: Gamification and escape rooms for learning. *International Journal of Environmental Research and Public Health, 17*(7), 1–12.

Lo, S. H., Peters, G. J. Y., & Kok, G. (2012). Energy-Related Behaviors in Office Buildings: A Qualitative Study on Individual and Organisational Determinants. *Applied Psychology, 61*(2), 227–249. doi:10.1111/j.1464-0597.2011.00464.x

Los, S. (2013). *Geografia dell'architettura. Progettazione Bioclimatica e disegno architettonico* [Geography of Architecture. Bioclimatic Design and Architechtural Design]. Il Poligrafo.

Lounis, S., Kotsopoulos, D., Bardaki, C., Papaioannou, T. G., & Pramatari, K. (2017). Waste No More: Gamification for Energy Efficient Behaviour at the Workplace. In *Proceedings of 1st International GamiFIN Conference* (pp. 129-134). Academic Press.

Luh, R., Temper, M., Tjoa, S., Schrittwieser, S., & Janicke, H. (2020). PenQuest: a gamified attacker/ defender meta model for cyber security assessment and education. *J. Comput Virol. Hack. Techn.*, 19-61. doi:10.1007/s11416-019-00342-x

Luhova, T. (2020). Narrative and storytelling in the knowledge structure of educational and business video games as factors of synergy of information technologies and spiritually-oriented pedagogy. *Open Educational E-Environment of Modern University,* (8), 42-59.

Luhova, T., Blazhko, O., Troianovska, Y., & Riashchenko, O. (2019). The Canvas-Oriented Formalization of the Game Design Processes. In *2019 IEEE 2nd Ukraine Conference on Electrical and Computer Engineering (UKRCON)* (pp. 1254-1259). Lviv, Ukraine: IEEE.

Luhova, T. (2021). Game design oriented approach to the development of academic disciplines of higher educational institutions. *Information Technologies and Learning Tools, 81*(1), 235–254.

Luhova, T. (2022). Serious Games for Recruitment in the New Humanism. In O. Bernardes & V. Amorim (Eds.), *Handbook of Research on Promoting Economic and Social Development Through Serious Games* (pp. 375–394). IGI Global. doi:10.4018/978-1-7998-9732-3.ch017

Luhova, T. A. (2021). Journalism education based on serious games. *OpenEdu [Internet]*, (11), 92–105.

Machinations, S. (2021). *Craft perfectly balanced games - Simulate game systems, before writing a single line of code.* https://machinations.io/

Machuca-Villegas, L., & Gasca-Hurtado, G. P. (2018). Gamification for improving software project management processes: A systematic literature review. In *International Conference on Software Process Improvement* (pp. 41-54). Springer.

MacKinnon, D. P. (2008). *Introduction to statistical mediation analysis.* Lawrence Erlbaum.

MacKinnon, D. P., & Pirlott, A. G. (2015). Statistical approaches for enhancing causal interpretation of the M to Y relation in mediation analysis. *Personality and Social Psychology Review, 19*(1), 30–43. doi:10.1177/1088868314542878 PubMed

Maclin, E. L., Mathewson, K. E., Low, K. A., Boot, W. R., Kramer, A. F., Fabiani, M., & Gratton, G. (2011). Learning to multitask: Effects of video game practice on electrophysiological indices of attention and resource allocation. *Psychophysiology, 48*(9), 1173–1183. doi:10.1111/j.1469-8986.2011.01189.x PMID:21388396

Maglogiannis, I., Kalatha, E., & Paraskevopoulou-Kollia, E. A. (2017). An Overview of Affective Computing from the Physiology and Biomedical Perspective. In E. Spyrou, D. Iakovidis, & P. Mylonas (Eds.), *Semantic Multimedia Analysis and Processing* (pp. 367–396). CRC Press. doi:10.1201/b17080-14

Mahey, M., Al-Abdulla, A., Ames, S., Bray, P., Candela, G., Chambers, S., & Wilms, L. (2019). *Open a GLAM lab*. QU Press.

Mahmud, S. (2014). *History & Re-convergence of Galleries, Libraries, Archives, Museums (GLAM) - A systematic literature review* [Master's Thesis]. Queensland University of Technology. https://bit.ly/3CMJ72k

Malone, T. W. (1981). Toward a theory of intrinsically motivating instruction. *Cognitive Science*, *4*(4), 333–369. doi:10.120715516709cog0504_2

Mandryk, R. L., Atkins, M. S., & Inkpen, K. M. (2006, April). A continuous and objective evaluation of emotional experience with interactive play environments. In *Proceedings of the SIGCHI Conference on Human Factors in computing systems* (pp. 1027-1036). 10.1145/1124772.1124926

Manzano-León, A., Camacho-Lazarraga, P., Guerrero, M. A., Guerrero-Puerta, L., Aguilar-Parra, J. M., Trigueros, R., & Alias, A. (2021). Between level up and game over: A systematic literature review of gamification in education. *Sustainability*, *13*(4), 2247. doi:10.3390u13042247

Mao, W., Cui, Y., Chiu, M. M., & Lei, H. (2022). Effects of Game-based learning on students' critical thinking: A meta-analysis. *Journal of Educational Computing Research*, *59*(8), 1682–1708. doi:10.1177/07356331211007098

Marcão, R. P., Pestana, G., & Sousa, M. J. (2017). Gamification in project management. *Conference: 2nd International Conference On Economic and Business Management (FEBM 2017)*. 10.2991/febm-17.2017.115

Marczewski, A. (2015a). Even Ninja Monkeys Like to Play: Gamification, Game Thinking and Motivational Design. In User Type Heaxd. CreateSpace Independent Publishing.

Marczewski, A. (2015b). Gamification mechanics and elements. In Even Ninja Monkeys Like to Play: Gamification, Game Thinking & Motivational Design (pp. 165–177). CreateSpace Independent Publishing Platform.

Marczewski, A. (2016). *6 tips for short term gamification*. Retrieved from Gamified UK: https://www.gamified.uk/2016/06/23/short-term-gamification

Marczewski, A. (2017). *Gamification elements and mechanics*. Retrieved from https://www.slideshare.net/daverage/gamification-elements-and-mechanics

Marczewski, A. (2018). *Gamification & user experience UX connect*. Retrieved from https://www.slideshare.net/daverage/gamification-user-experience-ux-connect?next_slideshow=1

Marczewski, A. (2017). The ethics of gamification. XRDS: Crossroads. *The ACM Magazine for Students*, *24*(1), 56–59.

Marczewski, A. (2018). *Even Ninja Monkeys Like To Play. Unicorn Edition*. Gamified UK Publishing.

Markov, O. I. (2004). *Scenario culture of directors of theatrical performances and holidays: a textbook for teachers, graduate students and students of universities of culture and arts*. KGUKI.

Marques, J. R. (2019). *Quais são os principais problemas organizacionais?* Instituto Brasileiro de Coaching - IBC. https://www.ibccoaching.com.br/portal/rh-gestao-pessoas/quais-sao-principais-problemas-organizacionais

Marshburn, D. (2018). Scrum retrospectives: Measuring and improving effectiveness. *Proceedings of the southern Association for Information systems conference.*

Marshburn, D., & Sieck, J. P. (2019). Don't Break the Build: Developing a Scrum Retrospective Game. *Proceedings of the 52nd Hawaii International conference on system sciences*. 10.24251/HICSS.2019.838

Martens, A., Diener, H., & Malo, S. (2008). Game-based learning with computers–learning, simulations, and games. In *Transactions on edutainment I* (pp. 172–190). Springer. doi:10.1007/978-3-540-69744-2_15

Maske, P. (2019, June 10). *Benefits of gamification in training.* eLearning Learning. https://www.elearninglearning. com/gamification/statistics/?open-article-id=10681320&article-title=benefits-of-gamification-in-training&blog-domain=paradisosolutions.com&blog-title=paradiso

Mastrocola, V. M. (2012). *Ludificador: um guia de referências para o game designer brasileiro.* Independente.

Matsumura, N., Fruchter, R., & Leifer, L. (2015). Shikakeology: Designing triggers for behavior change. *AI & Society, 30*(4), 419–429. doi:10.100700146-014-0556-5

Mattei, L., & Heinen, V. L. (2020). Impacts of the COVID-19 crisis on the Brazilian labor market. *Brazilian Journal of Political Economy, 40,* 647–668. doi:10.1590/0101-31572020-3200

Maturo, A., Mori, L., & Moretti, V. (2016). An ambiguous health education: The quantified self and the medicalization of the mental sphere. *Italian Journal of Sociology of Education, 8*(3), 248–268.

McCaul, K. D., & Glasgow, R. E. (1985). Preventing adolescent smoking: What have we learned about treatment construct validity? *Health Psychology, 4*(4), 361–387. doi:10.1037/0278-6133.4.4.361 PMID:4054080

McCord, A., Cocks, B., Barreiros, A. R., & Bizo, L. A. (2020). Short video game play improves executive function in the oldest old living in residential care. *Computers in Human Behavior, 108,* 106337. doi:10.1016/j.chb.2020.106337

McCoy, S. I., Buzdugan, R., Grimball, R., Natoli, L., Mejia, C. M., Klausner, J. D., & McGrath, M. R. (2018). Stick To It: Pilot study results of an intervention using gamification to increase HIV screening among young men who have sex with men in California. *mHealth, 4,* 40. Advance online publication. doi:10.21037/mhealth.2018.09.04 PMID:30363751

McKee, R. (1997). *Story: style, structure, substance, and the principles of screenwriting.* Harper Collins.

McLennan, M. (2021). *The Global Risks Report 2021.* T. W. E. Forum.

McQuiggan, S. W., Rowe, J. P., Lee, S., & Lester, J. C. (2008). Story-Based Learning: The Impact of Narrative on Learning Experiences and Outcomes. In B. P. Woolf, E. Aïmeur, R. Nkambou, & S. Lajoie (Eds.), *Intelligent Tutoring Systems* (pp. 530–539). Springer Berlin Heidelberg. doi:10.1007/978-3-540-69132-7_56

Medema, W., Mayer, I., Adamowski, J., Wals, A. E., & Chew, C. (2019). *The potential of serious games to solve water problems: Editorial to the special issue on game-based approaches to sustainable water governance.* Academic Press.

Mekler, E. D., Brühlmann, F., Tuch, A. N., & Opwis, K. (2017). Towards understanding the effects of individual gamification elements on intrinsic motivation and performance. *Computers in Human Behavior, 71,* 525–534. doi:10.1016/j.chb.2015.08.048

Melzer, A., Shafir, T., & Tsachor, R. P. (2019). How do we recognize emotion from movement? Specific motor components contribute to the recognition of each emotion. *Frontiers in Psychology, 10,* 1389. doi:10.3389/fpsyg.2019.01389 PMID:31333524

Merrick, J., & Parnell, G. S. (2011). A comparative analysis of PRA and intelligent adversary methods for counterterrorism risk management. *Risk Analysis: An International Journal, 31*(9), 1488–1510. doi:10.1111/j.1539-6924.2011.01590.x PMID:21418080

Messager Rota, V., & Tabaka, J. (2009). *Gestion de projet–vers les méthodes agiles* [Project Management Towards Agile Methods]. Eyrolles.

Metcalf, S. J., Reilly, J. M., Kamarainen, A. M., King, J., Grotzer, T. A., & Dede, C. (2018). Supports for deeper learning of inquiry-based ecosystem science in virtual environments - Comparing virtual and physical concept mapping. *Computers in Human Behavior, 87*, 459–469. doi:10.1016/j.chb.2018.03.018

Michael, D. R., & Chen, S. L. (2006). *Serious games: Games that educate, train, and inform*. Muska & Lipman/Premier-Trade.

Michie, S., Atkins, L., & West, R. (2014). *The behaviour change wheel. A guide to designing interventions*. Silverback Publishing.

Michie, S., Richardson, M., Johnston, M., Abraham, C., Francis, J., Hardeman, W., Eccles, M. P., Cane, J., & Wood, C. E. (2013). The behavior change technique taxonomy (v1) of 93 hierarchically clustered techniques: Building an international consensus for the reporting of behavior change interventions. *Annals of Behavioral Medicine, 46*(1), 81–95. doi:10.100712160-013-9486-6 PMID:23512568

Michie, S., Van Stralen, M. M., & West, R. (2011). The behaviour change wheel: A new method for characterising and designing behaviour change interventions. *Implementation Science; IS, 6*(1), 1–12. doi:10.1186/1748-5908-6-42 PMID:21513547

Microsoft. (2021). *Visual Studio Code*. Author.

Mildner, P., & Mueller, F. F. (2016). Design of Serious Games. In R. Dörner, S. Göbel, W. Effelsberg, & J. Wiemeyer (Eds.), *Serious games* (pp. 57–82). Springer International Publishing. doi:10.1007/978-3-319-40612-1_3

Mills, S., Yanes, M., & Casebeer, C. (2009). Perceptions of distance learning among faculty of a college of education. *Journal of Online Learning and Teaching, 5*(1).

Minbaeva, D., Pedersen, T., Björkman, I., Fey, C., & Park, H. (2003). MNC knowledge transfer, subsidiary Absorptive Capacity, and HRM. *Journal of International Business Studies, 34*(6), 586–599. doi:10.1057/palgrave.jibs.8400056

Ministério da Saúde (Brasil). (2020). *Plano nacional de operacionalização da vacinação contra a COVID-19* [National Plan for the Operationaliszation of Vaccination against COVID-19]. Author.

Mishamishutka. (2012, December 5th). *Unity3d. Getting started, practical advice*. Retrieved 03 30, 2021, from https://habr.com/ru/post/161463/

Mitchell, A., & Savill-Smith, C. (2004). *The use of computer and video games for learning. A review of the literature*. Academic Press.

Mitchell, B. L. (2012). *Game design essentials*. John Wiley & Sons.

Mitchell, R., Schuster, L., & Drennan, J. (2016). Understanding how gamification influences behaviour in social marketing. *Australasian Marketing Journal*. Advance online publication. doi:10.1016/j.ausmj.2016.12.001

MITRE Corporation. (n.d.). *Common Weakness Enumeration*. Retrieved January 12, 2021, from https://cwe.mitre.org/

MITRE. (2017). *CVE-2017-0144*. Retrieved May 14, 2021, from https://cve.mitre.org/cgi-bin/cvename.cgi?name=CVE-2017-0144

Mohr, D. C., Schueller, S. M., Montague, E., Burns, M. N., & Rashidi, P. (2014). The behavioral intervention technology model: An integrated conceptual and technological framework for eHealth and mHealth interventions. *Journal of Medical Internet Research, 16*(6), e146. doi:10.2196/jmir.3077 PMID:24905070

Molka-Danielsen, J., Prasolova-Førland, E., Hokstad, L. M., & Fominykh, M. (2015, November). Creating safe and effective learning environment for emergency management training using virtual reality. In Norsk konferanse for organisasjoners bruk at IT (Vol. 23, No. 1). Academic Press.

Moore, M. (n.d.). *Bringing gamification to cyber security training.* Retrieved from Global Sign: https://www.globalsign.com/en/blog/bringing-gamification-to-cybersecurity-training

Mora, A., Riera, D., Gonzalez, C., & Arnedo-Moreno, J. (2015). A Literature Review of Gamification Design Frameworks. *7th International Conference on Games and Virtual Worlds for Serious Applications (VS-Games),* 1-8. 10.1109/VS-GAMES.2015.7295760

Morganti, L., Pallavicini, F., Cadel, E., Candelieri, A., Archetti, F., & Mantovani, F. (2017). Gaming for Earth: Serious games and gamification to engage consumers in pro-environmental behaviours for energy efficiency. *Energy Research & Social Science, 29,* 95–102. doi:10.1016/j.erss.2017.05.001

Morganti, M., Vigoni, V., Currà, E., & Rogora, A. (2020). Energy Retrofit Cost-Optimal Design Solutions in Social Housing: The Case of Three Tower Buildings of the 1980s. In A. Sayigh (Ed.), *Green Buildings and Renewable Energy* (pp. 221–235). Springer. doi:10.1007/978-3-030-30841-4_16

Morine-Dershimer, G. (1993). Tracing conceptual change in preservice teachers. *Teaching and Teacher Education, 9*(1), 15–26. doi:10.1016/0742-051X(93)90012-6

Morschheuser, B., & Hamari, J. (2019). The Gamification of Work: Lessons From Crowdsourcing. *Journal of Management Inquiry, 28*(2), 145–148. doi:10.1177/1056492618790921

Morschheuser, B., Hassan, L., Werder, K., & Hamari, J. (2018). How to design gamification? A method for engineering gamified software. *Information and Software Technology, 95,* 219–237. doi:10.1016/j.infsof.2017.10.015

Morschheuser, B., Werder, K., Hamari, J., & Abe, J. (2017). How to gamify? Development of a method for gamification. *Proceedings of the 50th annual Hawaii international conference on system sciences (HICSS),* 4–7.

Mortara, M., Catalano, C. E., Bellotti, F., Fiucci, G., Houry-Panchetti, M., & Petridis, P. (2014). Learning cultural heritage by serious games. *Journal of Cultural Heritage, 15*(3), 318–325. doi:10.1016/j.culher.2013.04.004

Morton, A., Reeves, A., Bull, R., & Preston, S. (2020). Empowering and Engaging European building users for energy efficiency. *Energy Research & Social Science, 70,* 101772. doi:10.1016/j.erss.2020.101772

Moultrie, J. (2016). *Stakeholder analysis - lifecycle approach.* University of Cambridge. Management technology Policy. https://www.ifm.eng.cam.ac.uk/research/dmg/tools-and-techniques/stakeholder-analysis-lifecycle-approach/

Muller, M. J., & Druin, A. (2012). Participatory design: the third space in human–computer interaction. In *The Human–Computer Interaction Handbook* (pp. 1125–1153). CRC Press.

Mullins, J. K., & Sabherwal, R. (2020). Gamification: A cognitive-emotional view. *Journal of Business Research, 106*(October), 304–314. doi:10.1016/j.jbusres.2018.09.023

Mullins, J. K., & Sabherwal, R. (2018). Beyond Enjoyment: A Cognitive-Emotional Perspective of Gamification. *Proceedings of the 51st Hawaii International Conference on System Sciences,* 1237–1246. 10.24251/HICSS.2018.152

Murray, E., Hekler, E. B., Andersson, G., Collins, L. M., Doherty, A., Hollis, C., Rivera, D. E., West, R., & Wyatt, J. C. (2016). Evaluating digital health interventions: Key questions and approaches. *American Journal of Preventive Medicine, 51*(5), 843–851. doi:10.1016/j.amepre.2016.06.008 PMID:27745684

Myers, M. D., & Venable, J. R. (2014). A set of ethical principles for design science research in information systems. *Information & Management*, *51*(6), 801–809. doi:10.1016/j.im.2014.01.002

Mystakidis, S., & Berki, E. (2014). Participative Design of qMOOCs with Deep Learning and 3d Virtual Immersive Environments : The case of MOOCAgora. *Can MOOCs Save Europe's Unemployed Youth? Workshop. ECTEL 2014 Conference.*

Mystakidis, S., Cachafeiro, E., & Hatzilygeroudis, I. (2019). Enter the serious e-scape room: A cost-effective serious game model for deep and meaningful e-learning. *2019 10th International Conference on Information, Intelligence, Systems and Applications (IISA)*, 1–6. 10.1109/IISA.2019.8900673

Mystakidis, S. (2020). Distance Education Gamification in Social Virtual Reality: A Case Study on Student Engagement. *11th International Conference on Information, Intelligence, Systems and Applications (IISA 2020)*, 1–6. 10.1109/IISA50023.2020.9284417

Mystakidis, S. (2021). Combat tanking in education - The TANC model for playful distance learning in social virtual reality. *International Journal of Gaming and Computer-Mediated Simulations*, *13*(4), 1–20. doi:10.4018/IJGCMS.291539

Mystakidis, S. (2022). Metaverse. *Encyclopedia*, *2*(1), 486–497. doi:10.3390/encyclopedia2010031

Mystakidis, S., Berki, E., & Valtanen, J.-P. (2017a). Designing and Implementing a Big Open Online Course by Using a 3d Virtual Immersive Environment – Lessons Learned. *9th Annual International Conference on Education and New Learning Technologies (EDULEARN17)*, 8070–8079. 10.21125/edulearn.2017.0487

Mystakidis, S., Berki, E., & Valtanen, J.-P. (2017b). Toward Successfully Integrating Mini Learning Games into Social Virtual Reality Environments – Recommendations for Improving Open and Distance Learning. *9th Annual International Conference on Education and New Learning Technologies (EDULEARN17)*, 968–977. 10.21125/edulearn.2017.1203

Mystakidis, S., Berki, E., & Valtanen, J.-P. (2021). Deep and meaningful e-learning with social virtual reality environments in higher education: A systematic literature review. *Applied Sciences (Basel, Switzerland)*, *11*(5), 2412. doi:10.3390/app11052412

Mystakidis, S., Besharat, J., Papantzikos, G., Christopoulos, A., Stylios, C., Agorgianitis, S., & Tselentis, D. (2022). Design, development and evaluation of a virtual reality serious game for school fire preparedness training. *Education Sciences*, *12*(4), 281. doi:10.3390/educsci12040281

Mystakidis, S., Filippousis, G., Tolis, D., & Tseregkouni, E. (2021). Playful metaphors for narrative-driven e-learning. *Applied Sciences (Basel, Switzerland)*, *11*(24), 11682. doi:10.3390/app112411682

Mystakidis, S., Fragkaki, M., & Filippousis, G. (2021). Ready teacher one: Virtual and augmented reality online professional development for K-12 school teachers. *Computers*, *10*(10), 134. doi:10.3390/computers10100134

Mystakidis, S., Mourtzis, P., & Tseregkouni, E. (2022). *Collaborative Problem Solving for In-Depth Conceptual Knowledge in 3D Virtual Worlds. In 100+ Ideas for Active Learning.* Active Learning Network.

Mystakidis, S., Papantzikos, G., & Stylios, C. (2021). Virtual Reality Escape Rooms for STEM Education in Industry 4.0: Greek Teachers Perspectives. *2021 6th South-East Europe Design Automation, Computer Engineering, Computer Networks and Social Media Conference (SEEDA-CECNSM)*, 1–5. 10.1109/SEEDA-CECNSM53056.2021.9566265

Nacke, L. E., & Deterding, C. S. (2017). The maturing of gamification research. *Computers in Human Behaviour*, 450-454.

Nacke, L., & Deterding, S. (2017). The maturing of gamification research. *Computers in Human Behavior*, *71*, 450–454. doi:10.1016/j.chb.2016.11.062

Nagamachi, M. (2011). *Kansei / Affective Engineering*. CRC Press.

Nah, F. F. H., Eschenbrenner, B., Claybaugh, C. C., & Koob, P. B. (2019). Gamification of enterprise systems. *Systems*, 7(1), 13. doi:10.3390ystems7010013

Nguyen, T. A., & Aiello, M. (2013). Energy intelligent buildings based on user activity: A survey. *Energy and Building*, 56, 244–257. doi:10.1016/j.enbuild.2012.09.005

Nguyen, T. T. H., Ishmatova, D., Tapanainen, T., Liukkonen, T. N., Katajapuu, N., Makila, T., & Luimula, M. (2017, January). Impact of serious games on health and well-being of elderly: a systematic review. In *Proceedings of the 50th Hawaii International Conference on System Sciences*. 10.24251/HICSS.2017.447

Ng, Y. Y., Khong, C. W., & Thwaites, H. (2012). A review of affective design towards video games. *Procedia: Social and Behavioral Sciences*, 51, 687–691. doi:10.1016/j.sbspro.2012.08.225

Nicholson, S. (2012) A User-Centered Theoretical Framework for Meaningful Gamification. Paper Presented at Games+Learning+Society 8.0, Madison, WI.

Nicholson, S. (2015). A RECIPE for meaningful gamification. In T. Reiners & L. Wood (Eds.), Gamification in Education and Business (pp. 1–20). Academic Press.

Nicholson, S. (2016). *The State of the Escape: Escape Room Design and Facilities*. Paper Presented at Meaningful Play 2016. https://scottnicholson.com/pubs/stateofescape.pdf

Nicholson, S. (2015). A recipe for meaningful gamification. In T. Reiners & L. C. Wood (Eds.), *Gamification in business and education*. Springer. doi:10.1007/978-3-319-10208-5_1

Nicholson, S., & Cable, L. (2021). *Unlocking the potential of puzzle-based learning. Designing Escape Rooms + Games for the classroom*. CORWIN.

Nobre, H., & Ferreira, A. (2017). Gamification as a platform for brand co-creation experiences. *Journal of Brand Management*, 24(4), 349–361. doi:10.105741262-017-0055-3

Nonaka, I., & Takeuchi, H. (1995). *The knowledge-creating company: How Japanese companies create the dynamics of innovation*. Oxford university press.

Nørgård, R. T., Toft-Nielsen, C., & Whitton, N. (2017). Playful learning in higher education: Developing a signature pedagogy. *International Journal of Play*, 6(3), 272–282. doi:10.1080/21594937.2017.1382997

Norman, D. (1986). User centered system design. *New perspectives on human-computer interaction*.

Nwehouse, W., Keith, S., Scribner, B., & Witte, G. (2017). *National Initiative for Cybersecurity*. National Institute of Standards and Technology. doi:10.6028/NIST.SP.800-181

Nyström, T. (2021). Exploring the Darkness of Gamification: You Want It Darker? In K. Arai (Ed.), Intelligent Computing (pp. 491-506). Cham: Springer.

O'Donnell, C. (2014). *Developer's dilemma: The secret world of videogame creators*. MIT press. doi:10.7551/mitpress/9035.001.0001

O'Neil, H. F., Wainess, R., & Baker, E. L. (2005). Classification of learning outcomes: Evidence from the computer games literature. *Curriculum Journal*, 16(4), 455–474. doi:10.1080/09585170500384529

O'Sullivan, D., Stavrakakis, I., Gordon, D., Curley, A., Tierney, B., Murphy, E., Collins, M., & Becevel, A. (2021). "You Can't Lose a Game If You Don't Play the Game": Exploring the Ethics of Gamification in Education. *International Journal for Infonomics*, *14*(1), 2035–2045. doi:10.20533/iji.1742.4712.2021.0211

Odobašić, D., Medak, D., & Miler, M. (2013). Gamification of Geographic Data Collection. In *Proceedings of GI_Forum 2013 - Creating the GISociety* (pp. 328-337). Academic Press.

Office of Gas and Electricity Markets. (2018). *Typical domestic consumption values*. https://www.ofgem.gov.uk/gas/retail-market/monitoring-data-and-statistics/typical-domestic-consumption-values

Ogden, J. (2016). Celebrating variability and a call to limit systematisation: The example of the Behaviour Change Technique Taxonomy and the Behaviour Change Wheel. *Health Psychology Review*, *10*(3), 245–250. doi:10.1080/17437199.2016.1190291 PMID:27189585

Oliveira, V., Coelho, A., Guimarães, R., & Rebelo, C. (2012). Serious game in security: A solution for security trainees. *Procedia Computer Science*, *15*, 274–282. doi:10.1016/j.procs.2012.10.079

Oprescu, F., Jones, C., & Katsikitis, M. (2014). I PLAY AT WORK—Ten principles for transforming work processes through gamification. *Frontiers in Psychology*, *5*, 14. doi:10.3389/fpsyg.2014.00014 PMID:24523704

Oracle. (2021). *MySQL Database Service*. https://www.mysql.com

Østby, G., Berg, L., Kianpour, M., Katt, B., & Kowalski, S. J. (2019). A socio-technical framework to improve cyber security training. *Work (Reading, Mass.)*.

Ozkan, N., Gök, M. Ş., & Köse, B. Ö. (2020). Towards a Better Understanding of Agile Mindset by Using Principles of Agile Methods. In *Proceedings of the 15th Conference on Computer Science and Information Systems (FedCSIS)* (pp. 721-730). IEEE.

Pahl, G., & Beitz, W. (2013). *Engineering Design: A Systematic Approach*. Springer Science & Business Media.

Paone, A., & Bacher, J. P. (2018). The Impact of Building Occupant Behavior on Energy Efficiency and Methods to Influence It: A Review of the State of the Art. *Energies*, *11*(4), 953. doi:10.3390/en11040953

Papachristos, G. (2014). Towards multi-system sociotechnical transitions: Why simulate. *Technology Analysis and Strategic Management*, *26*(9), 1037–1055. doi:10.1080/09537325.2014.944148

Papaioannou, T., Dimitriou, N., Vasilakis, K., Schoofs, A., Nikiforakis, M., Pursche, F., Deliyski, N., Taha, A., Kotsopoulos, D., Bardaki, C., Kotsilitis, S., & Garbi, A. (2018). An IoT-Based Gamified Approach for Reducing Occupants' Energy Wastage in Public Buildings. *Sensors (Basel)*, *18*(2), 537. doi:10.339018020537 PMID:29439414

Parjanen, S., & Hyypiä, M. (2019). Innotin game supporting collective creativity in innovation activities. *Journal of Business Research*, *96*, 26–34. doi:10.1016/j.jbusres.2018.10.056

Park, S., & Kim, S. (2017). A Validation of differences in academic achievement among Bartle's player types in an educational gamification environments. *J. Korean Game Soc.*, *17*(4), 25–36. doi:10.7583/JKGS.2017.17.4.25

Parong, J., Mayer, R. E., Fiorella, L., MacNamara, A., Homer, B. D., & Plass, J. L. (2017). Learning executive function skills by playing focused video games. *Contemporary Educational Psychology*, *51*, 141–151. doi:10.1016/j.cedpsych.2017.07.002

Parra-González, M. E., López-Belmonte, J., Segura-Robles, A., & Fuentes-Cabrera, A. (2020). Active and emerging methodologies for ubiquitous education: Potentials of flipped learning and gamification. *Sustainability*, *2020*(12), 602. doi:10.3390u12020602

Pasini, D., Reda, F., & Häkkinen, T. (2017). User engaging practices for energy saving in buildings: Critical review and new enhanced procedure. *Energy and Building*, *148*, 74–88. doi:10.1016/j.enbuild.2017.05.010

Patel, S. (n.d.). *2019 Global Developer Report: DevSecOps finds security roadblocks divide teams.* Retrieved July 18, 2020, from https://about.gitlab.com /blog/2019/07/15/global-developer-report

Patricio, R., & Morozumi, R. (2018). Gamification for service design and Innovation: ideaChef® method and tool. In *ServDes2018. Service Design Proof of Concept, Proceedings of the ServDes. 2018 Conference, 18-20 June, Milano, Italy* (No. 150, pp. 1212-1228). Linköping University Electronic Press.

Patrício, R., Moreira, A. C., & Zurlo, F. (2018). Gamification approaches to the early stage of innovation. *Creativity and Innovation Management*, *27*(4), 499–511. doi:10.1111/caim.12284

Patrício, R., Moreira, A. C., & Zurlo, F. (2021). Enhancing design thinking approaches to innovation through gamification. *European Journal of Innovation Management*, *24*(5), 1569–1594. doi:10.1108/EJIM-06-2020-0239

Patrício, R., Moreira, A., Zurlo, F., & Melazzini, M. (2020). Co-creation of new solutions through gamification: A collaborative innovation practice. *Creativity and Innovation Management*, *29*(1), 146–160. doi:10.1111/caim.12356

Patti, I. (2018). *Serious Game Design: storia e teorie sull'esperienza ludica applicata* [Serious Game Design: History and Theories on the Applied Play Experience]. Franco Angeli.

Pazzi, L., & Pellicciari, M. (2017). From the Internet of Things to Cyber-Physical Systems: The Holonic Perspective. *Procedia Manufacturing*, *11*, 989–995. doi:10.1016/j.promfg.2017.07.204

Pea, R. D. (2004). The social and technological dimensions of scaffolding and related theoretical concepts for learning, education, and human activity. *Journal of the Learning Sciences*, *13*(3), 423–451. doi:10.120715327809jls1303_6

Pedreira, O., García, F., Brisaboa, F., & Piantinni, M. (2015). Gamification in software engineering –a systematic mapping. *Information ans Software Technology, 57*, 157–168.

Peffers, K., Rothenberger, M., Tuunanen, T., & Vaezi, R. (2012, May). Design science research evaluation. In *International Conference on Design Science Research in Information Systems* (pp. 398-410). Springer.

Peham, M., Breitfuss, G., & Michalczuk, R. (2014). The "ecoGator" app: gamification for enhanced energy efficiency in Europe. *Proceedings of the Second International Conference on Technological Ecosystems for Enhancing Multiculturality - TEEM '14*, 179–183. 10.1145/2669711.2669897

Pekrun, R. (2016). Academic Emotions. In K. Wentzl & D. B. Miele (Eds.), *Handbook of Motivation at School* (pp. 120–144). Routledge.

Pekrun, R., & Stephens, E. J. (2012). Academic emotions. In APA educational psychology handbook: Vol. 2. *Individual differences and cultural and contextual factors* (pp. 3–31). American Psychological Association.

Pellas, N., & Mystakidis, S. (2020). A systematic review of research about game-based learning in virtual worlds. *Journal of Universal Computer Science*, *26*(8), 1017–1042. doi:10.3897/jucs.2020.054

Pellas, N., Mystakidis, S., & Christopoulos, A. (2021). A systematic literature review on the user experience design for game-based interventions via 3D virtual worlds in K-12 education. *Multimodal Technologies and Interaction*, *5*(6), 28. doi:10.3390/mti5060028

Peng, L. H., & Bai, M. H. (2021). How Gameful Experience Affects Public Knowledge, Attitudes, and Practices Regarding COVID-19 Among the Taiwanese Public: Cross-sectional Study. *JMIR Serious Games*, *9*(2), e26216. doi:10.2196/26216 PMID:33737262

Pereira, I. M., Amorim, V. J., Cota, M. A., & Gonçalves, G. C. (2016). Gamification use in agile project management: an experience report. In *Brazilian workshop on agile methods* (pp. 28-38). Springer.

Pessoa, L. (2013). *The Cognitive-Emotional Brain. from Interactions to Integration*. MIT Press. doi:10.7551/mitpress/9780262019569.001.0001

Petruzzi, V. (2015). *Il potere della Gamification* [The Power of Gamification]. Franco Angeli.

Pfeffers, K., Tuunanen, T., Gengler, C. E., Rossi, M., Hui, W., Virtanen, V., & Bragge, J. (2006). The design science research process: A model for producing and presenting information systems research. In *Proceedings of the First International Conference on Design Science Research in Information Systems and Technology (DESRIST 2006), Claremont, CA, USA* (pp. 83-106). Academic Press.

Piaget, J. (1952). *The origins of intelligence*. International Universities Press. doi:10.1037/11494-000

Pickard, T. (2015). *5 Statistics That Prove Gamification is the Future of the Workplace*. Retrieved February 27, 2016, from https://www.business.com/management/5-statistics-that-prove-gamification-is-the-future-of-the-workplace/

Piligrimiene, Z., Dovaliene, A., & Virvilaite, R. (2015). Consumer engagement in value co-creation: What kind of value it creates for company? *The Engineering Economist*, *26*(4), 452–460. doi:10.5755/j01.ee.26.4.12502

Pine, J., & Gilmore, J. (1999). The Experience Economy. Harvard Business School Press.

Plass, J. L., Homer, B. D., & Kinzer, C. K. (2015). Foundations of game-based learning. *Educational Psychologist*, *50*(4), 258–283. doi:10.1080/00461520.2015.1122533

Plutchik, R. (2001). The nature of emotions: Human emotions have deep evolutionary roots, a fact that may explain their complexity and provide tools for clinical practice. *American Scientist*, *89*(4), 344–350. doi:10.1511/2001.4.344

Pogrebtsova, E., Tondello, G.F., Premsukh, H., & Nacke, L.E. (2017). Using Technology to Boost Employee Wellbeing? How Gamification Can Help or Hinder Results. *PGW@CHI PLAY*.

Porsse, A. A., Souza, K. D., Carvalho, T. S., & Vale, V. A. (2020). Impactos econômicos da COVID-19 no Brasil [Economic Impacts of COVID-19 in Brazil] *Nota Técnica NEDUR-UFPR*, *1*, 44.

Portnoy, C. B., Scott-Sheldon, L. A. J., Johnson, B. T., & Carey, M. P. (2008). Computer-delivered interventions for health promotion and behavioral risk reduction: A meta-analysis of 75 randomized controlled trials, 1988-2007. *Preventive Medicine*, *47*(1), 3–16. doi:10.1016/j.ypmed.2008.02.014 PMID:18403003

Pré. (2017). *Simapro LCA software 8.0*. http://www.pre-sustainability.com/simapro

Pré. (2018). *SimaPro Database Manual. Methods library*. https://www.pre-sustainability.com/download/DatabaseManualMethods.pdf

Prensky, M. (2003). Digital game-based learning. *Computers in Entertainment*, *1*(1), 21–21. doi:10.1145/950566.950596

Prins, P. J., Brink, E. T., Dovis, S., Ponsioen, A., Geurts, H. M., De Vries, M., & Van Der Oord, S. (2013). "Braingame Brian": Toward an executive function training program with game elements for children with ADHD and cognitive control problems. *GAMES FOR HEALTH: Research, Development, and Clinical Applications*, *2*(1), 44–49. doi:10.1089/g4h.2013.0004 PMID:26196554

Prochaska, J. O., & Velicer, W. F. (1997). The transtheoretical model of health behavior change. *American Journal of Health Promotion*, *12*(1), 38–48. doi:10.4278/0890-1171-12.1.38 PMID:10170434

Project Management Institute. (2017). *A guide to the Project Management Body of Knowledge (PMBOK guide)* (6th ed.). Project Management Institute.

Propp, V. I. (1976). *Folklore and reality: Selected articles*. Nauka.

Przegalinska, A. (2015). Gamification: Playing with Neuroscience. In Gamification Crital Approaches (pp. 40–55). University of Warsaw, Faculty of Artes Liberales.

Psaltis, A., Kaza, K., Stefanidis, K., Thermos, S., Apostolakis, K. C., Dimitropoulos, K., & Daras, P. (2016, October). Multimodal affective state recognition in serious games applications. In *2016 IEEE International Conference on Imaging Systems and Techniques (IST)* (pp. 435-439). IEEE. 10.1109/IST.2016.7738265

Pugh, B., & Hovemeyer, D. (n.d.). *Spotbugs*. Retrieved February 15, 2021, from https://spotbugs.github.io/

Puntambekar, S., & Hübscher, R. (2005). Tools for scaffolding students in a complex learning environment: What have we gained and what have we missed? *Educational Psychologist, 40*(1), 1–12. doi:10.120715326985ep4001_1

Purwandari, B., Sutoyo, M. A. H., Mishbah, M., & Dzulfikar, M. F. (2019, October). Gamification in e-Govemment: A Systematic Literature Review. In *2019 Fourth International Conference on Informatics and Computing (ICIC)* (pp. 1-5). IEEE. 10.1109/ICIC47613.2019.8985769

PwC. (n.d.). *Game of Threats*. Retrieved from https://www.pwc.ru/en/publications/game-of-threats.html

Qamar, A., Rahman, M. A., & Basalamah, S. (2014). Adding inverse kinematics for providing live feedback in a serious game-based rehabilitation system. In *Proceedings of the 5th International Conference: Intelligent Systems, Modelling and Simulation (ISMS)* (pp. 215–220). IEEE.

Qian, M., & Clark, K. R. (2016). Game-based learning and 21st century skills: A review of recdent research. *Computers in Human Behavior, 63*, 50–58. doi:10.1016/j.chb.2016.05.023

Quan, H., Li, S., & Hu, J. (2018). Product innovation design based on deep learning and Kansei engineering. *Applied Sciences (Switzerland), 8*(12), 1–17. doi:10.3390/app8122397

Radhakrishnan, K., Baranowski, T., O'Hair, M., Fournier, C. A., Spranger, C. B., & Kim, M. T. (2020a). Personalizing sensor-controlled digital gaming to self-management needs of older adults with heart failure: A qualitative study. *Games for Health Journal, 9*(4), 304–310. doi:10.1089/g4h.2019.0222 PMID:32155355

Radhakrishnan, K., Julien, C., Baranowski, T., O'Hair, M., Lee, G., De Main, A. S., ... Kim, M. (2021). Sensor-controlled digital game and heart failure self-management behaviors: A feasibility randomized controlled trial study. *JMIR Serious Games*, 1–37. doi:10.2196/29044 PMID:34747701

Radhakrishnan, K., Julien, C., O'Hair, M., Baranowski, T., Lee, G., Allen, C., Sagna, A., Thomaz, E., & Kim, M. (2020b). Usability testing of a sensor-controlled digital game to engage older adults with heart failure in physical activity and weight monitoring. *Applied Clinical Informatics, 11*(05), 873–881. doi:10.1055-0040-1721399 PMID:33378780

Radoff, J. (2011). *Energize your business with social media games*. Academic Press.

Raftopoulos, M. (2014). Towards gamification transparency: A conceptual framework for the development of responsible gamified enterprise systems. *Journal of Gaming & Virtual Worlds, 6*(2), 159–178. doi:10.1386/jgvw.6.2.159_1

Rapp, A., Hopfgartner, F., Hamari, J., Linehan, C., & Cena, F. (2019). *Strengthening gamification studies: Current trends and future opportunities of gamification research*. Academic Press.

Rayome, A. D. (2019, March 19). The 3 Least Secure Programming Languages. *TechRepulic*.

Rednic, E., Toma, A., & Apostu, A. (2013). Organize distributed work environments in a game-like fashion. In Z. Chen & E. Lopez-Neri (Eds.), *Recent Advances in Knowledge Engineering and Systems Science* (pp. 213–218). WSEAS Press.

Reeves, B., Cummings, J. J., Scarborough, J. K., & Yeykelis, L. (2015). Increasing energy efficiency with entertainment media: An experimental and field test of the influence of a social game on performance of energy behaviors. *Environment and Behavior, 47*(1), 102–115. doi:10.1177/0013916513506442

Reeves, B., & Read, J. L. (2009). *Total engagement: How games and virtual worlds are changing the way people work and businesses compete.* Harvard Business Press.

Reichle, R., Wagner, M., Khan, M. U., Geihs, K., Lorenzo, J., Valla, M., Fra, C., Paspallis, N., & Papadopoulos, G. A. (2008). A comprehensive context modeling framework for pervasive computing systems. In *Distributed Applications and Interoperable Systems* (pp. 281–295). Springer. doi:10.1007/978-3-540-68642-2_23

Reiners, T., & Wood, L. C. (2015). *Gamification in Education and Business.* Springer International Publishing. doi:10.1007/978-3-319-10208-5

Reis, A. C. B., Júnior, E. S., Gewehr, B. B., & Torres, M. H. (2020). Prospects for using gamification in industry 4.0. *Production, 30.* Advance online publication. doi:10.1590/0103-6513.20190094

Renshaw, C., & Liew, C. L. (2021). *Descriptive standards and collection management software for documentary heritage management: Attitudes and experiences of information professionals.* Global Knowledge, Memory and Communication.

Ricciardi, F., & De Paolis, L. T. (2014). A comprehensive review of serious games in health professions. *International Journal of Computer Games Technology.*

Ricci, F., Rokach, L., Shapira, B., & Kantor, P. B. (2011). *Recommender Systems Handbook.* Springer. doi:10.1007/978-0-387-85820-3

Rieckmann, M. (2012). Future-oriented higher education: Which key competencies should be fostered through university teaching and learning? *Futures, 44*(2), 127–135. doi:10.1016/j.futures.2011.09.005

Rieckmann, M. (2017). *Education for sustainable development goals: Learning objectives.* UNESCO Publishing.

Riedel, J. C., Feng, Y., & Azadegan, A. (2013). Serious Games Adoption in Organizations–An Exploratory Analysis. In *European Conference on Technology Enhanced Learning* (pp. 508-513). Springer.

Riedel, S. (2006). Bedarfe erheben oder Bedarfe wecken? Das Tiefeninterview der qualitativen Marktforschung – diskursanalytisch betrachtet. In M. Boenigk, D. Krieger, A. Belliger, & C. Hug (Eds.), *Innovative Wirtschaftskommunikation* (pp. 115–128). DUV. doi:10.1007/978-3-8350-9663-9_9

Rietz, T., & Maedche, A. (2019). LadderBot: A Requirements Self-Elicitation System. *27th International Requirements Engineering Conference (RE)*, 357-362.

Rios Insua, D., Couce-Vieira, A., Rubio, J. A., Pieters, W., Labunets, K., & Rasines, G., D. (. (2021). An adversarial risk analysis framework for cybersecurity. *Risk Analysis, 41*(1), 16–36. doi:10.1111/risa.13331 PMID:31183890

Rios Insua, D., Ríos, J., & Banks, D. (2009). Adversarial risk analysis. *Journal of the American Statistical Association, 104*(486), 841–854. doi:10.1198/jasa.2009.0155

Rix, K., Zeihlund, T., & Long, T. (2015) Double the sharing- the effects of gamification at one of the world's largest employers. *Strategic industrial applications of games and gamification: proceedings of the International Gamification for Business Conference 2015.*

Robert Koch-Institute. (2021). *Kennzahlen zur Corona-Warn-App* [Key Figures for the Corona-Warn-App]. https://www.rki.de/DE/Content/InfAZ/N/Neuartiges_Coronavirus/WarnApp/Archiv_Kennzahlen/Kennzahlen_21052021.pdf?__blob=publicationFile

Robinson, C. (n.d.). *Comparison of 15 leading gamification software systems*. Retrieved from Finances: https://financesonline.com/top-15-gamification-software-systems

Robson, K., Plangger, K., Kietzmann, J., McCarthy, I., & Pitt, L. (2014). Understanding the Gamification of Consumer Experiences. In A. Press (Ed.), Association for Consumer Research ACR North American Advances (Vol. 42, pp. 352–357). Academic Press.

Robson, K., Plangger, K., Kietzmann, J. H., McCarthy, I., & Pitt, L. (2015). Is it all a game? Understanding the principles of gamification. *Business Horizons*, *58*(4), 411–420. doi:10.1016/j.bushor.2015.03.006

Ro, M., Brauer, M., Kuntz, K., Shukla, R., & Bensch, I. (2017). Making Cool Choices for sustainability: Testing the effectiveness of a game-based approach to promoting pro-environmental behaviors. *Journal of Environmental Psychology*, *53*, 20–30.

Romero, M., Usart, M., & Ott, M. (2015). Can serious games contribute to developing and sustaining 21st century skills? *Games and Culture*, *10*(2), 148–177. doi:10.1177/1555412014548919

Romero-Rodríguez, L. M., Ramírez-Montoya, M. S., & Gonzalez, J. R. V. (2019). Gamification in MOOCs: Engagement application test in energy sustainability courses. *IEEE Access: Practical Innovations, Open Solutions*, *7*, 32093–32101. doi:10.1109/ACCESS.2019.2903230

Ronchi, S., Arcidiacono, A., & Pogliani, L. (2021). The New Urban Plan of Rescaldina Municipality. An Experience for Improving Ecosystem Services Provision. In A. Arcidiacono & S. Ronchi (Eds.), *Ecosystem Services and Green Infrastructure* (pp. 141–152). Springer. doi:10.1007/978-3-030-54345-7_11

Rosa, B. (2021). *Guia Completo de Customer Success (Sucesso do Cliente): Conceitos, Estratégias e Ferramentas: entenda a jornada do cliente no seu negócio*. Academic Press.

Rosso, B. D., Dekas, K. H., & Wrzesniewski, A. (2010). On the meaning of work: A theoretical integration and review. *Research in Organizational Behavior*, *30*, 91–127. doi:10.1016/j.riob.2010.09.001

Rozman, T., Maribor, S. S., Fistis, G., Luminosu, C., & Zwolinski, P. (2015). *Leadership in sustainability - Support your business towards sustainability - For educational purposes only*. LeadSUS Project Group. doi:10.13140/RG.2.2.20342.40001/1

Rubini, P. (2019). *A Fórmula da Satisfação do Cliente: como conquistar e manter clientes rentáveis*. Editora Autografia Edição e Comunicação Ltda.

Rubino, I., Barberis, C., Xhembulla, J., & Malnati, G. (2015). Integrating a location-based mobile game in the museum visit: Evaluating visitors' behaviour and learning. *Journal on Computing and Cultural Heritage*, *8*(3), 1–18. doi:10.1145/2724723

Rumelhart, D. E., & Norman, D. A. (1976). *Accretion, tuning and restructuring: Three modes of learning*. Academic Press.

Rumeser, D., & Emsley, M. (2019). Can serious games improve project management decision making under complexity? *Project Management Journal*, *50*(1), 23–39.

Ryan, R. M., & Deci, E. L. (2000). Self-determination theory and the facilitation of intrinsic motivation, social development, and well-being. *The American Psychologist*, *55*(1), 68–78. doi:10.1037/0003-066X.55.1.68 PMID:11392867

Ryan, R. M., Rigby, C. S., & Przybylski, A. (2006). The motivational pull of video games: A self-determination theory approach. *Motivation and Emotion, 30*(4), 347–363. doi:10.100711031-006-9051-8

Sadik, S., Ahmed, M., Sikos, L. F., & Islam, A. (2020). Toward a Sustainable Cybersecurity Ecosystem. *Computers, 9*(3), 74. doi:10.3390/computers9030074

Saeed, K., & Nagashima, T. (2012). *Biometrics and Kansei Engineering*. Springer-Verlag. doi:10.1007/978-1-4614-5608-7

Sahnoun, M., Xu, Y., Belgacem, B., Imen, B., David, B., & Louis, A. (2019). Fractal modeling of Cyber physical production system using multi-agent systems. *Proceedings - 2019 3rd International Conference on Applied Automation and Industrial Diagnostics, ICAAID 2019*. 10.1109/ICAAID.2019.8934976

Sailer, M., Hense, J. U., Mayr, S. K., & Mandl, H. (2017). How gamification motivates: An experimental study of the effects of specific game design elements on psychological need satisfaction. *Computers in Human Behavior, 69*, 371–380. doi:10.1016/j.chb.2016.12.033

Sakurazawa, S., Yoshida, N., & Munekata, N. (2004, September). Entertainment feature of a game using skin conductance response. In *Proceedings of the 2004 ACM SIGCHI international conference on advances in computer entertainment technology* (pp. 181-186). 10.1145/1067343.1067365

Salen, K. (2017). Designing a place called school: A case study of the public school quest to learn. *She Ji: The Journal of Design, Economics, and Innovation, 3*(1), 51–64. doi:10.1016/j.sheji.2017.08.002

Sanders, E. B. N. (2002). From user-centered to participatory design approaches. In *Design and the social sciences* (pp. 18–25). CRC Press. doi:10.1201/9780203301302.ch1

Sandoval-Almazan, R., & Valle-Cruz, D. (2017). Open innovation, living labs and public officials: The case of Mapaton in Mexico. *In Proceedings of the 10th International Conference on Theory and Practice of Electronic Governance* (pp. 260-265). New York, NY: ACM. 10.1145/3047273.3047308

Sanguinet, E. R., Alvim, A. M., Atienza, M., & Fochezatto, A. (2021). The subnational supply chain and the COVID-19 pandemic: Short-term impacts on the Brazilian regional economy. *Regional Science Policy & Practice, 13*(S1), 158–186. doi:10.1111/rsp3.12442

Sardi, L., Idri, A., & Fernández-Alemán, J. L. (2017). A systematic review of gamification in e-Health. *Journal of Biomedical Informatics, 71*, 31–48. doi:10.1016/j.jbi.2017.05.011 PMID:28536062

Sarkum, S. (2018). *A Strategy Engagement in Marketing: A Reviews of the Literature*. 10.31227/ doi:osf.io/kw9uz

Savery, J. R., & Duffy, T. M. (1995). Problem-based learning: An instructional model and its constructivist framework. *Educational Technology, 35*(5), 31–35.

Savin-Baden, M. (2014). Using problem-based learning: New constellations for the 21st century. *Journal on Excellence in College Teaching, 25*(3 & 4).

SC. (n.d.). *Gamification: A winning strategy for cybersecurity training*. Retrieved from Media: https://www.scmagazine.com/home/opinion/executive-insight/gamification-a-winning-strategy-for-cybersecurity-training

Scariot, C. A., Heemann, A., & Padovani, S. (2012). Understanding the collaborative-participatory design. *Work (Reading, Mass.), 41*(Supplement 1), 2701–2705. doi:10.3233/WOR-2012-0656-2701 PMID:22317129

Schachter, S., & Singer, J. (1962). Cognitive, social, and physiological determinants of emotional state. *Psychological Review, 69*(5), 379–399. doi:10.1037/h0046234 PMID:14497895

Schacter, D., Gilbert, D., Wegner, D., & Hood, B. M. (2011). *Psychology* (European Edition). Macmillan International Higher Education.

Schaufeli, W., & Bakker, A. (2003). *UWES Utrecht Work Engagement Scale, Preliminary Manual* [Version 1, November 2003]. Utrecht University: Occupational Health Psychology Unit.

Scheier, L. M. (2020). Adolescent drug misuse prevention: Challenges in school-based programming. In S. Y. Sussman (Ed.), *Cambridge handbook of substance and behavioral addictions* (pp. 1235–1324). Cambridge University Press. doi:10.1017/9781108632591.021

Scheiner, C., Haas, P., Bretschneider, U., Blohm, I., & Leimeister, J. M. (2017). Obstacles and challenges in the use of gamification for virtual idea communities. In *Gamification* (pp. 65–76). Springer. doi:10.1007/978-3-319-45557-0_5

Schell, J. (2008). *The Art of Game Design: A book of lenses.* CRC Press. https://www.amazon.es/Art-Game-Design-book-lenses/dp/0123694965

Schell, J. (2008). *The Art of Game Design: A book of lenses.* CRC press. doi:10.1201/9780080919171

Schelly, C., Cross, J. E., Franzen, W. S., Hall, P., & Reeve, S. (2011). Reducing energy consumption and creating a conservation culture in organizations: A case study of one public school district. *Environment and Behavior, 43*(3), 316–343. doi:10.1177/0013916510371754

Scherer, K. R. (2000). Psychological models of emotion. *The Neuropsychology of Emotion, 137*(3), 137-162.

Scherer, K. R. (2005). What are emotions? And how can they be measured? *Social Sciences Information. Information Sur les Sciences Sociales, 44*(4), 695–729. doi:10.1177/0539018405058216

Schneier, B. (n.d.). *Software Developers and Security.* Retrieved July 25, 2019, from https://www.schneier.com/blog/archives/2019/07/software_devel o.html

Scholefield, S., & Shepherd, L. A. (2019). Gamification Techniques for Raising Cyber Security Awareness. *HCII 2019: HCI for Cybersecurity, Privacy and Trust, 11594*, 191–203. doi:10.1007/978-3-030-22351-9_13

Schreiber, P. (2012). Kinderuniversitäten in der Welt – ein Vergleich. In B. Dernbach, C. Kleinert, & H. Münder (Eds.), *Handbuch Wissenschaftskommunikation* (pp. 107–115). Springer. doi:10.1007/978-3-531-18927-7_14

Schuller, B. W., Dunwell, I., Weninger, F., & Paletta, L. (2013). Serious gaming for behavior change: The state of play. *IEEE Pervasive Computing, 12*(3), 48–55.

Schultze, U. (2012). Performing embodied identity in virtual worlds. *European Journal of Information Systems, 23*(1), 84–95. doi:10.1057/ejis.2012.52

Schultz, R. B., & DeMers, M. N. (2020). Transitioning from emergency remote learning to deep online learning experiences in geography education. *The Journal of Geography, 119*(5), 142–146. doi:10.1080/00221341.2020.1813791

Schütte, S., Eklund, J., Axelsson, J., & Nagamachi, M. (2004). Concepts, methods and tools in Kansei Engineering. *Theoretical Issues in Ergonomics Science, 5*(3), 214–231. doi:10.1080/1463922021000049980

Schutz, P. A., & Lanehart, S. L. (2002). Introduction: Emotions in education. *Educational Psychologist, 37*(2), 67–68.

Schwaber, K., & Sutherland, J. (2011). The scrum guide. *Scrum Alliance, 21*(19), 1.

Schwarz, N. (2011). Feelings-as-information theory. In P. A. M. Van Lange, A. W. Kruglanski, & E. T. Higgins (Eds.), *Handbook of theories of social psychology* (pp. 289–308). Sage Publications Ltd.

Schwebel, D. C., & McClure, L. A. (2010). Using virtual reality to train children in safe street-crossing skills. *Injury Prevention, 16*(1), e1–e1. doi:10.1136/ip.2009.025288 PMID:20179024

Schwebel, D. C., & McClure, L. A. (2014). Training children in pedestrian safety: Distinguishing gains in knowledge from gains in safe behavior. *The Journal of Primary Prevention, 35*(3), 151–162. doi:10.100710935-014-0341-8 PMID:24573688

Schwebel, D. C., McClure, L. A., & Porter, B. E. (2017). Experiential exposure to texting and walking in virtual reality: A randomized trial to reduce distracted pedestrian behavior. *Accident; Analysis and Prevention, 102*, 116–122. doi:10.1016/j.aap.2017.02.026 PMID:28279843

Schwebel, D. C., McClure, L. A., & Severson, J. (2014). Usability and feasibility of an internet-based virtual pedestrian environment to teach children to cross streets safely. *Virtual Reality (Waltham Cross), 18*(1), 5–11. doi:10.100710055-013-0238-5 PMID:24678263

Schwebel, D. C., Severson, J., He, Y., & McClure, L. A. (2017). Virtual reality by mobile smartphone: Improving child pedestrian safety. *Injury Prevention, 23*(5), 357–357. doi:10.1136/injuryprev-2016-042168 PMID:27585563

Schwebel, D. C., Shen, J., & McClure, L. A. (2016). How do children learn to cross the street? The process of pedestrian safety training. *Traffic Injury Prevention, 17*(6), 573–579. doi:10.1080/15389588.2015.1125478 PMID:26760077

Schweitzer, F., & Tidd, J. (2018). *Innovation heroes: Understanding customers as a valuable innovation resource* (Vol. 31). World Scientific. doi:10.1142/q0158

Seaborn, K., & Fels, D. I. (2015). *Gamification in theory and action: A survery Int. J. Human-Comput. Stud.*, 9. doi:10.1016/j.ijhcs.2014.09.006

SEI-CERT. (n.d.). *Cert Secure Coding.* Retrieved January 8, 2021, from https://wiki.sei.cmu.edu/confluence/display/seccode

Sein, M., Henfridsson, O., Purao, S., Rossi, M., & Lindgren, R. (2011). Action Design Research. *Management Information Systems Quarterly, 35*(1), 37–56. doi:10.2307/23043488

Semchuk, S. (2014). Moral and spiritual development of the individual in the context of the influence of computer technology. *Scientific Bulletin of Melitopol State Pedagogical University named after Bohdan Khmelnytsky. Series. Pedagogy, 1*(12), 221–225.

Setiono, D., Saputra, D., Putra, K., Moniaga, J. V., & Chowanda, A. (2021). Enhancing Player Experience in Game With Affective Computing. *Procedia Computer Science, 179*, 781–788. doi:10.1016/j.procs.2021.01.066

Shackelford, S. J., Fort, T. L., & Charoen, D. (2016). Sustainable cybersecurity: Applying lessons from the green movement to managing Cyber Attacks. *U. Ill. L. Rev.*

Shackleton-Jones, N. (2019). *How People Learn: Designing Education and Training that Works to Improve Performance.* Kogan Page Publishers.

Shahri, A., Hosseini, M., Phalp, K., Taylor, J., & Ali, R. (2014). Towards a code of ethics for gamification at enterprise. In IFIP working conference on the practice of enterprise modeling (pp. 235-245). Springer. doi:10.1007/978-3-662-45501-2_17

Sharma, A. (2020, January 26). *Back To Basics: How Gamification Can Improve Employee Engagement In 2020.* eLearning Industry. https://elearningindustry.com/how-gamification-improve-employee-engagement-2020

Sheldon, L. (2011). *The Multiplayer Classroom: Designing Coursework as a Game.* Cengage Learning PTR.

Sheldon, L., & Seelow, D. (2017). The multiplayer classroom: The designer and the collaboration. *International Journal on Innovations in Online Education, 1*(4). Advance online publication. doi:10.1615/IntJInnovOnlineEdu.2017024959

Shen, E. Y.-T., Lieberman, H., & Davenport, G. (2009). What's next? Emergent storytelling from video collections. *Proceedings of the SIGCHI Conference on Human Factors in Computing Systems*, 809–818. 10.1145/1518701.1518825

Shiralkar, S. W. (2016). *IT through experiential learning: Learn, deploy and adopt IT through gamification.* Apress. doi:10.1007/978-1-4842-2421-2

Shirinian, A. (2010). *The uneasy merging of narrative and gameplay.* Academic Press.

Shiva, S., Roy, S., & Dasgupta, D. (2010). Game theory for cyber security. *Proceedings of the Sixth Annual Workshop on Cyber Security and Information Intelligence Research.*

Shpakova, A., Dörfler, V., & MacBryde, J. (2017). *Changing the game: a case for gamifying knowledge management. World Journal of Science, Technology and Sustainable Development.*

Shu, L., Xie, J., Yang, M., Li, Z., Li, Z., Liao, D., Xu, X., & Yang, X. (2018). A review of emotion recognition using physiological signals. *Sensors (Basel)*, *18*(7), 2074. doi:10.339018072074 PMID:29958457

Sicart, M. (2008). Defining Game Mechanics. *The International Journal of Computer Game Research*, *8*(2).

Sicart, M. (2009). *Ethics of computer games.* MIT Press. doi:10.7551/mitpress/9780262012652.001.0001

Sicart, M. (2015). Playing the good life: Gamification and ethics. In S. Waltz & S. Deterding (Eds.), *The gameful world: Approaches, issues, applications* (pp. 225–244). MIT Press.

Siegel, D. S., Waldman, D. A., Atwater, L. E., & Link, A. N. (2003). Commercial knowledge transfers from universities to firms: Improving the effectiveness of university–industry collaboration. *The Journal of High Technology Management Research*, *14*(1), 111–133. doi:10.1016/S1047-8310(03)00007-5

Silensec. (2020). Retrieved from https://www.silensec.com

Silva, R. J. R. D., Rodrigues, R. G., & Leal, C. T. P. (2019). Gamification in management education: A systematic literature review. *BAR - Brazilian Administration Review*, *16*(2), e180103. doi:10.1590/1807-7692bar2019180103

Simões, A., & Queirós, R. (2020). On the nature of programming exercises. *ICPEC - First International Computer Programming Education Conference*, 251-259.

Simon, H. A. (1996). *The sciences of the artificial.* MIT Press.

Sipiyaruk, K., Gallagher, J. E., Hatzipanagos, S., & Reynolds, P. A. (2018). A rapid review of serious games: From healthcare education to dental education. *European Journal of Dental Education*, *22*(4), 243–257.

Sipiyaruk, K., Hatzipanagos, S., Reynolds, P. A., & Gallagher, J. E. (2021). Serious games and the COVID-19 pandemic in dental education: An integrative review of the literature. *Computers*, *10*(4), 42. doi:10.3390/computers10040042

Sitas, E. (2017). Gamification as tool to raise sociocultural awareness. *International Conference on Open & Distance Education*, *9*, 275–281.

Sitzmann, T. (2011). A meta-analytic examination of the instructional effectiveness of computer-based simulation games. *Personnel Psychology*, *64*(2), 489–528. doi:10.1111/j.1744-6570.2011.01190.x

Sloman, A. (1999). Review of affective computing. *AI Magazine*, *20*(1), 127–127.

Smith, L. W. (2000). Stakeholder analysis: a pivotal practice of successful projects. *Project Management Institute Annual Seminars & Symposium.* https://www.pmi.org/learning/library/stakeholder-analysis-pivotal-practice-projects-8905

Software Engineering Institute. (n.d.). *SEI CERT Oracle Coding Standard for Java - FIO04-J. Release resources when they are no longer needed.* Retrieved January 22, 2021, from https://wiki.sei.cmu.edu/confluence/display/java/FIO04-J. +Release+resources+when+they+are+no+longer+needed

Soler-Dominguez, J. L., & Gonzalez, C. (2021). Using EEG and Gamified Neurofeedback Environments to Improve eSports Performance: Project Neuroprotrainer. *Proceedings of the 16th International Joint Conference on Computer Vision, Imaging and Computer Graphics Theory and Applications (VISIGRAPP 2021).* 10.5220/0010314502780283

SonarSource. (n.d.). *SonarQube.* Retrieved February 17, 2021, from https://www.sonarqube.org/

Souza, J. P., Zavan, A. R., & Flôr, D. E. (2016). Scrum hero: Gamifying the scrum framework. In *Brazilian Workshop on Agile Methods* (pp. 131-135). Springer.

Sovacool, B. K. (2014). What are we doing here? Analyzing fifteen years of energy scholarship and proposing a social science research agenda. *Energy Research & Social Science, 1,* 1–29. doi:10.1016/j.erss.2014.02.003

Sponge. (2019). *6 reasons why it's time to overhaul cybersecurity training.* Retrieved from https://wearesponge.com/insights/2019/10/6-reasons-why-its-time-to-overhaul-cybersecurity-training

Springer Nature Switzerland, A. G. (2021), *Pahl/Beitz Konstruktionslehre* [Pahl/Beitz Design Theory]. https://www.springer.com/de/book/9783662573020

Sproutel. (2021). *Jerry the Bear.* Retrieved from www.jerrythebear.com/

Squire, K., & Jenkins, H. (2003). Harnessing the power of games in education. *Vision (Basel), 3,* 7–33.

Staddon, S. C., Cycil, C., Goulden, M., Leygue, C., & Spence, A. (2016). Intervening to change behaviour and save energy in the workplace: A systematic review of available evidence. *Energy Research & Social Science, 17,* 30–51. doi:10.1016/j.erss.2016.03.027

Stanitsas, M., Kirytopoulos, K., & Vareilles, E. (2019). Facilitating sustainability transition through serious games: A systematic literature review. *Journal of Cleaner Production, 208,* 924–936.

State of the Global Workplace. (2017). *Gallup's state of the Global Workplace.* https://fundacionprolongar.org/wp-content/uploads/2019/07/State-of-the-Global-Workplace_Gallup-Report.pdf

Staton, R. (2015). *A Brief History of Video Games: From Atari to Xbox One.* Little, Brown Book Group Limited.

Stettina, C. J., Offerman, T., De Mooij, B., & Sidhu, I. (2018). Gaming for agility: using serious games to enable agile project & portfolio management capabilities in practice. In *2018 IEEE International Conference on Engineering, Technology and Innovation (ICE/ITMC)* (pp. 1-9). IEEE.

Stock, T., Obenaus, M., Kunz, S., & Kohl, H. (2018). Industry 4.0 as Enabler for a Sustainable Development: A Qualitative Assessment of its Ecological and Social Potential. *Process Safety and Environmental Protection, 118,* 254–267. doi:10.1016/j.psep.2018.06.026

Stofella, A., & Fadel, L. M. (2022). Fidelity and Play Model: Balancing Seriousness. In O. Bernardes & V. Amorim (Eds.), *Handbook of Research on Promoting Economic and Social Development Through Serious Games* (pp. 1–20). IGI Global. doi:10.4018/978-1-7998-9732-3.ch001

Stokrocki, M., & Chen, J. (2012). Taiwanese undergraduates' digital story quests for art treasures in Second Life. *Journal of Cultural Research in Art Education, 30*(13), 32–59.

Strenziok, M., Parasuraman, R., Clarke, E., Cisler, D. S., Thompson, J. C., & Greenwood, P. M. (2014). Neurocognitive enhancement in older adults: Comparison of three cognitive training tasks to test a hypothesis of training transfer in brain connectivity. *NeuroImage*, *85*, 1027–1039. doi:10.1016/j.neuroimage.2013.07.069 PMID:23933474

Su, C. H., & Cheng, C. H. (2015). A mobile gamification learning system for improving the learning motivation and achievements. *Journal of Computer Assisted Learning*, *31*(3), 268–286.

Sukale, R., & Pfaff, M. S. (2014). QuoDocs: Improving developer engagement in software documentation through gamification. In CHI'14 Extended Abstracts on Human Factors in Computing Systems (pp. 1531-1536). ACM.

Sullivan, P. H. (1998). *Profiting from Intellectual Capital: Extracting Value from Innovation*. John Wiley & Sons.

Sun, H., & Zhang, P. (2018). Causal Relationships between Perceived Enjoyment and Perceived Ease of Use: An Alternative Approach. *Journal of the Association for Information Systems*, *7*(9), 618–645. doi:10.17705/1jais.00100

Suppan, L., Abbas, M., Catho, G., Stuby, L., Regard, S., Harbarth, S., Achab, S., & Suppan, M. (2020). Impact of a serious game on the intention to change infection prevention and control practices in nursing homes during the COVID-19 pandemic: Protocol for a web-based randomized controlled trial. *JMIR Research Protocols*, *9*(12), e25595. doi:10.2196/25595 PMID:33296329

Suppan, M., Catho, G., Nunes, T. R., Sauvan, V., Perez, M., Graf, C., ... Suppan, L. (2020). A serious game designed to promote safe behaviors among health care workers during the COVID-19 pandemic: Development of "Escape COVID-19". *JMIR Serious Games*, *8*(4), e24986. doi:10.2196/24986 PMID:33242312

Susi, T., Johannesson, M., & Backlund, P. (2007). *Serious games: An overview*. Academic Press.

Sutherland, J., & Schwaber, K. (2017). *The Scrum Guide™ The Definitive Guide to Scrum: The Rules of the Game November 2017*. Academic Press.

Sutherland, J., & Sutherland, J. J. (2018). Scrum: A arte de fazer o dobro do trabalho na metade do tempo [Scrum: The Art of Doing Twice the Work in Half the Time] (3rd ed.). Rio de Janeiro: LeYa.

Sutton, A., Williams, H., & Allinson, C. (2015). A longitudinal, mixed method evaluation of self-awareness training in the workplace. *European Journal of Training and Development*, *39*(7), 610–627. doi:10.1108/EJTD-04-2015-0031

Sweetman, B. (2018, March 16). Increasing Engagement Using Product Gamification. *Headway.Io*. https://www.headway.io/blog/gamification-is-more-than-achievements

Swiss Centre for Life Cycle Inventories. (2018). *Ecoinvent database v3.4*. https://www.ecoinvent.org/database/

Sylvester, T. (2013). *A guide to engineering experiences. O'Reilly Media.*

Syrjälä, H., Kauppinen-Räisänen, H., Luomala, H. T., Joelsson, T. N., Könnölä, K., & Mäkilä, T. (2020). Gamified package: Consumer insights into multidimensional brand engagement. *Journal of Business Research*, *119*(January), 423–434. doi:10.1016/j.jbusres.2019.11.089

Tanenbaum, T. J., Antle, A. N., & Robinson, J. (2013, April). Three perspectives on behavior change for serious games. In *Proceedings of the SIGCHI Conference on Human Factors in Computing Systems* (pp. 3389-3392). ACM.

Tan, M., & Hew, K. F. (2016). Incorporating meaningful gamification in a blended learning research methods class: Examining student learning, engagement, and affective outcomes. *Australasian Journal of Educational Technology*, *32*(5).

Taylor, C. (2011, June 6). Counties honored for Web 2.0 innovations. *NaCO County Newsletter*.

Technologies, U. (2022). *VR & AR Engine*. https://unity.com

TechSci Research. (2019). *Global Gamification Market*. Available at: https://www.techsciresearch.com/sample-report.aspx?cid=3892

Teles, J. (2018). *O uso do Gamification como ferramenta de aprendizagem no treinamento e desenvolvimento de colaboradores*. Linkedin. https://www.linkedin.com/pulse/o-uso-do-gamification-como-ferramenta-de-aprendizagem-jenifer-teles/

Terno, S. (2011). Why is it important to develop students' critical thinking? *History in the Schools of Ukraine*, (10), 30-34.

Terno, S. (2016). Critical thinking: dynamics and scope. *Works of the Historical Faculty of Zaporizhia National University*, (46), 310-315.

Terzi, S., Bouras, A., Dutta, D., Garetti, M., & Kiritsis, D. (2010). Product lifecycle management - From its history to its new role. *International Journal of Product Lifecycle Management*, 4(4), 360–389. doi:10.1504/IJPLM.2010.036489

The Game Balancing Platform. Beta design, simulate & handoff game systems. (2022). Retrieved from Machinations: https://machinations.io/

Thibault, M., & Hamari, J. (2021). Seven points to reappropriate gamification. In Transforming Society and organizations through Gamification: From the Sustainable Development Goals to Inclusive Workplaces (pp. 11-28). Palgrave Macmillan. doi:10.1007/978-3-030-68207-1_2

Thomas, M. K., Shyjka, A., & Gjomemo, R. (2019). Educational Design Research for the Development of a Collectible Card Game for Cybersecurity Learning. *Journal of Formative Design in Learning*, 3(1), 27–38. doi:10.100741686-019-00027-0

Thompson, M., & Takabi, H. (2016). Effectiveness of Using Card Games to Teach Threat Modeling For Secure Web Application Developments. *Issues in Information Systems*, 17(3), 244–253. doi:10.48009/3_iis_2016_244-253

Thornton, D., & Francia, G. (2014). Gamification of Information Systems and Security Training: Issues and Case Studies. *Information Security Education Journal*, 1, 16–29.

Thorpe, A. S., & Roper, S. (2019). The ethics of gamification in a marketing context. *Journal of Business Ethics*, 155(2), 597–609. doi:10.100710551-017-3501-y

Thuan, N. H., Drechsler, A., & Antunes, P. (2019). Construction of design science research questions. *Communications of the Association for Information Systems*, 44(1), 20.

Thurner-Irmler, J., & Menner, M. (2020). The Development and Testing of a Self-designed Escape Room as a Concept of Knowledge Transfer into Society. In M. Ma, B. Fletcher, S. Göbel, J. Baalsrud Hauge, & T. Marsh (Eds.), *Serious games. JSCG 2020* (pp. 105–116). Lecture Notes in Computer Science. Springer. doi:10.1007/978-3-030-61814-8_9

Tidd, J., & Bessant, J. R. (2005). *Managing innovation: integrating technological, market and organizational change*. John Wiley & Sons.

Tobias, S., Fletcher, J. D., & Wind, A. P. (2014). Game-based learning. In Handbook of research on educational communications and technology (pp. 485-503). New York: Springer Science+Business Media. doi:10.1007/978-1-4614-3185-5_38

Tondello, G. F., Wehbe, R. R., Diamond, L., Busch, M., Marczewski, A., & Nacke, L. E. (2016). The gamification user types Hexad scale. *CHI PLAY 2016 - Proceedings of the 2016 Annual Symposium on Computer-Human Interaction in Play*, 229–243. 10.1145/2967934.2968082

Toth, F. L. (1988). Policy exercises: Objectives and design elements. *Simulation & Games*, 19(3), 235–255. doi:10.1177/0037550088193001

Totterdill, P., Dhondt, S., & Devons, N. (2016). The case for workplace innovation. Brussels: European Workplace Innovation Network (Euwin).

Touboulic, A., & Walker, H. (2016). A relational, transformative, and engaged approach to sustainable supply chain management: The potential of action research. *Human Relations*, *69*(2), 301–343. doi:10.1177/0018726715583364

Tovarnak, D. (2017). *KYPO Cyber Range Design and Use Cases*. Retrieved from CSIRT-MU: https://is.muni.cz/publication/1386573/2017-ICSOFT-kypo-cyber-range-design-presentation.pdf

Trullenque, V. R. (2013). *Game Design & Development (GDD)* [Bachelor's thesis]. Universitat Politècnica de Catalunya.

Tsourma, M., Zikos, S., Albanis, G., Apostolakis, K. C., Lithoxoidou, E. E., Drosou, A., Zarpalas, D., Daras, P., & Tzovaras, D. (2019). Gamification concepts for leveraging knowledge sharing in Industry 4.0. *International Journal of Serious Games*, *6*(2), 75–87. doi:10.17083/ijsg.v6i2.273

Tsunoda, M., & Yumoto, H. (2018). Applying gamification and posing to software development. In *2018 25th Asia-Pacific Software Engineering Conference (APSEC)* (pp. 638-642). IEEE. 10.1109/APSEC.2018.00081

Tsvyatkova, D., & Storni, C. (2019). Designing an educational interactive eBook for newly diagnosed children with type 1 diabetes: Mapping a new design space. *International Journal of Child-Computer Interaction*, *19*, 1–18. doi:10.1016/j.ijcci.2018.10.001

Turkle, S. (2005). *Video games and computer holding power*. Academic Press.

Tye-Murray, N. (2016). *A clEAR Solution to the Changing Climate of Hearing Healthcare*. Retrieved from www.clearworks4ears.com/static/media_relations/Audiology%20practices%20proofs.pdf

Tye-Murray, N. (2021b). *EARS Train the Brain*. Retrieved from www.clearworks4ears.com/

Tye-Murray, N. (2021a). A digital therapeutic and hearing health coach for enhancing first-time hearing aid experiences. *Hearing Review*, *28*(5), 25–26.

Tye-Murray, N., Spehar, B., Sommers, M., Mauzé, E., Barcroft, J., & Grantham, H. (2021). Teaching children with hearing loss to recognize speech: Gains made with computer-based auditory and/or speechreading training. *Ear and Hearing*. Advance online publication. doi:10.1097/AUD.0000000000001091 PMID:34225318

Ullman, D., Phillips, E., Aladia, S., Haas, P., Fowler, H. S., Iqbal, I. S., ... Malle, B. F. (2021). Evaluating psychosocial support provided by an augmented reality device for children with Type 1 diabetes. *Proceedings of the International Symposium on Human Factors and Ergonomics in Health Care*, *10*(1), 126-130. 10.1177/2327857921101117

UNESCO. (2010). *Tomorrow Today*. Tudor Rose.

UNFCCC. (2014). *United Nations Framework Convention on Climate Change: Status of Ratification of the Kyoto Protocol*. Retrieved October 30, 2016, from http://unfccc.int/kyoto_protocol/status_of_ratification/items/2613.php

UNFCCC. (2016). *United Nations Framework Convention on Climate Change: Paris Agreement - Status of Ratification*. Retrieved November 30, 2016, from http://unfccc.int/2860.php

Ungerleider, N. (2011, April 22). *Welcome To JihadVille*. Fast Company.

Unity Technologies. (2019). *Unity*. Author.

UniversityC. M. (2020). *PicoCTF*. Retrieved from https://picoctf.org/

US-CERT. (2020). *Department of Homeland Security. Software Assurance*. Retrieved September 27, 2020, from https://tinyurl.com/y6pr9v42

Uskov, A., & Sekar, B. (2015). Smart Gamification and Smart Serious Games. In Fusion of Smart, Multimedia and Computer Gaming Technology: Research, Systems and Perspectives (Vol. 84, pp. 7–36). Springer International Publishing. doi:10.1007/978-3-319-14645-4_2

Valacich, J. S., & Schneider, S. (2018). *Enhancing information system today: Managing in the digital world*. Pearson Education.

Valencia, K., Rusu, C., Quiñones, D., & Jamet, E. (2019). The impact of technology on people with autism spectrum disorder: A systematic literature review. *Sensors (Basel)*, *19*(20), 4485.

Van Rozen, R., & Dormans, J. (2014). Adapting game mechanics with micro-machinations. In Foundations of Digital Games. Society for the Advancement of the Science of Digital Games. Springer.

Vasconcelos, P., & Ribeiro, R. (2020). Using property-based testing to generate feedback for c programming exercises. *ICPEC - First International Computer Programming Education Conference*, 285-294.

Vasianovych, H. P. (2013). Spiritual and moral message of victorious multimedia at the beginning of the vicious process. *Science notes. Series. Pedagogyka*, (3), 20–26.

Vasiu, I., & Vasiu, L. (2018). Cybersecurity as an essential sustainable economic development factor. *European Journal of Sustainable Development*, *7*(4), 171–178. doi:10.14207/ejsd.2018.v7n4p171

Venable, J., Pries-Heje, J., & Baskerville, R. (2012). A comprehensive framework for evaluation in design science research. In *International conference on design science research in information systems* (pp. 423-438). Springer. 10.1007/978-3-642-29863-9_31

Venters, C., Lau, L., Griffiths, M., Holmes, V., Ward, R., Jay, C., Dibsdale, C., & Xu, J. (2014). The blind men and the elephant: Towards an empirical evaluation framework for software sustainability. *Journal of Open Research Software*, *2*(1). Advance online publication. doi:10.5334/jors.ao

Veretennikova, N., & Vaskiv, R. (2018). Application of the lean startup methodology in project management at launching new innovative products. In *2018 IEEE 13th International Scientific and Technical Conference on Computer Sciences and Information Technologies (CSIT)* (Vol. 2, pp. 169-172). IEEE.

Vermeulen, H., Gain, J., Marais, P., & O'Donovan, S. (2016). Reimagining gamification through the lens of Activity Theory. *49th Hawaii International Conference on System Sciences (HICSS)*. doi:10.1109/HICSS.2016.168

Versteeg, M. J. (2013). *Ethics & Gamification design: a moral framework for taking responsibility* [Master's thesis]. Universiteit Utrecht.

Vianna, Y., Vianna, M., Medina, B., & Tanaka, S. (2013). *Gamification, Inc. Como reinventar empresas a partir de jogos*. MVJ Press.

Viberg, O., Khalil, M., & Lioliopoulos, A. (2020). Facilitating Ideation and Knowledge Sharing in Workplaces: The Design and Use of Gamification in Virtual Platforms. In *International Conference on Human-Computer Interaction* (pp. 353-369). Springer. 10.1007/978-3-030-50506-6_25

Vilarinho, T., Farshchian, B., Floch, J., & Hansen, O. G. (2018). Participatory Ideation for Gamification: Bringing the User at the Heart of the Gamification Design Process. In *International Conference on Human-Centred Software Engineering* (pp. 51-61). Springer.

Viola, F. (2011). *Gamification - I Videogiochi nella Vita Quotidiana* [Gamificatio – Video Games in Everyday Life]. Arduino Viola.

VMware. (2022). *Messaging that just works - RabbitMQ*. https://www.rabbitmq.com

Vogel, J. J., Vogel, D. S., Cannon-Brower, J., Bowers, C. A., Muse, K., & Wright, M. (2006). Computer gaming and interactive simulations for learning: A meta-analysis. *Journal of Educational Computing Research*, *34*(3), 229–243. doi:10.2190/FLHV-K4WA-WPVQ-H0YM

VULDB. (2018). *The Community-Driven Vulnerability Database*. Retrieved July 28, 2021, from https://vuldb.com/

Vygotsky, L. S. (1978). *Mind in society: The development of higher psychological processes*. Harvard University Press.

Wagner, A., & Gałuszka, D. (2020). Let's play the future: Sociotechnical imaginaries, and energy transitions in serious digital games. *Energy Research & Social Science*, *70*, 101674.

Wang, H., & Sun, C. T. (2011). Game reward systems: Gaming experiences and social meanings. *Proc. 2011 DIGRA Int. Conf.: Think Design Play (DIGRA '11)*. Retrieved from http://gamelearninglab.nctu.edu.tw/ctsun/10.1.1.221.4931.pd

Wang, C., Lan, Y.-J., Tseng, W.-T., Lin, Y.-T. R., & Gupta, K. C.-L. (2020). On the effects of 3D virtual worlds in language learning – a meta-analysis. *Computer Assisted Language Learning*, *33*(8), 891–915. doi:10.1080/09588221.2019.1598444

Wang, C., & Zhao, H. (2020). The impact of COVID-19 on anxiety in Chinese university students. *Frontiers in Psychology*, *11*, 1168. doi:10.3389/fpsyg.2020.01168 PMID:32574244

Wanick, V., & Bui, H. (2019). Gamification in Management: A systematic review and research directions. *International Journal of Serious Games*, *6*(2), 57–74. doi:10.17083/ijsg.v6i2.282

Wardrip-Fruin, N., & Montfort, N. (Eds.). (2003). *The new media reader* (Vol. 1). MIT press.

Warmelink, H., van Elderen, J., & Mayer, I. (2021). Game Design Elements: Understanding the bricks and mortar of gamification. In Organizational Gamification (pp. 40-60). Routledge.

Warmelink, H., Koivisto, J., Mayer, I., Vesa, M., & Hamari, J. (2018). Gamification of the work floor: A literature review of gamifying production and logistics operations. *Journal of Business Research*, *106*, 331–340. doi:10.1016/j.jbusres.2018.09.011

Webb, E. N. (2013). Gamification : When It Works, When It Doesn't. Lecture Notes in Computer Science, 8013(2), 608–614.

Webster, J., & Martocchio, J. J. (1992). Microcomputer Playfulness: Development of a Measure With Workplace Implications. *Management Information Systems Quarterly*, *16*(2), 201–227. doi:10.2307/249576

Wee, S. C., & Choong, W. W. (2019). Gamification: Predicting the effectiveness of variety game design elements to intrinsically motivate users' energy conservation behaviour. *Journal of Environmental Management*, *233*, 97–106.

Weiland, K. M. (2017). *Creating Character Arcs: The Masterful Author's Guide to Uniting Story Structure, Plot, and Character Development*. PenForASword Publishing.

Wells, L. F. (2018). *Energy Explorer: A theory-informed design for a serious game with the purpose of promoting energy conservation behaviours* (Doctoral dissertation). University of Tasmania.

Wenzler, I. (1993). *Policy exercises: A new approach to policy development*. Instituut voor Toegepaste Wetenschappen.

Wenzler, I., & Chartier, D. (1999). Why do we bother with games and simulations: An organizational learning perspective. *Simulation & Gaming*, *30*(3), 375–384. doi:10.1177/104687819903000315

Werbach, K. (2014). (Re) defining gamification: A process approach. In *International conference on persuasive technology* (pp. 266-272). Springer. 10.1007/978-3-319-07127-5_23

Werbach, K., & Hunter, D. (2012). *For The Win: How Game Thinking can revolutionize your business*. Wharton Digital Press, The Wharton School, University of Pensylvania.

WeSpire. (2019). *WeSpire - Employee Engagement Platform Powered by Behavioral Science*. Retrieved February 14, 2019, from https://www.wespire.com/

Westera, W. (2017). How people learn while playing serious games: A computational modelling approach. *Journal of Computational Science, 18*, 32–45. doi:10.1016/j.jocs.2016.12.002

West, S. G., & Aiken, L. S. (1997). Toward understanding individual effects in multicomponent prevention programs: Design and analysis strategies. In K. J. Bryant, M. Windle, & S. G. West (Eds.), *The science of prevention: Methodological advances from alcohol and substance abuse research* (pp. 167–209). American Psychological Association. doi:10.1037/10222-006

Wetzel, R., Blum, L., & Oppermann, L. (2012, May). Tidy city: A location-based game supported by in-situ and web-based authoring tools to enable user-created content. In *Proceedings of the international conference on the foundations of digital games* (pp. 238-241). 10.1145/2282338.2282385

Wheaton, M. G., Messner, G. R., & Marks, J. B. (2021). Intolerance of uncertainty as a factor linking obsessive-compulsive symptoms, health anxiety and concerns about the spread of the novel coronavirus (COVID-19) in the United States. *Journal of Obsessive-Compulsive and Related Disorders, 28*, 100605. doi:10.1016/j.jocrd.2020.100605 PMID:33251098

Whiteley, L., Brown, L. K., Mena, L., Craker, L., & Arnold, T. (2018). Enhancing health among youth living with HIV using an iPhone game. *AIDS Care, 30*(sup4), 21-33. doi:10.1080/09540121.2018.1503224

Whiteley, L., Craker, L., Haubrick, K. K., Arnold, T., Mena, L., Olsen, E., & Brown, L. K. (2021). The impact of a mobile gaming intervention to increase adherence to pre-exposure prophylaxis. *AIDS and Behavior, 25*(6), 1884–1889. doi:10.100710461-020-03118-3 PMID:33483897

Whiteley, L., Olsen, E., Mena, L., Haubrick, K., Craker, L., Hershkowitz, D., & Brown, L. K. (2020). A mobile gaming intervention for persons on pre-exposure prophylaxis: Protocol for intervention development and randomized controlled trial. *JMIR Research Protocols, 9*(9), e18640. doi:10.2196/18640 PMID:32924954

White, R. W. (1959). Motivation reconsidered: The concept of competence. *Psychological Review, 66*(5), 297–333. doi:10.1037/h0040934 PMID:13844397

Wiek, A., Withycombe, L., & Redman, C. L. (2011). Key competencies in sustainability: A reference framework for academic program development. *Sustainability Science, 6*(2), 203–218. doi:10.100711625-011-0132-6

Wieringa, R. J. (2014). *Design Science Methodology for Information Systems and Software Engineering*. Springer.

Wijman, T. (2020, June). *Three Billion Players by 2023: Engagement and Revenues Continue to Thrive Across the Global Games Market*. https://newzoo.com/insights/articles/games-market-engagement-revenues-trends-2020-2023-gaming-report/

Wilson, K. A., Bedwell, W. L., Lazzara, E. H., Salas, E., Burke, S., Estock, J. L., Orvis, K. L., & Conkey, C. (2009). Relationships between game attributes and learning outcomes. *Simulation & Gaming, 40*(2), 217–266. doi:10.1177/1046878108321866

Winn, B. (2009). The Design, Play, and Experience Framework. In R. Ferdig (Ed.), *Handbook of Research on Effective Electronic Gaming in Education* (Vol. 3, pp. 1010–1024). IGI Global. doi:10.4018/978-1-59904-808-6.ch058

Witt, M., Scheiner, C. W., & Robra-Bissantz, S. (2011, October). Gamification of online idea competitions: insights from an explorative case. In GI-Jahrestagung (p. 392). Academic Press.

Wodke, P. (2020). *Wissenschaftskommunikation – Wissenschaftstransfer – Wissenstransfer. Im Dickicht der Begriffswelten.* https://kristinoswald.hypotheses.org/3044

Woo, J. C. (2014). Digital game-based learning supports student motivation, cognitive success, and performance outcomes. *Journal of Educational Technology & Society, 17*(3), 291–307.

Woo, Y., & Reeves, T. C. (2007). Meaningful interaction in web-based learning: A social constructivist perspective. *The Internet and Higher Education, 10*(1), 15–25. doi:10.1016/j.iheduc.2006.10.005

Wouters, P., van Nimwegen, C., van der Spek, E., & van Oostendorp, H. (2013). A meta-analysis of the cognitive and motivational effects of serious games. *Journal of Educational Psychology, 105*(2), 249–265. doi:10.1037/a0031311

Wu, C. H., Huang, Y. M., & Hwang, J. P. (2016). Review of affective computing in education/learning: Trends and challenges. *British Journal of Educational Technology, 47*(6), 1304–1323. doi:10.1111/bjet.12324

Wu, J., & Chen, V. D.-T. (2019). A systematic review of educational digital storytelling. *Computers & Education, 103786.* Advance online publication. doi:10.1016/j.compedu.2019.103786

Wu, J., & Lu, X. (2018). Effects of Extrinsic and Intrinsic Motivators on Using Utilitarian, Hedonic, and Dual-Purposed Information Systems: A Meta-Analysis. *Journal of the Association for Information Systems, 14*(3), 153–191. doi:10.17705/1jais.00325

Wu, X., Liu, S., & Shukla, A. (2020). Serious Games as an Engaging Medium on Building Energy Consumption: A Review of Trends, Categories and Approaches. *Sustainability, 12*(20), 8508.

Xi, N., & Hamari, J. (2019). Does gamification satisfy needs? A study on the relationship between gamification features and intrinsic need satisfaction. *International Journal of Information Management, 46*, 210–221.

Xu, F., Buhalis, D., & Weber, J. (2017). Serious games and the gamification of tourism. *Tourism Management, 60*, 244–256. doi:10.1016/j.tourman.2016.11.020

Xu, Y., Poole, E. S., Miller, A. D., Eiriksdottir, E., Kestranek, D., Catrambone, R., & Mynatt, E. D. (2012). This is not a one-horse race: Understanding player types in multiplayer pervasive health games for youth. *Proceedings of the ACM Conference on Computer Supported Cooperative Work, CSCW, April 2015*, 843–852. 10.1145/2145204.2145330

Yin, R. K. (2009). *Case Study Research: Design and Methods* (4th ed.). SAGE Publications.

Zhonggen, Y. (2019). A meta-analysis of use of serious games in education over a decade. *International Journal of Computer Games Technology, 2019*, 4797032. doi:10.1155/2019/4797032

Zichermann, G., & Cunningham, C. (2011). *Gamification by Design: Implementing Game Mechanics in Web and Mobile Apps.* OReilly Media, Inc.

Zimmerman, B. J. (2008). Investigating self-regulation and motivation: Historical background, methodological developments, and future prospects. *American Educational Research Journal, 45*(1), 166–183. doi:10.3102/0002831207312909

Zimmerman, M. (1995). Psychological empowerment: Issues and illustrations. *American Journal of Community Psychology, 23*(5), 581–599. doi:10.1007/BF02506983 PMID:8851341

Zimmermann, P., Guttormsen, S., Danuser, B., & Gomez, P. (2003). *AffectiveComputing - A Rationale for Measuring Mood with Mouse and Keyboard.* Swiss Federal Institute of Technology.

Zoto, E., Kianpour, M., Kowalski, S. J., & Lopez-Rojas, E. A. (2019). A socio-technical systems approach to design and support systems thinking in cybersecurity and risk management education. *Complex Systems Informatics and Modeling Quarterly*, (18), 65–75. doi:10.7250/csimq.2019-18.04

About the Contributors

Oscar Bernardes holds a Ph.D. in management, since 2013. He worked as management consultant for several years, in several organizations (social, profitable, and governmental). He is Invited Professor at Polytechnic Institute of Porto (P.Porto), Portugal, where he has been lecturing courses in the following areas: entrepreneurship, innovation, marketing and general management. His research interests include entrepreneurship, gamification, innovation, and marketing.

Vanessa Amorim is a Business and Economics Ph.D. student at the University of Aveiro - Portugal. She has a master's in Organizational Management - Specialization: Business Management and a Post-Graduation in Management Tools for Business Competitiveness from Institute Polytechnic of Porto - Portugal. Her main research interests are Innovation, Entrepreneurship, Marketing, and Business Management.

António Carrizo Moreira obtained a Bachelor's degree in Electrical Engineering and a Master's degree in Management, both from the University of Porto, Portugal. He received his Ph.D. in Management from the University of Manchester, England. He has a solid international background in industry leveraged working for a multinational company in Germany as well as in Portugal. He has also been involved in consultancy projects and research activities. He is an Associate Professor with Habilitation at the Department of Economics, Management, Industrial Engineering, and Tourism, University of Aveiro, Portugal, where he is the Director of the PhD program in Bisienss and Economics. He is member of GOVCOPP research unit and of INESCTEC.

* * *

Francisco Aguayo-González, B. Industrial Eng, Engineer, and Ph.D. Industrial Engineering, B. Psychology, Computer Science Engineering, MS. Quality, Environment, Security and Health, is a professor at the University of Seville (Department of design engineering, Field of Knowledge: engineering Project). He worked as a Project Manager for engineering projects for installations and products.

Assia Alexandrova holds a Ph.D. from The Open University, UK. Her research focuses on requirements engineering practices, serious games, and the gamification of Agile methods. She is a Certified Project Management Professional (PMI) and a product management practitioner at Accenture Interactive.

Leonardo Alves is a Ph.D. student in Computer Science. He holds a master's degree in Electrical and Computer Engineering from the Federal University of Goiás (2010), a degree in Administration from Unifan (2013), a degree in Pedagogical Training from the University of Southern Santa Catarina (2005), and a degree in Computer Science from the Pontifical Catholic University of Goiás (2001). He is currently a member of the Committee for the Democratization of Informatics of Goiás professor at UFG - Federal University of Goiás. He is also engineering, architecture, and quality of systems, administration, and auditing in companies. He is the author of Start Games courses and develops Games for PC, Mobile, Tablets and Xbox Console, and Playstation.

María Jesús Ávila-Gutiérrez received the PhD. in Manufacturing Eng. in 2017, a B. Eng. in Industrial Design in 2010, and an MS degree in Design and development of products and industrial installations in 2011. From 2010 to 2011, she worked for consulting companies within the aeronautical and agroindustrial sectors and, since 2011, for the University of Seville. She is an Assistant Professor of Project Area at the Design Department of the Higher Polytechnic School of Seville. Her thesis is about holonic architecture in manufacturing systems in the materials, manufacturing, and environmental engineering doctoral program. Her research interest includes holonic manufacturing systems, ecological modeling, and natural and industrial systems with an emphasis on environmental management and sustainability.

Cleopatra Bardaki holds a Ph.D. in Information Systems enabled by Internet-of-Things technologies in the Supply Chain from Athens University of Economics and Business (AUEB), an MSc in Information Systems from AUEB, and a BSc (with honors) in Informatics and Telecommunications from the University of Athens. Previously, she was a Research Coordinator and Senior Researcher at ELTRUN E-Business Research Center of AUEB with a long experience in the research coordination and project management of leading-edge research & development projects funded mainly by the EU. Her research interests include the Design & Evaluation of Internet of Things applications, Data Analytics to support Decision making, Information Systems (IS) Evaluation with an emphasis on Information Quality (IQ) evaluation, and Supply Chain Management. A 4-year scholarship has funded her doctoral research from Bodossaki Foundation, and she has received more academic distinctions and scholarships during her studies. She has published over fifty papers in academic journals, proceedings of international academic conferences, and edited books.

George Caridakis (http://ii.ct.aegean.gr/) serves as a faculty member, Assistant Professor at the Department of Cultural Technology & Communication, the University of the Aegean, where he founded and coordinated the Intelligent Interaction Research Group (ii.Aegean.gr), a recently established but dynamic research group already making an impact attracting Regional and National funding and participating in numerous International conferences and workshops. He is also affiliated as an Adjunct Professor at the Athena RC (athenarc.gr/en) and as a Senior Researcher with the Intelligent Systems, Content and Interaction Laboratory, National Technical University of Athens. He offers undergraduate and postgraduate-level courses in different institutions and supervises Ph.D., MSc, and undergraduate theses. He has served on boards and committees and as a reviewer in numerous international scientific journals, conferences, and workshops. He is a member of the Association for the Advancement of Affective Computing and the Greek ACM SIGCHI Special Interest Group board in Computer-Human Interaction. His research on various aspects of intelligent human-computer interaction, such as Affective Computing, Artificial Intelligence, Natural, Augmented, and Embodied Interaction, has been published in more than 25 journal articles and book chapters and more than 50 papers in conferences and workshops and has been well recognized by the scientific community by being cited more than 1500 times with an h-index of 20. He has served as an evaluator in many funding and grant frameworks. He has long experience in European and National funded R&D projects participating as a researcher, Principal Investigator, and Scientific Coordinator in over 20 projects during the past 15 years.

Paolo Carli, Architect and Ph.D., is a Researcher at the Department of Architecture and Urban Studies. He carries out research in the field of environmental design within settled areas at the urban, micro-urban, and building scales.

Breno Carvalho has a Doctorate in Design at UFPE (2020). Master's in Design at UFPE (2014). Specialist in Information Design UFPE (2002) and graduate in Social Communication at Unicap (1999). Currently, a researcher at CREATECH - Technologies Applied to the Development of Solutions and Products in Creative Industries, at the Institute for Media Convergence and Information Studies (Icinform), lecturer in the Postgraduate Program in Creative Industries, and coordinator of the Games Technology Course Digital of the Catholic University of Pernambuco. Coordinated the interactive solutions agency Combogó Unicap. Member of the Innovation, Creativity, and Entrepreneurship Laboratory at Unicap - LICEU. Responsible for the Column Cabra Nerd of the Algomais online magazine. Experience in the Communication area, with an emphasis on Visual Communication and Web Design, acting mainly on the following themes: creative industries, branding, mutant brand, playable mutant brand, games, gamification, UX, Virtual Reality, and 3D technologies.

Miquel Casals is a full professor of Construction Engineering at Universitat Politecnica de Catalunya, Head of Group of Research and Innovation in Construction. Principal researcher in numerous international and national research projects. Author of more than 50 referred journal papers, more than 100 conferences, and other publications. The main research topics are building performance, energy efficiency in buildings, construction management, and other related fields.

Luís Afonso Maia Rosa Casqueiro is a senior Computer Science and Business Management student at ISCTE- Lisbon University Institute. He received a bachelor's degree in Computer Science and Business Management in 2020, having enrolled in a master's course afterward. He is interested in understanding how gamification can impact learning within organizational contexts and how artificial intelligence can be used to enhance this experience further.

Carla Cavalcante has a Master's in Creative Industries at the Catholic University of Pernambuco (UNICAP, 2021), with a final Project that focused on peripheral entrepreneurship of the communities of Recife. Specialism in Business Management at the Faculdade dos Guararapes (FG, 2016), and graduated in Tourism at the Federal University of Pernambuco (UFPE, 2011). Currently, taking a course in Publicity and Advertising at UFPE and working in the area of Entrepreneurship and Digital Marketing.

Antonio Córdoba received a PhD. in Engineering and Architecture in 2017 from Cadiz University. Technical Engineer in Industrial Design and University Master in Installations and Product Design. Since 2010 he has been a professor and investigator at the University of Seville (Department of Design

Engineering, Field of Knowledge: Engineering Project for the University of Seville. His research interest includes product design, Kansei engineering, and ergonomics.

Fernando Costa is a Master's student in the Postgraduate Program in Sustainable Development in the Humid Tropics at the Center for Higher Amazonian Studies of the Federal University of Pará (NAEA/UFPA). Specialist in Scientific Communication in the Amazon by the International Program for Training Specialists in the Development of Amazonian Areas (NAEA/UFPA). Bachelor in Geography from the Federal Institute of Education, Science and Technology of Pará (IFPA), 2017. Bachelor's degree in Tourism from the Federal University of Pará (UFPA), 2010. He has publications in the areas of Computing and Scientific Communication and researches and works in the areas of Geography, Culture, Traditional Peoples and Communities of the Amazon, Social Cartography, Scientific Communication, facial expression recognition tools, and violence against women. Currently, she is developing research on violence in the metropolitan region of Belém from the perspective of Necropolitics. ORCID: https://orcid.org/0000-0002-0226-7505.

Kristy de Salas is an Associate Professor in the Information & Communication discipline in the School of Technology, Environments, and Design at the University of Tasmania in Australia. Kristy primarily teaches and researches in the domains of Business Process Management and Information Systems, with a specific focus on Small and Medium Sized Enterprises. Kristy also studies project management, identifying opportunities for improvement in methodology and implementation. Most recently, Kristy has commenced studies in human behaviour in the areas of health, education, and conservation and the opportunities to modify individual and group behaviours through technology-based interventions.

Jason Diakoumakos is a Ph.D. student at the University of Peloponnese, Department of Informatics and Telecommunications, researching gamification techniques used in cybersecurity.

Marcos Aurelio Domingues is currently a professor at the State University of Maringá, Brazil. He took a Ph.D. Degree (2010) in Computer Science at the University of Porto, Portugal; a Master's Degree in Computer Science and Computational Mathematics (2004) at the University of São Paulo, Brazil; and a Degree in Computer Science (2002) at the Federal University of Lavras, Brazil. He also has a postgraduate course in Linux Network Administration (2003) and a Master in Business Administration and Management (2007). His main research interests are Artificial Intelligence; Data Science; Machine Learning; Web, Text, and Data Mining; and Recommender Systems.

Tiago Espinha Gasiba is a security researcher at Siemens AG in Munich. He received his Engineering Degree in 2002 from Faculdade de Engenharia da Universidade do Porto, his Master of Science in Communications Engineering in 2004 from Technische Universität München, and his Ph.D. in 2021 from the Universität der Bundeswehr München, with distinction. He has published extensively on the topics of cyber security and the usage of serious games to raise awareness of software developers in the industry, which was also the topic of his dissertation.

Kati Fager (MA) worked as a research assistant at the Tampere University in Pori, Finland. Fager worked on research projects dealing with gamification and serious games. She majored in digital culture and did her thesis on gamification. Currently, Fager is working as a community manager at the business community Crazy Town in Pori, Finland.

Núria Forcada has an MSc in Industrial Engineering and an international Ph.D. in Construction Engineering from the Universitat Politècnica de Catalunya (UPC). She is a member of the Group of Construction Research and Innovation (GRIC) and has authored/co-authored 54 internationally refereed research papers, which have appeared in leading international journals. Dr. Forcada participates in many national and international research projects funded by the European Union and the Spanish research council. She has coordinated the ConTerMa project: Analysis of thermal comfort in nursing homes in the cross-border cooperation space of Spain-Portugal, (2018-2020), funded by the Programa de Cooperación Interreg V-A España – Portugal (POCTEP) and the FEDER funds. She is currently coordinating the Thecoelen project: "Implications of the thermal comfort of the elderly to energy consumption," funded by the state research agency under the program Challenges of society (2020-2023) Spanish Ministry of Economy, Industry, and Competitiveness (Retos Program). Her current interests focus on building management to improve occupants' thermal comfort and reduce energy consumption BIM and building performance. For this, Dr. Forcada is working on the integrated analysis (Big Data) of monitored environmental data and the characteristics of the occupants to develop adaptive thermal comfort models.

Marta Gangolells has been an industrial engineer and Ph.D. in construction engineering since 2010. She currently works as an associate professor in the Department of Projects and Construction Engineering at the Technical University of Catalonia. Her research expertise is related to improving the energy efficiency of buildings from multiple perspectives, including building renovation, applied ICT solutions for building automation, pro-environmental behaviors, and new building energy efficiency standards. She is also an expert on life-cycle environmental impact modelling and sustainability metrics. Within the Group of Construction Research and Innovation, she successfully led the EOFF research project (2016-2020), funded by the Spanish government and aimed at identifying sustainable and cost-optimal energy retrofitting solutions for the existing office building stock. Dr. Gangolells has also participated in several EU-funded research projects within the H2020 and FP7 programs devoted to reducing the buildings' energy consumption and the corresponding carbon footprint, such as the EnerGAware project (2015-2018) and the SEAM4US project (2011-2014). Dr. Gangolells has supervised three doctoral theses, published 49 papers in top-ranked international journals (H-index: 20 according to Scopus), and authored or co-authored several conference papers.

William B. Hansen is a social psychologist by training. He has developed, tested, and commercialized numerous interventions, notably the All Stars drug abuse prevention program. He has extensively published what makes drug prevention programs work, mediating mechanisms, and implementation factors that enhance program effectiveness. He is one of the leading prevention scientists worldwide and is currently evaluating a new version of Drug Abuse Resistance Education (DARE).

Diego Issicaba received the B.S. and M.S. degrees in electrical engineering from the Federal University of Santa Catarina, Santa Catarina, Brazil, in 2006 and 2008, respectively, and the Ph.D. degree in sustainable energy systems, under the MIT Doctoral Program, from the Faculty of Engineering, University of Porto, Portugal, in 2013. He was a Researcher with the Institute for Systems and Computer Engineering—Technology and Science (INESC TEC), Portugal, from 2009 to 2013. He is currently a

Professor with the Department of Electrical and Electronic Engineering, Federal University of Santa Catarina. He is also the Area Leader of INESC P&D Brasil. His research interests involve smart grids, multiagent systems, reliability evaluation, and wide area monitoring systems.

Eirini Kalatha is a Ph.D. candidate in the Department of Cultural Technology and Communication, University of the Aegean, in the field of Serious games with emotional awareness and their implementation in adult education and culture. In 2016, she received a Master of Arts in "Education and Disability. Le dinamiche emotivo-affettive" from the University of Rome Tor Vergata, and in 2013, she received a Master of Science in" Cultural Informatics and Communication" at the Department of Cultural Technology and Communication of the University of the Aegean. In 2012, she graduated from the Department of Computer Science and Biomedical Informatics of the University of Thessaly. Her research includes serious games, affective computing, human-computer interaction (HCI), educational technology, and cultural education.

Tim Katzwinkel studied Engineering Design at RWTH Aachen University. In his diploma thesis entitled "Computer-aided concept development using the Koller method," he dealt with the topic of the methodical development of innovative product concepts using catalog knowledge. From 2013 to 2017, Mr. Katzwinkel worked as a research assistant at the Chair and Institute for General Design Engineering of Mechanical Engineering (ikt). His research focus included software-supported product innovation and methods of virtual design synthesis. From 2017 to 2019, Tim Katzwinkel was promoted to head of the Virtual Product Development (VPE) and Product Lifecycle Management (PLM) research group at the Institute of Machine Elements and Systems Engineering (MSE) at RWTH Aachen University. The research group focuses on an end-to-end model-based PLM methodology for integrating methods, processes, and data from the individual lifecycle phases in the product development process and beyond. Dr. Katzwinkel completed his doctorate with honors in 2019 with the research topic "Methodology for software-supported initial design finding for new mechanical designs." Since 2019, Tim Katzwinkel has been working as managing director at the Institute for Product Innovation, University of Wuppertal. The research Focus of the Institute for Product Innovation includes Mechanical Design, Manufacturing Engineering, and Model-Based Systems. Dr. Katzwinkel has specific expertise in the field of sustainability, digitalization, and innovation of industrial components and products.

David Kessing holds an M.Sc. degree in Engineering Design from RWTH Aachen University. He completed his master's thesis in the engineering design department of Audi AG with a focus on sensor development. From 2017 to 2019, he worked as a research assistant at the Institute for Machine Elements and Systems Engineering (MSE) at RWTH Aachen University. His main topics were digitalization of teaching and research in additive manufacturing. In his teaching activities, David Kessing was responsible for lectures with up to 1500 students in the field of machine design and construction theory. Since 2019, he has been working at the Department for Product Safety and Quality Engineering (PSQ) at the University of Wuppertal (BUW). In addition to his responsibilities as a digital teaching consultant for the Faculty of Mechanical Engineering and Safety Engineering, he is a mentor for international teams in design thinking courses. Through his research, David Kessing has proven expertise in gamification, requirements management, and product innovation. He is currently writing his doctoral thesis in the area of "Gamification and Product Development" with a focus on "Improvement of Design-to-Customer."

Syrine Khelifi is a computer science engineering student. Her main research interest deals with video games, gamification, advanced HCI as AR and VR, and AI applications for Video Games.

Maha Khemaja is an assistant professor at the Computer Science Department of the Higher Institute of Applied Science and Technologies at the University of Sousse-Tunisia. Her research interest deals with Technology Enhanced Learning, including Intelligent Tutoring Systems, Game-Based Learning, and software engineering intended for TEL development and Semantic technologies. She received her Ph.D. in computer science from the University of Paul Sabatiers Toulouse, France, in 1993. She had been a dean of the Higher Institute of Management and computer science for seven years at the University of Kairouan - Tunisia. She also participated in several e-learning resource development and e-course tutoring with the Virtual University of Tunis.

Mazaher Kianpour is a Ph.D. candidate at NTNU. He holds a Bachelor's degree in Computer Engineering (Software) from Payame Noor University. He obtained his Master's degree in Architecture of Computer Systems from Shahid Beheshti University, Tehran, Iran. He started his Ph.D. in Information Security at NTNU in May 2018. His Ph.D. research lies at the intersection of economics and information security from a socio-technical perspective. He has several years of work experience at the Tehran University of Medical Sciences, and his professional training includes Computer Networks, Cybersecurity, and Risk Management.

Nicholas Kolokotronis is an Associate Professor and Director of the Cryptography and Security Group at the Department of Informatics and Telecommunications, University of Peloponnese. He received a B.Sc. degree in mathematics from the Aristotle University of Thessaloniki, Greece, in 1995, an M.Sc. degree (highest honors) in highly efficient algorithms in 1998, and a Ph.D. degree in cryptography in 2003, both from the National and Kapodistrian University of Athens. Since 2004, he has held visiting positions at the University of Piraeus, University of Peloponnese, National and Kapodistrian University of Athens, and Open University of Cyprus. During 2002-04, he was with the European Dynamics S.A., Greece, as a security consultant. He has been a member of working groups to provide professional cyber-security training to large organizations, including the Hellenic Telecommunications and Posts Commission. He has published more than 100 papers in international scientific journals, conferences, and books and has participated in more than 25 EU-funded and national research and innovation projects. He has been a co-chair of international conferences (IEEE CSR 2021-22), workshops (IEEE SecSoft 2019, 2021, IEEE CSRIoT 2019-20, and ACM EPESec 2020-22), and special sessions (GIIS 2018) focusing on IoT security. Moreover, he has been a TPC member in many international conferences, incl. IEEE ISIT, IEEE GLOBECOM, IEEE ICC, ISC, etc. He is co-editor and lead author of the books "Internet of things, threats, landscape, and countermeasures" and "Cyber-security threats, actors, and dynamic mitigation," released by CRC Press in mid-2021. He is currently a Guest Editor in the "Engineering - cyber security, digital forensics and resilience" area of Springer's Applied Sciences Journal (since 2019) and in the Reviewer Board of MDPI's Cryptography journal (since 2020), whereas he has been an Associate Editor of the EURASIP Journal on Wireless Communications and Networking (2009-17) and a regular reviewer for a number of prestigious journals, incl. IEEE TIFS, IEEE TIT, IEEE TETC, DCC (Springer), COSE (Elsevier), etc. His research interests span the broad areas of security, cryptography, and coding theory.

Dimosthenis Kotsopoulos is a post-doctoral researcher at the Department of Management Science and Technology at Athens University of Economics and Business (AUEB). He holds a Ph.D. in Management Science and Technology, an MBA from AUEB, and an MSc in Geographic Information Science from University College London (UCL). His research focuses on organizational behavior, pro-environmental behavior, IoT, information systems, gamification, and innovative entrepreneurship, while he has published research papers in academic journals and conferences. He has participated in various EU-funded projects focused on technologically innovative solutions and has significant work experience in a management role within an industrial setting.

Stewart Kowalski has over 35 years of industry and academic experience in information security. He has worked for several large international companies, including Ericsson, Telia Research, Huawei, Digital, and HP. He has also taught and researched information security at several universities, including the Royal Institute of Technology (KTH), Stockholm School of Economics, and Stockholm University Department of Computer and Systems Sciences. He is currently a Professor of Information Security at the Department of Information Security and Communication Technology, Norwegian University of Science and Technology, Norway. He is the current head of the Information Security Management Group at the Center for Cyber and Information Security, CCIS, www.ccis.no, and Program Director for 4 Master Programs and a Core Management 2013- 2018. Here is currently a Core Member of the Norwegian Cyber Range project between 2018- 2021. Norwegian Cyber Range Your Tube Video.

George Lepouras is a Professor at the Department of Informatics and Telecommunications, University of Peloponnese, and Vice-Rector for Finance, Planning, and Development at the same institution. He holds a first degree in Mathematics from the University of Athens, an MSc in Information Technology from the University of Strathclyde, Scotland, and a Ph.D. in Human-Computer Interaction from the University of Athens. Dr. Lepouras is a senior member of ACM and has served as the chairman of the Greek ACM SIGCHI. His research interests include game-based profiling, personal and task information management, multilingual interfaces, web-based interfaces, virtual reality and augmented reality applications and cultural technologies. He is an author and co-author of more than a hundred papers, of which more than forty appear in international journals. As a researcher, technical manager, or team coordinator, he has participated in many national and European research and technological development projects: SmartGov, DELOS, Experimedia, CROSSCULT, and FORESIGHT.

Manuel Löwer is the head of the Department for Product Safety and Quality Engineering (PSQ) at the University of Wuppertal (BUW) and CEO of the Institute for Product Innovations (IPI). His research and teaching focus on engineering design concerning safe and sustainable products, quality management, production and process safety, and Product Lifecycle Management (PLM). Before being appointed there, he has been the Executive Manager of the Institute for Engineering Design (ikt) at RWTH Aachen University, where he still holds teaching positions in the field of Systematic Engineering and Automotive Engineering. After his diploma in Mechanical Engineering and professional experience in the Automotive Industry, he achieved his Dr.-Ing. Degree in the field of Innovation and Product Lifecycle Management from RWTH Aachen University. From 2006 - 2017 he was associated with the Institute for Engineering Design and led the PLM and Systematic Engineering department before being appointed Executive Manager in 2010. Besides, he worked in a consultancy for innovation and development in Munich and

Aachen and is also the founder and CEO of the company ikt Syprac GmbH. He is a scientific committee member and reviewer for several journals and conferences.

Tetiana Luhova was born in 1978, Odesa city. Ph.D. in Art History, assistant professor of Information activities, and media communications chair of Odesa Polytechnic State University (Odesa city, Ukraine). Basic higher education - teaching. South Ukrainian State Pedagogical University. KD Ushinskogo. Thesis on specialty 17.00.01 - theory and history of culture "Evolution of East vertep puppet theater." Experience teaching activities in higher education - 15 years. More than 100 scientific papers. Industries of interest: gamification of education, creating an educational game environment, transforming education in the information society, knowledge management, consolidation of intellectual resources. Member of the Odesa International Project Team "GameHub - University-Enterprises Cooperation in Game Industry in Ukraine" (Project Number: 561728-EPP-1-2015-1-ES-EPPKA2-CBHE-JP) under the ERASMUS + program. Expert of the Project GISAP International Research Championship in Art History, History, Philosophy, Culturology, Physical Culture, and Sports (from 2013-2017 certificates). Member of the editorial boards of scientific publications: «Applied Aspects of Information Technology» (2018-2021); «Herald of Advanced Information Technology» (2018-2021); Ukrainian-German Conference "Information. Culture. Technology," 2018-2021; "Logos. The art of thought " (2020-2021).

Marcel Macarulla is an associate professor in the Department of Project and Construction Engineering at Universitat Politècnica de Catalunya BarcelonaTech (UPC). He is working in the energy efficiency field, focusing his research on the analysis of the building data coming from Energy Management Systems, the development of key performance indicators and their visualization, and developing strategies for user energy awareness in public buildings to reduce the building energy consumption and the development of predictive control strategies. In addition, he developed reduced-order models for indoor air quality, thermal comfort, and the whole building. During his career, Dr. Marcel Macarulla participated in 3 projects founded by the European Union and two projects launched by the Spanish government. As a result of his research, he has co-authored 34 internationally refereed research papers, which have appeared in leading international journals.

Gil Vicente Maia has a Master's in Creative Industries at UNICAP - Catholic University of Pernambuco (2021), with a research project on software for editing interactive films. Specialization in Narratives of Photography and Audiovisual (2018) and graduation in Journalism (1991), both at UNICAP. Experience in editorial photography, documentary film, and image bank management. Member of ABD/APECI - Brazilian Association of Documentarians / Pernambuco Association of Filmmakers.

Jari Multisilta is the President and Managing Director of Satakunta University of Applied Sciences. In his former position, he was a professor of Multimedia at the Tampere University of Technology and the director of the Pori University Consortium. He was a Visiting Fellow at Nokia Research Center on 2008-2009, Nokia Visiting Professor in 2012, and Visiting Scholar at Stanford University, H-STAR Institute from 2007-2014 (18 months). His research interests include mobile learning, mobile video storytelling, gamification and games, and teaching computer coding.

Stylianos Mystakidis is an education innovator, project manager (PMI/PMP), a researcher at the University of Patras, Greece, and a Professor-Counselor at the Hellenic Open University, Greece. He holds a Ph.D. in Cognitive Science from the Faculty of Information Technology at the University of Jyväskylä, Finland (2019), a Master of Arts in Education in Virtual Worlds at the University of the West of England Bristol, United Kingdom (2016), and a Master of Science in Mechanical Engineering at the National Technical University of Athens, Greece (1998). He actively participates in interdisciplinary projects, European policy, and international research. His professional practice, teaching, and research focus mainly on e-learning, distance education, open education, blended learning, game-based learning, and virtual and augmented reality.

Maria Pinto-Albuquerque is Assistant Professor at ISCTE - Instituto Universitário de Lisboa and researcher at Istar-Iscte. Her work focuses on the relation of the human, as a user or developer, with the computer system. Addressing this relation leads to work in cybersecurity awareness, alignment of security with usability, and requirements engineering. She has been developing tools and techniques, like serious games and creativity techniques, to promote an efficient, responsible, and secure use (by the users) and development (by software engineers, co-developing with all types of stakeholders) of computer systems.

Lucia Rapanotti, Ph.D., is a Senior Lecturer at The Open University, UK, and Editor for Wiley's Expert Systems - the Journal of Knowledge Engineering. She is a Chartered Engineer, a Fellow of the BCS, The Chartered Institute of IT, and a Senior Fellow of the Higher Education Academy. Lucia's main research is innovative theories, methods, and tools to address complex problems in organizations, and she has published over 90 articles in international fora.

Alessandro Rogora, Architect and Ph.D., is a Full Professor at Dipartimento DAStU of Politecnico di Milano (Italy). He is interested in the relationships between architectural design and energy, both from a methodological and instrumental point of view; in this context, he has developed tools and methods of analysis and representation of the environment for the project.

Mauro Augusto da Rosa received his B.Sc., and M.Sc. degrees from the Catholic University of Rio Grande do Sul (PUCRS), Porto Alegre, Brazil, in 1998 and 2003, respectively, all in Electrical Engineering. He worked as a lecturer at the FENG – Faculty of Engineering of PUCRS until 2005. From 1999 to 2004, he also worked as a planning engineer from RGE – Rio Grande Energia (Distribution System Company) in Brazil. During this period, he received another postgraduate degree as a distribution system planning specialist from Mackenzie University in São Paulo, Brazil. From 2005 to 2009, he worked with INESC Porto, Porto, Portugal. He received his Ph.D. degree from FEUP – Faculty of Engineering of Porto University in 2010 in Electrical and Computer Engineering. Porto University awarded it the title of European Ph.D.. From 2010 to 2013, he was a Senior Researcher at INESC Porto with Power Systems Unit and dedicated some hours as an invited assistant professor at the Faculty of Engineering of Porto University. Since 2013, he has been a professor at the Federal University of Santa Catarina (UFSC) in the Power System Area. Currently, he is with LABPLAN, where he has developed his research interests, including distributed artificial intelligence, intelligent agents, and power system reliability. Additionally, he is a Director of Science and Technology of INESC P&D Brazil.

Rogerio Salvini is an Associate Professor at the Institute of Informatics of the Federal University of Goiás (UFG). Graduated with a bachelor's degree in Mathematics from Fluminense Federal University (UFF) and a master's and a Ph.D. in Systems Engineering and Computer Science from the Federal University of Rio de Janeiro (COPPE-UFRJ). Has experience in Artificial Intelligence, acting on Machine Learning, and Data Mining.

Lawrence M. Scheier is President of LARS Research Institute, Inc., a not-for-profit company offering a full line of research services encompassing health promotion, program evaluation, program development, and behavioral science technology transfer. He is also Visiting Scholar in the Department of Public Health Education at the University of North Carolina, Greensboro, and a Senior Research Scientist, at Prevention Strategies, Greensboro, NC. Dr. Scheier is a developmental psychologist whose research emphasizes the causes and consequences of drug use and the evaluation of programs that promote positive youth adaptation. His specific interests include the role of social cognition in health behaviors, identity formation, self-concept, learning and motivation, and psychosocial factors that nurture developmental change.

Jenn Scott is a Clinical Psychologist with over two decades of experience working with patients and families to enhance coping with physical and mental illnesses and with organizations to improve staff mental health. She is the former Head of Discipline for the School of Psychological Sciences, University of Tasmania (Utas), and Deputy Chair of the Faculty Board, College of Health and Medicine, Utas. Her clinical interventions encompass multimedia approaches (video/DVD/Apps, mobile devices, telehealth, and face-to-face) and involve collaborations with peak international, national & state-based organizations. Her research has been funded by National Health and Medical Research Council (NHMRC), Australian Research Council (ARC), commonwealth and state government agencies, and non-profit organizations.

Marcos César da Rocha Seruffo has graduation in Data Processing Technology from the University Center of the State of Para (CESUPA, 2004), is a specialist in Computer Systems Technical Support from the Federal University of Para (UFPA, 2005), and has a Master in Computer Science (PPGCC, UFPA, 2008) and Doctor in Electrical Engineering with an emphasis in Applied Computing (PPGEE, UFPA, 2012) and Post Doctorate at the Pontifical Catholic University of Rio de Janeiro, in the Postgraduate Program in Electrical Engineering (PPGEE, PUC-RJ, 2020). He is an Associate Professor level I of the Federal University of Pará and a Professor of Anthropic Studies in the Amazon Graduate Program (PPGEAA) and Electrical Engineering Graduate Program (PPGEE). He was Principal of the School of Computing from Castanhal Campus (2013-2015). He was Principal of the Faculty of Computer Engineering and Telecommunications - Institute of Technology (2017-2019). He was vice-coordinator of the Postgraduate Program in Anthropic Studies in the Amazon (2017-2019). He is a researcher from Operational Research Laboratory (LPO). He is a project evaluator in several national funding agencies. He coordinates and participates in teaching, research, and extension activities through national and international projects in interdisciplinary areas: Social Technologies, User Experience, Data Mining, Computer Networks, Informatics in Education, Social Network Analysis, Anthropic Studies, and Natural Language Processing. He is a Productivity Scholarship in Technological Development and Innovative Extension - DT - Level 2 from CNPq.

Ammanda Silva has a Master's in Creative Industries at the Catholic University of Pernambuco (UNICAP), with a dissertation, focused on management models. MBA in IT Management at the Federal University of Pernambuco (UFPE) and Graduate in Computer Science at the Catholic University of Pernambuco (UNICAP). Currently Operations Superintendent at Neurotech and lecturer on the

Postgraduate course at the Catholic University of Pernambuco (UNICAP) in the discipline of Quality Management in Projects.

Susana Suarez-Fernandez de Miranda is a professor at the University of Seville. Ph.D. in Manufacturing, Materials, and Environmental Engineering. Author of "The challenge of integrating Industry 4.0 in the degree of Mechanical Engineering", "Life Cycle Engineering 4.0: A Proposal to Conceive Manufacturing Systems for Industry 4.0 Centred on the Human Factor (DfHFinI4.0)", "Neuro-Competence Approach for Sustainable Engineering," "Occupational Safety and Health 5.0—A Model for Multilevel Strategic Deployment Aligned with the Sustainable Development Goals of Agenda 2030" among other publications.

Alessandro Trevisan, Architect, is an energy and sustainability consultant for CasaClima, CasaClima auditor, ARCA designer for wooden buildings, Passive House designer, Blower Door Test technician for airtightness testing of buildings; urban planning and infrastructural expert.

Pauliina Tuomi (Ph.D.) is a postdoctoral researcher at Tampere University in Pori, Finland. Tuomi has worked on various research projects dealing with mobile learning, game-based learning innovations, serious games, robotics, and gamification. Tuomi has produced a wide range of national and international publications and reviewed articles for national and international journals.

Index

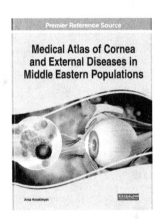

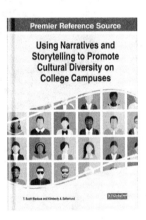

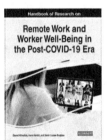

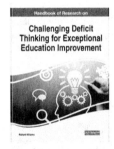

Printed in the United States
by Baker & Taylor Publisher Services